PETERSON FIELD GUIDE TO

BIRDS OF NORTHERN CENTRAL AMERICA

Belize, El Salvador, Guatemala, Honduras

MARINER

An Imprint of Harper Collins*Publishers*

Boston New York

PETERSON FIELD GUIDE TO

BIRDS OF NORTHERN CENTRAL AMERICA

Belize, El Salvador, Guatemala, Honduras

Jesse Fagan

AND

Oliver Komar

ILLUSTRATED BY
ROBERT DEAN AND PETER BURKE

MARINER

HarperCollins*Publishers*
Boston New York

Sponsored by the
Roger Tory Peterson Institute
and the National Wildlife Federation

Published by arrangement with Zona Tropical SA

Mariner Books
An Imprint of HarperCollins Publishers, registered in the United States of America and/or other jurisdictions.

www.marinerbooks.com

Library of Congress Cataloging-in-Publication Data is available.

ISBN 978-0-544-37326-6

Book design by Eugenie S. Delaney

Printed in Thailand

24 RRDA 10 9 8 7 6

We dedicate this book to our families, who withstood and supported our birding habits for so many years: Jesse's wife, Rocio, and Oliver's wife, Lorena, and daughter, Yvonne.

The legacy of America's greatest naturalist and creator of the field guide series, Roger Tory Peterson, is kept alive through the dedicated work of the Roger Tory Peterson Institute of Natural History (RTPI). Established in 1985, RTPI is located in Peterson's hometown of Jamestown, New York, near Chautauqua Institution in the southwestern part of the state.

Today RTPI is a national center for nature education that maintains, shares, and interprets Peterson's extraordinary archive of writings, art, and photography. The Institute, housed in a landmark building designed by world-class architect Robert A. M. Stern, continues to transmit Peterson's zest for teaching about the natural world through leadership programs in teacher development as well as outstanding exhibits of contemporary nature art, natural history, and the Peterson Collection.

Your participation as a steward of the Peterson Collection and supporter of the Peterson legacy is needed. Please consider joining RTPI at an introductory rate of 50 percent of the regular membership fee for the first year. Simply call RTPI's membership department at (800) 758-6841 ext. 226, or email membership@rtpi.org to take advantage of this special membership offered to purchasers of this book. For more information, please visit the Peterson Institute in person or virtually at www.rtpi.org.

CONTENTS

Topography and Bird Distribution in Northern Central America

For the purpose of this field guide, Northern Central America (NCA) includes the countries of Guatemala, Belize, Honduras, and El Salvador. The total area is roughly 164,000 square miles (265,000 square kilometers [km^2]), an area comparable to the state of Colorado (167,000 square miles [270,000 km^2]) or the country of Ecuador (176,000 square miles [284,000 km^2]). The largest country in NCA is Honduras (69,000 square miles [112,090 km^2]), followed by Guatemala (67,000 square miles [108,890 km^2]). Belize (14,000 square miles [22,966 km^2]) is much smaller, but the smallest is El Salvador (13,000 square miles [21,040 km^2]). NCA is located below the Tropic of Cancer, within the tropical belt between 18°N 89°W (Northern Belize) and 13°N 87°W (Southern Honduras). It is bordered to the north and east by the Caribbean Sea and in the south and west by the Pacific Ocean.

The Continental Divide splits NCA more or less down the middle, creating a Caribbean Slope (or drainage) and Pacific Slope (map on p. 9). This divide is important in understanding climate and habitat differences in NCA, which directly affect bird distribution in the region. In addition, NCA includes zones of convergence of three major tectonic plates: the Cocos (Pacific), North American, and Caribbean plates. Subduction of the Cocos Plate gave rise to dozens of volcanoes along the Pacific coasts of Guatemala and El Salvador, forming part of the infamous "Ring of Fire." The Motagua Fault (through which drains the Motagua River) cuts across southeastern Guatemala and is a major, active strike-slip fault formed along the boundary between the North American and Caribbean plates. Ancient and modern seismic activity (creating peaks and intermontane valleys), including the division between Caribbean and Pacific Slopes, and combined with the prevailing winds and weather patterns of two oceans, has helped create a region rich in plant and animal life and species endemism. The Motagua Fault in particular appears to have been an important avian divide separating distinctive subspecies and limiting species expansion north and south.

Considering the biogeographic region from southern Mexico (south of the Isthmus of Tehuantepec) to northern Nicaragua, without considering political boundaries, we find 41 range-restricted ("endemic") bird species with ranges estimated at less than 19,000 square miles (50,000 km^2) occurrence area (Table I). A majority (25 species) are located in the interior and volcanic highlands, but several are endemic to the lowlands of the Petén rainforests and the Yucatán Peninsula (12 species), and a smaller number are confined to the Pacific Slope foothills and lowlands (3 species). One is endemic to just a few dry valleys on the Caribbean Slope of Honduras. Several additional species can be considered endemic to the tropical lowlands that extend from northeastern Honduras to western Panama, species such as Tawny-chested Flycatcher, Snowy Cotinga, White-throated Shrike-Tanager, and Gray-headed Piprites.

The Caribbean Slope

The Continental Divide splits the countries of Guatemala and Honduras and, as a result, the Caribbean Slope includes large areas of Guatemala, Honduras, and the entire country of Belize. Generally speaking, in comparison to the Pacific Slope, the Caribbean Slope of NCA is a more humid region (especially nearer the coast) receiving larger amounts of rainfall for a longer period of the year. Some areas remain quite dry, however, and exceptions include the rainshadow valleys of Honduras (for example, the Aguán and Agalta Valleys), the Motagua River Valley (Guatemala), the semiarid interior highlands, northern Belize and northern Guatemala (which belong biogeographically to the Yucatán Peninsula), and extreme eastern Honduras.

The Caribbean Slope has two large lowland landmasses containing primary and near-primary rainforest: the Petén (of northern Guatemala; pronounced Pay-tén, with the second syllable stressed) and La Moskitia (of eastern Honduras). Some mountains in La Moskitia may receive in excess of 13 feet (4 meters) of rainfall a year! The Petén rainforests are drier, with less than half that amount of annual precipitation. These two important landmasses, once connected by vast tracts of lowland rainforest that ran along the north coast of Honduras through southern Belize and across northern Guatemala, are now isolated, and the remaining forest is fragmented and restricted to national parks and similar protected areas.

The avifauna of the lowland Caribbean Slope includes many species that range into South America. Many southern tropical species reach their northern limits on the Caribbean Slope of Honduras, northern Guatemala, or southern Mexico. Some examples are Great Green Macaw; Great Potoo; several species of hummingbird, including Band-tailed Barbthroat, Brown Violetear, and Purple-crowned Fairy; White-whiskered Puffbird; Scaly-throated Leaftosser; Cocoa Woodcreeper; most NCA antbirds, including Plain Antvireo, Slaty Antwren, Bare-crowned Antbird, and Ocellated Antbird; Gray-headed Piprites; Shining Honeycreeper; White-vented Euphonia; and Passerini's Tanager.

There are other important large land features located on the Caribbean Slope. Northern Central America includes approximately 620 miles (1,000 km) of Caribbean coastline, made up of narrow sandy beaches, mangrove estuaries, and some rocky shoreline. Offshore are numerous islands and keys, such as the Bay Islands of Honduras (which have a distinctly Yucatán-influenced avifauna). Many keys (or cayes) are associated with the Mesoamerican Barrier Reef, the second largest coral reef in the world (after the Great Barrier Reef of Australia). Some of the keys and rocky islets are home to breeding colonies of seabirds, such as Red-footed Booby, Magnificent Frigatebird, Least Tern, Roseate Tern, and Bridled Tern.

The interior portion of the Caribbean Slope forms part of the Crystalline Highlands, a complex series of ancient mountain ranges and high plateaus composed primarily of metamorphic, sedimentary, and igneous rocks, and also karstic (limestone) formations. This area stretches from southern Mexico (Chiapas) to northern Nicaragua at elevations ranging from 2,620 feet (800 meters) to well over 9,840 feet (3,000 meters) in the Sierra de los Cuchumatanes in western Guatemala in the departments of Huehuetenango and El Quiché. Habitats found in the interior highlands include pine savanna, pine-oak forest, cloud forest, elfin woodlands, semideciduous forest, and grasslands. Most of the NCA endemics (see Table I) are found in the interior highlands, including Ocellated Quail, Bearded Screech-Owl, Bushy-crested Jay, Pink-headed Warbler, and Black-capped Siskin. Some temperate bird species reach their southern limits in this biome,

TABLE I. **BIRD SPECIES ENDEMIC TO THE NCA BIOGEOGRAPHIC REGION**

COMMON NAME	SCIENTIFIC NAME	SLOPE	GEOGRAPHICAL REGION
White-bellied Chachalaca	*Ortalis leucogastra*	P	PL
Highland Guan	*Penelopina nigra*	CP	H, V
Horned Guan	*Oreophasis derbianus*	CP	H, V
Ocellated Turkey	*Meleagris ocellata*	C	Y
Black-throated Bobwhite	*Colinus nigrogularis*	C	Y, M
Ocellated Quail	*Cyrtonyx ocellatus*	CP	H, V
Atitlan Grebe[1]	*Podilymbus gigas*	P	V
Pacific Parakeet	*Psittacara stenuus*	P	PL
Red-throated Parakeet	*Psittacara rubritorquis*	CP	H, V, PL
Yellow-lored Parrot	*Amazona xantholora*	C	Y
Bearded Screech-Owl	*Megascops barbarus*	CP	H
Guatemalan Pygmy-Owl	*Glaucidium cobanense*	CP	H, V
Yucatan Poorwill	*Nyctiphrynus yucatanicus*	C	Y
Yucatan Nightjar	*Antrostomus badius*	C	Y
Rufous Sabrewing	*Campylopterus rufus*	CP	V
Honduran Emerald	*Amazilia luciae*	C	D
Green-throated Mountain-gem	*Lampornis viridipallens*	CP	H, V
Green-breasted Mountain-gem	*Lampornis sybillae*	CP	H
Slender Sheartail	*Doricha enicura*	CP	H, V
Wine-throated Hummingbird	*Atthis ellioti*	CP	H, V
Blue-throated Motmot	*Aspatha gularis*	CP	H, V
Yucatan Woodpecker	*Melanerpes pygmaeus*	C	Y

COMMON NAME	SCIENTIFIC NAME	SLOPE	GEOGRAPHICAL REGION
Belted Flycatcher	*Xenotriccus callizonus*	CP	H, V
Yucatan Flycatcher	*Myiarchus yucatanensis*	C	Y
Bushy-crested Jay	*Cyanocorax melanocyaneus*	CP	H, V
Yucatan Jay	*Cyanocorax yucatanicus*	C	Y
Black-throated Jay	*Cyanolyca pumilo*	CP	H, V
Giant Wren	*Campylorhynchus chiapensis*	P	PL
Rufous-browed Wren	*Troglodytes rufociliatus*	CP	H, V
Black-capped Swallow	*Notiochelidon pileata*	CP	H, V
Rufous-collared Robin	*Turdus rufitorques*	CP	H, V
Black Catbird	*Melanoptila glabrirostris*	C	Y
Blue-and-white Mockingbird	*Melanotis hypoleucus*	CP	H, V
Goldman's Warbler	*Setophaga goldmani*	CP	H
Pink-headed Warbler	*Ergaticus versicolor*	CP	H, V
Azure-rumped Tanager	*Tangara cabanisi*	C	V
Green-backed Sparrow	*Arremonops chloronotus*	C	Y, CL
Rose-throated Tanager	*Piranga roseogularis*	C	Y
Bar-winged Oriole	*Icterus maculialatus*	CP	H, V
Orange Oriole	*Icterus auratus*	C	Y
Black-capped Siskin	*Carduelis atriceps*	CP	H, V

C = Caribbean Slope
P = Pacific Slope
CP = both slopes
CL = Caribbean Coast lowlands
D = interior dry valleys
H = interior highlands
M = La Moskitia
PL = Pacific Coast lowlands
V = Pacific Coast volcanic highlands
Y = Yucatán Peninsula
1 = (last documented records from 1980s)

including Buff-breasted Flycatcher, Greater Pewee, Common Raven, Golden-crowned Kinglet, Bushtit, Olive Warbler, Spotted Towhee, and Red Crossbill.

The isolated Mayan Mountains of central Belize and northern Guatemala are a karst landscape and the northernmost extension of the Crystalline Highlands in NCA. Their highest point is Doyle's Delight at 3,690 feet (1,124 meters). Several species associated with the interior highlands also have isolated ranges here, such as Acorn Woodpecker, Plumbeous Vireo, Slate-colored Solitaire, Rufous-capped Warbler, Common Chlorospingus, Red Crossbill, and Elegant Euphonia.

The Yucatán Peninsula ecoregions, which extend south from Mexico to include the northern portions of Guatemala (Petén) and northern Belize, have drier climates. Habitats include grassland, pine savanna, and semideciduous or deciduous forest and scrub. Species found only in this area (within NCA) include Yucatan Poorwill, Yucatan Nightjar, Yucatan Woodpecker, Yucatan Flycatcher, Black Catbird, and Gray-throated Chat. Interestingly, the La Moskitia pine savanna of extreme eastern Honduras has many similarities to the pine savanna of Belize, not only in appearance, but in bird species (including Black-throated Bobwhite, Grace's Warbler, Chipping Sparrow, and Botteri's Sparrow).

The Pacific Slope

The long Pacific coastline of NCA stretches roughly 745 miles (1,200 km) from southwestern Guatemala to southern Honduras. It is a relatively flat coastal plain that is bounded on the north by the Crystalline Highlands and the Volcanic Highlands. In fact, there are no fewer than 14 recently active volcanoes between Guatemala and El Salvador, and in total around 55 active since the end of the last ice age (approximately 12,000 years ago). In Guatemala, the coastal plain is quite wide (more than 12 miles, or 20 kilometers), but in western El Salvador, the Balsam mountains come down to the ocean, forming a rocky coastline with impressive sea cliffs. Constant volcanic activity has created a region rich in fertile lands and, indeed, the coastal plains were once covered in lush, tall semideciduous forest. Sadly, this forest has long since disappeared; much was cleared in the mid-twentieth century for vast plantations of cotton and now sugarcane. A few small forest patches still can be found in El Salvador, for example at Walter T. Deininger National Park and Nancuchiname Natural Protected Area. Species once fairly common along the Pacific coastal plain (and associated with taller forests) are now extirpated or extremely rare, such as King Vulture, White Hawk, Ornate Hawk-Eagle, Sungrebe, Scarlet Macaw, White-necked Puffbird, and Royal Flycatcher.

The picturesque conical shapes of volcanoes dot the landscape. The highest point in NCA, Tajumulco Volcano, is located in southwestern Guatemala at 13,850 feet (4,220 meters). The string of foothills and volcanoes along the Pacific Slope form the Volcanic Highlands. Most of these hillsides are now dotted with shade-grown coffee plantations (usually good habitat for observing birds) and patches of semideciduous forest, and the higher elevations still contain intact cloud forest and pine-oak forest. White-bellied Chachalaca, Pacific Parakeet, and Giant Wren are found only along the Pacific coastal plain, while other regional endemics found in the Volcanic Highlands include Horned Guan, Ocellated Quail, Guatemalan Pygmy-Owl, Rufous Sabrewing, Blue-throated Motmot, Pink-headed Warbler, Azure-rumped Tanager, Bar-winged Oriole, and Black-capped Siskin. The extinct Atitlan Grebe was found only on a single caldera lake (Lake Atitlán) in the Volcanic Highlands.

Along the Pacific Slope there are two prevailing seasons: wet and dry. Though the Caribbean Slope can be said to have the same seasonal pattern, it is less pronounced, with humidity and moisture occurring throughout the year. In contrast, on the Pacific Slope, nearly 95 percent of the annual precipitation falls between the months of April and October.

North-South Divide

The Motagua River Valley of southeastern Guatemala is a strike-slip boundary between the North American and Caribbean plates, and forms a major avian north-south divide. The landmass south of the valley is called the Chortis Block. Several northern species reach their southernmost terminus here, including Bearded Screech-Owl, Russet-crowned Motmot, Yellow Grosbeak, and Varied Bunting. Others are found from the valley southward, such as Olivaceous Piculet, Cocoa Woodcreeper, and Gray-headed Piprites. Expansion to the north (or south) around the Motagua boundary occurs along the narrow Caribbean coastal plain in Guatemala, or along the Pacific Slope skirting the Volcanic Highlands. The valley division seems to explain the distribution of species like Elegant Trogon, Turquoise-browed Motmot, Rufous-and-white Wren, and Spot-breasted Oriole. The division is no more obvious than with the distinctive subspecies

of Rufous-capped Warbler, the *rufifrons* group occurring north of the valley, while the *delattrii* group is found south of this boundary.

Another important division occurs at the Honduran Depression. The Honduran Depression runs from northwestern Honduras, beginning in the Sula Valley, south through Lake Yojoa, the Comayagua Valley, and along the border of Honduras and El Salvador to the western edge of the Gulf of Fonseca. The depression includes a series of geological faults and also represents an east-west divide for several species, including a number of NCA regional endemics. A few of these species include both Green-throated and Green-breasted Mountain-gems, Blue-throated Motmot, Belted Flycatcher, Brown-backed Solitaire, and Black-capped Swallow.

NCA Species by the Numbers

There have been 849 species recorded in NCA. Included in this list are approximately 43 "vagrant" species. Thus about 806 species occur regularly in NCA. Twenty-two vagrants, species with only one or two documented reports from NCA (such as Peruvian Pelican and Northern Mockingbird), are not covered in the Species Accounts but are listed in the Appendix. Vagrants that occur more frequently, such as California Gull and Yellow-headed Caracara, are illustrated and covered in the main text. Therefore, the guide contains maps, text, and illustrations for 827 species of birds. Not included in the spe-

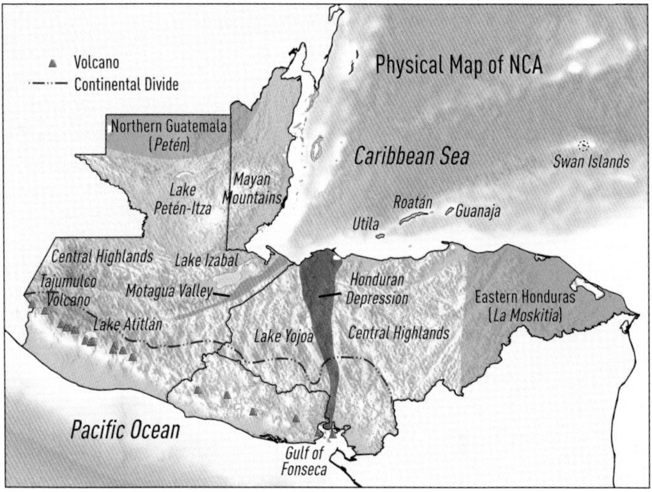

cies totals (or texts and plates) are 20 hypothetical species, reported by reliable observers but lacking adequate documentation, such as a photograph or a specimen; these species are also listed in the Appendix, as well as another 20 species that are expected to occur but have not yet been reported. There is one living species endemic to NCA, the Honduran Emerald, and one extinct endemic species (Atitlan Grebe). Honduras has the highest species total (763) and the highest number of species found only within its borders (75); though the highest number of regional NCA endemics belongs to Guatemala (38) (Table II).

How to Use This Guide

This guide is laid out in a relatively straightforward "field guide" manner, following the tradition of the Peterson Field Guide series. Complete species accounts and the associated illustrations of each species appear on facing pages, so there is no need to look in separate sections to find illustrations, texts, and range maps. The text of each species account begins with the species' size, followed by a brief description of the male, female, and immature (or juvenile) plumage, with key field marks highlighted in boldface text. A reference to similar species follows. Next, we provide a brief summary of the range in Northern Central America (referred to throughout the guide as NCA), a note on

TABLE II. SPECIES RICHNESS BY COUNTRY IN NCA

(hypothetical reports not included in counts)

COUNTRY	TOTAL SPECIES	UNIQUE TO ONE COUNTRY WITHIN NCA	NCA REGIONAL ENDEMICS
Belize	587	3	12
Guatemala	727	23	38
El Salvador	556	0	18
Honduras	763	75	21
NCA Region	849		

preferred habitats and noteworthy behavior, a description of vocalizations, and, finally, the species' worldwide distribution.

Family Accounts

A short text describes each bird family treated in the book. The text includes general characteristics common to the species within the family, global distribution, and other interesting facts. The total number of species (and genera) found within NCA appears in bold text.

Range Maps

Each map shows the political borders of Belize, Honduras, Guatemala, and El Salvador, and includes the outlying Bay Islands of Honduras (Utila, Roatán, and Guanaja), as well as the Turneffe Islands and Ambergris Caye of Belize. Neighboring countries, not labeled on the maps, are Mexico to the west and north, and Nicaragua to the east and south. The oceans are also not labeled. To the west (left) is the Pacific Ocean, and to the east (right) is the Caribbean Sea. The distribution of each species in NCA is indicated with colored ranges. Colored dots represent local populations or, in the case of a green dot, a single observation.

RED = BREEDING VISITOR. Species are present, generally, from April to October. This is a relatively small group of migrants. Examples include Swallow-tailed and Plumbeous Kites (both of which arrive earlier, in January or February), Sulphur-bellied and Streaked Flycatchers, and Yellow-green Vireo. All breed in NCA and winter in South America.

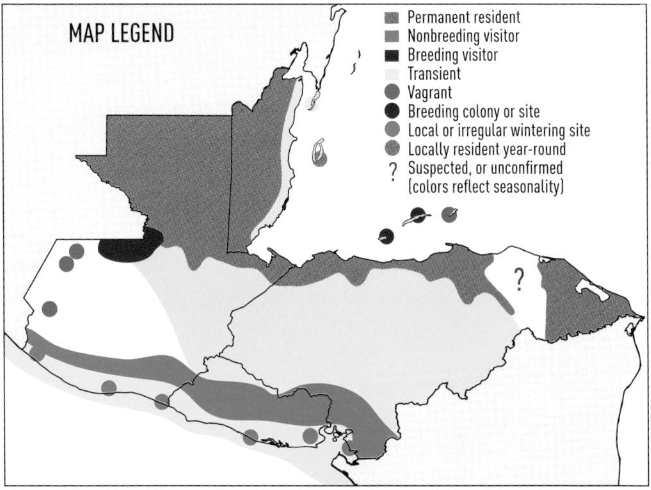

BLUE = WINTER OR NONBREEDING VISITOR. Species are generally present from November to March in NCA. Some species arrive earlier; Orchard Oriole and Louisiana Waterthrush begin to arrive in July every year, as do several species of shorebirds. Many migratory warblers have arrived by September. Many species can still be found in April or even May, but by then, most of the migrants observed are actually transients passing through from farther south. A few winter visitors may remain present on the wintering grounds throughout the year in low numbers, especially immature waterbirds (herons, sandpipers), and raptors (Osprey) associated with water. Some pelagic visitors (such as Wedge-rumped Storm-Petrel) are austral migrants, which breed in the Southern Hemisphere and spend the nonbreeding season (the southern winter) in the Northern Hemisphere. They may be present roughly from May through November.

PURPLE = RESIDENT. Species are present year-round and breed in NCA. Some resident species are augmented in the nonbreeding season by migrants. Examples of such "partial" migrants include many species of herons and egrets, Turkey Vulture, Red-tailed Hawk, American Kestrel, Vaux's Swift, and Northern Rough-winged Swallow; for these species, the purple color is used to represent the resident population, rather than blue for the visitors. In many of these cases, it is difficult or impossible to separate the migrants from the permanent residents.

YELLOW = TRANSIENT. Species are migrants who spend just a few days or weeks in NCA as they move north or south through the region. Most of these species migrate in the fall (August to November) and spring (March to May). The majority of transients are migrating from the temperate North (Canada, U.S.) in fall to south Central America or South America. They make the return trip in the spring. Examples include Upland Sandpiper, Eastern Kingbird, and Red-eyed Vireo.

GREEN = VAGRANT OR AN EXTRALIMITAL OBSERVATION. Green dots indicate single observations. A vagrant is a wanderer that has strayed outside its normal range.

Species Accounts

Each account begins with the species' common and scientific name. These names follow the current nomenclature of eBird/*Clement's Checklist of Birds of the World* (v6.9), but in a few cases they follow other published taxonomies, according to the authors' best judgment (White-breasted Hawk, Red-throated Parakeet, Guatemalan Pygmy-Owl, and Goldman's Warbler). The arrangement of species and families follows closely that of eBird/*Clement's*, but some rearrangements were necessary (such as for terns, flamingos, tropicbirds, and some shorebirds) so that similar-looking species could be placed together on plates. Measurements are noted at the beginning of each account in inches (in.) and centimeters (cm) and correspond to the species' average length from tip of bill to tip of tail. In some cases, when sexes or ages differ significantly in length, a range or sex-specific measurement is given. In other cases—for example, with birds of prey—a wingspan measurement (WS, wingtip to wingtip) is given for the purpose of making comparisons between species in flight.

PLUMAGE AND FIELD MARKS

Plumage characteristics are described for each species, including differences among male, female, and immature (or juvenile) plumages. Breeding and nonbreeding plumages are described where applicable, with the plumage most often seen in NCA described first. Important field marks are noted in bold text; these will provide the most useful aid in field identification. Where useful, separation from similar species is discussed following the plumage description. Terms used to describe specific feather tracts or body parts are included in the figure opposite of a typical bird's "topography."

TOPOGRAPHY OF A BIRD

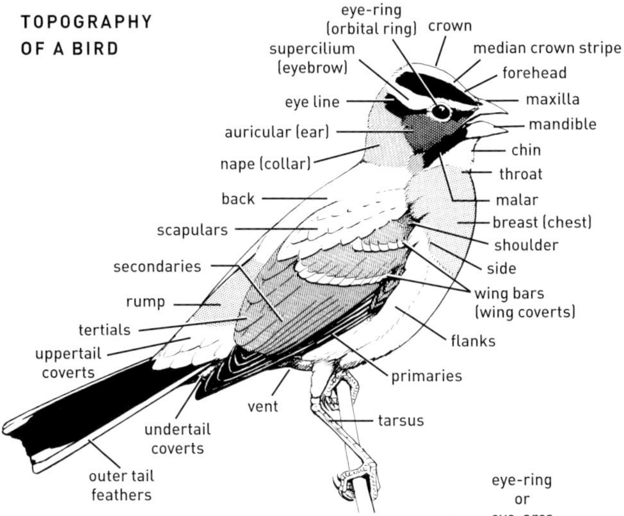

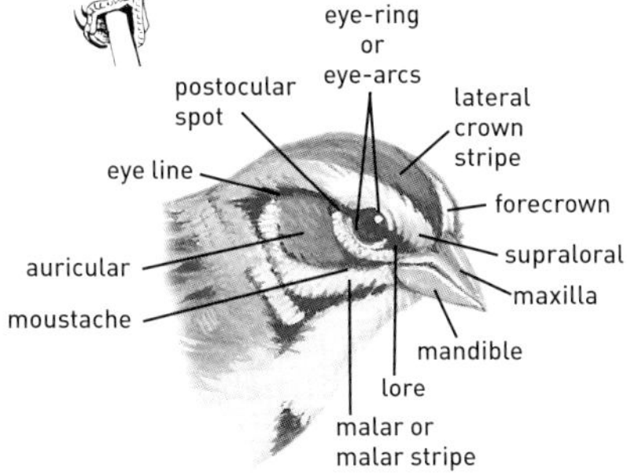

UNDERSURFACE OF WING

On the upper surface of the secondaries, some waterfowl have a bright-colored patch, called a *speculum.*

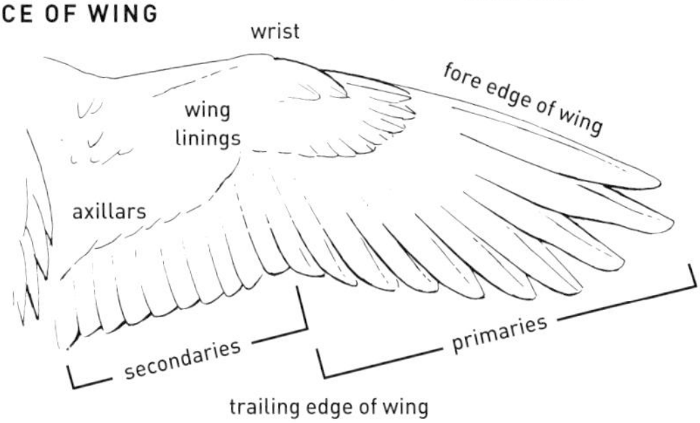

RELATIVE ABUNDANCE

In the species accounts, we describe relative abundance with the terms "abundant," "common," "fairly common," "uncommon," and "rare." These terms describe roughly the likelihood of encountering a species (either by sight or sound) during a full day in the field within its stated habitat and elevational range, inside the geographical area prescribed on its range map. A 50 percent chance of seeing a species can be interpreted as finding the bird on 5 out of 10 days in the proper habitat. For the purpose of this guide, we make the following definitions:

ABUNDANT = A SPECIES THAT IS HARD TO MISS. A near 100 percent chance of encountering the species. Usually, "abundant" implies not only that the species is easy to find, but also that it is usually found in large numbers (large groups or flocks). Few species are actually "abundant."

COMMON = A SPECIES THAT SHOULD BE FOUND WITH RELATIVE EASE. More than 75 percent chance of encountering this species. This species is encountered nearly daily in moderate or good numbers.

FAIRLY COMMON = A SPECIES THAT IS USUALLY FOUND IN THE PROPER HABITAT. Between 50 percent and 75 percent chance of encountering the species.

UNCOMMON = A SPECIES THAT COULD BE MISSED ON ANY GIVEN VISIT. From 10 percent to 50 percent chance of encountering the species. Usually found in low numbers.

RARE = NOT TO BE EXPECTED. Less than 10 percent chance of encountering the species. Usually present in low numbers or at irregular intervals (some migrants). Possibly difficult to detect, and easily missed. "Very rare" refers to species that are as difficult to find as vagrants, but occur with regularity; they would be found on less than .5 percent of field days spent in the appropriate habitat.

VAGRANT = ONLY A FEW RECORDS FOR NCA. A species that does not occur regularly in NCA and should not be expected.

HABITATS

Most terms used to describe habitats are self-explanatory (for example, rainforest, coastal scrub, coffee plantations, urban parks, and gardens). A complete explanation of every habitat term used is available in Ecosystems in Northern Central America, on page 17. Here we provide a few explanations that may not be obvious to many readers.

We refer to oceanic habitat, beyond 2 miles (3.2 km) from shore, as "pelagic." We describe forest habitats with just nine principal forest types. In order from driest to wettest, we used the following classification: thorn forest, semideciduous forest, pine savanna, pine-oak forest, riparian forest, rainforest, cloud forest, and swamps. Semideciduous forest can refer to dry forest in moist soils on coastal plains (floodplain forest) or to moist montane forests in areas that are not wet enough to qualify as cloud forest; semideciduous forests feature trees that partially or completely lose their leaves during dry spells, but unlike temperate deciduous forests, some trees bear foliage at any given time. Riparian forest is also known as gallery forest, and refers to the narrow strip of taller, evergreen broadleaf trees that grow near the banks of streams and rivers. Cloud forests are very wet montane forests that receive much of their moisture directly from clouds (or horizontal precipitation). For this reason, such forests are characterized by abundant air-growing plants (epiphytes), including mosses, ferns, orchids, and even cacti that mat the trunks and larger branches of cloud forest trees. Many mountaintops of NCA are home to cloud forests. Finally, swamps include several types of inundated forest, which vary depending on the salinity of the soil and the water in which the trees grow. Among the most distinctive classes of swamp forest is the mangrove forest, which occupies many tidal river estuaries and some seacoasts on both the Pacific and Caribbean shores of NCA.

VOCALIZATIONS

Virtually every bird species can be identified by its unique vocalizations. Many species have multiple vocalizations, and for most, the call or song may be a key to field identification. We attempted to describe the vocalizations of many species found in this guide, especially when they are useful for identification. Some explanation is necessary to understand the basic terminology we used for describing bird sounds.

There are basically two types of bird vocalizations: calls and songs. A call is a simple vocalization, often a single note, used to sound an alarm (for example, a predator in the area), to make contact with another individual (for example, between male and female, an "I am here and okay"), to maintain unity within a flock (often flight calls), or to beg for food. On the other hand, a song is a more complex, longer vocalization used (mostly by males) to proclaim territories (a defense against other intruding males) and to attract mates. In some cases, males and females sing together in duets.

In most orders and families, vocalizations are genetically hardwired, and every individual sounds virtually identical to others within the same species. In the oscine passerines (songbirds listed in the taxonomic order following the manakins [Pipridae], beginning with the shrikes [Laniidae] and the vireos [Vireonidae] and including all families through the end of the Passeriformes, such as the mockingbirds, wrens, thrushes, warblers, tanagers, blackbirds, and finches), however, the songs (but not the calls) are not fixed genetically, but rather are learned during juvenile development. In these species, there is great individual variation in the song, and local dialects develop among populations within a species.

In some species accounts, we have included a phonetic description of a song or call. In these descriptions, we used an exclamation point to indicate sharpness or explosiveness (for example, *seeeeet!*). Loudness is denoted with capital letters (*Seeeeet!* and *SEEEEET!*). For length of a song, we often give timings (in seconds or minutes) for especially long notes, intervals, or series. We abbreviate seconds as "sec."

For series, the separation of notes is indicated by apostrophes, hyphens, and dashes, such as *Zee-Zee-Zee-Zee-Zee-zeeeee*. Here, six evenly spaced notes are separated by hyphens, the first five notes are louder than the last (indicated by their capitalization), and the last note is longer in duration than the other notes. Longer pauses between notes in a series are depicted with a longer dash and shorter pauses with an apostrophe (*Zee'Zee'Zee'Zee'Zee—zeeeee* or *Zee—Zee—Zee—Zee—Zee'zeeeee*).

We recognize that phonetic descriptions are limited in their usefulness. We encourage readers to use apps that include bird songs, such as BirdsEye, and to visit audio libraries on the Internet, such as xeno-canto.org and the Macaulay Library of Natural Sounds at the Cornell Lab of Ornithology (macaulaylibrary.org), to hear reference recordings with the actual sounds.

WORLDWIDE DISTRIBUTIONS

Finally, the last section of the species account provides the species' worldwide distribution. A species that is "endemic to the region" is a species whose worldwide distribution falls between southern Mexico (including the states of Chiapas, Tabasco, Quintana Roo, and Yucatán) and northern Nicaragua. A list of these species is found in Table I.

Ecosystems in Northern Central America: A Lexicon of Habitats Mentioned in the Guide

Aquatic Ecosystems

LAKES, LAGOONS, PONDS, AND RESERVOIRS: Inland bodies of still freshwater, either naturally created (a caldera lake) or manmade (reservoirs, aquaculture tanks, or a sewage treatment facility). Lagoons are shallow waters with surface and overhanging edge vegetation. Important lakes and reservoirs in NCA include Lake Atitlán and Lake Petén-Itza (Guatemala), Lake Yojoa (Honduras), and Cerrón Grande Reservoir and Lake Olomega (El Salvador).

RIVERS AND STREAMS: Rivers are large, natural flowing systems of water that eventually connect with another river or flow directly into the ocean or sea at an estuary or "mouth." Streams are small rivers that are usually not very wide, are often shallow, and can be swift or slow moving. Several large rivers in NCA form political boundaries, such as Río Paz (border between El Salvador and Guatemala) and Río Segovia (border between Honduras and Nicaragua).

SWAMPS: A wetland system of standing freshwater, usually under a canopy of often dense woody vegetation with plant and tree species adapted to living in flooded environments.

MARSHES: Wetland areas (freshwater or brackish) with standing or slow-moving water, filled with non-woody aquatic vegetation such as cattails, sedges, and other grasses.

COASTAL BEACHES AND ESTUARIES: Coastal beaches are the sandy ocean shorelines of NCA. An estuary is a nearly enclosed body of water with one or more rivers flowing into it and at least a partial connection to the ocean. Estuaries are transitional zones subject to tidal fluctuations and influxes of both freshwater and salt water. Estuary habitats may include river mouths, mudflats, sandy beaches, and edge vegetation communities (such as mangroves).

MANGROVES: Found along both coasts in NCA, mangroves are tree species that form dense stands of flooded forests in saline waters. Some mangrove forests are of low stature, under 13 feet (4 meters) tall and scrubby, while others (even made up of the same species) are tall and majestic, reaching a canopy 100 feet (30 meters) aboveground. "Mangrove" can refer to the habitat type or to one of several tree species. Red mangrove (*Rhizophora mangle*) is adapted to the highest water levels, while white mangrove (*Laguncularia racemosa*) generally grows above the high-tide mark.

PELAGIC WATERS: Open ocean or sea waters far from the coastline. "Pelagic waters" refers to ocean areas more than 2 miles (3.2 km) from shore. In this guide, "Pacific or Ca-

ribbean waters," without specifying "pelagic," refers to the inshore habitat roughly 0 to 2 miles (0–3 km) from shore. Few truly pelagic species occur on the Caribbean side of NCA.

Terrestrial Ecosystems

COASTAL SCRUB: Also known as "littoral scrub." This is any sort of low, dense vegetation that grows in sandy areas near the coastline. This vegetation is usually windswept and adapted to harsh, dry, saline environments.

THORN FOREST: A type of dry forest vegetation adapted to environments with little annual precipitation; generally low in stature with a dense, often impenetrable, scrubby understory. The plants have sharp thorns and less green leafy material, which is an adaptation against foliage-eating predators. Some thorn forests are deciduous, losing their leaves entirely during the dry season. Columnar cacti and prickly-pear cactus can be common in this habitat. Thorn forest often occurs in intermontane valleys where there is a significant rain shadow effect. Good examples of this type of forest include the Motagua River Valley (Guatemala) and the Aguán Valley (Honduras).

SEMIDECIDUOUS FOREST: Sometimes called "tropical dry broadleaf forest" or "tropical dry forest," semideciduous forest is found on both slopes from sea level up to 5,910 feet (1,800 meters). This forest is generally tall in stature and characterized by buttressed trees, long hanging vines or lianas, and some epiphytic growth (air-growing plants). A semideciduous forest may receive the majority of its annual precipitation during the wet season (in most of NCA, this occurs between April and early November) where the forest will appear green and vegetation grows rapidly. In the dry season, many plants and trees drop their leaves and the forest appears dry and brown. Good representations can be found in Tikal National Park (Guatemala) and at El Imposible National Park (El Salvador).

RAINFOREST

RAINFOREST: Found on the Caribbean Slope from sea level up to 5,000 feet (1,500 meters). Rainforests receive large amounts of regular annual precipitation. They are composed of tall, semideciduous or evergreen trees with large buttressed trunks, lianas, and varying amounts of epiphytic growth. Depending on the amount of light penetration, several vegetative layers may exist, including understory, midlevel vegetation, and subcanopy vegetation, along with emergent trees. The heavily forested area of the northern Petén region (Guatemala) represents a transition zone, described as "quasi-rainforest," where the southern, more humid rainforest is transitioning into a drier, more seasonal forest typical of the Yucatán Peninsula. In this sense, the northern Petén could be viewed as either semideciduous forest or rainforest. Good examples of rainforest include the Río Plátano Biosphere Reserve and Pico Bonito National Park (both in Honduras).

CLOUD FOREST

CLOUD FOREST: A humid habitat found at higher elevations, typically between 6,000 and 8,200 feet (1,800 and 2,500 meters), characterized by the constant presence of air moisture in the form of either clouds or light (misty) precipitation. Abundant epiphytes, including bromeliads, orchids, arboreal ferns, and a variety of mosses, form dense mats on tree trunks and major branches. Trees are very tall and gnarly with large buttresses and generally narrow canopies. Little light penetrates the thick canopy, and as a result understory growth is limited. Good examples of cloud forest can be found in the Sierra de Agalta (Honduras), at La Tigra National Park (Honduras), Sierra de Las Minas (Guatemala), and in Montecristo National Park (El Salvador).

RIPARIAN FOREST: Also known as "gallery forest." Medium to tall forest found along rivers and large streams. Riparian forest grows year-round because of its nearly constant water supply. The trees are often taller and greener than in surrounding "upland" areas, and the understory is often dense.

RIPARIAN FOREST

GRASSLANDS AND SAVANNA

PINE SAVANNA

GRASSLANDS AND SAVANNA: Grasslands are open areas with extensive native bunch grasses. Savannas are grasslands with scattered taller trees and bushes. Natural grasslands are fairly rare in NCA, but good examples exist in western Guatemala. Savanna is a common feature of northern Belize and eastern Honduras (La Moskitia).

PINE SAVANNA: A habitat dominated by pine trees (genus *Pinus*) with a grassy or brushy understory. Within undisturbed or mature pine savanna, the trees are evenly spaced, and at least historically, this habitat would have been maintained by frequent natural fires (caused by lightning strikes or indigenous peoples). Pine savanna is found throughout NCA on both slopes. It is particularly prominent in parts of central Belize and eastern Honduras (*P. caribaea*), and in the interior highlands (where *P. oocarpa* is the most common species). Pine savanna ranges from sea level up to at least 9,840 feet (3,000 meters); however, in the interior highlands it is generally found above 2,620 feet (800 meters).

PINE-OAK FOREST: A semiarid forest habitat dominated by pine (*Pinus* spp.) and oak trees (*Quercus* spp.) occurring above 2,620 feet (800 meters) on the Pacific Slope, but also at lower elevations on the Caribbean Slope. Some epiphytes are present, as well as shrubs in the understory. Pine-oak forest (along with pine savanna) is a major habitat type within the interior highlands of NCA. Good examples are found in the Sierra de Las Minas (Guatemala), Montecristo National Park (El Salvador), and at Celaque and La Tigra national parks (Honduras).

PINE-OAK FOREST

DISTURBED HABITAT: This refers to any heavily altered land, with or without regenerating vegetation. This habitat is generally patchy, scrubby, and open, with large amounts of penetrating sunlight. In most instances, the land has been altered by human disturbance, although some disturbances are natural, such as landslides and treefall gaps. In the case of human disturbance, some of the emerging plant species may not be part of the original native habitat. Examples include city parks and gardens, hedgerows, agricultural fields, plantations, and farms. Coffee and cocoa plantations are common along the Pacific Coast and in the interior highlands of NCA. They represent a special type of disturbed habitat that can maintain diverse and abundant bird populations depending on canopy diversity and local management.

A Note About eBird and BirdsEye

We encourage all practicing bird observers to use eBird and BirdsEye, free apps that offer unique birding resources and permit you to share your own observations with others. eBird is a global database for bird observations, to which any bird observer can contribute sightings by visiting eBird.org or by downloading the free eBird app to a smartphone. The eBird database and Internet portal is run by the Cornell Lab of Ornithology. An extensive network of expert volunteer collaborators helps review the database for accuracy and quality control. BirdsEye is a free app, developed by Birds in the Hand L.L.C. (birdseyebirding.com), that helps you find local hot spots and learn about the common birds that are present near your location. Paying subscribers have access to information about all bird species. BirdsEye uses the observation data that has been shared to the eBird database in real time. Thus, if an eBird user reports a Scarlet Macaw in Belize at 10:00 A.M., a BirdsEye subscriber in Belize can know about it immediately.

Much of the distribution information in this book was generated by eBird users. In fact, virtually every species account and range map was vetted by reviewing information in eBird. One of the great benefits of eBird is that it generates up-to-date information constantly. And the information comes from hundreds or thousands of users, rather than a single expert. Furthermore, information is available at multiple scales. Bird reporters can create points on range maps to represent specific observations of a species, which are associated with the observer's name, the date, a georeferenced location, and the complete original report, which may include descriptive texts, photographs, audio, and even video recordings.

As the eBird database grows, both eBird and BirdsEye come closer and closer to functioning as a birding site guide as well. Hundreds of birding sites across Northern Central America are registered in eBird, and as time goes by, eBird assembles ever more complete checklists and bar charts (weekly reports of bird abundance) for each of these sites.

Range and abundance information for birds is always more up-to-date on eBird than in any published field guide. Future updates of the information in this guide will greatly benefit, and increase in accuracy, if bird observers share their observations, bird lists from site visits, audio recordings, and/or digital photos and videos with the public, through eBird.org. The Central American portal to eBird can be found on the Internet at eBird.org/camerica.

SPECIES ACCOUNTS

TINAMOUS

TINAMIDAE (Order: Tinamiformes). These fowl-like, terrestrial birds occur only in the Americas, from Mex. to s. South America. They are heavy-bodied, practically tailless, and have small heads and short bills. Cryptic in coloration (and therefore difficult to see), they are detected most often by call. There are only slight differences in plumage between the sexes. **4 species (2 genera)**

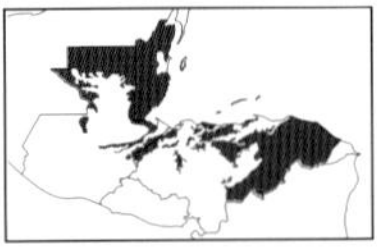

GREAT TINAMOU *Tinamus major*

16 in. (41 cm). **Largest tinamou in NCA.** Above gray brown with dark barring; **head pale gray with broad postocular stripe**; chest brown, remaining underparts light brown washed with buff; **dark barring on flanks**; **legs grayish**. Distinguished from other tinamous by large size and gray legs. Fairly common on Caribbean Slope; to 3,960 ft. (1,200 m). Prefers humid habitats; found in rainforest and semideciduous forest. Difficult to see, but sometimes sighted on trails and roads at dawn or dusk; unlike other tinamous, may fly when disturbed. Call is a series of long quavering notes on a single pitch: *wheuu-whooo'o'o'o'o-wheuu-whooo'o'o'o'o*. Mex. to Brazil.

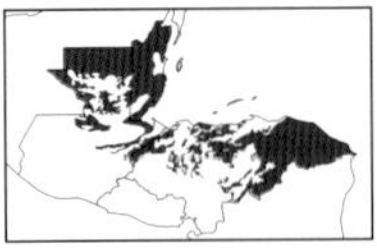

LITTLE TINAMOU *Crypturellus soui*

8.5 in. (22 cm). **Smallest tinamou in NCA. Brownish gray upperparts lack barring**; head pale gray; underparts tawny to grayish tawny; **legs dull greenish yellow**. Fairly common on Caribbean Slope; to 4,620 ft. (1,400 m). Prefers drier habitats; found at edge of rainforest and within disturbed habitat, including scrub. Call is a series of high-pitched, quavering whistles: *wheuu-wheuu-WHEUUU-WHEUUU'WHEUUU'WHEUUU'WHEUUU* (the last notes accelerate and rise in pitch); also makes a quavering whistle that rises and falls: *whuueeeu'u'u'u'u*. Mex. to Brazil.

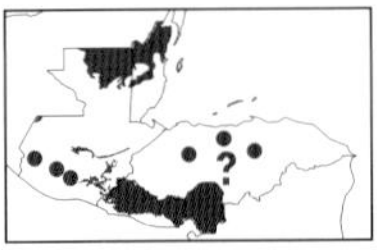

THICKET TINAMOU *Crypturellus cinnamomeus*

10.5 in. (27 cm). **Upperparts heavily barred**; crown dark; **face, neck, and underparts tawny**; sides and flanks with heavy black barring; **legs orange** (similar to those of Slaty-breasted Tinamou). On male, chest unmarked. On female, chest with fine grayish black barring. Male very similar to female Slaty-breasted Tinamou, but is darker above and has tawny chest (not gray) and more barring on flanks and thighs. Fairly common on both slopes; to 6,435 ft. (1,950 m). Found in semideciduous forest, thorn forest, and coffee plantations. Difficult to see. Call is a single, high-pitched, slightly quavering and ringing whistle (less than 1 sec.). Reported to hybridize with Slaty-breasted Tinamou in n. Honduras. Mex. to Costa Rica.

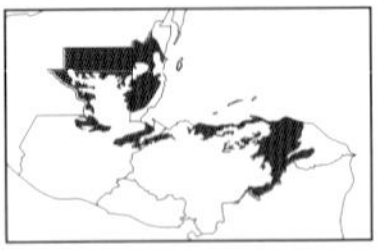

SLATY-BREASTED TINAMOU *Crypturellus boucardi*

10.5 in. (27 cm). On male, **upperparts grayish brown with little barring**; neck, head, and chest gray; throat white; flanks and undertail coverts buffy with dark brown barring. On female, upperparts with heavy barring; neck and head browner than male's. On **both sexes, legs orange** (similar to those of Thicket Tinamou). Female Slaty-breasted Tinamou very similar to male Thicket Tinamou, but paler above and has gray chest (not tawny) and less barring on flanks and thighs. Fairly common on Caribbean Slope; to 1,980 ft. (600 m). Found in rainforest and semideciduous forest, generally in dense undergrowth; occasionally sighted on trails and roads at dawn or dusk. Call composed of 2 notes: *whooaaaaa-whooo* (resembles call of *Leptotila* doves, [p. 52]). Reported to hybridize with Thicket Tinamou in n. Honduras. Mex. to Costa Rica.

GREAT
TINAMOU
LITTLE
TINAMOU
female
THICKET
TINAMOU
male
female
SLATY-BREASTED
TINAMOU
male

WHISTLING-DUCKS, GEESE, AND MUSCOVY DUCK

ANATIDAE (Order: Anseriformes). Ducks and geese are waterfowl with large bodies, short tails, fully webbed feet, and short, stubby bills. Some species feed on aquatic vegetation, while others eat small fish and invertebrates. Most species are sexually dimorphic. Of these, adult males are generally more brightly patterned than females; however, after breeding, some males temporarily molt into a drab "eclipse" plumage. Most of the species found in NCA are winter visitors from the north. Ducks are highly gregarious, frequently forming large flocks. **19 species (8 genera)**

BLACK-BELLIED WHISTLING-DUCK *Dendrocygna autumnalis*

19 in. (48 cm). **Bill and legs pinkish red**; chestnut body contrasts with grayish brown face and foreneck; **belly and vent black**. In flight, shows **large white patches on wings**. Juvenile duller brown with bill and legs bluish gray. Compare juvenile with Fulvous Whistling-Duck, but is duskier overall and lacks banding on neck and back. Fairly common to common on both slopes; to 6,600 ft. (2,000 m). Found on and near freshwater lagoons, marshes, lakes, and reservoirs. Nests in tree cavities near water's edge. Often in groups of 10 to 50 or more individuals. Quite vocal in flight; also vocalizes at night when feeding. Often kept as a pet. Call is a series of whistled squeaks and piping screams: *weeeeee-weeeeee'teeee'tee'teeee!*; alarm call is a loud *peek!* U.S. to Argentina.

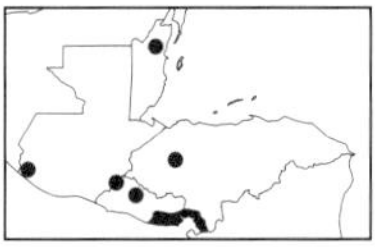

FULVOUS WHISTLING-DUCK *Dendrocygna bicolor*

20 in. (51 cm). **Head and underparts bright fulvous**; **blackish back** has pale tawny barring; note **buffy white feathering on sides and on neck**; **bill bluish gray**. In flight, shows **black wings** and **white base to tail**. Compare with juvenile Black-bellied Whistling-Duck, but is brighter tawny overall and has banding on neck and back. Locally common in wetlands; to 2,600 ft. (800 m). Found on and near freshwater lagoons, marshes, lakes, and reservoirs. Nests in tree cavities near water's edge. Sometimes congregates in groups numbering in the thousands. Vocalizes in flight and also at night when feeding. Call is a distinctive *pit-cheeeah!* U.S. and Caribbean to Argentina.

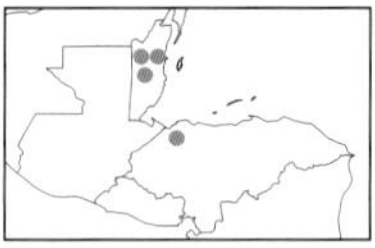

SNOW GOOSE *Chen caerulescens*

30 in. (76 cm). A large waterfowl. On white morph, **body snow white**; primaries black; on **pinkish bill note black pattern that suggests a grin**. On blue morph, **body sooty gray**; **neck and head white**; varying amounts of white on belly and vent. Very rare winter visitor (Nov.–Feb.). Found in agricultural fields (including rice paddies) and at edges of lakes and reservoirs. Canada (breeding) to Mex. (winter).

MUSCOVY DUCK *Cairina moschata*

30 in. (76 cm). A large waterfowl. Male larger than female, immature smaller. Adult **blackish overall** with green and purple glossy highlights; in flight, from above and below, adult shows **large white wing patch** (immature shows very small patch, usually just a white spot on upperwing). Bill pinkish with black markings. On male, note **pink warts at base of bill and around eye** (absent in female). Domesticated birds often show white patches on body and generally occur near human habitation. Uncommon throughout NCA; to 3,300 ft. (1,000 m). Found on and around secluded freshwater lakes, marshes, lagoons, reservoirs, and rivers. Usually solitary or in pairs, although occasionally forms large foraging flocks of up to hundreds of birds. Generally silent. U.S. to Argentina.

two Fulvous with Black-bellieds

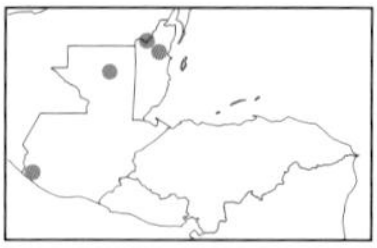

GADWALL *Anas strepera*

20 in. (51 cm). Male **silvery gray overall** with dark eye line, copper-pink–edged scapulars, and black rear end; in flight or while dabbling note white speculum; bill is black. Female similar to female Mallard (below), but has black bill with orange edging and lacks buffy stripe along tail. Gadwall has square-looking head. Rare winter visitor to Belize, Guatemala; however, reports increasing; to 2,460 ft. (750 m). Found on freshwater lakes and lagoons, flooded fields; occasionally more coastal. Temperate N. America, Europe, and Asia. Winters to Mex. (and NCA).

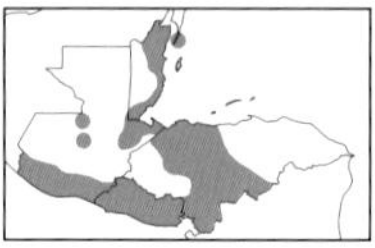

AMERICAN WIGEON *Anas americana*

20 in. (51 cm). On both sexes, **bill grayish white**; body pinkish. On male, note combination of **postocular green stripe and white crown**; in flight, **large white patch on forewing**. On female, pale gray head with fine black streaks or spotting. Uncommon winter visitor (early Oct.–early Apr.); to 4,950 ft. (1,500 m). Found on lakes, lagoons, estuaries, and reservoirs. Usually in groups of 5 to 20 individuals, but sometimes numbers in the hundreds. U.S. and Canada (breeding) to Colombia (winter).

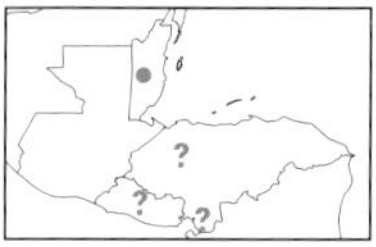

MALLARD *Anas platyrhynchos*

23 in. (58 cm). On male, thin white necklace separates **green head and neck** from **chestnut chest**; **bright yellow bill**; blue speculum bordered by white. On female, creamy buff chevrons on dark brown body; **bill orange with black smudge on top**. Female similar to female Gadwall. Individuals found near human habitation may be domesticated variety, which may show up anywhere. Reports of wild birds should be well documented. Very rare or vagrant winter visitor to NCA. Found on lakes, lagoons, estuaries, and reservoirs. U.S. and Canada (breeding) to Mex. (winter).

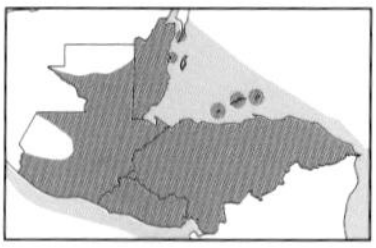

BLUE-WINGED TEAL *Anas discors*

15.5 in. (39 cm). On male, **white crescent on face**; dark gray head; black spotting on body. On female, pale face, dark eye line, and **small white patch at base of bill**. In flight, both sexes show **pale blue patch on upperwing** and **silver wing lining**. Female similar to female Cinnamon Teal, but has obvious eye line, pale patch at base of bill, smaller bill, more distinctive markings on flanks, and is duller brown; female also similar to female Green-winged Teal, but has larger paler body, larger bill, orange legs, and lacks creamy tail stripe. Common transient and winter visitor (Aug.–mid-May); to 6,600 ft. (2,000 m). Found on large lakes, lagoons, estuaries, reservoirs, and in mangroves. Flocks often number in the thousands. U.S. and Canada (breeding) to Brazil (winter).

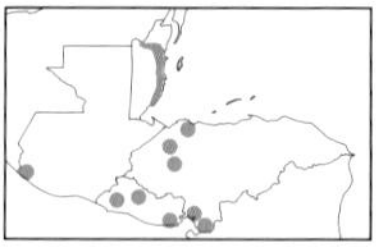

CINNAMON TEAL *Anas cyanoptera*

16 in. (41 cm). Distinctive male has **rich chestnut-cinnamon plumage** and **red eyes**. Female similar to female Blue-winged Teal, but lacks eye line and pale patch at base of bill, has a larger bill, more subtle markings on flanks, and is richer brown; female similar to female Northern Shoveler (p. 32), but has dark bill (not orange) and less distinctive markings on flanks; female similar to female Green-winged Teal (p. 32) but has larger body and bill, and orangish legs. Very rare to rare winter visitor (Sept.–Apr.); to 1,650 ft. (500 m). Found on lakes, lagoons, estuaries, and reservoirs. Usually solitary or in pairs. Canada to Argentina.

Dabbling ducks (genus Anas*) forage on the water's surface or tip their bodies forward to sift for food just below the surface.*

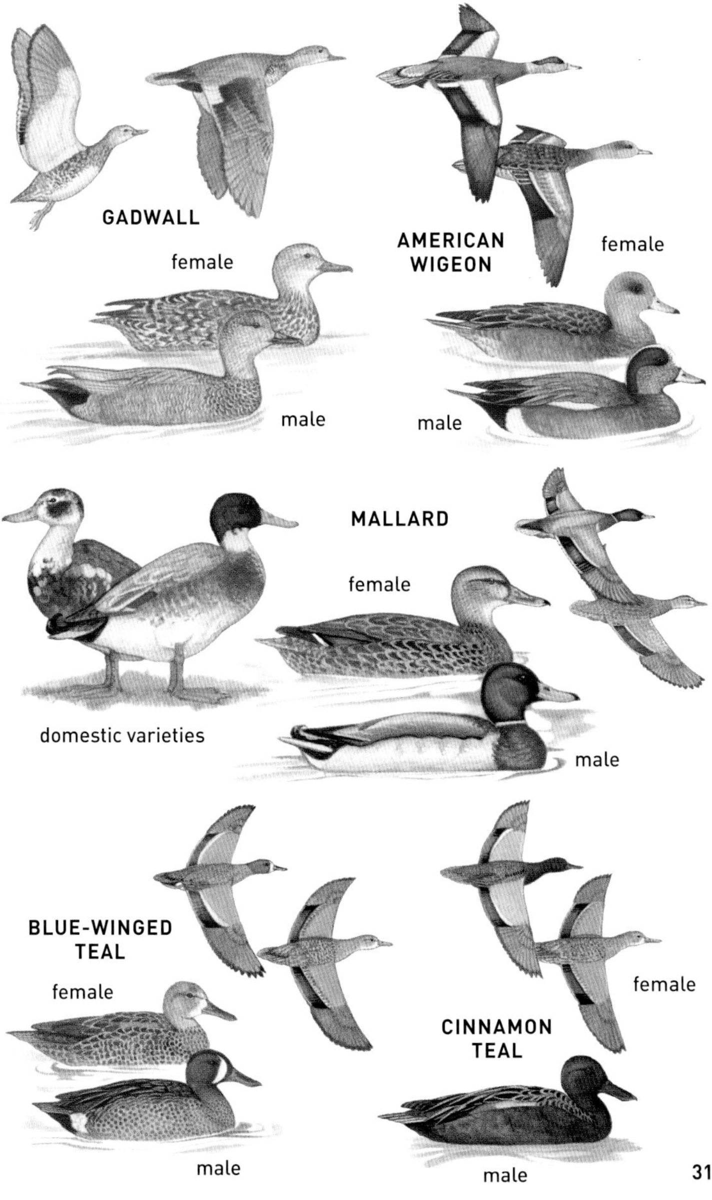

SOME DABBLING DUCKS AND DIVING DUCKS

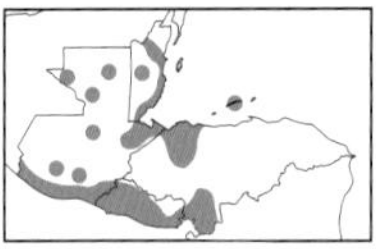

NORTHERN SHOVELER *Anas clypeata*

19 in. (48 cm). On both sexes, note **long shovel-like bill** (black on male, orange on female). On male, combination of **green head, white chest, and chestnut sides** is distinctive. On female, creamy chevrons on body; similar to female Cinnamon Teal (p. 30), but has mainly orange bill (dark on female Cinnamon Teal) and more distinctive markings on flanks. Uncommon transient and winter visitor (late Sept.–mid-May); to 4,950 ft. (1,500 m). Found on lakes, lagoons, estuaries, and reservoirs. Flocks range in size from just a few birds to several hundred. U.S. and Canada (breeding) to Colombia (winter).

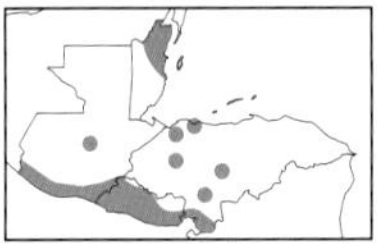

NORTHERN PINTAIL *Anas acuta*

Male: 25 in. (64 cm); female: 21 in. (53 cm). Long neck and slender build; **thin bill with grayish blue sides**. On male, combination of **dark brown head and white stripe extending up side of neck** is unique; **long thin tail** (shorter on female). Female brown with thin creamy chevrons above and on sides; pale below. Rare transient and winter visitor (early Oct.–Mar.); to 6,600 ft. (2,000 m). Found on lakes, lagoons, estuaries, and reservoirs. Flocks range in size from just a few birds to several hundred. U.S. and Canada (breeding) to Colombia (winter).

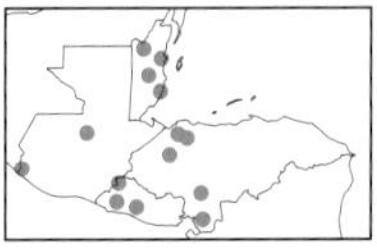

GREEN-WINGED TEAL *Anas crecca*

14 in. (36 cm). A small dabbling duck. On both sexes, note **creamy stripe on tail**. On male, **chestnut head with green postocular stripe**; also note **vertical white slash** on side of pale gray body. Female has dark crown and eye line and brown body with dark chevrons; similar to female Blue-winged Teal (p. 30), but has smaller darker body, smaller bill, dusky green legs, and creamy tail stripe (absent on female Blue-winged Teal). Female similar to female Cinnamon Teal (p. 30) but has smaller body and bill, green legs. Rare winter visitor (late Sept.–Mar.); to 6,600 ft. (2,000 m). Found on lakes, lagoons, rivers, reservoirs, and estuaries. U.S. and Canada (breeding) to Caribbean and NCA (winter); also Old World.

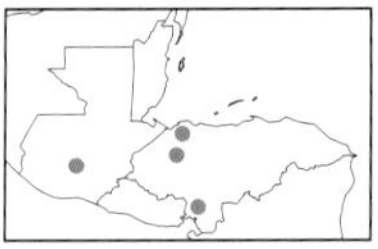

CANVASBACK *Aythya valisineria*

21 in. (53 cm). Male has **rufous-chestnut head and neck**, black chest, and silver body; also note black undertail coverts and red eyes. Female drabber, with brownish head, **pale area around eye**; body silver with brown sheen. On both sexes, note **sloping forehead** and **long sloping bill**. Very rare winter visitor (Nov.–Feb.); to 3,900 ft. (1,200 m). Found on lakes, lagoons, rivers, reservoirs, and estuaries. U.S. and Canada (breeding) to Mex. (winter).

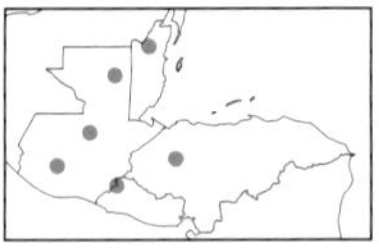

REDHEAD *Aythya americana*

19 in. (48 cm). Male has **reddish head**, black chest, and silver body; also note black undertail coverts and yellow eyes; **bluish bill has dark tip**. Female warm brown overall; note **buffy eye-ring and thin postocular stripe**. Very rare winter visitor in NCA (Dec.–Mar.). Found on lakes, lagoons, rivers, reservoirs, and estuaries. U.S. and Canada (breeding) to Mex. (winter).

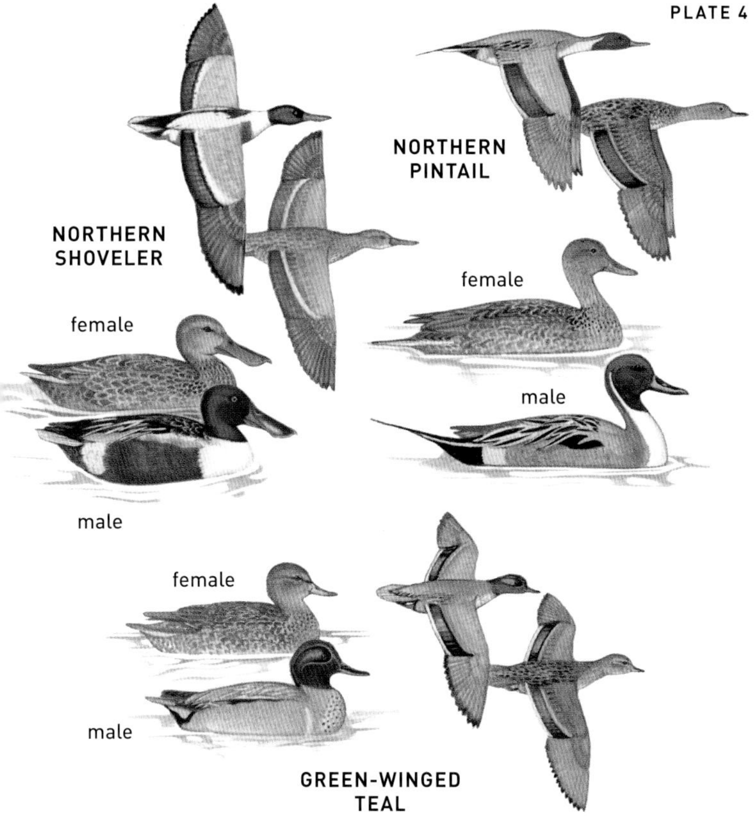

Diving ducks (genus Aythya*) dive several feet below the water's surface to search for food.*

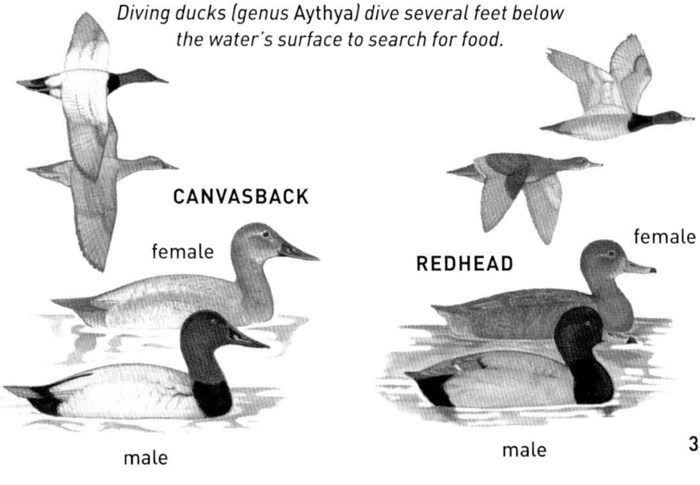

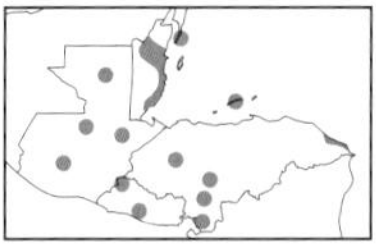

RING-NECKED DUCK *Aythya collaris*

17 in. (43 cm). Rear of crown peaked; **white band near tip of bill**. On male, head and neck show iridescent purple; **upperparts black**; sides with **white vertical slash**; eyes yellow. Female drab brown overall; **white wash at base of bill** and **thin pale line behind eye**. Male similar to male Lesser Scaup, but has black back (not silver gray), white band on bill, and vertical white slash on sides. Female similar to female Lesser Scaup, but has white band on bill and lacks white patch at base of bill. Winter visitor (late Oct.–early Apr.). Uncommon on Caribbean Slope, rare to uncommon on Pacific Slope; to 5,900 ft. (1,800 m). Found on lakes, lagoons, estuaries, and reservoirs; also found on inland brackish waters along both coasts. Flocks often number in the dozens. U.S. and Canada (breeding) to Panama (winter).

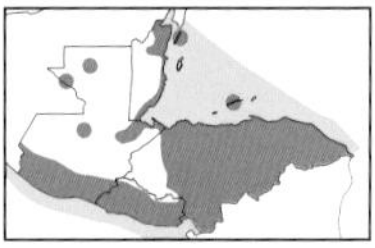

LESSER SCAUP *Aythya affinis*

17 in. (43 cm). Rear of crown slightly peaked; bill grayish; in flight, note **white stripe that extends from secondaries to inner primaries**. On adult male, head and neck show purplish green gloss; **sides and back silver gray**; eyes yellow. Female and immature male mostly drab brown; note **white patch at base of bill**. Adult male similar to male Ring-necked Duck, but has silver gray back (not black), all-gray bill, and lacks vertical white slash on sides. Female similar to female Ring-necked, but has unmarked bill, and white patch at base of bill. Transient and winter visitor (mid-Oct.–mid-May). Common on Caribbean Slope, less common on Pacific Slope; to 5,900 ft. (1,800 m). Found on lakes, lagoons, estuaries, and reservoirs. Flocks may number in the hundreds. U.S. and Canada (breeding) to Ecuador (winter).

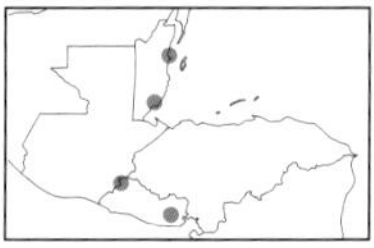

RED-BREASTED MERGANSER *Mergus serrator*

21.5 in. (55 cm). Male has dark green head with **contrasting white collar and dark reddish brown chest**; also note **wispy crest**. Female has orange-brown head. On both sexes, note thin red-orange bill. Very rare winter visitor in NCA; to 2,600 ft. (800 m). Found on lakes and reservoirs as well as inshore coastal waters. U.S. and Canada (breeding) to Mex. (winter).

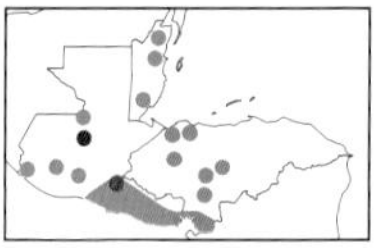

RUDDY DUCK *Oxyura jamaicensis*

15 in. (38 cm). Male has **black crown and white cheeks**; blue bill. Nonbreeding male has grayish body; breeding male (not illustrated) is bright rufous all over, contrasting with white cheeks and black crown. Female grayish overall; has **single dark line across face** (female Masked Duck is buffy with 2 dark lines across face). Nonbreeding male (Sept.–Mar.) similar to female, but shows white cheeks. Rare to uncommon winter visitor (Oct.–Apr.), and occasional summer breeder; to 5,115 ft. (1,550 m). Found on freshwater lakes and reservoirs. Forages with tail cocked or fanned. Sometimes occurs in flocks of up to several hundred individuals. Canada to NCA.

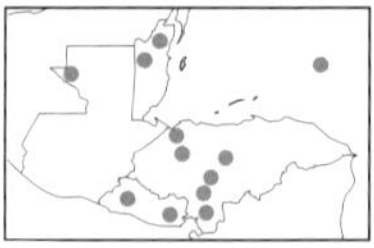

MASKED DUCK *Nomonyx dominicus*

14 in. (36 cm). Male has **black face**; blue bill **with dark tip**. Female similar to female Ruddy Duck, but has **parallel black stripes across buffy face** (not a single dark stripe across cheek). Rare on both slopes; to 3,600 ft. (1,100 m). Nomadic; makes erratic movements within NCA, partially due to fluctuating water levels; occasionally breeds. Found at edges of lakes, ponds, and lagoons. Difficult to observe, as it often seeks cover in aquatic vegetation. Frequently submarines with just its head above water. Forages with tail cocked or fanned. Solitary or in pairs. Mex. and Caribbean to Argentina.

a pair of Ring-necked Ducks with male Lesser Scaup and American Coots

CHACHALACAS AND SMALL GUANS

CRACIDAE (Order: Galliformes). A family of large, long-tailed birds, many with distinctive crests and colorful soft parts. Cracids generally forage alone or in small groups, and can be found at all levels of the forest. Chachalacas are the easiest of the cracids to detect, with raucous groups calling back and forth to each other. Guans are more difficult to observe, as they are quieter and more secretive, and move in smaller groups. As with quails (p. 40), the cracids of NCA face the twin threat of hunting and habitat loss. **7 species (5 genera)**

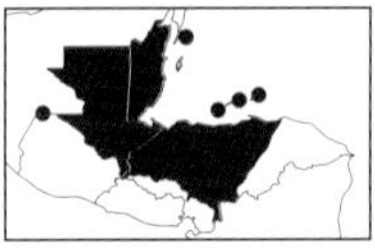

PLAIN CHACHALACA *Ortalis vetula*

18.5 in. (47 cm). **Belly, vent, and undertail coverts washed tawny or cinnamon**; long tail dusky with buffy cinnamon tip; head and neck grayish; small red gular. Little overlap with other species of chachalacas in NCA. Common in Belize, fairly common on Caribbean Slope of Guatemala and Honduras, expanding onto Pacific Slope; to 5,910 ft. (1,800 m). Forages at mid- and upper levels of thorn forest and semideciduous forest; also occurs in disturbed habitat, pine forest, and coastal scrub. Generally in small groups. Loud and raucous; groups frequently call back and forth to each other. Call is a loud, scratchy *CHALK'ALOT!-CHALK'ALOT!-CHALK'ALOT!-CHALK'ALOT!* (series repeated every few seconds; very similar to call of White-bellied Chachalaca, but harsher); when alarmed, makes a *chek'chek'chek'chek' chek'chek'chek'chek*. U.S. to Costa Rica.

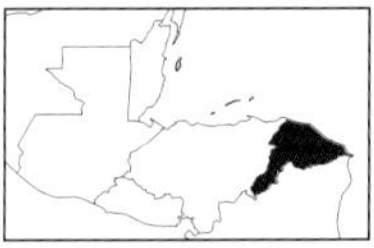

GRAY-HEADED CHACHALACA *Ortalis cinereiceps*

22 in. (56 cm). Grayish head contrasts with brown neck and upperparts; belly, vent, and undertail coverts washed grayish brown; note **rufous primaries and secondaries** (visible on closed wing); tail tipped buffy white; small red gular. Almost no overlap with other species of chachalacas in NCA. Fairly common in e. Honduras; to 3,280 ft. (1,000 m). Forages at mid- and upper levels at edge of rainforest; also occurs in disturbed habitat. Generally in small groups. Loud and raucous. Calls include a loud, ringing *Wee'chuck!-Wee'chuck!-Wee'chuck!-Wee'chuck! . . .* (quite parrotlike and different from other chachalacas); also makes a *Weeek!-Weeek!-Weeek! . . .* ; and a soft whining, twittering trill. Honduras to Colombia.

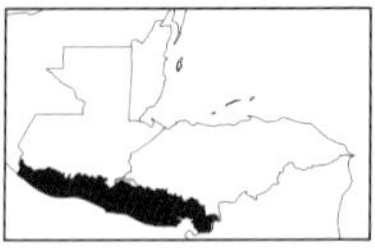

WHITE-BELLIED CHACHALACA *Ortalis leucogastra*

20.5 in. (52 cm). **White belly, vent, and undertail coverts** distinctive; grayish brown head and neck contrast lightly with warm brown upperparts; **whitish tail tips**; small red gular. Little overlap with other species of chachalacas in NCA. Uncommon to fairly common on Pacific Slope; to 5,500 ft. (1,700 m). Forages at midlevels at edge of disturbed habitat, thorn forest, and semideciduous forest; also occurs in coastal scrub and coffee plantations. Generally in small groups. Loud and raucous. Call is very similar to call of Plain Chachalaca, but is slightly thinner. Endemic to region.

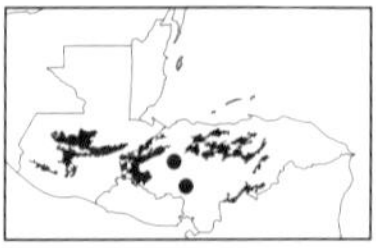

HIGHLAND GUAN *Penelopina nigra*

24.5 in. (62 cm). Male black overall with **bright red bill, legs, and throat wattle**. Female brown overall with **heavy black barring**. Uncommon in Guatemala, Honduras, and El Salvador; 3,940 to 9,510 ft. (1,200–2,900 m), and locally near sea level on the Caribbean Slope. Forages at all levels of cloud forest and pine-oak forest. Generally solitary; male defends territory during breeding period. Call is a high-pitched whistle that rises in volume and pitch and lasts about 2 sec.: *weeeeeeeeeeEEEEEEEEEE!* Also produces a loud mechanical noise from wings, typically during the breeding period (Mar.–Aug.): *kek-kr-kar'r'r'r'r'r'r'r'r'r'r'r*. Endemic to region.

PLAIN
CHACHALACA
GRAY-HEADED
CHACHALACA
WHITE-BELLIED
CHACHALACA
HIGHLAND
GUAN
male
female

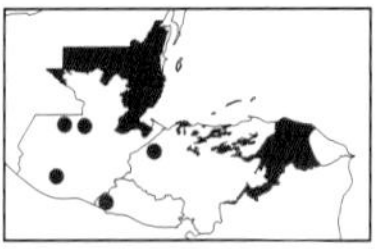

GREAT CURASSOW *Crax rubra*

33 in. (84 cm). Very large, with long tail and **extravagant crest**. Male **black overall** with solid black crest and yellow knob on bill. On female, **upperparts rufous brown**; head and neck speckled black and white; **crest and tail with thin white bands**. Rare to uncommon on Caribbean Slope, very rare on Pacific Slope; to 4,920 ft. (1,500 m). Forages on ground in rainforest and semideciduous forest; roosts in trees. Solitary or in pairs. Secretive; most often detected by voice. Call from male is a soft, booming, very low-pitched *Wheuuuuuup!*; also both sexes may make a loud *Peek!* or a soft upslurred whistle when alarmed. Mex. to Ecuador.

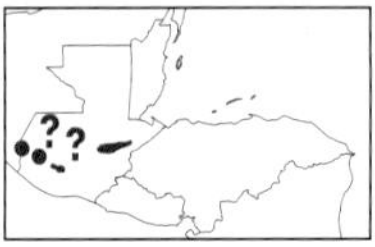

HORNED GUAN *Oreophasis derbianus*

33 in. (84 cm). Very large; **bright red horn** on crown is distinctive; **dark upperparts** contrast with **white underparts**; long, broad **tail with single white band**; small yellow bill and white eyes. Rare and local in Guatemala; 4,920 to 7,550 ft. (1,500–2,300 m). Forages at all levels of pine-oak forest and cloud forest. Solitary or in small groups. Calls include a crackling *kr'r'r'rack-kr'r'r'rack-kr'r'r'rack-* . . . ; also makes a low, growling *uh-ROOO-ehhhhh*; and a nasal, begging *eh-eh eh-eh-eh-eh-eh-eh-eh-uh-ROOO-ahhhh!* Endemic to Guatemala and Mex. (Chiapas).

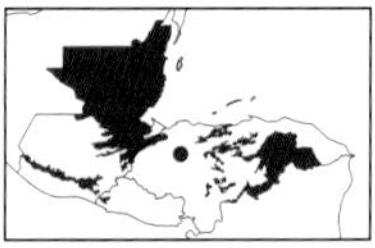

CRESTED GUAN *Penelope purpurascens*

34 in. (86 cm). Notably **large body** and **long tail**; blackish brown overall with **dull white streaking on chest**; also note prominent crest, bluish bare skin around eye, and striking **red throat wattle**. Uncommon on both slopes; to 8,200 ft. (2,500 m). Forages at mid- to upper levels of rainforest, cloud forest, semideciduous forest, and riparian forest. Generally solitary or in pairs. Often secretive; may be difficult to detect when not vocalizing. Calls include a loud, far-carrying, honking *WOK!-WOK!-WOK!-WOK!-WOK!-WOOAK!-WOOAK!-WOOAK!* . . . ; a piping *POK!-POK!-POK!* . . . ; and a low, nasal, grunting *aahhnk-aahhnk*. Mex. to Peru.

PHASIANIDAE (Order: Galliformes). A cosmopolitan family of chickenlike game birds that includes pheasants, partridges, turkeys, Old World quail, and others. Members of this family vary greatly in size, but most have a plump rounded body, a small head, and strong feet (some with spurs). They are nonmigratory and mainly terrestrial, though some are good fliers. A well-known member of this family is the Red Junglefowl (*Gallus gallus*) of southeast Asia, the wild ancestor of the domesticated chicken. The Ocellated Turkey is closely related to the Wild Turkey (*Meleagris gallopavo*) of North America. **1 species (1 genus)**

OCELLATED TURKEY *Meleagris ocellata*

Male: 38 in. (97 cm); female: 29.5 in. (75 cm). Male unmistakable. Female and immature similar to male, but are duller overall and lack fleshy horn on crown. Uncommon in Belize and n. Guatemala; to 980 ft. (300 m). Roosts low in trees and forages on ground in open areas of thorn forest, semideciduous forest, and pine savanna. Often in small or medium-sized groups. Call is a liquid, bubbling clucking that grows louder, then chokes at the end: *cuk-cuk-cuk-CUK'K'K'K'K'K'K'KAAAH'GUH!* At dusk, makes a low, nasal barking: *poak—poak—poak—poak—poak*. Endemic to region.

GREAT
CURASSOW
female
male
HORNED
GUAN
CRESTED
GUAN
female
OCELLATED
TURKEY
male

WOOD-PARTRIDGES AND QUAILS (BOBWHITES)

ODONTOPHORIDAE (Order: Galliformes). These ground-dwelling birds have rounded bodies, small crests, and short tails. They generally occur in small groups called coveys. Quails forage secretively in grasslands and on the forest floor, flying only in short bursts to escape when threatened. Generally difficult to observe, they often reveal their presence with loud, rollicking calls. As with cracids (p. 36), the quails of NCA face the twin threat of hunting and habitat loss. **9 species (6 genera)**

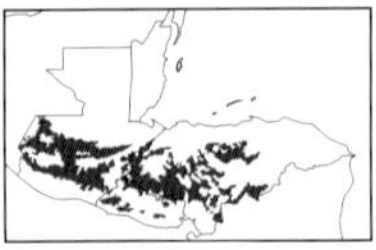

BUFFY-CROWNED WOOD-PARTRIDGE *Dendrortyx leucophrys*

13 in. (33 cm). Underparts bluish gray; wings chestnut; combination of **buffy white forecrown, supercilium, and throat** is diagnostic; also note relatively **long tail,** red legs, and reddish bare skin around eye. Fairly common locally in NCA; 1,980 to 9,570 ft. (600–2,900 m). Found on ground in semideciduous forest, pine-oak forest, and coffee and tea plantations. Moves in pairs or coveys of 3 to 8 individuals. Secretive and often difficult to observe. Call is a boisterous, repeated *woah-woah-WOAH!-WOAH!-K'WOAH!-K'WOAH!-K'WOAH! . . .* or *K'WOAH!-weet!-K'WOAH!-weet!-K'WOAH!-weet! . . .* ; also chirps when agitated. Mex. to Costa Rica.

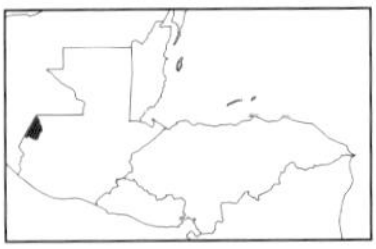

NORTHERN BOBWHITE *Colinus virginianus*

8 in. (21 cm). Male **rufous overall** with dark feather edging and white spotting above; **black head** and **subtle white supercilium**. Female shows large white spots below. Rare and local in w. Guatemala; 2,970 to 6,105 ft. (900–1,850 m). Found on ground in grasslands, savannas, and semiarid open areas. Call is an emphatic *bob-Wheeet!* U.S. to Guatemala.

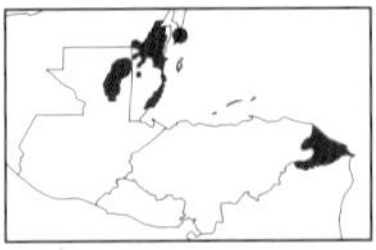

BLACK-THROATED BOBWHITE *Colinus nigrogularis*

8 in. (20 cm). On male, note **bold white scaling below** (scaling on chest and belly edged with black; scaling on sides and flanks edged with rufous); also note **thick black eye line** and **black throat**. Fairly common to common in Belize and e. Honduras, rare and local in n. Guatemala; to 660 ft. (200 m). Occurs in pine savannas, grasslands, and other open areas. Male sometimes calls from an elevated perch. Call is either an emphatic *bob-Wheeet!* (similar to call of Northern Bobwhite) or *bob-Wha'eeet!* Endemic to region.

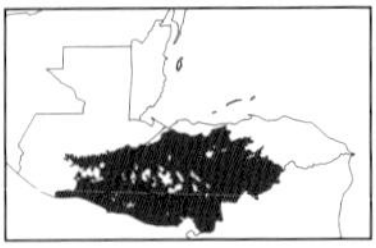

CRESTED BOBWHITE *Colinus cristatus*

8 in. (21 cm). Two subspecies identified in NCA: *C.c. hypoleucus* and *C.c. leucopogon*, both known as Spot-bellied Bobwhite. Subspecies overlap in range, and intergrading can complicate identification. *C.c. hypoleucus* (e. Guatemala to cen. El Salvador) has **white throat and chest**; sides and flanks with brown mottling; **lower belly and undertail coverts with white spots** edged brownish black. *C.c. leucopogon* (Guatemala, Honduras, and e. El Salvador) has **underparts rusty brown with heavy white to buff spotting**; **throat black on male**. Fairly common in NCA; to 5,940 ft. (1,800 m). Occurs in grasslands, pine savannas, agricultural fields, and other semiarid open areas. Male sometimes calls from an elevated perch. Call is a 3-part *whert-were-Wheeet!* or *bob-per-Wheeet!* When agitated, it makes a soft, piping *pip-pip-pip-pip . . .* Guatemala to Brazil.

Bobwhites. *Males of the 3 bobwhite species of NCA are more distinct than females (which are very similar, with tawny supercilium and throat); all have similar calls. They appear to have no range overlap, however, so identifying them shouldn't be a problem.*

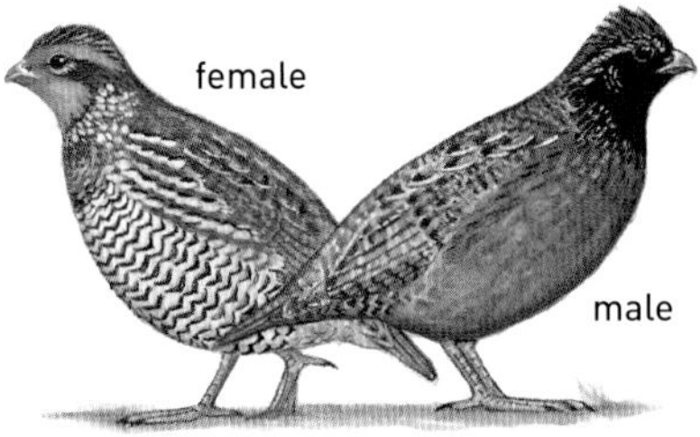

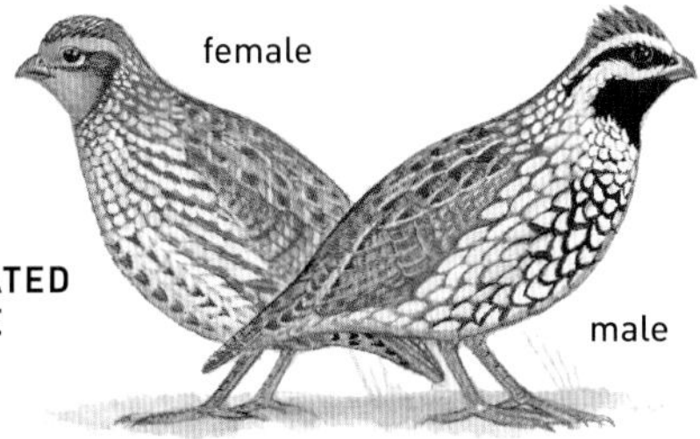

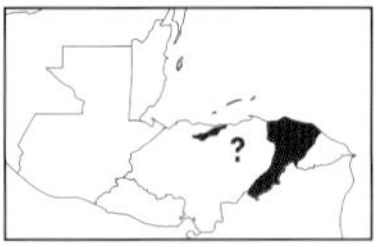

BLACK-EARED WOOD-QUAIL *Odontophorus melanotis*
9.5 in. (24 cm). Sexes similar. **Face and throat black; underparts deep rufous**; bluish bare skin around eye. Rare to uncommon in n. and e. Honduras; to 1,650 ft. (500 m). Found on ground in rainforest. Secretive and difficult to observe. Call is a fast, rollicking *kooLAWK-kooLAWK-kooLAWK-kooLAWK . . .* Honduras to Panama.

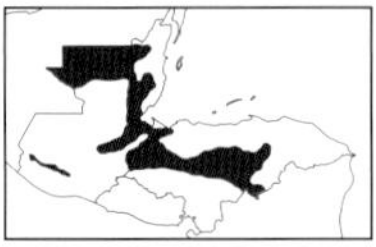

SPOTTED WOOD-QUAIL *Odontophorus guttatus*
9.5 in. (24 cm). On male, **rufous underparts** with **white spots; throat black with white streaking**; rufous orange in crest. Female similar to male but has completely dark crest (lacks rufous orange). Uncommon to fairly common in NCA; 1,650 to 6,600 ft. (500–2,000 m). Found in semideciduous forest, pine-oak forest, and cloud forest. Found on ground in pairs or small coveys. Secretive and difficult to observe; loud call often a key to detection. Call is rollicking (often with multiple birds calling together): *Kool'UP-Cheer'hump-Kool'UP-Cheer'hump-Kool'UP-Cheer'hump . . .*; also makes a low, mournful whistle. Mex. to Panama.

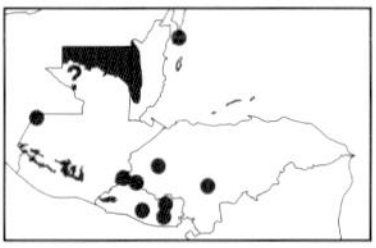

SINGING QUAIL *Dactylortyx thoracicus*
8.5 in. (22 cm). On male, **supercilium and throat tawny orange**; underparts olive gray with fine whitish streaking. On female, **supercilium and throat gray; underparts rufous**. Uncommon to fairly common locally in Guatemala, Honduras, and El Salvador; rare in Belize; 800 to 9,405 ft. (250–2,850 m). Found in mature semideciduous forest, pine-oak forest, and cloud forest. Found on ground, almost always in pairs or small coveys. Secretive and difficult to observe; loud call often a key to detection. Call begins slowly with low, mournful whistles and escalates to a fast, rollicking finale (often with multiple birds calling together): *weeuu-weeuu-weeuu-weeuu-weu'u'u'u-Pwr'r'r'e'e'e'e-Pwr'r'r'r'e'e'e'e-PEEP'tierra!-PEEP'tierra!-PEEP'tierra!-PEEP'tierra!*; also makes a low, mournful (and slightly trilled) *peeuuu'r'r'r'r'r*. Mex. to Honduras.

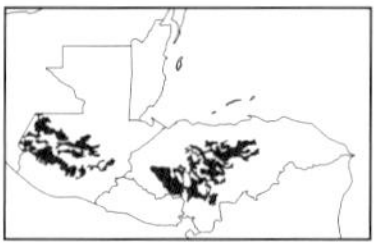

OCELLATED QUAIL *Cyrtonyx ocellatus*
8.5 in. (22 cm). On male, **face pattern is distinctive; rounded head has slight crest in back**; tawny spotting on upper chest and sides of neck. Female drab brown overall; facial pattern reminiscent of male. Rare to locally uncommon in NCA; 2,475 to 10,065 ft. (750–3,050 m). Found on ground in pine savannas, pine-oak forest, grasslands, and abandoned fields. Almost always in pairs. Secretive and difficult to observe. Seldom calls; call is a long, quavering, descending, high-pitched whistle; also sings *tee-tee-teu-teu'teu* (descends in pitch toward the end). Endemic to region.

TAWNY-FACED QUAIL *Rhynchortyx cinctus*
8 in. (20 cm). On male, note **bright tawny-orange face** with bold eye line; crown dark brown; **chest gray**. On female, supercilium and throat whitish; chest tawny brown. Rare to uncommon in n. and e. Honduras; to 2,475 ft. (750 m). Pairs and small coveys found on ground in rainforest. Secretive and difficult to observe. Call is a series of low, soft, mournful whistles followed by a 2-part element: *whaaao!-whaaao!-whaaao!-whaaao!-wee'ear-wee'ear-wee'ear-whaaao! . . .* Honduras to Ecuador.

BLACK-EARED WOOD-QUAIL
SPOTTED WOOD-QUAIL
SINGING QUAIL
female
male
OCELLATED QUAIL
female
male
TAWNY-FACED QUAIL
female
male

GREBES

PODICIPEDIDAE (Order: Podicipediformes). Small to medium-sized aquatic birds with rounded bodies and thin necks. Grebes have large lobed toes ideal for swimming, but they are virtually unable to walk because their legs are set so far back on their bodies. Skilled divers, they feed on aquatic vegetation, small fish, and amphibians. They construct floating platform nests out of muddy vegetation. Despite their size and short, rounded wings, grebes are good fliers capable of making long-distance migrations. **4 species (3 genera)**

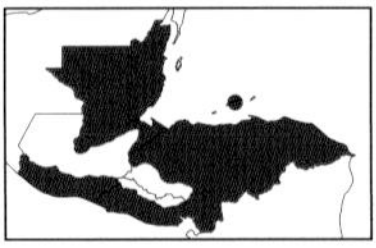

LEAST GREBE *Tachybaptus dominicus*

9 in. (23 cm). Smallest grebe in NCA. **Slate gray overall** with **puffy white undertail coverts**; note thin dark bill and **yellow eyes**. Fairly common on both slopes; to 4,920 ft. (1,500 m). Prefers secluded areas of aquatic habitats; found on lakes, ponds, streams, and tree-lined rivers. Call is a churring rattle (similar to but shorter than call of Ruddy Crake [p. 106]); also makes a nasal, piercing *weeenk!* Juvenile makes soft, high-pitched begging notes: *psii-psii-psii-psii-psii-psii-psii-psii . . .* U.S. and Caribbean to Argentina.

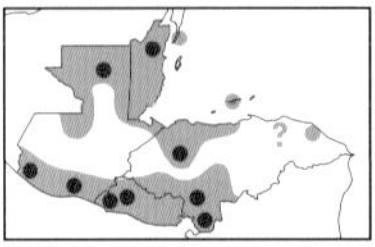

PIED-BILLED GREBE *Podilymbus podiceps*

12 in. (31 cm). Breeding adult has brown body with rusty highlights; neck washed with silver gray; throat black; **stout silvery bill with black band**. On nonbreeding adult, body, neck, and head brown with rusty highlights; throat whitish; creamy bill lacks black band. Resident populations joined by winter visitors and transients (Aug.–May). Fairly common on Caribbean Slope, locally uncommon on Pacific Slope (where mainly winter visitors occur); to 6,560 ft. (2,000 m). Found on lakes, ponds, reservoirs, and lagoons. Generally quite confiding; feeds in the open. Call is a nasal, agitated *pek!-pek!-pek!-pek!-pek!-pek!-pek! . . .* ; also a low *caow—caow—caow—caow-caow-caow-caow-caow-caow—caow—caow—caow—caow—caow* (accelerates, then trails off). Canada to Argentina.

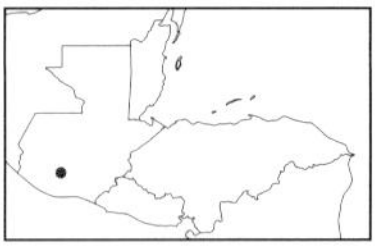

ATITLAN GREBE *Podilymbus gigas*

14.5 in. (37 cm). Extinct. Similar to Pied-billed Grebe, but was larger and flightless, and had a heavier, stout bill. Found only on Lake Atitlán, Guatemala (5,090 ft./1,550 m). Several factors contributed to this species' extinction, beginning with the introduction of black bass (*Micropterus* spp.) to Lake Atitlán in 1958. The bass were introduced to boost tourism, but the predatory bass competed with the grebes for small native fish. During the 1970s and 1980s, shoreline development and water pollution damaged the reeds used by grebes for nesting. The massive 1976 earthquake led to a permanent drop in water levels, and ultimately the grebe could not survive the many threats it faced. The last confirmed sighting was in 1986.

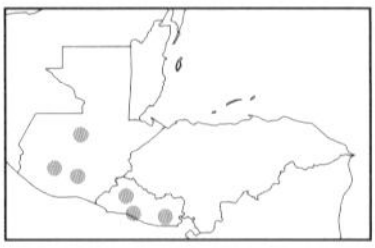

EARED GREBE *Podiceps nigricollis*

12 in. (31 cm). Note **peaked crown** and red eyes. Breeding adult black with rusty sides; broad fan of golden plumes behind eye is suggestive of ears. Nonbreeding adult has blackish upperparts, hindneck, and crown; **broad white malar stripe extends to back of neck**. Winter visitor (Oct.–late Mar.). Rare in Guatemala and El Salvador (records in NCA have decreased drastically since the 1980s); to 5,090 ft. (1,550 m). Found on lakes, ponds, reservoirs, and lagoons. Generally silent in NCA. Canada (breeding) to El Salvador (winter); also in Old World, where known as Black-necked Grebe.

LEAST
GREBE
nonbreeding
PIED-BILLED
GREBE
nonbreeding
ATITLAN
GREBE
EARED
GREBE
breeding
nonbreeding

PIGEONS

COLUMBIDAE (Order: Columbiformes). In general, pigeons and doves are small (doves) to medium-sized (pigeons) birds, with plump, rounded bodies, small heads, and short tails. They feed mostly on fruit, seeds, flowers, and young leaves, and have large crops for food storage. Pigeons have strong, falconlike flight. Calls are often low-pitched whistles of only a few syllables. The columbids of NCA are a diverse group, with both forest-dwelling species and species of open country. Some species occur in large flocks, while others are solitary or in pairs. **22 species (9 genera)**

ROCK PIGEON (FERAL PIGEON) *Columba livia*

13 in. (33 cm). The common city pigeon. Highly variable; of the many color morphs, the closest to original wild plumage is gray overall with dark purplish head and neck, **iridescent green patch on neck**, and **2 wide black wing bars**. Common in NCA; to 8,200 ft. (2,500 m). Found near human habitation (many individuals are only semiferal); forages on ground and on rooftops. Generally in flocks, but may be solitary; often glides with wings held in deep V. Call is a deep, slightly reedy *whoooooa* (often repeated). Introduced. Cosmopolitan (native to Eurasia).

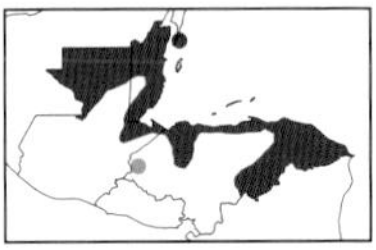

PALE-VENTED PIGEON *Patagioenas cayennensis*

12.5 in. (32 cm). Back, shoulder, and chest washed rufous purple; head grayish; **belly and vent whitish**. Distinguished from Red-billed Pigeon by **dark bill** (yellow on Red-billed) and paler underparts. Fairly common on Caribbean Slope; to 2,460 ft. (750 m). Found in towns, cities, and open country; often perches on wires and in trees. Solitary or in pairs. Call is a 3-part *who-cooks-youuu?* (typically 3 notes; similar to call of Red-billed Pigeon, but lacks extra note). Mex. to Argentina.

RED-BILLED PIGEON *Patagioenas flavirostris*

13 in. (33 cm). **Head, chest, and shoulder purplish rufous**. Distinguished from Pale-vented Pigeon by **yellow bill with red base** (dark in Pale-vented) and darker underparts. Fairly common on both slopes; to 5,910 ft. (1,800 m). Found at edges of semideciduous forest, pine savanna, plantations, and other open habitat; also occurs in cities and towns; perches at upper levels. Solitary or in pairs. Call is fairly low *whooooa—woa-woa'wo-whooo* (typically 4–5 notes; similar to call of Pale-vented Pigeon, but with extra note). U.S. to Costa Rica.

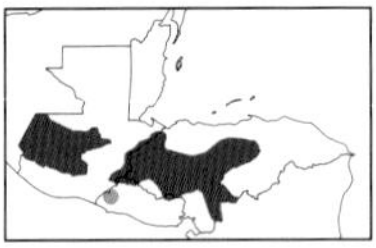

BAND-TAILED PIGEON *Patagioenas fasciata*

14 in. (36 cm). A large, grayish pigeon distinguished by narrow **white band on nape** and **yellow bill with dark tip**. Fairly common on both slopes; 2,460 to 9,510 ft. (750–2,900 m) but generally above 5,580 ft. (1,700 m). Found in pine-oak forest and pine savanna; often flies in small flocks of 5 to 15 individuals. Call is a low *woooo-woo'whoo-woo'whoo*; or *woooo-woooo-woooo* . . . Canada to Argentina.

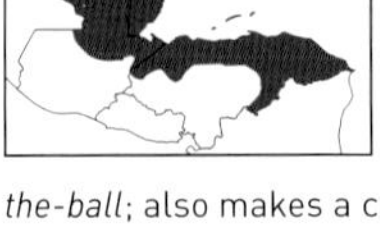

SHORT-BILLED PIGEON *Patagioenas nigrirostris*

11.5 in. (29 cm). Overall plumage a **soft reddish brown**; wings and tail darker; **short black bill**. Uncommon to fairly common on Caribbean Slope; to 5,910 ft. (1,800 m). Perches at midlevels to canopy in rainforest interior; generally shy and difficult to see. Solitary or in pairs. Call is loud, fairly low *who-kicks-the-ball*; also makes a catlike purring. Mex. to Colombia.

ROCK PIGEON

feral pigeons have variable plumage

PALE-VENTED PIGEON

RED-BILLED PIGEON

BAND-TAILED PIGEON

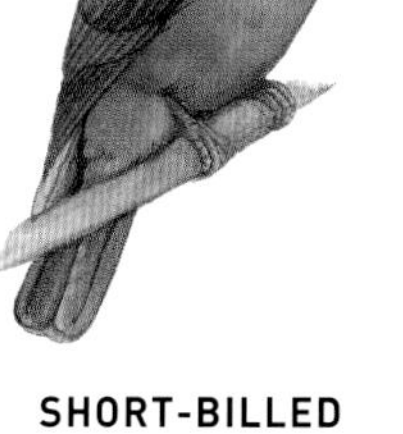

SHORT-BILLED PIGEON

MORE PIGEONS, QUAIL-DOVES, AND A GROUND-DOVE

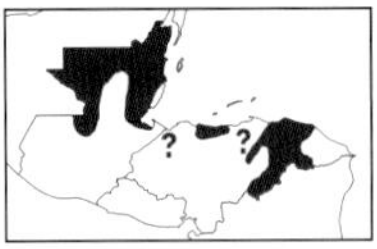

SCALED PIGEON *Patagioenas speciosa*

13 in. (33 cm). **Heavy scaling on neck and underparts is diagnostic**; bill red with yellow tip. Uncommon to fairly common locally on Caribbean Slope; to 2,950 ft. (900 m). Often perches and forages in canopy of rainforest interior, semideciduous woodlands, and occasionally in pine savanna; solitary or in pairs. Call is a low, 3-note *whoooooa'whooo-weeuuuu*; also makes a faster *who'who-whooooo* and a 2-note *who'whoooooo*. Mex. to Argentina.

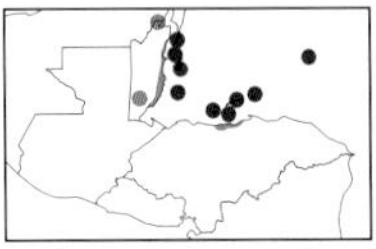

WHITE-CROWNED PIGEON *Patagioenas leucocephala*

14 in. (36 cm). Dark grayish blue overall with contrasting **white crown**; iridescent green scaling on hindneck. NCA resident populations appear to migrate locally; uncommon to fairly common on islands and cayes of Belize and Honduras (some localities late Feb.–mid-Oct.), rare (Honduras) to uncommon (Belize) winter visitor on mainland (Nov.–Feb.), but some birds may commute to and from mainland during breeding period (a few summer records from mainland Belize); to 660 ft. (200 m). Found in coastal scrub, gardens, around towns; often perches at tops of trees or on telephone poles. Call is a low, muddled *whooooa-who-hoooo*; also makes a low, strong purring. Caribbean islands, Yucatán (Mex.), and Caribbean coast of Central America.

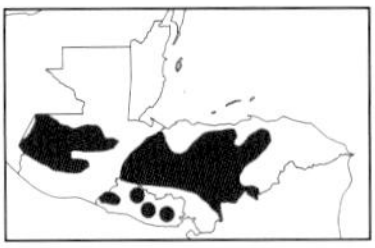

WHITE-FACED QUAIL-DOVE *Zentrygon albifacies*

12 in. (31 cm). Adult has **purplish bronze wings and back**, **buff-gray scaling on nape and sides of neck**. Juvenile has dark barring above and below; scaling less obvious on nape and neck. Uncommon to fairly common in interior highlands on both slopes from 4,920 to 8,200 ft. (1,500–2,500 m); more rarely, found as low as 1,640 ft. (500 m). Forages on ground in pine-oak forest, cloud forest, semideciduous forest, and (less commonly) coffee plantations. Solitary. Call, often given from a midlevel perch, is a low, slightly rising *weeuuuuuu* repeated every 4 sec. (similar to call of Ruddy Quail-Dove, but is longer, slower, and slightly lower-pitched; most similar to Gray-chested Dove [p. 52], but little or no range overlap). Mex. to Nicaragua.

RUDDY QUAIL-DOVE *Geotrygon montana*

9.5 in. (24 cm). **Male has dark ruddy-bronze upperparts**; iridescent pink on nape; **cream-colored malar slash**; base of bill and eye-ring red. Female similar to male, but duller brown overall and lacking ruddy-bronze upperparts. Uncommon on Caribbean Slope, rare on Pacific Slope; to 6,400 ft. (1,950 m). Found in rainforest and semideciduous forest, and on plantations. Forages at lower levels; perches at midlevels when calling. Solitary. Call is a low *weeuuuu* repeated every 1.5 to 2 sec. (similar to call of White-faced Quail-Dove, but is shorter, faster, and slightly higher-pitched). Mex. and Caribbean to Argentina.

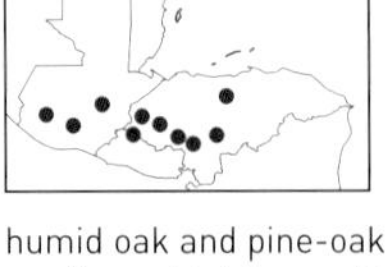

MAROON-CHESTED GROUND-DOVE *Claravis mondetoura*

8 in. (20 cm). Male dark gray-blue above with **purplish red chest**; note **2 purplish blue bands on folded wing** and **white outer tail feathers**. Female tawny-brown overall with redder tail. Very rare and local in NCA; 3,940 to 8,200 ft. (1,200–2,500 m). Found in or around stands of native bamboo at edges of humid oak and pine-oak forests and cloud forest; may be more evident when bamboo is seeding, which is a cyclic event. Forages on ground, but may perch and call at midlevels. Call is a low, 2-syllable *wha'whoop!* (repeated at 1-sec. intervals). Mex. to Bolivia.

SCALED
PIGEON
immature
WHITE-CROWNED
PIGEON
WHITE-FACED
QUAIL-DOVE
female
RUDDY
QUAIL-DOVE
male
MAROON-CHESTED
GROUND-DOVE
male
female

BLUE GROUND-DOVE *Claravis pretiosa*

8.5 in. (22 cm). Male **grayish blue overall** with conspicuous purple spotting on folded wing. Female similarly patterned, but **tawny-brown overall**. Distinguished from other doves by **yellow bill**. Uncommon on Caribbean Slope, rare on Pacific Slope; to 3,280 ft. (1,000 m). Found in semiopen and wooded habitats, including mangroves, plantations, and botanical gardens; perches at all levels. Solitary or in pairs. Call is deep, far-carrying *boop!* (repeated every 1.5 sec. or slower). Mex. to Argentina.

COMMON GROUND-DOVE *Columbina passerina*

6.5 in. (17 cm). Note **dark scaling on chest, nape, and crown** (lacking in Ruddy Ground-Dove). **Pink base to bill** is diagnostic. Male has **pinkish wash to wings, chest, and face** (lacking in female). Fairly common on Pacific Slope, increasingly common in interior dry valleys and on Caribbean Slope; to 7,710 ft. (2,350 m). Found in semiarid to arid habitats, including coastal scrub, thorn forest, and pine savanna. Forages on ground and makes low, short flights when flushed. Solitary or in pairs. Call is a repeated, low, rising *whuuup* (similar to call of Ruddy Ground-Dove, but slower). U.S. and Caribbean to Venezuela.

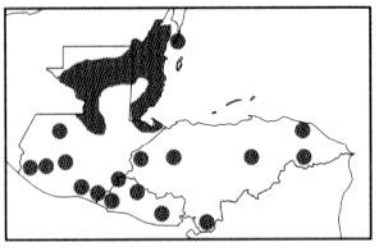

PLAIN-BREASTED GROUND-DOVE *Columbina minuta*

6 in. (15 cm). A very small columbid. Male has whitish head and **unmarked pale gray underparts**. Female similar to male but duller and browner overall. Both sexes similar to female and immature Ruddy Ground-Dove, but have less rufous to wings and tail, and purplish blue (not black) spotting on wings. Uncommon in Belize, rare in Guatemala, Honduras, and El Salvador; to 2,460 ft. (750 m). Found in semiarid open country and along roadsides; forages on ground. Solitary or in pairs. Call is rapid *hu'oop-hu'oop-hu'oop-hu'oop-* . . . Mex. to Paraguay.

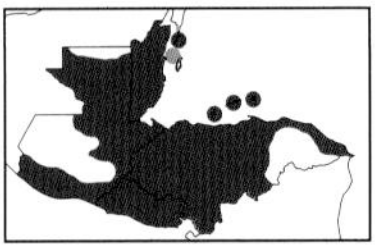

RUDDY GROUND-DOVE *Columbina talpacoti*

6.5 in. (17 cm). On male, **rufous upperparts contrast with gray head**; underparts warm pink; wings have black spots or slashes. Female similar but duller overall. Female and immature similar to Plain-breasted Ground-Dove, but have more rufous on wings and tail, and black (not purplish blue) spotting on wings. Common on both slopes; to 4,430 ft. (1,350 m). Found in open areas and disturbed habitats. Forages on ground in coastal scrub, thorn forest, farmland, cities, and towns. Solitary or in pairs, sometimes flocks of dozens. Call is a low, slightly rising *woo'up-woo'up-woo'up-woo'up* . . . (similar to call of Common Ground-Dove, but faster). Mex. to Argentina.

INCA DOVE *Columbina inca*

8.5 in. (22 cm). A small columbid with a relatively **long tail** and **distinctive scaling over entire body**; in flight, note rufous primaries and **mostly white outer tail feathers**. Fairly common to common on Pacific Slope and in interior Guatemala and Honduras; absent or vagrant in n. Guatemala and Belize; to 8,040 ft. (2,450 m). Found in arid and semiarid habitats; forages on ground and makes low, short flights when flushed. Usually in pairs or small groups. Calls frequently with a sad *no hope!*; also makes a distinctive rattling sound from wings when flushed. U.S. to Costa Rica.

PLATE 13

BLUE GROUND-DOVE
male
female
COMMON GROUND-DOVE
male
female
male
PLAIN-BREASTED GROUND-DOVE
female
male
RUDDY GROUND-DOVE
female
INCA DOVE

WHITE-TIPPED DOVE *Leptotila verreauxi*

11.5 in. (29 cm). Overall light brown dove with **pinkish wash to hindcrown and nape** (may be difficult to see in deep shade); forecrown and throat whitish; axillaries and wing linings chestnut (visible in flight); eye-ring color mainly red, but some individuals show varying amounts of blue; legs and feet are reddish pink; in flight, **obvious white tips to tail feathers**. Most similar to Caribbean Dove, but lacks rosy wash to side of face and chest, is darker below, has less white in tail, lacks white border at bend of wing, and has less chestnut on the underwing; also note differences in call and range. Common on both slopes (only *Leptotila* dove found on Pacific Slope); to 6,560 ft. (2,000 m). Individuals forage on the ground in semideciduous forest, rainforest, thorn forest, and coffee plantations. Calls from elevated perch at low to midlevels; makes a very low (as if blowing over the top of a bottle), 2-syllable *who'huuuuuuuu*; occasional variations on this call include a higher-pitched, 3-syllable *who-hu'huuuuuuuu*. U.S. to Argentina.

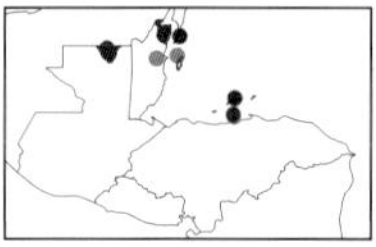

CARIBBEAN DOVE *Leptotila jamaicensis*

11.5 in. (29 cm). Similar to White-tipped Dove, but has **extensive rosy wash to sides of neck and chest**; paler below; note **obvious white border to bend of wing** (absent on White-tipped); more chestnut on underwing; also **more extensive white tips to tail feathers**. Fairly common within its limited NCA range (n. Belize, n. Guatemala, Bay Is.). Found in coastal scrub and forest; perches at low to midlevels. Call is a low, 4-part *who-wheeu'coo-cooooo*. Caribbean islands, Yucatán (Mex.) to n. Belize and Guatemala including Bay Is.

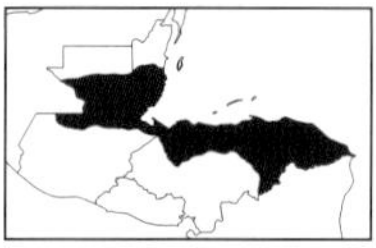

GRAY-CHESTED DOVE *Leptotila cassini*

10.5 in. (27 cm). Distinguished from other *Leptotila* doves in NCA by **golden brown nape and hindcrown** and **dark gray chest**; shows the least amount of white in tail of the NCA *Leptotila* doves. Fairly common on Caribbean Slope; to 4,590 ft. (1,400 m). Found in rainforest and adjacent clearings; forages on ground and perches at low to midlevels. Solitary or in pairs. Call is a low, drawn-out *weeeuuuuuu* (repeated every 3.5 to 4 sec.). Mex. to Colombia.

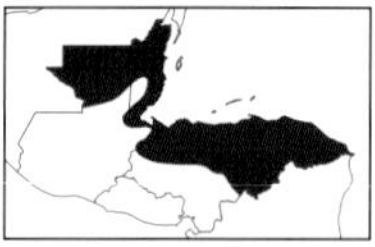

GRAY-HEADED DOVE *Leptotila plumbeiceps*

10.5 in. (27 cm). **Gray wash to crown and nape** contrasts with **buffy cheeks and chest**; white in tail tips is less extensive than on White-tipped Dove. Uncommon to fairly common on Caribbean Slope; to 4,920 ft. (1,500 m). Found in rainforest; perches at lower to midlevels. Solitary. Call is a low, short *wheeuu* (repeated every 1.5 to 2 sec.). Mex. to Colombia.

Leptotila. *A genus of similarly plumaged, medium-sized, terrestrial doves. They are generally solitary and are often seen briefly, walking along the edge of shady forest trails or roads. The best key to identifying species is by their calls.*

Tail patterns of Leptotila *doves*

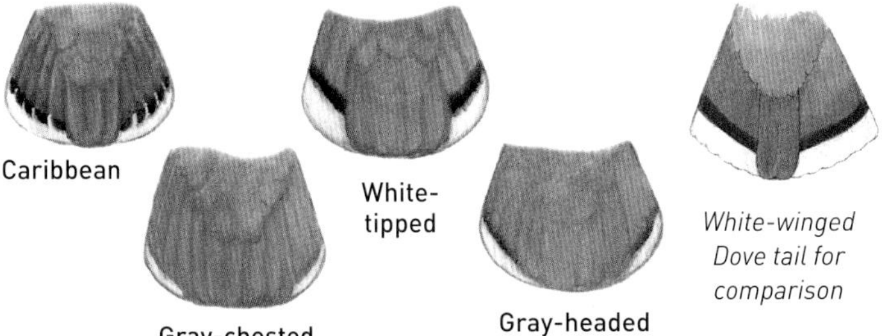

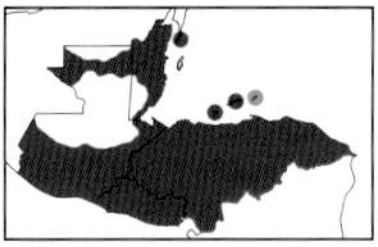

WHITE-WINGED DOVE *Zenaida asiatica*

10.5 in. (27 cm). **White crescent on wing** (also visible on folded wing; Mourning Dove does not show white wing); iridescent pink tones on nape and upper back; black slash on neck; **bluish orbital skin**. Common on both slopes (less common in n. Guatemala and ne. Honduras); to 9,020 ft. (2,750 m). Found at edge of open unforested habitats, and in cities and towns; forages on ground and perches at all levels. Large flocks (more than 50 individuals) are often seen flying to feeding sites at dawn. Call is a frequently heard *who-huuu-who—who-huuu-who—huuuuu-who—huuuuu*; or a *who-cooks-for-youuu?* U.S. to Panama.

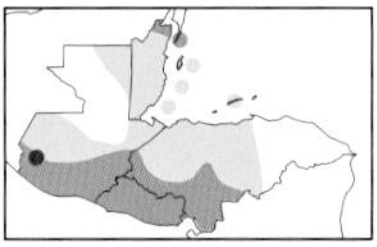

MOURNING DOVE *Zenaida macroura*

11 in. (28 cm). Somewhat similar to White-winged Dove, but lacks the white crescents in wings; shows **large black spots on folded wing**; **tail pointed** with broad white tips. Locally common winter visitor on both slopes (mid-Oct.–Apr., but records from all months in Guatemala where breeding status unclear); to 10,500 ft. (3,200 m). Found in arid and semiarid habitats, including pine savanna, pine-oak forest, clearings, and agricultural fields. Large flocks of hundreds may be encountered during the nonbreeding season. Call is a low, mournful *weeeuuu-huuuu!-whooo-who'who*; also makes a distinctive whistling sound in flight. Canada to Panama.

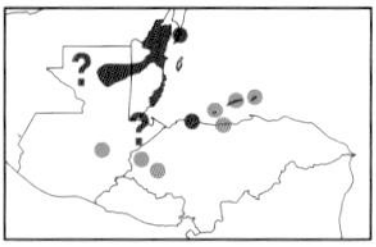

EURASIAN COLLARED-DOVE *Streptopelia decaocto*

12.5 in. (32 cm). A **large pale columbid**; note dark primaries and base to tail; **thin black band on nape**. On immature, pale edging gives scaled effect on wing coverts. Recently colonized mainland and some cayes in Belize, n. Guatemala, and north coast of Honduras, including Bay Is. Likely to colonize new areas soon. Found in urban and agricultural areas; perches on power lines and rooftops, forages on ground. Call is fairly low *whooa-wooooo-who* (repeated); also makes a grating, catlike *rhheeaaaa*. Introduced. U.S. and Caribbean islands to NCA (native to Eurasia).

CUCULIDAE (Order: Cuculiformes). A family of arboreal and terrestrial species. Most cuckoos have long tails and rounded wings, and all have zygodactyl feet (2 toes forward and 2 toes backward, like parrots). Three species make long-distance migrations. Cuckoos are aggressive feeders that consume insects, fruit, bird eggs, nestlings, and small reptiles and mammals; the anis are also known for picking ticks off the backs of cattle. Several species are quite secretive and difficult to observe. Their vocalizations range from simple whistles and moans to drawn-out cackles. **11 species (8 genera)**

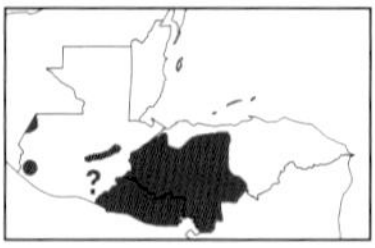

LESSER GROUND-CUCKOO *Morococcyx erythropygus*

10.5 in. (27 cm). A striking bird when seen clearly. **Underparts rich tawny**; **rich iridescent blue behind eye** bordered in black; **bill mostly yellow**. Fairly common on both slopes; up to 6,070 ft. (1,850 m) but less common above 4,920 ft. (1,500 m). Found in understory (on or near ground) of thorn forest and semideciduous forest; also occurs in pine savanna and scrub. Secretive; very difficult to see well, vocalizes infrequently. Call is reminiscent of an overly eager referee whistle: *WEER-WEER-WEER-WEER-WEER-Wee'tah-Wee'tah-Wee'tah—Wee'tah—Wee'tah—Wee'tah——Wee'tah* (slows at the end); also makes a single mournful whistle (*weuuur*). Mex. to Costa Rica.

WHITE-WINGED
DOVE
MOURNING
DOVE
EURASIAN
COLLARED-DOVE
LESSER
GROUND-CUCKOO

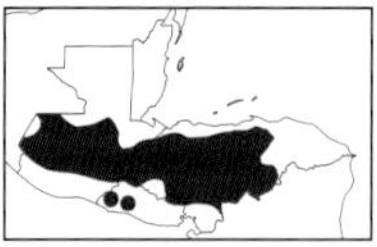

LESSER ROADRUNNER *Geococcyx velox*

18 in. (46 cm). **Upperparts streaked**; underparts tawny buff with streaking on chest and belly; crest may be lowered; note **very long, graduated tail**. Uncommon on both slopes; 980 to 7,220 ft. (300–2,200 m). Found in understory, at edge, or along roads within arid to semiarid thorn forest; pine savanna; or within pine-oak forest. Forages on the ground. Calls from low perch with a low, mournful *WOOA-WOOA-Whoo-Who-whoo* (as if crying out in pain). Mex. to Nicaragua.

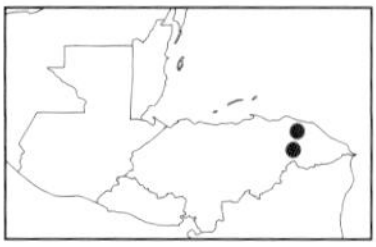

RUFOUS-VENTED GROUND-CUCKOO *Neomorphus geoffroyi*

19 in. (48 cm). Not likely to be mistaken. Large bodied with **long tail**, long legs, and **short spiky crest**; also note **black chest band** and stout yellowish bill. Very rare in e. Honduras; to 2,950 ft. (900 m). Found on ground in rainforest interior; often follows army ant swarms. Extremely shy and difficult to observe. Call is a low, mournful wail: *Weuuuuuuuoooooo!* (rises slightly at end). Also makes loud, sharp bill snaps. Honduras to Brazil.

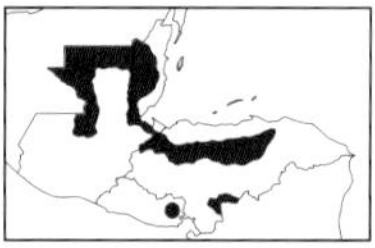

PHEASANT CUCKOO *Dromococcyx phasianellus*

15 in. (38 cm). Similar to smaller Striped Cuckoo, but has **spotted breast** (unmarked in Striped); darker above, **long tail graduated and often flared** (narrower and shorter on Striped) with white tips on undertail; maxilla is dark. Rare to uncommon on both slopes; to 4,920 ft. (1,500 m). Forages at lower and middle levels of thorn forest and semideciduous forest; also occurs in pine savanna and more humid habitats, but nearly always in dense undergrowth; perches higher when singing. Secretive; seldom seen or heard. Call is similar to longer call of Striped Cuckoo, but ends in a trill: *tree-tree-tree'e'e'e'e-up*. Also makes a mechanical, wind-up toylike noise while performing display on ground. Mex. to Argentina.

STRIPED CUCKOO *Tapera naevia*

11.5 in. (29 cm). Creamy buff overall with paler underparts and **heavy blackish streaking on back**; note **short rufous crest** and **black mask**; bill mostly yellow. Similar to larger Pheasant Cuckoo, but has unmarked breast, paler above, and narrower tail with small white tips. Uncommon on both slopes; to 5,250 ft. (1,600 m). Found in thorn forest, scrubby areas, plantations, and agricultural fields. Somewhat secretive, often detected first by voice. Calls from an exposed perch with a high-pitched, monotone, whistled *tree-tree*; also makes a longer, rising *tree-tree-Tree-Tree'tu* (similar to call of Pheasant Cuckoo, but does not end with a trill). Mex. to Argentina.

SQUIRREL CUCKOO *Piaya cayana*

18 in. (46 cm). **Rufous above** and gray below with pink wash to head and upper chest; **long, graduated tail**; undertail black with broad white tips; bill, lores, and orbital skin yellow-green. Common on both slopes; to 7,220 ft. (2,200 m). Perches at mid-levels of rainforest, semideciduous forest, and thorn forest; also occurs in mangroves. Vocalizes often; common call is an emphatic *kick!-burrr*; also makes a single *medar!*; song is a repeated, piping *medar—pip-pip-pip-pip-pip-pip-pip-pip…* (series lasts up to 30 sec.). Mex. to Argentina.

LESSER ROADRUNNER

RUFOUS-VENTED GROUND-CUCKOO

PHEASANT CUCKOO

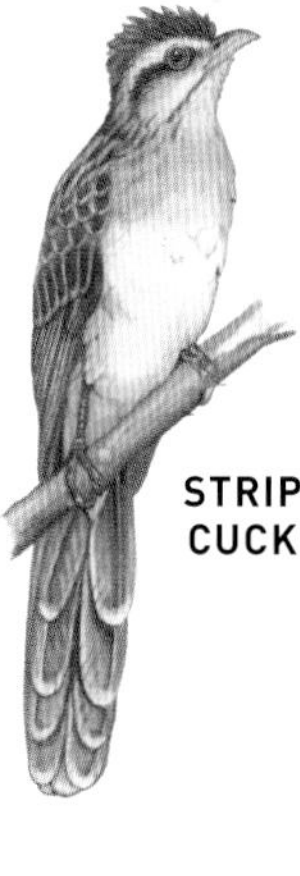

STRIPED CUCKOO

SQUIRREL CUCKOO

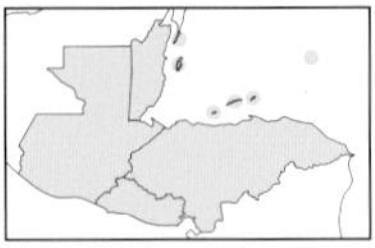

YELLOW-BILLED CUCKOO *Coccyzus americanus*

12 in. (31 cm). Distinguished from Mangrove Cuckoo and Black-billed Cuckoo by combination of **rufous in primaries** (visible on folded wing), **broad white tips to undertail**, and **mostly yellow mandible**. Note clean white underparts and yellow eye-ring. Uncommon transient in region (both slopes), including Swan and Bay Is. (Apr.–mid-June; late Aug.–late Nov.), but less common on Pacific Slope in spring; very rare or irregular winter visitor (Dec. and Jan.); to 9,350 ft. (2,850 m). Found at all levels in rainforest, riparian forest, semideciduous forest, mangroves, woodlots, and wooded fencerows. Generally silent away from breeding grounds. U.S. to Argentina.

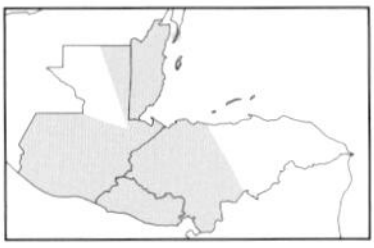

BLACK-BILLED CUCKOO *Coccyzus erythropthalmus*

12 in. (31 cm). Similar to Yellow-billed Cuckoo and Mangrove Cuckoo, but has **thin, all-dark bill** and **red eye-ring**; also note **narrow whitish tips to undertail**. Transient (Apr.–May, Sept.–Nov.). Uncommon on Caribbean Slope, rare on Pacific Slope; to 9,350 ft. (2,850 m). Found at all levels in rainforest, semideciduous forest, mangroves, and plantations. Generally silent in migration. Canada to Bolivia.

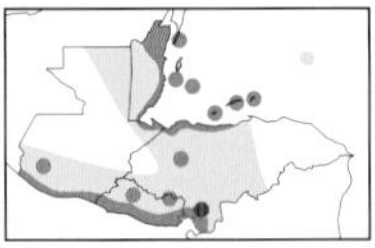

MANGROVE CUCKOO *Coccyzus minor*

12 in. (31 cm). Most similar to Yellow-billed Cuckoo but is **tawny buff below** (not white); distinguish from Black-billed Cuckoo by yellow mandible, tawny buff underparts, broad white tips to undertail, and yellow eye-ring. Uncommon transient and winter visitor on both slopes; rare and local breeder; to 4,920 ft. (1,500 m). Generally found near the coast in semideciduous forest, thorn forest, scrubby areas, and mangroves; also plantations and wooded fencerows. Usually quite secretive, and vocalizes infrequently. Call is a chattering *ke'ke'ke'ke'ke'k'r'r'rrrrrr*; also makes a longer *k'k'k'k'ke'ke'ke'ke'ke'ke'ke'coh'coh'hhh*. U.S. to Suriname; also in Caribbean.

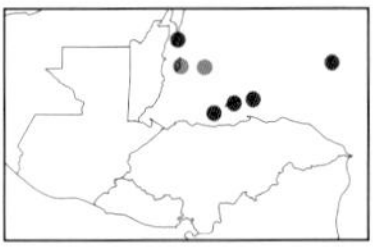

SMOOTH-BILLED ANI *Crotophaga ani*

14 in. (36 cm). Glossy black overall with long, graduated tail. Distinguished from smaller Groove-billed Ani by **more highly arched culmen that lacks grooves**; also note range difference. Fairly common on Swan Is. and Bay Is. (Honduras) and cayes of Belize; mainly winter records from Belize, but breeding suspected on Ambergris Caye; to 660 ft. (200 m). Found in open fields, coastal scrub, and at edge of disturbed forest and mangroves. Call is a loud, wailing *Rheeeeyy-up!* (reminiscent of a military siren). U.S. to Argentina; also in Caribbean.

GROOVE-BILLED ANI *Crotophaga sulcirostris*

13 in. (33 cm). Very similar to larger Smooth-billed Ani, but has **less-arched culmen** and **grooves on maxilla** (grooves absent on immature); also note range difference. Common on both slopes; to 6,730 ft. (2,050 m). Forages at lower and middle levels of thorn forest; also found in disturbed habitats and open areas, even in cities. Often in small groups. Call is an emphatic *Peet-weur!* (with a slight bell-like quality); also makes a *Peet-jeu!* U.S. to Peru.

Groove-billed Anis on barbed wire fence

SWIFTS I

APODIDAE (Order: Apodiformes). Although superficially similar to swallows (p. 296), swifts are related to hummingbirds (p. 64). Among the best fliers in the world, they make rapid and frequent turns and dives. Swifts' wide gapes enable them to consume insects on the wing. They use their small feet to cling to vertical surfaces, but they cannot walk. Many species nest in tree hollows or behind waterfalls. Most often observed high in the air, this group is notoriously difficult to identify. Flight behavior and vocalizations are useful keys to identification. **10 species (5 genera)**

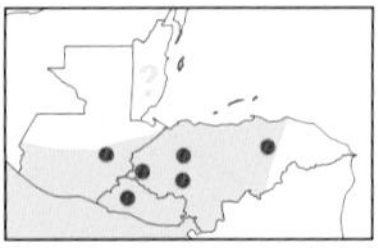

BLACK SWIFT *Cypseloides niger*

6 in. (15 cm). **Pale edging on vent** and inconspicuous **pale lores**. In flight, sharp **bend at wrist** gives wings a swept-back appearance. Flight profile is similar to that of Chestnut-collared Swift; often glides or soars without flapping while tail is held closed (may show small cleft). Plumage blacker and wings longer than Chestnut-collared Swift's; also similar to White-chinned Swift, but forehead whiter and chin darker; note vocalization differences. Uncommon transient throughout; status of breeding populations (*costaricensis*) in NCA uncertain (but reported Apr.–Nov.); to 9,350 ft. (2,850 m). Northern populations (*borealis*) pass through the region, including well offshore. Usually near gorges, river valleys, or behind waterfalls where it nests. Calls (*borealis*) include rich *pit* or *chit* notes in flight, or a longer series *pit'pit'pit'pit'pit'peet'see!-pit'pit'pit* . . . Canada (breeding) to Brazil (winter).

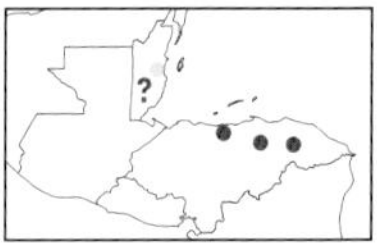

WHITE-CHINNED SWIFT *Cypseloides cryptus*

5.5 in. (14 cm). Similar to Black Swift and Chestnut-collared Swift, but intermediate in size and has **white scaling on chin** and sides of forehead (visible in ideal viewing conditions); also note difference in vocalizations and distribution. Flight profile similar to that of Black Swift, but wings are less pointed; flight more fluttery (less soaring). Apparently rare on Caribbean Slope but status uncertain; better documentation needed; to 9,350 ft. (2,850 m). Call is a hard, scratchy ticking or chattering series: *tzcheet'tzeeet'cheet'cheet'cheet'zeeet'zeeet'zeeet* . . . Mex. to Venezuela.

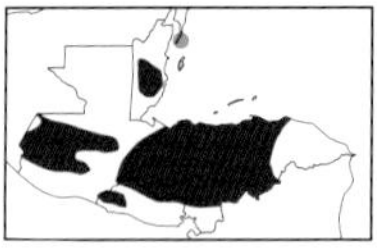

CHESTNUT-COLLARED SWIFT *Streptoprocne rutila*

5 in. (13 cm). On adult male, note **rich chestnut collar** (although backlit birds appear all-dark). Most adult females and juveniles lack chestnut collar. Many individuals appear similar to Black Swift and White-chinned Swift, but are smaller and browner, and have different vocalizations. In flight, often glides. Uncommon resident on both slopes; to 9,350 ft. (2,850 m). Found over semideciduous forest, pine savanna, pine-oak forest, and coffee plantations; generally in areas of varying relief, such as gorges, mountains, and volcanoes. Often in groups up to 80 birds. Call is a thin, electric crackling chatter: *chit'chit'chit'chit'chit'zit'zit'zit'zit'zit'* . . . Mex. to Bolivia.

WHITE-COLLARED SWIFT *Streptoprocne zonaris*

8.5 in. (22 cm). The second largest swift in the world. Black overall with **bold white collar**; in flight, note falconlike wings and notched tail. On juvenile, forecollar is reduced to a narrow band of whitish scaling. Fairly common on both slopes; to 8,200 ft. (2,500 m). Found over cloud forest, semideciduous forest, thorn forest, pine-oak forest, pine savanna, and coffee plantations. May travel many kilometers from roosting site in search of prey (wasps). Often seen in large, kettling flocks of more than 100 individuals. Mainly soars, flapping occasionally. Call is a series of screams: *pleet-pleet-pleet-PLEET'PLEET'PLEET'PLEET-pleet-pleet-pleet* . . . Mex. to Argentina.

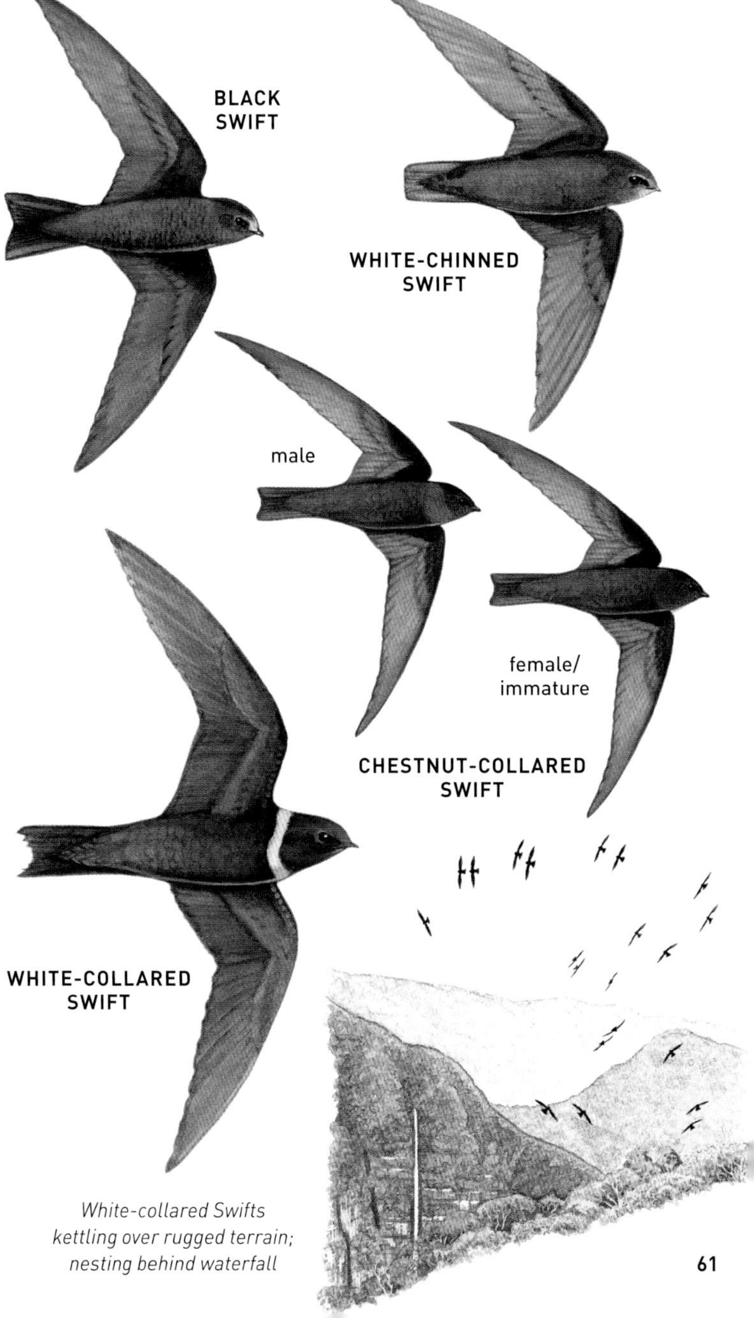

White-collared Swifts kettling over rugged terrain; nesting behind waterfall

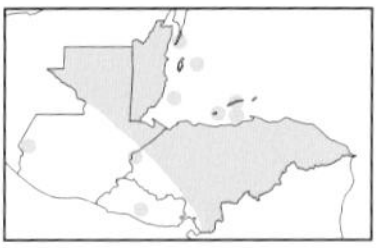

CHIMNEY SWIFT *Chaetura pelagica*

4.5 in. (12 cm). Sooty brown overall with **paler throat**; rapid flight with constant fluttering and intervals of soaring. Similar to Vaux's Swift, but larger, shows little contrast between rump and back; in flight, has slightly longer, pointier, more angled wings, **slower wingbeats**, and longer tail; soars more often. Common transient in most of NCA, rare on parts of Pacific Slope (late Mar.–late Apr., late Sept.–early Nov.); to 4,920 ft. (1,500 m). Migrating flocks are usually small, but may number in the hundreds. Generally silent in migration, but rarely gives a chipping and twittering *tip* call, similar to Vaux's Swift but richer and slower. Canada to Peru.

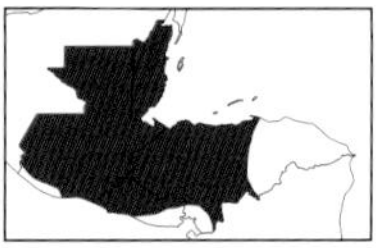

VAUX'S SWIFT *Chaetura vauxi*

4 in. (10 cm). Similar to Chimney Swift, but smaller, has **paler throat and underparts**, and more **contrasting pale rump**; in flight, Vaux's Swift has shorter, stubbier wings; soars less often than Chimney Swift and has **faster wingbeats**. Common on both slopes; resident population is augmented by migrants from the north (mid-Sept.–May); to 9,350 ft. (2,850 m). Found in airspace above any habitat, from woodlands to cities. Often in flocks of dozens. Nests in tree cavities and occasionally in chimneys. Call is a thin, fast twittering (faster than calls of Chimney Swift). AK to Venezuela.

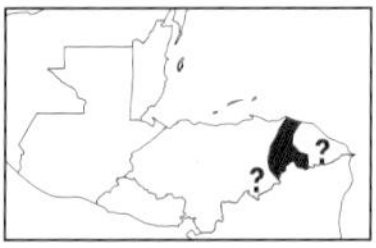

GRAY-RUMPED SWIFT *Chaetura cinereiventris*

4 in. (10 cm). Most obvious feature is **pale gray rump and uppertail coverts**. Uncommon in La Moskitia of e. Honduras. Flies over rainforest and riparian forest; rapid flight with short glides. Call is a rapid twittering series, *tit'tit'tit'tit'tit'tit'tit'tit'tit'tit*. Honduras to Argentina.

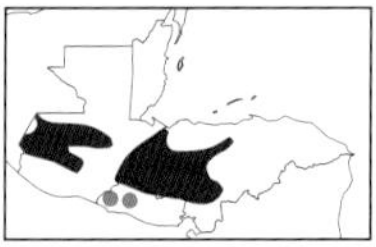

WHITE-THROATED SWIFT *Aeronautes saxatalis*

6 in. (15 cm). A **large** swift; **white throat and belly** are distinctive. Uncommon in NCA; from 1,640 to 8,200 ft. (500–2,500 m). Found over pine-oak forest and near deep gorges, cliffs, and tall waterfalls. Generally in small flocks. Flies high and fast with near constant soaring. Call is a high-pitched, nasal, complaining chatter: *peet!-peet!-peet!-peet!-pzeeet!-pzeeet!-pzeeet!-pzeeet!* . . . Canada to Honduras.

LESSER SWALLOW-TAILED SWIFT *Panyptila cayennensis*

5 in. (13 cm). A lean, angular swift with prominent **white throat**; note **long, deeply forked tail** (often held closed in flight). Similar to Great Swallow-tailed Swift, but much smaller and white trailing edge to wing is reduced or absent; also, prefers more humid habitats and lower elevations. Uncommon in NCA; to 6,230 ft. (1,900 m). Soars over forest and plantations. Flies with quick flaps and short glides. Nest is a hanging basket attached to a cliff overhang or large tree branch. Call is a thin, sometimes buzzy twittering: *pee'pee'pee'pee'zeeet'zeeet'zeeet'zeeet* . . . Mex. to Brazil.

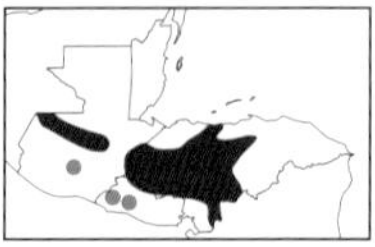

GREAT SWALLOW-TAILED SWIFT *Panyptila sanctihieronymi*

8 in. (20 cm). Similar to Lesser Swallow-tailed Swift, but much larger and has more notable **white trailing edge to wing**; also, prefers drier habitats and higher elevations. Rare in NCA; from 1,640 to 7,870 ft. (500–2,400 m). Patrols skies over cloud forest, pine-oak forest, pine savanna, and scrub. Flies high with frequent long glides. Call is a high-pitched *keel'dee!-keel'dee* . . . (similar to call of Killdeer [p. 116]). Mex. to Nicaragua.

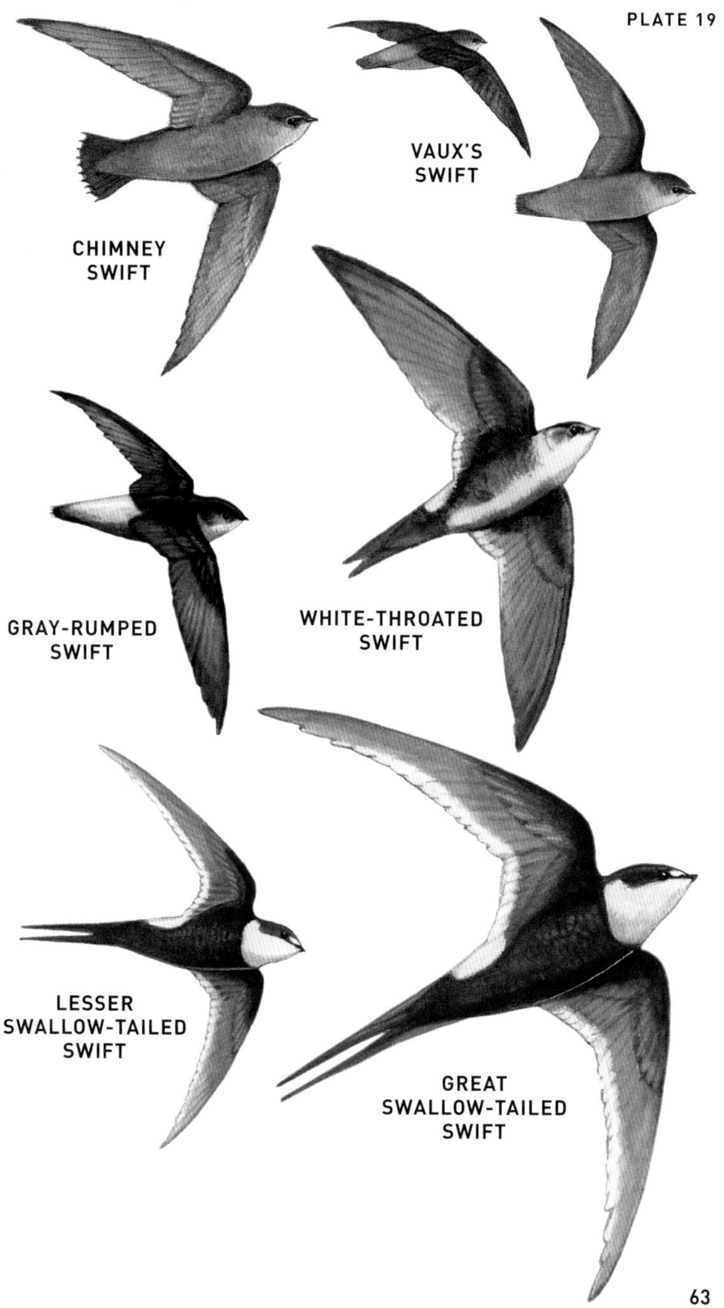
CHIMNEY SWIFT
VAUX'S SWIFT
GRAY-RUMPED SWIFT
WHITE-THROATED SWIFT
LESSER SWALLOW-TAILED SWIFT
GREAT SWALLOW-TAILED SWIFT

LARGE HUMMINGBIRDS

TROCHILIDAE (Order: Apodiformes). A New World family, easily recognized by their small size, brilliant colors, and remarkable flight abilities. Hummingbirds are the only birds capable of flying backward, and they frequently hover in place. They feed on nectar; their bills evolved to fit the shapes of specific flowers they feed from. With extremely high metabolism, hummingbirds are constantly on the move in search of nectar (some species also eat insects). They are active only during the day. Sexual dimorphism is common; males often show spectacular iridescent plumage and eye-catching gorgets (visible in the proper light, but often appearing dark) while females are generally drabber. On the Pacific Slope of NCA, where there are just 2 seasons, the breeding period for most hummingbirds is in Oct. and Nov. after the end of the rainy season, when flowers are most abundant. **45 species (28 genera)**

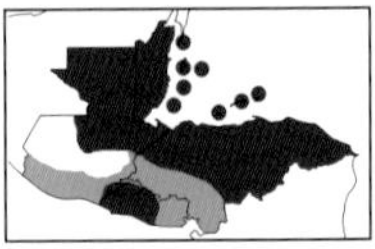

GREEN-BREASTED MANGO *Anthracothorax prevostii*

4.5 in. (12 cm). Male green overall with **blackish blue stripe down throat and center of chest**; note **purple tail** and **decurved bill**. Female and immature **white below** with **dark green stripe from chin to belly**; immature shows buff on side of throat. Fairly common on Caribbean Slope, uncommon winter visitor and local breeding resident on Pacific Slope; to 5,410 ft. (1,650 m). Found in rainforest, semideciduous forest, thorn forest, disturbed forest, and gardens; forages at large flowers and hawks for insects. Often perches high in canopy. Song is a high warble, often given in flight; call is a warbler-like chip. Mex. to Peru.

WHITE-NECKED JACOBIN *Florisuga mellivora*

4.5 in. (12 cm). Male has **iridescent blue hood**, white nape, **pure white belly**, and **mostly white tail**. Female similar to Scaly-breasted Hummingbird (p. 78), but has more distinctive scaling on throat and breast, brighter white on belly, and darker undertail coverts. Fairly common on Caribbean Slope; to 2,460 ft. (750 m). Forages at lower levels in rainforest edge and adjacent clearings, and in gardens. Call is a repeated, high-pitched *tseet*; when perched, also makes a fast *tsip-tsip-tsip-tsip-tsip* . . . Mex. to Brazil.

PLAIN-CAPPED STARTHROAT *Heliomaster constantii*

5 in. (13 cm). Glittering **red gorget** may appear black in poor light. Similar to Long-billed Starthroat, but crown lacks iridescence, has **white postocular stripe** (not spot) and whitish flanks (not grayish green). Uncommon on Pacific Slope; to 6,400 ft. (1,950 m). Found at edge of thorn forest, semideciduous forest, and coastal scrub. Forages at mid to upper levels and at banana flowers; hawks insects. Call is a repeated, ringing *tseeep*. Mex. to Costa Rica.

LONG-BILLED STARTHROAT *Heliomaster longirostris*

4.5 in. (12 cm). **Long straight bill**; on male iridescent **blue crown** and **rose pink gorget** appear dark in poor light; note white tail corners. Female distinguished from male by greenish tones in crown and narrower gorget. Differs from Plain-capped Starthroat by iridescence in crown, **white postocular spot** (not stripe) and grayish green sides (not whitish). Uncommon on both slopes (very rare in Belize); distribution in region is patchy; to 6,070 ft. (1,850 m). Found in disturbed habitat, thorn forests, coastal scrub, coffee plantations, and gardens; in more humid forest on the Caribbean Slope, including rainforest; generally at forest edge. Forages at midlevels to canopy; hawks insects. Call is a squeaky, slightly nasal *tseek*. Mex. to Brazil.

male
immature
female
GREEN-BREASTED
MANGO
female/
immature
male
WHITE-NECKED
JACOBIN
PLAIN-CAPPED
STARTHROAT
LONG-BILLED
STARTHROAT
male

BRONZY HERMIT *Glaucis aeneus*

4 in. (10 cm). Distinguished from Band-tailed Barbthroat by **rufous throat and underparts, rufous in tail**, and more **decurved bill**; note dark submalar stripe. Common in e. Honduras; to 2,460 ft. (750 m). Forages at lower levels at rainforest edge, older disturbed forest, and along riparian corridors. Often visits *Heliconia* and banana plants. Calls include a soft, high-pitched *tseew* or *tseet*; also makes a twittering *tsew'ew'ew'ew'ew'ew'ew'ew*. Honduras to Ecuador.

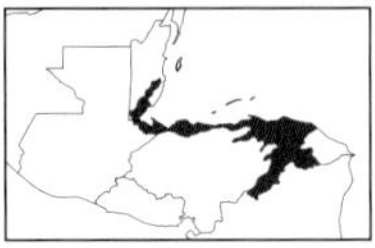

BAND-TAILED BARBTHROAT *Threnetes ruckeri*

4 in. (10 cm). Distinguished from Bronzy Hermit by **dark throat**, gray underparts, **black-and-white tail**, and less decurved bill. Uncommon in Belize and n. Honduras, rare in n. Guatemala; to 1,640 ft. (500 m). Forages at lower levels in rainforest and second-growth thickets, often visiting *Heliconia* and banana plants. Song is a high-pitched series: *sue'e'e'e'e'e'e'e-sisisi-seeee-sue'sue'sue-sweet*. Guatemala to Ecuador.

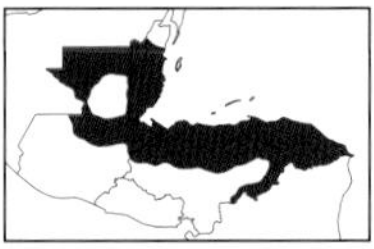

LONG-BILLED HERMIT *Phaethornis longirostris*

6.5 in. (17 cm). **Brownish upperparts** and **long white central tail feathers** are distinctive. Similar to Stripe-throated Hermit, but is much larger and has longer central tail feathers. Fairly common on Caribbean Slope; to 4,920 ft. (1,500 m). Forages at lower levels in lowland and foothill rainforest; forages inside or at forest edge; often visits *Heliconia* and banana plants. Flight call is a loud, squeaky *seeek!* (often heard as it zips by); lekking males perch just a few centimeters aboveground and make a repeated *seeek* or a mixed series of high-pitched notes (*seeek-seet-seeek-seet-saweet-seet . . .*). Mex. to Ecuador.

STRIPE-THROATED HERMIT *Phaethornis striigularis*

4 in. (10 cm). A **small** hermit; **upperparts tawny green**; **pale rufous underparts**; graduated tail is mainly dark with **elongated white central feathers**. Similar to Long-billed Hermit, but is much smaller and has shorter central tail feathers. Fairly common on Caribbean Slope; to 5,250 ft. (1,600 m). Forages at lower levels in rainforest and gardens; flight is slow and methodical. Lekking song is a high-pitched, squeaky *seet-seet-seet-suit-se'saweet'-seet-seet- . . .* or *sweet-sweet-see'aweet-sweet-see'aweet-see'ah'weeee-sweet . . .* Mex. to Ecuador.

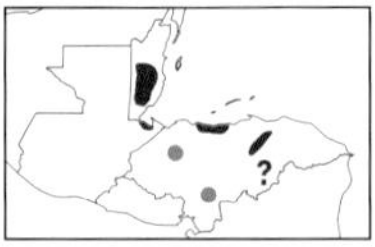

BROWN VIOLETEAR *Colibri delphinae*

4 in. (10 cm). **Brownish overall** with **iridescent purple ear patch**. Uncommon on Caribbean Slope; to 5,410 ft. (1,650 m); on n. coast of Honduras, appears to be an altitudinal migrant, visiting lowlands June–Aug. Forages at midlevels in rainforest. Appears to wander seasonally; may be common at a site and then absent. Song is a loud, fairly rich *t'chip-t'chip-t'chip-t'chip . . .* Mex. to Brazil.

Hermits (genera Glaucis, Threnetes, Phaethornis): *Hermits are known for trap-lining, in which they travel a circuit of the same nectar sources repeatedly. They are also a lekking group, thus small groups of males congregate to sing from nearby perches low in the forest understory. Several species have long central tail feathers and long, decurved bills.*

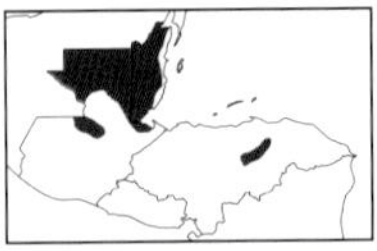

WEDGE-TAILED SABREWING *Campylopterus curvipennis*
5 in. (13 cm). On male, **long graduated tail turquoise-green**; face and underparts gray; **blue-purple crown** visible in good light; note **white postocular spot**. Female similar to male, but has shorter tail with large white tips. All sabrewings are named for the broad sabre-shaped quills of the outer primary feathers of males. Fairly common in n. Guatemala and Belize; also locally in e. Honduras; to 4,590 ft. (1,400 m). Found in semideciduous forest, rainforest, riparian forest, in the interior, at clearings or forest edge; forages and perches at lower and middle levels. Perched call is a rapid, twittering series: *tip-tip-tip-tip-tip-tip-tip'tip'tip'tip'tip'tip'tip'tip-tip-tip-...* (may go on for minutes). Lekking males sing a soft, warbling series of squeaky chips, seeps, and nasal twitters and buzzes. Mex. to Honduras.

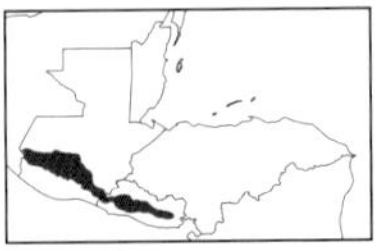

RUFOUS SABREWING *Campylopterus rufus*
5 in. (13 cm). **Underparts rufous**; long black bill is slightly decurved. Similar to Cinnamon Hummingbird (p. 82), but is larger, has all-black bill (not red), green central tail feathers (not rufous), and **white postocular spot**; also note differences in distribution and habitat. Fairly common in the volcanic range of the Pacific Slope; 2,950 to 7,870 ft. (900–2,400 m). Found primarily in oak and pine-oak forest, at edge and in adjacent clearings; generally at lower and middle levels. Call is a sharp, rich *tzip*, sometimes in a rapid machine-gun manner (*tzip-tzip-tz'z'z'z'ip-tzip-tz'z'z'z'ip-tzip . . .*); song (given while perched) is a rich, slightly ringing *tsip-tsip-tsip'tsip-tsip-tsip-tsip . . .* of a different quality from call. Endemic to region.

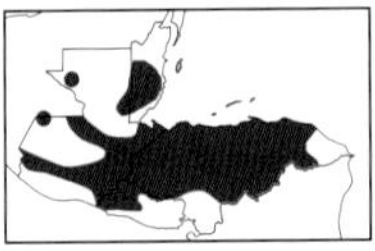

VIOLET SABREWING *Campylopterus hemileucurus*
6 in. (15 cm). A **large** hummingbird. On male, **iridescent purple plumage** is distinctive (may show green on wing coverts and uppertail coverts). Female and immature green above and gray below with purple speckling on throat. Both sexes with **large white patches on outer tail feathers**, white postocular spot, and long **heavily decurved bill**. Uncommon to fairly common on both slopes; to 8,200 ft. (2,500 m). Found in rainforest, riparian forest, semideciduous forest, and gardens; feeds at lower levels, often at banana plants, heliconias, and other ornamentals. Flight call is like rapid machine-gun fire: *tit'it'it-tit'it'it-tit'it'it-tit'it'it . . .* Perched song is a series of sharp, high-pitched squeaks: *sip!-tseeuu!-sip!-sip!-sip!-sip!-tseeuu!-sip! . . .* (as recorded in Guatemala). Mex. to Panama.

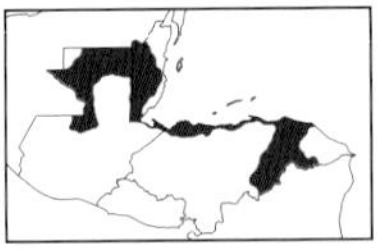

PURPLE-CROWNED FAIRY *Heliothryx barroti*
5 in. (13 cm). A large flashy hummingbird with long tail, unmistakable **clean white underparts**; crown is a glittering purple; female similar but has green forecrown. Rare to uncommon on Caribbean Slope; to 3,770 ft. (1,150 m). Found in edge and interior of rainforest, along streams, and in gardens; forages at midlevels of canopy. Makes quick, erratic flights; often flashes white in tail. Generally silent. Mex. to Ecuador.

WEDGE-TAILED SABREWING
RUFOUS SABREWING
female
VIOLET SABREWING
male
female
male
PURPLE-CROWNED FAIRY

MOUNTAIN HUMMINGBIRDS I

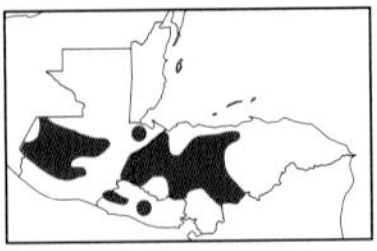

MEXICAN VIOLETEAR *Colibri thalassinus*

4 in. (10 cm). Adult iridescent **green overall** with **purple ear patch**. Immature drabber with buff edging to head and upperparts. Fairly common in highlands of NCA; 1,640 to 11,150 ft. (500–3,400 m). Found in clearings and edge of pine-oak forest and cloud forest; forages at all levels. Sings from a perch with a loud series of chips and twitters with individual or local variation: *sip-tip-sip-tip-sip-ti'chip-sip-ti'chip-sip-tip-ti'chip* . . . Mex. to Nicaragua. This species was formerly known as Green Violetear.

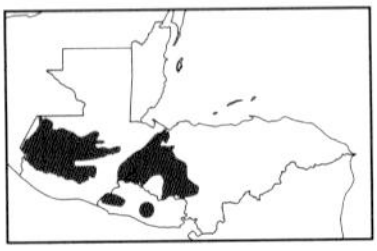

GREEN-THROATED MOUNTAIN-GEM *Lampornis viridipallens*

4.5 in. (12 cm). Sides grayish green; tail dark with **gray outer tail feathers**. Male has iridescent **bluish green scaling on throat** (absent on female). Immature similar to female, but has buff edging to head. In all plumages, similar to Green-breasted Mountain-gem, but no range overlap. Adult male similar to female White-eared Hummingbird (p. 74), but is much larger, and has a dark bill, less scaling on throat, and gray outer tail feathers. Adult female is distinguished from female Amethyst-throated Hummingbird by broader postocular stripe, different tail pattern, and whiter underparts. Fairly common; 2,950 to 8,860 ft. (900–2,700 m). Found in pine-oak forest, cloud forest, and seasonally in coffee plantations; forages at lower and middle levels; often flashes gray outer tail feathers while foraging. Some individuals make altitudinal migrations. Flight call is a thin, buzzy *dzzzzzzrt*; perched call is a high-pitched *seet*; song is a weak, jumbled series of electric buzzes and a plucking guitarlike chatter (sings from a low perch). Endemic to region.

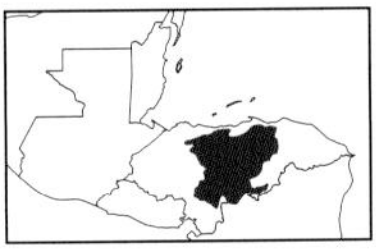

GREEN-BREASTED MOUNTAIN-GEM *Lampornis sybillae*

4.5 in. (12 cm). Tail dark with **whitish outer tail feathers**. On male, **throat, chest, and sides scaled iridescent bluish green**. On female, **throat whitish to buff** (lacks scaling). Immatures resemble their parents but have buff edging to head. In all plumages, similar to Green-throated Mountain-gem, but no range overlap. Similar to female White-eared Hummingbird (p. 74) but much larger, has a black mandible, and different tail pattern. Separate female from Amethyst-throated Hummingbird by broader postocular stripe, different tail pattern, and whiter underparts. Fairly common in cen. and se. Honduras; 2,460 to 7,870 ft. (750–2,400 m). Forages at lower and middle levels in pine-oak forest, cloud forest, coffee plantations, and gardens. Often flashes white outer tail feathers while foraging. Vocalizations similar to Green-throated Mountain-gem's. Endemic to Honduras and Nicaragua.

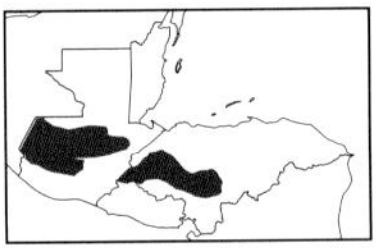

AMETHYST-THROATED HUMMINGBIRD

Lampornis amethystinus

4.5 in. (12 cm). Male has **thin white to buff moustachial stripe**; **glittering rose pink gorget**; **underparts dark brown to smoky gray**; tail dark with pale grayish tips to outer tail feathers. Female and immatures have buff gray throat. Female similar to female Green-breasted and Green-throated Mountain-gems, but note thinner postocular stripe, different tail pattern, and grayer underparts. Female also similar to Magnificent Hummingbird (p. 72), but has buffy throat (not whitish), darker underparts, and lacks bold white tail corners. Locally common in interior highlands on both slopes; 2,950 to 10,010 ft. (900–3,050 m) but mostly above 6,560 ft. (2,000 m). Found in pine-oak forest and cloud forest; also in disturbed habitat, brush, and gardens; forages at lower and middle levels. Flight call is a rapid, flat *thick'ic'ic'ic'ic'ic'ic'ic'ic-thic'ic'ic* . . . ; also makes a high-pitched *tseeet!* or *tseet-tseet*; call from perch is a rapid *ti'ti'ti'ti'ti'ti'ti'ti'ti'* . . . ; song is a high-pitched, squeaky *siip-siip-seet-siip-seet-seet-seet-siip* . . . Mex. to Honduras.

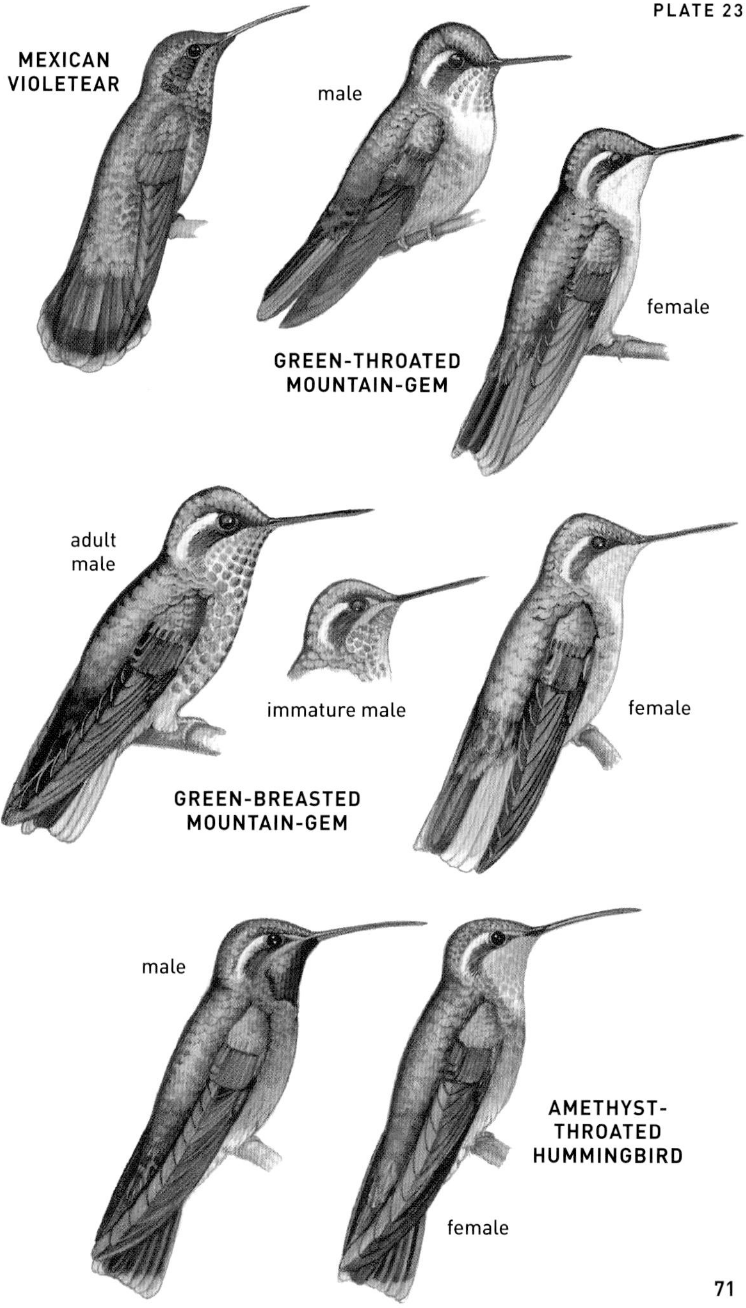
MEXICAN VIOLETEAR
male
female
GREEN-THROATED MOUNTAIN-GEM
adult male
immature male
female
GREEN-BREASTED MOUNTAIN-GEM
male
AMETHYST-THROATED HUMMINGBIRD
female

MOUNTAIN HUMMINGBIRDS II

GARNET-THROATED HUMMINGBIRD *Lamprolaima rhami*

4.5 in. (12 cm). Only **large** hummingbird in NCA with **extensive rufous in wings** and a **short straight bill**. Female has white postocular stripe, grayish underparts, and white tail corners. Uncommon locally in NCA; 2,950 to 9,680 ft. (900–2,950 m) but mostly above 6,560 ft. (2,000 m). Found in pine savanna, pine-oak forest, and cloud forest; usually forages in bromeliads at lower and middle levels. A fast flier; rufous wings are conspicuous in flight. Flight call is a thin, buzzy *zit'tit'tit'tit-zit'tit'tit-zit'tit'tit'tit* . . . Mex. to Honduras.

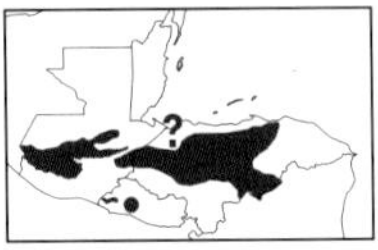

EMERALD-CHINNED HUMMINGBIRD *Abeillia abeillei*

3 in. (8 cm). A small hummingbird. Short black bill; small **white postocular spot**. Male has **iridescent green gorget and blackish breast**; female has gray throat. Uncommon in NCA; 3,280 to 7,220 ft. (1,000–2,200 m). Found in cloud forest and pine-oak forest, and at flowering edges. Forages at lower levels; feeds slowly, often with tail fanned, and frequent calling. Males known for lekking. Call in flight is a fast, sputtering *tip-tip'ip'ip'ip-tip-tip'ip-tip-tip'ip'ip'ip* . . . ; song is a high-pitched series of whistles, reminiscent of a squeaky wheel (*tsee'saw'seee-tsee'saw'seee tsee'saw'seee-tsee'saw'seee* . . .). Mex. to Nicaragua.

MAGNIFICENT HUMMINGBIRD *Eugenes fulgens*

5 in. (13 cm). A **large** hummingbird with a **long, black bill**. Male shows **purple forecrown**, glittering **green gorget**, and white **postocular spot**. Female similar to female Amethyst-throated Hummingbird (p. 70), but has whitish throat (not buffy), gray underparts, and white tail corners. Fairly common to common in central highlands; 3,280 to 9,510 ft. (1,000–2,900 m). Found at edge of pine savanna, pine-oak forest, and cloud forest; forages at all levels. Feeds from large tubular flowers, such as those of century plants. Call is a fairly rich *tsip!* (given in flight, and repeated at perch); also makes harsh chatters; song is a repeated *tseee'tsup-tseee'tsup-tseee'tsup-tseee'tsup-* . . . U.S. to Panama.

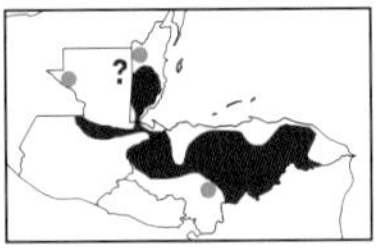

STRIPE-TAILED HUMMINGBIRD *Eupherusa eximia*

4 in. (10 cm). Male **emerald green overall**; **tail flashes white** when feeding; **rufous in wing** visible at rest and in flight. Female grayish below and shows small postocular spot and more extensive white in tail. Fairly common in foothills on Caribbean Slope; up to 5,910 ft. (1,800 m) but mainly from 980 to 3,610 ft. (300–1,100 m). Found in rainforest and cloud forest; feeds at lower and middle levels. Flight call is a liquid buzz: *zeep-zeep-zeep-zeep* . . . Mex. to Panama.

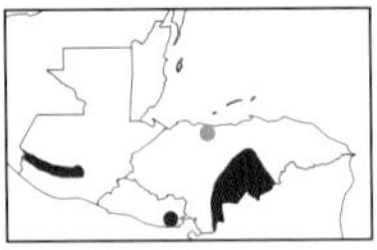

BLUE-TAILED HUMMINGBIRD *Amazilia cyanura*

4 in. (10 cm). Two NCA subspecies: *A.c. cyanura* (e. Honduras and e. El Salvador) and *A.c. guatemalae* (Guatemala). *A.c. cyanura* male **glittery green**; **rufous in wing** visible in flight or at rest; **tail and all tail coverts steely blue**; white leggings obvious when perched. *A.c. guatemalae* very similar, but rufous in wings is reduced or absent on female. Hybridizes with Berylline Hummingbird (p. 82) in Guatemala and e. El Salvador. Fairly common in Guatemala; uncommon in Honduras and El Salvador; to 3,940 ft. (1,200 m). Both subspecies make seasonal movements and may wander out of the usual range. Found in semideciduous forest, montane forest, riparian forest, coffee plantations, and coastal scrub; forages at lower and middle levels. *A.c. cyanura* call is a loud, ringing, slightly buzzy *tzzeet! A.c. guatemalae* makes a *tseet'tah* and a thin, buzzy *dzzzzzrt*. Song (of *guatemalae*) is a long rattle that rises slightly in pitch and then falls off midway (reminiscent of Yellow-winged Tanager [p. 366]). Mex. to Costa Rica.

GARNET-THROATED HUMMINGBIRD
male
female
male
female
EMERALD-CHINNED HUMMINGBIRD
male
male
MAGNIFICENT HUMMINGBIRD
female
female
STRIPE-TAILED HUMMINGBIRD
BLUE-TAILED HUMMINGBIRD
male

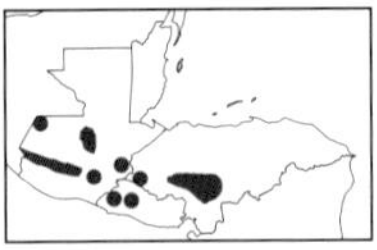

SLENDER SHEARTAIL *Doricha enicura*

3–4.5 in. (8–12 cm). On male, **long, deeply forked black tail** is distinctive; note iridescent purple gorget. Female has cinnamon underparts; rufous tail is short and slightly forked, with black band and white corners. Male similar to male Sparkling-tailed Hummingbird but tail all-black (lacks white tips). Female similar to female Sparkling-tailed Hummingbird but lacks white patches on rump, and has longer, decurved bill and rufous tail. Rare in Guatemala, Honduras, and El Salvador; 3,280 to 7,220 ft. (1,000–2,200 m). Found in pine-oak forest edge, brushy hillsides, and ornamental gardens; forages at lower and middle levels. Slow in flight. Call described as hard, rapid chips (often repeated or slightly trilled). Endemic to region.

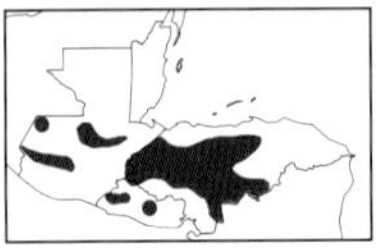

SPARKLING-TAILED HUMMINGBIRD *Tilmatura dupontii*

2.5–3.5 in. (6–9 cm). A **small** hummingbird; note **white patches on sides of rump**. Male has iridescent purplish gorget and **long, deeply forked tail with white tips**. Female **rufous below** and has short tail. Male similar to Slender Sheartail but tail shorter and not solid black. Female similar to female Slender Sheartail but has white patches on rump, shorter bill, and no rufous in tail. Uncommon in Guatemala, Honduras, and El Salvador; 1,310 to 6,400 ft. (400–1,950 m) but generally above 3,280 ft. (1,000 m). Found at edge of pine-oak forest and cloud forest, and in ornamental gardens; forages at lower levels. Flight is slow and insectlike, often with tail cocked. Generally silent. Mex. to Nicaragua.

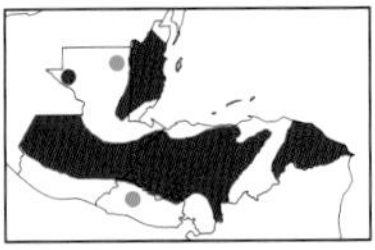

AZURE-CROWNED HUMMINGBIRD *Amazilia cyanocephala*

4.3 in. (11 cm). Subspecies *cyanocephala* has **iridescent blue crown** visible in good light (subspecies *A.c. chlorostephana* from e. Honduras has emerald green to turquoise-green crown); throat white with speckled border; **sides and flanks dusky green**; **rump and tail bronzy green**. Similar to White-bellied Emerald (p. 80), but lacks subterminal tail band, and has iridescent blue crown (in *cyanocephala*), bronzier rump, duskier sides and flanks, and longer bill. Fairly common to common on both slopes; to 9,510 ft. (2,900 m); on Pacific Slope above 3,610 ft. (1,100 m). Found in pine savanna, semideciduous forest, and coffee plantations; on Caribbean Slope, also found at edge of rainforest. Forages at all levels. Perched call is a harsh, buzzy *tzip* (often repeated in a long, chattering series). Mex. to Nicaragua.

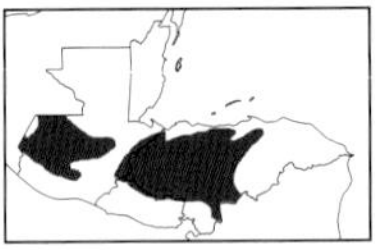

WHITE-EARED HUMMINGBIRD *Hylocharis leucotis*

3.7 in. (9 cm). On male, **iridescent blue-purple crown and gorget** appear black in poor light; note broad **white postocular stripe**; underparts grayish with dusky green sides; **bill bright red with dark tip**. Female similar to male but has brown crown, speckled throat, and dark maxilla. Immature similar to female, but has buffy edging to crown and back. Common in Guatemala, Honduras, and El Salvador highlands; 3,610 to 9,510 ft. (1,100–2,900 m). Found at edge of pine-oak and oak forest, and at highland clearings with flowers; forages at lower levels and sings from perches at lower and middle levels. Song is a chirping series of paired notes (repeated at 3.5-sec. intervals), and may include rapid buzzy, electric elements: *chea'tip-chea'tip-chea'tip-chea'tip-chea'tip*. Flight call is a rapid, repeated *ti'it'it'it'it'it*. Mex. to Nicaragua.

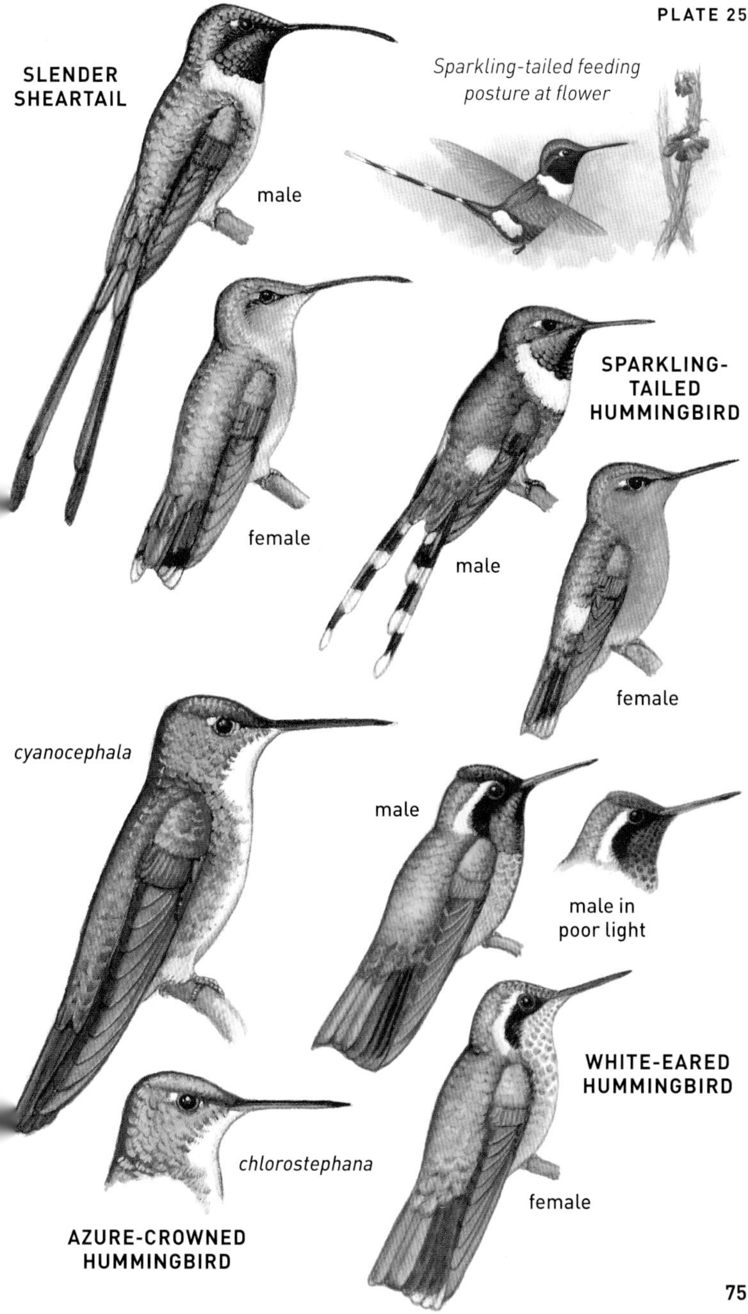
SLENDER SHEARTAIL
male
female
Sparkling-tailed feeding posture at flower
SPARKLING-TAILED HUMMINGBIRD
male
female
cyanocephala
chlorostephana
AZURE-CROWNED HUMMINGBIRD
male
male in poor light
female
WHITE-EARED HUMMINGBIRD

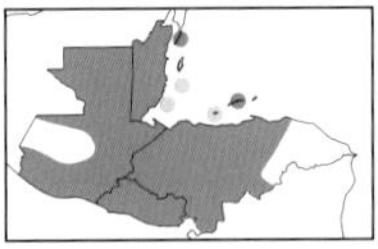

RUBY-THROATED HUMMINGBIRD *Archilochus colubris*

3 in. (8 cm). On male, note small white postocular spot, **glittering ruby red gorget** (appears blackish in poor light), green on flanks, white chest, **and black forked tail**. Female and immature similar to male, but have **clean white throat** and underparts (immature male with speckled throat), and white tips to tail. Both sexes distinguished from larger Broad-tailed Hummingbird by **black cheeks** (not olive gray), green on flanks (not tawny), and **black tail** (lacks rufous). Transient and nonbreeding winter visitor (early Sept.–early May). Fairly common to common on both slopes; to 9,350 ft. (2,850 m). Found in thorn forest, semideciduous forest, scrub, coffee plantations, clearings, gardens, and towns; forages at all levels. Flight call is a thin, buzzy *tzzit'tit'tit'tit-tzzit-tzzit'tit'tit'tit-tzzit-tzzit* . . . Canada to Panama.

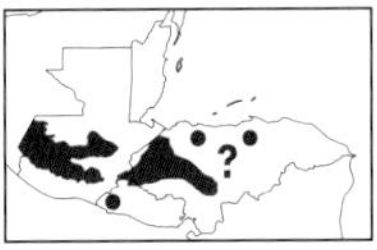

WINE-THROATED HUMMINGBIRD *Atthis ellioti*

2.7 in. (7 cm). A **small** hummingbird. Male's **extravagant magenta gorget** spreads at the corners; female has speckled throat. On both sexes, light rufous on sides; **tail rufous** with **dark subterminal band**; note **very short, dark bill**. Uncommon in Guatemala, Honduras, and El Salvador; 4,920 to 9,510 ft. (1,500–2,900 m). Forages at lower levels in clearings and edge of pine-oak forest and cloud forest; may make altitudinal migrations. Flight is slow and insectlike; males defend territories and sing vigorously from low perches. Song is a complicated jumble of buzzes, chips, and electric, guitar-plucking noises: *tew-tew-tew-tew-wi'see-wi'see-wi'see-tew-tew-tew-wi'see-wi'see-wi'see-ti'ti'ti'ti'ti'ti-see-see* . . . Endemic to region.

CANIVET'S EMERALD *Chlorostilbon canivetii*

3–3.5 in. (8–9 cm). Two subspecies identified in NCA: *C.c. canivetii* and *C.c. osberti*. On *C c. canivetii* (n. Guatemala, Belize, and Bay Is.), male is **iridescent green overall** with white vent; **blue-black tail deeply forked**; note slightly decurved **red bill with black tip**. Female has black cheek and white postocular stripe; underparts grayish; tail forked with black subterminal band and white tips. *C.c. osberti* (s. Guatemala, mainland Honduras, and El Salvador) similar, but smaller and has shorter tail (both sexes). Both subspecies uncommon to fairly common in region; to 6,230 ft. (1,900 m). Found in edge of semideciduous forest, thorn forest, and coastal scrub; forages at lower levels. Flight call is a rapid twittering series: *chit'it'it'it'it-chit-chit'it'it'it'it-chit-chit'it'it-chit* . . . The subspecies *osberti* is sometimes considered a separate species called Salvin's Emerald. Mex. to Costa Rica.

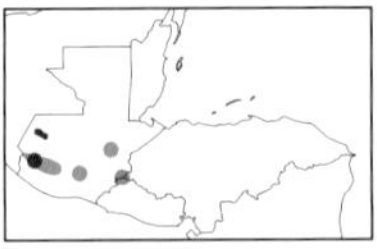

BROAD-TAILED HUMMINGBIRD *Selasphorus platycercus*

4 in. (10 cm). Male has rose red gorget; female has white throat speckled green. Both sexes distinguished from smaller Ruby-throated Hummingbird by **olive gray cheeks** (not black), **tawny tones on flanks** (heavier in female), and **rufous at base of outer tail feathers**. Uncommon to fairly common in w. Guatemala, presumed vagrants reported in El Salvador; from 2,620 to 10,990 ft. (800–3,350 m) but generally above 8,040 ft. (2,450 m). Found at edge of pine savanna and pine-oak forest, and also in grasslands; forages at lower and middle levels. Perched call is sharp *tsip* or *tzip*; male makes a distinctive humming with wings in flight. U.S. to El Salvador.

male
RUBY-THROATED HUMMINGBIRD
female
male
WINE-THROATED HUMMINGBIRD
female
osberti
male
CANIVET'S EMERALD
female
caniveti
osberti
male
BROAD-TAILED HUMMINGBIRD
female
open tail

SOME CARIBBEAN SLOPE HUMMINGBIRDS

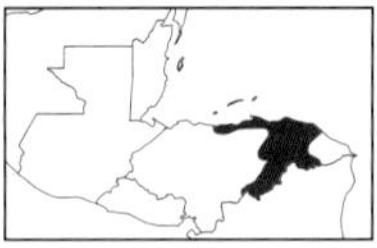

VIOLET-HEADED HUMMINGBIRD *Klais guimeti*

3 in. (8 cm). Male has **purple forecrown and throat**; female has bluish forecrown and gray throat; note **white spot behind eye** (both sexes). Rare to uncommon in Honduras; to 3,940 ft. (1,200 m). Found in rainforest; forages at all levels. In flight, body held horizontal and tail cocked up. In flight, makes a hard, high-pitched *teet!* and a flatter *tit!*; song is an extremely high-pitched series of sharp whistles (*tsee'ti'tsee-tsee'ti'tsee . . .*). Honduras to Brazil.

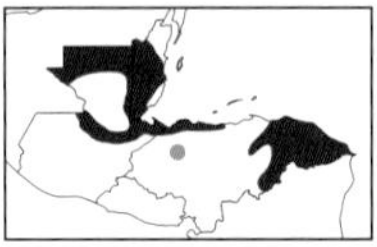

SCALY-BREASTED HUMMINGBIRD *Phaeochroa cuvierii*

4.5 in. (12 cm). Throat and chest mainly green with **subtle scaling**; **large white tips to outer tail feathers**; mandible pinkish. Similar to female White-necked Jacobin (p. 64), but scaling on chest more subtle, belly drab (not bright white), and undertail coverts paler. Fairly common in humid areas of Caribbean Slope; to 3,940 ft. (1,200 m). Found in open areas and edge habitat of rainforest or semideciduous forest; feeds at lower and middle levels at flowering trees (especially *Inga* species). Song mixed with variable calls and chatters (may be reminiscent of a Euphonia call), sometimes well-spaced: *seet—seet—tsip-tseeu-seet—seet-tsip-tseeu-tsee* . . . Guatemala to Colombia.

BRONZE-TAILED PLUMELETEER *Chalybura urochrysia*

4 in. (10 cm). Male **emerald green overall** with purplish bronze tail. Female grayish below; has white tail corners. Note **pink feet** on both sexes. Uncommon to fairly common in e. Honduras; to 2,460 ft. (750 m). Found at edge of rainforest, disturbed forest; forages at lower and middle levels. Calls include a flat, repeated *peet!* or *pit!*; in flight, makes a distinctive harsh, woodpecker-like *chit* or *chit'chit'chit'chit*. Song is a series of harsh, electronic elements repeated rapidly: *peet!-pitpitpitpitpitpitpitpit-pitpitpit-pitpit*. Honduras to Ecuador.

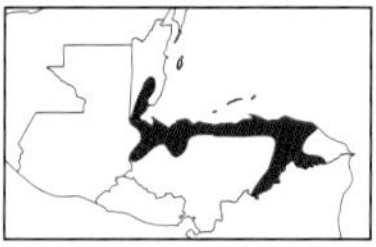

CROWNED WOODNYMPH *Thalurania colombica*

4 in. (10 cm). On male, **glittering purple-blue crown, shoulders, and belly** contrast with **iridescent green gorget**; fairly long, forked tail projects beyond wings. Female mostly white below; note **purple-blue shoulders**; tail has white tips. Uncommon on Caribbean Slope; to 3,610 ft. (1,100 m). Found in the interior of rainforest, riparian forest, along streams in forest; forages at lower and middle levels. Call is a rich *tip!* (often repeated at song perch); also makes a rapid twitter of flat *pit* notes mixed with other buzzy, electric-sounding elements. Guatemala to Colombia.

SNOWCAP *Microchera albocoronata*

3 in. (8 cm). A **small hummingbird**. Male unmistakable. Female emerald green above and grayish below; tail pattern similar to male's (often flashes white in tail). Uncommon in e. Honduras; to 2,460 ft. (750 m). Found in rainforest; forages at lower levels with slow, insectlike flight. Generally silent, but sometimes makes a sputtering *tz'e'e'e'p* in flight. Honduras to Panama.

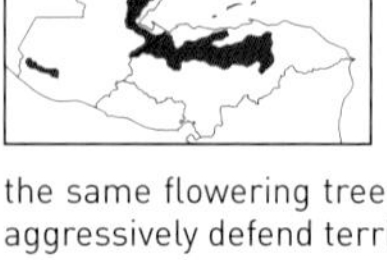

BLACK-CRESTED COQUETTE *Lophornis helenae*

3 in. (8 cm). Note **white band on rump** and **short, straight red bill**. Male has **long black filamentous feathers on crown and throat**. Female has pale throat. Rare and local on both slopes; to 5,910 ft. (1,800 m). Found at all levels in rainforest, semideciduous forest, coffee plantations, and gardens. Often visits the same flowering trees or bushes for long periods. Flight is slow and beelike; males aggressively defend territories from rivals. Generally silent. Mex. to Costa Rica.

male
VIOLET-HEADED HUMMINGBIRD
female
SCALY-BREASTED HUMMINGBIRD
male
BRONZE-TAILED PLUMELETEER
female
male
female
CROWNED WOODNYMPH
male
SNOWCAP
female
male
BLACK-CRESTED COQUETTE
female

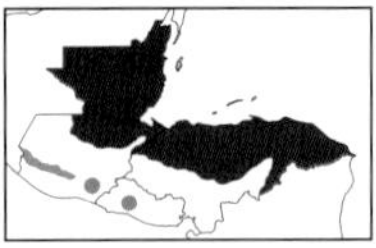

WHITE-BELLIED EMERALD *Amazilia candida*

3.5 in. (9 cm). **Clean white underparts**; tail with **dark subterminal band**. Similar to Azure-crowned Hummingbird (p. 74), but has green crown, greener rump, whiter flanks, shorter bill, and subterminal tail band. Fairly common on Caribbean Slope, rare to uncommon in winter on Pacific Slope (w. Guatemala only); to 4,920 ft. (1,500 m). Found at edge of rainforest and semideciduous forest, and in coffee plantations and gardens; forages at lower and middle levels and sings from perch at midlevels. Song is similar in quality to song of Blue-throated Goldentail (p. 82), but the elements vary; makes a repeated *wit-pea'tea*; also a *wi'wi'wi'wi-tah'pea*; and a *chick!-pea'pea'pea*. Mex. to Nicaragua.

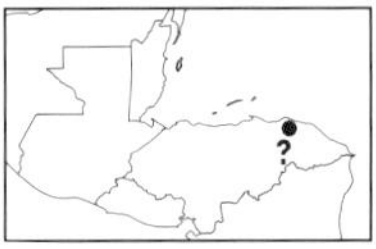

BLUE-CHESTED HUMMINGBIRD *Amazilia amabilis*

4 in. (10 cm). On male, **chest and lower throat iridescent blue and purple**. Female has spotting on chest with some iridescent blue-purple. Tail blackish and notched. Rare to uncommon in e. Honduras; to 1,970 ft. (600 m). Found at edge or within clearings of rainforest. Forages at low levels. Song is a sharp, high-pitched *Pseet!-Pseet!-Pseet!-Pseet!* . . . ; call is a thin, nasal *tseeeuuu*. Honduras to Ecuador.

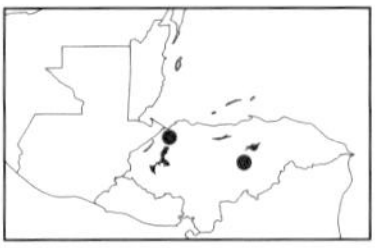

HONDURAN EMERALD *Amazilia luciae*

3.5 in. (9 cm). **Gray postocular spot**; **iridescent blue-green gorget**; **chest has slightly scaled appearance**. Note large, deeply-notched tail. Similar to Blue-throated Goldentail (p. 82), but little range overlap; larger with darker bill, less yellow in tail, and has postocular spot. Locally uncommon in Honduras; patchily distributed in dry interior valleys of the Caribbean Slope; from 660 to 2,800 ft. (200–850 m). Found in thorn forest and semideciduous forest. Forages at lower and middle levels. Calls include a scolding chatter *chi'chi'chi'chi'chi'chi* (similar to Azure-crowned Hummingbird [p. 74]). Song is a very soft series of trills, whistles, and *tic* notes. Endemic to Honduras.

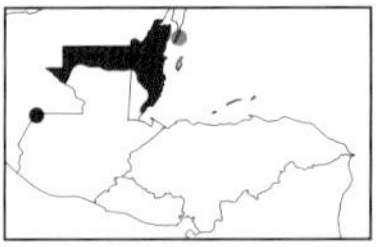

BUFF-BELLIED HUMMINGBIRD *Amazilia yucatanensis*

4 in. (10 cm). Similar to Rufous-tailed Hummingbird, but has **cinnamon belly**, tail with cleft, and **green on central tail feathers**. Fairly common in Belize, uncommon in n. Guatemala; to 3,940 ft. (1,200 m). Found in thorn forest, disturbed habitat, pine savanna, and semideciduous forest; forages at lower and middle levels. Flight call is similar to Rufous-tailed Hummingbird; song is a high-pitched, thin *peet'tseuu-peet'tseuu-peet'tseuu* . . . Cinnamon and Rufous-tailed Hummingbirds may hybridize, with offspring resembling Buff-bellied Hummingbird. U.S. to Belize.

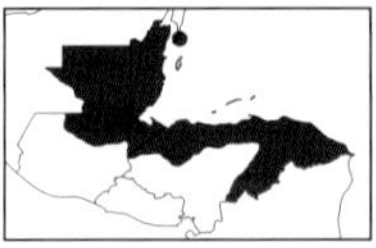

RUFOUS-TAILED HUMMINGBIRD *Amazilia tzacatl*

4 in. (10 cm). **Uppertail coverts and tail rufous**; male has iridescent green throat and chest; **belly and vent grayish**; female similar to male, but belly and vent paler. Similar to Berylline Hummingbird (p. 82), but has blackish wings and rufous tail (not bronzy purple); little range overlap. Similar to Buff-bellied Hummingbird, but has grayish belly and all-rufous tail. Common on Caribbean Slope; to 3,940 ft. (1,200 m). Found at edge of semideciduous forest and rainforest, in disturbed habitat, plantations, gardens, and towns; forages at lower and middle levels. Flight call is a buzzy *zzzzt* (similar to call of Buff-bellied); song is a series of high-pitched elements, repeated every 4 to 5 sec. (*tseee-tee'tah-tee-tee-tee*). Hybrid Cinnamon x Rufous-tailed Hummingbird may resemble Buff-bellied Hummingbird. Mex. to Ecuador.

BLUE-CHESTED
HUMMINGBIRD
female
WHITE-BELLIED
EMERALD
male
HONDURAN
EMERALD
feeding at
Euphorbia
"pie de niño"
RUFOUS-TAILED
HUMMINGBIRD
BUFF-BELLIED
HUMMINGBIRD

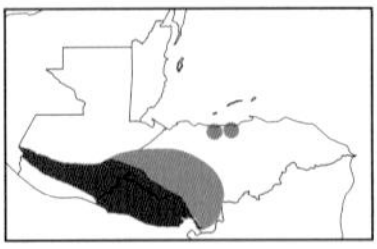

BERYLLINE HUMMINGBIRD *Amazilia beryllina devillei*

4 in. (10 cm). Male **glittery green overall** (dark in poor light); **uppertail coverts and tail bronzy purple**; **rufous in wing** visible in flight and at rest; **undertail coverts have dark rufous centers**; white leggings obvious when perched. Female similar to male but lower chest and belly are edged gray; similar to Rufous-tailed Hummingbird (p. 80), which overlaps in a few areas, but has rufous in wings and no rufous in tail. Berylline x Blue-tailed hybrids have been reported in Guatemala and e. El Salvador. Common resident on Pacific Slope where breeds Oct.–Mar., and uncommon locally on Caribbean Slope outside the breeding season, Apr.–Aug.; to 6,560 ft. (2,000 m). Found in edge and interior of semideciduous forest, thorn forest, riparian forest, and coffee plantations; forages at lower and middle levels. Flight call is a ringing *tssi'tea'tea'tea'tea'tea'tea'tea*; while foraging, gives a buzzy, rapid chatter (*tzzzi'i'i'i'i'i'i*). Sings from a perch at mid- or upper levels; song is similar to flight call, but is a slower, ringing series given at 2.5-sec. intervals: *tsssi-tea'ah'tea'ah'tea'ah'tea'ah'tea'ah*. Mex. to Honduras.

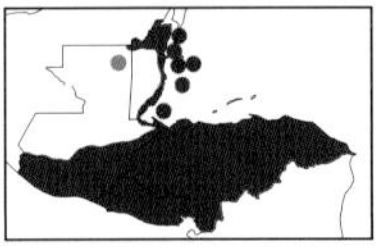

CINNAMON HUMMINGBIRD *Amazilia rutila*

4.5 in. (12 cm). **Underparts cinnamon**; tail rufous with dark tips. Similar to Rufous Sabrewing (p. 68), but is smaller, has **bright red bill with dark tip**, has all-rufous tail, and lacks postocular spot; also note differences in distribution and habitat. Common on both slopes; to 5,580 ft. (1,700 m). Found in dry scrub, thorn forest, coastal scrub, coffee plantations, and mangroves; generally prefers edge habitat and lower to middle levels. Call is an agitated, repeated *tip*; also makes a jumble of squeaky, buzzy notes. Song is a series of high-pitched elements: *tsee-tsee-tsi'tsee-tsee-tsi-tsee*. Mex. to Costa Rica.

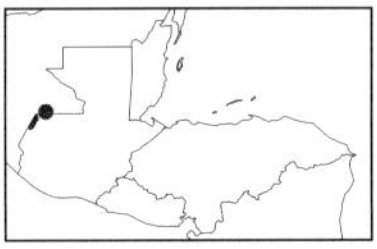

GREEN-FRONTED HUMMINGBIRD *Amazilia viridifrons*

4 in. (10 cm). Male has **blackish green crown**, **coppery rump and tail**, and **clean white underparts**. Female similar to male, but rump and tail have greenish gold tones. Locally common at several sites in w. Guatemala; from 2,950 to 4,590 ft. (900–1,400 m). Found in thorn forest, dry scrub, and riparian forest; feeds and perches at mid- and upper levels. Calls include a dry, chattering *chit-chit-chit-chit*; song is a high-pitched *tsee'tsee'tsee-tsee-tsee*. Mex. and Guatemala.

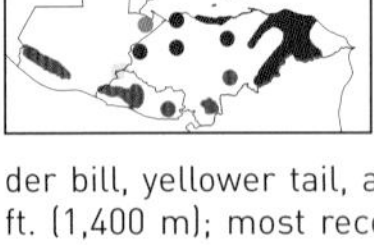

BLUE-THROATED GOLDENTAIL *Hylocharis eliciae*

3.5 in. (9 cm). On male, **iridescent blue gorget** appears dark in poor light; belly grayish; **tail greenish gold**; **bill is bright red with dark tip**. Female similar to male, but maxilla is darker with scaly gorget (appears more grayish). Similar to Honduran Emerald (p. 80), but little range overlap; smaller with redder bill, yellower tail, and lacks postocular spot. Uncommon on both slopes; to 4,590 ft. (1,400 m); most records on Pacific Slope are from Aug.–Apr. when breeding takes place. Found in rainforest and semideciduous forest, also coffee plantations; forages at all levels, and sings from perches at mid- and upper levels. Song is a fairly loud, slightly metallic chatter repeated at 2.5-sec. intervals: *tip-tea'tea'tea'tea'tea—tip'ti'ti*; also a *tip-tear'tear'tear'tear'tear* and a *tip-tea'dew'tea'dew'tea'dew*, all songs similar in quality to songs of White-bellied Emerald (p. 80). Mex. to Colombia.

PLATE 29

BERYLLINE
HUMMINGBIRD
male
Berylline/Blue-tailed hybrid
tail pattern
CINNAMON
HUMMINGBIRD
GREEN-FRONTED
HUMMINGBIRD
female
BLUE-THROATED
GOLDENTAIL
male

STORKS, FLAMINGOS, AND SPOONBILLS

CICONIIDAE (Order: Ciconiiformes). Storks are a mainly Old World group of wading birds. Most species have white plumage and bare necks and heads. Their large, pointed bills allow for a varied diet of fish, frogs, snakes, small mammals, and birds. Storks' broad wings are well adapted for soaring, and most migrate or wander after breeding. **2 species (2 genera)**

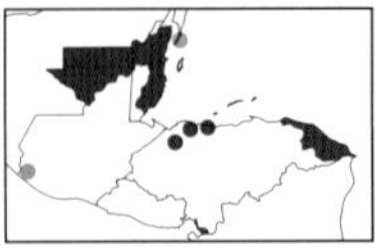

JABIRU *Jabiru mycteria*

56 in. (142 cm). Large size and **massive, slightly recurved bill** make this bird unmistakable. All-white body contrasts with **bare black neck and head**; note **bare red patch at base of neck**. Rare to uncommon on Caribbean Slope, rare and local on Pacific Slope; to 330 ft. (100 m). Found in and near flooded fields, shrimp farms, swamps, rivers, streams, estuaries, and lagoons; builds very large stick nests high in trees. Generally solitary or in pairs; may occur in large groups where food supply is abundant. Mex. to Uruguay.

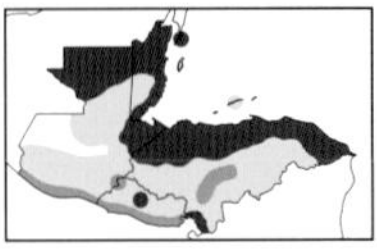

WOOD STORK *Mycteria americana*

37.5 in. (95 cm). A large white wader with **bare blackish head and neck**. In flight, similar to American White Pelican (p. 92), but **all flight feathers are black**, neck is longer (extended, not curved), and legs project well beyond **black tail**. Fairly common on both slopes; to 2,950 ft. (900 m). Populations fluctuate as resident individuals disperse from colonies after breeding, and northern populations enter NCA (late Nov.–Apr.). Found in marshes, swamps, estuaries, flooded fields, and shrimp farms. Nests in large colonies; often seen soaring in groups of 10 to 20 individuals. Occasionally soars with Black Vultures (p. 152). U.S. to Argentina.

PHOENICOPTERIDAE (Order: Phoenicopteriformes). Flamingos are tall and thin waders with extremely long legs and long necks. Adults have rosy pink plumage, a product of bacteria and beta carotene consumption (brighter individuals have better diets). Of four New World species of flamingos, only one naturally occurs in NCA. **1 species (1 genus)**

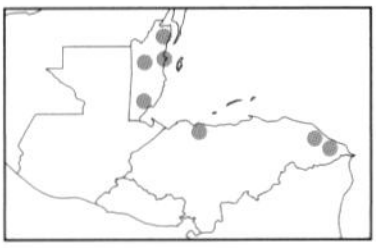

AMERICAN FLAMINGO *Phoenicopterus ruber*

46 in. (117 cm). Adult is **pink overall**; **very long dull pink legs and long neck**; pale pink bill with dark tip. In flight, **black flight feathers** contrast with pink body. Juvenile grayish overall and subadult duller pink. Rare visitor on Caribbean coast of Belize and Honduras; at or near sea level. Found in saline environments such as estuaries, coastal mudflats, and salt pans. Mex. (Yucatán) and Caribbean to Venezuela.

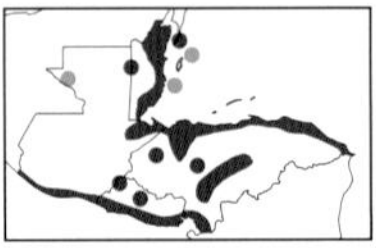

ROSEATE SPOONBILL *Platalea ajaja*

32 in. (81 cm). Part of the Threskiornithidae family (ibises [p. 102]). Unmistakable **rosy pink plumage**; flat **spoon-shaped bill**. Immature similar to adult but is paler overall. In flight, distinguish from American Flamingo by all-rosy wings (no black flight feathers). Fairly common on both slopes to 3,280 ft. (1,000 m). Found in freshwater and saltwater wetlands, including lakes, ponds, marshes, lagoons, estuaries, and mangroves. Solitary or in small flocks. An active forager; swings bill side to side through the water and mud or sand in a unique sifting motion. Generally silent away from breeding site. U.S. to Argentina.

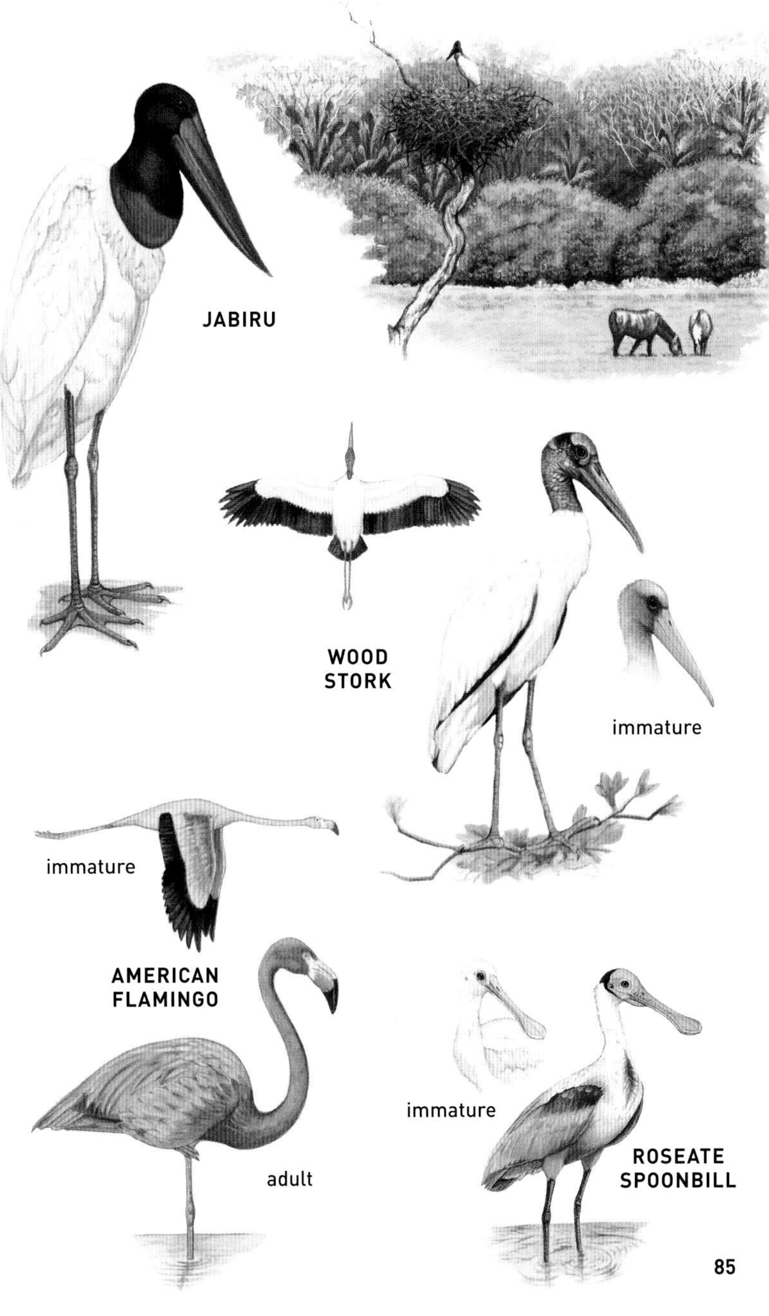
JABIRU
WOOD
STORK
immature
immature
AMERICAN
FLAMINGO
adult
immature
ROSEATE
SPOONBILL

TROPICBIRDS AND "MASKED" BOOBIES

PHAETHONTIDAE (Order: Phaethontiformes). Tropicbirds are elegant pelagic birds of warm tropical oceans. Adults have extended central tail feathers that form their distinctive streaming tails. Their feet are totipalmate (webbed between all four toes). Tropicbirds fly high and make great plunge-dives to capture their prey (primarily squid and small fish). They nest in burrows and crevices on sea cliffs and rocky islands. **2 species (1 genus)**

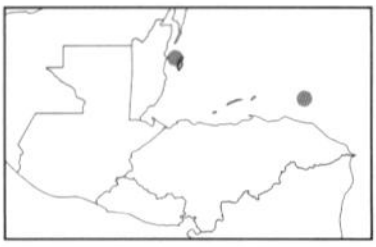

WHITE-TAILED TROPICBIRD *Phaethon lepturus*

36 in. (92 cm), including tail streamers. Adult white overall with small black mask; bill orange in Atlantic populations (greenish yellow in Pacific populations); in flight, **black slashes on upperwings form a broken M**. Juvenile similar but has black dorsal markings and lacks tail streamers. Juvenile similar to Red-billed Tropicbird, but has sparser dorsal markings and slimmer body, wings, and bill. Vagrant in NCA Caribbean pelagic waters, but likely to reoccur since it breeds widely throughout the Caribbean. No Pacific records in NCA. Pacific, Atlantic, and Indian Oceans.

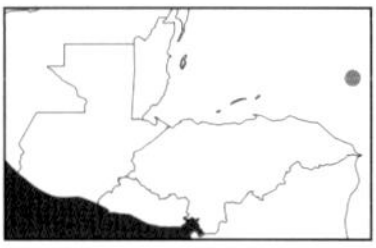

RED-BILLED TROPICBIRD *Phaethon aethereus*

42 in. (107 cm), including tail streamers. Adult white overall with **black outer primaries**; **black dorsal markings** (**including uppertail coverts**); small black mask; **red bill**. Juvenile similar, but has greenish yellow bill (not red) and lacks tail streamers; juvenile similar to White-tailed Tropicbird, but is larger overall and has heavier dorsal markings. Uncommon in NCA Pacific pelagic waters, occasionally near shore; vagrant in Caribbean. Flies high in search of prey, or sits on water with tail cocked. Solitary. Pacific, Atlantic, and Indian Oceans.

SULIDAE (Order: Suliformes). Boobies are large seabirds with heavy pointed bills. In flight, their wings and tails are long and pointed. When feeding, primarily on squid and flying fish, they make spectacular plunge-dives into the water. Boobies breed on rocky islands, where they perform courtship dances and show off their colorful feet. Usually solitary or in pairs. **5 species (1 genus)**

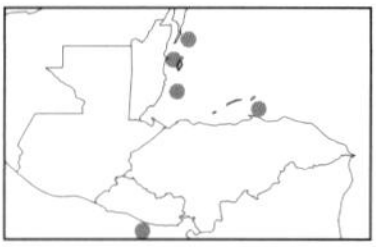

MASKED BOOBY *Sula dactylatra*

34 in. (86 cm). White body and black flight feathers; black bare skin at base of **greenish yellow bill**. On juvenile, upperparts dark overall and bill dull yellowish. Very similar to Nazca Booby but has greenish yellow bill (not pinkish orange). Juvenile sometimes has broader white hindcollar than Nazca, but may not be separable in the field. Compare juvenile also to the smaller and darker-billed juvenile Blue-footed Booby. Very rare in NCA Caribbean waters and Pacific waters (where it's far outnumbered by Nazca Booby). Skims low over water and also flies high; floats on water and perches on buoys or flotsam. Pantropical.

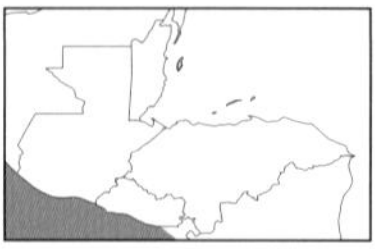

NAZCA BOOBY *Sula granti*

34 in. (86 cm). Adult very similar to Masked Booby, but has **pinkish orange bill** (not greenish yellow). Juvenile grayish brown above; yellowish bill; very similar to juvenile Masked Booby but paler and generally **lacks complete white hindcollar**. Juvenile similar also to the smaller and darker-billed juvenile Blue-footed Booby. Uncommon to fairly common in NCA Pacific pelagic waters (where it far outnumbers Masked Booby). Skims low over water and also flies high; floats on water and perches on buoys, flotsam, or the backs of sea turtles. E. Tropical Pacific Ocean.

WHITE-TAILED TROPICBIRD
adult
immature
RED-BILLED TROPICBIRD
adult
immature
adult
immature
MASKED BOOBY
immature
NAZCA BOOBY
adult

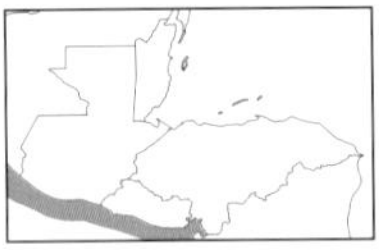

BLUE-FOOTED BOOBY *Sula nebouxii*

32 in. (81 cm). Adult has white body with **brownish streaks on head and neck**; mantle, wings, and tail blackish brown; **bill dark**; **sky blue feet** are diagnostic. Juvenile has gray legs and feet; dark brown head, neck, and chest; **white at base of hindneck, whitish rump,** and white axillaries. Juvenile similar to juvenile Brown Booby but has dark feet (not yellowish) and pale underparts (not brown). Juvenile similar to juvenile Nazca and Masked Boobies, but is smaller and has dark bill (not yellow); also has dark hindneck (lacks white collar of Masked). Uncommon in NCA Pacific waters (no confirmed reports of its breeding in NCA). Found close to shore; skims low over water and also flies high. E. Tropical Pacific Ocean.

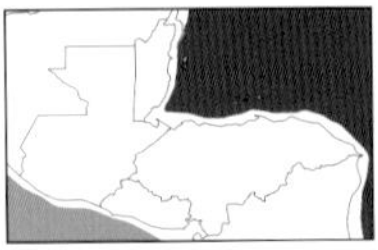

RED-FOOTED BOOBY *Sula sula*

27 in. (68 cm). Smallest booby in NCA. Adult has **red feet**; blue to greenish blue bill with pinkish red base. Several color morphs occur. White morph **striking white overall**; outer primaries and secondaries black; **tail white**. Brown morph chocolate brown overall but darker on mantle and wings; **tail tip whitish**. Juvenile sooty brown and similar to juvenile Brown Booby but has white-tipped tail and pinkish red feet (not yellowish). Fairly common in NCA Caribbean waters (historically bred on Little Swan I., Honduras, and currently breeding on Half Moon Caye, Belize); rare in NCA Pacific pelagic waters. Nearly always seen away from shore; may perch on buoys or ship rigging. Flight graceful (reminiscent of a large tropicbird). Over 95 percent of Caribbean individuals are white morph. Pantropical.

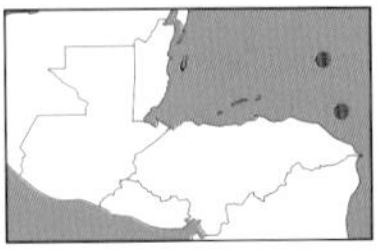

BROWN BOOBY *Sula leucogaster*

28 in. (71 cm). **Dark brown upperparts and breast** contrast sharply with **white underparts**; **bill and feet yellow**. Juvenile **dark brown overall** (paler below); bill dark; **feet yellowish**. Juvenile similar to juvenile Red-footed Booby but has yellowish feet (not pinkish red) and lacks white-tipped tail. Juvenile similar to juvenile Blue-footed Booby but has yellowish feet (not dark), and brown underparts (not pale). Fairly common in NCA Caribbean waters (breeding confirmed in Honduras on Little Swan I. and at Cayos Vivorillos); uncommon in NCA Pacific waters (bred historically in Gulf of Fonseca). Found close to shore and far out at sea. Skims low over water and also flies high; will float on water and perch on buoys, flotsam, and rigging of fishing boats. Pantropical.

adult
immature
BLUE-FOOTED
BOOBY
adult
light
morph
RED-FOOTED
BOOBY
dark
morph
immature Brown Booby (L) with adult Nazca Booby
adults
immature
BROWN
BOOBY
adult

CORMORANTS AND ANHINGAS

PHALACROCORACIDAE (Order: Suliformes). Large aquatic birds with long necks, fairly long tails, and dark plumage. Cormorants have fully webbed feet (totipalmate), and dive from the water's surface to capture fish, crustaceans, and amphibians. They often sun themselves with their wings open in an effort to dry their plumage (which is not fully waterproof). Cormorants fly in ragged groups, often forming broken V formations that dissolve and re-form. They breed colonially and vocalize very little except for grunting noises while at breeding grounds. **2 species (1 genus)**

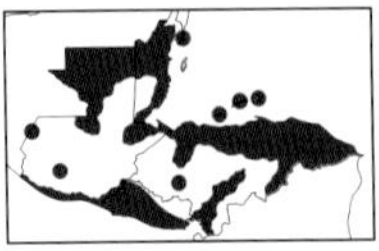

NEOTROPIC CORMORANT *Phalacrocorax brasilianus*

26 in. (66 cm). A **slim** cormorant with a **long tail**. Adult has **white border to posterior edge of bare skin on throat**. Breeding adult has thin white plumes on side of head, which may be difficult to see from a distance (lacking in nonbreeding). Immature brownish black overall with paler (occasionally white) chest. Adult similar to adult Double-crested Cormorant, but is smaller and slimmer, and has dark lores (not orange), longer tail, and white border to throat. Immature very similar to immature Double-crested Cormorant, but is smaller and slimmer, has dark lores (not orange), and longer tail. Note sharper angle to bare skin on throat (rounded in Double-crested). Fairly common to abundant in NCA; to 2,460 ft. (750 m). Found on lakes, reservoirs, rivers, estuaries, shrimp farms, and in water treatment facilities. Occurs in small to very large groups; breeding colonies may number hundreds or thousands of individuals. U.S. to Argentina and Chile.

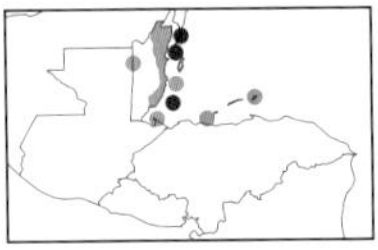

DOUBLE-CRESTED CORMORANT *Phalacrocorax auritus*

30 in. (76 cm). A **stocky** cormorant with a **short tail**. Adult has **orange skin on throat and lores**. Breeding adult has black ear tufts (lacking in nonbreeding). Immature brown overall with paler chest. Adult similar to adult Neotropic Cormorant but is larger and heavier, has a shorter tail, orange lores (not dark), and lacks white border to throat. Immature very similar to immature Neotropic Cormorant, but is larger and heavier, and has shorter tail and orange lores. Note rounded base to bare skin on throat (not pointed). In Belize, fairly common to common on cayes (where breeds) and in coastal areas, rare farther inland; recent records in nearby Guatemala; vagrant to Bay Is. (Honduras); to 160 ft. (50 m). Prefers mangroves, coastal beaches, lagoons, and estuaries; where inland, found on lakes, reservoirs, and shrimp farms. U.S. to Belize.

ANHINGIDAE (Order: Suliformes). A pantropical family of large aquatic birds known as darters in the Old World. Only one species occurs in the New World. Anhingas are slender with long, thin necks; sharply pointed bills; long tails; and webbed feet (totipalmate). They are found in freshwater and brackish habitats and often submerge their bodies so that only their heads and necks remain above the water (giving a serpentine appearance that has earned them the nickname "snakebirds"). **1 species (1 genus)**

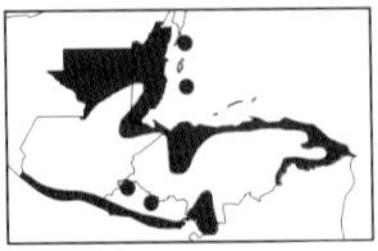

ANHINGA *Anhinga anhinga*

35 in. (89 cm). **Slender** with **long tail** and **sharply pointed bill** (used to spear fish). Male with **silver upperwing coverts and scapulars**; tail with cinnamon tip. On female and immature, note **creamy buff head and neck**; tail with buffy tip. Uncommon to fairly common on both slopes; to 2,950 ft. (900 m). Resident populations augmented by northern migrants. Found primarily in freshwater habitats and marshy surrounding areas; prefers still or slow-moving water of lakes, reservoirs, rivers, streams, swamps, and mangroves. Soars often (in-flight appearance likened to a flying cross); also seen sunning itself on a log with wings open. U.S. to Argentina.

NEOTROPIC CORMORANT

DOUBLE-CRESTED CORMORANT

Neotropics in flight with two Double-crested

ANHINGA

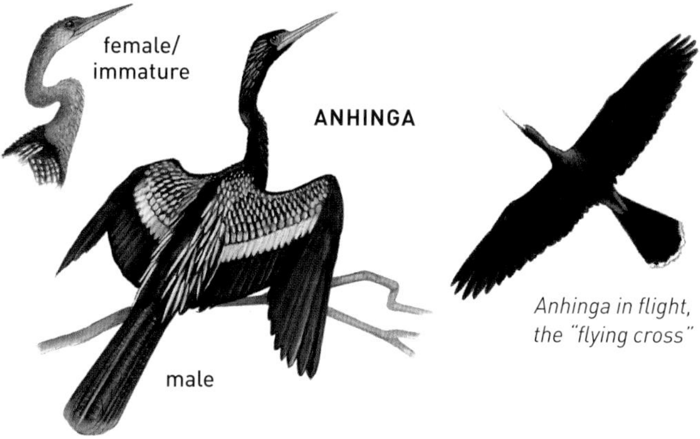

Anhinga in flight, the "flying cross"

FREGATIDAE (Order: Suliformes). This pantropical family of pelagic seabirds comprises five species, one of which occurs in NCA. Frigatebirds have the largest wingspan-to-body-weight ratio of any bird, and can sustain long, soaring flights for a week or more. They avoid landing on water because their plumage isn't waterproof. Agile fliers, they snatch prey items such as fish, jellyfish, and squid from the surface of the water. They also steal prey from other birds, a strategy known as *kleptoparasitism*, which has earned them the nickname "man o' war bird." Males have a red gular pouch that they inflate into a large throat balloon during breeding season. Frigatebirds nest on islands and rocky cliffs, where they build stick platform nests in low vegetation. **1 species (1 genus)**

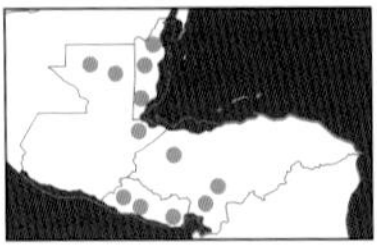

MAGNIFICENT FRIGATEBIRD *Fregata magnificens*

38.5 in. (98 cm); WS: 88.5 in. (225 cm). Large and angular; notably **long, thin wings strongly bent at wrists**; **long forked tail** generally held closed in flight. Male **blackish overall** with **red gular pouch** (inflated on breeding grounds). Female also black overall, but has **white chest** and lacks red gular pouch. Juvenile black with **white chest and head**. Common along both coasts over pelagic waters; rare more than a few kilometers inland. Often soars high; may perch on fishing boats. E. Pacific and w. Atlantic Oceans.

PELECANIDAE (Order: Pelecaniformes). Very large aquatic birds. Pelicans have long wings and bills, short tails, and fully webbed feet. Their characteristic five-gallon bill pouch is used to scoop up fish and other prey, but hunting methods vary between species. **2 species (1 genus)**

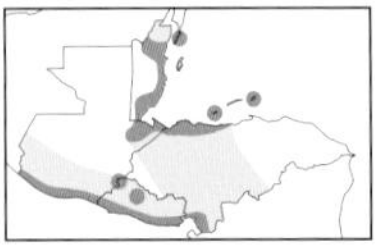

AMERICAN WHITE PELICAN *Pelecanus erythrorhynchos*

61 in. (155 cm). Very large and heavy. **White overall** with **black primaries and outer secondaries** (inner secondaries white); **large yellow or orange bill**. In flight, note enormous wingspan, short tail, and heavy body; distinguished from Wood Stork (p. 84) by shorter neck (curved, not extended), white tail and inner secondaries (not black), and feet barely extending beyond the tail. Nonbreeding, winter visitor and transient, with occasional summering flocks. Birds in breeding condition grow a "hump" on the top of the bill. Uncommon to fairly common at freshwater wetlands on Pacific Slope; rare to uncommon in n. Belize (including on cayes) and n. Honduras; to 1,310 ft. (400 m). Generally prefers freshwater habitats; found on lakes, reservoirs, river sandbars, and occasionally in estuaries and river mouths. In migration, soars very high in groups of 10 to 100 individuals and often circles slowly on thermals. Often works cooperatively in flocks to stir up fish and other prey. Canada (breeding) to Nicaragua (winter).

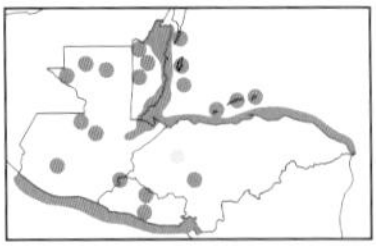

BROWN PELICAN *Pelecanus occidentalis*

49 in. (125 cm). A **large coastal seabird** with grayish brown body and wings. Breeding-plumaged adult has **broad chestnut stripe along hindneck**, contrasting with whitish foreneck and head (top of head washed yellow). Bill pouch can be bright red (Pacific population) or blackish (Atlantic/Caribbean population). Nonbreeding adult has all-white neck and dark pouch. Immature has grayish brown head and neck and pale underparts. Adult plumage is acquired in the third year. Fairly common to common on both coasts (breeds on Bay Is. and cayes of Belize and Honduras); rare inland. Resident populations are augmented with migrants from N. America. Found on coastal beaches, estuaries, and open waters. Plunge-dives for prey; also sits on water, perches on fishing boats, and roosts in trees at edge of water. U.S. to Venezuela. The similar but much larger **Peruvian Pelican (*Pelecanus thagus*)**, not illustrated, is a vagrant to the Pacific coast.

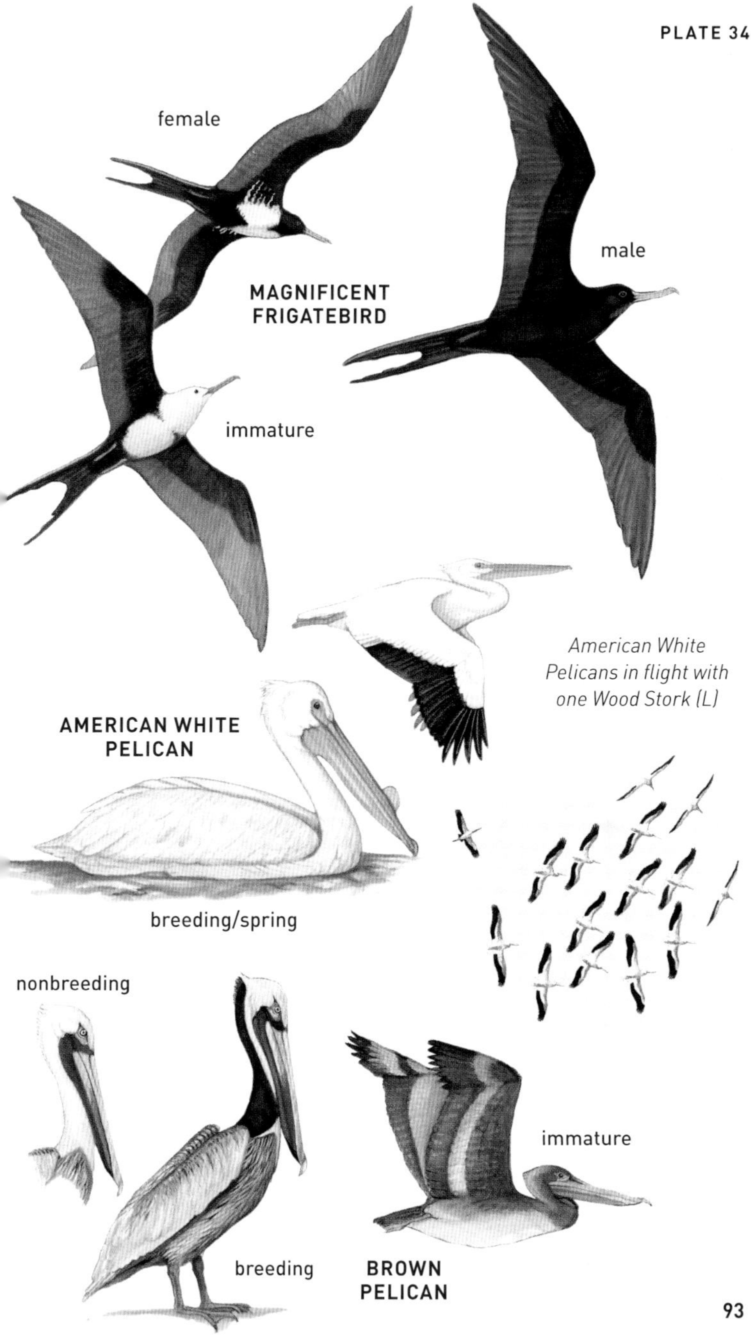
female
male
MAGNIFICENT
FRIGATEBIRD
immature
American White
Pelicans in flight with
one Wood Stork (L)
AMERICAN WHITE
PELICAN
breeding/spring
nonbreeding
immature
breeding
BROWN
PELICAN

BITTERNS AND GREEN HERON

ARDEIDAE (Order: Pelecaniformes). Herons are typically found in wetland and aquatic habitats. Most species feed by using their long, pointed bills to spear fish, crustaceans, and occasionally small snakes, lizards, mice, and birds. Many roost and breed colonially, often in mixed-species groups. Egrets are usually white, herons slaty blue, while bitterns have shades of brown. Briefly worn breeding plumage may include long, elegant plumes, or brightly colored bills and bare skin. Head plumes are known as *aigrettes*, named for the egret, a generic term for white heron. **18 species (11 genera)**

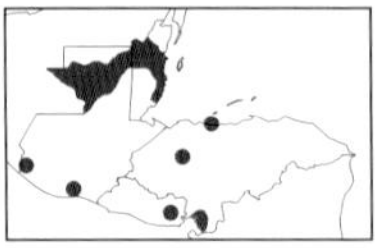

PINNATED BITTERN *Botaurus pinnatus*
27.5 in. (70 cm). **Upperparts buff with dark streaking and barring**; underparts pale. Similar to American Bittern, but larger and buff overall (not chestnut), has **fine black barring on neck** (not streaking) and on crown, and lacks dark malar. Uncommon in n. Belize, rare elsewhere in NCA; to 2,130 ft. (650 m). Found in freshwater marshes and wet grass fields. Cryptic plumage and upright posture make detection difficult. Call is a series of pumping notes followed by a deeper boom: *plick-plick-OOMMM!* Also a croaking alarm call in flight. Mex. to Brazil.

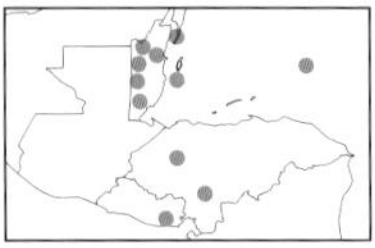

AMERICAN BITTERN *Botaurus lentiginosus*
22 in. (56 cm). **Upperparts chestnut with dark barring**; underparts pale. Similar to Pinnated Bittern, but smaller and darker overall, and has long **tawny-chestnut streaks on throat and chest** (not barring), **solid dark crown**, and **dark malar**. Winter visitor (Oct.–Apr.). Very rare (Pacific Slope) to rare (Caribbean Slope) in NCA including Swan Is. and Belizean cayes; to 4,430 ft. (1,350 m). Found in freshwater marshes and wet grass fields. Difficult to detect owing to cryptic plumage and upright posture; remains still for long periods. In flight, note hunchback appearance. Call is a throaty *auk*, given when flushed. Canada (breeding) to Nicaragua (winter).

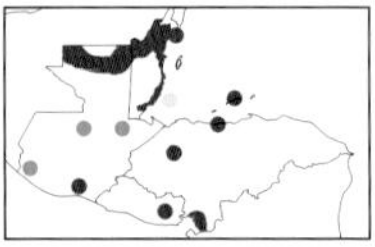

LEAST BITTERN *Ixobrychus exilis*
11.5 in. (29 cm). **Smallest heron in NCA.** On male, upperparts and crown black; **face and neck rich tawny**; throat and chest white with tawny streaking; note **creamy wing panel**. Female similar to male but is drabber overall. Similar in form to Green Heron. Rare to uncommon resident locally throughout NCA; some migrants augment the population Nov. to Mar.; to 6,560 ft. (2,000 m). Found in freshwater wetlands with tall grasses or reeds; forages from perches in cattails or marsh grass; cryptic plumage pattern can make it difficult to detect. Call is a low *poe-poe'poe'poe* (accelerates slightly toward the end); also makes a throaty *wrrroooaa*; flight call is a *kek*. U.S. to Colombia.

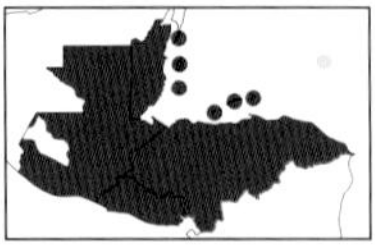

GREEN HERON *Butorides virescens*
17 in. (43 cm). Adult has **dark green upperparts**; dark crown; **maroon neck**. Immature similar to adult, but is browner above and has pale edging and spots on wing coverts, streaks on throat. Adult similar to adult Least Bittern in size and posture, but has maroon neck (not tawny) and greenish upperparts (not black), and lacks pale wing panel. Fairly common resident on both slopes and Bay Is.; common transient and winter visitor in NCA (Sept.–May), rare transient on Swan Is.; to 6,560 ft. (2,000 m). Found in lakes, ponds, marshes, rivers, streams, mangroves, and estuaries. Generally solitary. Occasionally nests in urban areas. When flushed, alarm call is an explosive *Kiuuuew!*; also makes a low territorial growl (*kaaaw*). U.S. to Panama.

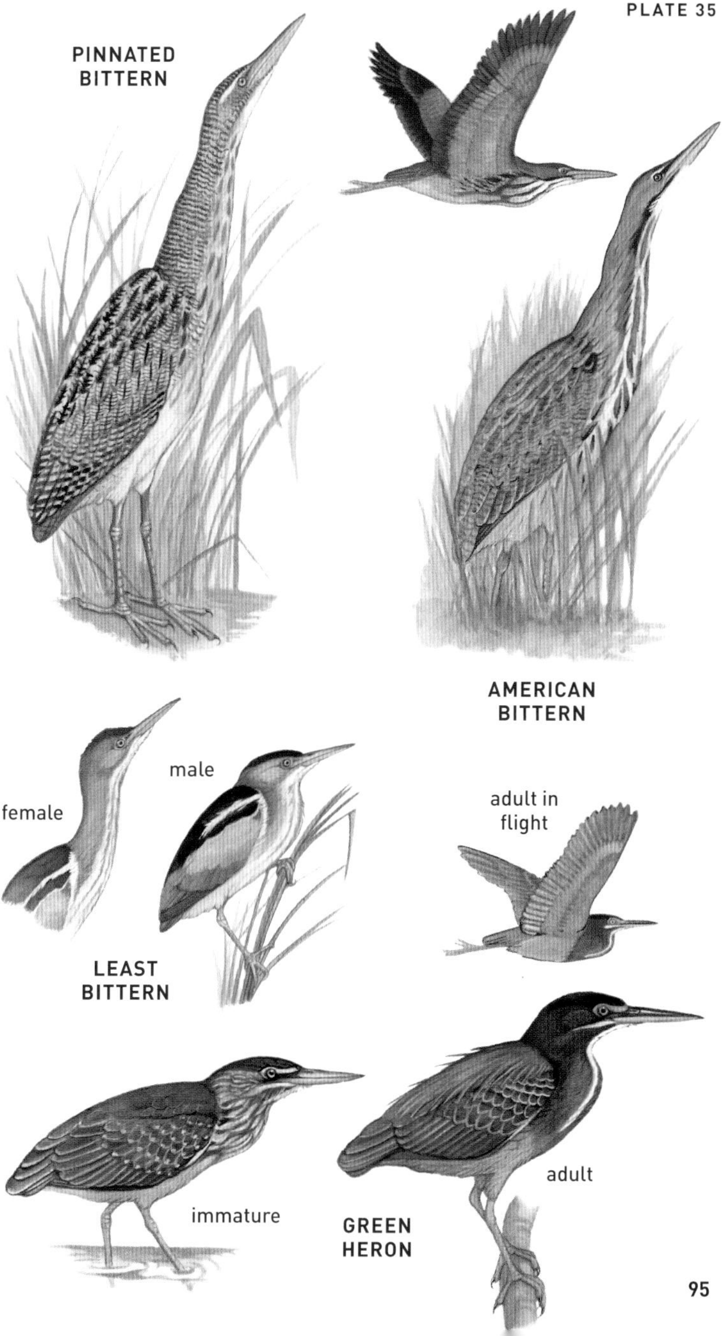
PINNATED
BITTERN
AMERICAN
BITTERN
male
female
LEAST
BITTERN
adult in
flight
immature
GREEN
HERON
adult

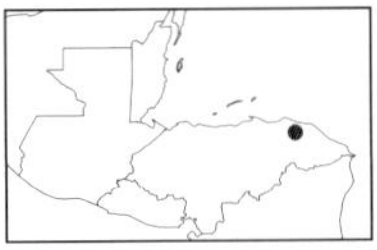

FASCIATED TIGER-HERON *Tigrisoma fasciatum*

25 in. (64 cm). On adult, **upperparts dark sooty gray**; dark crown; **relatively short bill**; **white chin and throat**. On juvenile, neck tawny orange with bold black barring. Distinguish from juvenile Rufescent Tiger-Heron by smaller body and bill, and barring on neck (not chevrons); also note habitat. Uncommon in e. Honduras; to 2,950 ft. (900 m). Found along swift streams within rainforest. Forages among boulders, often waits motionless. Generally silent. Honduras to Brazil.

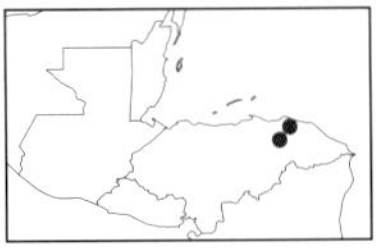

RUFESCENT TIGER-HERON *Tigrisoma lineatum*

27 in. (69 cm). Adult has **rufous head and neck**. Juvenile like Bare-throated Tiger-Heron, but has black chevrons on neck and feathered throat; also like Fasciated Tiger-Heron, but has larger body and bill, and chevrons on neck; note habitat differences. Rare in e. Honduras; to 660 ft. (200 m). Found near streams and swamps within rainforest; moves slowly or stands motionless. Call is a throaty *rah-rah-raaaahhhh!*; also a repeated *rah*. Honduras to Argentina.

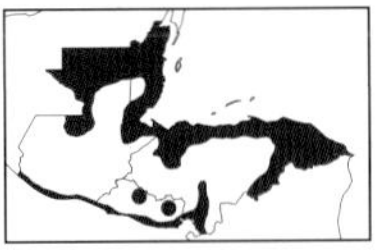

BARE-THROATED TIGER-HERON *Tigrisoma mexicanum*

30 in. (76 cm). **Bare yellow throat**. On adult, **face and crown grayish**; **neck with fine black barring**. Distinguish juvenile from Rufescent Tiger-Heron by thin barring (not chevrons) on neck, and unfeathered throat. Fairly common on both slopes; to 3,280 ft. (1,000 m). Forages at edges of lakes, marshes, and rivers; also in mangroves. Sometimes perches in trees. Generally solitary. Crepuscular call is a low, barking *woa-woa-woa-woa-woa-*. . . ; when flushed or agitated, makes a gruff, throaty *rhaw-rhaw-rhaw-*. . . Mex. to Colombia.

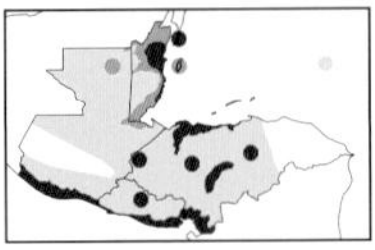

BLACK-CROWNED NIGHT-HERON *Nycticorax nycticorax*

25 in. (64 cm). Adult has **black crown and back**. Immature brown overall with pale streaking and **large white spots on wing coverts**; yellow mandible. Distinguish immature from Yellow-crowned Night-Heron by larger white spots on wing coverts, yellow mandible (not dark), and shorter legs that extend only slightly beyond the tail in flight. Locally uncommon resident on both slopes; to 6,560 ft. (2,000 m). Populations augmented by migrants Sept. to May. Found near any wetland habitat. Hunts at night; leaves roost at twilight. Solitary or in small groups. Call is a throaty *rrraaah!* Cosmopolitan.

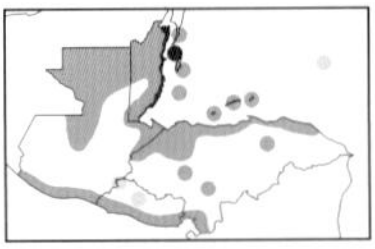

YELLOW-CROWNED NIGHT-HERON *Nyctanassa violacea*

24 in. (61 cm). Adult with **distinctive black-and-white face pattern.** Immature like Black-crowned Night-Heron, but has smaller spots on wing coverts, all-dark bill, and longer legs that project well beyond the tail in flight. Fairly common resident on Caribbean Slope and Bay Is., rare resident on Pacific Slope; winter visitors disperse widely on both slopes (Sept.–Apr.); to 2,460 ft. (750 m). Found near any wetland habitat. Hunts day and night. Solitary or in small groups. Call similar to call of Black-crowned Night-Heron but slightly reedier. U.S. to Brazil.

BOAT-BILLED HERON *Cochlearius cochlearius*

19.5 in. (50 cm). **Shovel-shaped bill** is distinctive. Immature similar to adult, but has a dirtier look. Fairly common on both slopes, and Belizean cayes; to 2,950 ft. (900 m). Found on riverbanks, at edges of lakes and ponds, and in mangroves. Hunts at night. Solitary or in small groups. Call is a nasal barking (similar to chuckling). Mex. to Argentina.

FASCIATED
TIGER-HERON
adult
immature
RUFESCENT
TIGER-HERON
adult
immature
adult
immature
BARE-
THROATED
TIGER-HERON
adult in
flight
adult
BLACK-CROWNED
NIGHT-HERON
immature
YELLOW-
CROWNED
NIGHT-HERON
adult
immature
BOAT-BILLED
HERON
adult
immature

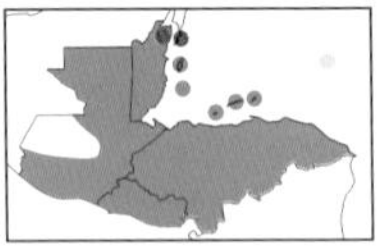

GREAT BLUE HERON *Ardea herodias*

47 in. (120 cm). **Largest heron in NCA**. On adult, upperparts gray; **head whitish with long black plumes**; thighs rufous; in flight, note dark flight feathers. Immature darker overall and has dark cap; paler thighs. White morph (known as Great White Heron) similar to Great Egret, but is larger and has heavier bill and yellow-gray legs (not black). Fairly common winter visitor on Caribbean Slope, including cayes, Bay Is., and Swan Is.; common winter visitor on Pacific Slope (late Aug.–early May); rare summer visitor (breeding; June–Aug.) in Belize; white morph is uncommon on n. cayes of Belize; to 6,560 ft. (2,000 m). Found in lakes, ponds, marshes, mangroves, estuaries, and coastal beaches. Usually solitary, although small groups can be seen migrating at high altitudes. Makes a deep, hoarse *Braaahk!* when flushed. Canada (breeding) to Venezuela (winter).

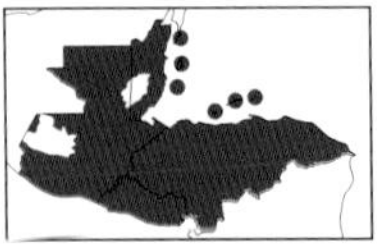

GREAT EGRET *Ardea alba*

38 in. (97 cm). **Large, slender white wader**; legs black. Breeding adult has long, flowing white plumes on back, and lime green lores. Similar to white-morph Great Blue Heron (n. Belize only), but is smaller, and has black legs (not yellow-gray). Larger than white-morph Reddish Egret and has **bright yellow bill**. Common resident throughout, with population augmented by northern migrants (Oct.–May); to 6,560 ft. (2,000 m). Found in wetland environments, including lakes, ponds, marshes, drainage ditches, rice fields, estuaries, and beaches. Forages alone or with other long-legged waders. Breeds in colonies. Call is a deep, throaty *aaahhhh!* Cosmopolitan.

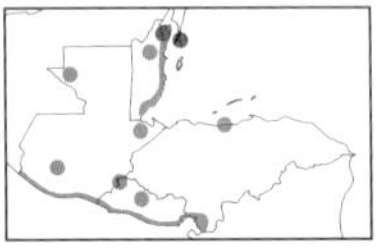

REDDISH EGRET *Egretta rufescens*

31 in. (79 cm). On dark-morph adult, dark blue-gray upperparts contrast with **reddish neck**; breeding **bill with pinkish base and dark tip** (nonbreeding bill dark). Juvenile dark morph has duller, chalky coloration and dark gray bill and lores. Light morph all-white but retains pinkish bill with dark tip, and black legs (juvenile has dark gray bill and lores). Distinguished from other herons by colors of bill and legs, dark lores, and contrasting **white eyes**. Uncommon resident on cayes of n. Belize; rare visitor along both coasts, but more common on Pacific coast (late July–Apr.); to 130 ft. (40 m). Found on coastal beaches and mudflats. Actively forages by shadowing with open wings, with quick bursts of running. Solitary (except at breeding colonies). Generally silent. U.S. and Caribbean to Venezuela.

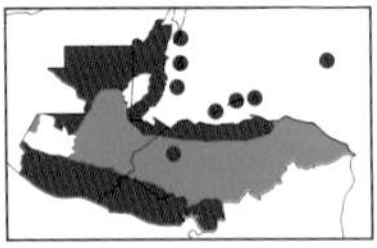

SNOWY EGRET *Egretta thula*

24 in. (61 cm). A medium-sized wader with a slender, graceful build. On nonbreeding adult and immature, note **dark bill** and **yellow lores**; **black legs** (yellowish on back of leg); **yellow feet**. Breeding adult similar, but has long, shaggy white breeding plumes on crown, lower back, and chest; lores are reddish pink at peak breeding time. Immature similar to first-year Little Blue Heron, but has darker bill and legs and yellow lores (not gray). Common resident along both coasts (and slightly inland), and on Swan Is. and Bay Is.; winter visitors disperse widely on both slopes (Oct.–May); to 6,560 ft. (2,000 m). Coastal populations frequent mangroves, estuaries, and beaches; also occurs inland in lakes, ponds, swamps, marshes, rivers, and even drainage ditches. Forages with other long-legged waders; sometimes hunts by dancing in pools and shadowing. Call is a forced *aahhh!* (higher-pitched than Great Egret's). U.S. to Argentina.

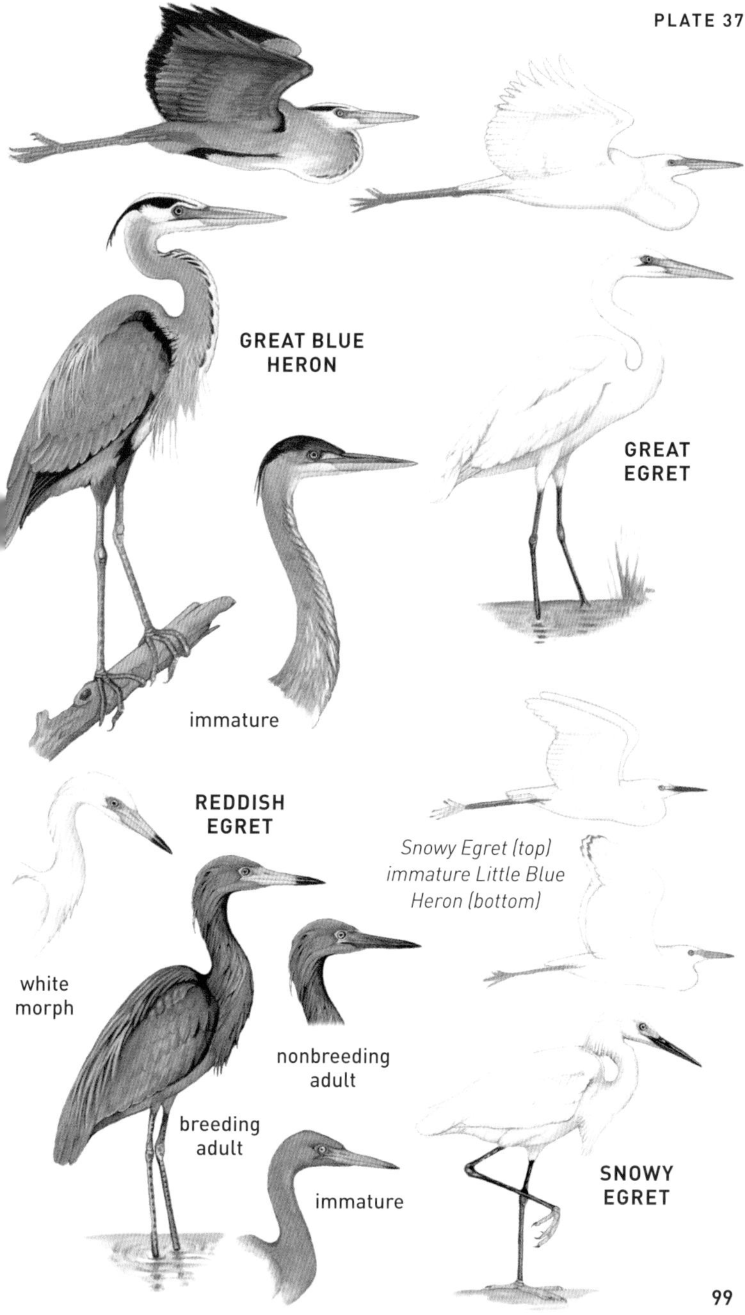
GREAT BLUE HERON
immature
GREAT EGRET
REDDISH EGRET
white morph
Snowy Egret (top)
immature Little Blue
Heron (bottom)
nonbreeding adult
breeding adult
immature
SNOWY EGRET

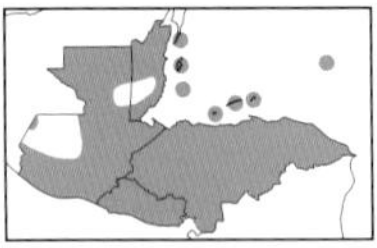

LITTLE BLUE HERON *Egretta caerulea*

24 in. (61 cm). Adult **slaty blue overall**; **head and neck violet maroon**; bill blue-gray with dark tip. First-year plumage all-white; bill gray with dark tip; similar to immature Snowy Egret, but has dull greenish gray legs, gray lores (not yellow), paler bill, and dusky tips to primaries (see plate 37 for in-flight comparison). Second-year plumage white with patches of purplish blue feathers (known as calico plumage). Common nonbreeding resident along both coasts (although not known to nest), and on Swan Is. and Bay Is.; winter visitors and transients disperse widely on both slopes (Oct.–May); to 6,560 ft. (2,000 m). Found on coastal beaches and around lakes, ponds, marshes, swamps, mangroves, and estuaries; also along rivers. Commonly forages with other long-legged waders; less active feeder than Snowy Egret. Call is a throaty *ehhh!* or *aahh!* (similar to call of Snowy Egret). U.S. to Brazil.

TRICOLORED HERON *Egretta tricolor*

26 in. (66 cm). Attractive **2-tone plumage**. Adult **purplish blue overall** with purplish maroon tones on neck; note **white belly**; **long, pointed bill**; creamy head plumes. Immature plumage similar to adult's, but with reddish brown neck and upper back; immature similar to immature Agami Heron, but has shorter bill, pale yellowish legs, and white underparts (no streaking). Uncommon resident along both coasts (and slightly inland), and on Bay Is.; fairly common as winter visitors and transients dispersing widely on both slopes (Oct.–May); to 6,560 ft. (2,000 m). Found on coastal beaches and in lakes, ponds, marshes, mangroves, and estuaries. Solitary. Generally silent. U.S. to Brazil.

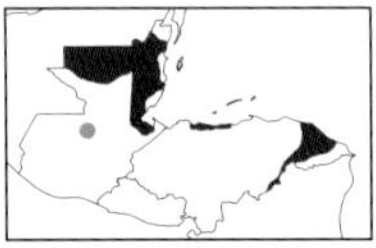

AGAMI HERON *Agamia agami*

28 in. (71 cm). Slightly iridescent dark green upperparts; **neck and underparts chestnut**; note **silver edging on neck** and long silver plumes on crown; **very long, thin bill**. Immature brown to rufous brown above; underparts white with brown streaking; immature similar to immature Tricolored Heron but has longer bill, more brown overall, and streaking below. Rare to locally uncommon on Caribbean Slope; to 2,130 ft. (650 m). Found along quiet rivers and streams within rainforest. Secretive; seldom encountered. Generally silent away from breeding colony. Mex. to Brazil.

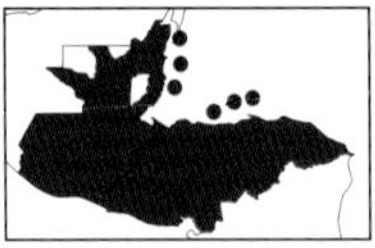

CATTLE EGRET *Bubulcus ibis*

19 in. (48 cm). Nonbreeding adult has all-white plumage, yellow bill and lores, and dark legs. Breeding adult similar, but shows **orange patches on back, chest, and crown**; lores reddish pink during peak breeding time; legs yellowish orange. Immature similar to nonbreeding adult, but may show darker bill. Cattle Egret populations expanded naturally into NCA in the 1950s; now abundant on both slopes; to 6,560 ft. (2,000 m). The only NCA heron that spends much of its time in dry habitats; found in open areas, including pastures, agricultural fields, and roadways. While foraging, methodically follows in the footsteps of grazing animals; often perches on the backs of resting cattle. Large flocks can be seen in fields and in flight. Forms nighttime roosts by the thousands. Call at colony is a short, throaty *rah* or *aah*; generally silent away from roost or breeding site. Cosmopolitan.

Cattle Egrets foraging with cow

THRESKIORNITHIDAE (Order: Pelecaniformes). Large long-legged wading birds with long necks, and long, decurved or spoon-shaped bills. Ibises forage by probing soft mud or sand, while spoonbills sift through the water with rapid side-to-side motions. These birds are often seen foraging in small flocks, or flying overhead in irregular V formations. They roost and breed colonially, often in mixed-species groups. (See p. 84 for the spoonbill species account.) **5 species (4 genera)**

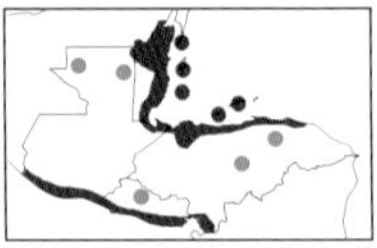

WHITE IBIS *Eudocimus albus*

25 in. (64 cm). Adult **white overall** with long, heavily decurved red bill; legs red; in flight, note **black tips to primaries**. On immature, back and upperwings dark brown; legs grayish pink. Fairly common in coastal areas on both slopes, and occasional on the Bay Is. Found in low-lying lakes, ponds, marshes, mangroves, and estuaries; rarely to 3,280 ft. (1,000 m). Almost always encountered in flocks. Generally silent. U.S. to Peru.

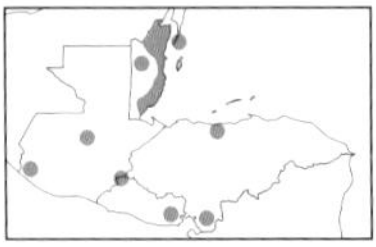

GLOSSY IBIS *Plegadis falcinellus*

23 in. (59 cm). Breeding adult has **dark maroon plumage** with **iridescent green and purple wing coverts**; at base of bill, note grayish facial area with **thin white border**; bill is long and heavily decurved; **eyes dark**. Nonbreeding adult similar to breeding, but is drabber overall and lacks iridescent plumage. Immature similar to nonbreeding adult, but sometimes lacks white border on face; immature indistinguishable from some immature White-faced Ibis until latter species shows red eyes or facial skin. Uncommon and local winter visitor in Belize (mid-Sept.–May); winter vagrant in El Salvador, Honduras, and Guatemala. Found in flooded fields, along lakes, ponds, or reservoirs, marshes, and estuaries, up to 4,590 ft. (1,400 m). Usually in small flocks. Generally silent. Cosmopolitan.

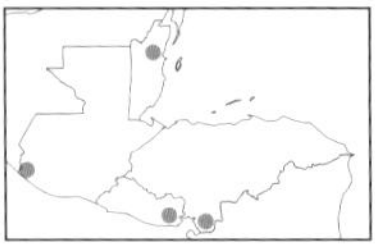

WHITE-FACED IBIS *Plegadis chihi*

23.5 in. (60 cm). Breeding adult has **red facial area at base of bill bordered heavily in white that wraps behind the eye; irides are red**. Nonbreeding adult still retains the red eye and red facial area, but lacks white on face. Immature indistinguishable from immature Glossy Ibis until it shows red eyes or facial skin. Winter vagrant (Dec., Jan.) to NCA. Found in flooded fields, along lakes, ponds, or reservoirs, marshes, and estuaries, up to 980 ft. (300 m). Usually in small flocks. Generally silent. Canada to Argentina.

GREEN IBIS *Mesembrinibis cayennensis*

21 in. (53 cm). **Glossy green overall**; eyes dark. Uncommon in e. Honduras. Found in rainforest; along forested streams and meadows; to 660 ft. (200 m). Crepuscular call is a hollow, rolling *krwa-krwa-krwa-krwa*. Honduras to Brazil.

WHITE
IBIS
adult
immature
nonbreeding/
immature
WHITE-FACED
IBIS
GLOSSY
IBIS
breeding
nonbreeding/
immature
GREEN
IBIS

LIMPKIN AND WOOD-RAILS

ARAMIDAE (Order: Gruiformes). Although similar in structure to herons and ibises, the Limpkin is more closely related to rails (p. 108) and cranes, but is in a monotypic family. It is a tropical wading bird found only in the New World. It feeds primarily at night on freshwater snails (genus *Pomacea*). **1 species (1 genus)**

LIMPKIN *Aramus guarauna*

24 in. (61 cm). Long-legged with a rather **long, slightly decurved bill**; brown overall with **large white spots on wing**; fine white streaking on neck. Uncommon to fairly common on Caribbean Slope, rare to uncommon on Pacific Slope; to 4,920 ft. (1,500 m). Found in freshwater wetlands such as marshes, swamps, and lagoons, where large apple snails can be found. Usually solitary. Call is a loud, raucous *KEH-R'R'R'E'EEA!*; also makes a *WREAAH!* and a softer *kek*. U.S. to Argentina.

RALLIDAE (Order: Gruiformes). Crakes and rails are small, thin-bodied birds that generally stay hidden in thick vegetation of wetland habitats; they are among the most difficult birds to observe. Their relatively long legs and toes are adapted for walking on aquatic vegetation. They feed on small invertebrates, amphibians, and plant matter. Despite their propensity for walking, rails are good fliers (some are migratory). Gallinules and coots are larger-bodied and easier to observe, as they forage at the water's edge, often swimming in the open. **16 species (10 genera)**

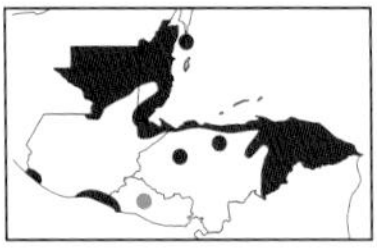

RUSSET-NAPED WOOD-RAIL *Aramides albiventris*

16 in. (41 cm). Largest rail in NCA. **Gray face and neck** contrast strongly with rufous crown and chest. Fairly common but local on Caribbean Slope, uncommon and local on Pacific Slope; to 2,950 ft. (900 m). Found in mangroves, swamp forest, and wet areas of rainforest and semideciduous forest. Secretive, but sometimes forages in the open. Often detected by voice—a very loud, laughing *KOOK-KOOK-KOOK-KWAY!-KWAY!-KWAY!-KWAY!*; also makes an agitated clucking. Mex. to Argentina. Formerly considered a subspecies of Gray-necked Wood-Rail (*Aramides cajaneus*).

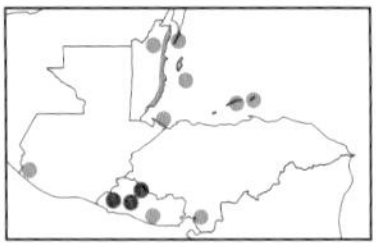

RUFOUS-NECKED WOOD-RAIL *Aramides axillaris*

12 in. (31 cm). **Bright rufous head, neck, and underparts**. Rare to uncommon locally in NCA, including Bay Is.; winter visitor to Belize (mid-Sept.–late May); seasonal occurrence in coastal areas and montane breeding habitats suggests altitudinal migration; to 3,280 ft. (1,000 m). Found in mangroves; breeds in semideciduous forest on Pacific Slope. Secretive, but sometimes forages in the open on mudflats. Call is a loud, ringing *KOW!-KOW!-KIP!-KIP'KOW!-KIP'KOW!-KOW-KOW-KOW-KIP'KOW!* . . . , given during crepuscular flights during breeding season; also makes a lower *Kee'oh!* and an agitated, hard *Tik!* On breeding grounds, makes a soft, low-pitched, *poo-poo-poo-poo-poo-poo*, like tapping on a drum. Mex. to Ecuador.

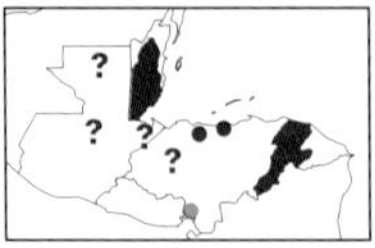

UNIFORM CRAKE *Amaurolimnas concolor*

8.5 in. (22 cm). **Uniformly rufous brown**. Uncommon locally on Caribbean Slope; to 2,620 ft. (800 m). Found in rainforest and swamp forest; forages on ground in thick low vegetation at edge of forest pools. Difficult to see. Calls infrequently, a high-pitched, winnowing *Curreee-Cureee-Curree-Curree-CREEP-Curree-CREEP-Curree-CREEP* . . . (ventriloquial; often given in duet). Mex. to Brazil.

LIMPKIN

RUSSET-NAPED
WOOD-RAIL

RUFOUS-NECKED
WOOD-RAIL

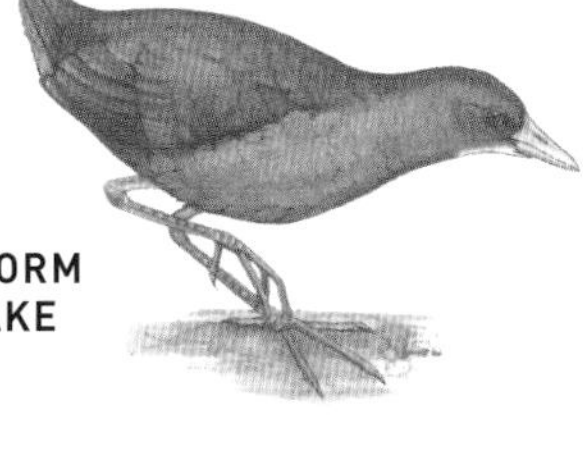

UNIFORM
CRAKE

RUDDY CRAKE *Laterallus ruber*

6 in. (15 cm). **Grayish black head** contrasts with **rufous nape and underparts**; bill dark, legs dark yellow-green; eyes red. Similar to White-throated Crake, but lacks black-and-white barring below. Fairly common on Caribbean Slope, locally rare to uncommon on Pacific Slope; to 4,920 ft. (1,500 m). Found in freshwater marshes and flooded fields (including swampy edge habitat); prefers the cover of tall grasses and reeds. Secretive and difficult to observe, but occasionally forages in the open. Most often detected by voice. Call is a loud, scratchy, churring *CHI' CHI'CHI'CHI'CH'R'R'R'R'R'R'R'R'r'r'r'r'r'r'r'r* (descends in volume toward the end); also makes agitated chirps (*tic!*) and barks (*arrf!*). Mex. to Nicaragua.

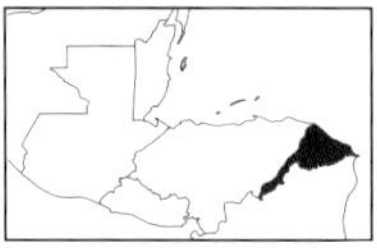

WHITE-THROATED CRAKE *Laterallus albigularis*

6 in. (15 cm). Nape and **chest rufous**; throat whitish (may be difficult to see); **black-and-white barring on sides, flanks, and undertail coverts**. Bill dark (with lime green base to mandible) and legs dark yellow-green. Similar to Ruddy Crake but has black-and-white barring below. Similar to Gray-breasted Crake but has rufous chest (not gray). Uncommon in e. Honduras; to 2,460 ft. (750 m). Found in freshwater marshes, flooded fields, and swampy edge habitat. Most often detected by voice. Long churring call is similar to call of Ruddy Crake; also a *kek* contact call. Honduras to Ecuador.

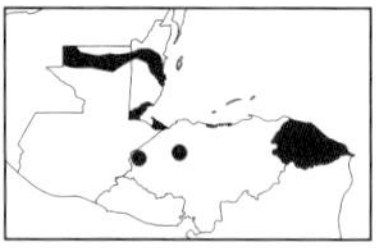

GRAY-BREASTED CRAKE *Laterallus exilis*

6 in. (15 cm). **Gray head and chest** contrast with rufous nape and whitish throat; **flanks and undertail coverts with black-and-white barring**. Base of mandible lime green. Legs and feet yellow-green. Very similar to White-throated Crake, but has gray chest (not rufous). Similar to Black Rail, but is paler overall and lacks thin white barring above. Rare to uncommon locally on Caribbean Slope; to 2,130 ft. (650 m). Found in wet meadows, rice fields, freshwater marshes, and weedy lake edges. Calls infrequently; makes a mechanical froglike *tink-ti'ti'ti'ti'ti'ti* and a *tink-tink-tink-tink*. Mex. to Brazil.

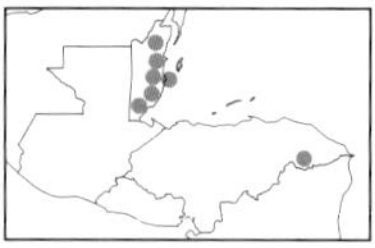

BLACK RAIL *Laterallus jamaicensis*

5 in. (13 cm). A very small rail. Similar to Gray-breasted Crake, but is sooty black on head and underparts and has **thin white barring above**; **bill all-dark**. Very rare winter visitor to NCA (Nov.–Mar.) with few, scattered records; possibly breeds in Belize and coastal Moskitia region of e. Honduras; to 4,430 ft. (1,350 m). Found in seasonally flooded savannas, freshwater marshes, and wet fields. Rarely seen. Calls infrequently. Call is a slightly nasal *kii-kii-kurrr*; also makes an agitated, scolding *chir'chir'chir'chir'chir'chir'chir'r'r'r'r'r'r'r'r'r'r'r*. U.S. to Chile.

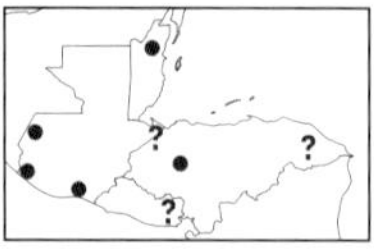

YELLOW-BREASTED CRAKE *Hapalocrex flaviventer*

5 in. (13 cm). A very small rail. **Buffy yellow breast** contrasts with dark upperparts; note **thin white supercilium** and **dark eye line**; flanks and sides heavily barred black and white. Similar to juvenile Sora (p. 108), but is smaller, has bold white supercilium, dark eye line, and thin dark bill. Very rare and local in NCA; to 2,950 ft. (900 m). Found in freshwater marshes, wet meadows, rice fields, and weedy lake edges. Secretive and difficult to observe; however, occasionally forages at edge. Call is a soft, nasal *chik'chik'chik'chik'chik*. Mex. to Argentina.

RUDDY
CRAKE

WHITE-THROATED
CRAKE

GRAY-BREASTED
CRAKE

YELLOW-BREASTED
CRAKE

BLACK
RAIL

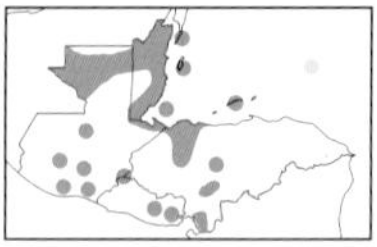

SORA *Porzana carolina*

8.5 in. (22 cm). A small rail. Note grayish face and underparts with contrasting **black at base of bill, black throat, and bright yellow bill**; also, thin black-and-white barring on flanks. Juvenile (plumage kept until Dec.) lacks black in face and on throat; compare with Yellow-breasted Crake (p. 106), but juvenile Sora lacks a bold white supercilium and dark eye line, plus note heavier yellow bill (thin and dark on crake). Winter visitor (mid-Sept.–mid-Apr.). Uncommon to fairly common on Caribbean Slope, rare to uncommon locally on Pacific Slope; to 6,560 ft. (2,000 m). Found in wet meadows, rice fields, freshwater marshes, and weedy lake edges. May forage at edge in open. Call is an inquisitive, nasal *Kurreee?*; also makes a high-pitched *Weep!* and a descending, whinnylike *keek-kik!'kik!'kik!'kik!'kik!'kik'k'r'r'r'r'r'r'r'r'r.* Canada to S. America.

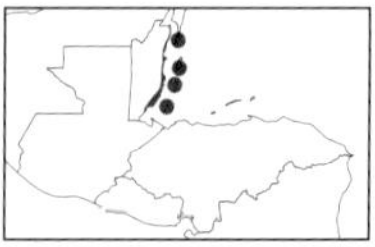

CLAPPER RAIL *Rallus crepitans*

13.5 in. (34 cm). Virtually identical to Mangrove Rail, but no range overlap. Grayish brown overall with bold, dark streaking on upperparts; **flanks, belly, and undertail coverts barred black and white**; note pale supercilium and **long yellow-orange bill**. Similar to Virginia Rail, but much larger, and less obvious barring on flanks; also note differences in range and habitat. Fairly common in Belize; to 160 ft. (50 m). Found in coastal marshes, mangrove scrub, and estuaries. Calls infrequently; call is a rough, scratchy, laughing *kik'kik'kik'kik'kik'kik'kik'kik'kik'kik'kik'kik'k'k'k'k'k* (drops in pitch and volume toward the end); also makes a slower *kek-kek-kek-kek-kek-kek . . .* (roughly 2 notes per sec.) and a grating *craaake!* U.S. and Caribbean to Belize.

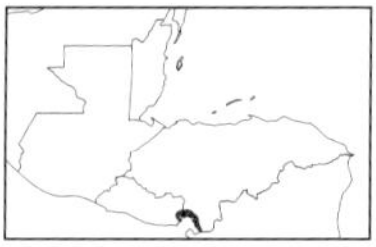

MANGROVE RAIL *Rallus longirostris*

13.5 in. (34 cm). Virtually identical to Clapper Rail, with differing vocalizations and different range. Uncommon in s. Honduras and El Salvador around Gulf of Fonseca. Found in mangrove scrub. Sometimes forages at edge of mudflats. Calls include a rapid *kik'kik'keeer-kik'kik'keeer-kik'kik'keeer-kik'kik'keeer . . .*; also a 2-part *kit'keeeeahh!* and a harder *kik-kik*. El Salvador to Brazil and Ecuador.

VIRGINIA RAIL *Rallus limicola*

9 in. (23 cm). Similar to Clapper Rail, but is much smaller with **brighter tawny-rufous edging to upperparts and chest**; also, **more obvious black-and-white barring on flanks and undertail coverts**. Also note range and habitat differences. Very rare autumn visitor (recorded Sept. and Oct.) in Guatemala, but possibly resident; from 4,430 to 5,090 ft. (1,350–1,550 m). Found in freshwater marshes and wet fields. Call is a scratchy, slightly nasal, barking *Rahnk!-Rahnk!-Rahnk!-Rahnk!-Rahnk!-Rahnk!-Rahnk!-k'k'k'r'r'r* (drops in pitch and volume toward the end); also makes a thin, ticking *kek-kek-kek-kedek-kedek-kedek . . .* Canada to Peru.

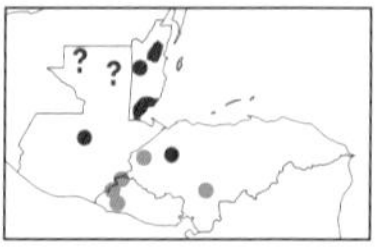

SPOTTED RAIL *Pardirallus maculatus*

10.5 in. (27 cm). Distinctive **black-and-white spotting on neck and chest** turns to barring on belly, sides, and flanks; upperparts brown with black-and-white markings; **long, greenish yellow bill has red spot at base**; legs orange red. Rare and local in NCA, but prone to wandering; to 2,460 ft. (750 m). Found in freshwater marshes and marshy edges of lakes and reservoirs. Secretive. Calls infrequently with a harsh, scratchy *KEK!* or *KEK'KEK'KEK'KEK*; also makes a *KREEEEAH!* Mex. to Argentina.

SORA
adult
immature
CLAPPER/
MANGROVE RAIL
VIRGINIA
RAIL
SPOTTED
RAIL

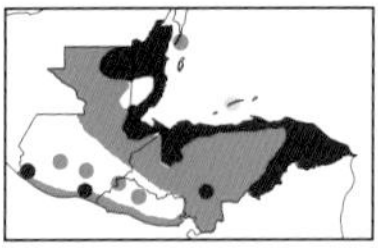

PURPLE GALLINULE *Porphyrio martinicus*

12.5 in. (32 cm). Adult unmistakable, with **purple-blue head, neck, and underparts**; **sky blue frontal shield**; **red bill with yellow tip**; large feet are bright yellow. Juvenile drab overall; distinguished from juvenile Common Gallinule by greenish brown tones to upperparts, and paler, tawny underparts (not gray). Uncommon resident throughout, although nearly absent from NCA in October; populations augmented by winter visitors Nov. to early Mar.; to 2,950 ft. (900 m). Found in freshwater marshes and rice fields, and at marshy edges of lakes and reservoirs; walks on lily pads and surface vegetation. Calls include a nasal, begging *caw-ka'ka'ka'ka'ka'caw!* or a single *Caw!*; also makes a thinner *keh-keh-keh-* . . . U.S. to Argentina.

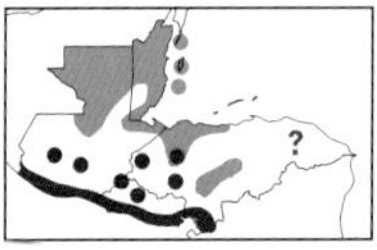

COMMON GALLINULE *Gallinula galeata*

13.5 in. (34 cm). On breeding adult, **dark gray head, neck, and underparts** separated from chestnut brown wings and tail by **choppy white stripe across side**; legs yellow (bare red thighs often not visible); note **red frontal shield and bill** (yellow tip to bill); plumage and bill color duller on nonbreeding adults. Juvenile has dull gray head and underparts, white belly; juvenile similar to juvenile Purple Gallinule, but is dull gray below (not tawny), and lacks greenish brown tones above. Resident with influx of winter visitors late Nov. to early Mar. Fairly common in NCA; to 6,560 ft. (2,000 m). Found in freshwater marshes, rice fields, lagoons, and marshy edges of lakes and reservoirs; walks on lily pads and surface vegetation. Call is a rapid, nasal, cackling *keh'keh'keh'keh'keh'keh'keh'* . . . ; also makes a louder, thin bark (*Kep!*). U.S. to Argentina.

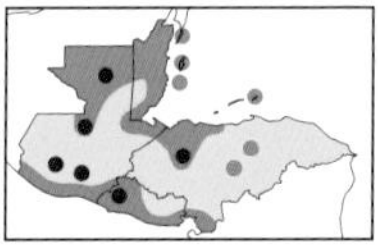

AMERICAN COOT *Fulica americana*

15 in. (38 cm). Adult **dark slate gray** overall with black head; **white frontal shield** with reddish spot; **bill white with reddish band**; legs yellow green; feet grayish with large, lobed toes. Juvenile and first-winter birds similar to adult, but paler overall and lack white frontal shield. Winter visitor (Sept.–Apr.; some individuals linger through summer, and occasionally breed). Fairly common in NCA; to 6,560 ft. (2,000 m). Found in freshwater marshes and on lakes, lagoons, reservoirs, rice fields, and brackish waters, including estuaries and coastal marshes. Calls include a thin, nasal piping or clucking (*kek-kek-kek-kek-kek* . . . or *kak-kak-kak-kak* . . .); also makes a more grating *kraaah*. AK and Canada to Colombia.

HELIORNITHIDAE (Order: Gruiformes). A tropical family of only 3 species, with 1 representative in the New World. Each species is in its own genus. These aquatic birds are known collectively as *finfoots* for their lobed toes; they prefer secluded aquatic habitats with abundant vegetation. Male finfoots are unique in that they have skin pockets on the underside of their wings, which they use to transport young chicks (even while flying). **1 species (1 genus)**

SUNGREBE *Heliornis fulica*

11 in. (28 cm). **Black-and-white striping on face and neck**; bill of male pinkish. Female distinguished from male by **tawny-orange cheek patch**, and brighter reddish orange bill. Uncommon and somewhat local in NCA; to 1,640 ft. (500 m). Found on slow-moving rivers and streams, secluded lakes and reservoirs, lagoons and mangrove swamps. Secretive; sits low in water. Usually solitary or in pairs. Call is a nasal, low-pitched *Woah!-Woah!-Woah!-Whaoh!*; also makes a quacking *Wree!-Wree!-Wree!* Mex. to Brazil.

adult
PURPLE
GALLINULE
immature
adult
immature
COMMON
GALLINULE
adult
immature
AMERICAN
COOT
SUNGREBE
female
male

SUNBITTERN, THICK-KNEES, AND STILTS

EURYPYGIDAE (Order: Eurypygiformes). A monotypic order; the Sunbittern, a unique Neotropical species that recalls a large rail, is generally found along quick-moving rivers or larger streams, but also in the open understory of lowland rainforest. Was once placed in the order Gruiformes (which includes rails, Limpkin, and Sungrebe), but recent taxonomic work shows a closer relationship with the Kagu (*Rhynochetos jubatus*) of New Caledonia. **1 species (1 genus)**

SUNBITTERN *Eurypyga helias*

18 in. (46 cm). Unlikely to be mistaken with other species; on open wings, note **"sun" spots**. Uncommon on Caribbean Slope; to 4,100 ft. (1,250 m). Found along fast-moving streams in rainforest; also in understory. Forages among large rocks and in leaf litter in search of insects, frogs, and small fish. Cryptic, difficult to detect despite size. Sits motionless for long periods. Walks on ground and may be seen flying along rivers. Call is a clear whistle, *Weeeeeeuuuuu!* (falling in pitch at end); also a rapid, rattling *ti'ti'ti'ti'ti'ti'ti'ti'ti'teu'u'u.*

BURHINIDAE (Order: Charadriiformes). Thick-knees are terrestrial waders found throughout tropical and temperate parts of the world, but just one representative lives in NCA. Thick-knees (also known as dikkops or stone-curlews) prefer arid to semiarid open habitats; they are nocturnal foragers (note large eyes), and seek cover under bushes or in tall grass during the day. **1 species (1 genus)**

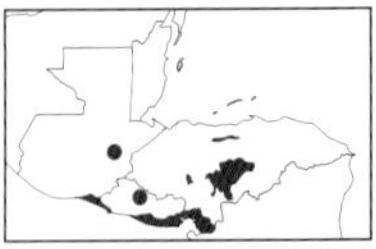

DOUBLE-STRIPED THICK-KNEE *Burhinus bistriatus*

19 in. (48 cm). Long legs, thin neck, and small head; **white supercilium** and **broad black lateral crown stripes**; large yellow eyes. Rare to uncommon on Pacific Slope and in interior dry valleys on Caribbean Slope; to 4,920 ft. (1,500 m). Found in dry grasslands, coastal scrub, and cattle pastures. Can be difficult to observe owing to cryptic plumage and tendency to sit motionless. Call, often heard at night, recalls Southern Lapwing (p. 114) and Ferruginous Pygmy-Owl (p. 178) but usually faster: *heyr-heyr-heyr-heyr-* . . . Mex. to Brazil.

RECURVIROSTRIDAE (Order: Charadriiformes). A cosmopolitan family of long-legged, thin-billed waders. Stilts are named for their long legs, which allow them to forage in deeper water than other shorebirds. Avocets have a distinctive upturned bill (hence the genus name *Recurvirostra*), which they sweep from side to side in the soft mud while foraging in shallows. **2 species (2 genera)**

BLACK-NECKED STILT *Himantopus mexicanus*

14 in. (36 cm). **Long red legs**; thin black bill; **striking pied appearance**. Uncommon and local resident on both slopes, including Bay Is.; resident population augmented by winter visitors July to mid-Apr., when the species can be locally abundant; to 2,950 ft. (900 m). Found in coastal habitats; also occurs inland around lakes and on wet fields. Forages in shallow pools or on mudflats. Call is an agitated, insistent *keh'keh'keh'keh'keh'keh* . . . ; also a hard *kek*. Canada to S. America.

AMERICAN AVOCET *Recurvirostra americana*

18 in. (46 cm). **Long, thin, recurved bill**; black-and-white pattern on upperparts. On breeding adult, **head and neck tawny orange**. On juvenile and nonbreeding adult, **neck and head grayish white**. Winter visitor (Oct.–early Apr.). Rare but increasing on both slopes; to 2,460 ft. (750 m). Found in coastal habitats; also inland around lakes. Forages in shallow pools or on mudflats. Call is a high-pitched, ringing *peep!* or *peep!-peep!-peep!* . . . Canada to Costa Rica.

SUNBITTERN

Sunbittern flashing "sun" spots

Thick-knees in a traditional setting

DOUBLE-STRIPED THICK-KNEE

BLACK-NECKED STILT

AMERICAN AVOCET

nonbreeding

breeding

OYSTERCATCHERS, LAPWINGS, AND *PLUVIALIS* PLOVERS

HAEMATOPODIDAE (Order: Charadriiformes). A cosmopolitan family with 1 genus consisting of 12 species (1 extinct). Among waders, oystercatchers most resemble plovers but they have unique, brightly colored bills adapted for smashing and prying open mollusks. Oystercatchers also probe for worms or other invertebrates. **1 species (1 genus)**

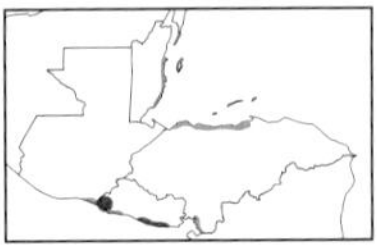

AMERICAN OYSTERCATCHER *Haematopus palliatus*

17.5 in. (45 cm). **Long bright red bill** and **black hood** distinctive. Rare to uncommon winter visitor on both coasts (mid-July–mid-Apr.); breeds locally on Pacific coast, Apr. to July. Restricted to coastal shorelines, where it feeds on mudflats, sandbars, exposed rock, and at oyster beds. Call is a nasal *Weeurrr!* (may be given in flight); also makes a more agitated *pip'pip'pip'pip'* . . . U.S. to Chile.

CHARADRIIDAE (Order: Charadriiformes). A cosmopolitan family of plump, small-headed, long-legged shorebirds with upright postures. Sexes are similar, but there are marked differences between breeding and nonbreeding plumages, as well as between immature and adult plumages. Plovers are found in both wet and dry habitats. **8 species (3 genera)**

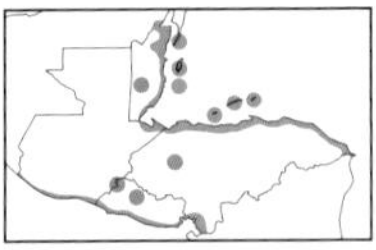

BLACK-BELLIED PLOVER *Pluvialis squatarola*

11.5 in. (29 cm). Breeding adult shows **black-and-white checkerboard pattern** above; face and most of underparts solid black. Nonbreeding adult grayish overall. Juvenile shows spotting on chest, dark crown, and a few golden feathers on upperparts. Juvenile and nonbreeding adult similar to nonbreeding American Golden-Plover, but is larger overall (including bill), shows **black axillaries and white tail** in flight, and has shorter primary projections. Fairly common visitor to NCA (late June–late May); some juveniles may oversummer; to 2,300 ft. (700 m). Found mostly in coastal habitats, rarely on inland lakes and reservoirs; forages on mudflats and sandbars. May be solitary or in flocks; mixes with other species. Flight call is a whistled *Peeer-ooh-weee!* (rising, falling, then rising again). Canada (breeding) to S. America (winter); also Old World.

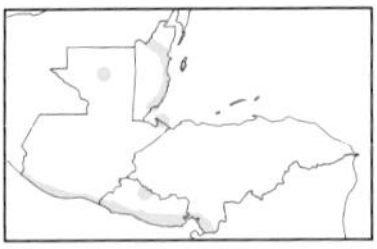

AMERICAN GOLDEN-PLOVER *Pluvialis dominica*

10.5 in. (27 cm). **Breeding adult has rich golden tones to upperparts. In flight, pale axillaries and brown rump.** Nonbreeding adult and juveniles have lightly spotted underparts, streaked crowns, and warm golden flecking on upperparts. Similar to Black-bellied Plover, but smaller, bill shorter and thinner, more golden above, lacks black axillaries and white tail in flight, and has longer primary projection (visible on standing bird). Rare transient (late July–early Dec., Feb.–late May); some individuals may overwinter; few fall records; to 6,560 ft. (2,000 m). Found in coastal habitats, and inland on wet fields, grasslands, and savannas. Solitary or in small flocks. Call is a thin, high-pitched *suuu'weeet!* AK (breeding) to S. America (winter).

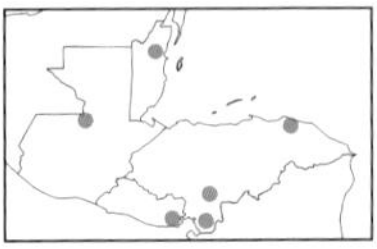

SOUTHERN LAPWING *Vanellus chilensis*

14 in. (36 cm). Note **black patch at base of bill**, **black chest**, and thin crest. Vagrant to NCA (records in all countries; expected to expand north into NCA). Found in pastures, savannas, agricultural fields, and other open country. Call is a loud, agitated *KEEEAH—KEEAAH—* . . . ; also *eh!-eh!-eh!-eh!-eh!* . . . (in flight), similar to Double-striped Thick-knee (p. 112). Nicaragua to S. America.

AMERICAN
OYSTERCATCHER
breeding
nonbreeding
BLACK-BELLIED
PLOVER
breeding
nonbreeding
AMERICAN
GOLDEN-PLOVER
SOUTHERN
LAPWING

CHARADRIUS PLOVERS

COLLARED PLOVER *Charadrius collaris*

6 in. (15 cm). **Thin black chestband**; **thin black bill**. Brown nape (not white as in other *Charadrius* species). Juvenile may show broken breast-band like Snowy Plover, but is smaller, has fleshy pink legs, dark nape, and is darker above. Uncommon on both slopes; to 2,460 ft. (750 m). Found on coastal beaches and estuaries; less commonly on inland lakes and sandbars in rivers. Calls include a single *pip* (also given in flight) and a rapid, sputtering *pee'rrrip!-pee'rrrip!-pee'rrrip!* Mex. to Chile.

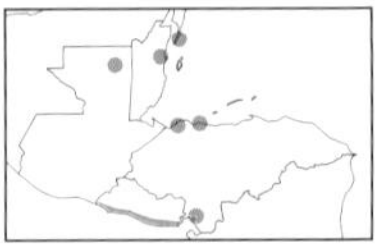

SNOWY PLOVER *Charadrius nivosus*

6.5 in. (17 cm). Breeding adult male has pale brown-gray upperparts, black auriculars, and **incomplete black chest band**; also note **thin, black bill** and **gray legs**. Female typically duller, washed brown. Juvenile and nonbreeding adult similar to female, but paler still and lack black on face. Winter visitor (Aug.–Mar.). Rare to uncommon on both slopes; to 330 ft. (100 m). Found on coastal beaches, estuaries, and shrimp farms. Call is an emphatic, rising *tour'Wheep!*; also makes an agitated sputter: *prrrt'prrt'prrrrt'pp'p'p'prrrt* . . . U.S. to S. America.

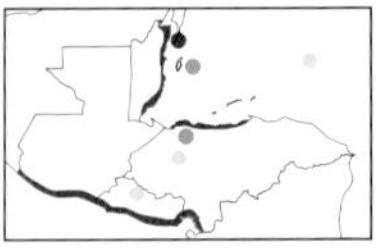

WILSON'S PLOVER *Charadrius wilsonia*

8 in. (20 cm). Breeding male has brown upperparts; **heavy black breast-band**; **long, thick black bill** (no other *Charadrius* plover has such a heavy bill); **pinkish legs**. Female has dark brown breast-band and head markings. Juvenile and nonbreeding adult similar to female, but drabber still and chest band sometimes slightly broken. Uncommon to fairly common resident on both slopes, including cayes and Swan Is.; to 330 ft. (100 m). Populations augmented in fall and winter by migrants from N. America. Found on coastal beaches, estuaries, and shrimp farms. Alarm call near nest is a hard *peep!*; also makes a softer *pip*. U.S. to Brazil.

SEMIPALMATED PLOVER *Charadrius semipalmatus*

7 in. (18 cm). Brown upperparts. On breeding adult, note fairly **heavy black breast-band**; **short, stubby orange bill with black tip**; and **yellow-orange legs**. Nonbreeding adult and juvenile similar to breeding male, but drabber and may show nearly all-black bill. Transient and winter visitor (late July–late June); some individuals may oversummer. Fairly common in NCA; to 330 ft. (100 m). Often in flocks. Found on coastal beaches, estuaries, and shrimp farms. Call is a rich, emphatic *ka'reep!* (often given in flight). AK and Canada to Argentina.

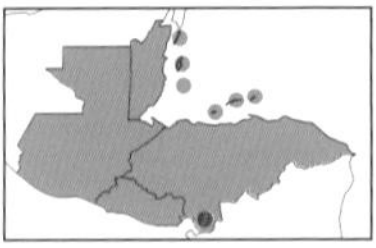

KILLDEER *Charadrius vociferus*

10.5 in. (27 cm). **Double black breast-band and tawny rump (in flight) are distinctive**. Winter visitor (early Oct.–late Apr.), rarely oversummering. Fairly common in NCA; to 10,170 ft. (3,100 m). Found in open areas such as grasslands, agricultural fields, wet meadows, and even lawns and parking lots, often in loose flocks. Call (for which it is named) is a loud, insistent *deee, dee'dee'dee, kill-DEEA!*; also makes a longer, single *deeeeeee!* AK and Canada to S. America.

Charadrius. *Four of the five* Charadrius *plovers found in NCA have very similar field marks (Killdeer is the exception). Pay special attention to the bills' size, structure, and colors. Chest band (wide or thin, complete or broken) and leg color also aid in identification.*

JACANIDAE (Order: Charadriiformes). These tropical shorebirds have extremely long toes, which enable them to walk on aquatic surface vegetation. Jacanas have colorful bills and fleshy areas of bare skin around the base of the bill. Interestingly, only the males incubate the eggs. Both sexes have forewings with bony spurs that they use in combat. The name *jaçanã* is derived from the name given by the Tupi people of Brazil. **1 species (1 genus)**

NORTHERN JACANA *Jacana spinosa*

9 in. (23 cm). Upperparts and belly deep chestnut; head and neck black; note **bright yellow bill and frontal shield.** Immature white below and with white eye line; distinguished from similar shorebirds by very long toes and yellowish bill. Fairly common in NCA; to 3,940 ft. (1,200 m). Found in marshes, lagoons, lakes, and ponds (at edge), wet fields, and roadside ditches. Contact call is a gruff, throaty *eeehhh!*; also makes an *ehk-ehk-ehk-ehk-* . . . Mex. to Panama.

SCOLOPACIDAE (Order: Charadriiformes). A diverse, cosmopolitan family of shorebirds. Most species occur in wetland habitats, although a few species prefer dry fields. Sandpipers have medium to long legs for wading, and a horizontal feeding posture. Their bills are often adapted for probing mudflats in search of invertebrates. Sexes are generally similar, but there are marked differences between breeding and nonbreeding plumages (and juveniles often appear brighter than adults). Most species make long-distance migrations from northern breeding grounds to the coasts and savannas of Cen. and S. America. **30 species (10 genera)**

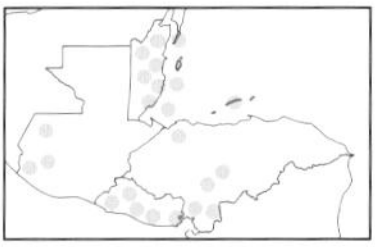

UPLAND SANDPIPER *Bartramia longicauda*

12 in. (31 cm). **Thin neck** and **small head** are distinctive; note **small, thin bill**. Buffy brown overall; **dark chevrons below**. Transient (mid-Mar.–May, late July–early Oct.). Rare in NCA, including Bay Is.; to 9,510 ft. (2,900 m). Found in grasslands and agricultural fields; may perch on fenceposts. Migrates at night, when it is often heard calling. Flight call is a bubbly, whistled *wee-di'di-pup!* or just *whip-pup*. AK and Canada (breeding) to Argentina (winter).

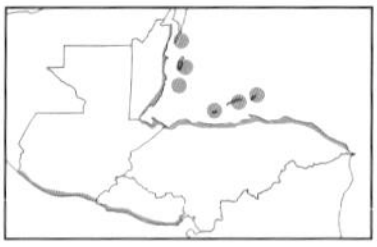

WHIMBREL *Numenius phaeopus*

18 in. (46 cm). **Long, decurved bill**; note **dark eye line** and **lateral crown stripes**. Winter visitor; records from all months, as it arrives early, departs late, and some individuals oversummer. Fairly common on both slopes. Restricted to coasts, where it forages on mudflats, sandbars, and beaches. Roosts in flocks on lower branches of mangroves and on beaches. Alarm call is ringing *pip-pip-pip-PIP-PIP-pip-pip*. Cosmopolitan.

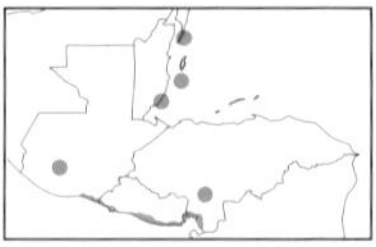

LONG-BILLED CURLEW *Numenius americanus*

23 in. (59 cm). **Very long, thin, decurved bill.** In flight, note golden brown flight feathers and underwing, similar to Marbled Godwit (p. 122) but bill shape different. Rare visitor (records from all months) on both slopes; to 4,430 ft. (1,350 m). Found in coastal areas on sandbars and mudflats. Call is a high-pitched, ringing *Keh'weeu'weeu'weeu!*; also makes a longer *cur-lewww!* Canada (breeding) to Panama (winter).

NORTHERN
JACANA

immature

UPLAND
SANDPIPER

WHIMBREL

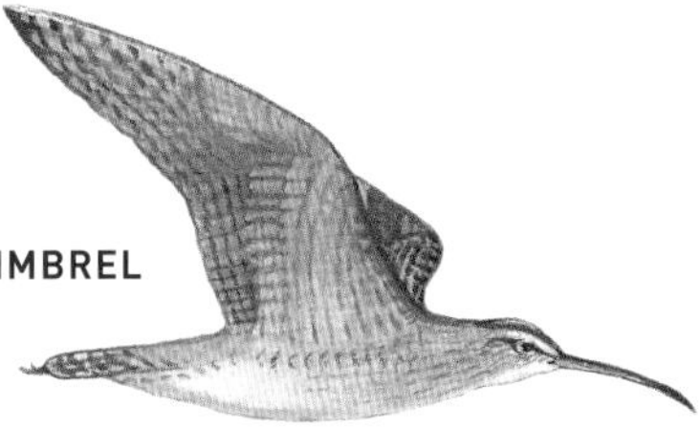

LONG-BILLED
CURLEW

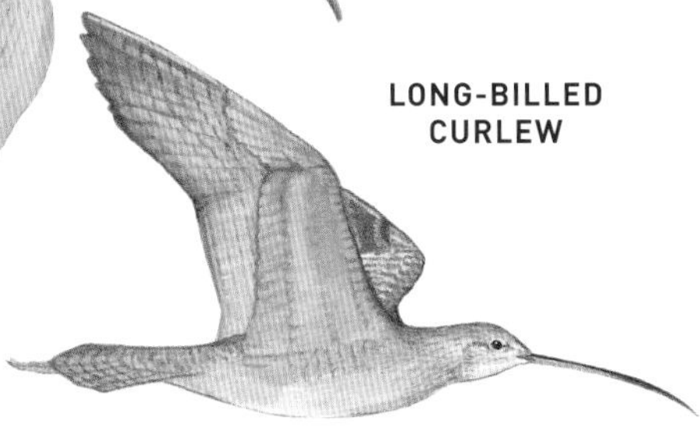

WANDERING TATTLER *Tringa incana*

11 in. (28 cm). Grayish overall; **dark eye line** and **white supercilium**; fairly long, stout bill; **legs yellow**. Breeding adult shows **zigzag barring below**. Nonbreeding adult **unmarked below**. Similar to Willet but legs shorter and bright yellow; in flight shows solid gray wings and upperparts. Similar to Surfbird (p. 122) but has much longer bill, dark eye line, and white supercilium. Uncommon on Pacific Slope; at sea level. Found in rocky coastal areas and on jetties. Call is a high-pitched, whistled *tea'e'e'e'e* or *deedeedeedee*. AK and Canada (breeding) to Peru (winter).

WILLET *Tringa semipalmata*

15 in. (38 cm). **Large gray sandpiper** with long stout bill and long gray legs. **Wings show wide white stripe**. Distinguished from yellowlegs species and Wandering Tattler by larger size, larger bill, and gray legs, and in flight, shows wide white stripe. Uncommon to fairly common transient and winter visitor in NCA, including Belizean cayes (early July–mid-May). Restricted to coastal areas; to 330 ft. (100 m). Found in estuaries, mudflats, and sandbars. Roosts in flocks of dozens on beaches or in mangroves. Call is a nasal, ringing *Will-lit-lit!* (often repeated); also makes a *keereah!* or *karack-karack-karack* . . . Canada (breeding) to S. America (winter).

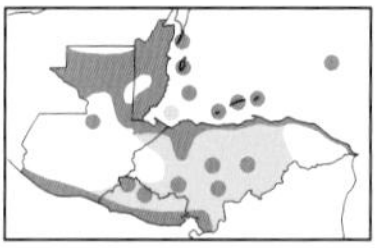

LESSER YELLOWLEGS *Tringa flavipes*

10.5 in. (27 cm). Very similar to Greater Yellowlegs, but smaller and has thinner, straighter bill. Also note differences in call. May be confused with nonbreeding Wilson's Phalarope (p. 130), but is larger, has longer legs, streaky breast, and dusky face. Transient and winter visitor (early July–mid-May). Fairly common to common on Caribbean Slope; uncommon on Pacific Slope; to 7,220 ft. (2,200 m). Found in coastal and interior wetland habitats, including lakes, reservoirs, lagoons, marshes, estuaries, and mangroves. Often forages with other shorebirds and long-legged waders. When flushed, alarm call is a single or doubled *tew* (may be repeated). AK and Canada (breeding) to Argentina (winter).

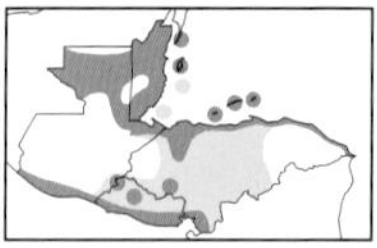

GREATER YELLOWLEGS *Tringa melanoleuca*

14 in. (36 cm). **Long yellow legs**; head, neck, and breast streaked or spotted; white eye-ring. **Dark bill (often paler at base) is long, thin, and slightly recurved**. Breeding adult shows dark barring on sides and flanks. Very similar to Lesser Yellowlegs, but larger (need side-to-side comparison) and bill is thicker at base and slightly recurved; also note calls. Transient and winter visitor, some individuals may oversummer (records from all months). Fairly common in NCA; to 6,560 ft. (2,000 m). Found in coastal and interior wetlands, particularly lakes, lagoons, marshes, reservoirs, estuaries, mangroves, and beaches. Often forages with other shorebirds and egrets or herons. When flushed, alarm call is a *Tee!-tew-tew* (3 or more notes). AK and Canada (breeding) to S. America (winter).

SOLITARY SANDPIPER *Tringa solitaria*

8.5 in. (22 cm). **White eye-ring, greenish legs,** and thin straight bill. In flight, note **solid blackish wings, dark rump, and dark central tail feathers**. Other *Tringa* species are larger and differ in leg color. In nonbreeding plumage, similar to Spotted Sandpiper (p. 126) but bobs head more than tail, has prominent eye-ring and white speckling on upperparts. Transient and winter visitor (late July–early May). Locally fairly common; to 6,560 ft. (2,000 m). Found mainly in freshwater wetlands, including marshes, lagoons, and edges of lakes and reservoirs. Call is sharp *pit* or *peet-peet!* (often given in flight). AK and Canada (breeding) to Argentina (winter).

breeding
WANDERING
TATTLER
nonbreeding
"Western" Willet
nonbreeding
WILLET
"Eastern" Willet
nonbreeding
nonbreeding
LESSER
YELLOWLEGS
nonbreeding
SOLITARY
SANDPIPER
GREATER
YELLOWLEGS
nonbreeding

HUDSONIAN GODWIT *Limosa haemastica*

15.5 in. (40 cm). On breeding adult, **deep chestnut underparts with dark barring contrast with pale face**. **Bill is very long and slightly recurved with pinkish base**. In flight, note **black underwing coverts** and tail. Spring transient (late Apr. and May). Very rare on both slopes; to 820 ft. (250 m). Found in lagoons, sewage ponds, rice fields, estuaries, and shrimp farms. A long-distance migrant that makes few stops between breeding and winter grounds; fall migration is largely over the Atlantic Ocean so bypasses NCA. AK and Canada to Argentina.

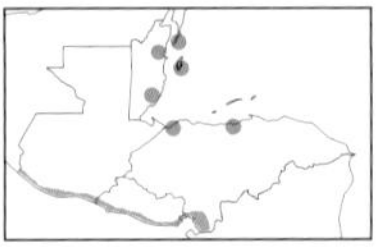

MARBLED GODWIT *Limosa fedoa*

18 in. (46 cm). **Warm golden brown** overall with dark markings on upperparts; **very long, slightly recurved bill is pinkish with dusky tip**. In flight, similar wing pattern and color to Long-billed Curlew (p. 118), but note bill differences. Transient and winter visitor (mid-July–mid-May). Rare to uncommon on Caribbean Slope; uncommon on Pacific Slope; to 330 ft. (100 m). Found in coastal habitats, particularly estuaries, mudflats, and sandbars. Alarm call is a loud *Keer'aack!* (may be repeated in a series); also makes a *care-whew'whew!* Canada to Chile.

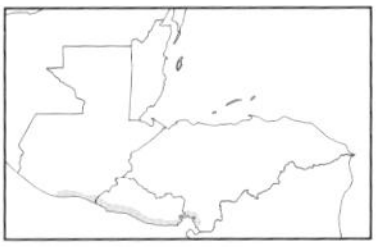

SURFBIRD *Calidris virgata*

10 in. (26 cm). Note **yellow legs**; short, stout bill; narrow **white eye-ring**. Breeding adult shows streaking and spotting on head and chest, and **rufous scapulars**. Nonbreeding adult **solid dark gray above** with **paler, speckled belly**. In flight, shows white wing stripe and broad black tips to tail. Similar to Wandering Tattler (p. 120) but has shorter bill and lacks dark eye line and supercilium. Transient (Mar.–Apr., July–Sept.); should also be watched for in winter. Uncommon on Pacific Slope; near sea level. Found along the coast on mudflats, sandbars, rocky jetties, and exposed oyster beds. When flushed, alarm call is a hard *pip!* AK to Chile.

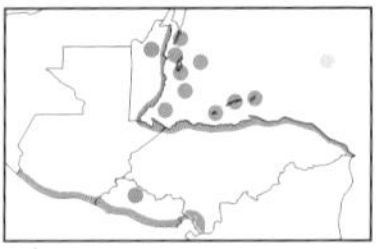

RUDDY TURNSTONE *Arenaria interpres*

9.5 in. (24 cm). Nonbreeding adult and juvenile brownish black above with lighter crown, and **dark brown patches on sides of chest**. Breeding adult rich **rufous-brown above**; note striking **black-and-white pattern on head and chest**. In flight, note white down center of back, white base of tail, and white wing stripes. **Legs orange**. Transient and winter visitor (late July–early June); some individuals may oversummer. Common on both slopes; near sea level. Found along the coast on mudflats, sandbars, rocky jetties, and exposed oyster beds. Flight call is a hard *pip'pip'pip!* Cosmopolitan.

RED KNOT *Calidris canutus*

10.5 in. (27 cm). Chunky body makes head look relatively small. Breeding adult **rufous below**. Nonbreeding adult **unmarked gray above**; grayish chest contrasts with paler belly; dark barring on flanks; note **dark eye line** and **pale supercilium**. Juvenile similar to nonbreeding adult, but has pale-edged scapulars. Nonbreeding adult and juvenile similar to Wandering Tattler, but bill shorter, legs dull green (not bright yellow), and found on beaches (not on rocks).Transient and winter visitor (late July–mid-Apr.). Uncommon and local on both slopes; near sea level. Found strictly in coastal areas on estuaries, mudflats, sandbars, and beaches; also occurs on shrimp farms. Cosmopolitan.

breeding
nonbreeding
HUDSONIAN GODWIT
nonbreeding in flight
MARBLED GODWIT
SURFBIRD
breeding
nonbreeding
breeding
nonbreeding
RUDDY TURNSTONE
breeding
nonbreeding
RED KNOT
molting
two Ruddy Turnstones with Sanderlings and Black-bellied Plover

PEEPS (SMALL *CALIDRIS* SANDPIPERS)

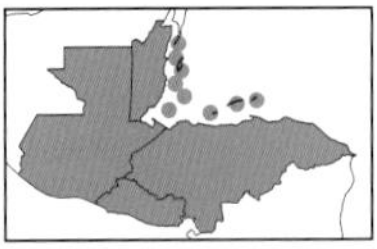

LEAST SANDPIPER *Calidris minutilla*

6 in. (15 cm). **Brownish gray above and on chest** with **yellowish legs** (which distinguish it from similar species) and **relatively short**, blackish bill. On breeding adult, note rufous edging on upperparts; juvenile brighter on upperparts. Winter visitor (late July–May); some oversummer. Common on both slopes; to 4,430 ft. (1,350 m). Found mainly in freshwater habitats. Flight call is *kreeet-kreeet!* AK and Canada (breeding) to Chile (winter).

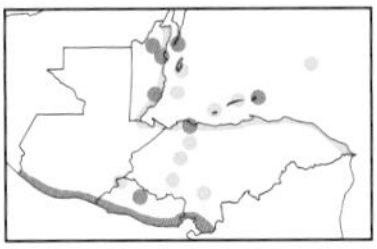

SEMIPALMATED SANDPIPER *Calidris pusilla*

6.5 in. (17 cm). **Straight black bill is relatively short**; legs black. Nonbreeding adult grayish above; note pale supercilium and lightly marked chest. Breeding adult grayish brown overall with streaked chest, dark scapulars, and reddish brown wash to cap and face. Juvenile similar to nonbreeding adult, but has dark cap and dark scapulars with gold edging. Very similar to Western Sandpiper but has shorter, straighter bill. Fairly common transient and uncommon winter visitor on both slopes (early Aug.–May); to 4,000 ft. (1,200 m). Found on coastal beaches, sandbars, and mudflats; also at shrimp farms and water treatment facilities. Flight call is a thin, reedy *preeet!* AK and Canada (breeding) to Argentina (winter).

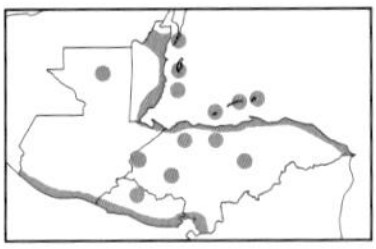

WESTERN SANDPIPER *Calidris mauri*

6.5 in. (17 cm). **Fairly long black bill with slight droop**; legs black. On breeding adult, note **reddish scapulars, wing coverts, cap, and face**; chest and sides with **dark chevrons**. Juvenile similar to nonbreeding adult, but has reddish scapulars and buffy tones to head and chest. Adult similar to Semipalmated Sandpiper, but more streaking on sides, and more rufous on head and scapulars (breeding); also note longer bill and larger head. Common visitor on both slopes (late July–mid-May), some may oversummer; to 1,150 ft. (350 m). Found on beaches, sandbars, and mudflats; also at shrimp farms. Call (similar to Least Sandpiper) is a high-pitched, slightly reedy *cheeeat* or *pweeep*. AK and Canada (breeding) to Chile (winter).

BAIRD'S SANDPIPER *Calidris bairdii*

7.5 in. (19 cm). **Wingtips project beyond tail**. Breeding adult shows dark-centered scapulars and moderate streaking on chest (resembling a small Pectoral Sandpiper [p. 126]). On juvenile, note buffy breast-band and scaled look to upperparts. Distinguish from White-rumped Sandpiper by straight, **all-dark bill**, unstreaked flanks, and dark center to rump. Rare transient (Apr.–early May, late Oct.–early Dec.); to 2,640 ft. (800 m). May be found in pastures or fields, even cowpens, far from water, but also at shrimp farms or sewage treatment plants. Call is a sputtering *pe'e'e'e'ep!*; alarm call is an inflected *peeee'up!* AK and Canada (breeding) to Argentina (winter).

WHITE-RUMPED SANDPIPER *Calidris fuscicollis*

7.5 in. (19 cm). **Wingtips project beyond tail. Rump entirely white (visible in flight).** Breeding adult shows rufous in cheeks and caps; **heavily streaked below, including sides and flanks**. Juveniles washed brightly above in rufous and gold with dark-centered scapulars. Distinguished from Baird's Sandpiper by reddish base to mandible and presence of streaking on sides and flanks (in all plumages). Common spring transient on Caribbean Slope (mid-Apr.–early June); very rare fall transient (Oct.; Belize); to 4,590 ft. (1,400 m). Found in wetland habitats (primarily freshwater). Call is a distinctive, reedy, insectlike *teeeet!* Canada (breeding) to S. America (winter).

Identifying "peeps" (small *Calidris* sandpipers). *Habitat, foraging behavior, and size are all useful for field identification. Western, Semipalmated, and Least are the most common "peeps" in NCA. The less common White-rumped and Baird's Sandpipers are larger and have longer wings. The Sanderling, also larger, is common and usually stays close to sandy beaches and the surf's edge.*

LARGE *CALIDRIS* SANDPIPERS

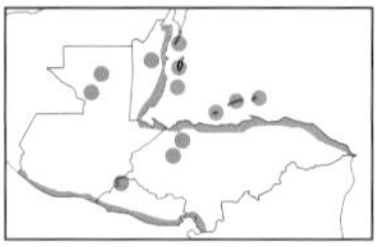

SANDERLING *Calidris alba*

8 in. (20 cm). Nonbreeding adult pale gray above with **pale supercilium** and **black at bend of folded wing** (sometimes hidden). Breeding adult shows **brick red upperparts, head, and chest**; note **dark-centered scapulars**. Juvenile similar to nonbreeding adult, but has dark scapulars and buffy, golden tones to head and sides. Note straight black bill of medium length. Transient and winter visitor (early Aug.–early May); some individuals may oversummer in NCA. Fairly common along both coasts; near sea level. Found on coastal beaches and sandbars; almost always near water's edge. Flight call is a thin, nasal *pwit-pwit!* Cosmopolitan.

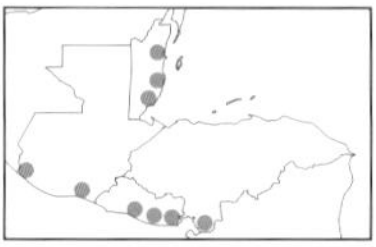

DUNLIN *Calidris alpina*

8.5 in. (22 cm). **Long bill droops at tip**. Nonbreeding adult grayish above; **light grayish wash to chest contrasts with white belly**. On breeding adult, note bright rufous upperparts and **black belly patch**. Compare with more common Stilt Sandpiper (p. 128), but Dunlin is very rare, lacks obvious white supercilium, has shorter, black legs, and bill has heavier droop. Very rare transient and winter visitor (Oct.–May); to 160 ft. (50 m). Found on coastal mudflats, sandbars, and shrimp farms. AK and Canada to Mex., rarely to Costa Rica and Colombia.

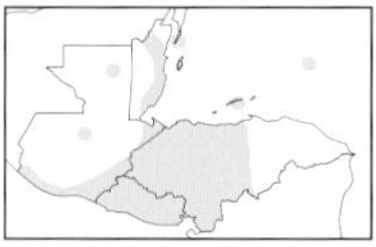

PECTORAL SANDPIPER *Calidris melanotos*

8.5 in. (22 cm). Looks like a large Least Sandpiper (p. 124). Note golden-edged feathers on upperparts, dark eye line and pale supercilium, and **streaked throat and chest contrasting markedly with white belly**. Legs yellowish; bill with reddish orange base and slight droop. Transient (mid-Aug.–early Nov., early Feb.–late May). Fairly common on both slopes to 4,430 ft. (1,350 m). Found in wetland habitats (usually freshwater), including wet fields, lakes, reservoirs, and shrimp ponds. When flushed or in flight, call is a sputtering, slightly reedy *pwi'i'i'i'i'p!* AK, Canada, and Asia to Brazil and Australia.

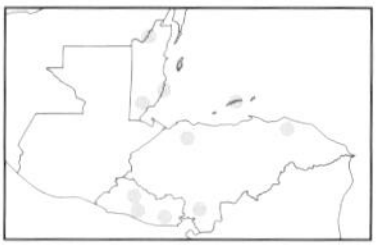

BUFF-BREASTED SANDPIPER *Calidris subruficollis*

8.5 in. (22 cm). **Rich buffy yellow overall** (darker above); plain face; small head and **thin short bill**; yellow legs; in flight, note **white wing lining**. Rare transient (late Aug.–late Sept.; mid-Apr.–early May), more records from Caribbean Slope (including Roatán) than from Pacific Slope; to 3,280 ft. (1,000 m). Generally found in short-grass pastures or fields, often away from water, but also at shrimp farms and sewage treatment plants. AK and Canada to Argentina.

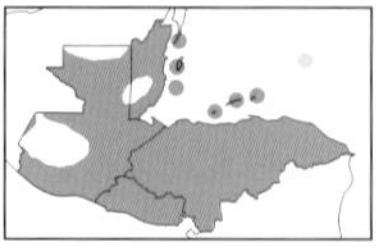

SPOTTED SANDPIPER *Actitis macularius*

7.5 in. (19 cm). Breeding adult with **dark eye line** and **white supercilium**; also note **dark spotting on underparts**; yellow legs and mandible. Nonbreeding adult similar, but **unspotted below**. Transient and winter visitor (early July–late May). Common in NCA; to 7,220 ft. (2,200 m). Found in both freshwater and saltwater wetland habitats, including marshes, lakes, lagoons, riverbanks, coastal beaches, mudflats, and mangroves. Distinctive bobbing motion when foraging or walking; in flight, has rapid, fluttering wingbeats as it flies low over water; both bobbing and wing flutter distinguish it from other shorebirds. When flushed, alarm call is a high-pitched *pee-peat!* or *pee-weet!* AK and Canada (breeding) to Chile (winter).

SANDERLING
breeding
nonbreeding
DUNLIN
breeding
nonbreeding
PECTORAL SANDPIPER
BUFF-BREASTED SANDPIPER
breeding
SPOTTED SANDPIPER
nonbreeding
"bobbing"
Spotted Sandpiper

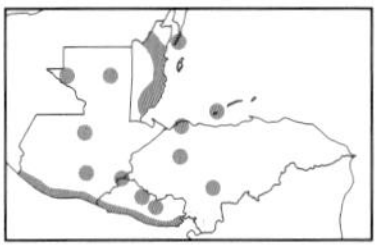

STILT SANDPIPER *Calidris himantopus*

8.5 in. (22 cm). Note combination of **yellowish green legs** and **fairly long, slightly drooping bill**. Nonbreeding adult grayish above with **dark eye line and white supercilium**. On breeding adult, **heavy dark barring below is distinctive**; note rufous-washed cheeks and crown. Similar to nonbreeding dowitchers (*Limnodromus* spp.), but smaller, leaner (not "plump"), shorter bill, and lacks white stripe down back (visible on dowitchers in flight). Similar to the very rare Dunlin (p. 126), but has obvious white supercilium, has longer, greenish legs, and bill has less droop. Transient and winter visitor (Aug.–May). Uncommon to fairly common on both slopes; to 4,430 ft. (1,350 m). Found in wetlands (usually freshwater), including lakes, reservoirs, shrimp ponds, estuaries, and mudflats. AK and Canada (breeding) to Argentina (winter).

SHORT-BILLED DOWITCHER *Limnodromus griseus*

11 in. (28 cm). Very similar to Long-billed Dowitcher; dowitchers in general have a distinctive "sewing machine" foraging manner and differ from other shorebirds by showing a white stripe on back in flight. Two subspecies identified in NCA: *L.g. hendersoni* and *L.g. caurinus*. In both subspecies, nonbreeding adult grayish above, paler below, with barred or spotted flanks; breast speckled. **Black and white bars of even width on tail.** Juvenile has buffy breast, rufous edging above, and **dark tertials with buffy orange or rufous barring and edges**. Breeding adult *hendersoni* is buffy orange below with spotting on sides of neck; **throat and upper chest relatively unmarked** (most similar to breeding Long-billed Dowitcher). Breeding adult *caurinus* has **whitish belly** with dense orange spotting on throat and chest; darker above than *hendersoni*. Nonbreeding dowitchers similar to nonbreeding Stilt Sandpiper, but dowitchers are larger, "plumper," have longer, straighter bill, and white stripe on back in flight. Winter visitor (early July–late Apr.). Uncommon on both slopes; to 330 ft. (100 m). Found in saline habitats, including coastal mudflats, sandbars, and marshes; also on shrimp farms. Call is rapid, flat *tew-tew-tew-tew*. See Long-billed Dowitcher. AK and Canada (breeding) to Brazil (winter).

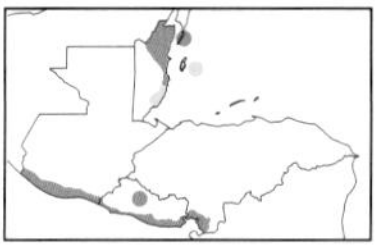

LONG-BILLED DOWITCHER *Limnodromus scolopaceus*

11.5 in. (29 cm). Nonbreeding adult very similar to nonbreeding Short-billed Dowitcher, but darker above and has fewer markings on face and chest; **on tail, black bars are wider than white bars**. Compared to Short-billed, bill length overlaps and is not a reliable field mark, but Long-billed body shape is bulkier and appears more hunchbacked while feeding (for all ages). Juvenile similar to juvenile Short-billed Dowitcher, but **tertials lack barring (rusty edges only)**. Breeding adult is similar to Short-billed Dowitcher (*hendersoni*), but darker above, richer orange and more heavily marked below, and has darker tail. Winter visitor (late Aug.–late Apr.). Sometimes in large flocks of hundreds; to 4,430 ft. (1,350 m). Prefers freshwater wetlands; also found in shrimp ponds and sewage treatment facilities. Call is a sharp *pweek*, singly or in a rapid series (different from Short-billed Dowitcher). AK and Canada (breeding) to Costa Rica (winter).

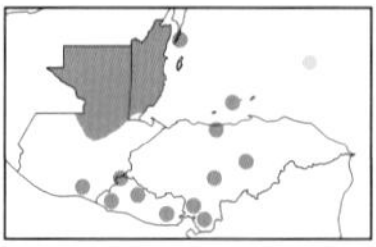

WILSON'S SNIPE *Gallinago delicata*

10.5 in. (27 cm). Distinctive **striped pattern on head and back**; barring on sides; **very long, straight bill**. Winter visitor (mid-Sept.–early Apr.). Rare to uncommon on both slopes; to 10,170 ft. (3,100 m). Found at edges of freshwater marshes and lagoons; also in drainage ditches, wet agricultural fields, wet meadows, and bogs. Difficult to detect because of cryptic plumage and tendency to sit quietly. Call is a gruff, throaty *eeeehk!* AK and Canada (breeding) to Colombia (winter).

feeding postures of dowitchers: two Short-billed (left) and three Long-billed (right)

tertials of juvenile dowitchers, Short-billed (top) and Long-billed

WILSON'S PHALAROPE *Phalaropus tricolor*

9 in. (23 cm). Nonbreeding adult grayish above with **white face, gray cap,** and **very thin, black bill**. Nonbreeding similar to nonbreeding Red-necked Phalarope, but paler above, lacks black mask, and has longer bill. Nonbreeding adult may also be confused with nonbreeding Stilt Sandpiper (p. 128) or Lesser Yellowlegs (p. 120), but is shorter legged, relatively unmarked below (both Stilt and Yellowlegs show some streaking below), and paler overall. Breeding female has **bold black stripe on face and down side of neck**; foreneck orange-chestnut. Breeding male similar to breeding female, but drabber overall. Transient (late Aug.–mid-Oct.; late Apr.–mid-May). Small numbers may overwinter in s. Honduras. Rare on both slopes; to 4,430 ft. (1,350 m). Prefers freshwater wetlands; found in lakes, reservoirs, shrimp ponds, and sewage treatment facilities. Occasionally seen swimming and spinning (less so than the other phalaropes), forming a small whirlpool ("vortexing"), which aids in raising food items from the bottom of shallow waters. An active feeder. Canada to Chile.

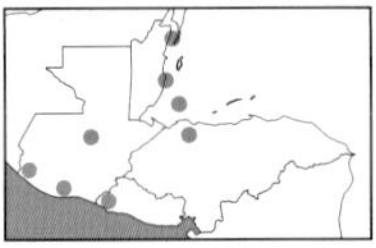

RED-NECKED PHALAROPE *Phalaropus lobatus*

8 in. (20 cm). Nonbreeding adult similar to nonbreeding Wilson's Phalarope, but has darker upperparts (including cap), **black mask**, and shorter bill. Breeding adult female shows **white throat bordered by rufous chestnut**. Breeding male similar to breeding female, but drabber overall. Transient and winter visitor (late Aug.–mid-Apr.). Uncommon on Pacific Slope, very rare on Caribbean Slope. Generally occurs in pelagic waters, but closer to shore than Red Phalarope. Storm-driven individuals may be found along the coast, or inland on lakes, reservoirs, and shrimp farms. Often seen swimming and spinning ("vortexing"), which is a behavior unique to phalaropes and aids in raising food items to the water's surface. AK and Canada to Chile; Greenland and Russia to Africa and se. Asia.

RED PHALAROPE *Phalaropus fulicarius*

8.5 in. (22 cm). **Bill heavier and thicker-based** than in other phalaropes; often shows **yellow base in nonbreeding individuals**. Nonbreeding adult grayish above with **black eye patch**. On breeding adult female bright white cheeks contrast with black head and **rufous underparts**; bill yellow with small dark tip. Breeding male similar to breeding female but drabber overall. Transient and winter visitor (Oct.–mid-Apr.). Rare to uncommon in Pacific pelagic waters; occasionally found near the coast. Often seen swimming and spinning ("vortexing"), which aids in raising food items to the water's surface, a behavior unique to phalaropes. AK and Canada to Chile; Greenland and Russia to South Africa.

Phalaropes exhibit a rare case of sexual dimorphism, in which traditional roles are reversed: females are brighter than males; males incubate the eggs and raise the young.

JAEGERS

STERCORARIIDAE (Order: Charadriiformes). Jaegers are superficially similar to gulls (p. 134) but have darker plumage, more strongly hooked bills, and hooked claws. Jaegers were once thought to be part of the gull family Laridae. The name *jaeger* is derived from the German *jäger* (hunter); these species often steal food from other birds (kleptoparasitism), but also pick food from the water's surface. Plumages are complicated because of color morphs, individual variation, and feather wear. Juvenile plumages are very similar among species (size and structure may be more useful for identification). This group is highly pelagic, and all species make long-distance offshore migrations from Arctic breeding grounds to wintering grounds in S. America. Two large stercorariids, the Great Skua (*Stercorarius skua*) and the South Polar Skua (*S. maccormicki*), are likely to visit the region occasionally (see the Appendix). **3 species (1 genus)**

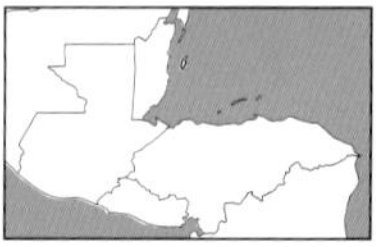

POMARINE JAEGER *Stercorarius pomarinus*

18.5 in. (47 cm). A **large-bodied** jaeger with a stout, hooked bill. Complex plumage includes several cycles and color morphs. In all ages and plumages, pale base to both primaries and primary coverts gives appearance of **2 pale crescents on each underwing** (visible in flight). Dark-morph adult all-dark with **long, spoon-shaped central tail feathers**. Light-morph adult has dark cap that extends to malar, and a dark, well-defined breast-band. Juvenile light to dark brown, lacking rufous tones seen in juvenile Parasitic Jaeger; also note short rounded central tail tips. Transient and winter visitor (Oct.–early May; a few may oversummer). Uncommon to fairly common in NCA pelagic waters; occasionally near shore. Cosmopolitan.

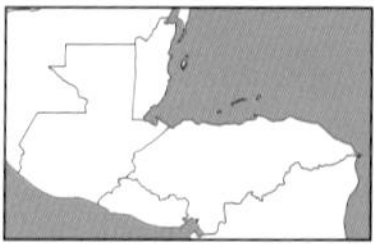

PARASITIC JAEGER *Stercorarius parasiticus*

16.5 in. (42 cm). **Smaller-bodied** than Pomarine Jaeger; note **small, peaked head** and **slender bill**. In all ages and plumages, pale base to primaries gives appearance of **single pale crescent on underwing** (visible in flight); upperwing shows pale shaft to 4 or 5 outer primaries. Dark-morph adult is all-dark, with **pointed, extended central tail feathers**. Light-morph adult has less extensive dark cap (extending only to top of bill) and white underparts with faint, less-defined breast-band than Pomarine. Juveniles are dark to light, but generally show some **rufous tones to body** (lacking in other juvenile jaegers); also note darker bill (less 2-toned than on Pomarine). Transient and winter visitor (early July–mid-June; a few may oversummer). Uncommon in NCA pelagic waters; occasionally near shore. Cosmopolitan.

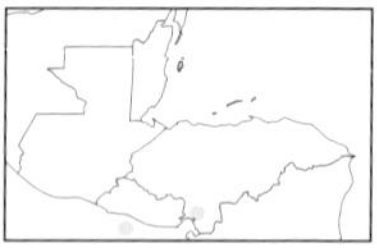

LONG-TAILED JAEGER *Stercorarius longicaudus*

15 in. (38 cm). Compared to the other jaegers, Long-tailed is smaller and slimmer, and has narrower wings. In all ages and plumages, pale base to primaries gives appearance of single pale crescent on underwing (visible in flight); **upperwing shows pale shafts on 2 or 3 outermost primaries**; also note **stubby bill**. In spring, breeding plumaged adult has small black cap and clean, **yellow-gray underparts** (lacks breast-band seen in other jaegers), and **very long, pointed central tail feathers**. Nonbreeding adult (fall, winter) lacks tail streamers. Juvenile dark to light, generally with whitish edging and barring to upperparts, some individuals with pale belly, and long tail shows rounded central tail feathers; lacks rufous tones seen in juvenile Parasitic Jaeger. Very rare transient in NCA Pacific pelagic waters; no records from NCA Caribbean waters. Occasionally found on beaches or inland. Cosmopolitan.

immature
adult
breeding
growth stages of tail
nonbreeding adult
POMARINE JAEGER
immature
adult
breeding
growth stages of tail
nonbreeding adult
PARASITIC JAEGER
immature
LONG-TAILED JAEGER
breeding
growth stages of tail
nonbreeding adult

BLACK-HEADED GULLS

LARIDAE (Order: Charadriiformes). This family includes the gulls and terns found in coastal areas and pelagic waters. Gull identification is complicated because young gulls go through a series of plumages called *cycles* before acquiring adult plumage. A cycle is roughly equivalent to one year; smaller gulls generally have 2 cycles whereas larger gulls have 3 or 4. Body size, eye and leg color, and bill pattern and structure are helpful for identification. Gulls have bills adapted for tearing flesh (including carrion). Terns are leaner and have more pointed bills than gulls, and their sharp bills are adapted for spearing fish. **26 species (13 genera)**

SABINE'S GULL *Xema sabini*

14 in. (36 cm). In flight, wing pattern is distinctive. On adult, **bill black with yellow tip**. Nonbreeding adult has partial black hood; breeding adult has dark gray hood with black border. Juvenile and first-cycle birds brown to blackish above with **distinctive pale edging to upperparts (scaling)**; all-dark bill. Transient and winter visitor (late July–early May). Rare to uncommon in Pacific pelagic waters. Call is a thin, whining *peeep!* AK (breeding) to Chile and sw. Africa (winter).

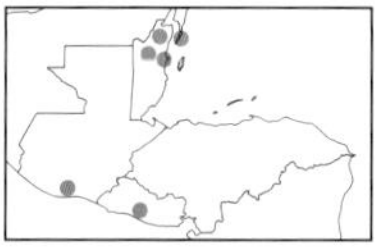

BONAPARTE'S GULL *Chroicocephalus philadelphia*

13 in. (33 cm). A small gull with a small, all-black bill. Nonbreeding adult has **small black spot behind eye**; breeding adult has black hood. **In flight, white leading edge to primaries forms thin white triangle** (tips to primaries black). In flight, first-cycle individuals similar in appearance to nonbreeding adult, but show a **dark M across upperwings** and note **dark tail tips**. Wings more pointed than on most gulls, giving a ternlike appearance in flight. Very rare winter visitor (late Dec.–early June). Found in coastal waters, estuaries, and lagoons. AK and Canada (breeding) to Mex. (occasionally Central America) (winter).

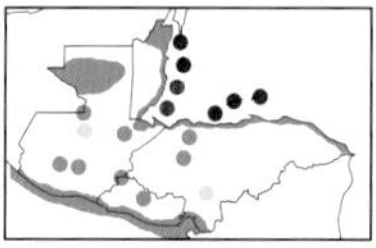

LAUGHING GULL *Leucophaeus atricilla*

16 in. (41 cm). Nonbreeding adult has white head; **dusky smudge around and behind eye**, white eye crescents; in flight, shows **all-dark primaries**, sometimes with white tips. First-cycle bird shows brown wing coverts, complete dark tail band. Breeding adult has black hood, deep red bill. Similar to Franklin's Gull but larger, has thinner eye crescents, lacks obvious white wingtips (in adults), and bill is larger; also, trace of hood (nonbreeding) is less obvious. On first cycle, note complete tail band. Winter visitor, but nonbreeders can be found throughout the year. Breeds locally in Belize. Common on both slopes; to 5,580 ft. (1,700 m). Found in coastal areas on beaches, sandbars, and mudflats; also inland at shrimp farms, and on lakes and reservoirs. Calls include a nasal *ehh-ah!* and a growling *eeehrrr!*; also makes a cackling *eh'eh'eh'eh'eh'ehhhh'ehhhhh'ehhhhh!* U.S. (breeding) to Peru (winter).

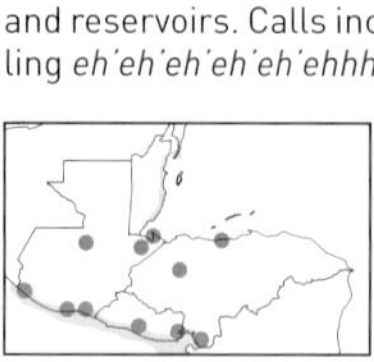

FRANKLIN'S GULL *Leucophaeus pipixcan*

15 in. (38 cm). Similar to Laughing Gull, but is smaller, has shorter bill, shows **bolder eye crescents**, and has **white tips and subterminal band on primaries** (in adults); nonbreeding has **more pronounced black hood**. Often shows **pinkish wash to breast**. First cycle has incomplete black subterminal tail band (complete in Laughing Gull first cycle). Common transient and uncommon winter visitor on Pacific Slope (mid-Oct.–early July); rare transient on Caribbean Slope (mid-Oct.–early Dec., late Mar.–late May). Found in coastal areas on beaches, sandbars, and mudflats; rare on inland lakes and reservoirs. Groups of hundreds migrate along the Pacific coast, and roost at river mouths. Call is higher-pitched than that of Laughing Gull. Canada (breeding) to Chile (winter).

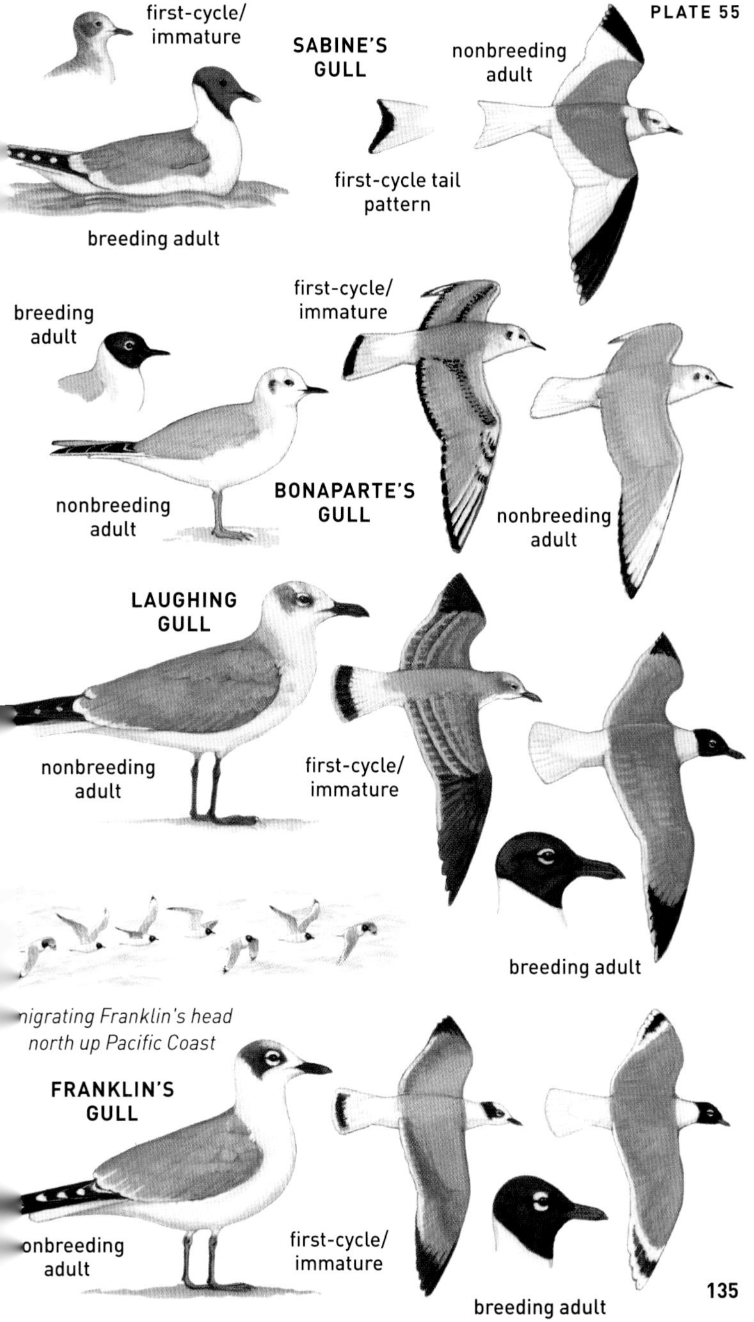
first-cycle/
immature
SABINE'S
GULL
nonbreeding
adult
first-cycle tail
pattern
breeding adult
breeding
adult
first-cycle/
immature
nonbreeding
adult
BONAPARTE'S
GULL
nonbreeding
adult
LAUGHING
GULL
nonbreeding
adult
first-cycle/
immature
breeding adult
migrating Franklin's head
north up Pacific Coast
FRANKLIN'S
GULL
nonbreeding
adult
first-cycle/
immature
breeding adult

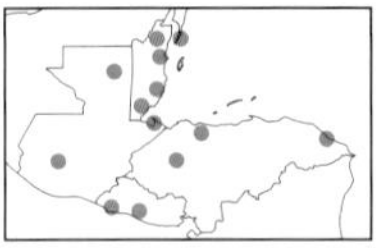

RING-BILLED GULL *Larus delawarensis*

17 in. (43 cm). On adult, **bill greenish yellow with black band near tip**; **legs yellow**; wingtip black with white spot; eyes dark. Nape streaked on nonbreeding adult, unmarked on breeding adult. On first-cycle bird, **bill is pink with dark tip**; legs pinkish; wing coverts and tertials dark brown; streaking on head and chest; dark tail band. Similar to the much larger second- and third-cycle Herring Gull, but note yellow legs (not pink) and less streaking on neck and head. Winter visitor (mid-Aug.–mid-Apr.). Rare on both slopes; to 2,300 ft. (700 m). Found in coastal areas on beaches, sandbars, and mudflats; occurs occasionally on inland lakes and reservoirs. Canada to Panama.

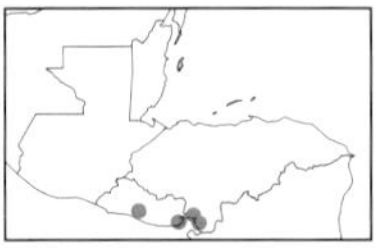

CALIFORNIA GULL *Larus californicus*

21 in. (53 cm). **Eyes dark in all ages.** On adult, **bill yellow with red-and-black mark at tip**; dark wingtip shows large white spot; legs yellow; nape and crown streaked in nonbreeding adult, unmarked in breeding adult. First- and second-cycle birds have dark-centered wing coverts, secondaries, and primaries; dark tail band; bill yellow to grayish green with black tip. In second cycle, begins to show gray on mantle and wing coverts. First-cycle similar to second-cycle Herring Gull, but is smaller overall, and has all-dark primaries (lacking pale window; visible in flight) and dark eyes (not pale yellow). Adult similar to adult Herring Gull, but note bill tip color, dark eyes (not yellow), and gray secondaries on underwing in flight (not pale like Herring). Vagrant on Pacific Coast on sandbars and mudflats. Canada to Mex.

HERRING GULL *Larus argentatus*

25 in. (64 cm). **A large gull.** On adult, note **heavy yellow bill with red spot near tip; eyes yellow; legs pink**; wingtip black with white spots; nape and crown extensively streaked in nonbreeding plumage, unmarked in breeding plumage. First-cycle bird dark brownish gray overall with black primaries; in flight, note **pale wing panel** and black tail band; **bill all-dark**; eyes dark. Through second and third cycles, mantle and wing coverts become gray; dark eyes become yellow; dark bill becomes pink to yellow with dark tip. Second- and third-cycle birds similar to the much smaller Ring-billed Gull, but have pink legs (not yellow) and more streaking on neck and head. Transient and winter visitor. Uncommon on Caribbean Slope (mid-Oct.–late Apr.); rare on Pacific Slope (mid-Nov.–early Feb.); to 330 ft. (100 m). Found in coastal areas on beaches, sandbars, and mudflats; rarely inland. AK and Canada to Panama.

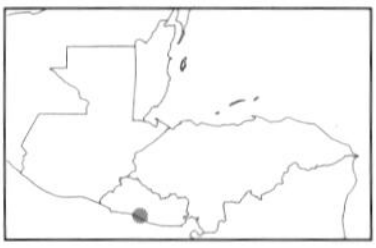

GLAUCOUS-WINGED GULL *Larus glaucescens*

26 in. (66 cm). **A very large gull.** On nonbreeding adult, **faint brown barring on neck** is distinctive; eyes dark; bill yellow with red spot near tip; legs pink; **mantle and upperwing soft pale gray with white tips to primaries.** Breeding adult similar to nonbreeding, but has clean white head and neck. First- and second-cycle birds **uniformly pale gray** (possibly with soft browns) and have **all-dark bill**. Third-cycle plumage resembles that of nonbreeding adult, but bill has dark tip. Vagrant to El Salvador (Jan.); to be looked for on Pacific Coast beaches, sandbars, and mudflats. AK and Canada to Mex.

nonbreeding
adult
breeding
adult
first-cycle/
immature
first-cycle/
immature
nonbreeding
adult
RING-BILLED
GULL
first-cycle/
immature
nonbreeding
adult
CALIFORNIA
GULL
HERRING
GULL
nonbreeding
adult
breeding
adult
first-cycle/
immature
nonbreeding
adult
third-cycle/
immature
first-cycle/
immature
nonbreeding
adult
breeding adult
GLAUCOUS-WINGED
GULL

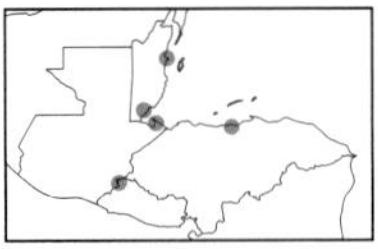

LESSER BLACK-BACKED GULL *Larus fuscus*

21 in. (53 cm). Nonbreeding adult shows **dark gray mantle** and **black smudge around yellow eye**; bill yellow with red spot near tip; **legs yellow**. Breeding adult similar, but has clean white head. First-cycle bird has black-and-white pattern above (dark greater coverts) with dark tail band and all-dark bill, but still shows black smudge around eye; legs pink. Nonbreeding adult similar to nonbreeding Kelp Gull, but has **paler back** (not blackish), smaller body and bill, and yellow legs (not greenish yellow). Very rare winter visitor to NCA; to 2,460 ft. (750 m). Found in coastal areas on beaches, sandbars, and mudflats; less commonly inland, on lakes and reservoirs. Canada and U.S. to Caribbean and Colombia; Europe to Africa.

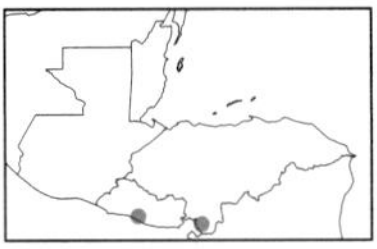

KELP GULL *Larus dominicanus*

23 in. (59 cm). **A large gull.** Nonbreeding adult similar to nonbreeding adult Lesser Black-backed Gull, but is larger, has heavier body and bill, **darker back** (nearly black), and greenish yellow legs (not yellow). In flight, note dark primaries and dark trailing edge to underwing. First-cycle similar to first-cycle Lesser Black-backed, but has heavier bill and darker tail. Vagrant winter visitor on Pacific Coast (to be looked for also on Caribbean coast) on beaches, sandbars, and mudflats. Confusing large gulls may be hybrids of Kelp x Herring Gull (known as "Chandeleur Gull"), as they interbreed on the Gulf shore of U.S. Colombia to Chile; S. Africa and Australasia.

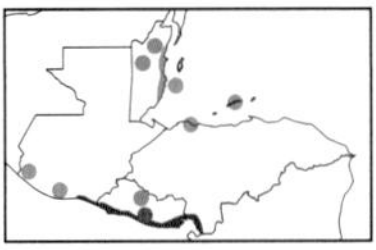

BLACK SKIMMER *Rynchops niger*

18 in. (46 cm). **Black-and-red bill with extended lower mandible** makes this species unmistakable. On juvenile, upperparts brownish black. Uncommon resident on Pacific Slope (breeds locally in El Salvador), uncommon transient and winter visitor on Caribbean and Pacific Slope (Aug.–June); to 820 ft. (250 m). Generally found in coastal areas (and along major rivers farther inland); large flocks roost on sandbars and mudflats during the day. Feeds mostly at night; flies low over water and uses its long bill to skim the surface of the water for small fish or invertebrates. This is the only species of bird in which the mandible is longer than the maxilla. Call is a loud, nasal *EH-EH-EH-EH-EH-EH-* . . . U.S. to Argentina.

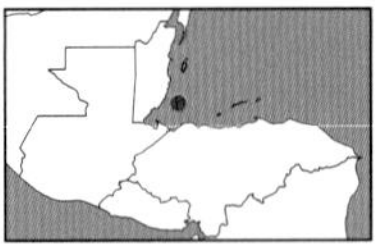

BROWN NODDY *Anous stolidus*

15 in. (38 cm). **Dark brown overall** with **silvery white forehead and crown**. Immature and worn adults show paler brown wing coverts. Similar to Black Noddy, but is larger and has proportionately shorter, thicker bill; also note differences in distribution. Uncommon to fairly common visitor in NCA Caribbean pelagic waters (primarily mid-Apr.–mid-Sept., but records from every month); uncommon visitor in NCA Pacific pelagic waters (mid-May–Oct.). Breeds locally on Belizean cayes. Pantropical.

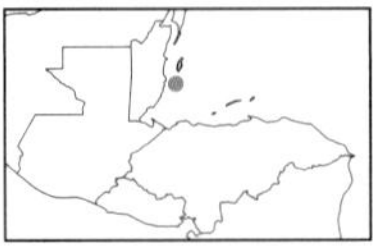

BLACK NODDY *Anous minutus*

13.5 in. (34 cm). Similar to Brown Noddy but smaller, appears **black in fresh plumage** (brownish in worn birds), and has proportionately longer, more slender bill; also note differences in distribution. Very rare in NCA Caribbean waters. Historically bred on Belizean cayes, now extirpated. Pantropical.

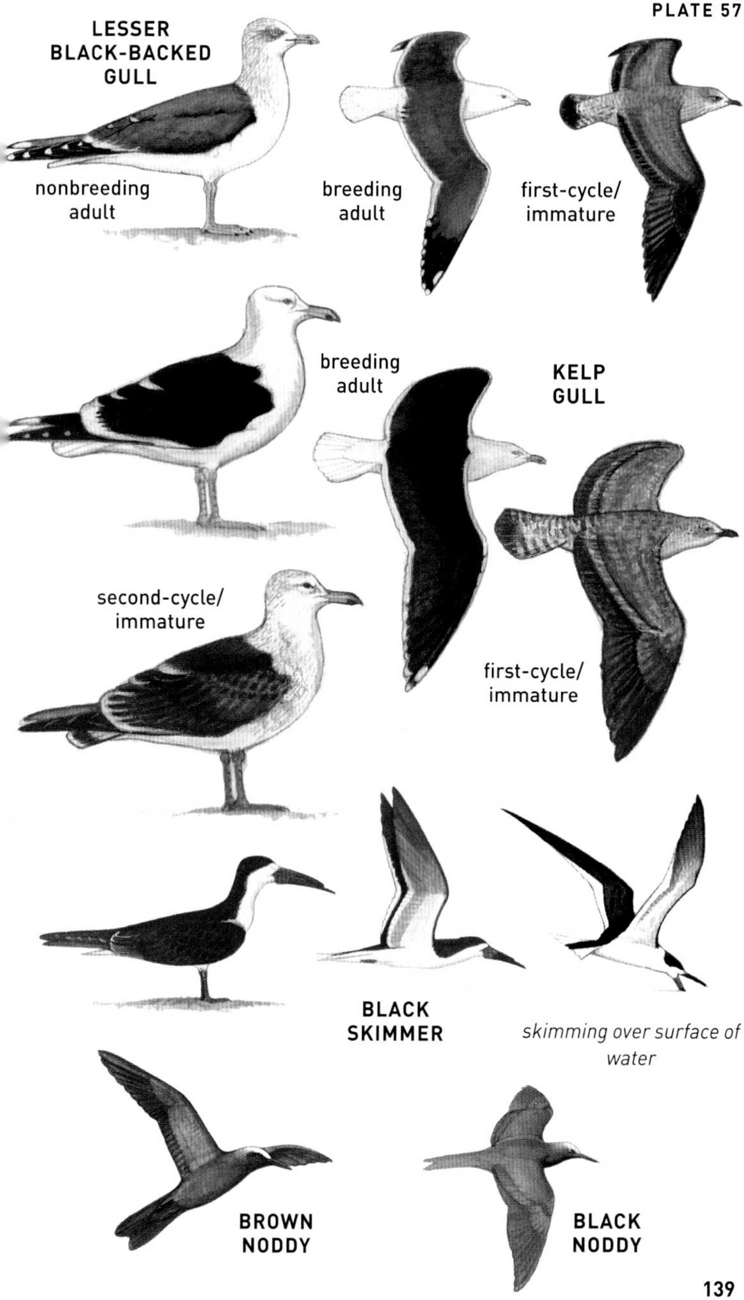
LESSER BLACK-BACKED GULL
nonbreeding adult
breeding adult
first-cycle/ immature
breeding adult
KELP GULL
second-cycle/ immature
first-cycle/ immature
BLACK SKIMMER
skimming over surface of water
BROWN NODDY
BLACK NODDY

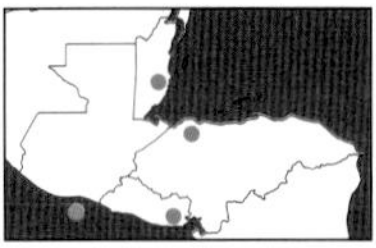

SOOTY TERN *Onychoprion fuscatus*

16 in. (41 cm). Adult **blackish above** with white forehead that extends only as far as the eye. In flight, underwing shows **dark primaries** and **dark trailing edge to secondaries**. Juvenile all-black with white-tipped upperwing coverts. Adult similar to adult Bridled Tern, but is blackish above (not dark gray), has less extensive white forehead, no collar, darker underwing pattern, and less white in tail. Uncommon summer visitor in NCA Caribbean pelagic waters (Feb.–mid-Aug.), rare summer visitor in NCA Pacific pelagic waters (mid-Apr.–early Oct.). Breeds on at least one Belizean caye (Middle Snake). Storm-driven birds occasionally found far inland. Pantropical.

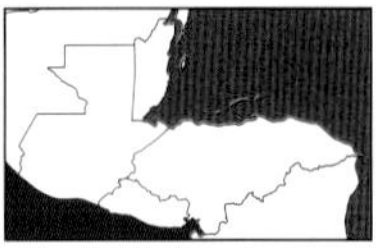

BRIDLED TERN *Onychoprion anaethetus*

15 in. (38 cm). Similar to Sooty Tern, but has **dark gray upperparts** that contrast with **pale collar** (lacking on Sooty), **black cap**, white forehead that extends beyond the eye, **paler underwing pattern**, and extensive white in tail. Juvenile and immature similar to adult, but have whitish head and pale edging above that gives a scaled appearance. Fairly common summer visitor in NCA Caribbean pelagic waters (early Apr.–mid-Sept.), uncommon year-round visitor in NCA Pacific pelagic waters. Breeding occurs on smaller Belizean cayes and Cayos Cochinos (Honduras). Breeding also in Gulf of Fonseca (Nicaragua), very close to Honduras and El Salvador waters. Pantropical.

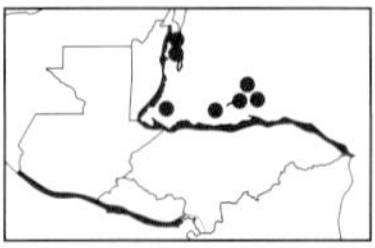

LEAST TERN *Sternula antillarum*

9 in. (23 cm). **A small, delicate tern.** Nonbreeding adult has black cap and nape, thin white forehead, and dark bill; breeding adult similar, but **bill is yellow** (unique to small terns). On standing birds, legs appear short. **In flight, note 2 or 3 dark outer primaries.** Immature similar to nonbreeding adult, but has dark carpal bar. Uncommon to fairly common on Caribbean Slope, uncommon on Pacific Slope; breeds locally on both slopes; to 160 ft. (50 m). Found in coastal areas on beaches, sandbars, and mudflats; occasionally in pelagic waters. In flight, note rapid wingbeats (similar to Roseate Tern [p. 144]) and frequent short aerial dives, surface dips, and kiting behavior. Call is a thin, high-pitched *key'e'e'e'e'e'e!* U.S. to Colombia.

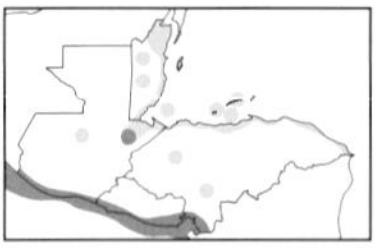

BLACK TERN *Chlidonias niger*

9.5 in. (24 cm). Nonbreeding adult dark gray above and pale below, with **dark patch on side of breast**; also note dark crown and **black spot behind eye**. Breeding adult is distinctive, with **all-black body, grayish wings**, and white vent; in flight, note all-gray underwing. Note that in all plumages, upper surface of wings, tail, and back are darker gray than all other terns (except Sooty, Bridled, and noddies, p. 138). Common transient and winter visitor on Pacific Slope (July–early May, but present year-round), fairly common to common transient on Caribbean Slope (late Apr.–late May, early Aug.–early Nov.); to 2,620 ft. (800 m). Generally found in pelagic waters; also occurs along the coast, where large flocks roost on sandbars and mudflats; also occasionally inland at lakes and reservoirs. One of the most common birds in NCA Pacific pelagic waters, where it often perches on the backs of sea turtles to rest. Canada to Peru; also Europe to Africa.

adult
SOOTY
TERN
immature
BRIDLED
TERN
adult
immature
LEAST
TERN
breeding
adult
nonbreeding
adult
immature
breeding
adult
BLACK
TERN
molting
nonbreeding
adult

CASPIAN TERN *Hydroprogne caspia*

21 in. (53 cm). **A large tern.** Distinguished from Royal Tern by less shaggy crest; more **stout, deep red bill with dark tip**; more **extensive black in primaries** (visible in flight), and less white on forecrown (on nonbreeding). Transient and winter visitor (mid-Aug.–early May; however, records from all months). Uncommon to fairly common on both slopes; to 330 ft. (100 m). Found in coastal areas on beaches, sandbars, and mudflats; also at coastal and inland marshes, lagoons, and at shrimp farms. More frequent in freshwater areas (where Royal Tern is very rare) and uncommon to rare in coastal areas (where far outnumbered by Royal Tern). Flight call is a thin, high-pitched whistle (*weeeeeeeur!*) and a rail-like squawking. Cosmopolitan except S. America.

ROYAL TERN *Thalasseus maximus*

20 in. (51 cm). **A large tern.** Distinguished from Caspian Tern by shaggier crest; slimmer, **orange bill**; less extensive black in primaries (visible in flight); and more extensive **white on forecrown** (on nonbreeding). Similar to Elegant Tern, but is larger and heavier overall, and has less shaggy crest and thicker, straighter bill. Common transient and winter visitor on both slopes; records from all months; to 160 ft. (50 m). Found on coastal beaches and sandbars, as well as in marshes and lagoons. Call is a somewhat harsh *kah'r'r'e'e'e't!* (similar to calls of Sandwich Tern, but less harsh and scratchy). U.S. to Argentina; Africa.

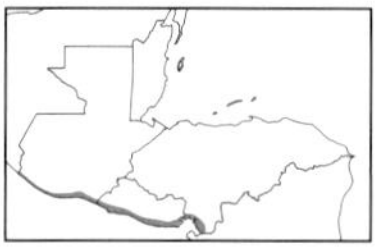

ELEGANT TERN *Thalasseus elegans*

17 in. (43 cm). Similar to Royal Tern, but overall smaller, yellow-orange **bill is long and thin (and slightly decurved)**, and **crest is longer and shaggier**. Breeding adult has all-black crown and may show rosy tones on underparts. Transient and winter visitor (probably year-round, but most reports Oct.–Dec. and Mar.–May). Uncommon on Pacific Slope; to 160 ft. (50 m). Found in coastal areas on beaches and sandbars, and in marshes and lagoons; also in near-shore pelagic waters. Flight call is a thin *kre'e'e'e'e't!* U.S. to Chile.

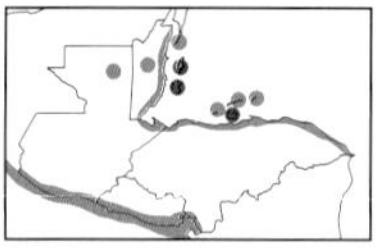

SANDWICH TERN *Thalasseus sandvicensis*

15 in. (38 cm). **Thin black bill has small yellow tip.** Nonbreeding adult has whitish forecrown with black mask and shaggy crest. Breeding adult has all-black crown. In all plumages, similar to Gull-billed Tern, but has longer, thinner bill with yellow tip (dark tip in Gull-billed) and shaggier crest. Fairly common nonbreeding visitor year-round on both slopes; has bred on Caribbean cayes; near sea level. Found in coastal areas on beaches and sandbars, also in marshes and lagoons. Call is a thin, scratchy *kah'r'r'e'e'e't!*; also makes a harsher *Kar'r'ak!* (both calls are similar to call of Royal Tern, but slightly harsher). U.S. to Argentina; Europe to Africa.

GULL-BILLED TERN *Gelochelidon nilotica*

14 in. (36 cm). **Pale overall**, with slightly gray upperparts and **stout, all-black bill**. Breeding adult has black crown and nape. Nonbreeding adult has pale head and thin, dark mask. In all plumages, similar to Sandwich Tern, but has shorter, heavier bill (and lacks yellow tip to bill). Uncommon transient and winter visitor on both slopes (observations from all months); to 160 ft. (50 m). Found in coastal areas on beaches, sandbars, and mudflats; also, coastal marshes, lagoons, and at shrimp farms. Call is a harsh *eh-rack!* or a repeated *ehk-ehk-ehk-ehk-ehk-* . . . Cosmopolitan.

CASPIAN TERN
breeding adult
nonbreeding adult
breeding adult
nonbreeding adult
ROYAL TERN
juvenile
Elegant and Royal terns on beach
breeding adult
nonbreeding adult
ELEGANT TERN
nonbreeding adult
GULL-BILLED TERN
nonbreeding adult
SANDWICH TERN
breeding adult
breeding adult

STERNA TERNS

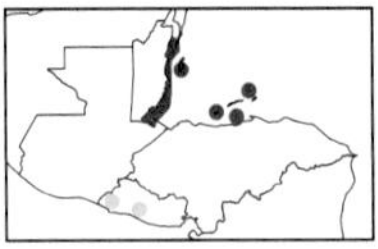

ROSEATE TERN *Sterna dougallii*

12.5 in. (32 cm). An elegant, **strikingly pale** medium-sized tern with short legs (knees barely visible) and a **very long tail** that extends well beyond wingtips. Thin bill is generally black (Caribbean population shows extensive orange base) in both breeding and nonbreeding birds. Breeding adult is often **washed with rose below**; orange-red legs. In flight, note dark gray outer primaries. Juvenile has dark, scaly pattern above with dark crown. Uncommon to fairly common summer visitor on Caribbean Slope (Apr.–Nov.), very rare transient on Pacific Slope (May and Nov.); to 160 ft. (50 m). Found on coastal beaches and sandbars; also observed offshore in NCA Caribbean waters. Breeding colonies found on Tobacco Caye (Belize), and the Bay Is. and Cayos Cochinos (Honduras). The smallest of the *Sterna* terns, it flies with stiff and rapid wingbeats (like the Least Tern [p. 140]). Flight call is a thin, 2-part *khe-reeet!* Pantropical and subtropical waters.

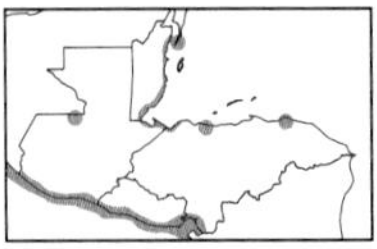

COMMON TERN *Sterna hirundo*

14 in. (36 cm). **Wingtips generally project beyond tail** in standing birds; also note long legs (knees visible). Nonbreeding adult has whitish forecrown, black bill, and **dark carpal bar**. **Dark outer web of outer tail feathers** is fairly obvious on standing birds (compare with Forster's Tern). Breeding adult has all-dark cap, contrasting **underparts are grayer (slightly paler than Arctic Tern)**, and bill is **red with dark tip**. In flight, **upperwing pattern uniformly gray** (from mantle to primaries) with dark wedge at primaries. Immature similar to nonbreeding adult, but with more extensive black on outer primaries and shorter tail. Fairly common transient and winter visitor on Pacific Slope (records year-round, seasonal abundance peaks still not fully understood), uncommon on Caribbean Slope (early Sept.–late May); to 160 ft. (50 m). Found in coastal areas on beaches, sandbars, and mudflats; storm-driven birds may be found farther inland. Call is a harsh *keeey-rat!* Cosmopolitan.

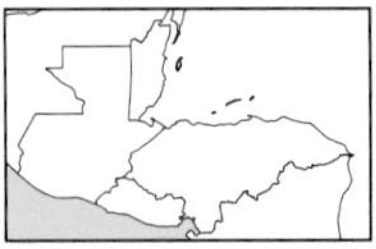

ARCTIC TERN *Sterna paradisaea*

15 in. (38 cm). Tail projects slightly beyond wingtips; **bill is short; legs appear very short on standing birds** (knees not visible). Nonbreeding adult has whitish forehead and **weak carpal bar**. Breeding adult has all-dark cap, reddish orange bill and legs, and gray underparts (on average, darker than on Common Tern). In flight, **upperwing uniformly pale gray**. Head more rounded than on other similar terns. Few records, but presumed to be a rare transient in NCA Pacific pelagic waters. Calls are similar to Common Tern. Holarctic to Antarctica.

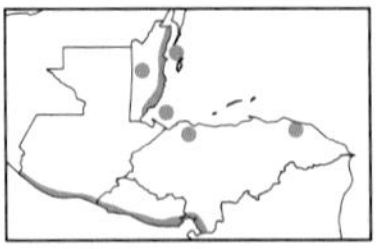

FORSTER'S TERN *Sterna forsteri*

14 in. (36 cm). On standing bird, **tail projects well beyond wingtips** and **legs are long** (knees easily visible). On nonbreeding adult, **"bandit mask"** is distinctive. Breeding adult has **orange bill** with black tip and **orange legs** (not reddish as in Common or Arctic). In flight, **pale gray mantle and upperwing coverts contrast with whitish secondaries and primaries**. Rare winter visitor (late Aug.–early May); to 4,430 ft. (1,350 m). Found on coastal beaches and sandbars; also in marshes and lagoons. Call is a harsh, throaty *aaaaaak!* Canada to Costa Rica.

Sterna. *After breeding, most* Sterna *terns lose color in their bills and legs, which change from orange or deep red to black. Juveniles usually resemble nonbreeding adults, but also show brown and black edging on upperparts and dark carpal bars. Bill structure, leg length, and wingtip projection beyond tail are useful field marks.*

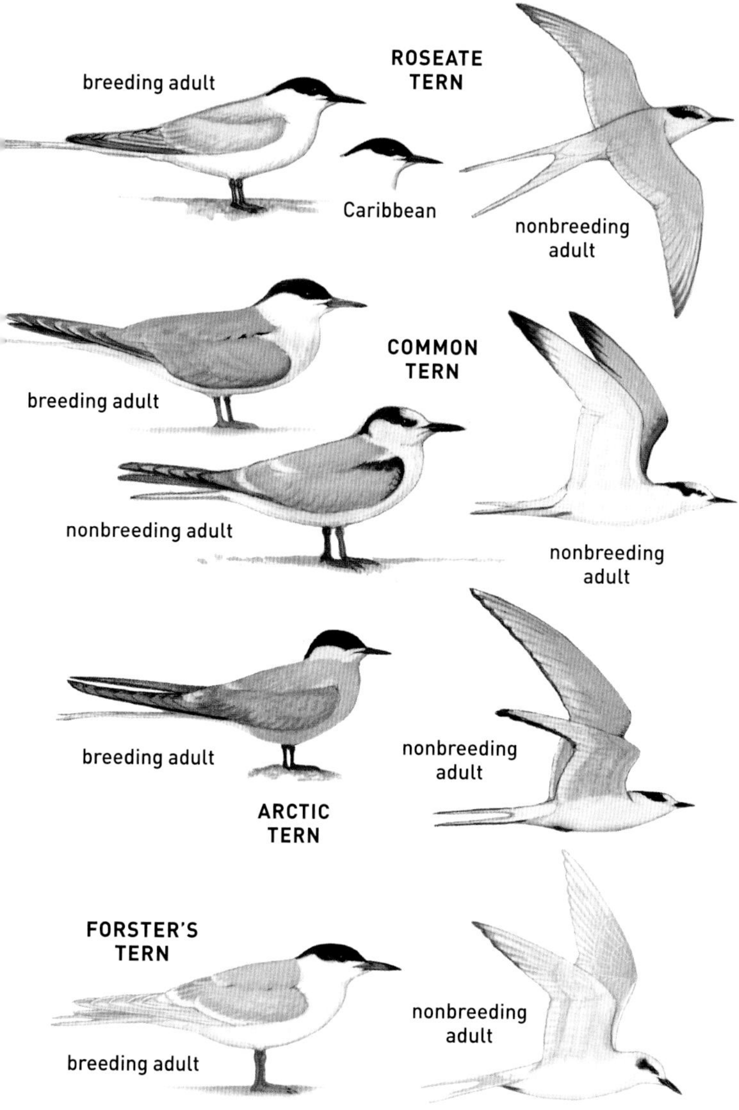

DARK SHEARWATERS

PROCELLARIIDAE (Order: Procellariiformes). Petrels and shearwaters, a cosmopolitan family of pelagic seabirds, spend most of their lives over open waters; many can soar for hours without flapping, and some rarely land on the water (feeding on the wing). They catch fish and squid by dipping their bills into the water's surface while on the wing or by plunge-diving; also they sift for plankton, and scavenge scraps of prey items. Like albatrosses and storm-petrels (p. 150), procellarids have a naricorn, a tube positioned along the culmen that allows them to detect scents and expel salt extracted from sea water by the salt glands (hence the collective nickname *tubenoses*). Most species come to land only to breed, which they may do irregularly, or in 1- to 4-year cycles. They generally breed in remote coastal cliff sides and mountains, often in burrows. Most species are silent at sea. **7 species (2 genera)**

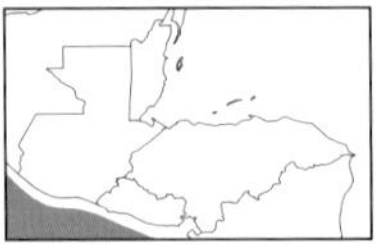

WEDGE-TAILED SHEARWATER *Ardenna pacifica*

17.5 in. (45 cm). **Bill pale gray with dark tip**; note long, fairly broad wings (in flight, **noticeably bent at wrist**) and **long, wedge-shaped tail**; feet pinkish. Light morph sooty gray-brown above **with pale scalloping to wing coverts and mantle**; **may show a subtle dark M across wings**. Underparts whitish with gray-brown smudging on face, neck, sides, and undertail coverts; underwing whitish with dark trailing edge. Light morph similar to Black-vented Shearwater, but is larger and leaner, and has long-necked, long-tailed appearance; also note darker face and more angled wings in flight. Dark morph (rare in NCA waters) sooty brown overall with pale edging to wing coverts and mantle; underwing shows pale base to primaries; dark morph distinguished from Sooty Shearwater by paler bill, all-dark underwing, and pinkish legs (gray in Sooty). Also compare with Christmas Shearwater, but larger overall, paler (not sooty black), and gray bill with dark tip. Uncommon in NCA Pacific pelagic waters (recorded all months). Solitary or in groups of up to 1,000; often in mixed-species flocks. Flight is slow and unhurried; wings are pressed forward and bowed above body plane. Tropical Pacific and Indian Oceans; breeds in Hawaii and on islands in Mex.

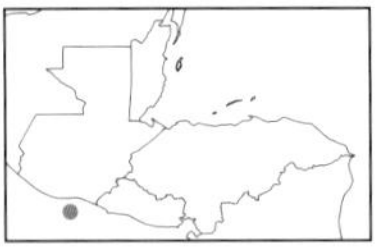

CHRISTMAS SHEARWATER *Puffinus nativitatis*

14.5 in. (37 cm). Sooty black overall with **dark underwings**; note **thin dark bill**. Compare with Sooty Shearwater, but is darker overall (not sooty brown) and has dark underwings. Also compare with dark-morph Wedge-tailed Shearwater, but smaller overall, and darker (not sooty brown), and all-dark bill (not gray with dark tip). One record from Guatemalan pelagic waters, but possibly regular. Tropical Pacific Ocean; breeds in Hawaii, Marshall Is., Kiritimati (Christmas I.).

SOOTY SHEARWATER *Ardenna grisea*

17.5 in. (45 cm). **Dark sooty brown** overall; **bill and legs dark**; underwing dark with **pale wing lining**. Similar to dark-morph Wedge-tailed Shearwater, but has darker bill, pale underwing coverts, and gray legs (not pinkish). Compare with Christmas Shearwater, but is paler overall (not sooty black) and has pale underwings. One record in NCA Pacific pelagic waters (Guatemala), but possibly regular. Flight is strong and direct; frequently soars high between flaps. Feet project only slightly beyond long tail in flight. Pacific, Atlantic, and Southern Oceans; sub-Arctic waters; breeds in Australia, New Zealand, and s. South America.

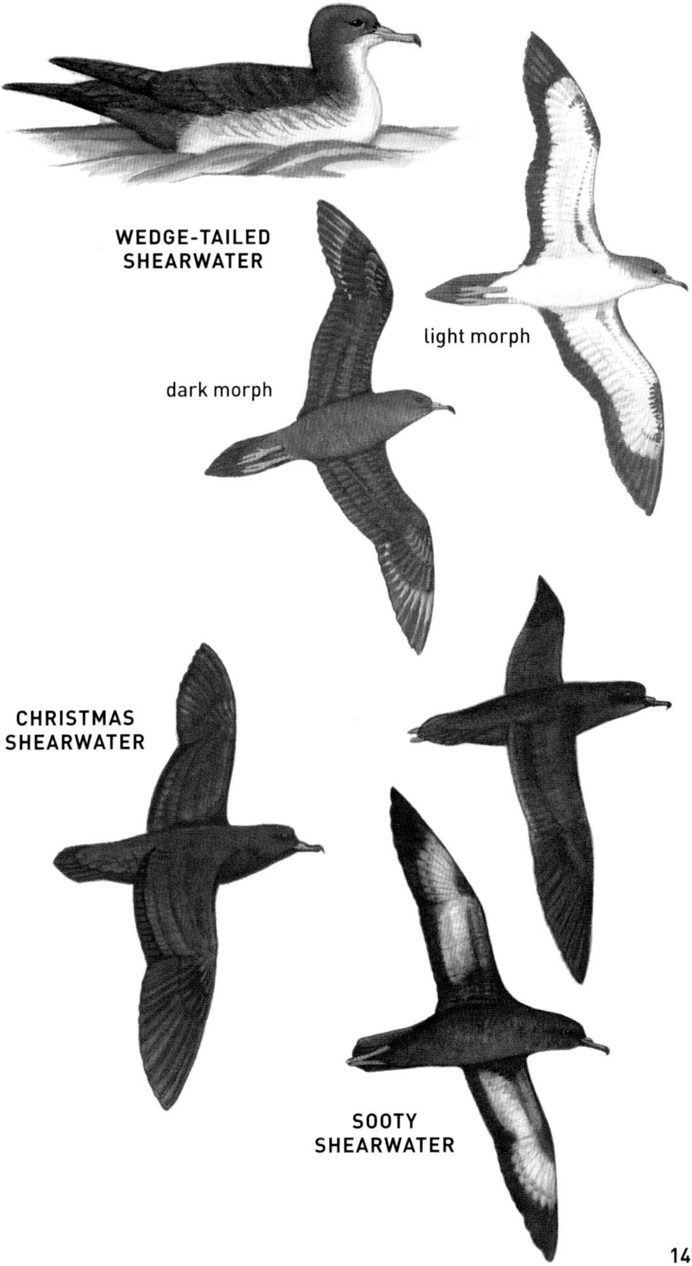
WEDGE-TAILED SHEARWATER
light morph
dark morph
CHRISTMAS SHEARWATER
SOOTY SHEARWATER

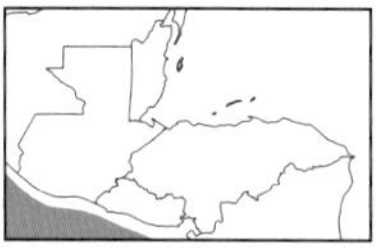

PINK-FOOTED SHEARWATER *Ardenna creatopus*

18.5 in. (47 cm). A **large, stocky shearwater** with a barrel chest and **broad wings**. Upperparts **uniformly brownish gray** (fresh-plumaged individuals show pale fringes or scalloping to mantle, rump, and wing coverts); sides of face smudgy brown. Underparts variable: chin and throat whitish, but may be washed brown; **belly white**; underwing pale with dark axillaries; **undertail coverts brownish**. **Bill pinkish yellow with dark tip**; feet pinkish. Rare to uncommon in NCA Pacific pelagic waters year-round. Generally solitary or in small groups. Flight is leisurely; generally flaps twice and then glides for several seconds. Eastern Pacific Ocean; breeds on islands in Chile.

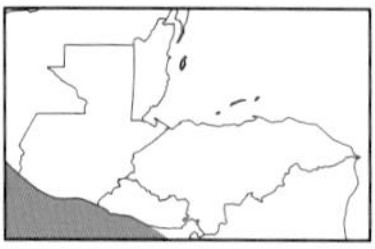

BLACK-VENTED SHEARWATER *Puffinus opisthomelas*

14.5 in. (37 cm). **Fairly small, stocky shearwater**. Upperparts grayish brown; underparts white, with grayish brown undertail coverts; smudgy markings on face and **sides of upper chest**; underwing white with dark trailing edge; bill sooty gray; tail wedge-shaped. Similar to light-morph Wedge-tailed Shearwater but is smaller and stockier, and has shorter neck and tail; also note paler face and less-angled wings in flight. Rare in NCA Pacific pelagic waters (records from Oct. to Jan.). Generally solitary, occasionally in groups of up to 20 individuals. Eastern Pacific Ocean; breeds on islands in Mex.

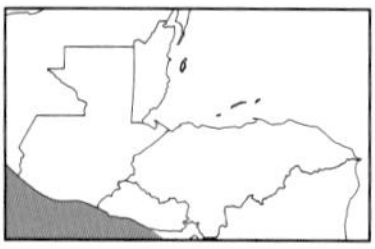

GALAPAGOS SHEARWATER *Puffinus subalaris*

12 in. (31 cm). Small and compact with **short, rounded wings**; note **contrast of dark brown upperparts and white underparts**. Dark brown on face extends below eye and is **cleanly separated from white throat**; note thin white crescents above and below eye. Undertail coverts dark; underwing mostly white, but tips of primaries dark. Dark bill is relatively long and thin. Formerly considered conspecific with the similar Audubon's Shearwater, but no range overlap. Fairly common in NCA Pacific pelagic waters (recorded in all months, but mainly Aug.–Apr.). Gregarious; often in small groups of 3 to 25 individuals, but also in mixed-species groups of up to several thousand. Often sits on water. E. Pacific Ocean; breeds on the Galápagos Is.

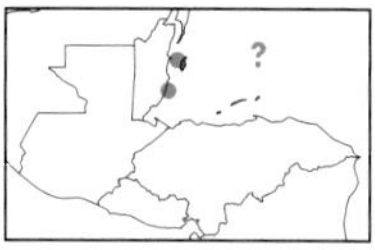

AUDUBON'S SHEARWATER *Puffinus lherminieri*

12 in. (31 cm). Very similar (almost identical) to Galapagos Shearwater, but no range overlap. Very rare vagrant in Belize but may be regular in pelagic waters of the western Caribbean. W. tropical and subtropical Atlantic Ocean; breeds in the Caribbean and on islets off of Tobago, Venezuela, and Panama.

PINK-FOOTED SHEARWATER
BLACK-VENTED SHEARWATER
GALAPAGOS/AUDUBON'S SHEARWATER

STORM-PETRELS

HYDROBATIDAE (Order: Procellariiformes). As with other members of this order, storm-petrels have a naricorn (see Procellariidae [p. 146]). These small, dark seabirds are similar to shearwaters in diet and breeding habits, but are more active; they tend to have fluttering wingbeats, and some species "tiptoe" on the surface of the water with their relatively long legs when foraging. The genus name *Oceanodroma* means "ocean runner." **4 species (1 genus)**

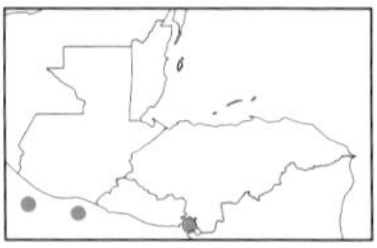

LEACH'S STORM-PETREL *Oceanodroma leucorhoa*

8.5 in. (22 cm). The nominate form (*O.l. leucorhoa*) is a **large, long-winged storm-petrel** with a **deeply forked tail**. Sooty brown overall with pale upperwing band; **rump patch mostly white** with **variable dusky markings down the center** (dark-rumped individuals are very rare). Flight is bounding and unpredictable, reminiscent of nighthawk flight. The "Chapman's" Storm-Petrel (*O.l. chapmani*) is smaller (7 in., 18 cm), has **mostly dark rump** with varying amounts of white on sides of rump, and **more deeply forked tail**; wings shorter, broader, and more rounded than Black Storm-Petrel's. Pacific Ocean; breeds on Coronado Is. and San Benito Is. (Mex.), and photographed in August 2015 off s. Honduras. Reports off s. Guatemala (Apr. and Oct.) have not been assigned to subspecies. N. Pacific and Atlantic Oceans.

WEDGE-RUMPED STORM-PETREL *Oceanodroma tethys*

7.5 in. (19 cm). Sooty brown-black overall with silvery upperwing band; distinctive **broad white rump patch extends nearly to tip of notched tail**. In flight, **short legs do not extend beyond tail**. Uncommon visitor to NCA Pacific pelagic waters (May–Dec.). Solitary or in small groups. Flight is direct with strong, choppy wingbeats. When foraging, likes to "tiptoe" across the surface of the water while fluttering wings. E. Tropical Pacific Ocean; breeds on Galapagos Is. and along coast of Peru.

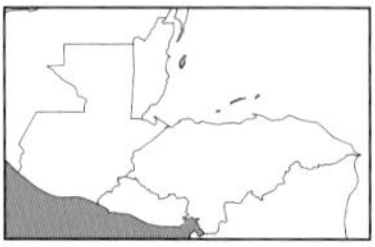

BLACK STORM-PETREL *Oceanodroma melania*

9 in. (23 cm). **Largest storm-petrel in NCA waters**. Sooty brown-black overall; note **long, pointed wings**, **bent at the wrist** (resembling wings of a small falcon or nighthawk); tail deeply forked. Similar to dark-rumped individuals of Leach's Storm-Petrel, but is larger and darker, and has longer, narrower, more pointed wings. Uncommon to fairly common in NCA Pacific pelagic waters (recorded in all months, but less common in May and June). Flight is ternlike and powerful, fairly relaxed, alternating deep wingbeats with lengthy glides. Ne. Pacific Ocean; breeds on islands in California and Mex.

LEAST STORM-PETREL *Oceanodroma microsoma*

5.5 in. (14 cm). **Smallest storm-petrel in NCA waters**. Note **rounded tail** (not forked), unmarked dark rump (lacks white patches), and **short, rounded wings** with pale upperwing bands. Uncommon in NCA Pacific pelagic and near-shore waters year-round, but presumed to be a nonbreeding visitor. Most likely storm-petrel to be seen from shore. Mixes with other storm-petrel species when feeding. Batlike flight. Subtropical e. Pacific Ocean; breeds on islands in Mex.

LEACH'S STORM-PETREL
leucorhoa
chapmani
WEDGE-RUMPED STORM-PETREL
BLACK STORM-PETREL
LEAST STORM-PETREL
storm-petrels in flight
Least
Black
Leach's
Wedge-rumped

VULTURES

CATHARTIDAE (Order: Accipitriformes). Large, soaring birds characterized by their featherless heads and necks and carrion-based diet. Vultures fly to great heights and distances in search of food, which they can detect using their keen sense of smell. Of the NCA vultures, the Turkey Vulture stands out for its spectacular long-distance, diurnal migrations (often traveling in groups of thousands of individuals). Species are silent away from breeding sites, where they are limited to harsh grunts and calls. The taxonomic placement of this family is still debated; it was formerly placed in the order Ciconiiformes (with storks), but some authorities now suggest placing it in its own order. **4 species (3 genera)**

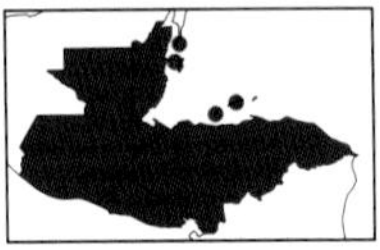

BLACK VULTURE *Coragyps atratus*

24 in. (61 cm); WS: 58.5 in. (149 cm). Large and black, with **bare black head**. In flight, note **silvery primaries** and short tail. In flight, distinguished from Turkey Vulture by black secondaries (grayish on Turkey) and short square tail (long and wedge shaped on Turkey). Common in NCA; to 11,480 ft. (3,500 m). Found in a variety of habitats, but generally around open and disturbed habitats, including cities and towns; normally seen soaring, often in large groups. Roosts communally. Often scavenges in garbage dumps. U.S. to S. America.

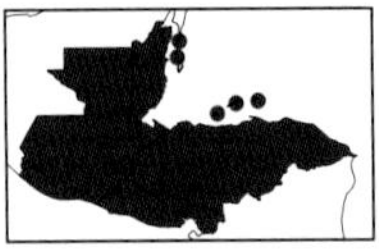

TURKEY VULTURE *Cathartes aura*

28 in. (71 cm); WS: 69 in. (170 cm). Adult has **bare red head**. Immature has bare dark gray head, like Black Vulture. In flight, **grayish primaries and secondaries contrast with dark wing lining and body**. Very similar to Lesser Yellow-headed Vulture, but has red head (not multicolored), grayish (not silver) primaries and secondaries, and slightly wedge-shaped tail (not square). In flight, appears to rock on the wind, a behavior mimicked by Zone-tailed Hawk (p. 166). Told from the hawk by unfeathered head, lack of barring on underwing, and lack of tail bands. Common resident and transient (Oct.–Nov., Mar.–Apr.) in NCA; to 13,120 ft. (4,000 m). Found in a wide variety of open habitat types. Groups of several thousand can be seen migrating in riverlike formations or kettling in a thermal. Canada to S. America.

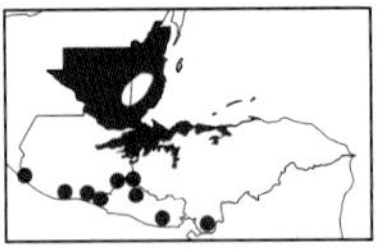

LESSER YELLOW-HEADED VULTURE *Cathartes burrovianus*

24.5 in. (62 cm); WS: 61 in. (154 cm). Very similar to Turkey Vulture, but has **bare red, yellow, and blue head**; in flight, note **silver secondaries and primaries** (more contrasting than Turkey Vulture) and **relatively square tail**. Immature similar to immature Turkey Vulture, but with more extensive feathering on hindneck. Uncommon on Caribbean Slope; very rare on Pacific Slope; to 1,490 ft. (454 m). Found in lowland open country, often near marshes, lagoons, rivers, and estuaries. Soars and forages much lower than other vultures; rarely soars high. Mex. to Argentina.

KING VULTURE *Sarcoramphus papa*

28.5 in. (73 cm); WS: 73 in. (178 cm). Very large. Adult distinctive; **white overall with contrasting black flight feathers**; bare neck and bill washed with red and orange; pearly white eyes. Juvenile sooty black overall. Uncommon on Caribbean Slope; rare and local on Pacific Slope; to 8,370 ft. (2,550 m). Found in mature pine-oak forest, humid semideciduous forest, and pine savanna. Soars high over forest; in flight, note broad wings, spread primaries, and relatively short tail. Solitary or in pairs. Mex. to Argentina.

BLACK VULTURE

ventral and dorsal views of Lesser Yellow-headed (L) and Turkey

LESSER YELLOW-HEADED VULTURE

TURKEY VULTURE

KING VULTURE

adult

juvenile in flight

OSPREY AND EAGLES

PANDIONIDAE (Order: Accipitriformes). A family of only one species, which occurs on all continents except Antarctica. The Osprey is also known as the *fish hawk*, as it feeds almost exclusively on fish. It is distinguished from other diurnal birds of prey by several unique morphological adaptations, including a reversible outer toe, spicules on the underside of its toes (to aid in grasping slippery fish), rounded talons (not grooved), and closable nostrils that can keep water out during dives. Some northern populations are migratory. **1 species (1 genus)**

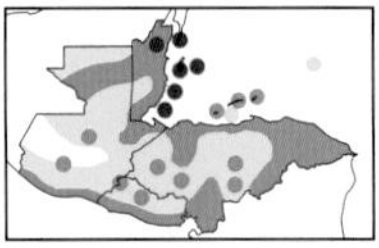

OSPREY *Pandion haliaetus*

23 in. (59 cm). **White head with broad black eye line**. In-flight appearance distinctive; note **long, narrow wings bent at wrists, spread primaries**, and **dark carpal patches**. Both slopes: uncommon transient and winter visitor (Oct.–Apr.); some young birds oversummer; to 2,940 ft. (896 m). Found along both coasts, and inland near lakes and rivers. Captures fish with impressive dives; may be seen carrying fish in flight. Calls include a drawn-out, rising *tewp-tewp-tewp-TEWP-TEWP-tewp-tewp* and a shrill, begging *teeeeeah*. Cosmopolitan. The resident Caribbean subspecies, *P. h. ridgwayi*, breeds on Belizean cayes and locally along the Belize coastline, and is distinguished by a nearly all-white head.

ACCIPITRIDAE (Order: Accipitriformes). A large, cosmopolitan family well represented in NCA. Kites, hawks, eagles, and allies are part of the group collectively known as *raptors* (birds of prey). This family comprises large and medium-sized birds with sharp bills and talons used to rip and tear the flesh of their prey. They are primarily diurnal hunters, and prey on insects, fish, reptiles, amphibians, birds, and small to medium mammals (including monkeys). Pair bonding is strong and may be for life. Some species exhibit sexual dimorphism in terms of plumage and/or size; in many species, females are larger than males. Several species migrate by the millions through NCA, and it is not uncommon to see daytime flights of tens of thousands of individuals passing within hours; indeed, there are few things more spectacular than watching a "river of raptors" moving south to their wintering grounds. **35 species (22 genera)**

HARPY EAGLE *Harpia harpyja*

40 in. (102 cm); WS: 80 in. (194 cm). **Largest raptor in NCA**. Adult similar to adult Crested Eagle, but has **broad black chest band, forked crest, black barring on thighs**, and **massive, thick legs and talons**. Distinguish immature from immature Crested by size and thickness of legs. Very rare in NCA; to 1,640 ft. (500 m). Found only in primary rainforest. Usually stays deep in forest interior; does not soar and is rarely seen. Call is a loud, scratchy scream: *EEEEEAAAAAhhhhhhh!* (descends at the end). Mex. to Argentina.

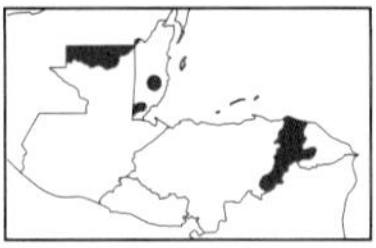

CRESTED EAGLE *Morphnus guianensis*

33 in. (84 cm); WS: 66.5 in. (169 cm). **A large raptor.** Adult has **grayish hood**; **short crest** (not forked); whitish below with soft chestnut barring. Immature similar to adult, but paler overall and has white head (lacks gray hood). Adult similar to adult Harpy Eagle, but slightly smaller with thinner legs, has gray (not black) chest, and unbarred thighs; immature distinguished from very similar immature Harpy by smaller size and thinner legs. Very rare in NCA; to 1,640 ft. (500 m). Found only in primary rainforest. Perches at mid- and upper levels of interior forest; rarely soars and is seldom observed. Call is a sharp, high-pitched shrill whistle, *Wreee-aaEEEEEEEE!* (rising in pitch and volume toward end), lasting approximately 1.5 sec.; also from juvenile a *Wheeer!-Wheeer!* and other piping whistles. Guatemala to Argentina.

PLATE 65

OSPREY
Osprey diving for fish
HARPY EAGLE
immature
adult
CRESTED EAGLE
adult
adult dark morph
immature

BLACK HAWK-EAGLE *Spizaetus tyrannus*

25.5 in. (65 cm); WS: 55.5 in. (141 cm). Adult **black overall; legs barred white; tail with 2 to 3 obvious pale gray bands and tip**. In flight, primaries heavily barred black; similar to dark-morph Hook-billed Kite (p. 166), but larger and paler (especially on secondaries and underwing coverts). Uncommon in NCA; to 6,560 ft. (2,000 m). Found in rainforest, semideciduous forest, riparian forest, humid montane forest, and pine-oak forest. Rarely seen perched; soars over forest canopy with wings held flat and pressed forward; often calls in flight. Call is a loud, whistled *wie-wie-wha'weeeeeeeee!* (similar in quality to Ornate Hawk-Eagle's). Mex. to Argentina.

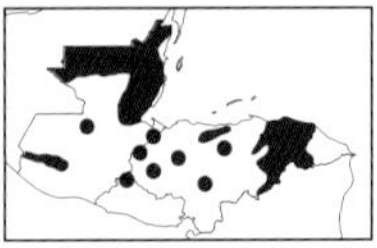

ORNATE HAWK-EAGLE *Spizaetus ornatus*

24 in. (61 cm); WS: 51 in. (130 cm). Adult with **long black crest; bold rufous down sides and back of neck**; black barring below; tail with 3 black bands; legs barred black. Immature plumage dark brown above; head and underparts white; note crest. First year similar to immature Gray-headed Kite, but has yellow eyes (not dark), longer crest, and feathered legs. Immature Ornate Hawk-Eagle similar to immature Black Hawk-Eagle, but has less obvious barring on legs and flanks, yellow cere, and a longer crest; immature also similar to Black-and-white Hawk-Eagle, but shows barring on legs and flanks, has yellowish cere, and longer crest. Rare to uncommon on Caribbean Slope, very rare on Pacific Slope; to 5,910 ft. (1,800 m). Found in rainforest, semideciduous forest, riparian forest, and occasionally in pine forest. Often detected by call, repeated while flying above forest canopy; call is loud, richly whistled *wie-weeeeeeee-wie'wha!—weeeeeeer-wie'wie'wie . . .* (similar in quality to call of Black Hawk-Eagle). Mex. to Argentina.

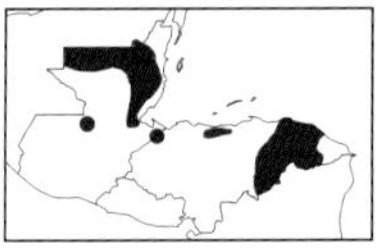

BLACK-AND-WHITE HAWK-EAGLE *Spizaetus melanoleucus*

23 in. (59 cm): WS: 51 in. (130 cm). Striking **2-tone pattern** (blackish brown above, white below); **small black crest**; note yellow-brown eyes and **orange cere**; in flight, **white leading edge of wings** visible from above (visible at bend of wing when perched). Similar to juvenile light-morph Gray-headed Kite, but has long feathered legs, orange cere (not yellow), dark mask, and yellow-brown eyes (not dark); immature similar to immature Ornate Hawk-Eagle, but lacks barring on legs and flanks, has orange cere, and shorter crest. Rare on Caribbean Slope; to 3,940 ft. (1,200 m). Found in primary rainforest. Call is a loud, piping whistle, *Weeer!-Weeer!-Weeer!-Weeer!* Mex. to Argentina.

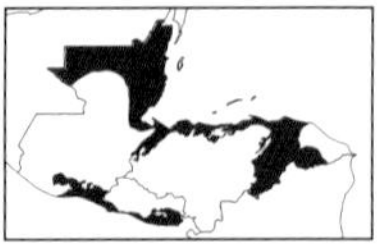

GRAY-HEADED KITE *Leptodon cayanensis*

20 in. (51 cm); WS: 39 in. (99 cm). **Head pale gray**; in flight, note **black underwing coverts** contrasting with white body and **barred primaries**. Juvenile plumage is variable: light morph similar to adult Black-and-white Hawk-Eagle, but has bare legs (not feathered), lacks dark mask, has dark eye (not yellow-brown), and yellow cere (not orange). Light-morph juvenile also similar to first-year Ornate Hawk-Eagle, but has dark eyes, shorter crest, and bare legs. Rare dark-morph juvenile has blackish brown head with dark streaking below. Uncommon on Caribbean Slope, rare on Pacific Slope; to 4,920 ft. (1,500 m). A solitary forest dweller; found in coastal semideciduous forest and swamp forest on Pacific Slope; on Caribbean Slope in rainforest and riparian forest. Calls include a repeating nasal scream: *reh!-reh!-reh!-reh!-reh!-reh'reh'reh'reh'reh* (accelerates toward the end) or simply *reh'reh'reh'reh'reh' . . .* Mex. to Argentina.

Spizaetus. *Hawk-eagles are large raptors with long, feathered legs; long tails; and conspicuous crests. Sexes are similar, and immature birds are generally paler versions of adults. They spend much of their time in the forest, hunting snakes and birds. They are often first detected by voice; they call while soaring high above the forest canopy on broad, paddle-shaped wings.*

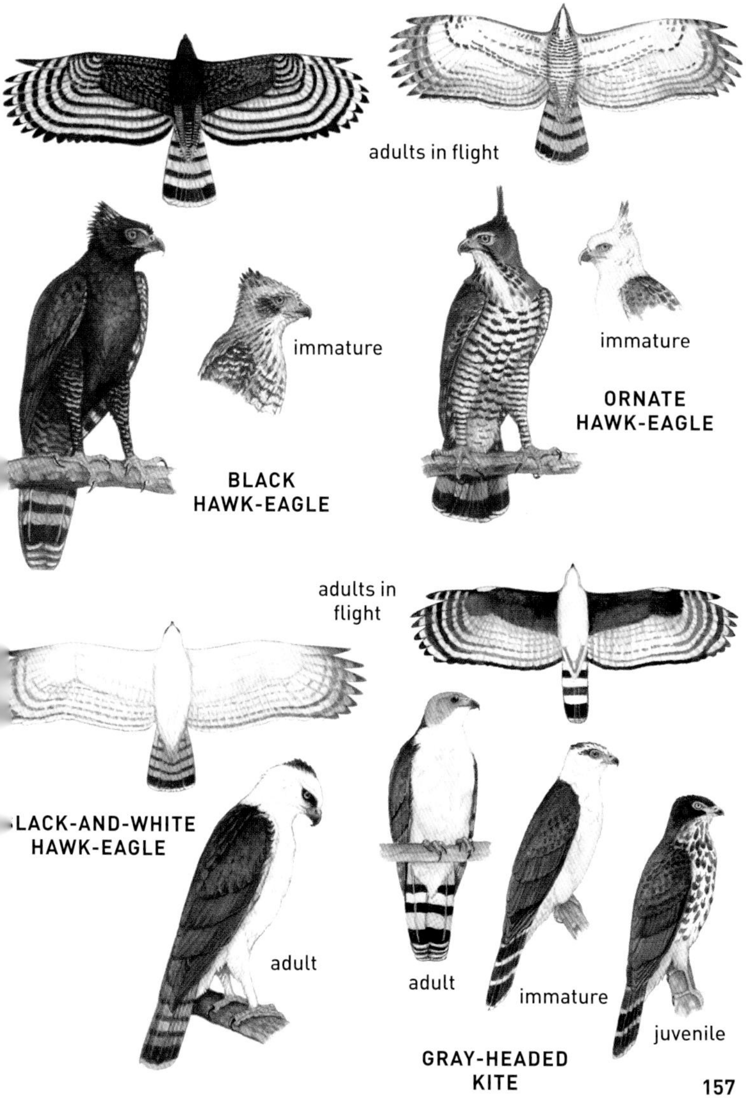

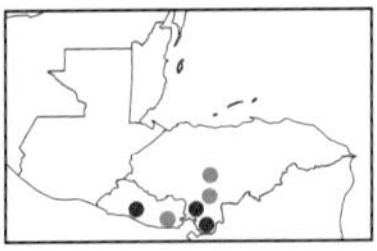

PEARL KITE *Gampsonyx swainsonii*

9 in. (23 cm); WS: 19.5 in. (50 cm). Very small raptor. **Forecrown creamy white**; upperparts bluish gray; **sides and thighs washed pale rufous**; eyes red. First recorded in NCA in 2009 near the Gulf of Fonseca, but appears to be expanding; to 4,920 ft. (1,500 m). Prefers open habitat; found in disturbed forest edges, agricultural fields, and coastal scrub. Often soars. Calls include a high-pitched, begging *si'si'si'si'si'si'si'si'si'si'si . . .* ; and a trilled *si'he'si'he'si'he'si'he'si' . . .* Honduras and El Salvador to S. America.

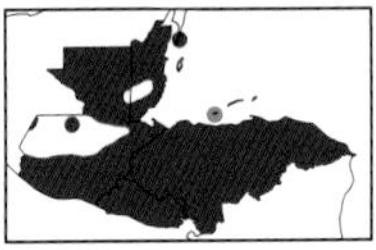

WHITE-TAILED KITE *Elanus leucurus*

15 in. (38 cm); WS: 37 in. (94 cm). Note combination of **white tail** and **black shoulders**. In flight, underwing shows **black carpal patch** and dark primaries. Juvenile resembles adult (including black shoulders), but has buffy smudges on breast, also light tawny-brown above. Fairly common on both slopes; to 4,920 ft. (1,500 m). Prefers open habitat; found in agricultural fields and disturbed habitat; also marshes and grasslands. Frequently "hover hunts" in open fields and savanna for insects and rodents; often seen perched on telephone poles, electric wires, and small trees. Calls include a somber, descending *peuuurr*, and a soft, repeated *peuuuh*. U.S. to Argentina.

SWALLOW-TAILED KITE *Elanoides forficatus*

22 in. (56 cm); WS: 49 in. (125 cm). Distinctive in flight. Fairly common breeding visitor and transient on Caribbean Slope (Feb.–Sept.), very rare transient on Pacific Slope; breeds up to 4,590 ft. (1,400 m); transients found up to 6,890 ft. (2,100 m). Occurs in semideciduous forest, rainforest, swamp forest, and pine savanna. Soars gracefully in lazy circles during migration and while hunting insects; also feeds on small reptiles and amphibians. Call is a high-pitched, whistling scream: *sah-weeet!—sa'wheet!—sa'wheet!* U.S. to S. America.

MISSISSIPPI KITE *Ictinia mississippiensis*

14 in. (36 cm); WS: 35 in. (89 cm). Adult mostly gray; **tail all-dark**; long pointed **wings reach to tip of tail when perched**; **secondaries whitish above**; primaries show a little rufous. Adult similar to Plumbeous Kite, but lacks tail bands and has less rufous on primaries. Immature very similar to immature Plumbeous Kite, but paler overall, shows little or no rufous in primaries, and, in flight, has longer tail, more rounded wings. Uncommon transient on both slopes (Apr.–May, mid-Sept.–late Oct.); to 4,920 ft. (1,500 m). Generally migrates at lower altitudes than other raptors, passing over almost any habitat. U.S. to S. America.

PLUMBEOUS KITE *Ictinia plumbea*

14 in. (36 cm); WS: 35 in. (89 cm). Adult **dark gray above**; long pointed **wings extend beyond tail when perched**; extensive **rufous on primaries**; **tail with thin white bands**. Adult similar to Mississippi Kite, but darker overall, has dark secondaries, extensive rufous on primaries, and white bands on tail. Immature similar to immature Mississippi Kite (take care in separating), but shows rufous in primaries, and, in flight, tail is shorter and wings more pointed. Uncommon summer visitor (Feb.–Aug.); to 4,430 ft. (1,350 m). Breeds in mangroves, swamp forest, also disturbed habitat, savannas, semideciduous forest, and pine forest. Often perches on exposed treetops. Soars lazily, catching insects in flight; performs aerial acrobatics during courtship. Calls include a high-pitched, 2-note *tea-heeee!* Mex. to S. America.

PEARL
KITE
WHITE-TAILED
KITE
immature
adult
SWALLOW-TAILED
KITE
adults in flight
adult
immature
MISSISSIPPI
KITE
adult
immature
PLUMBEOUS
KITE

SNAIL KITE *Rostrhamus sociabilis*

19 in. (48 cm); WS: 44 in. (112 cm). In all plumages, note sharply hooked, black bill (adapted for eating aquatic snails) and long white tail that shows slight cleft with **broad black subterminal band**. Male **slaty black overall** with **orange-red cere and legs**. Female dark brown with whitish throat and buffy streaking below. Juvenile similar to adult female, but paler overall, showing more pronounced buffy white supercilium, face, and underparts; also lacks orange-red cere and legs. Adult male similar to Crane Hawk (p. 166), but has orange-red cere (not gray) and different tail pattern; in flight, lacks pale crescent at base of primaries. Fairly common to common locally on both slopes, but may be absent from seemingly good habitat; to 2,130 ft. (650 m). Found near lakes and freshwater marshes, where it plucks snails from reeds or from the water's surface. Flies with wings bowed and tail spread, often low over water. Generally silent, but immature calls include a begging, toadlike *rrre'e'e'e'e'e'ahhhhh*. U.S. to Argentina.

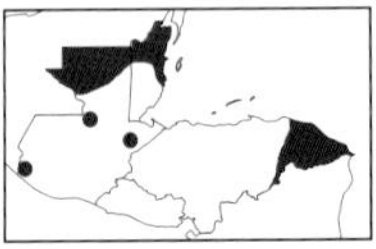

BLACK-COLLARED HAWK *Busarellus nigricollis*

19.5 in. (50 cm); WS: 48.5 in. (123 cm). **Rufous overall** with **whitish head** and **black collar in front of neck**; also note broad black subterminal band on a tawny tail. Immature has similar pattern but lacks rufous tones of adult and shows some barring below. Flies on flat, broad wings. Uncommon to rare on Caribbean Slope, rare or extirpated on Pacific Slope; to 2,460 ft. (750 m). Found in swamps and marshes, and near lakes (often perches at low levels along lake edge). Call is a loud, throaty, froglike *baaaaaahhhhh*; also makes a high-pitched, scratchy, screamed *rhheeeeeeaaa—rhheeeeeaaa—rhheeeeeaaa*. Mex. to Argentina.

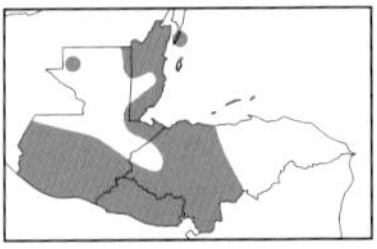

NORTHERN HARRIER *Circus cyaneus*

20 in. (51 cm); WS: 42.5 in. (108 cm). In all plumages, note facial disk and **white uppertail coverts**. Male has gray upperparts and hood, white underparts; in flight, note **white underwing with dark trailing edge and dark primaries**. Adult female **streaked below, tawny overall**. Immature similar but has less streaking and is richer tawny below. Uncommon transient and rare winter visitor in NCA (late Sept.–mid-Apr.); to 7,710 ft. (2,350 m). Found in grasslands and other open habitats; hunts low over fields. Narrow wings usually held in a dihedral when hunting or soaring; in migration or moderate glide, may resemble an *Accipiter* owing to long tail and bent wings. AK and Canada to S. America; also Europe and Asia (where known as Hen Harrier).

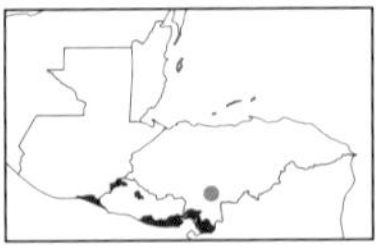

HARRIS'S HAWK *Parabuteo unicinctus*

20.5 in. (52 cm); WS: 43.5 in. (111 cm). Adult dark brown overall with **rufous shoulders and thighs**; note **white undertail coverts** and long **white** tail with **wide black tail band**. Rare year-round on Pacific Slope; to 1,480 ft. (450 m), rarely higher. Found in open country, such as agricultural areas and savannas; also occurs in marshes and coastal scrub. Often perches in the open, on or near the ground. Social; usually in pairs or small groups, hunts cooperatively. U.S. to Argentina.

adult female
BLACK-COLLARED HAWK
adult male
SNAIL KITE
immature
adult
immature
adult male
immature
adult females
immature
adult
NORTHERN HARRIER
HARRIS'S HAWK

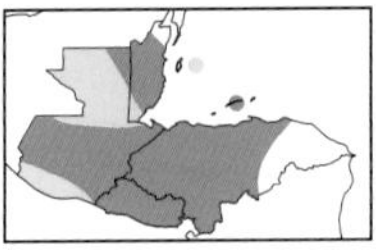

SHARP-SHINNED HAWK *Accipiter striatus*

11–14 in. (28–36 cm); WS: 20–25 in. (51–64 cm). In flight, long **squared tail** and **wrist bent at leading edge of wing**; on perched birds, small head and thin legs. Adult slaty gray above; barred rufous below; **little contrast in color between nape and crown**. Immature brown above; heavily streaked below, including belly. Similar to Cooper's Hawk in all ages and plumages, but Sharp-shinned is smaller with thinner legs; squared tail in flight (not rounded); bent leading edge of wing (not straight). Also adult Sharp-shinned has dark gray nape (not pale gray); on immature note heavily streaked belly (not lightly streaked). In flight, shape similar to that of White-breasted Hawk, but note marked underparts. Fairly common winter visitor in NCA (Sept.–Apr.); to 9,350 ft. (2,850 m). Found in a variety of woodland habitats; from semideciduous forest to pine and pine-oak forest; hunts inside the forest at all levels. AK and Canada (breeding) to Panama (winter).

WHITE-BREASTED HAWK *Accipiter chionogaster*

10.5–14.5 in. (27–37 cm); WS: 20–25 in. (51–64 cm). **Face and underparts a striking white**; eyes red. Immature slate gray above with rusty feather edging; very thin streaks on underparts noticeable at close range; eyes orangish yellow. In flight, like Sharp-shinned Hawk, but note bright white underparts. Uncommon to fairly common in NCA; 2,130 to 9,840 ft. (650–3,000 m); rarely lower (to 660 ft./200 m). Found in pine savanna and pine-oak forest; also cloud forest; and less commonly into nearby farmlands. Perches at midlevels in forest; soars over forest canopy. Courtship behavior includes puffing out breast and undertail coverts, and exaggerated, deep undulating flight that exposes the white underparts. Calls include a chattering (alarm) series of high-pitched notes given as *tu-tu-tu-tu-tu-tu-tu-tu-tu . . .* ; also a longer wailing call, *eeeeeee—eeeeeee—eeeeeee— . . .* ; birds vocalize mainly near nest. Mex. to Nicaragua. Considered by some authors to be a subspecies of Sharp-shinned Hawk.

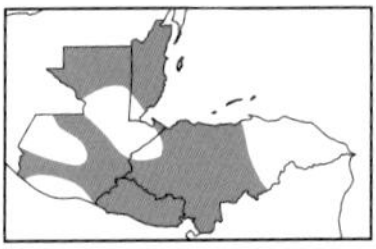

COOPER'S HAWK *Accipiter cooperii*

15–18 in. (38–46 cm); WS: 27–34 in. (69–86 cm). In all ages and plumages, similar to Sharp-shinned Hawk, but larger, has thicker legs, and in flight, a **rounded tail** and **straight leading edge** to wing (not bent). Adult has **pale nape** (giving a capped appearance). Immature similar to Sharp-shinned, but has sparser and crisper streaking on chest and belly, and rounded tail. Compare also with immature Gray Hawk (p. 168) and with immature Double-toothed Kite (p. 172). Winter visitor (Sept.–Apr.). Uncommon in NCA; to 9,350 ft. (2,850 m). Hunts at all levels of semideciduous forest, pine savanna, and pine-oak forest; often seen soaring and flapping on morning thermals. Canada (breeding) to Costa Rica (winter).

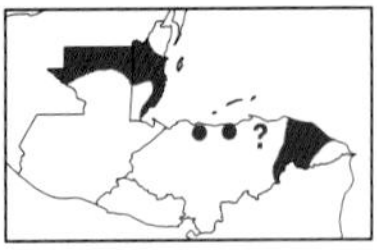

BICOLORED HAWK *Accipiter bicolor*

14–17 in. (36–43 cm); WS: 25–30 in. (64–76 cm). Adult slate gray above with **pale nape** and **dark crown**; **rufous thighs** (often concealed); long legs. Immature similarly patterned, but brownish above and buff or whitish below; thighs may be spotted brown or rufous. Immature similar to Barred and Collared Forest-Falcons (p. 216), but lacks yellow orbital skin present on forest-falcons; Collared Forest-Falcon has dark eyes (not pale). Rare to uncommon on Caribbean Slope; to 4,590 ft. (1,400 m). Found in rainforest interior; secretive. Call is a growling *rreeeahh!* Mex. to Argentina.

Accipiter. *Small and medium-sized raptors that hunt birds and reptiles. Their short, broad wings and long tails are ideal for hunting in forest interior, allowing quick corrections in pursuit of aerial prey. They are also accomplished migrants. Flight appears labored, with short bursts of flapping followed by gliding. Accipiters usually migrate at lower levels than larger raptors. Females are larger than males.*

BUTEOGALLUS BLACK-HAWKS

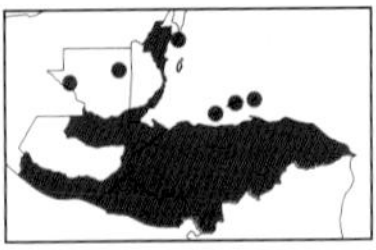

COMMON BLACK-HAWK *Buteogallus anthracinus*

20 in. (51 cm); WS: 46.5 in. (118 cm). Adult has **single wide white tail band**; **yellow cere, base of bill, and orbital ring**. First-year has face with **dark eye line and malar stripe**; underside of tail shows 4 or 5 dark bands. In flight, note broad wings held slightly forward, with straight leading edge. Adult similar to Great Black-Hawk, but smaller and has more yellow around eyes, all-gray thighs, dark uppertail coverts, and, in flight, legs barely reach white tail band. Adult similar to Solitary Eagle, but is smaller, and has thinner legs. Distinguish adult from Zone-tailed Hawk (p. 166) by broader wings, darker flight feathers (barred in Zone-tailed), yellow base of bill, tail pattern, and shorter tail; also, doesn't soar in dihedral as Zone-tailed does. First-year similar to immature Great Black-Hawk, but has more facial markings, fewer tail bands (on average) and lacks broad subterminal band. Fairly common in NCA, including Bay Is.; to 6,560 ft. (2,000 m). Perches at all levels in edge of rainforest, semideciduous forest, and pine savanna, usually near streams; also found in mangroves and near other aquatic habitats. Hunts on ground in mudflats and on beaches, running after crabs. Soars regularly. Call is a repeated, high-pitched, piping: *wheeep!* or *wreeeep!*, with a typical series of 10 to 12 notes rising slowly, then falling quickly. U.S. to S. America.

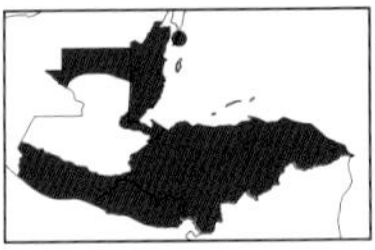

GREAT BLACK-HAWK *Buteogallus urubitinga*

23 in. (59 cm); WS: 50.5 in. (128 cm). Adult blackish overall; **uppertail coverts, 2 tail bands are white** (basal band is difficult to see); thighs with **fine white barring**. Immature head pale with dark eye line (**malar stripe faint or absent**); underside of tail with 4 to 7 thin, dark bands and **broad subterminal band**. Adult similar to Common Black-Hawk and Solitary Eagle, but differs in size, has **gray or yellowish gray lores (not yellow)**, white barring on thighs, white basal tail band and uppertail coverts, and longer legs that extend to middle of white tail band in flight. Immature similar to first-year Common Black-Hawk, but has more tail bands and broad subterminal band; also lacks a distinct malar stripe and eye line. Uncommon in NCA; to 5,910 ft. (1,800 m). Found in a variety of habitats; at rainforest or semideciduous edge, pine savanna, swamp forest, and mangroves. In flight, repeats a nasal scream, *wreep!-wreep!-wreep!-wreep!-wreep!-wreep!-wiiiir* (similar to call of Common Black-Hawk); also makes a loud, drawn-out, whistling scream, *wrrreeeeeeeeeep!*; and a series of *auk* notes that rises slightly in pitch and volume and lasts 6 to 8 sec. Mex. to Argentina.

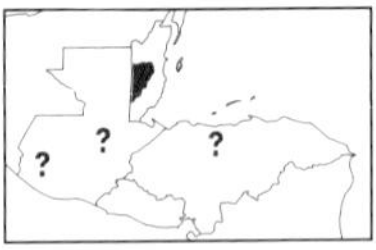

SOLITARY EAGLE *Buteogallus solitarius*

28 in. (71 cm); WS: 67 in. (170 cm). **A large raptor**. Adult blackish overall **with grayish cast**. In flight, leading edge of wing is nearly straight, head extending well beyond; **"bulging" wings (secondaries) extend nearly to the trailing edge of the tail**; short tail shows one bold white band (feet extend beyond band in flight). When perched, wingtips reach tip of tail. Immature dark brown above; buffy white below with heavy streaking (**solid brown patches on sides of chest extend into malar**); **all-dark thighs**; head heavily patterned with dark cap, bold black eye line. Adult Solitary Eagle similar to Common Black-Hawk but is much larger, has thicker legs and broader wings. Distinguish adult from perched Great Black-Hawk by unmarked thighs, and yellow base to bill; in flight, note broad wings, also tail lacks white basal band, and uppertail coverts are dark. Very rare in NCA; 1,970 to 6,230 ft. (600–1,900 m). Found in pine savanna, mature semideciduous forest, and pine-oak forest; prefers mountainous terrain. In flight, makes slow wingbeats and takes long periods to circle (because of its size). Call is a rising *wheeeo* followed by a higher-pitched, 3-part *wha-eeeee-ah*. Mex. to Argentina.

adults in flight
COMMON
BLACK-HAWK
adult
immature
adult
immature
GREAT
BLACK-HAWK
adult in flight
SOLITARY
EAGLE
adult
immature

HOOK-BILLED KITE *Chondrohierax uncinatus*

18 in. (46 cm); WS: 34.5 in. (88 cm). In all plumages, identified by **sharply hooked bill** and orangish supraloral mark; adult has white eyes. Light-morph male gray overall; **underparts whitish with gray barring**. Light-morph female similarly patterned but brown above with **rufous barring below**. Dark morph **slaty black overall** with **single broad white tail band**. Flight profile is distinctive: note broad paddle-shaped wings pressed slightly forward, and spread primaries. Uncommon resident and possible transient on both slopes (Oct.–Nov.) where small southbound groups have been observed; to 6,560 ft. (2,000 m). Found in rainforest, semideciduous forest, thorn forest, swamp forest, mangroves, and even coffee plantations. Call is a 3- or 4-note *chu-chu-chu-chu*; also makes a clucking, chattering *ke'ke'ke'ke'ke'ke'ke'ke'ke* (slightly descending in pitch). U.S. to Argentina.

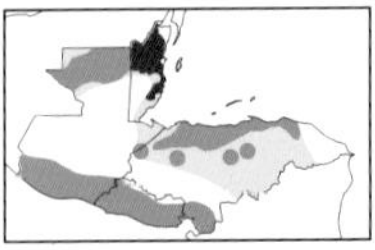

CRANE HAWK *Geranospiza caerulescens*

19 in. (48 cm); WS: 38.5 in. (98 cm). All ages, note long tail with white bands and pale crescent in primaries (slightly barred in immatures). Adult **dark gray overall**; light barring on vent and thighs; **note long orange-red legs and red eyes**. Immature has pale face and heavier barring below; **eyes brownish red**. Adult male similar to Snail Kite (p. 160), but has gray cere (not orange-red) and different tail pattern. In comparison with black-hawks, Crane Hawk is smaller, has a proportionately longer tail, red legs (not yellow), and gray cere (yellow in black-hawks). Uncommon on Caribbean Slope, rare and local on Pacific Slope; to 4,920 ft. (1,500 m). Found in coastal swamp forest, wet savanna, mangroves, and along rivers. Call is a loud, piercing *wee'urrrrrrr!* (similar to call of Roadside Hawk). Mex. to Argentina.

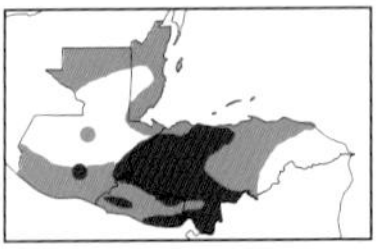

ZONE-TAILED HAWK *Buteo albonotatus*

20 in. (51 cm); WS: 51 in. (130 cm). Adult slaty black; shows 1 obvious broad white distal tail band and **2 thinner inner bands on tail**; cere and feet yellow. Immature similar, but has whitish spots on chest and lacks the white bands in tail. In flight, **2-tone underwing pattern** and **dihedral wing angle** are similar to Turkey Vulture (p. 152), but note black feathered head with yellow cere, barring on flight feathers, and banded tail. In flight, also similar to adult Common Black-Hawk, but has narrower wings, longer tail, and dihedral wing angle (not flat). Uncommon in NCA but easily overlooked because of similarity to Turkey Vulture in flight, which it mimics as a hunting strategy; to 9,350 ft. (2,850 m). Breeds at mid- to upper elevations in pine-oak forest and pine savanna, and occasionally in mangroves along the coast; more common in lowlands during nonbreeding season; in some areas, only a winter visitor found mid-Oct. to mid-Apr. (for example, in Belize). Calls include a slightly nasal, drawn-out *kee-ahrrrrrr* (similar to call of Red-tailed Hawk); also makes a short, less-rising *keee* (repeated). U.S. to Brazil.

HOOK-BILLED
KITE
light-morph
female
light-morph male
dark morph
immature
CRANE
HAWK
immature
adult
ZONE-TAILED
HAWK
adult
immature

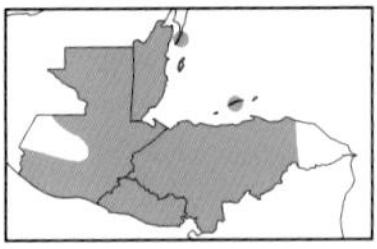

BROAD-WINGED HAWK *Buteo platypterus*

15.5 in. (40 cm); WS: 34 in. (86 cm). Light-morph adult dark brown above; shows **chestnut splotches and barring below**; **tail with 2 bold white bands** (inner band is narrower, difficult to detect); eyes pale brown; in flight, note tail pattern and **dark trailing edge of wings**. On immature light morph, **face relatively unpatterned**; underparts heavily streaked (with variable barring); tail with 4 to 5 dark brown bands. Dark morph rarely reported in NCA (but migrates over region); has dark brown head, underparts, and wing linings. Immature light morph similar to immature Gray and Roadside Hawks (see below and p. 172), but has unmarked face, white underparts with crisp streaking (Roadside shows demarcation between streaking and barring), unbarred thighs, and pale brown eyes. Immature light morph similar to immature Double-toothed Kite (p. 172), but streaking below larger and bolder, thighs unbarred, multiple dark brown tail bands from above, and different eye color. Compare dark morph with more common dark-morph Short-tailed Hawk, but tail pattern and dark trailing edge on wing are always diagnostic. Common winter visitor and transient on Pacific Slope; rare to uncommon on Caribbean Slope (Sept.–May); to 6,560 ft. (2,000 m). In migration, soars high overhead; migrates by the thousands over NCA (mainly on Pacific Slope), often mixing with other raptors. Winter visitors occur in a variety of tall woodlands, including semideciduous forest, rainforest, riparian forest, pine-oak forest, and cloud forest. Call (heard regularly in NCA) is a high-pitched, 2-part whistle: *pi-teeeeeeeee!* Canada (breeding) to S. America (winter).

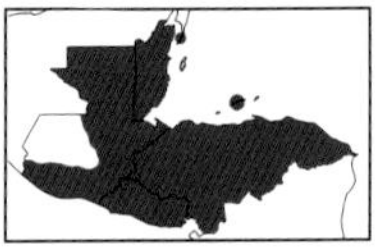

GRAY HAWK *Buteo plagiatus*

16.5 in. (42 cm); WS: 35 in. (89 cm). **Adult gray overall**; tail with 2 or 3 white bands. Immature dark brown above; **white cheek and supercilium separated by dark eye line**; **barred thighs**; underside of tail shows 4 or 5 dark bands (subterminal band is broader). Immature similar to light-morph immature Broad-winged Hawk, but shows white on face and barring on thighs. Also compare to immature Roadside and Cooper's Hawks (p. 172 and p. 162), but Gray Hawk has a well-marked face, streaking below (with no barring), and dark eyes (not orange-brown). Fairly common on both slopes, including Roatán (Bay Is.); occurs up to 6,230 ft. (1,900 m) but generally below 3,280 ft. (1,000 m). Habitat includes disturbed areas, edge of semideciduous forest, thorn forest, rarely pine-oak forest; often seen on roadside telephone poles or on wires; soars frequently. Call is a long, high-pitched, scream, similar to Roadside Hawk's (p. 172) but thinner: *weeeuuuuuuuuuuu!*; also a longer series with a quetzal-like quality, *were'eee-were'eee-were'eee-were'eee*. U.S. to Argentina.

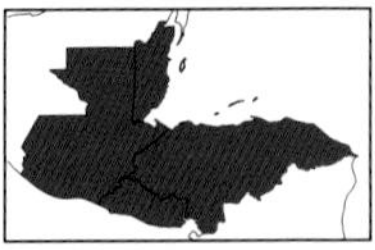

SHORT-TAILED HAWK *Buteo brachyurus*

16.5 in. (42 cm); WS: 35 in. (89 cm). Two color morphs, both common in NCA. Dark morph is blackish overall with **white lores and forehead**; light morph is brown above and white below with **hooded appearance**. In flight, both morphs show **shaded secondaries** and **dark subterminal tail band**. In flight, light-morph adult similar to light morph of adult Swainson's Hawk (p. 170), but is smaller, has white upper chest (not dark bib), and wings are more rounded and less pointed. Dark-morph adult is similar to dark-morph Broad-winged Hawk, but tail pattern lacks bold white bands. Uncommon to fairly common in NCA; to 6,560 ft. (2,000 m). Found in semideciduous forest, pine savanna, and pine-oak forest; soars regularly. Call is a thin, nasal scream: *reeeeeeaahhh!* U.S. to Argentina.

Buteo. *These raptors are the common soaring hawks, and this genus is well represented in NCA with 7 species. They are found in a variety of open and semiopen habitats, often perched on a telephone pole, or soaring high on thermals during the midday heat. Buteos have the "classic" raptor shape in soaring flight, with fairly broad wings pressed slightly forward, a straight leading edge, and short fanned tails.*

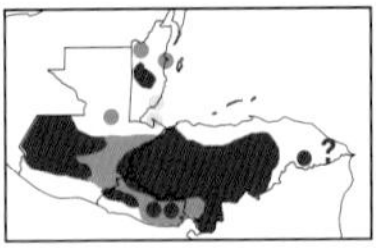

RED-TAILED HAWK *Buteo jamaicensis*

21 in. (53 cm); WS: 50 in. (127 cm). Several races and color morphs in NCA. In all races and morphs, **rufous tail** is diagnostic. Adult light morph dark brown above with **paler scapulars** (forming a V across the back); **underparts white**; variable **dark streaking may form a band across belly** (generally absent on resident birds). In flight, note **dark marks at the wrists and on the leading edge of the wing**. Immature light morph paler than adults (belly band usually present) with pale, thinly banded tail. Immature light morph distinguished from other immature raptors by its large size, broad wings, smudge on leading edge of wing, and faint belly band. Adult dark morph blackish brown; note 2-tone appearance in flight (pale flight feathers contrast with dark body and wing linings). Fairly common in NCA; 160 to 9,840 ft. (50–3,000 m). Found in semideciduous forest, cloud forest, pine-oak forest, pine savanna, and other open areas. Often seen soaring on long, broad wings with tail open; circles lazily on thermals; may hover motionless in the wind. Large numbers of migrants invade NCA from Oct. to Apr. Common call is a long scream lasting roughly 2.5 sec.: *keeee-uhrrrrrrrrrr!* (similar to Zone-tailed Hawk). AK and Canada to Panama.

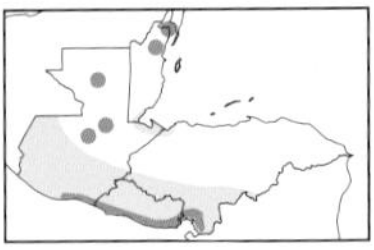

SWAINSON'S HAWK *Buteo swainsoni*

20 in. (51 cm); WS: 52 in. (132 cm). Polymorphic. Adult light morph has **white throat and belly separated by dark chestnut bib**. In flight, note white wing lining and **dark flight feathers**; tail barred with **thin black subterminal band**. Intermediate and dark-morph adults variably dark below; tail pattern similar to light-morph adult. Immature pale below with streaking (heavier on dark morph) and dark sides to chest (on all morphs); face is paler than that of adult; may lack subterminal band. On all ages and morphs, note distinctive in-flight silhouette with long, relatively narrow, pointed wings. In flight, light-morph adult similar to corresponding morph of adult Short-tailed Hawk (p. 168), but is larger, has dark bib, and wings are long and narrow, pointed. In flight, adult is similar to White-tailed Hawk but has narrower wings and longer tail. Fairly common to common transient on Pacific Slope (late Mar.–Apr., late Sept.–Nov.); very rare transient in Caribbean lowlands; and locally uncommon winter visitor along Pacific Coast; to 6,560 ft. (2,000 m). Migrants can be seen high overhead in groups of hundreds or thousands, often mixed with other diurnal migrants; mainly migrates along the foothills and volcanic highlands of the Pacific Slope. Canada (breeding) to S. America (winter).

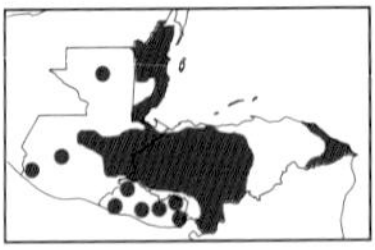

WHITE-TAILED HAWK *Geranoaetus albicaudatus*

20.5 in. (52 cm); WS: 50 in. (127 cm). Adult slate gray above with **chestnut shoulders**; **all-white below**; in flight, note shaded flight feathers and **broad wings**; **rump and tail white with black subterminal band**. First-year plumage blackish brown above; note **white chest** and **dark throat**; thin white supercilium. In flight, adult is similar to Swainson's Hawk but has broader wings and shorter tail. Uncommon in Belize and e. Honduras, rare on Pacific Slope; to 4,920 ft. (1,500 m). Occurs in semiarid open areas, coastal scrub, and pine savanna; often seen soaring or kiting. Call is a slightly nasal scream: *reeeeeaaaaaah-reahah'reahah'reahah'reahah.* U.S. to Argentina.

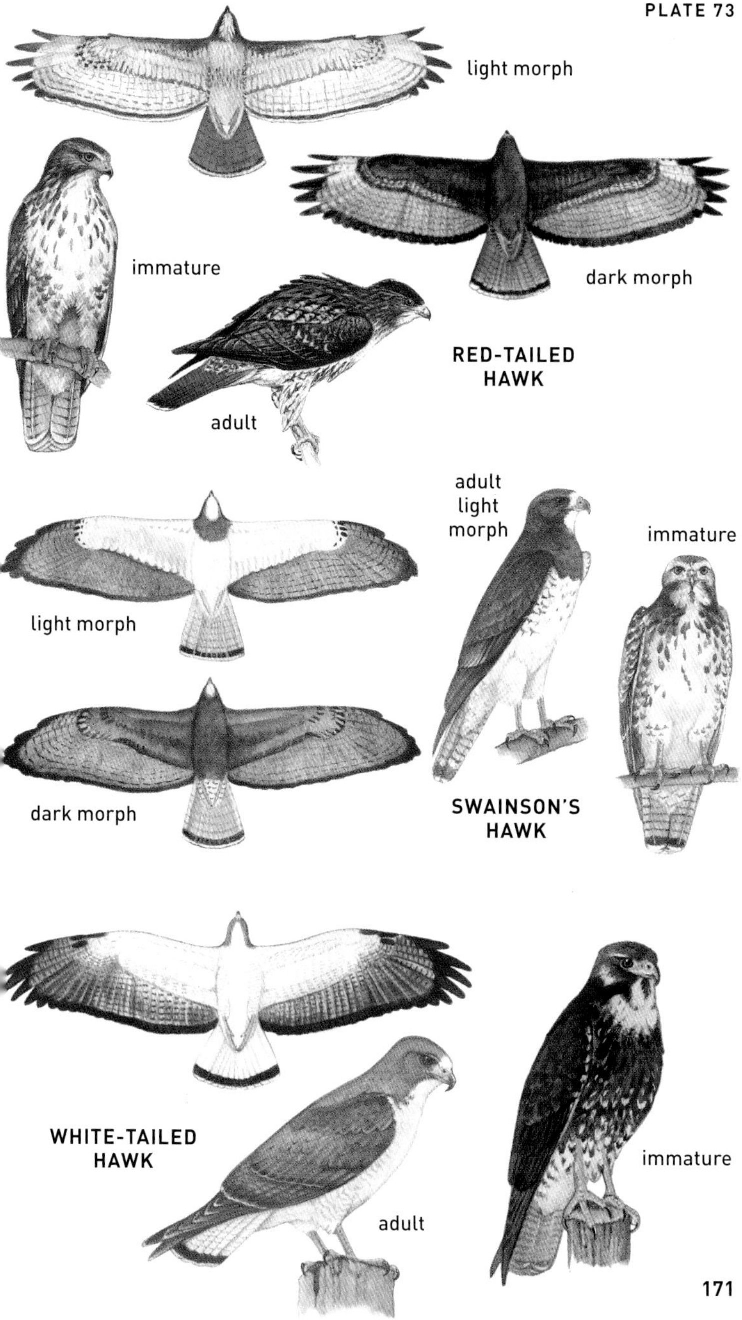
light morph
immature
dark morph
adult
RED-TAILED HAWK
adult light morph
immature
light morph
dark morph
SWAINSON'S HAWK
WHITE-TAILED HAWK
adult
immature

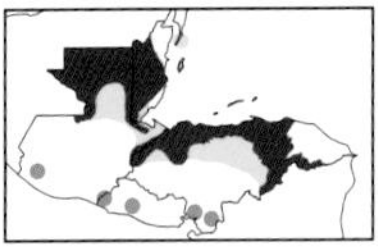

DOUBLE-TOOTHED KITE *Harpagus bidentatus*

13.5 in. (34 cm); WS: 27 in. (69 cm). In all plumages, shows **white throat with dark median stripe** and **long dark tail with 3 pale, thin bands**. On adult, **head gray**; **chest dark rufous with variable barring**. Immature has dark face with light eye-ring; underparts white with **crisp dark streaks or spots on chest** and some barring on flanks. In flight, similar to *Accipiter* species, but has longer wings and white undertail coverts. Immature similar to Broad-winged (p. 168) and Roadside Hawks, but has crisp spotting on breast, barring on thighs, different tail pattern, and reddish orange eyes. Immature also similar to Barred Forest-Falcon (p. 216) but has different breast markings. Uncommon resident on Caribbean; rare elsewhere Oct. to Mar.; to 4,920 ft. (1,500 m). Migrating flocks observed in Mar. in e. Guatemala. Found in semideciduous forest, rainforest, and riparian forest interiors; occasionally soars. Call is a rich *tseeu-tseeu-tseeu-tseeu-tseeu-tseeu*; also makes a *tseeu-wheeuu* and a *peeet!-wheeuu*. Mex. to Brazil.

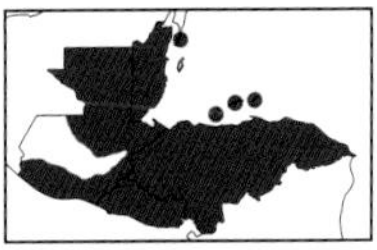

ROADSIDE HAWK *Rupornis magnirostris*

14.5 in. (37 cm); WS: 29 in. (74 cm). Adult has **gray hood**; **chestnut barring below**; eyes yellow; in flight, note **rufous in primaries**. Immature browner overall, has narrow **pale supercilium**, orange-brown eyes, and **streaking on chest with barring below**. Immature told from Double-toothed Kite by heavy streaking and barring below and tail pattern. Immature resembles immature Broad-winged and Gray Hawks (p. 168), but has different pattern of markings on underparts, fine barring on thighs (lacking on Broad-winged Hawk), rufous primaries, different uppertail pattern (similar to Broad-winged), and yellow eyes. Common on both slopes; may occur up to 6,890 ft. (2,100 m) but generally below 4,920 ft. (1,500 m). Occurs in open areas, such as agricultural fields and disturbed habitat, and along roads; often seen perched on telephone poles, fences, and in trees in open pasture (where it hunts insects and small reptiles and amphibians). Typical call is a nasal, slurred *ree-ahhhh* that lasts 2.5 sec. (similar to Gray Hawk [p. 168]); also makes a repeated series, *reh-reh-reh-reh* . . . (similar to Lineated Woodpecker [p. 206]). Mex. to Argentina.

SEMIPLUMBEOUS HAWK *Leucopternis semiplumbeus*

15 in. (38 cm); WS: 23 in. (59 cm). **Two-tone pattern** of dark above and **white below** in combination with **red cere** and **red-orange legs** is diagnostic. Rare in e. Honduras; to 2,460 ft. (750 m). Found in rainforest and riparian forest. Seldom seen; perches quietly in forest, does not soar. Honduras to Colombia.

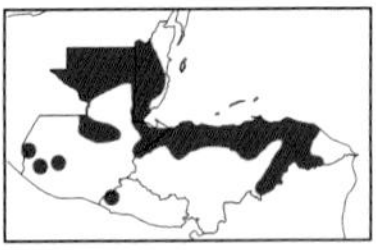

WHITE HAWK *Pseudastur albicollis*

23 in. (59 cm); WS: 48.5 in. (123 cm). Unmistakable. Amount of black on wings varies from paler birds on Pacific Slope and Belize (*ghiesbreghti*; white secondaries) to darker birds along the north coast of Honduras (*costaricensis*; dark markings on secondaries and inner primaries). Uncommon on Caribbean Slope, rare and local on Pacific Slope; may occur up to 5,910 ft. (1,800 m) but generally below 3,280 ft. (1,000 m). Perches at midlevels of interior rainforest, riparian forest, or semideciduous forest. Soars often. Call is a drawn-out, high-pitched whistle: *wheeeeeeeeeet*. Mex. to South America.

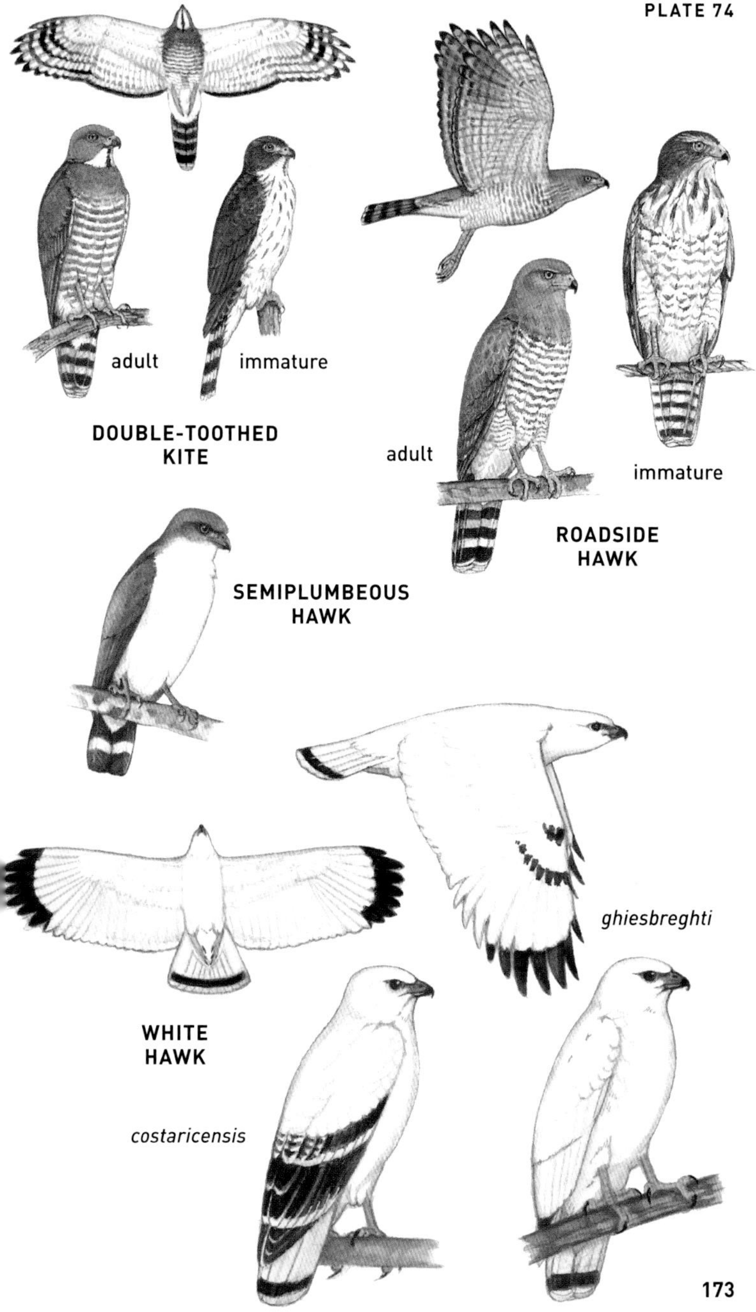
adult
immature
DOUBLE-TOOTHED KITE
adult
immature
ROADSIDE HAWK
SEMIPLUMBEOUS HAWK
ghiesbreghti
WHITE HAWK
costaricensis

BARN OWLS AND OWLS I

TYTONIDAE (Order: Strigiformes). Of the roughly 16 species of *Tyto* owls found worldwide, only 2 occur in the New World (1 on the mainland). Barn Owls differ from other owls by lacking "hooting" calls and ear tufts. They have a heart-shaped facial disk and fairly small oval eyes. They are strictly nocturnal. Sexes are similar. **1 species (1 genus)**

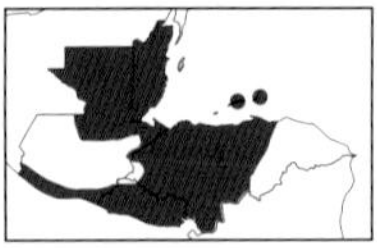

BARN OWL *Tyto alba*

15 in. (38 cm). A fairly large, pale owl with **heart-shaped facial disk**. Upperparts creamy brown with gray edging and white spots; **underparts white** (often buffy on female); **face whitish to tawny**. Uncommon on both slopes; to at least 6,560 ft. (2,000 m). Found in open and semiopen habitats, including pine savanna, palm plantations, disturbed woodlands, towns and cities. May rest and nest in buildings. Call (often given in flight) is a drawn-out, hissing screech *shreeeee* (lasts 2–5 sec.). Cosmopolitan.

STRIGIDAE (Order: Strigiformes). This group of mostly nocturnal predators have rounded faces, large forward-facing eyes, short legs and tail, and many have low-pitched voices. Screech-owls (*Megascops*) and pygmy-owls (*Glaucidium*) are tiny in comparison to several larger species. The "ear" tufts (or horns) of several species are feathers that extend above the crown of the head, but are neither ears nor made of horn. Sexes are similar, but females in several species are larger than males. Voice is useful for identification. **17 species (11 genera)**

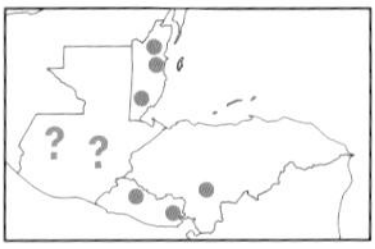

BURROWING OWL *Athene cunicularia*

10 in. (26 cm). **Brownish overall**: upperparts with **large pale spots**; brown facial disk rimmed in white with white throat; **underparts with dark barring and white spots**; bill and eyes yellow. Very rare winter visitor to NCA; to 820 ft. (250 m). A terrestrial diurnal owl that inhabits open country and grasslands. Stands on ground often near burrows or rock cavities where it roosts; flies short distances when flushed. Calls from region unknown; outside region gives a mournful *hu-paaaaw*; also a scream followed by barking *pip* notes. Canada to Argentina.

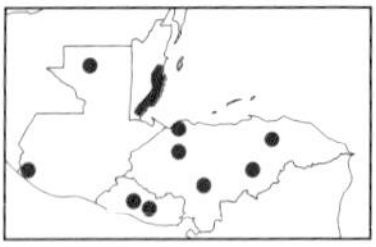

STRIPED OWL *Pseudoscops clamator*

14 in. (36 cm). **Facial disk buffy white rimmed in black**; **long dark ear tufts edged buff** extend from center of forecrown; underparts buffy white with large black streaks (densest on chest); black bill; **eyes dark**. Rare on Pacific Slope; uncommon on Caribbean Slope; to 2,950 ft. (900 m). Nests on the ground and perches often on fenceposts, wires, or in scattered trees in open savanna grasslands, pastures, marshes, and palm plantations. Call is a high-pitched *weeeeeeere!* Mex. to Argentina.

CRESTED OWL *Lophostrix cristata*

16 in. (41 cm). A distinctive-looking medium-sized owl. **Bold white eyebrows combined with 2 large white ear tufts above eyes** creates "crested" look; yellowish bill; eyes yellowish orange. Rare to uncommon on Caribbean Slope; very rare on Pacific Slope; to 6,560 ft. (2,000 m); rarely higher. Found in taller humid woodlands: rainforest up to cloud forest. Call is a deep, vibrating *whu'whu'whu-whooooah*. Mex. to Brazil.

BARN OWL

tawny-faced variant

BURROWING OWL

dark morph (left) and pale morph (bottom)

CRESTED OWL

STRIPED OWL

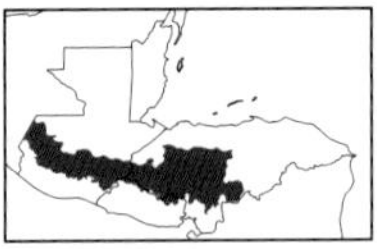

WHISKERED SCREECH-OWL *Megascops trichopsis*

7 in. (18 cm). Face whitish (gray morph) to rufous-brown (rufous morph), but in both cases face **shows obvious black border**; underparts white or grayish with **bold black vertical streaks and weaker cross bars** (in rufous morph cross bars are edged in rufous-brown). Overlaps in Guatemala with Bearded Screech-Owl, but compare pattern of underparts and voice. Fairly common in NCA central highlands; above 2,640 ft. (800 m). Found in pine savanna or pine-oak forest. Two calls; one call (approx. 6 sec.) is a steady *wo'wo-wo-wo-wo-wo-wo-wo-wo*; second call is a "Morse-code"–like series, slightly gruffer overall. U.S. to Nicaragua.

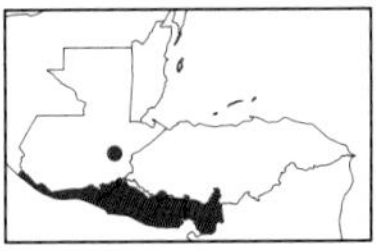

PACIFIC SCREECH-OWL *Megascops cooperi*

9.5 in. (24 cm). A **small grayish brown owl**; rufous morph rare; pale face **weakly bordered gray-brown**; paler upperparts generally light brown-gray with white tips to scapulars; underparts grayish with very **thin dark vertical lines and weak cross bars**. Little range overlap with similar Vermiculated Screech-Owl. Fairly common on Pacific Slope; to 3,440 ft. (1,050 m). Found mainly in dry forest and scrub, open semideciduous forest, and disturbed habitat. Call is a soft low-pitched bouncing *wudrrr-wud'd'd'd'd'd'd'd'd'drr* (rising in middle) or *who'who-who'who'who'who'who-who*; also an agitated growl *raaaaw!* Mex. to Costa Rica.

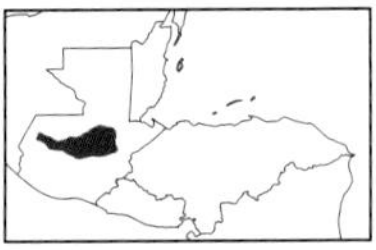

BEARDED SCREECH-OWL *Megascops barbarus*

7 in. (18 cm). Rufous morph has rich tawny facial disks (whitish or light brown in gray morph) bordered by black; note small whitish eyebrows; underparts whitish **with black vertical lines and black crossbars that curl upward** (crossbars edged rufous-brown in rufous morph), creating a **scalloped appearance below**; has **naked toes**. Overlaps in Guatemala with Whiskered Screech-Owl, but compare pattern of underparts and voice. Rare in highlands of Guatemala; above 4,920 ft. (1,500 m). Found at mid- to upper levels in humid pine-oak and cloud forest. Call is a froglike trill lasting about 5 sec. Endemic to region.

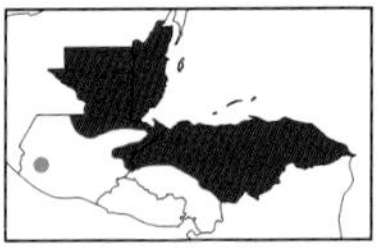

VERMICULATED SCREECH-OWL *Megascops guatemalae*

8.5 in. (22 cm). **Face generally rufous-brown (paler in gray morph) and bordered with black**; also with paler contrasting white eyebrows; underparts whitish (darker gray or rufous-brown on chest) with **thin dark vertical lines and weak cross bars**. Almost no range overlap with similar Pacific Screech-Owl. Fairly common on Caribbean Slope (vagrant or very rare on Pacific Slope); to 5,910 ft. (1,800 m). Seems to be found in a variety of habitat types, including plantations, dry forest, and semideciduous forest to edge of rainforest (a few reports from cloud forest). Call (approximately 9 sec.) is all on same pitch and volume, a fast trill easily confused with the nocturnal call of the terrestrial Cane Toad, *Rhinella marina*. Northern populations (*guatemalae*; Mex. to Nicaragua) are sometimes considered a separate species, Middle American Screech-Owl. Mex. to S. America.

Megascops. *The screech-owls are very similar in appearance: small; gray or rufous morphs; yellow eyes; green-yellow bills; and ear tufts. The biggest differences in plumage are the patterns of underparts. However, most species can be separated by habitat and elevation, range (Caribbean vs. Pacific Slope), and, in all cases, by voice.*

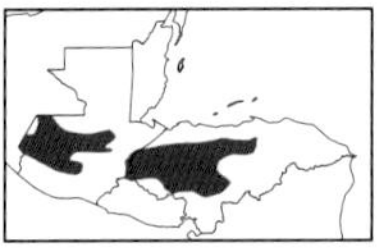

GUATEMALAN PYGMY-OWL *Glaucidium cobanense*

6.5 in. (17 cm). Two color morphs (some may be intermediates): more common **bright rufous morph** has **small buffy spots on forecrown** (nape and crown may be gray in some individuals); gray morph similarly patterned, but with darker gray or gray-brown upperparts; note **4 pale bands on undertail**. Locally uncommon in central highlands; above 5,250 ft. (1,600 m). Found at edge or in openings within pine savanna, pine-oak, and cloud forest. Call is a rapid series of *toot* notes, sometimes paired, with little or no pause in between notes, *toot-toot-toot-toot'toot-toot'toot-toot-toot-toot-toot-toot . . .* Endemic to region. Some authorities treat it as a subspecies of Northern Pygmy-Owl (*G. gnoma*).

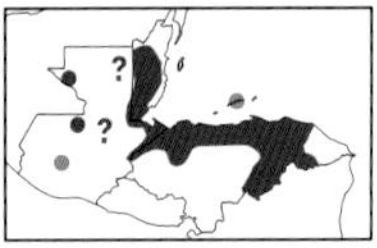

CENTRAL AMERICAN PYGMY-OWL *Glaucidium griseiceps*

6 in. (15 cm). **Gray crown with dense white spotting**; small white eyebrows; underparts white with chestnut sides and broad chestnut streaking across lower chest; note **2 pale bands on undertail**. Uncommon on Caribbean Slope (vagrant to Pacific Slope of Guatemala and to Bay Is.); to 3,940 ft. (1,200 m). Found in mid- to upper levels inside rainforest. Calls infrequently and difficult to locate. Call is a series of 4 to 16 monotypic whistled notes repeated every 5 to 7 sec.: *too-too-too-too-too-too*. Often the series is extended as the calling continues, such that it repeats 4 whistles several times, then increases to 5 for several repetitions, then 6, and so on. Mex. to Panama.

FERRUGINOUS PYGMY-OWL *Glaucidium brasilianum*

7 in. (18 cm). Rufous and brown color morphs. **Rufous or brown overall** with **pale streaking on forecrown** (note that immatures have weak spotting on forecrown); small white eyebrows; underparts white with rufous or brown sides and broad rufous or brown streaking across lower chest; note variable banding on undertail, ranging from unbanded rufous tail to 5 or 6 narrow pale bands on a dark brown tail; other *Glaucidium* have spotting on forecrown (not streaks). Common in NCA; to 6,560 ft. (2,000 m). Found in gardens and at edges in a variety of semiopen woodland habitats, including disturbed habitat, semideciduous forest, pine savanna and pine-oak forest, mangroves, and urban areas. Call is repeated whistle the entire series, generally lasting from 3 sec. or longer: *wet-wet-wet-wet-wet-wet . . .* U.S. to Argentina.

UNSPOTTED SAW-WHET OWL *Aegolius ridgwayi*

8 in. (20 cm). A small owl. **Uniform brown upperparts**; warm brown facial disks rimmed in white; **underparts tawny (lack markings)**; bill black; eyes golden brown. Rare and local in highlands of NCA; above 4,430 ft. (1,350 m). Found at edges or in clearings within pine-oak and cloud forest. Call is a high-pitched piping *hoo-hoo-hoo-hoo-hoo . . .* ; and a faster *ho'ho'ho'ho'ho'ho'ho'ho'ho*. Mex. to Panama.

Glaucidium. *The 3 species of pygmy-owls in NCA are small diurnal owls, nearly identical in plumage: small and mainly rufous; yellow eyes and bill; lacking ear tufts; streaked on underparts; and with false "eyes" on back of head. Some plumage differences do exist between species, and it is important to note spots vs. streaking on crown and the number of visible tail bands. However, the species separate well by habitat and range (Caribbean vs. Pacific Slope), elevation, and, in all cases, by voice.*

MOTTLED OWL *Ciccaba virgata*

14 in. (36 cm). Dark brown upperparts with tawny spots and bars; crown and sides of head with small pale spots; tawny facial disks with pale border; **upper chest densely marked**; **remaining underparts with heavy dark streaks**; bill yellow; **eyes dark**. Juvenile smaller than adult and has rich tawny down underparts. Common in NCA; to 7,220 ft. (2,200 m). Found in a variety of habitat types, including semideciduous forest, pine-oak forest, riparian forest, rainforest, orchards and coffee plantations, mangroves, and even urban parks and gardens. Fulvous Owl (sympatric at higher elevations) similar but note smaller size of Mottled Owl and dark facial disk, and lack of horizontal barring on chest. Calls include a gruff *WHOA-WHOA-whu* or *whu-whu-WHOA-WHOA-WHOA-whu*, the last note less inflected than the previous; also an eerie agitated growl *WHOA!*; or a longer drawn-out *whoooooa*, almost mammal-like in quality; pairs often duet. Mottled Owls are highly territorial; will often respond during the day and respond aggressively to calls of Black-and-white Owl. Mex. to Argentina.

BLACK-AND-WHITE OWL *Ciccaba nigrolineata*

15.5 in. (39 cm). A striking owl. **Black facial disk**; whitish underparts and sides of head **heavily barred black**; bright yellow bill; **eyes dark**. Uncommon on Caribbean Slope; rare and local on Pacific Slope; to 3,940 ft. (1,200 m). Found in rainforest, riparian forest, taller semideciduous forest, shaded coffee plantations, and city parks. Calls include a rapid *whu-whu-whu-WHOA!*, the entire series rising in volume; or a *whu-WHOA!*; also an agitated *wruuh-wruuh-wruuh-wruuh-wruuh*; pairs may duet. Mex. to Peru.

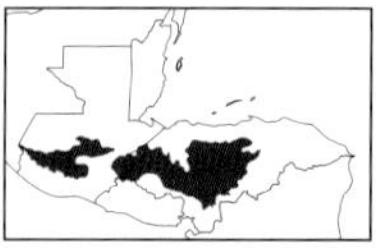

FULVOUS OWL *Strix fulvescens*

16 in. (41 cm). A large owl. **Pale facial disk rimmed black**; **upper chest with horizontal dark brown markings**; remaining **underparts buffy white with large crisp dark brown streaks**; yellow bill; **eyes dark**; female Mottled Owl (sympatric at lower elevations) similar but note larger size of Fulvous Owl and pale facial disks with black borders, also horizontal barring on chest. Uncommon to fairly common in highlands of NCA; above 5,580 ft. (1,700 m). Found in pine-oak and cloud forest; also taller humid semideciduous forest. Male call is a low gruff *whru-ru'wruh-wruh-wruh*; female call is higher-pitched, a cackling *ahh-uh-ooh-ahh-ahh*; pairs may duet; also gives a loud terrifying scream *SCAAAAAHHSSS!* Mex. to Honduras.

SPECTACLED OWL *Pulsatrix perspicillata*

18 in. (46 cm). A large owl. Distinctive facial pattern: note **bold white eyebrows** and **broad white or buffy collar**; also dark chest band and **buffy underparts**. Eyes yellow; bill yellowish green. Rare and local on Pacific Slope; uncommon on Caribbean Slope; to 2,790 ft. (850 m). Found in rainforest or taller semideciduous forest; riparian forest; often near water. Call is a resonating, vibrating *wu 'WU'WU'WU'WU'WU'wu'wu'wu'wu'wu'wu'wu'wu* (like someone shaking a piece of metal siding). Mex. to Argentina.

MOTTLED OWL

BLACK-AND-WHITE OWL

FULVOUS OWL

SPECTACLED OWL

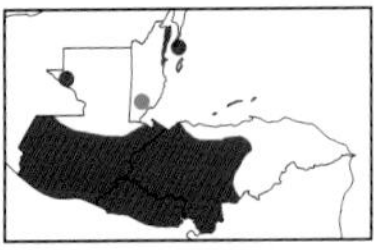

GREAT HORNED OWL *Bubo virginianus*

21 in. (53 cm). **Largest owl in NCA.** Note **large ear tufts extending from crown**; face tawny; **underparts heavily barred**; eyes yellow. Compare with Stygian Owl, but is larger, has tawny facial disks and fine barring below (not blotches and streaks), also tufts on crown are spaced farther apart. Local in NCA: uncommon in Belize and interior highlands of NCA; rare to uncommon on Pacific Slope; occurs at nearly all elevations. Found in a variety of woodland types from disturbed habitats, semideciduous forest, coffee plantations, pine savanna, edge of rainforest to near cloud forest. Call is a low, deep *Hoo-Hoo'Hoo Hoo-Hoo*; pairs may duet (Oct.–Mar.); call is usually given at dawn and dusk. AK to Argentina.

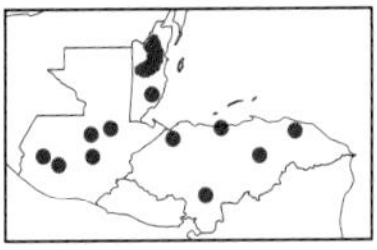

STYGIAN OWL *Asio stygius*

16 in. (41 cm). A large owl. **Dark sooty facial disks; long dark ear tufts** extend from center of forecrown; underparts whitish with bold dark blotches and streaks; bill greenish yellow; **eyes yellowish orange**. Compare with Great Horned Owl, but is smaller, has sooty facial disks (not tawny) and streaks below (not fine barring); also ear tufts on crown are spaced closer together. Rare throughout NCA; to 6,070 ft. (1,850 m). Generally found in pine savanna, but also semideciduous rainforest, open plantations, and coffee farms. Call is a series of deep *wooh* notes, each note separated by roughly 4 sec. Mex. to Brazil.

NYCTIBIIDAE (Order: Caprimulgiformes). A Neotropical family of 7 species (2 represented in NCA). Potoos are odd-looking nocturnal birds that resemble nightjars (p. 188) and owls, but have a vertical posture and cryptic plumage that gives them the appearance of a vertical snag or branch. During the day they remain perched motionless, often with head and bill pointed up. At night they hunt much like pewees (p. 256), making sallies for large insects and bats, and returning to the same perch. Although superficially similar to owls, potoos and other caprimulgiform birds are more closely related to swifts (p. 60) and hummingbirds (p. 64). **2 species (1 genus)**

GREAT POTOO *Nyctibius grandis*

21 in. (53 cm). A large potoo; **pale snowy gray overall** with **thin black chest band or necklace**; some individuals are rusty brown. Similar to Northern Potoo, but is larger and has paler upperparts and **dark eyes** (not yellow). Rare on Caribbean Slope; to 1,640 ft. (500 m). Found in clearings or edge of rainforest, and near large rivers. Roosts in an upright position on tall snags and vertical branches; cryptic in both coloration and perching behavior. Calls loudly with a nasal, somewhat rattling, painful scream: *WHA'A'A'A'A'A'A'A'A'AOHHH!* Shorter call given in flight. Mex. to Brazil.

NORTHERN POTOO *Nyctibius jamaicensis*

16 in. (41 cm). Similar to Great Potoo, but is **smaller** and has irregular splotchy black chest band, **darker upperparts**, and **yellow eyes** (not dark). Uncommon on both slopes; to 4,920 ft. (1,500 m). Found in clearings and edge of semideciduous forest, rainforest, mangroves, and plantations. Roosts in an upright position on tall snags and vertical branches; cryptic in both coloration and perching behavior. Call is a loud, nasal scream with a broken ending: *WHAAAAAAAAAH!-'WHA'WHA'WAH!* (harsher than call of Great Potoo). Short call of similar quality given in flight. Mex. and Caribbean to Costa Rica.

GREAT
HORNED OWL
STYGIAN OWL
GREAT
POTOO
NORTHERN
POTOO

NIGHTHAWKS

CAPRIMULGIDAE (Order: Caprimulgiformes). Known popularly as nightjars or goatsuckers, this is a group of cryptically plumaged nocturnal or crepuscular insectivores with large mouths, rather long wings and tails, and short bills and legs. Although plumages are superficially similar to owls (p. 174), nightjars and other caprimulgiform birds are more closely related to swifts (p. 60) and hummingbirds (p. 64). Nightjars roost on the ground or a low perch, and sally forth after their insect prey. Nighthawks generally feed high in the sky. Several species are migratory. The nighthawks migrate in large flocks by day, like raptors. Vocalizations are a key to locating and identifying. **13 species (6 genera)**

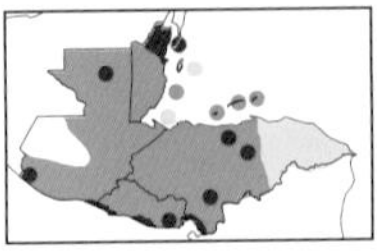

LESSER NIGHTHAWK *Chordeiles acutipennis*

8.5 in. (22 cm). On perched bird, **white band on primaries projects past tertial tips,** and **wings reach just to tail tip**; in flight, note slightly **rounded wingtips, and white band close to wingtip**. Adult female has buffy throat and band on wings, and lacks white on tail. Compared to Common Nighthawk, wingtip is less pointed and wing band is closer to wingtip. Common visitor in NCA, including Bay Is. (early Sept.–mid-May); uncommon local resident in NCA, especially along Pacific beaches where it nests on sand above high-tide line; to 8,200 ft. (2,500 m). Found at a variety of habitats: pine savanna, mangroves, pasturelands, and near cities and towns. Flight is erratic: quick, flicking wingbeats followed by faster fluttering and glides. Wings are held in a dihedral. Generally silent outside breeding period. Call is a long trill (like some *Megascops* screech-owls and toads), ending drops slightly in pitch (lasts 7 sec. or more). U.S. to Chile.

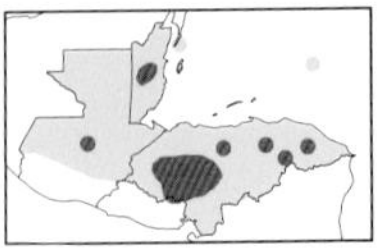

COMMON NIGHTHAWK *Chordeiles minor*

9.5 in. (24 cm). Female similar to male, but lacks white throat and white subterminal tail band. Very similar to Lesser Nighthawk, but larger and **plumage is often darker**; on perched birds, **white band on wing does not extend beyond tertial tips**, and **wings extend beyond tip of tail**. In flight, note more **pointed wings** and **white band closer to base of primaries**. Best distinguished from Antillean Nighthawk (Swan Is. only) by voice. Uncommon transient on Caribbean Slope (Aug.–Nov., Feb.–May); very rare transient on Pacific Slope; uncommon and local breeding visitor in central highlands (pine-oak belt); to 6,560 ft. (2,000 m). Found in semideciduous forest, thorn forest, pine savanna, pine-oak forest, and in cities and towns. Usually flies higher than Lesser Nighthawk, at dawn and dusk. Migrating flocks of hundreds are not unusual. Call (given in flight) is a nasal, insectlike *Peeeent!* "Booming" courtship display consists of great U-shaped dives generating a whooshing sound (made by wings). Canada to Argentina.

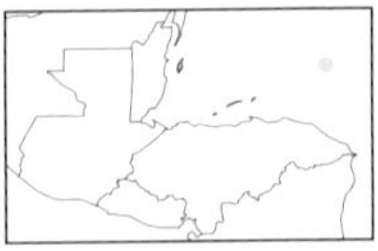

ANTILLEAN NIGHTHAWK *Chordeiles gundlachii*

8.5 in. (22 cm). Very similar to Common Nighthawk but smaller and has narrower wings. Best separated by voice. Rare (?) transient or summer visitor in Swan Is. (Honduras); near sea level. Status in NCA unclear. Flight and behavior similar to Common Nighthawk. Call is a dry, nasal (generally 3-part) *pilly-pee-pik!* U.S. (FL) and Caribbean (breeding) to unknown wintering grounds.

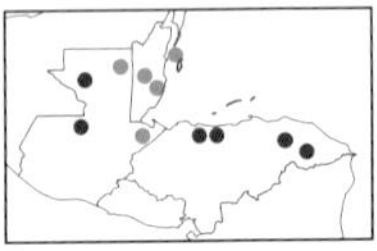

SHORT-TAILED NIGHTHAWK *Lurocalis semitorquatus*

8.5 in. (22 cm). In flight, note **short tail and all-dark wings**; white throat is often not visible on perched birds. Rare on Caribbean Slope; to 1,640 ft. (500 m). Seasonal status in much of the region is uncertain. Found in rainforest and riparian forest. Daytime roost is in subcanopy; at dawn and dusk flies low over canopy or forest streams with bounding, butterfly-like flight. Call is a sharp, liquid whistle *g'wick!*; also *whick-whick-whick-whick*; and a gruff growl, *chur'r'r'rrrr*. Mex. to Brazil.

LESSER
NIGHTHAWK
male
COMMON
NIGHTHAWK
male
male
ANTILLEAN
NIGHTHAWK
SHORT-TAILED
NIGHTHAWK

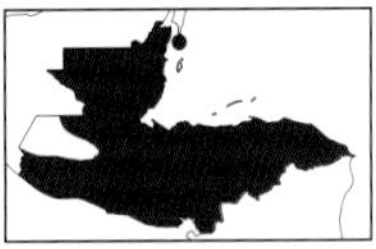

COMMON PAURAQUE *Nyctidromus albicollis*

11.5 in. (29 cm). Obvious pale **buffy white or cinnamon spotting on wing coverts**; face is rufous-brown; adult has white lower throat (often not visible); long tail extends well beyond primaries; in flight, adult male has **white outer tail feathers and large white bands across primaries**; female has reduced white in tail (only corners) and pale buff or cinnamon band on wing. Similar to Chuck-will's-Widow (p. 188), but lacks rufous in wings and tail and male has much more extensive white in tail. Common in NCA; to 6,070 ft. (1,850 m). Found at edge in a variety of taller woodland habitats: semideciduous forest, pine-oak forest, thorn forest, mangroves, disturbed habitat, pine savanna, and coffee plantations. Roosts on ground during day at edge of forest or along interior clearing. Feeds by making short sallies from ground to hawk insects from the air. Calls include a distinctive, sharp *Purr-WEER!* or *weu-Woop-Woop-Woop-Weu'WEER!* and agitated growls. U.S. to Brazil.

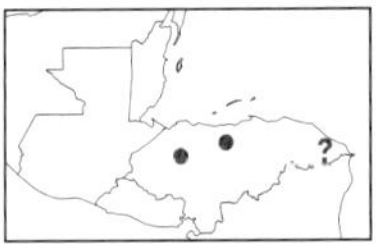

SPOT-TAILED NIGHTJAR *Hydropsalis maculicaudus*

8 in. (20 cm). A distinctive-looking nightjar. Dark gray overall with contrasting **pale buff scapular braces** and **pale buff spotting on wing coverts; tertials and secondaries have cinnamon brown tips**; note also **pale buff supercilium and moustachial stripe** outlining brownish face and contrasting with dark crown and malar stripe; broad hindcollar is cinnamon brown. Adult male has white tips to outer tail feathers and spotting on undertail (difficult to see); female tail is rufous-brown with light black barring. Rare transient and summer resident in Honduras; few confirmed records and status unclear; to 1,970 ft. (600 m). Found in pine savanna and savanna grasslands. Calls from ground or low perch. Call is a loud, clear whistled *Pitz!-Tzeeeuu'wee!* Mex. to Brazil.

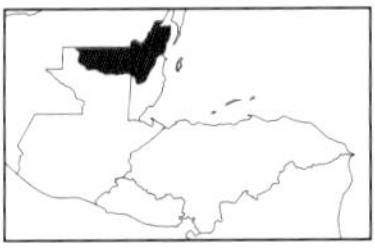

YUCATAN POORWILL *Nyctiphrynus yucatanicus*

8.5 in. (22 cm). **Dark overall** with dark brown face; **thin white forecollar** (often not visible on perched birds); relatively unmarked above, but note **dark-centered scapulars** and small white spots on wing coverts; **short tail has outer tail feathers tipped white**. Some individuals are paler rufous overall. Uncommon to fairly common in n. Guatemala and n. Belize; to 820 ft. (250 m). Found at edge in thorn forest and semideciduous forest. Roosts and perches in trees at low to midlevels. Call is a sharp, slightly rattling *WEUR'R'R'!* Endemic to region.

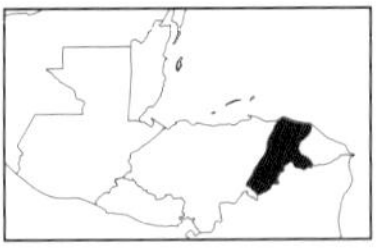

OCELLATED POORWILL *Nyctiphrynus ocellatus*

8.5 in. (22 cm). Distinctive in that it is relatively unmarked overall with a heavy-browed appearance; males are sooty brown (females are more rufous) with **black spots on scapulars** and white spots on belly; also white forecollar (often not visible on perched birds) and black and white tips to outer tail feathers. Uncommon in e. Honduras; to 2,460 ft. (750 m). Found at edges of rainforest. Daytime roost is on forest floor (sometimes low branch) where it blends in with heavy leaf litter. Call is very similar to that of Yucatan Poorwill (no range overlap). Honduras to Argentina.

COMMON PAURAQUE
male
male
SPOT-TAILED
NIGHTJAR
YUCATAN
POORWILL
male
male
OCELLATED
POORWILL

CHUCK-WILL'S-WIDOW *Antrostomus carolinensis*

12 in. (31 cm). **A large, long-tailed nightjar.** Rufous-brown face contrasts with grayer crown; whitish to pale buff forecollar; **rufous wings and tail with black banding**; tail flashes white in outer tail feathers (female lacks white in tail). Similar to Common Pauraque (p. 186), but note rufous wings and tail and males with much less white in tail. Uncommon transient and winter visitor in NCA; to 4,920 ft. (1,500 m). Found in woodland habitats: semideciduous forest, coffee plantations, and rainforest. Day roosts at low to midlevels on branches in trees. Hunts from ground or on perches; may hawk insects above forest canopy similar to nighthawks. Generally silent on winter grounds, but may call in spring prior to northbound migration. Call is a 3-part, *Chuck-wills-WIDOW!* or *Tuk-weeoo-WEEDOO!* U.S. (breeding) to Colombia (winter).

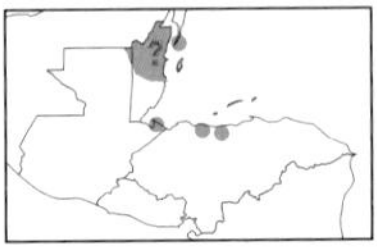

YUCATAN NIGHTJAR *Antrostomus badius*

10 in. (26 cm). **Tawny-cinnamon hindcollar and white spotting on underparts**; dark-centered scapulars with silver edging. Male has broad white corners to tail (female less). Similar to Eastern Whip-poor-will, but more rufous overall with more white in tail, heavier spotting on chest, and hindcollar prominent; note restricted distribution. Uncommon in Belize, including cayes; rare in ne. Guatemala; rare winter visitor to nw. Honduras; majority of individuals in NCA may be transients and winter visitors (mid-Oct.–late Apr.); near sea level. Found in a variety of woodland habitats. Perches at low to midlevels in forest. Call is a 3-part, *Peer-weeer-weeEU!* Endemic to region.

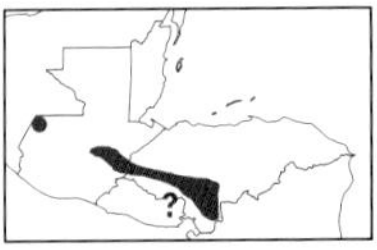

BUFF-COLLARED NIGHTJAR *Antrostomus ridgwayi*

8.5 in. (22 cm). **Tawny-cinnamon hindcollar.** Male has broad white tail corners (female reduced buffy white). Rare to uncommon in interior foothills and highlands; 490 to 5,410 ft. (150–1,650 m). Found on rocky hillsides and at edge in arid to semiarid thorn forest and scrub. Hunts from ground or near ground. Call is an accelerating series of dripping-water-like elements, *tok-tok-tok-tok'tok'tok'tue-tu'Leak!* U.S. to Honduras.

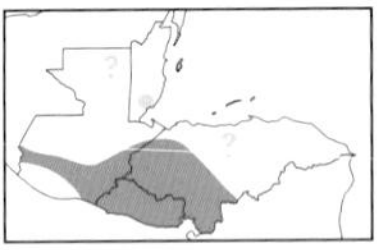

EASTERN WHIP-POOR-WILL *Antrostomus vociferus*

9.5 in. (24 cm). Similar to Yucatan Nightjar, but paler gray overall with less white in tail; hindcollar absent. Also similar to Mexican Whip-poor-will, but paler overall with more white in tail. Uncommon winter visitor in NCA (Oct.–early Mar.); to 7,710 ft. (2,350 m). Found in woodland habitats, including rainforest, dry forest, coastal scrub, pine-oak, cloud forest, and coffee plantations. Often flies over forest canopy at dusk. Generally silent on winter grounds; call similar to Mexican Whip-poor-will's, but with faster delivery. U.S. (breeding) to Panama (winter).

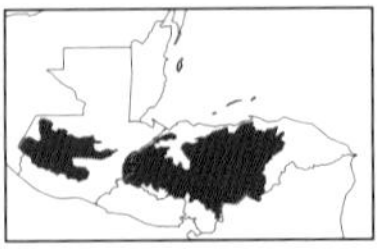

MEXICAN WHIP-POOR-WILL *Antrostomus arizonae*

9.5 in. (24 cm). Similar to Eastern Whip-poor-will, but darker overall with less white in tail. Uncommon resident in NCA; from 1,970 to 8,200 ft. (600–2,500 m). Found at edge of semideciduous forest, pine-oak forest, and pine savanna; also coffee plantations. Call is a repeated *weu'u'p-poor'Reeer!* (slower delivery than Eastern at less than 0.5 sec. per series and overall with more trill); generally more vocal from Mar. to Aug. U.S. to Honduras.

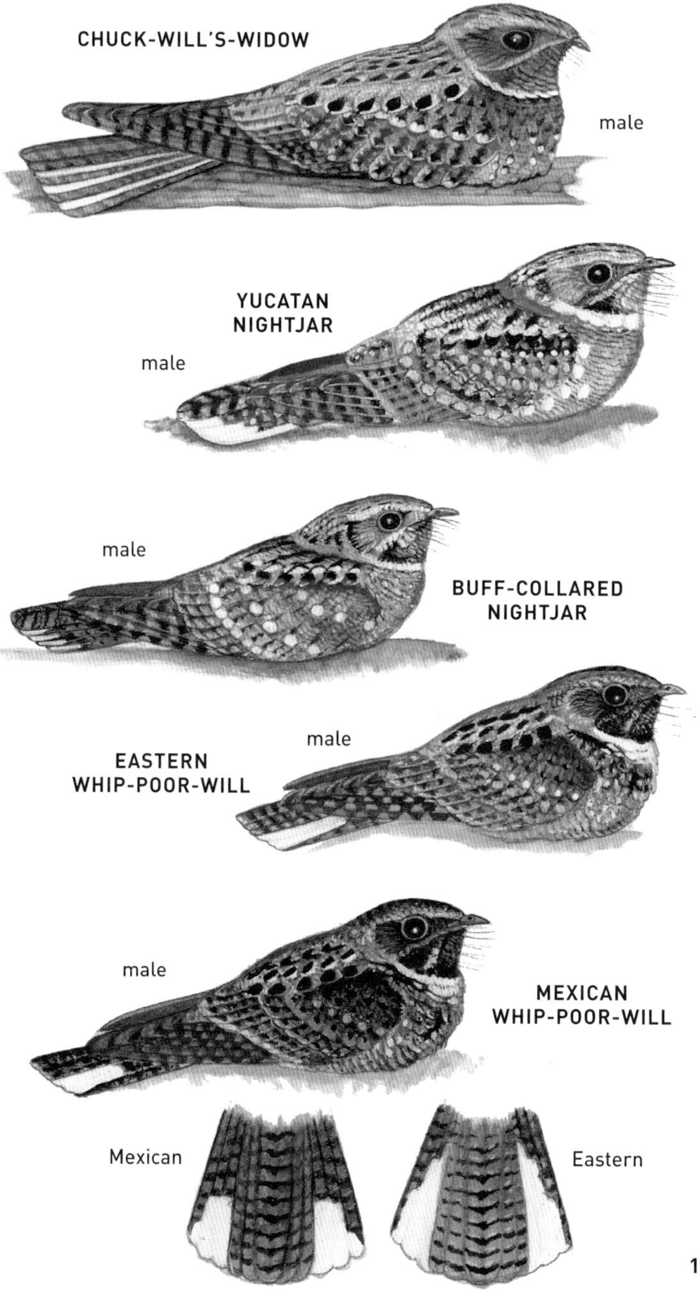
CHUCK-WILL'S-WIDOW
male
YUCATAN NIGHTJAR
male
male
BUFF-COLLARED NIGHTJAR
male
EASTERN WHIP-POOR-WILL
male
MEXICAN WHIP-POOR-WILL
Mexican
Eastern

QUETZALS AND RED-BELLIED TROGONS

TROGONIDAE (Order: Trogoniformes). Trogons and quetzals are tropical birds characterized by a vertical perching posture and colorful iridescent plumage. They feed mainly on fruits and berries, but feed insects or small lizards to their young. Trogons are cavity nesters and often excavate and use abandoned termitaria (arboreal termite nests) for nesting. For identification, it's useful to consider vocalizations, habitat, distribution, belly color, and undertail pattern. **8 species (2 genera)**

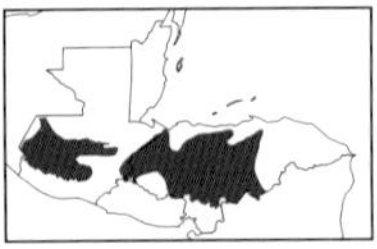

RESPLENDENT QUETZAL *Pharomachrus mocinno*

14.5 in. (37 cm); male up to 30 in. (76 cm) with tail plumes. Striking male with **extended uppertail coverts (plumes)** is unmistakable. Female lacks streaming plumes and is drabber overall. Uncommon and local in interior highlands; from 3,280 to 9,350 ft. (1,000–2,850 m). Generally found at mid- and upper elevations in pine-oak forest and cloud forest, but descends in search of fruiting avocado trees. Male performs an impressive aerial display from the forest canopy, making a high vertical flight and then a soft, angled descent with tail plumes quavering in the wind. Long call of male is a wailing *kaw-kuay-kaw-kuay-kaw-kuay-* . . . ; both sexes make an agitated, nasal *kah'rak!-kah'rak!-kah'rak!-kah'rak!* . . . ; shorter call is a *kwar-ahrr-rrak!* Also a short barking *kow* similar to Barred Forest-Falcon (p. 216). National bird of Guatemala. Mex. to Panama.

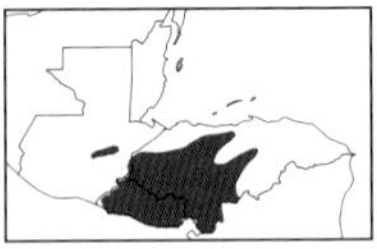

ELEGANT TROGON *Trogon elegans*

11.5 in. (29 cm). Male told from Collared and Mountain Trogons by **bronzy green uppertail** and undertail with **black-and-white barring** and **broad white tips**. Female distinguished from other trogons by bold **white mark behind eye**. Immature male similar to female, but shows some green on upperparts. Locally fairly common in NCA (except Belize); to 6,230 ft. (1,900 m). Found in semideciduous forest, riparian forest, thorn forest, also coffee plantations; forages at midlevels. Call is a hoarse barking *Kou'wee Kou'wee*, repeated 2 to 10 times in each series; also makes a low, forced, growling. Mex. to Costa Rica.

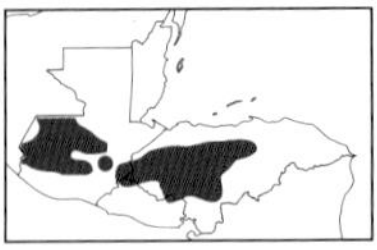

MOUNTAIN TROGON *Trogon mexicanus*

12 in. (31 cm). Male told from Elegant and Collared Trogons by darker gray wing panel and undertail pattern of **black feathers with broad white tips**. Female distinguished from other trogons also by undertail pattern, and from Elegant by dark maxilla. Uncommon in Guatemala and Honduras; 1,970 to 9,510 ft. (600–2,900 m) but generally above 5,580 ft. (1,700 m). Found in pine-oak forest and cloud forest; rarely semideciduous forest and rainforest. Forages at mid- and upper levels. Call is a slightly nasal *Kweow! Kweow! Kweow!* repeated 3 to 10 times; also makes a hard *Chup!* and an agitated *che'eh'eh'eh'eh'eh!* Mex. to Honduras.

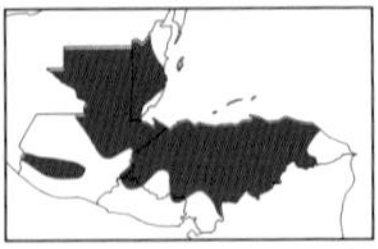

COLLARED TROGON *Trogon collaris*

11 in. (28 cm). Both sexes similar to Mountain and Elegant Trogons: distinguished by undertail pattern and wing panel with **fine black-and-white barring**. Female most similar to female Mountain, but more extensive red belly (meets the white breast-band) and undertail pattern is nearly all-white. Some individuals with orange bellies have been documented in NCA. Fairly common on both slopes; to 7,870 ft. (2,400 m). Found in semideciduous forest, rainforest, pine-oak forest, plantations, pine savanna, and cloud forest. Forages at mid- and upper levels. Call is a 2-part, slightly nasal *Kow-Kow* (may be repeated 3 or more times); also makes a trilling growl: *keea'r'r'r'r'r'r*. Mex. to Brazil.

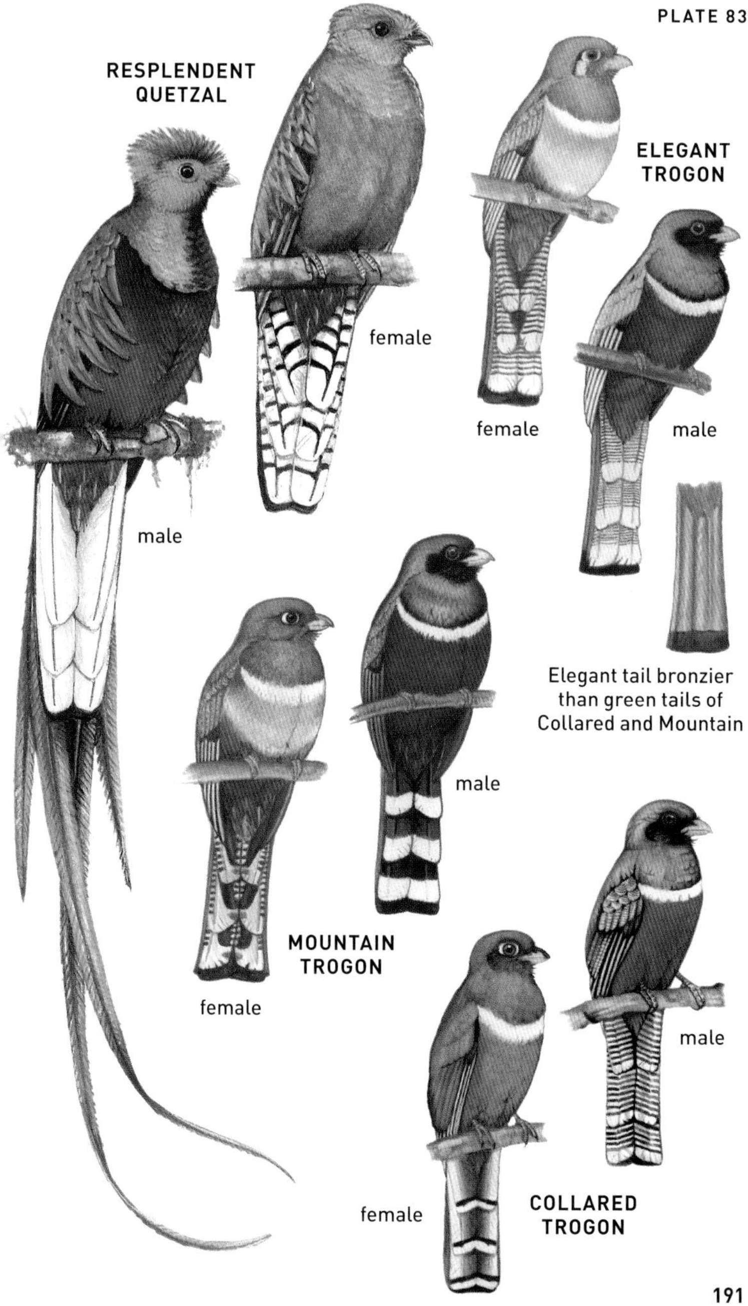
RESPLENDENT QUETZAL
female
male
ELEGANT TROGON
female
male
Elegant tail bronzier than green tails of Collared and Mountain
male
MOUNTAIN TROGON
female
male
COLLARED TROGON
female

SLATY-TAILED AND YELLOW-BELLIED TROGONS

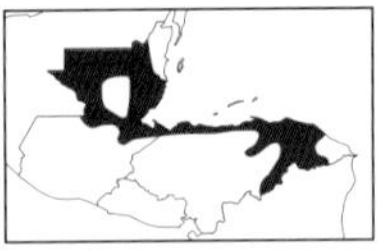

SLATY-TAILED TROGON *Trogon massena*

13.5 in. (34 cm). A large trogon. On male, dark green upperparts; gray wing panel; **undertail solid slaty gray**; note **orange-red bill** and eye-ring. Female similar to male, but is sooty gray above, lacks contrasting wing panel, and shows dark maxilla. Fairly common on Caribbean Slope; to 3,280 ft. (1,000 m). Found in rainforest, semideciduous forest, and taller plantations. Forages at midlevels in forest interior. Call is a long series of monotypic, nasal barking notes that begins softly and grows louder: *kaw-kaw-Kaw-Kaw-KAW-KAW-KAW-KAW-KAW-KAW-KAW-KAW* . . . (lasts up to 14 sec.); also makes a faster and more agitated *kaw'kaw'kaw'kaw'kaw'* . . . Mex. to Ecuador.

BLACK-HEADED TROGON *Trogon melanocephalus*

10.5 in. (27 cm). Distinguished from other **yellow-bellied** trogons by **broad white tips** on underside of tail feathers; also note combination of **sky blue eye-ring** and bluish gray bill. Male has blackish blue head and chest; iridescent blue-green upperparts and tail (dark in poor light); on wing, outer primaries usually show white shafts. Female and immature similar to male, but head, chest, and upperparts dull gray; immature undertail shows black-and-white barring at base. Fairly common, and somewhat local on both slopes; to 3,280 ft. (1,000 m). Found in rainforest, semideciduous forest, mangroves, and plantations; often near water. Forages at midlevels at edge or interior of forest. Call is a series of nasal barks that rises and accelerates, then rises slightly in pitch at end: *cheu—cheu—cheu-cheu-cheu-cheu-cheu 'cheu'cheu'cha'cha'CHA'CHA'CHA'CHA'cha*; also makes a shorter *cheu-cheu-cheu-cheu-cheu'cheu'cheu'cheu*. Males sometimes call simultaneously. Mex. to Costa Rica.

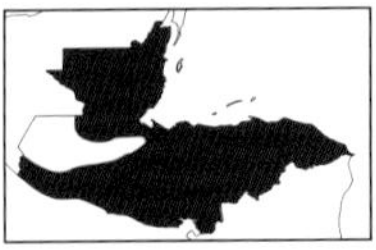

GARTERED TROGON *Trogon caligatus*

10 in. (26 cm). Male distinguished from other NCA trogons by **yellow eye-ring**; further distinguished from male Black-headed Trogon by **light gray wing panel** and extensive **black-and-white barring on undertail**. Also note iridescent green upperparts (dark in poor light) and horn gray bill. Female has sooty gray upperparts; undertail shows primarily black tail feathers with small white tips and black-and-white barring at edges; distinguished from female Black-headed Trogon by pale, **incomplete eye-ring** (broken above and below eye) and **black-and-white barring on wing**. Fairly common on both slopes; to 6,070 ft. (1,850 m). Found in interior and edge of rainforest, semideciduous forest, thorn forest, disturbed habitat, plantations, and mangroves; forages at midlevels. Call is a long, accelerating series of monotypic nasal toots, similar to call of Ferruginous Pygmy-Owl (p. 178): *kow-kow-kow-kow-kow-kow-kow-kow'kow'kow'kow'kow'kow* (lasts roughly 6 sec.). Also makes short growls: *kur'r'r'r'r'r'r'r*. Mex. to Ecuador.

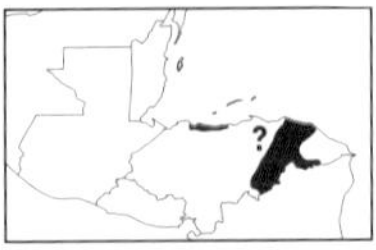

BLACK-THROATED TROGON *Trogon rufus*

10 in. (26 cm). Male distinguished from other yellow-bellied trogons by combination of **green head**, **blue eye-ring**, and **yellow bill**. Also note **black face and throat**; gray wing panel with fine black barring; undertail feathers with even **black-and-white barring** and **broad white tips**. Female distinguished by **brown head and upperparts**; also note pale, broken eye-ring. Uncommon on Caribbean Slope; to 4,100 ft. (1,250 m). Prefers humid environments; found in interior of rainforest and riparian forest. Forages at lower and middle levels. Call is very similar to call of Collared Trogon, but is slower, descends in pitch, and may have more elements: *Kow-Kow-Kow-Kow*. Female alarm call also similar to that of Collared Trogon (*teea'r'r'r'r'r'r'r*). Honduras to Argentina.

Black-headed Trogon flying into termitarium cavity
male
female
SLATY-TAILED TROGON
male
female
BLACK-HEADED TROGON
male
female
GARTERED TROGON
male
female
BLACK-THROATED TROGON

MOMOTIDAE (Order: Coraciiformes). Honduras alone has 7 species of motmots, which is more than any other country in the world. Members of this strictly Neotropical family have several unique features, including syndactyl feet (anterior toes fused at base) and, in 6 of the species, central tail feathers with spatulate tips, which lend the tail a racketlike shape. Although motmots have brightly colored plumages, they often remain still for long periods (though they frequently twitch their tails back and forth in a pendulum motion) in thick vegetation while hunting for butterflies and other large insects, and thus can be difficult to observe; most species, however, are quite vocal, which helps in locating and identifying them. Diet also includes fruits (including hot peppers). Sexes are similar. Motmots nest in earthen banks, where they hollow out a cavity for raising young. **8 species (6 genera)**

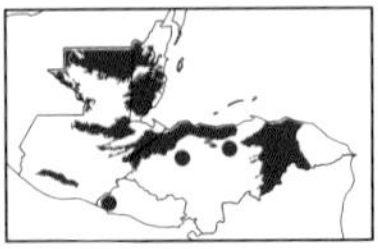

TODY MOTMOT *Hylomanes momotula*

6.5 in. (17 cm). Smallest motmot. Face has obvious **white moustachial stripe**, **turquoise supercilium**, and **black behind eye**; rufous crown; **short tail lacks rackets**. Uncommon on Caribbean Slope; on Pacific Slope, uncommon in Guatemala, and rare in extreme w. El Salvador; 330 to 5,250 ft. (100–1,600 m). Found at lower levels, in thick vegetation of rainforest and semideciduous forest. Call is a *bop* note, repeated every 1.5 sec. (very similar to call of Blue-throated Motmot); also makes an agitated, slightly growling *wha'wha'wha'wha'wha* . . . Mex. to Colombia.

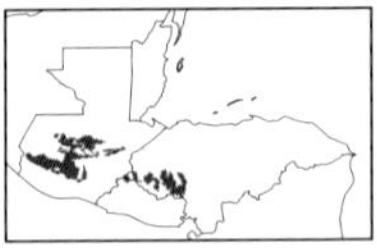

BLUE-THROATED MOTMOT *Aspatha gularis*

10.5 in. (27 cm). Note **blue throat**; tawny face with **black spot on auricular**; mostly pale bill; **no tail rackets**. Uncommon in Guatemala; rare and local in Honduras and El Salvador; above 4,920 to 9,840 ft. (1,500–3,000 m). Found in thick understory vegetation and at midlevels of mixed pine and oak forest, Mexican cypress forests and plantations, and cloud forest. Call is a *bop!* note repeated every 3 sec. (very similar to call of Tody Motmot); also makes an excited *whada-whada-whada-whada-whada-whada*. Endemic to the region.

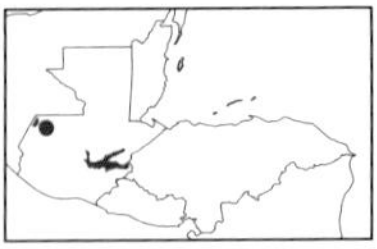

RUSSET-CROWNED MOTMOT *Momotus mexicanus*

13 in. (33 cm). **Bright rufous crown and nape**; **black mask** edged with iridescent purplish blue; dark "stickpin" on center of chest (actually 2 dark spots that often appear as 1); long tail has short rackets. Fairly common in interior dry valleys of Guatemala; 660 to 1,970 ft. (200–600 m). Prefers arid habitats. Perches at lower and middle levels in thorn forest and semideciduous forest. Call is a single reedy *woop* or a slightly higher *wup!*; when excited, pairs often call simultaneously. Mex. to Guatemala.

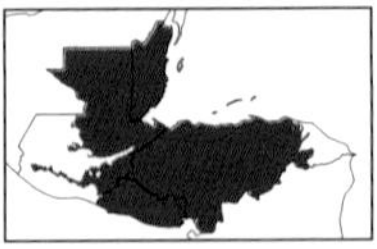

LESSON'S MOTMOT *Momotus lessonii*

16 in. (41 cm). **Black crown bordered by electric blue**; black mask edged in blue; 2 small black spots on chest; long tail with short rackets. Distinguished from Keel-billed Motmot (p. 196) by black crown (greenish on Keel-billed). Common on both slopes in NCA; to 5,910 ft. (1,800 m), rarely higher. Found at lower and middle levels in almost any forest habitat; also occurs in city parks and coffee plantations. Call a deep *woot-woot* (reminiscent of a distant barking dog), and sometimes a longer series of 5 *woot* notes; at dawn and dusk, birds often call back and forth to each other. Mex. to Panama. Formerly considered a subspecies of Blue-crowned Motmot (*Momotus momota*).

TODY
MOTMOT
BLUE-THROATED
MOTMOT
RUSSET-CROWNED
MOTMOT
LESSON'S
MOTMOT

RUFOUS MOTMOT *Baryphthengus martii*

19 in. (48 cm). A large motmot; mainly **rufous head and underparts** with **broad black mask**; greenish blue wings, belly, and undertail coverts; **small dark spot on chest**; long tail with short tail rackets; **heavy black bill**. Very similar to Broad-billed Motmot, but note much larger size, rufous chin, larger mask, and smaller spot on chest. Uncommon to fairly common in lowlands of e. Honduras; to 2,460 ft. (750 m). Found at midlevels of rainforest. Call is a low, bouncy *who-do'do'do* or often just a *who-do*; also makes a *whup-whup*. Honduras to S. America.

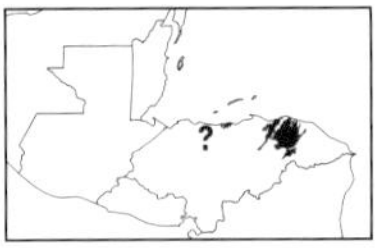

BROAD-BILLED MOTMOT *Electron platyrhynchum*

12.5 in. (32 cm). Rufous head and chest; long tail with short rackets. Similar to Rufous Motmot (ranges overlap in e. Honduras), but note much smaller size, **narrow dark mask**, **blue-green chin**, and **large smudgy spot on chest**. Compare with Keel-billed Motmot; hybrids of the 2 species have been reported in Costa Rica and elsewhere. Rare to uncommon in lowlands and foothills of Caribbean Slope of Honduras; to 3,610 ft. (1,100 m). Found at midlevels of rainforest. Call is a repeated *ahhh* (nearly identical to call of Keel-billed Motmot, and higher-pitched than call of Turquoise-browed Motmot); also makes a *wha-ah-ah-ah-ah-ah-ah*. Honduras to Brazil.

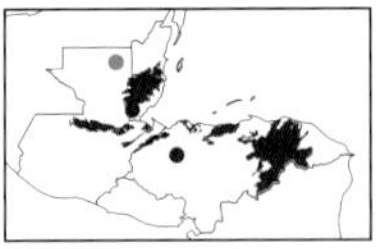

KEEL-BILLED MOTMOT *Electron carinatum*

12.5 in. (32 cm). **Aqua blue chin and supercilium**; greenish crown and dark mask; forehead and underparts vary from rufous to green; most individuals in NCA are **rufous below** (few are green below, as in more southern populations); **large smudgy black spot on chest**; long tail with short rackets. Compare with Broad-billed Motmot; hybrids of the 2 species have been reported in Costa Rica and elsewhere. Rare to uncommon in lowlands and foothills of Caribbean Slope; to 5,250 ft. (1,600 m). Found at midlevels of rainforest. Common call is a repeated *ahhh* (nearly identical to call of Broad-billed Motmot, and higher-pitched than call of Turquoise-browed Motmot); also makes a repeated, more drawn-out *araank* (rarely heard). Mex. to Costa Rica.

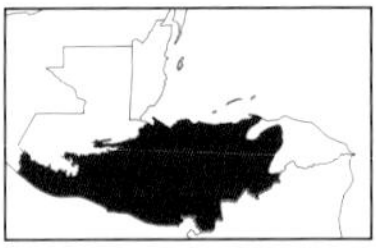

TURQUOISE-BROWED MOTMOT *Eumomota superciliosa*

14 in. (36 cm). A flashy motmot; bright blue flight feathers (visible in flight); russet back; **turquoise eyebrow** and **large black throat patch bordered in turquoise**; note long tail with **long rackets**. Common on Pacific Slope of Guatemala and El Salvador; fairly common on Caribbean Slope of Honduras; to 3,940 ft. (1,200 m) and sometimes at higher elevations in disturbed habitat. Found at lower and middle levels of forest edge, including disturbed forest, semideciduous forest, and thorn forest; also occurs in open agricultural areas, gardens, and urban areas. Frequently seen perched on power lines. Call is a hoarse *auk*, sometimes repeated (similar to calls of Keel-billed and Broad-billed Motmots, but lower in pitch); also makes a rapid *torogoz-torogoz-torogoz-torogoz*. National bird of El Salvador (and Nicaragua). Mex. to Costa Rica.

Turquoise-browed leaving nest cavity

KINGFISHERS I

ALCEDINIDAE (Order: Coraciiformes). In NCA, this is a small family of aquatic diving birds. Kingfishers sit motionless for periods, making short or medium dives into water for fish, amphibians, and insects. They are fairly heavy-bodied, but short legged with small feet. They use their large daggerlike bills to spear prey. They are generally plumaged with green or blue-gray upperparts and varying amounts of rufous and white below. They nest in cavities in earthy embankments along rivers and streams. **6 species (2 genera)**

RINGED KINGFISHER *Megaceryle torquata*

15.5 in. (40 cm). **Largest kingfisher in NCA**, with exceptionally large, heavy bill. Male has blue-gray upperparts, head, and tail; **rufous-chestnut underparts** bordered by **broad white collar**; note shaggy crest and white supraloral spot. Female similar, but has blue-gray chest separated from chestnut underparts by thin white band. In flight on both sexes, note white slashes in primaries of upperwing. Uncommon to fairly common on Caribbean Slope, rare but increasing on Pacific Slope; to 4,920 ft. (1,500 m). Perches at midlevels near water; found along large rivers, and in swamps, lagoons, and mangroves. Sometimes perches on power lines. Call is a loud, rattling *Kek!-Kek!-Kek!-Kek!-Kek!-Kek! . . .* ; also makes a 2-part *Kek'ek!* U.S. to Argentina.

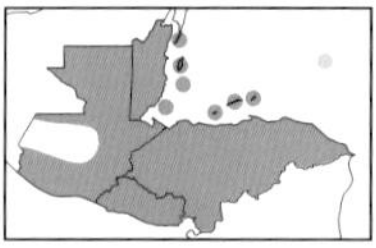

BELTED KINGFISHER *Megaceryle alcyon*

13 in. (33 cm). Male has blue-gray upperparts, head, and tail; underparts white with **blue-gray chest band**; note **broad white collar**, white supraloral spot, and large shaggy crest. Female similar to male, but has **rufous flanks and belly band**. Transient and winter visitor (mid-Aug.–late Apr.). Uncommon to fairly common on both slopes, including cayes and Bay Is.; to 6,560 ft. (2,000 m). Perches at lower and middle levels near water; found at edges of rivers and lakes, and in swamps, shrimp ponds, and mangroves. Sometimes perches on power lines. Generally silent in NCA, but in flight may give a rapid, rattling *chit!'chit!'chit!'chit!'chit!'chit!'chit! . . .* U.S. and Canada, Caribbean, to Venezuela.

AMAZON KINGFISHER *Chloroceryle amazona*

11.5 in. (29 cm). Male has **emerald green upperparts**, tail, and head; broad white collar; underparts with **emerald green sides of chest and rufous-chestnut on chest.** Female similar, but lacks rufous-chestnut on chest. Similar to Green Kingfisher, but is larger and has completely dark wings that lack any white spotting. Fairly common on Caribbean Slope; rare to uncommon (but increasing) on Pacific Slope; to 3,940 ft. (1,200 m). Found at edges of rivers and lakes; also in mangroves, marshes, and lagoons. Perches at lower and middle levels. Long call (song) begins rapidly, then slows and drops in pitch: *ti'ti'ti'ti'ti'ti'ti'ti'ti'ti'ti'teu'teu'teu'teu'teu'teu'teu'teu'teu-teu-teu*. Also makes hard rattles (*Kek!-Kek!*) and buzzes (*krrrik*). Mex. to Uruguay.

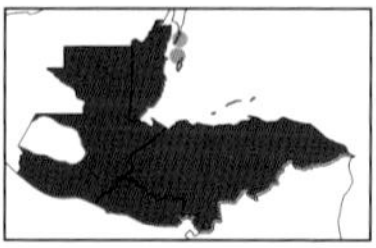

GREEN KINGFISHER *Chloroceryle americana*

8 in. (20 cm). Similar to Amazon Kingfisher, but is smaller and has **small white spots on wing**. Male has rufous breast; female lacks rufous on breast but shows green chest bands (the lower one often incomplete). Fairly common on both slopes; to 6,890 ft. (2,100 m). Perches at lower levels near water; frequents swamps, shrimp ponds, forest streams, rivers, lakes, lagoons, and mangroves. Call is a hard *tick-tick-tick*. U.S. to Argentina.

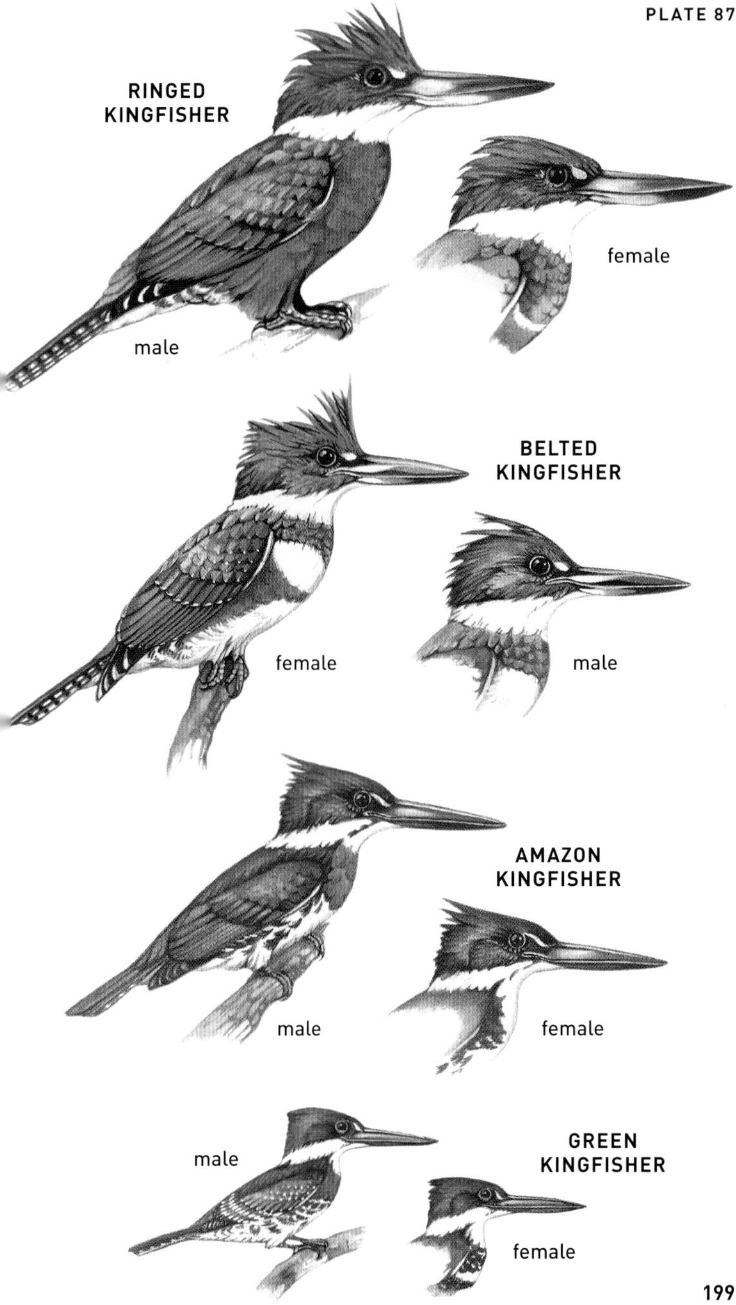
RINGED
KINGFISHER
female
male
BELTED
KINGFISHER
female
male
AMAZON
KINGFISHER
male
female
GREEN
KINGFISHER
male
female

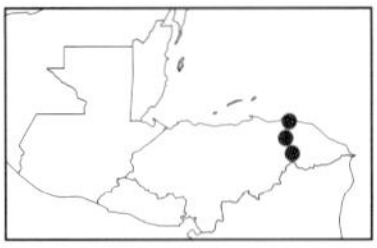

GREEN-AND-RUFOUS KINGFISHER *Chloroceryle inda*

8.5 in. (22 cm). **Buff collar** and **extensive rufous on underparts** are distinctive. American Pygmy Kingfisher has similar pattern, but is much smaller and has white on belly (both sexes). Rare in e. Honduras; to 660 ft. (200 m). Found near streams and wetlands within rainforest; perches at lower and middle levels. Flight call is a distinctive buzzy rattle: *Zeeuur'r'r't!* Longer call is a series of high-pitched whistles: *tseeuuu-tseeu-tseeuuu-Tseeup!* Honduras to Brazil.

AMERICAN PYGMY KINGFISHER *Chloroceryle aenea*

5 in. (13 cm). **A tiny kingfisher.** Both sexes distinguished from Green-and-rufous Kingfisher by small size and **white on belly and vent**. Uncommon on Caribbean Slope; rare on Pacific Slope; to 2,460 ft. (750 m). Found at edge of shallow forest pools; also swamps, roadside ditches, and other slow-moving waters (such as in mangroves). Perches at lower levels in the shade of overhanging branches. Calls include a high-pitched *Tseeup!* and soft *tik* notes (like 2 pebbles being tapped together). Mex. to Brazil.

GALBULIDAE (Order: Piciformes). A Neotropical family of the rainforest. Jacamars have long, pointed bills for catching moths, butterflies, and other flying insects. They are sit-and-wait predators, and will remain motionless and quiet for a long period before sallying out for their aerial prey. They are closely related to puffbirds and woodpeckers, and, like those groups, nest in cavities. **2 species (2 genera)**

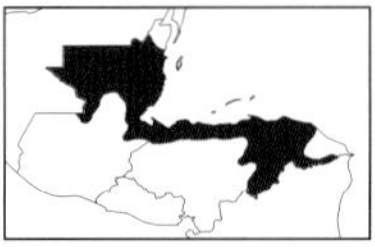

RUFOUS-TAILED JACAMAR *Galbula ruficauda*

9 in. (23 cm). Male **emerald green above** with iridescent golden sheen; throat white; **underparts rufous**; note long tail and **long, thin, sharply pointed bill**. Female similar to male, but throat cinnamon to buff. Distinguished from Great Jacamar by smaller size, **green chest band**, and rufous undertail. Uncommon to fairly common on Caribbean Slope; to 3,280 ft. (1,000 m). Found at edges and in interior of rainforest. Perches quietly and remains motionless for long periods; often detected by voice. Call is a sharp, squeaky *Weeek!*; also makes a longer, accelerating *Weeeeek!-Weeeeek!-Weeeek!-Week!-Week!-Wee'ee'ee'ee'ee'ee'eek!* Mex. to Argentina.

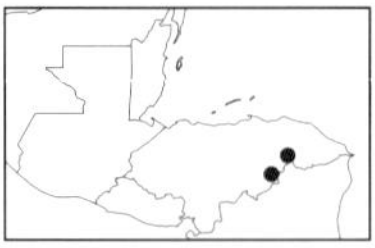

GREAT JACAMAR *Jacamerops aureus*

12 in. (31 cm). Distinguished from Rufous-tailed Jacamar by larger size, **rufous chest** (not green), and **dark undertail** (not rufous). Rare in e. Honduras (only recently discovered to occur in NCA); to 3,940 ft. (1,200 m). Perches quietly in rainforest. Song is a long, melancholy whistle: *heeeeeee'oooooooooo*. Also makes low groaning and whining noises. Honduras to Venezuela.

male
female
GREEN-AND-RUFOUS
KINGFISHER
male
AMERICAN PYGMY
KINGFISHER
female
male
male
GREAT
JACAMAR
female
female
RUFOUS-TAILED
JACAMAR

PUFFBIRDS

BUCCONIDAE (Order: Piciformes). A Neotropical group of heavy-bodied birds with stout hooked bills, short legs, and small feet. These forest-dwellers are sit-and wait-predators, and will remain motionless for long periods before making quick sallies for prey. Puffbirds are usually shy and quiet. Nunbirds form small groups that can be quite vocal and loud; they also associate with mixed-species flocks. **3 species (3 genera)**

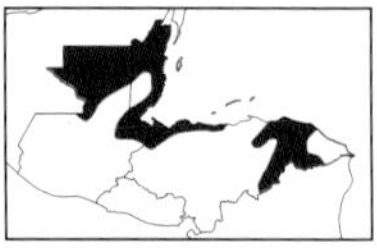

WHITE-NECKED PUFFBIRD *Notharchus hyperrhynchus*

10 in. (26 cm). Note **white forecrown** and **broad white collar**; white below with **broad black chest band** and black on flanks. Uncommon on Caribbean Slope, appears to be extirpated from the Pacific Slope; to 2,460 ft. (750 m). Found in rainforest on Caribbean Slope (formerly in semideciduous forest on Pacific Slope). Perches in canopy on bare limbs and exposed snags. Easily missed, as it sits motionless for long periods and rarely vocalizes. Call is a long, rapid, piping series: *wip!-Pea'Pea'Pea'Pea'Pea'Pea'Pea'Pea . . .* (lasts about 7 sec.). Mex. to Argentina.

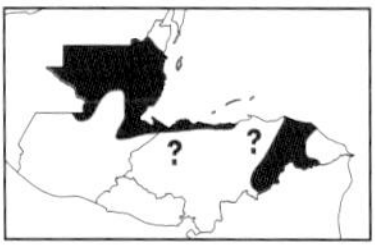

WHITE-WHISKERED PUFFBIRD *Malacoptila panamensis*

8 in. (20 cm). Male rufous brown above; **tawny face streaked buff** and broad buff malar stripe; **tawny-brown and black streaking on chest**. Female has similar pattern, but gray-brown coloration. On both sexes, erect feathers at base of bill give the appearance of whiskers; also note red eyes. Uncommon on Caribbean Slope; to 3,610 ft. (1,100 m). Found along edges and in interior of rainforest. Shy and reclusive. Easily missed, as it sits motionless in the forest for long periods and rarely vocalizes. Call is a thin, high-pitched, rattling whistle: *tseeeeu'u'u'u'u'u'u'u'u'u'u*. Mex. to Ecuador.

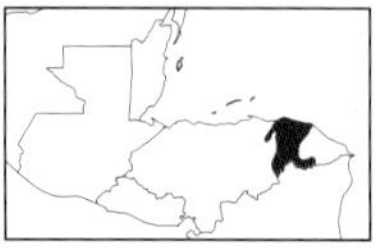

WHITE-FRONTED NUNBIRD *Monasa morphoeus*

11.5 in. (29 cm). **Blackish blue overall**; face blacker than body, with white at base of **orange-red bill**. Uncommon in e. Honduras; to 2,460 ft. (750 m). Found along edges and in interior of rainforest. Often in small groups, which vocalize loudly; also associates with mixed-species flocks. Calls include a loud, barking, complaining chatter: *Peep!-Cheet!'Cheet!'Cheet!-Reep!'Peet'Reep!'Peet-Peep!'Peep!'Peep! . . .* ; also a *Peer!-p'r'r'r'r'r'r'r'r* (second part a long trill). Honduras to Brazil.

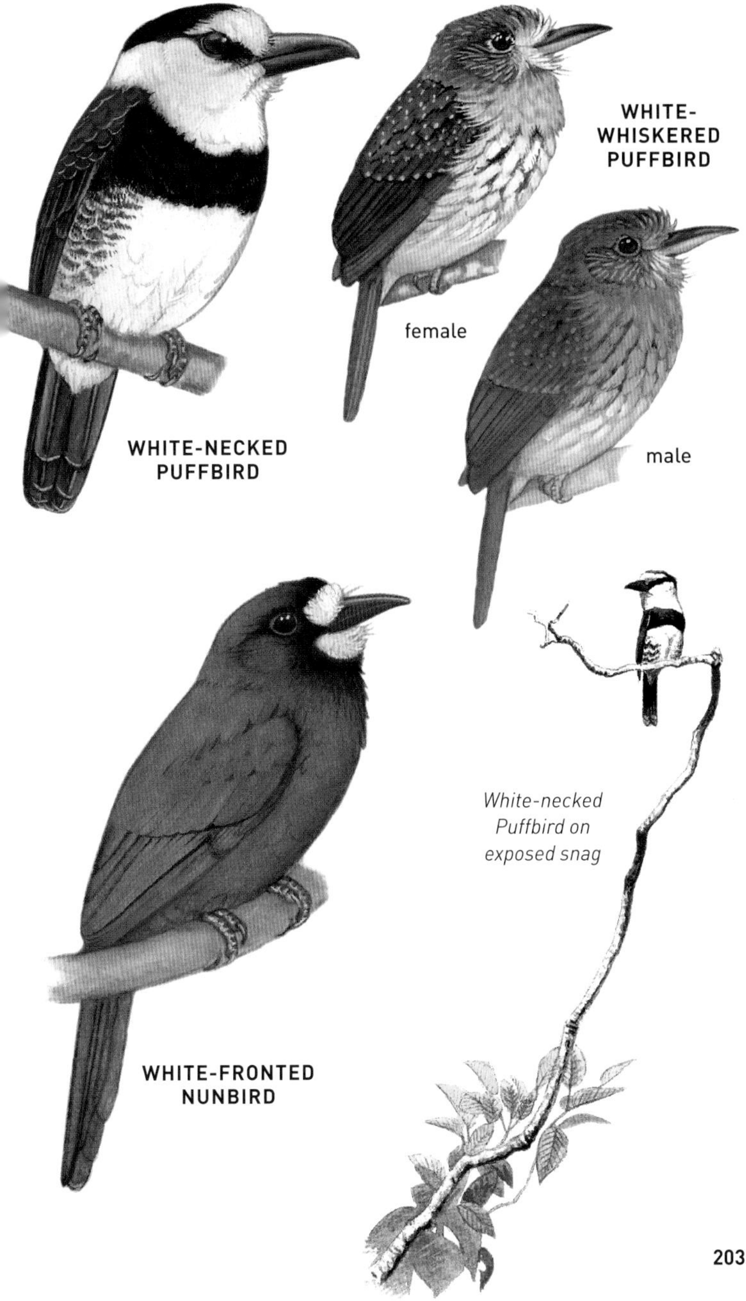
WHITE-WHISKERED PUFFBIRD
female
male
WHITE-NECKED PUFFBIRD
White-necked Puffbird on exposed snag
WHITE-FRONTED NUNBIRD

TOUCANS

RAMPHASTIDAE (Order: Piciformes). Toucans and araçaris are fairly large, heavy-bodied Neotropical birds. Their most characteristic feature is their long, stout decurved bills. These colorful bills are serrated and used most often for cutting and opening fruit. Members of this family are omnivores, however, and will devour amphibians, reptiles, and even young birds in nests. They have loud growling or barking calls and nest in cavities. **5 species (4 genera)**

EMERALD TOUCANET *Aulacorhynchus prasinus*

14 in. (36 cm). **Emerald green** overall; **white on throat**; undertail with rufous-brown tips; **maxilla mainly yellow**; mandible dark. Bare skin around eye black (or reddish brown in some Pacific Slope populations). Fairly common on both slopes; 660 to 9,510 ft. (200–2,900 m); on Pacific Slope mainly above 2,300 ft. (700 m). Found in semideciduous forest, pine-oak forest, and cloud forest. Forages at mid- and upper levels, but will go lower where fruit is available. Solitary or in small groups. Often detected by voice. Call is a nasal, barking *Wok!-Wok!-Wok!-Wok!-Wok!-Wok!-Wok!* . . . ; also makes a growling, throaty *wra'a'a'a'a'a'ak*. Mex. to Bolivia.

COLLARED ARAÇARI *Pteroglossus torquatus*

16 in. (41 cm). Distinctive. Underparts yellow with **reddish brown belly band and dark spot on chest**; eyes yellow. Fairly common on both slopes; to 5,410 ft. (1,650 m). Found in a variety of wooded and semiopen areas, including semideciduous forest, rainforest, plantations, and even city parks. Forages at mid- and upper levels. Almost always occurs in groups of 3 to 5 individuals. Call is a sharp, 2-part *Pe'TEET!* Mex. to Ecuador.

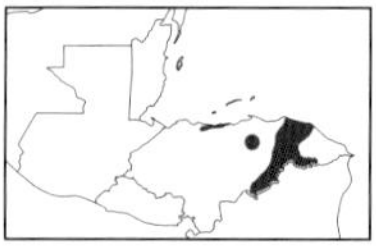

YELLOW-EARED TOUCANET *Selenidera spectabilis*

15.5 in. (40 cm). **Olive upperparts** contrast with **black head and underparts**; bill yellow above, with large chestnut triangle below. On male, note long **yellow ear patch**; on female, **reddish purple crown**. Rare to uncommon in n. and e. Honduras; to 3,280 ft. (1,000 m). Forages at mid- and upper levels of rainforest (including edge). Often solitary. Call is a loud, snapping *Tee-KAK!* Honduras to Colombia.

YELLOW-THROATED TOUCAN *Ramphastos ambiguus*

22.5 in. (57 cm). Mainly blackish overall; **yellow chest bordered below with thin red-white band**; undertail coverts red. Bill yellow on top with **broad chestnut triangle on lower part**. Uncommon in e. Honduras; to 2,460 ft. (750 m). Found in edge and semiopen areas of rainforest. Forages at mid- and upper levels. Solitary or in small groups. Call is a loud, nasal, and slightly scratchy *CHEER-UP!-GET-UP-GET-UP!* Honduras to Peru. Formerly known as Black-mandibled Toucan, and as Chestnut-mandibled Toucan (*Ramphastos swainsonii*).

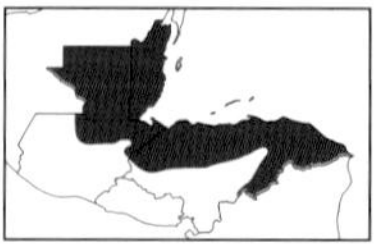

KEEL-BILLED TOUCAN *Ramphastos sulfuratus*

21.5 in. (55 cm). Unmistakable bill pattern. Fairly common on Caribbean Slope; to 4,590 ft. (1,400 m). Found in edge and semiopen areas of rainforest; also occurs in plantations. Forages at mid- and upper levels, and often perches on exposed canopy branches or tall snags. Solitary or in small groups. Call is a loud froglike croaking: *Kreeek!-Kreeek!-Kreeek!-Kreeek!-Kreeek!* . . . Mex. to Colombia. National bird of Belize.

a group of araçaris
leaving Cecropia tree
female
Caribbean
Slope
EMERALD
TOUCANET
Pacific
Slope
COLLARED
ARAÇARI
male
YELLOW-EARED
TOUCANET
YELLOW-THROATED
TOUCAN
KEEL-BILLED
TOUCAN

LARGE WOODPECKERS

PICIDAE (Order: Piciformes). With stiffened central tail feathers and zygodactyl feet, woodpeckers are well adapted for hitching up trees in search of food. They chip away at the bark with their chisel-like bills, and use their long barb-tipped tongues to extract beetle larvae, grubs, and other wood-boring insects that feed on softened heartwood. Woodpeckers are often detected by their loud territorial drumming (often machine gun–like). Although they are skillful tree climbers, woodpeckers are generally weak fliers and can be recognized by their distinctive bounding flight. Only the Yellow-bellied Sapsucker is a long-distance migrant. All species nest in tree cavities. **16 species (9 genera)**

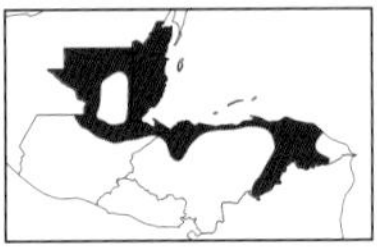

CHESTNUT-COLORED WOODPECKER *Celeus castaneus*

9 in. (23 cm). Upperparts and underparts **warm chestnut with black barring**; note **cream-colored head** with **shaggy crest**; ivory-colored bill may be washed yellow. Uncommon to fairly common on Caribbean Slope; to 3,610 ft. (1,100 m). Found in semideciduous forest and rainforest. Call is a sharp 2-part *wi-kah*; also makes a nasal *peahh* (like from a squeeze toy), sometimes followed by a *heh-he-he*; drum is short series of rapid hollow taps. Mex. to Panama.

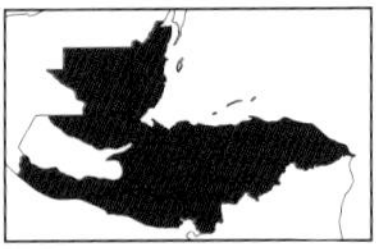

LINEATED WOODPECKER *Dryocopus lineatus*

13 in. (33 cm). A **large woodpecker**; **black overall** with **white line down the wing** (formed by scapulars); note **shaggy red crest**; pale eyes; heavy, ivory-colored bill. Male has red malar stripe; female has black forecrown. Distinguished from Pale-billed Woodpecker by white stripe across face (face entirely red in Pale-billed). Fairly common on both slopes; to 6,560 ft. (2,000 m). Found in wooded habitats, including rainforest, thorn forest, semideciduous forest, riparian forest, mangroves, disturbed habitat, pine savanna, and coffee plantations. Long call is a *wick-wick-wick-wick-wick-wick . . .* that lasts about 4 sec. (similar to call of Roadside Hawk [p. 172]); also makes an aggressive drumming that lasts about 2 sec. and accelerates toward the end. Mex. to Argentina.

PALE-BILLED WOODPECKER *Campephilus guatemalensis*

14.5 in. (37 cm). **Largest woodpecker in NCA**; wings black; **2 bold white lines beginning at nape converge in a V on black back**; heavy ivory-colored bill (sometimes washed with yellow); pale yellow eyes surrounded by dark orbital skin. Male has all-red face and crest; female similar to male but has black throat and black forecrown. Distinguished from Lineated Woodpecker by **all-red face** (lacks white stripe). Uncommon in NCA on both slopes; to 6,560 ft. (2,000 m). Found in rainforest, humid montane forest, semideciduous forest, riparian zones, and tall mangrove forest. Most common sound made is an emphatic double rap (*du-dump!*); calls include a nasal (like squeeze toy) *kip kip kip kip-hey'eh'eh*. Mex. to Panama.

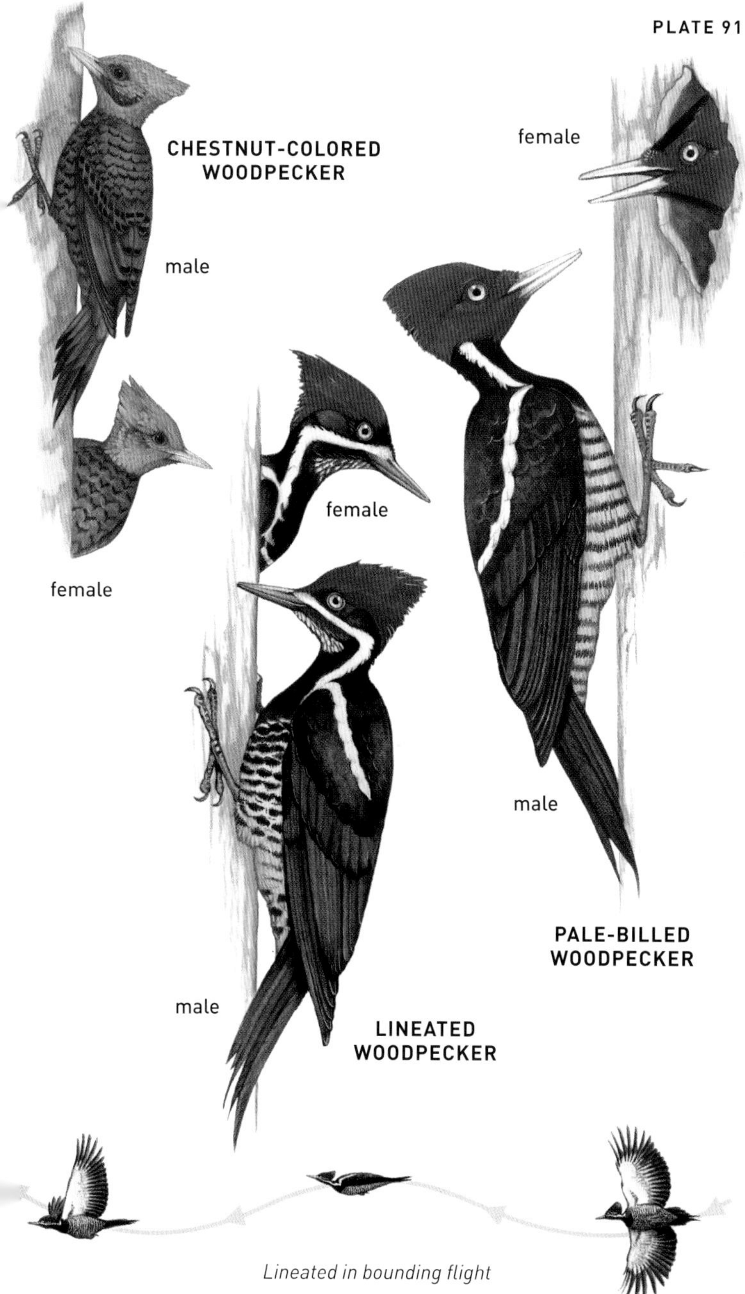

Lineated in bounding flight

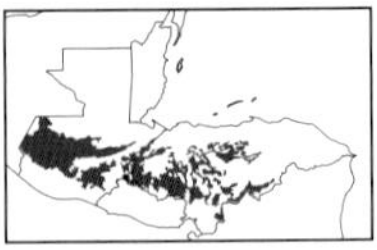

NORTHERN FLICKER *Colaptes auratus*

11 in. (28 cm). *C.a. mexicanoides*, the subspecies known as Guatemalan Flicker, is endemic to the region. **Upperparts with black-and-brown barring**; rump white; malar stripe red in male, cinnamon in female; **broad black chest band**; **flight feather shafts are reddish orange**. Fairly common in interior highlands; 2,460 to 11,500 ft. (750–3,500 m). Found mainly in pine savanna and pine-oak forest; may be seen on the ground feeding on ants. Long call is a raptorlike *keh-keh-keh-keh-keh-keh . . .* ; also makes a *wik'a-wik'a-wik'a-wik'a-wik'a*; drum is series of soft taps that lasts about 1 second. U.S. and Canada to Nicaragua.

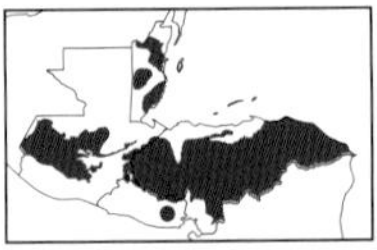

ACORN WOODPECKER *Melanerpes formicivorus*

8.5 in. (22 cm). Two subspecies in NCA: both have **solid black upperparts**; **distinctive "clown" face**; **white eyes**; on male, bright red crown borders white forecrown; on female, separated by black band. *M.f. lineatus* (interior highlands) has heavy **dark streaking on chest, sides, and flanks**; *M.f. albeolus* (Belize) has less dense, crisper streaking below. Fairly common in NCA; above 980 ft. (300 m) in the interior highlands; from near sea level to 4,270 ft. (1,300 m) in Belize and e. Honduras. Found in pine savanna, pine-oak forest, and oak forest. Forages in close-knit groups; caches acorns in drilled holes for later consumption. Call is a laughing, somewhat scratchy *wheh-he-he he-he-he*; also makes a chattering *rhe-e-e-e-e-e*, similar to parakeets. U.S. to Colombia.

HAIRY WOODPECKER *Picoides villosus*

8 in. (20 cm). **Black above** with **white band down center of back**; primaries with faint white spotting; **underparts vary from whitish to buffy brown**. Rear crown red on male, black on female. Fairly common in interior highlands; 1,970 to 11,500 ft. (600–3,500 m). Found in pine savanna, pine-oak, and cloud forest; forages at all levels. Single call is a loud *peek!*; flight call is a quick rattle that lasts about 2 sec.; drum is a 1-sec. series of rapid taps. U.S. and Canada to Panama.

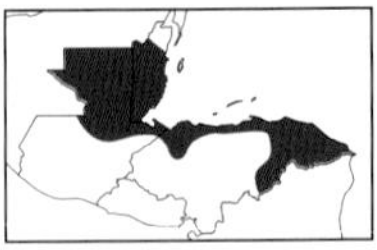

BLACK-CHEEKED WOODPECKER *Melanerpes pucherani*

7.5 in. (19 cm). **Black postocular stripe** with **white postocular spot**. Male has red crown and nape; female has red nape only. Fairly common on Caribbean Slope; to 2,460 ft. (750 m). Found in open areas of disturbed habitat and rainforest; forages at all levels. Call is a loud, slightly nasal *kair-r-r-r*, repeated about 5 times (similar to calls of Golden-fronted and Yucatan woodpeckers [p. 210]); also makes a more agitated *chuir'r'r*. Mex. to Ecuador.

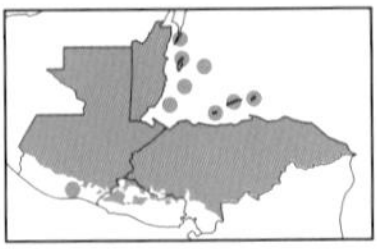

YELLOW-BELLIED SAPSUCKER *Sphyrapicus varius*

8 in. (20 cm). Male has uneven black-and-white barring on back; **long white wing patch** (visible on closed wing); **broad black eye line**; red crown and **red throat** both bordered in black; remaining underparts soft yellow. Female similar, but has **white throat**. Immature similar to female, but has dark crown and mottled brown-and-gray plumage overall. Winter visitor (Oct.–Apr.). Uncommon on both slopes; to 13,780 ft. (4,250 m). Found in semideciduous forest, pine-oak forest, pine savanna, cloud forest, open disturbed habitat, and urban gardens. Forages at low to midlevels; feeding behavior involves creating distinctive rows of resin wells on tree trunks. Generally silent on wintering grounds, but sometimes makes a whiny *meeah* (reminiscent of Gray Catbird [p. 324]). U.S. and Canada (breeding) to Panama (winter).

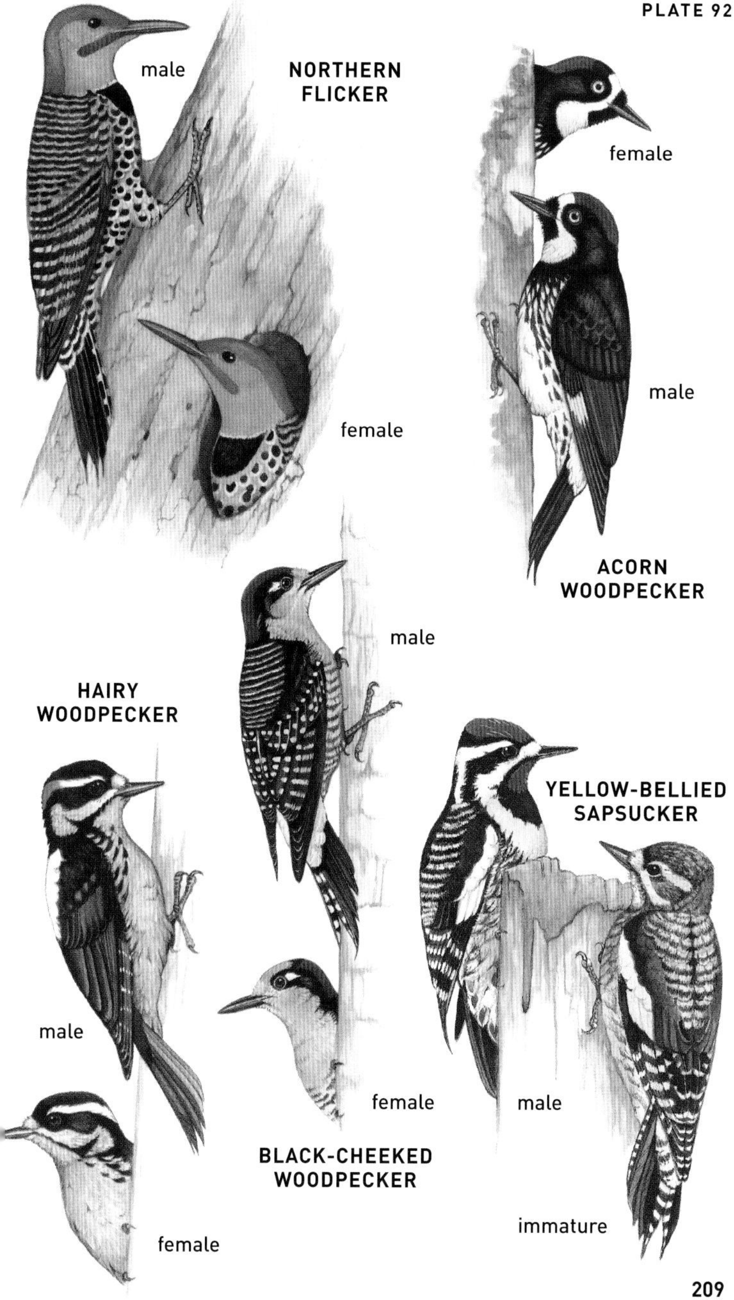
NORTHERN FLICKER
male
female
ACORN WOODPECKER
female
male
HAIRY WOODPECKER
male
female
BLACK-CHEEKED WOODPECKER
male
female
YELLOW-BELLIED SAPSUCKER
male
immature

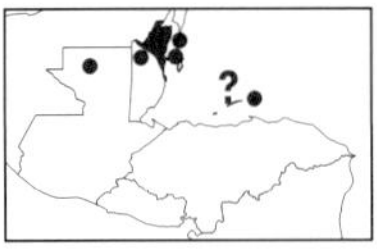

YUCATAN WOODPECKER *Melanerpes pygmaeus*

6.5 in. (17 cm). Back with **even black-and-white barring**; face and underparts grayish, **but both sexes show yellow forehead**; vent red; flanks and undertail coverts with faint black barring. Male has red crown and nape; female has red nape only. Distinguished from Golden-fronted Woodpecker by smaller size, shorter bill, **short tail**, and yellow forehead. Fairly common in n. Belize and on Guanaja I. (rare on other Bay Is. of Honduras); to 1,000 ft. (300 m). Found in disturbed habitat, rainforest, and pine-oak forest. Call is a loud nasal *kehr-r-r-r*, repeated about 5 times (similar to Black-cheeked Woodpecker, but slower and lower in pitch); also an agitated *cheh-rrr-rrr-rrr-rrr*. Endemic to the region.

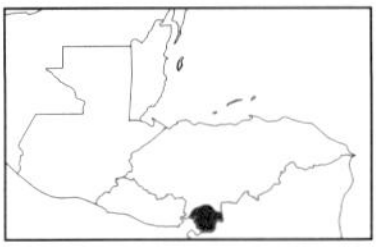

HOFFMANN'S WOODPECKER *Melanerpes hoffmannii*

8 in. (20 cm). Back and wings with **even black-and-white barring**; nape and forehead yellow; vent washed yellow. Both sexes distinguished from Golden-fronted Woodpecker by yellow nape, and in male, **red crown does not connect to yellow nape**. Fairly common in s. Honduras; to 4,100 ft. (1,250 m). Found in disturbed habitat and at edge of thorn forest and semideciduous forest. Call is a whiny, high-pitched *ehh-h-h-h*, repeated 5 or 6 times; also makes a long chattering *che'he'he'he'he'he'he'he*. Drums at about 10 taps per sec. Hybrids of Hoffmann's and Golden-fronted Woodpecker have been reported around the El Salvador–Honduras border and near the Nacaome River (Valle, Honduras). Honduras to Costa Rica.

GOLDEN-FRONTED WOODPECKER *Melanerpes aurifrons*

9.5 in. (24 cm). Two subspecies groups identified in NCA: *santacruzi* (interior highlands and Pacific Slope) and *dubius* (n. Guatemala, Belize, and the Bay Is.). Both subspecies show black-and-white barring above (**black bars are wider**), and dingy face and underparts. On *santacruzi*, **forehead and vent yellow**; lower nape red to yellowish orange, **upper nape red to orange red**; on male, nape joins **bright red crown**; on female, crown grayish. Similar Hoffmann's Woodpecker has all-yellow nape. On *dubius*, both sexes show **forehead, nape, and vent red**; on male, crown bright red; on female, crown grayish. Similar Yucatan Woodpecker is much smaller and has yellow forehead and shorter bill. Common up to 4,270 ft. (1,300 m), rare to 6,230 ft. (1,900 m). Found in open woodlands, including thorn forest, semideciduous forest, and pine savanna; also occurs in towns. Call is a loud, slightly nasal *che'e'e'e*, repeated 3 to 5 times; also makes a lower-pitched *che-huh*. Hybridizes with Hoffmann's where ranges meet in s. Honduras. Some authors treat all NCA subspecies as a separate species, Velásquez's Woodpecker (*M. santacruzi*). U.S. to Nicaragua.

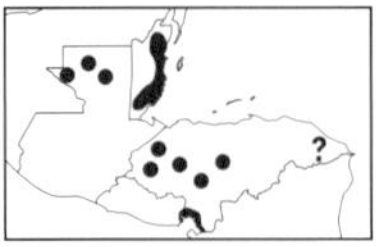

LADDER-BACKED WOODPECKER *Picoides scalaris*

7 in. (18 cm). On male, **crown is red**; bold **black postocular line connects to malar stripe behind auriculars**; underparts white with **black spotting on sides of upper chest** and barring on flanks. Female similar, but crown is black. Very local in NCA: fairly common around the Gulf of Fonseca; uncommon in Belize; rare in Guatemala; to 5,910 ft. (1,800 m). Found in thorn forest, pine savanna and pine-oak forest, and mangroves (Gulf of Fonseca). Call is sharp *pick!* (similar to call of Smoky-brown Woodpecker [p. 212]); also makes a fast rattling that drops in pitch at the end. U.S. to Nicaragua.

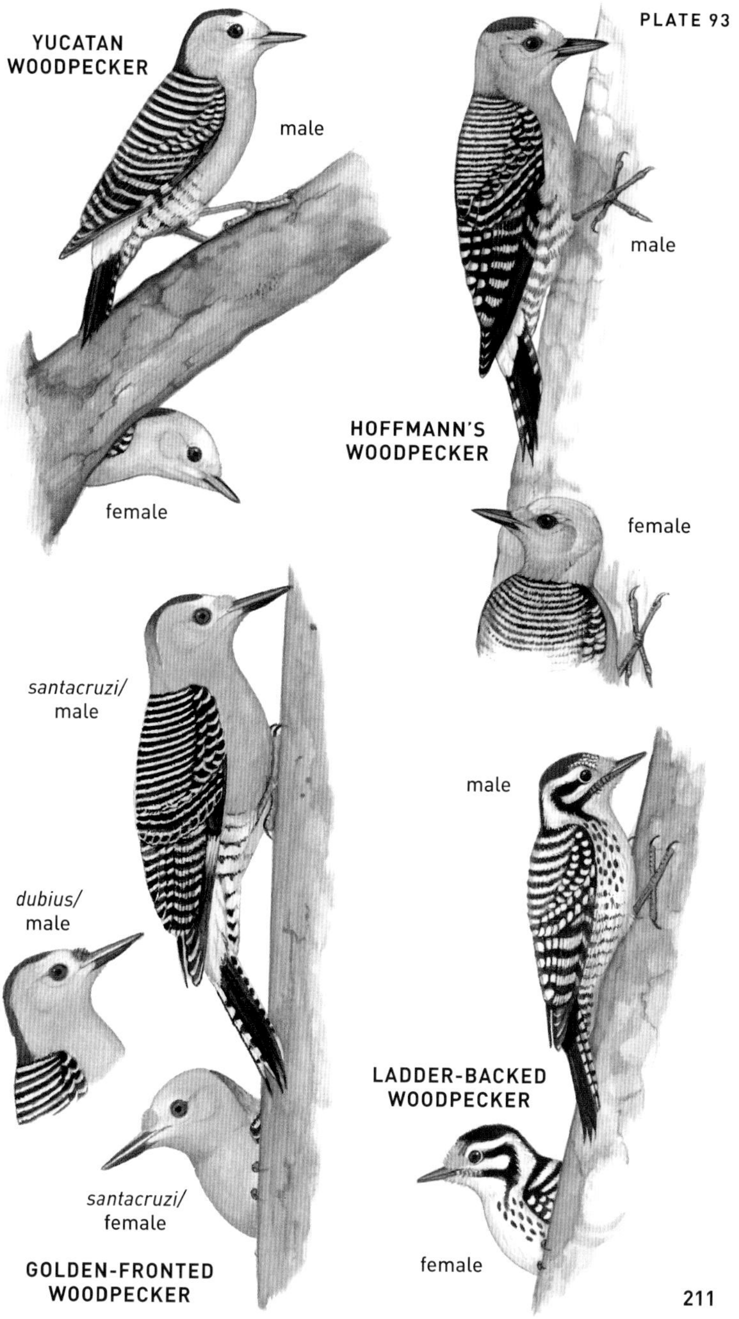
YUCATAN WOODPECKER
male
female
HOFFMANN'S WOODPECKER
male
female
santacruzi/ male
dubius/ male
santacruzi/ female
GOLDEN-FRONTED WOODPECKER
male
female
LADDER-BACKED WOODPECKER

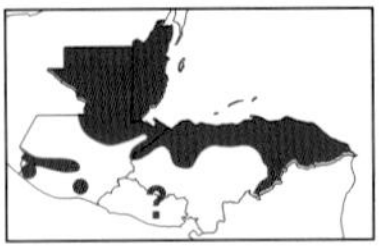

SMOKY-BROWN WOODPECKER *Picoides fumigatus*

6 in. (15 cm). A **small woodpecker**; **olive-brown overall**; male has red crown. Somewhat similar to Rufous-winged Woodpecker, but lacks red malar stripe (in males) and pale eyes. Fairly common on Caribbean Slope, uncommon on Pacific Slope of Guatemala, rare (possibly extirpated) in El Salvador; to 3,940 ft. (1,200 m). Found in taller semideciduous forest, rainforest, riparian forest, and coffee plantations; forages at all levels. Call is a *pick!* (similar to call of Ladder-backed Woodpecker [p. 210], but note differences in habitat); frequently makes a rattling *pic—wrr'wrr'wrr'wrr'wrr'wrr'wrr'wrr'wrr*; drum is a 1-sec. series of rapid heavy taps (machine gun–like). Mex. to Argentina.

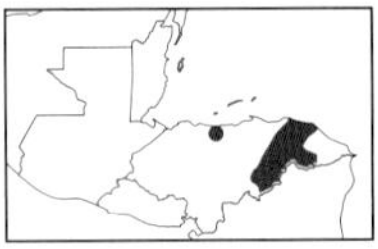

RUFOUS-WINGED WOODPECKER *Piculus simplex*

7.5 in. (19 cm). Olive-yellow upperparts and wing (rufous edging may be visible on folded wing); buffy underparts with olive barring; **bill pale**; **eyes pale blue**. Male has **red crown, nape, and malar stripe**; on female, only rear crown and nape are red. Similar to Smoky-brown Woodpecker (above), but has red malar stripe (in males) and pale blue eyes. Also similar to the larger Golden-olive Woodpecker (below), but that species has gray forecrown, black-and-white stippling on throat, dark eyes, and darker bill. Rare on Caribbean Slope of Honduras (nearly extirpated on north coast where few recent records); up to 1,310 ft. (400 m). Found in rainforest. Call is a drawn-out *keeahh* (similar to Brown Jay, p. 292); young in cavity make an agitated rattling *tek-tek-tek-tek-tek-tek-ke-ke-ke-ke* . . . Honduras to Panama.

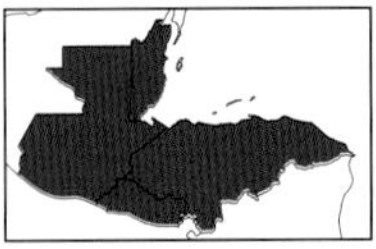

GOLDEN-OLIVE WOODPECKER *Colaptes rubiginosus*

8.5 in. (22 cm). Upperparts and wing olive-yellow; **face dingy white**; throat stippled black; buffy underparts with heavy olive barring; **eyes dark**; bill dark. On male, note red nape and malar stripe; **crown gray bordered below in red**. On female, red rear crown and nape only. Similar to the smaller Rufous-winged Woodpecker, but that species has red forecrown (males) and pale bill and eyes. Common in NCA on both slopes; to 7,380 ft. (2,250 m). Found in wooded and open areas, including semideciduous forest, thorn forest, pine-oak forest, disturbed habitat, coffee plantations, mangroves, and urban gardens. Frequently heard call is a single *k'yaah!* (similar to Great Kiskadee, p. 268); also makes a trill that lasts about 2 sec. (*pier'r'r'r'r'r'r'r'r'r'r'r'r*); drum is a quick series of hollow taps. Mex. to Argentina.

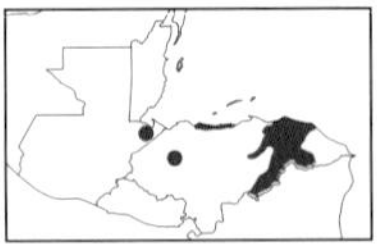

OLIVACEOUS PICULET *Picumnus olivaceus*

4 in. (10 cm). **A tiny woodpecker**; note **short tail** and **small wedge-shaped bill**. Both sexes show black crown with **white spotting**; male has red forecrown. Uncommon to fairly common on Caribbean Slope; to 2,460 ft. (750 m). Forages at lower and middle levels in rainforest; clings to small branches and vines. Long call is a rattling *tsuueew'w'w'w'w'w* that rises in pitch initially, then descends toward the end; call is a sharp *tsit*. Guatemala to Ecuador.

male
female
SMOKY-BROWN
WOODPECKER
male
RUFOUS-WINGED
WOODPECKER
female
female
male
GOLDEN-OLIVE
WOODPECKER
female
male
OLIVACEOUS
PICULET

FALCONS I

FALCONIDAE (Order: Falconiformes). Falcons (genus *Falco*) are open-country predators that use their sharp talons and powerfully fast flying to catch birds and large insects. Falcons are the fastest birds in the world; the Peregrine Falcon has been clocked at over 200 mph. Forest-falcons (*Micrastur*), found in woodland interiors, have rounded wings for maneuvering between branches and long legs for grasping prey. Caracaras are birds of open country. They eat carrion, among other prey items, and often walk or run on the ground. Caracaras form socially cooperative groups. For many species, females are larger than males. **12 species (6 genera)**

APLOMADO FALCON *Falco femoralis*

16.5 in. (42 cm). A large falcon; **distinctly patterned**. Uncommon in Belize; rare in Honduras; vagrant elsewhere in NCA; to 3,610 ft. (1,100 m). Found in semiopen country with scattered bushes and trees, savanna grasslands, and pine savanna. Perches on fenceposts and power poles. Feeds on a variety of prey items, but mostly birds and large insects. Calls include a sharp, piping *kek!* U.S. to Argentina.

BAT FALCON *Falco rufigularis*

10 in. (26 cm). A small falcon. **Dark head** contrasts with **buffy white collar**; chest dark steely gray with thin white barring; remaining underparts tawny-chestnut. Juvenile warmer cinnamon below with undertail coverts barred black. Juvenile similar to Orange-breasted Falcon, but much smaller in size with only light wash of tawny-chestnut on chest and sides of neck. Fairly common in most of region, including Bay Is., but rare on Pacific Slope; to 5,280 ft. (1,600 m). Found at edge of semideciduous forest, mangroves, and rainforest; also in secondary forest and plantations. Perches at mid- to upper levels conspicuously on snags and manmade towers. Solitary or in pairs. Crepuscular; hunts bats, small birds, and large insects. Flight is fast and direct. Calls include a thin, high-pitched *kee-kee-kee-kee-kee-kee-kee* . . . Mex. to Argentina.

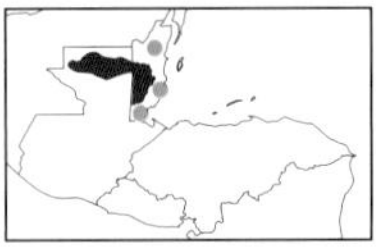

ORANGE-BREASTED FALCON *Falco deiroleucus*

13.5 in. (34 cm). Similar to juvenile Bat Falcon, but much larger and darker overall; shows extensive **tawny-chestnut on collar**. **Very large feet.** Rare and local in Guatemala and Belize; to 4,920 ft. (1,500 m). Found at edge of rainforest and in pine savanna. Eyries are located on large cliff faces, tall rocky limestone outcroppings, and Mayan temples. Perches at upper levels often on exposed branch or snag. Solitary or in pairs. Hunts mainly birds. Flight is powerful and direct (recalling Peregrine Falcon). Calls include a raspy, nasal high-pitched *Kek!-Kek!-Kek!-Kek!-Kek!-Kek!-Kek!-Kek!* (not as thin as Bat Falcon's). Mex. to Argentina.

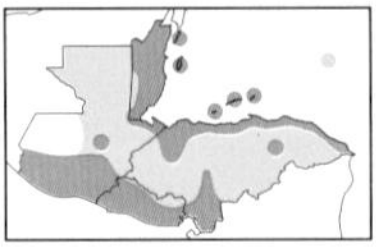

PEREGRINE FALCON *Falco peregrinus*

18 in. (46 cm). **A large falcon.** Note **bold "teardrop" on face** contrasting with whitish neck; **underparts are thinly barred**. Juvenile dark brown overall with heavy dark streaking below. Flight is strong, powerful, and direct. Uncommon transient and winter visitor to region, including islands (late Sept.–mid-May); occasionally summers and bred in Guatemala City in 2015; to 8,200 ft. (2,500 m). Found primarily in coastal areas; frequently near water. Perches at mid- to upper levels on exposed limbs, snags, or on top of telephone poles and cell phone towers. Also perches on window ledges of tall buildings in cities, where it feeds on Rock Pigeons (p. 46). Solitary. Feeds mainly on birds. Generally silent in NCA. Cosmopolitan.

Bat Falcon
perched
above forest
BAT
FALCON
APLOMADO
FALCON
PEREGRINE
FALCON
ORANGE-BREASTED
FALCON
immature
adult

AMERICAN KESTREL *Falco sparverius*

11 in. (28 cm). Two resident subspecies (*tropicalis* and *nicaraguensis*) and migrant/winter visitors. In general, a small falcon; adult male has **rufous upperparts contrasting with bluish wings**; note **2 dark slashes on face**; tawny underparts with heavy black spotting; in flight, **rufous tail has broad black subterminal band**. Male *tropicalis* (NCA highlands) and *nicaraguensis* (e. Honduras) are smaller than northern populations, have little or no rufous in crown, and underparts of male are more whitish, less marked on chest. Female has **rufous wings with heavy black barring** (more slaty blue in *nicaraguensis*) and are **heavily streaked below on chest and sides**; also, in flight, tail is paler rufous with **multiple thin dark bands**. Uncommon transient and winter visitor to both slopes and Bay and Swan Is. (mid-Sept.–early Apr.); uncommon to fairly common resident in region; to 10,990 ft. (3,350 m). Found in semiopen country with scattered trees and bushes. Breeds in pine savanna. Forages at all levels. Often perches on telephone poles or on wires. Preys on small reptiles, amphibians, birds, mammals, and also large insects. Generally solitary or in pairs. Call is a shrill *Klee!-Klee!-Klee!-Klee!* . . . AK to Argentina.

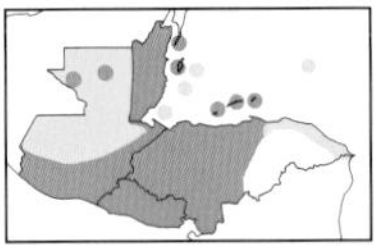

MERLIN *Falco columbarius*

12 in. (31 cm). Two subspecies winter in NCA. *F.c. columbarius* (Taiga Merlin) is **steely gray above** with **well-marked face** showing dark eye line and single black slash below eye; **underparts heavily streaked with brown**. *F.c. richardsoni* (Prairie Merlin, not illustrated) has **softer gray upperparts**, is much paler below, and has **paler, nearly unmarked face**. In flight, both subspecies have dark tails with 5 to 6 thin white bands. Females and immatures have brown to dark brown upperparts. Taiga Merlin uncommon to fairly common transient and winter visitor throughout NCA (mid-Sept.–early May); to 6,890 ft. (2,100 m). Prairie Merlin rare winter visitor to NCA; has been found inland to 5,600 ft. (1,700 m). Perches in open on tops of telephone polls and fenceposts. Solitary. Generally silent. AK (breeding) to Peru (winter).

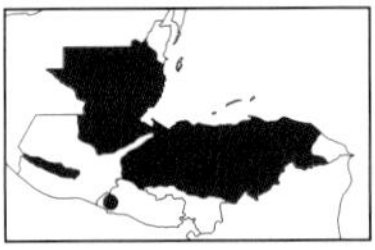

BARRED FOREST-FALCON *Micrastur ruficollis*

14 in. (36 cm). Adult **white below with thin gray barring**; tail is long with 3 to 4 thin white bands; note **bare yellowish orange area around eyes and lores**; **eyes pale yellow**. Immature brownish above with whitish collar; various amounts of dark barring below; eyes dark. Immature similar to immature Collared Forest-Falcon, but smaller, with less barring below. Uncommon to fairly common in NCA; to 8,530 ft. (2,600 m). Found in interior of mature woodlands. Secretive and difficult to observe. Call (often given at dawn or dusk) is a steady nasal, barking *koaw-koaw-koaw-koaw-koaw-koaw-koaw* . . . ; also an agitated *koawp!—koawp'kaow'kaow'kaow-kaow'kaow-kaowp*. Mex. to Argentina.

COLLARED FOREST-FALCON *Micrastur semitorquatus*

21.5 in. (55 cm). Adult dark sooty brown or blackish above with **contrasting white collar and dark slash across face**; underparts white (to buffy or rarely black); tail with 4 to 5 white bands; also note **bare yellow-green area around eyes and lores**; **eyes dark**. Immature larger than immature Barred Forest-Falcon, more barring below, and with darker eyes. Immature possibly confused with Hook-billed Kite (p. 166), but note longer tail with thin white bands, much longer legs, dark eye (adult Hook-billed has pale eye), also lacks colorful bare crescent in front of eye. Fairly common in NCA; to 6,560 ft. (2,000 m). Found in a variety of woodland habitats. Perches quietly at mid- to upper levels. Preys on snakes and small birds. Call is a far-carrying, patiently delivered, mournful *KAH!—KAH!—KAH!—KAH!—KAH!*; also a climaxing *Howh!-Howh!-Howh!-Howh!'Howh!'Howh!'Howh!-Hoooowh!-Hoooowh-Hoooooowh*. Mex. to Argentina.

male in flight
male
female
AMERICAN KESTREL
male in flight
MERLIN
male
female/immature
BARRED FOREST-FALCON
adult
immature
adults
COLLARED FOREST-FALCON
immature

LAUGHING FALCON *Herpetotheres cachinnans*
20 in. (51 cm). Distinctive appearance; note large creamy buff head with **black "bandito" mask**. Uncommon to fairly common in NCA; to 5,910 ft. (1,800 m). Found at edge in a variety of semiopen woodlands: semideciduous forest, disturbed habitat, pine savanna, mangroves, and at edge of rainforest. Perches in open on tops of trees. Hunts snakes; frequently seen in flight carrying snake in talons. Often heard calling. Call is a loud, laughing cackle, slow to start, but building in volume and pace, *wok—wok—wok—Wok-Wok-Wok-WOK!-WOK!-WOK!-WOK!-WOK!-WOK!-WOK!-* . . . or a 2-part *WOK'COW!* (pairs may call together in duet). Mex. to Argentina.

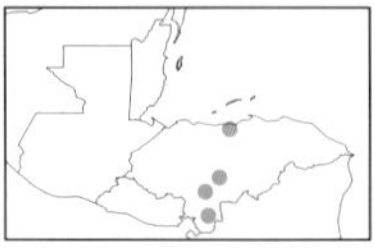

YELLOW-HEADED CARACARA *Milvago chimachima*
17.5 in. (45 cm). On adult, note broad dark postocular stripe; **neck and head, including underparts, buffy white**; upperparts, including wing and tail, dark brown (tail with multiple whitish bands near base). Facial skin yellow. Juvenile buffy brown with dark streaking on head and underparts. Recent visitor to Honduras and expanding in s. Central America; should be watched for throughout NCA, to 6,890 ft. (2,100 m). Found in open habitats often near water. Solitary or in small groups. Often perches on tops of fenceposts or feeds on ground. Call is a raspy, high-pitched *Pyeeer!* (though generally silent). Honduras to Bolivia.

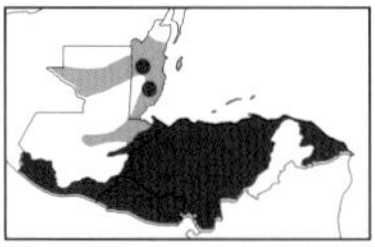

CRESTED CARACARA *Caracara cheriway*
21.5 in. (55 cm). On adult, **blackish brown crown** contrasts with **whitish neck and chest**; in flight, upperwing shows white base to primaries and base of tail; **base of bill and facial skin near eye is bright orange**. Juvenile buffy white with heavy brown streaking on foreneck and chest. Uncommon to fairly common in NCA; to 6,560 ft. (2,000 m). Found in open to semiopen habitat: agricultural fields or plantations with scattered bushes, disturbed habitat, and thorn forest; also along highways in forested regions, where it scavenges on roadkill. Solitary or in pairs during the day, but forms nighttime roosts of dozens of birds. Feeds on carrion, including bones. Often perches on tops of fenceposts or feeds on ground. Mostly silent. U.S. to Brazil.

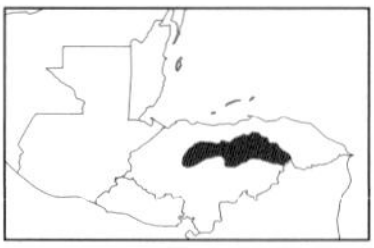

RED-THROATED CARACARA *Ibycter americanus*
23 in. (59 cm). **Distinctive black-and-white plumage** and **bare reddish face, gular, and legs**. Rare and local (declining) in Honduras; extirpated from Guatemalan Pacific lowlands; from 1,640 to 3,280 ft. (500–1,000 m). Found at edge of rainforest and in pine savanna. Flies with slow, deep wingbeats; often in pairs or small groups. Gregarious and noisy. Feeds on wasp larvae, which it extracts from hives. Calls include loud, throaty, raucous screams, *Graaaah!-Graaaah!-Graaaah!'Graaaah!'Graaaah!*; also a *Kek'Kek'Kek-kow!* or *Kek'cow!* or *Cacao!* Honduras to Brazil; extirpated from Guatemala and Mex.

LAUGHING
FALCON
YELLOW-HEADED
CARACARA
immature
adult
CRESTED
CARACARA
immature
adult
RED-THROATED
CARACARA

SMALL AND MEDIUM PARROTS

PSITTACIDAE (Order: Psittaciformes). This group includes the large, long-tailed macaws; the square-tailed parrots; and the smaller parakeets, with their notably pointed wings and tails. Their feet are zygodactyl (2 toes forward and 2 point backward), which makes it easy for them to grip branches while also holding the fruits, nuts, and seeds they feed on. In the wild, their vocalizations consist of loud shrieks, raucous calls, and babylike wails. These species are long-lived and highly intelligent. **16 species (8 genera)**

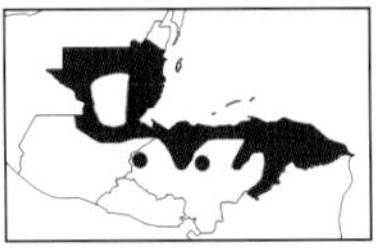

BROWN-HOODED PARROT *Pyrilia haematotis*

8.5 in. (22 cm). **Dark brown throat and cheeks and red ear patch are distinctive**; in flight, note bluish underwing and **red axillaries**. Common in Belize and n. Guatemala, uncommon on Caribbean Slope of Honduras; to 3,940 ft. (1,200 m). Found in rainforest; generally in small flocks (fewer than 15 individuals). Call is a harsh, scratchy, 2-part *kah'rack!* (similar to White-crowned Parrot, but harsher with less metallic quality); also makes a thin *kah'reeet* or *kreeet*. Mex. to Colombia.

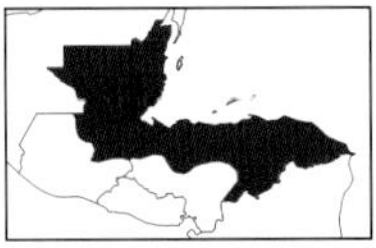

WHITE-CROWNED PARROT *Pionus senilis*

9.5 in. (24 cm). Mainly **blue head** with large **white forecrown** and white throat (not always visible); orbital skin pinkish white; note golden wing patch and **red undertail coverts**. Common on Caribbean Slope; to 6,560 ft. (2,000 m). Found in rainforest and riparian forest; generally in small flocks. Note deep wingbeats characteristic of *Pionus* parrots. Call is a loud, scratchy *kah'rat!* (similar to Brown-hooded Parrot, but less harsh with a more metallic quality); also makes a thin *kreeet!*; also in flight a raucous *kek'kek'kek'kek* . . . Mex. to Panama.

WHITE-FRONTED PARROT *Amazona albifrons*

9.5 in. (24 cm). **White forecrown** and **extensive red around eye**; bill mainly yellow; in flight, male shows red patch in outer wing (absent on female); female has less white in forecrown. Similar to Yellow-lored Parrot (ranges overlap in n. Guatemala and Belize), but White-fronted has red lores and lacks dark ear patch. Common on Caribbean Slope, local and declining on Pacific Slope; to 6,070 ft. (1,850 m). Found at edge of rainforest and semideciduous forest; also occurs in thorn forest, pine savanna, mangroves, and near agricultural fields. Often in medium to large flocks. Calls include a thin *keeat-keeat!* and a harsher *raaa'ke-ke-ke-ke!* Mex. to Costa Rica.

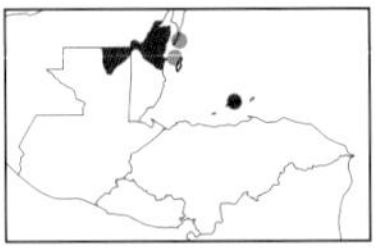

YELLOW-LORED PARROT *Amazona xantholora*

10.5 in. (27 cm). Respective sexes similar to White-fronted Parrot, but note **yellow lores** (more obvious in male), **dark ear patch** (darker in male), and often has red at bend of wing; female differs from male by absence of white forecrown and red in wing. Common in n. Belize, rare to uncommon in n. Guatemala (Petén); rare on Roatán (Bay Is.); to 820 ft. (250 m). Found at rainforest edge, in mangroves, and in disturbed habitat and savannas. Solitary or in large flocks. Calls like White-fronted Parrot. Endemic to region.

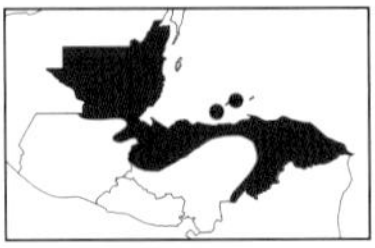

RED-LORED PARROT *Amazona autumnalis*

13.5 in. (34 cm). The only NCA parrot with **yellow cheeks** and **red lores**. Common on Caribbean Slope; to 3,610 ft. (1,100 m). Found at rainforest edge, and in disturbed habitat, plantations, mangroves, and pine savannas. Escaped individuals or pairs may be found in large cities outside the normal range, such as San Salvador. Flight is direct with shallow wingbeats; normally found in pairs. Call is a 2-part *peet-krahk!* (first syllable thin, second syllable harsh), often given in flight; perched call is a loud, throaty *Ra'a'a'ck!* Mex. to Brazil.

BROWN-HOODED PARROT
note deep wingbeats of Pionus
WHITE-CROWNED PARROT
WHITE-FRONTED PARROT
male
note shallow wingbeats of Amazona
male
male in flight
female/immature
YELLOW-LORED PARROT
RED-LORED PARROT

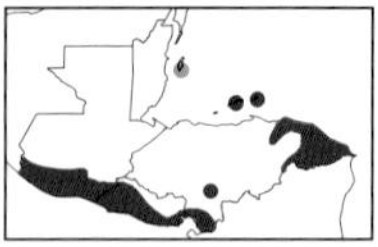

YELLOW-NAPED PARROT *Amazona auropalliata*

14.5 in. (37 cm). The nominate subspecies (*A.a. auropalliata*; Pacific Slope) is similar to Yellow-headed Parrot, but has **yellow nape** (may also show small yellow patch just above bill) and **lacks red at bend of wing; bill steely gray**. Individuals on Bay Is. (*caribaea*) and individuals of e. Honduras (*parvipes*) have head pattern of Yellow-naped, but red shoulders like Yellow-headed Parrot. Some have yellowish bills like Yellow-headed Parrot and others have grayish bills like *auropalliata*. Further study is needed to determine the taxonomic affinities of these populations. Uncommon and local on Pacific Slope; to 2,460 ft. (750 m). Common in ne. Honduras; rare on Roatán, but common on Guanaja in Bay Is. Found in lowland coastal disturbed habitat, semideciduous and thorn forest, and mangroves. Solitary or in pairs. Calls similar to Yellow-headed Parrot's. Mex. to Costa Rica.

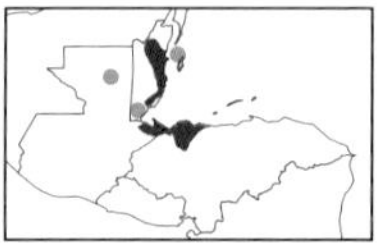

YELLOW-HEADED PARROT *Amazona oratrix*

14.5 in. (37 cm). Note **yellow on crown and eye area**, and **yellow flecking on nape** (yellow on head of immature more restricted); red at bend of wing; **yellow thighs; bill and cere pale pinkish to brown**. Individuals of the Sula Valley (*A.o. hondurensis*) have yellow restricted to napes and forecrown; their appearance is intermediate between Yellow-headed and Yellow-naped Parrot and very similar to *A. auropalliata caribaea* of the Bay Is.; further study is needed to determine the closest taxonomic affinities of the Sula Valley parrots, which, unfortunately, are close to extinction. Fairly common in Belize, rare in ne. Guatemala and extreme nw. Honduras; to 660 ft. (200 m). Found in pine savanna, mangroves, rainforest edge, thorn forest, and other open areas with some taller trees. Calls include babylike chatter and cries similar to calls of Yellow-naped Parrot. Mex. to Honduras.

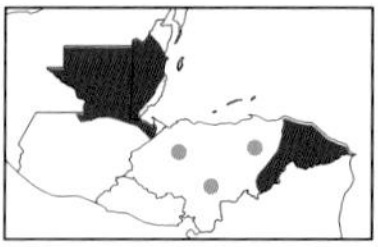

MEALY PARROT *Amazona farinosa*

16 in. (41 cm). **Scaly blue nape and crown**; broad white eyering. Uncommon on Caribbean Slope; to 3,940 ft. (1,200 m). Found in rainforest, riparian forest, disturbed habitat, and pine savanna; often seen perched in treetops. Found in pairs or large flocks. Call is a distinctive, squealing *chack!* or *chack-chack!*; also makes a shrieking *eeee'awwww!* Mex. to Brazil.

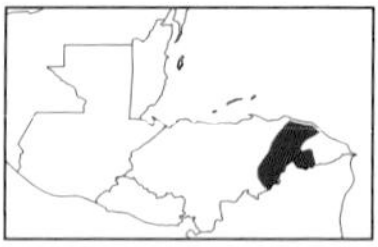

GREAT GREEN MACAW *Ara ambiguus*

33 in. (84 cm). Greenish overall with **bare pinkish face**; **forecrown red**; **tail mostly red**. Fairly common (but declining) in e. Honduras; to 2,460 ft. (750 m). Found in rainforest. Solitary or in pairs. Often heard before seen; call is a loud, harsh *wraaahh!* (similar to Scarlet Macaw). Honduras to Ecuador.

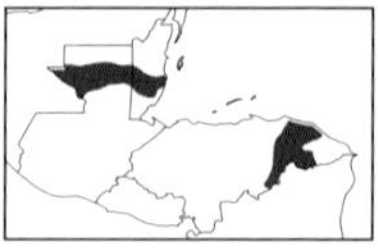

SCARLET MACAW *Ara macao*

35 in. (89 cm). Brilliant scarlet-red body with bright yellow and blue wings. Fairly common (but declining) in e. Honduras, rare in Belize and n. Guatemala (extirpated from Pacific Slope); reintroduced around Copán Ruins, Amapala Is. in s. Honduras, Barbareta in Bay Is., and a few other sites in the region; to 3,610 ft. (1,100 m). Found in rainforest, taller semideciduous forest, and pine savanna. Usually in pairs or small groups. Often heard before seen; call is a loud, harsh *wraaaahh!* (similar to Great Green Macaw). National bird of Honduras. Mex. to Brazil.

YELLOW-NAPED PARROT
YELLOW-HEADED PARROT
hondurensis
MEALY PARROT
GREAT GREEN MACAW
SCARLET MACAW

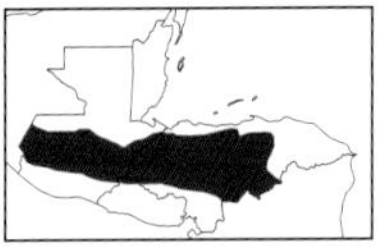

BARRED PARAKEET *Bolborhynchus lineola*

6.5 in. (17 cm). **Uniformly green** with fine black barring. Rare to uncommon in interior highlands; from 1,970 to 7,870 ft. (600–2,400 m). Found mostly in mature forest. Presence at lower elevations is erratic and may be seasonal. Pairs and sometimes large groups (fewer than 50 individuals) are generally seen in swift flight. Often heard before seen; call is a fairly distinctive, scratchy, thin *chirr'it* (numerous birds calling together can sound chirpy). Mex. to Peru.

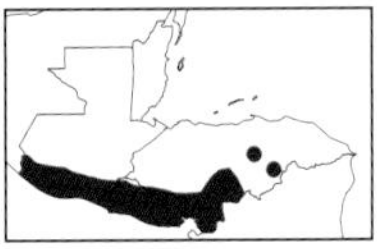

ORANGE-CHINNED PARAKEET *Brotogeris jugularis*

7 in. (18 cm). Note **orange-brown wing patch** on folded wing; **orange chin** can be difficult to see. Common on Pacific Slope (locally common on Caribbean Slope); to 4,920 ft. (1,500 m). Found in a variety of woodland types. Generally in pairs and small groups; flight is swift and direct with rapid wingbeats. Call is a thin, slightly whiny *kaa'reeet* (sometimes scratchy); perched call is a harsh *chet'chet'chet'chet* . . . Mex. to Venezuela.

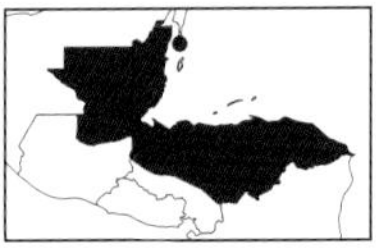

OLIVE-THROATED PARAKEET *Eupsittula nana*

9 in. (23 cm). Dark blue in wings; **golden olive throat and chest**. Common on Caribbean Slope; to 3,940 ft. (1,200 m). Found in rainforest, thorn forest, plantations, and open areas with some trees. Forms small flocks of 5 to 15 individuals. Call is a scratchy, high-pitched *keea-keea-keea-keea-* . . . ; also makes a whining *ehhhh-ehhhh* . . . and a *chet'chet'chet'chet* (some calls are similar to Orange-chinned Parakeet). Mex. to Panama; also in the Caribbean.

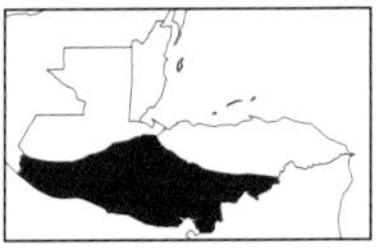

ORANGE-FRONTED PARAKEET *Eupsittula canicularis*

9.5 in. (24 cm). The Pacific Slope counterpart of Olive-throated Parakeet. Note **blue crown** and **orange forecrown**. Common on Pacific Slope; to 4,920 ft. (1,500 m). Found in a variety of open woodlands. Forms small flocks of 5 to 15 individuals, and roosts of several hundred birds. Calls include a scratchy, high-pitched *keea'ah!-keea'ah!* and a lower *keh'keh'keh'keh'keh*; also makes a whining *ehhhhh*. Mex. to Costa Rica.

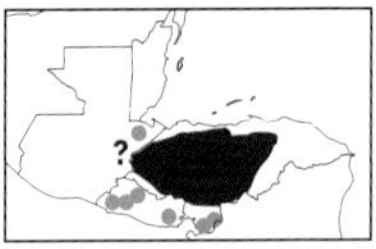

RED-THROATED PARAKEET *Psittacara rubritorquis*

11 in. (28 cm). Variable amounts of **orange-red on throat and upper chest** (absent on some juveniles). Uncommon on both slopes from e. Guatemala to n.-cen. Nicaragua; nonbreeding individuals disperse from highlands to lowland coastal areas; to 8,530 ft. (2,600 m). Found in a variety of woodlands; also cities and towns. Flocks may include more than 100 individuals; in El Salvador, forms large roosts with Pacific Parakeets, but the species remain segregated. Calls are very similar to Pacific Parakeet, but higher pitched. Endemic to region. Sometimes considered conspecific with **Green Parakeet** (*Psittacara holochlorus*) of Mexico.

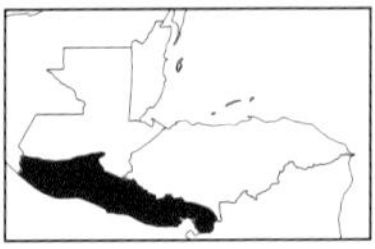

PACIFIC PARAKEET *Psittacara strenuus*

12.5 in. (32 cm). A **large green parakeet** with **horn-colored bill**; a few show small red flecks on neck. Fairly common on Pacific Slope; to 5,910 ft. (1,800 m). Found in all forest types and plantations, as well as in urban parks and gardens. Flocks may include more than 100 individuals. Perched calls include a scratchy *kreeh-kreeh-kreeh-kreeh-kreeei-kreeei* (very similar to Red-throated Parakeet, but lower pitched); in flight, makes a thinner, higher-pitched *kreh!—kreh!—kreh!—kreh!* . . . Endemic to region.

ORANGE-CHINNED PARAKEET
BARRED PARAKEET
OLIVE-THROATED PARAKEET
ORANGE-FRONTED PARAKEET
PACIFIC PARAKEET
juvenile
adult
RED-THROATED PARAKEET

ANTSHRIKES

THAMNOPHILIDAE (Order: Passeriformes). This is a diverse group of small to medium-sized passerines with stout, hooked bills. The antshrikes prefer scrubby edge habitat. Antwrens and antbirds are found in the humid forest interior, often associating with mixed-species flocks or following army ant swarms. **18 species (15 genera)**

FASCIATED ANTSHRIKE *Cymbilaimus lineatus*

7 in. (18 cm). Male with **black-and-white barring** (white barring thinner than black); **crown blackish**; red eyes. Female similarly patterned, but washed tawny and has rufous crown. Rare to uncommon in e. Honduras; to 1,320 ft. (400 m). Found in low scrubby vegetation at edge of disturbed habitat or rainforest. Secretive in movements and difficult to observe. Call is a series of 4 to 5 somewhat sharp, low mournful whistles, *Wheuuu—Wreee-Wreee-Wreee-Wreeeu*. Honduras to Brazil.

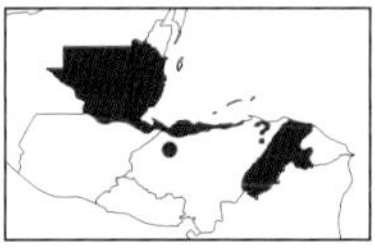

GREAT ANTSHRIKE *Taraba major*

8 in. (20 cm). A large antshrike: male is strikingly patterned in **black upperparts and white underparts**; eyes red. Female similarly patterned, but **rufous above**. Uncommon and local on Caribbean Slope; to 2,475 ft. (750 m). Found at edge in a variety of scrubby disturbed habitat or at edge of rainforest. Secretive, but often detected by voice. Calls include long series of whistled barks, dropping in end like a bouncing ball (lasting about 4.5 sec.; longer, slower, and lower-pitched than call of Barred Antshrike); also a low, long growl, *grrra'a'a'a'a'a!* (this call may directly follow the long call). An outlying population in mountains along the Nicaraguan border, discovered only in 2013 and still under study, is all-black (all rufous-brown in female). Mex. to Uruguay.

BARRED ANTSHRIKE *Thamnophilus doliatus*

6.5 in. (17 cm). Male **barred black and white overall**; **shaggy crest** black with white base. Female has unbarred **rufous upperparts**, tawny underparts, with black-and-white streaking on face; eyes in both sexes yellow. Fairly common in NCA on both slopes; to 5,910 ft. (1,800 m). Found at edge in a variety of disturbed habitats and second-growth vegetation. Somewhat secretive, but more confiding than other antshrikes; often detected by voice. Long call (from both sexes) is an accelerating series of nasal barked whistles ending with a sharp inflection, *wha-wha-Wha-WHA-WHA-WHA-WHA'WHA'WHA'WHA'WHA'WHA-WRAY!* (lasting about 3.5 sec.); long call is shorter, faster, and higher-pitched than Great Antshrike and also with hard inflection at end; long call is most similar to call of Black-crowned Antshrike (p. 228), but longer and accelerating with a harder inflection at end. Mex. to Argentina.

FASCIATED ANTSHRIKE

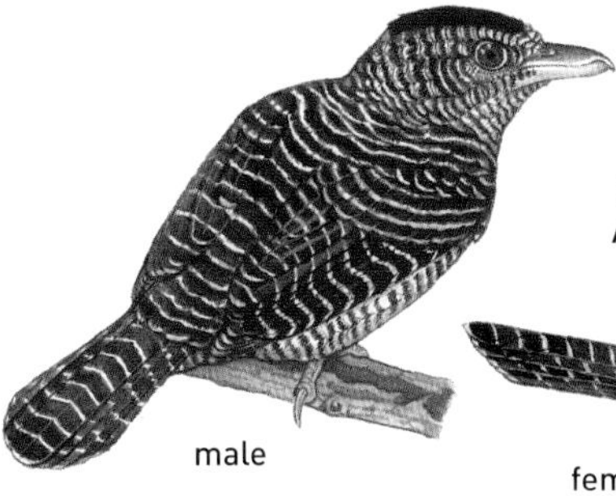

male

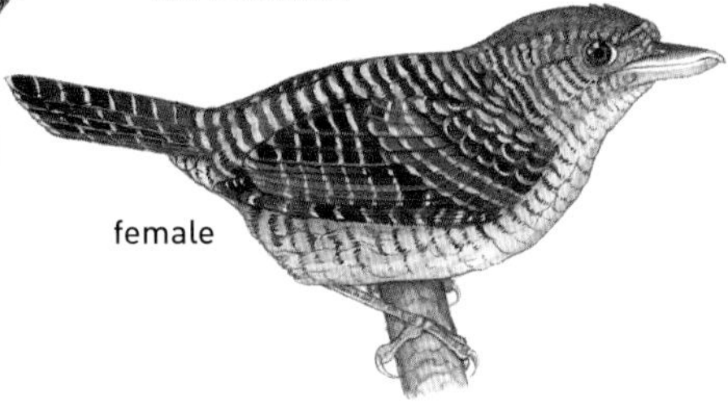

female

GREAT ANTSHRIKE

male

female

BARRED ANTSHRIKE

male

female

MORE ANTSHRIKES AND ANTVIREOS

BLACK-CROWNED ANTSHRIKE *Thamnophilus atrinucha*
6 in. (15 cm). Male **grayish overall with black crown**; blackish wings with **white spotting (forms 2 broken wing bars)**; scapulars also lightly edged with white; concealed white back patch is displayed in courtship or aggression; female similarly patterned but **tawny-brown overall**. Uncommon to fairly common and local on Caribbean Slope; to 1,640 ft. (500 m). Found in rainforest and semideciduous forest. At edge or interior, but arboreal and generally forages at mid- to upper levels. Call is similar to Barred Antshrike, but shorter, less accelerated, more strident with a softer inflection at end, *wha-wha-wha-Wha-Wha-Wha-Wha-Wha-Wha-Wha-Wha-Wha-Wray!* (lasting about 2.5 sec.). NCA to Ecuador.

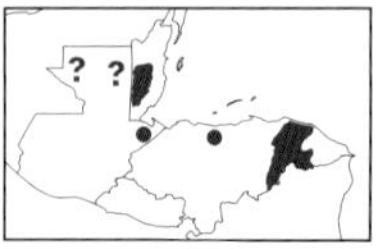

RUSSET ANTSHRIKE *Thamnistes anabatinus*
6 in. (15 cm). Sexes similar; rusty brown overall with paler tawny face and **obvious darker eye line**; fairly heavy, hooked bill. Uncommon and local on Caribbean Slope; to 1,320 ft. (400 m). Found in rainforest and semideciduous forest. Arboreal; forages at mid- to upper levels; often associates with mixed-species flocks. Call is a series of similar thin high-pitched whistles, *Tzeeeuuuuu-tseuu'tseuu'tseuu*. Mex. to Bolivia.

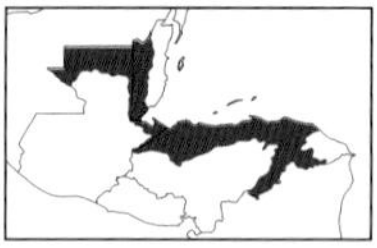

PLAIN ANTVIREO *Dysithamnus mentalis*
4.5 in. (11 cm). Small and chunky; male dark gray overall with yellowish wash to paler underparts; **blackish auriculars**; 2 thin wing bars. Female tawny-brown above with **rufous cap** and **white eye-ring**. Uncommon on Caribbean Slope; to 4,920 ft. (1,500 m). Found in interior of rainforest. Forages at low to midlevels; often in pairs; may associate with mixed-species flocks. Sluggish movement. Male gives a longer nasal barking series (similar in quality to Great Antshrike, but faster, shorter, and accelerating), *weu-weu-weu-Weu-Weu-Weu-Weu-Weu'weu'weu'weu'u'u'u* (lasting about 3 sec.); also female gives a single soft bark, *aarf!* Mex. to Argentina.

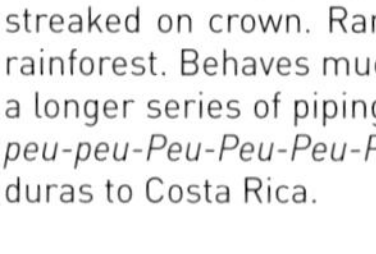

STREAK-CROWNED ANTVIREO *Dysithamnus striaticeps*
4 in. (10 cm). Small and chunky; male has olive-brown upperparts; paler below with **heavy gray streaking on chest and sides**; note **coarse dark spotting or streaking on crown**; 2 thin spotted wing bars. Female patterned similarly to male, but brown above with **tawny underparts** and **rufous cap**. Female similar to female Checker-throated Antwren (p. 230), but has streaks on chest and lightly streaked on crown. Rare to uncommon in e. Honduras; to 1,310 ft. (400 m). Found in rainforest. Behaves much like Plain Antvireo. Forages at low to midlevels. Calls include a longer series of piping, similar high-pitched whistled barks, accelerating at end, *peu-peu-peu-Peu-Peu-Peu-Pip-Pip-Pip-Pip'Pip'Pip'Pip'Pip'peu* (lasting approx. 4 sec.). Honduras to Costa Rica.

BLACK-CROWNED
ANTSHRIKE
male
female
RUSSET
ANTSHRIKE
female
male
PLAIN
ANTVIREO
male
STREAK-CROWNED
ANTVIREO
female

CHECKER-THROATED ANTWREN *Epinecrophylla fulviventris*
4.5 in. (11 cm). Male olive-brown above with **whitish or buffy cinnamon spotting on wing coverts**; below note **black throat with white spotting** (sometimes difficult to see in poor light); tawny belly and vent. Female duskier below with an unstreaked tawny throat and upper chest; eyes in both sexes pale yellow. Female similar to female Streak-crowned Antvireo (p. 228), but has unstreaked throat and chest, and unstreaked crown. Uncommon in e. Honduras; to 2,460 ft. (750 m). Found in rainforest. Forages at low to midlevels primarily in dead leaf clusters; often in pairs or small groups of 3 to 5 individuals. Calls include sharp *tip!;* also a flatter *tseet-tseet-tseet-tseet*. Honduras to Ecuador.

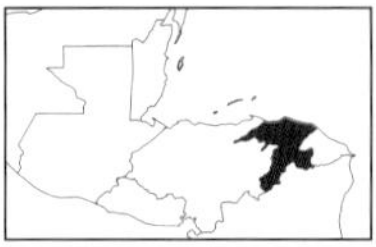

WHITE-FLANKED ANTWREN *Myrmotherula axillaris*
4 in. (10 cm). Small, delicate, with short tail; male **velvet black overall**; clean white spotting on wing coverts; thin white edging to scapulars; **fluffy white flanks** (sometimes difficult to see); white tips to tail. Female olive-brown above; tawny below with **dull cinnamon tips to wing coverts**. Compare male with male Dot-winged Antwren; compare female with female Dusky Antbird (p. 232). Rare in e. Honduras; to 2,475 ft. (750 m). Found in rainforest. Forages at low to midlevels, often in pairs; fairly arboreal; often associates with mixed-species flocks. Call is a slow series of sweet whistles, descending at end, *wee-wee-wee-Wee-Wee-Wee-Weu-weu-weu*; also thin, nasal, slightly buzzy *Tzzeeeup!* or *tzeee-tzeeeu*. Honduras to Brazil.

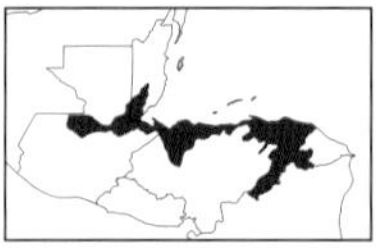

SLATY ANTWREN *Myrmotherula schisticolor*
4.5 in. (11 cm). Male **sooty gray overall** with white spotting on wing coverts; **blackish throat and chest**. Female olive-brown above; paler tawny below; indistinct eye-ring; lacks spots on wing coverts. Compare male with the larger male Dusky Antbird (p. 232), but Slaty Antwren has black throat and chest; also note habitat, behavior, and voice differences. Female recalls Rufous-browed Wren (p. 304), but no known range overlap. Rare and local on Caribbean Slope; to 4,920 ft. (1,500 m). Found in interior of rainforest. Forages at low to midlevels; fairly arboreal; often in pairs. Calls include harsh, buzzy elements, *nreeeeah!*, and softer, sweet whistles, *wreet!-wreet!-wreet!* Mex. to Peru.

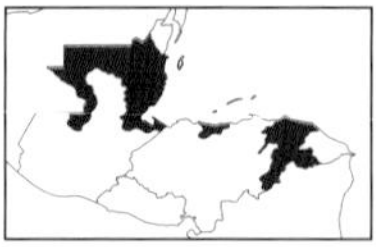

DOT-WINGED ANTWREN *Microrhopias quixensis*
4.5 in. (11 cm). Male **velvety black overall**; white spotting on wing coverts; **obvious, bold white lower wing bar**. Female similarly patterned but olive-brown above and **chestnut below**. Male similar to White-flanked Antwren but note bold wing bar and black flanks. Fairly common but local on Caribbean Slope; to 3,610 ft. (1,100 m). Found in rainforest. Fairly arboreal; forages at low to midlevels; often in pairs or small groups of 3 to 5 individuals. Call is a thin, nasal *pseeuuuu!* and a longer, slightly accelerating *tip-tip-Tip-Tip-Tip-Tip-Tip-Tip-Tip-teu-teu-teu-teu-teu'teu* (lasting approx. 2 sec.). Mex. to Bolivia.

CHECKER-THROATED
ANTWREN
female
male
WHITE-FLANKED
ANTWREN
female
male
female
male
SLATY
ANTWREN
female
male
DOT-WINGED
ANTWREN

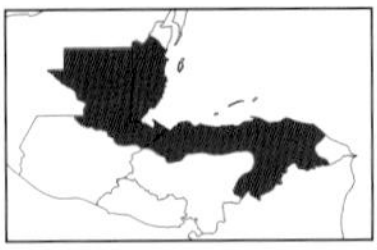

DUSKY ANTBIRD *Cercomacroides tyrannina*

5 in. (13 cm). Male **sooty gray overall**. Female olive-brown above; **rich tawny below**. Compare both sexes with the smaller Slaty Antwren (p. 230); male Dusky Antbird lacks black throat and chest (present on male Slaty), female Dusky richer tawny below; also note habitat and behavioral differences, as well as voice. Locally common on Caribbean Slope; to 3,610 ft. (1,100 m). Found in scrubby undergrowth, tangles, and secondary edge in rainforest and semideciduous forest. Forages at low levels; solitary or in pairs. Calls from male include a slightly rising and accelerating *teu-teu-teu-teu-Teu'Teu'Teu'Teu'Teu'Teu'Teu* (lasting approx. 2.5 sec.); and a stronger, rising *Peur-Peur-Peur-Pea-Pea-Pea-Pea'Pea*; both sexes give a harsh, scratchy, agitated *cheaa'r'r'r'r'r*. Mex. to Brazil.

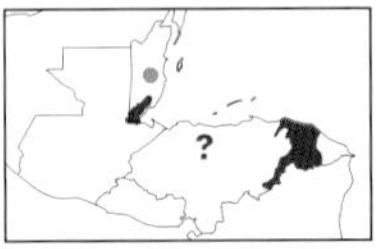

BARE-CROWNED ANTBIRD *Gymnocichla nudiceps*

6.5 in. (17 cm). Male **velvet black overall** with **large bare bluish region around eyes and lores;** 2 thin white wing bars. Female patterned similarly to male, but blackish brown above; tawny-brown underparts; wing bars buffy cinnamon. Uncommon on Caribbean Slope; to 820 ft. (250 m). Found in understory of rainforest. Forages at low levels; secretive; sometimes encountered at army ant swarms. More often detected by voice. Long call is a series of clear sweet whistles, rising in middle and accelerating slightly at end, *Teuu-tip-Tip-Tip-Tip-Tip-Tip-Tip-Tip-Tip'Tip'Tip'Tip'Tip*; call is a sharp *Peeet!* NCA to Colombia.

BICOLORED ANTBIRD *Gymnopithys leucaspis*

6 in. (15 cm). Sexes similar. Blackish face with blue orbital skin; **clean white below with blackish cheeks, sides, and flanks**. Uncommon on Caribbean Slope of Honduras; to 2,475 ft. (750 m). Found in interior of rainforest. Forages on or near the ground; secretive, but sometimes encountered at army ant swarms. More often detected by voice. Long call is a series of short, sharp repeated whistles, accelerating at end (lasting approx. 3.5 sec.); also a thin, whining *cheaaar'r'r'r'r*. Honduras to Brazil.

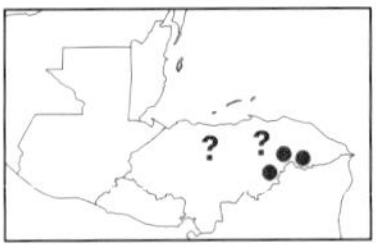

CHESTNUT-BACKED ANTBIRD *Myrmeciza exsul*

6 in. (15 cm). Male **head and underparts sooty black** with **chestnut back, wings, and tail**; note **blue orbital skin**. Female similar, but washed brown. Rare to uncommon in e. Honduras; to 3,940 ft. (1,200 m). Found in interior of rainforest. Forages on or near the ground; secretive, but sometimes encountered at army ant swarms. Most easily detected by voice. Call is a loud, ringing series of 2 or 3 clear whistles, *pee-peeeu!* or *pee-pee-peeeu!* Honduras to Ecuador.

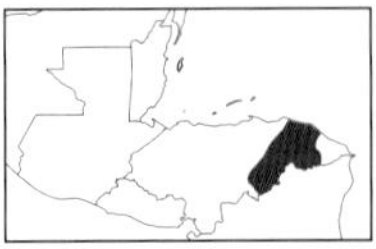

SPOTTED ANTBIRD *Hylophylax naevioides*

4.5 in. (11 cm). Male underparts clean white with **broad dark streaks and spots forming a necklace across chest; throat black**. Female similar to male, but head brown (not gray) and throat whitish. Fairly common in e. Honduras; to 3,300 ft. (1,000 m). Found in interior of rainforest. Forages on or near ground; secretive, but sometimes encountered at army ant swarms. More often detected by voice. Long call is a rolling series of unsteady nasal whistles, accelerating, then slowing at end, *Wee'tee'Wee'tee'WEE'TEE'WEE'TEE'WEE'TEE-Wee'tee-Wee'tee-Wee'tee—Wee'tee* (lasting approx. 4 sec.); also an agitated scratchy scream, *rea'a'a'a'a'a'zzzz*. Honduras to Ecuador.

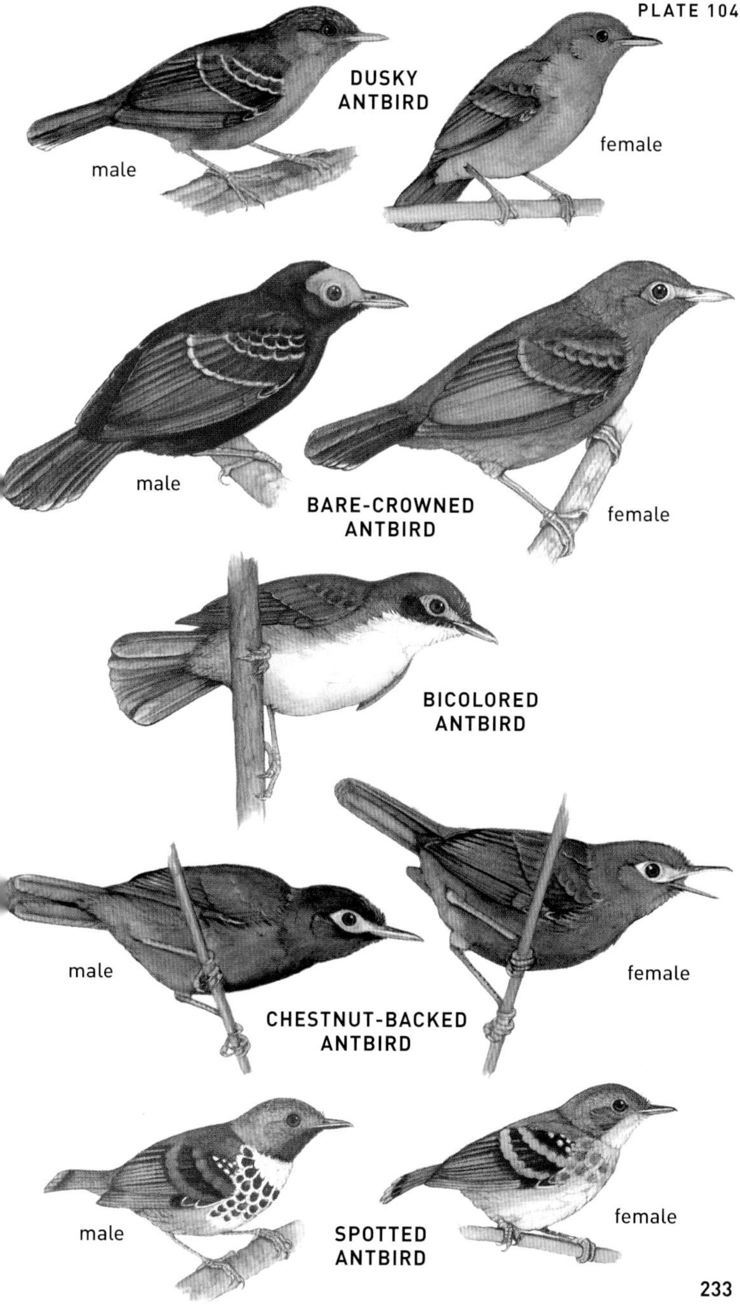
DUSKY ANTBIRD
male
female
male
BARE-CROWNED ANTBIRD
female
BICOLORED ANTBIRD
male
CHESTNUT-BACKED ANTBIRD
female
male
SPOTTED ANTBIRD
female

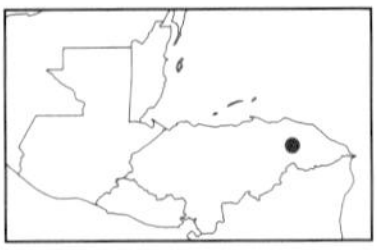

WING-BANDED ANTBIRD *Myrmornis torquata*

6 in. (15 cm). Male has combination **buffy wing bars** and **black throat**. Female has **tawny throat**. Both sexes with **extremely short tails**. Very rare in e. Honduras; only recently discovered in NCA; to 3,940 ft. (1,200 m). Found in rainforest where it forages on or near ground. Secretive and difficult to detect, if not for voice. Song is a series of sweet, clear, evenly spaced whistles, *Pwee-Pwee-Pwee-Pwee-Pwee-Pwee!-Pwee!-Pwee!-Pwee!-Pwee!PweePwee,* gaining volume toward middle and slightly accelerating at end; call is a *tear'r'r'r'r'r* (similar in quality to some trogon calls). Honduras to Brazil.

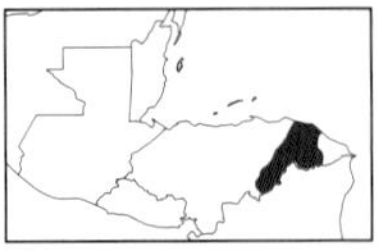

OCELLATED ANTBIRD *Phaenostictus mcleannani*

8.5 in. (22 cm). Sharply patterned and distinctive looking. Rare to uncommon in e. Honduras; to 3,300 ft. (1,000 m). Found in interior of rainforest. Forages on or near the ground; follows army ant swarms. More often detected by voice. Long call is a series of sharp, clear whistles, slightly accelerating and rising in pitch toward end, *PREE!-pea-pea-pea-pea-PEA-PEA-PEA'PEA'PEA!* (lasting approx. 3 sec.); also a short, buzzy, agitated *tseeur'r'r'r'r'r'r*. Honduras to Ecuador.

GRALLARIIDAE (Order: Passeriformes). The antpittas are oddly shaped birds fondly referred to as "eggs on legs" (short-tailed, short-winged with rounded bodies and long legs). Antpittas generally prefer shaded humid forests, where they hop on the ground and forage in the leaf litter. They can be incredibly difficult to observe and are more often heard than seen. Best key to detection and identification is by voice. **3 species (2 genera)**

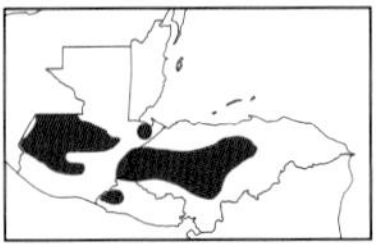

SCALED ANTPITTA *Grallaria guatimalensis*

7.5 in. (19 cm). Largest antpitta in NCA and only species outside of e. Honduras. Black edging to upperparts gives **scaled appearance**; head grayish; **underparts tawny**. Rare to uncommon in NCA; from 1,640 to 9,350 ft. (500–2,850 m). Found in shady interior of humid semideciduous forest, pine-oak forest, and cloud forest. May come to forest edge in early morning or late evening. Rarely heard singing in NCA. Song is a long series of pulsating, low-pitched whistles (the series accelerating in middle and slowing at end), *peu'peu'peu'peu'peu'PEUPEUPEUPEUPEU-WEU-WEU-WEU-WEU-WEU-WEU-weu'weu'weu* (lasting about 2.5 sec.). Mex. to Peru.

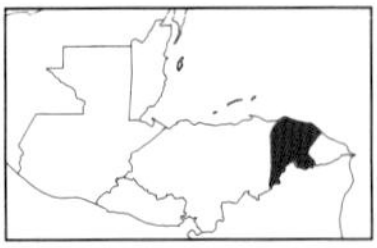

STREAK-CHESTED ANTPITTA *Hylopezus perspicillatus*

5.5 in. (14 cm). Somewhat similar to Thicket Antpitta, but has buffy eye-ring and heavier streaking below; also note voice. Uncommon in e. Honduras; to 660 ft. (200 m). Found in shady understory of rainforest. Song is a sharply pitched, slow, resonating series of clear whistles, *Sueet-Seu'teu'teu'teu'teu'teu'teu.* Honduras to Ecuador.

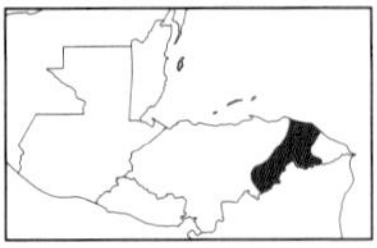

THICKET ANTPITTA *Hylopezus dives*

5.5 in. (14 cm). Somewhat similar to Streak-chested Antpitta, but lacks bold buffy eye-ring, streaking lighter below and near absent on sides and flanks; also, usually shows more **tawny or fulvous chest and sides contrasting with whitish belly and throat**; voices different. Uncommon to fairly common in e. Honduras; to 3,440 ft. (1,050 m). Found at edge or interior of rainforest or riparian forest, and in thickets in deforested areas. Song is a resonating series of piping whistles intensifying and ending abruptly, *poe'poe'poe'POE'POE'POE'POE'WUE'WUE* (lasting approx. 2 sec.). Honduras to Ecuador.

male

female

WING-BANDED ANTBIRD

OCELLATED ANTBIRD

STREAK-CHESTED ANTPITTA

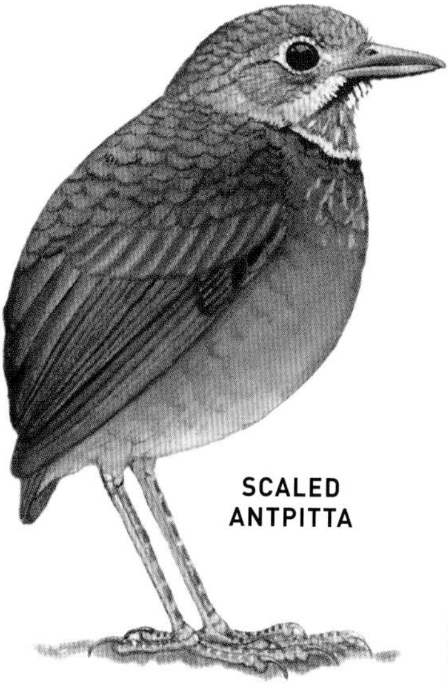

SCALED ANTPITTA

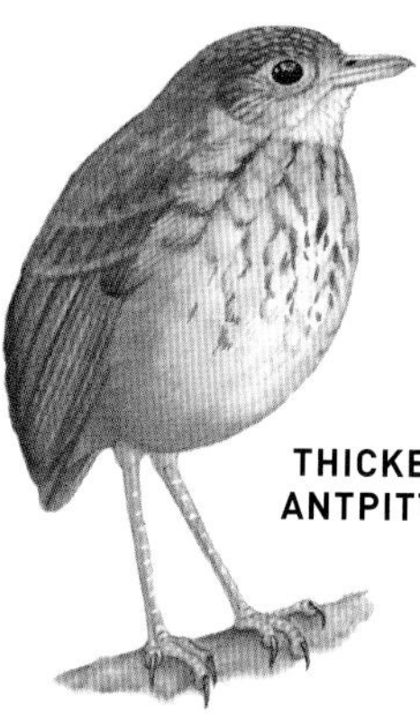

THICKET ANTPITTA

ANTTHRUSHES, LEAFTOSSERS, AND XENOPS

FORMICARIIDAE (Order: Passeriformes). Just 1 representative of this mainly S. American family in NCA. Antthrushes behave and appear like rails but are not closely related. They walk the floor of the rainforest, foraging in the damp leaf litter, calling frequently. They are subtly colored and extremely difficult to see. Detection is most often by voice. **1 species (1 genus)**

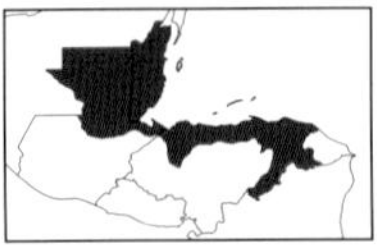

BLACK-FACED ANTTHRUSH *Formicarius analis*

7.5 in. (19 cm). Northern and southern forms differ in voice and appearance and are sometimes treated as 2 species. "Mayan Antthrush" (*moniliger* group; s. Mex. to cen. Honduras) has blackish throat with **rufous forecollar**. "Central American Antthrush" (*analis* group; e. Honduras to Colombia) similar but lacks rufous forecollar. Uncommon to fairly common on Caribbean Slope; to 5,910 ft. (1,800 m). Found in rainforest and humid semideciduous forest. Forages by walking on ground with short tail cocked. Secretive; often detected by voice. Voice of *moniliger* group is a loud series of ringing, clear, repeated whistles (second part faster), *PEEP!-Pee'peu' peu'peu'peu'peu'peu'peu'peu*; call of *analis* group is much slower and shorter with only 2 to 4 elements, *PEEP!-peu-peu*. Mex. to Brazil.

FURNARIIDAE (Order: Passeriformes). This diverse group is characterized by brown or rufous bodies and spiky tails. Leaftossers spend their time on the ground, in shady understory, flipping and tossing forest compost in search of small insects and worms. The woodcreepers are like woodpeckers (though not closely related) as they forage by moving up trunks of trees or out on limbs, using their long tails for leverage. Woodcreepers do not drill holes. Instead they forage by delicately probing the bark layers for insects and grubs. Songs and calls can be key to detection and identification. **22 species (14 genera)**

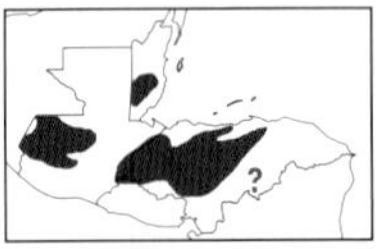

TAWNY-THROATED LEAFTOSSER *Sclerurus mexicanus*

6.5 in. (17 cm). Overall dark reddish brown; paler **tawny throat**, short tail, and long slender bill. Uncommon in NCA; 2,300 to 7,220 ft. (700–2,200 m). Found in shady understory of semideciduous forest, cloud forest, and foothill rainforest. Forages on ground in leaf litter; tosses leaves. Calls from low perch. Long call is a thin, high-pitched *seeuuu!-seeuuu!-seeuuu!-seeuuu!-seeuuu!* (sometimes dropping in volume or slowing down at end); or a *Seeu-seeuuu-seeuuu-seeu-tip'tip'tip'tip'tip'tip*; short call is a squeaky *Peeeu!* Mex. to Bolivia.

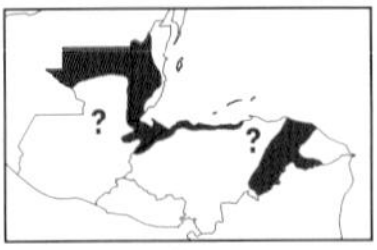

SCALY-THROATED LEAFTOSSER *Sclerurus guatemalensis*

7 in. (18 cm). Overall grayish brown; contrasting **whitish throat** with dark scaling (difficult to see). Rare to uncommon on Caribbean Slope (in lowlands and foothills); to 3,940 ft. (1,200 m). Found in shady understory of rainforest. Forages on ground in leaf litter; tosses leaves. Calls from low perch. Call is an emphatic series of squeaky *peep* notes: *Peep!-Peep!-Peep!-Peep!-Peep!-peuu-peuu-peuu-peep-peep-peep-Peep!-Peep!-Peep!-pea'pea'pea'pi'pi'pi'pi'pi'pi'pi* (the last part accelerated and agitated); also a loud, sharp *Week!* Mex. to Colombia.

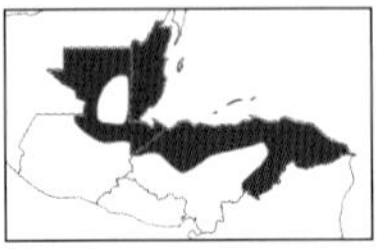

PLAIN XENOPS *Xenops minutus*

4.5 in. (11 cm). **Small**; buffy spectacles and **white malar stripe**; rufous wing pattern and small upturned **chisel-like bill**. Fairly common on Caribbean Slope; to 4,270 ft. (1,300 m). Found at edge in rainforest and taller disturbed habitat. Forages at low to midlevels; along vines and thin branches; often upside down. Call is a short *Peek!*; also a fairly long, squeaky trill, fastest in the middle. Mex. to Argentina.

BLACK-FACED ANTTHRUSH

analis

Antthrushes forage on ground with tail cocked

TAWNY-THROATED LEAFTOSSER

PLAIN XENOPS

SCALY-THROATED LEAFTOSSER

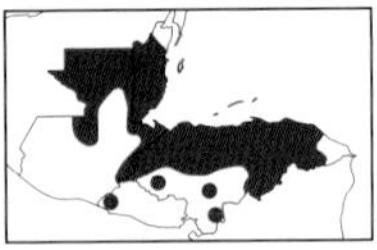

OLIVACEOUS WOODCREEPER *Sittasomus griseicapillus*

6.5 in. (17 cm). **A small woodcreeper**; unmarked greenish gray body with contrasting rufous in wings and tail; in flight, shows tawny wing stripe. Fairly common on Caribbean Slope; uncommon and local on Pacific Slope; to 6,400 ft. (1,950 m). Found in rainforest, semideciduous forest, and coffee plantations. Forages at low to midlevels. Call is a flat, rapid trill, rising in volume (lasting about 1.5 sec.). Mex. to Argentina.

WEDGE-BILLED WOODCREEPER *Glyphorynchus spirurus*

6 in. (15 cm). **A small woodcreeper** with **rounded head** and **pale, buffy supercilium; short blackish bill sharply pointed**. Fairly common on Caribbean Slope; to 4,430 ft. (1,350 m). Found in rainforest, semideciduous forest, and taller disturbed forest. Forages at all levels. Short call is a sharp *Pweek!* or *Teek!*; long call rises in the middle and sputters at the end, *weet-weet-WEEET-WEEET-weet-peet-peeet't't't't't'teu* (lasting about 2 sec.). Mex. to Brazil.

LONG-TAILED WOODCREEPER *Deconychura longicauda*

8 in. (20 cm). **A slender-bodied woodcreeper**; weak buffy streaking on crown and neck; plain back; light spotting on upper chest; throat buff; straight blackish bill. Similar to Cocoa Woodcreeper (p. 240), but is much smaller and has a much shorter bill; also different vocalizations. Rare in e. Honduras; to 1,310 ft. (400 m). Found in rainforest. Forages at midlevels. Rarely vocalizes. Long call is a loud, complaining *weet!-weet!-WEEEET!-WEEEET!-WEEEET!-weet-weet-weet . . .* (rising and falling in volume); also a long flat rattle. Honduras to Brazil.

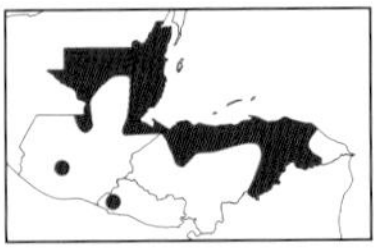

RUDDY WOODCREEPER *Dendrocincla homochroa*

8 in. (20 cm). The only woodcreeper with **uniform bright rufous plumage**; pale grayish lores; feathers at base of bill and throat often slightly raised. Uncommon and local in NCA; to 5,410 ft. (1,650 m). Found in rainforest, semideciduous forest, and coffee plantations. Forages at low to midlevels; often at ant swarms. Seldom vocalizes. Calls include a thin, nasal, whinny *tzeeeuuu!* and a long rattle like other *Dendrocincla* woodcreepers. Mex. to Venezuela.

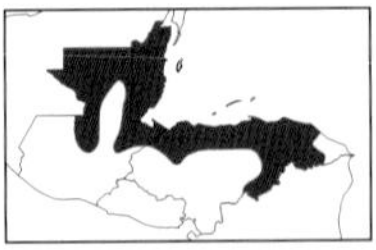

TAWNY-WINGED WOODCREEPER *Dendrocincla anabatina*

7.5 in. (19 cm). Overall rufous brown with **contrasting paler tawny wing panel**. Grayish face with buff supercilium and **buff malar stripe**. Similar to Plain-brown Woodcreeper, but shows contrasting tawny wing panel. Fairly common on Caribbean Slope; to 3,940 ft. (1,200 m). Found in rainforest. Forages at low to midlevels; often visits ant swarms. Short call is an emphatic *TEAURRR!*; also a long rattle similar to other *Dendrocincla* woodcreepers. Mex. to Panama.

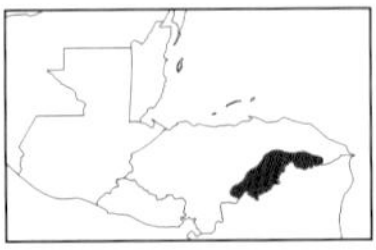

PLAIN-BROWN WOODCREEPER *Dendrocincla fuliginosa*

8 in. (20 cm). Distinctive **grayish face with contrasting black malar stripe**; note **pale eye** and straight blackish bill. Similar to Tawny-winged Woodcreeper, but lacks contrasting tawny wing panel. Rare in Honduras; to 2,475 ft. (750 m). Found in rainforest. Forages at low to midlevels; often visits ant swarms. Short calls include a loud, squeaky *PWEEK!* and an agitated *churrrrr*; long call is a flat trill slightly rising in volume and descending in pitch toward the end (lasting around 6 sec.); also a long rattle similar to that of other *Dendrocincla* woodcreepers. Honduras to Argentina.

OLIVACEOUS WOODCREEPER

WEDGE-BILLED WOODCREEPER

LONG-TAILED WOODCREEPER

army ant swarm attended by Ruddy, Tawny-winged, and Northern Barred-Woodcreeper

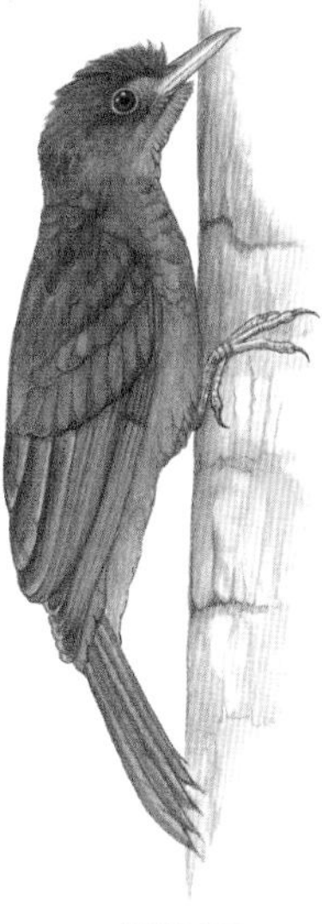

RUDDY WOODCREEPER

TAWNY-WINGED WOODCREEPER

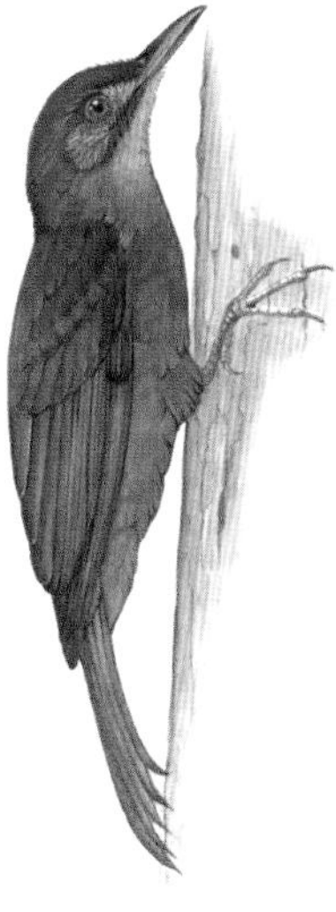

PLAIN-BROWN WOODCREEPER

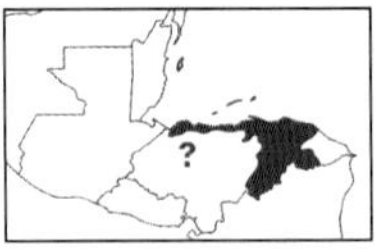

COCOA WOODCREEPER *Xiphorhynchus susurrans*
9 in. (23 cm). **A large woodcreeper**; **heavy buffy white spotting on chest** and **buffy white or whitish throat**; **bill is long and slightly decurved** with paler mandible and dark maxilla. Similar to Ivory-billed Woodcreeper (sympatric in n. Honduras), but has darker bill and less intense streaking below; also note vocal differences. Also similar to Long-tailed Woodcreeper (p. 238), but is much larger and has heavier, decurved bill, and different vocalizations. Fairly common on Caribbean Slope; to 3,280 ft. (1,000 m). Found in interior or at edge of rainforest, taller disturbed forest, and mangroves. Forages at midlevels; may associate with ant swarms. Long call is a steady rolling laughter on one pitch, but rising in volume toward middle and end, *weet-weet-WEET-WEET-WEET-WEET-WEET-WEET-WEET-WEET* (similar to long call of Ivory-billed Woodcreeper, but doesn't accelerate and is shorter in length); also an explosive *CHEAUU!* and a double *Chyrrrr!-Chyrrr!* Guatemala to Venezuela.

IVORY-BILLED WOODCREEPER *Xiphorhynchus flavigaster*
9.5 in. (24 cm). Similar to Cocoa Woodcreeper, but is slightly larger, **bill horn-colored**, and note more **extensive and bolder streaking below**. Fairly common to common on Pacific Slope; fairly common on Caribbean Slope in n. Guatemala and Belize, becoming less common in n. Honduras (where sympatric with Cocoa Woodcreeper); to 6,230 ft. (1,900 m). Found in interior and at edge of a variety of woodland types: semideciduous forest, riparian forest, mangroves, coffee plantations, taller disturbed forest, and rainforest. Calls include a rapid *WEET!-Wit-Wit-Wit-Wit* and a longer accelerating rolling laughter lasting approx. 4.5 sec. (See long call of Cocoa Woodcreeper, which doesn't accelerate and is shorter in duration.) Mex. to Costa Rica.

STREAK-HEADED WOODCREEPER *Lepidocolaptes souleyetii*
8 in. (20 cm). Appearance similar to a small Ivory-billed Woodcreeper; however, bill **shorter, thinner, more decurved, and pinkish**; at closer distances, note **fine streaking on crown**. Very similar to Spot-crowned Woodcreeper, but has fine streaking on crown rather than spots; also note differences in elevation and habitat, and vocalizations. The 2 species rarely overlap. Common on both slopes; to 6,070 ft. (1,850 m). Found at edge in a variety of woodland habitats: disturbed habitat, semideciduous forest, mangroves, and plantations; also pine-oak forest (rare). Forages at midlevels. Long call is rapid trill, descending slightly in pitch at end (lasting approx. 1.5 sec.). Mex. to Brazil.

SPOT-CROWNED WOODCREEPER *Lepidocolaptes affinis*
8 in. (21 cm). Very similar to Streak-headed Woodcreeper, but has **fine spotting on crown** (rather than streaking) and note elevation and habitat differences, vocalizations. The 2 species rarely overlap. Uncommon to common in NCA; from 3,280 to 9,510 ft. (1,000–2,900 m). Found in interior of pine-oak forest and cloud forest. Forages at mid- to upper levels. Often secretive; calls infrequently. Call is a very thin, rising *Tseeeuuu!* (similar in quality to call of Rose-throated Becard [p. 282]); also a shorter *Tseep!* and higher-pitched, thin *tseeeeeeeeee*. Mex. to Bolivia.

COCOA WOODCREEPER

IVORY-BILLED WOODCREEPER

STREAK-HEADED WOODCREEPER

SPOT-CROWNED WOODCREEPER

LARGE WOODCREEPERS

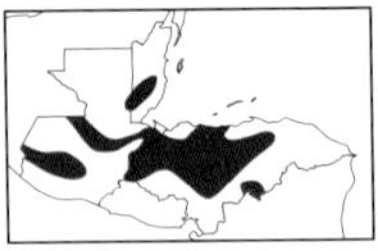

SPOTTED WOODCREEPER *Xiphorhynchus erythropygius*

9.5 in. (24 cm). Note **buffy eye-ring** and obvious **large buffy spots on chest**; stout, fairly long bill with darker maxilla and paler mandible. Uncommon in NCA (mostly Caribbean Slope); from 980 to 9,510 ft. (300–2,900 m). Found in foothills and highlands, including humid semideciduous forest, cloud forest, pine-oak, and coffee plantations. Forages at mid- to upper levels. Can be secretive; calls infrequently. Long call includes several rapidly delivered, nasal descending whistles, *t't't't't'TSEEUUU!—Seeeuuu—Seeeuuu*; short call is a *p'p'p'p'peeuuuu!* Mex. to Ecuador.

NORTHERN BARRED-WOODCREEPER

Dendrocolaptes sanctithomae

10.5 in. (27 cm). A large woodcreeper; rufous-chestnut to rufous-olive overall with **fine black barring on body** (may be difficult to see in poor light); grayish lores; **long straight blackish bill**. Fairly common on Caribbean Slope; locally uncommon on Pacific Slope; to 5,910 ft. (1,800 m). Found in rainforest, taller disturbed habitat, semideciduous forest, and coffee plantations. Forages at low to midlevels in forest. Often associates with ant swarms and mixed-species flocks. Short calls include an agitated, gruff *CHAAIII!*; long call is slightly nasal *pwee-PWEE-PWEE-PWEE-peeeurr* (lasting about 2 sec.; rising in volume at middle). Mex. to Ecuador.

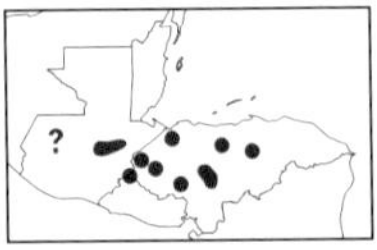

BLACK-BANDED WOODCREEPER *Dendrocolaptes picumnus*

10.5 in. (27 cm). Head, neck, and chest heavily streaked buffy white with pale buffy supercilium; **fine black barring on flanks, vent, and undertail coverts** (difficult to see in the field); note **fairly long, stout bill with dark maxilla**. Rare in NCA (absent from Belize; 1 record from El Salvador); from 2,460 to 9,510 ft. (750–2,900 m). Found in interior highlands; pine-oak forest and cloud forest. Forages at mid- to upper levels. Somewhat secretive; mostly silent. Call is a slow rolling laughter, descending at end, *teu-teu-TEU-TEU-TEE-TEE-TEE-TEE-tee-tee-teu-teu-teu* and an explosive *WEE!'WEE!'WEE!'WEE!'wee'wee'weu'weu'weu*; also a steady *Wee'Wee'Wee'Wee'Wee'Wee'Wee'Wee'Wee.* Mex. to Argentina.

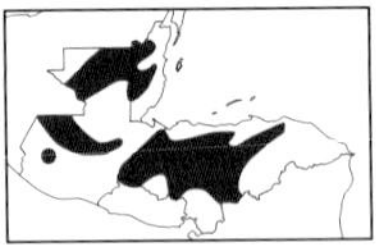

STRONG-BILLED WOODCREEPER

Xiphocolaptes promeropirhynchus

12 in. (31 cm). **Largest woodcreeper in NCA**; olive-brown overall with faint, fine buff streaking on chest and head; shows weak buffy supercilium and malar stripe; **long, stout blackish bill**. Rare to uncommon on both slopes (mainly interior foothills and highlands); to 9,350 ft. (2,850 m). Found in taller semideciduous forest, foothill rainforest, pine-oak, and cloud forest; highest abundance appears to be in pine-oak. Forages at mid- to upper levels. Generally solitary or occasionally associates with mixed-species flocks. Short call is a thin, nasal, rising *teeeeuuuuu'WEEEK!*; long call repeats short call into longer series, *teeu'WEEK!-teeu'WEEK!-teeu'WEEK!-teu'WEEK!-teu'WEEK!-teu'week-teu'week-teu'week-weeuuuu* (falling in volume toward end). Mex. to Bolivia.

SPOTTED
WOODCREEPER

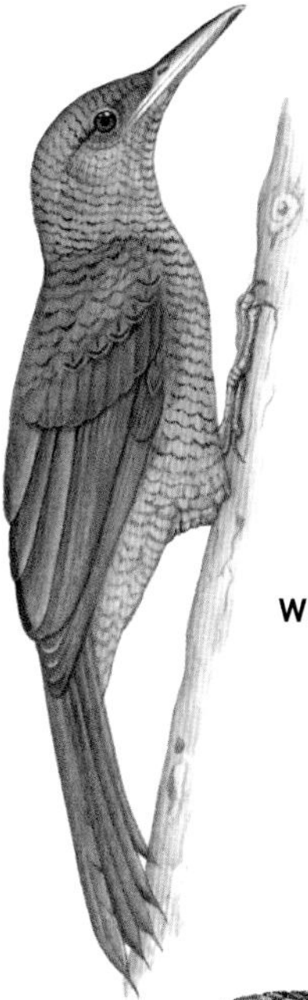

NORTHERN
BARRED-
WOODCREEPER

BLACK-BANDED
WOODCREEPER

STRONG-BILLED
WOODCREEPER

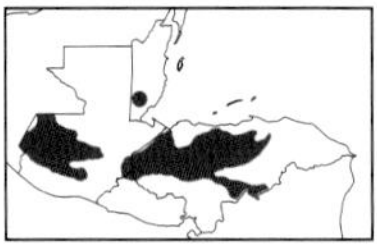

SCALY-THROATED FOLIAGE-GLEANER

Anabacerthia variegaticeps

6.5 in. (17 cm). Contrasting **buff "spectacles" on face**; light scaling on throat is difficult to see; rufous tail contrasts with reddish brown body. Smaller than Buff-throated Foliage-gleaner, also less buffy spectacles and throat; more arboreal, but also note elevation and distribution. Uncommon and local on both slopes (mainly in highlands); from 1,150 to 8,200 ft. (350–2,500 m). Found in semideciduous forest, cloud forest, and rainforest. Forages at low and (more frequently) midlevels. Probes along vines and in dead leaf clusters, often while upside down. Calls include an emphatic, high-pitched squeak, *Pseeek!* and a trilling *tseu'u'u'u'u!*; also from immature, a nasal bark, *Back!* Mex. to Ecuador.

BUFF-THROATED FOLIAGE-GLEANER

Automolus ochrolaemus

8 in. (20 cm). Large and heavy billed; note **buffy spectacles and throat**; tail and wings more rufous. Larger than Scaly-throated Foliage-gleaner, also more buffy spectacles and throat; not arboreal, but also note elevation and distribution. Uncommon on Caribbean Slope; to 4,920 ft. (1,500 m). Found in rainforest. Usually forages in dense tangles near ground, but occasionally at midlevels. Probes along vines and in dead leaf clusters. Call is a loud raspy rattle (lasting approx. 1.5 sec.). Mex. to Bolivia.

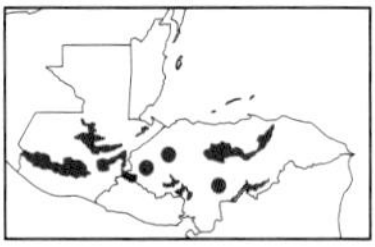

RUDDY FOLIAGE-GLEANER *Clibanornis rubiginosus*

8 in. (20 cm). Overall **reddish brown** with slightly paler tawny throat; **lacks buffy spectacles**; note thin orbital ring of bare bluish skin. Uncommon to fairly common on both slopes; from 1,150 to 8,200 ft. (350–2,500 m). Found in a variety of wooded habitats: semideciduous forest, pine-oak forest, cloud forest, and coffee plantations. Forages at low to midlevels. Can be quite secretive; most often detected by voice. Nests in earthen embankments. Call is a burry, scratchy *Churee!-Churee!-Churee!* (sometimes more notes). Mex. to Bolivia.

SLATY SPINETAIL *Synallaxis brachyura*

6 in. (15 cm). Slate gray overall with **contrasting rufous crown and wings**; note long spiky tail. Rare to uncommon in e. Honduras; to 2,460 ft. (750 m). Found in coastal scrub and disturbed habitat. Forages at low levels in thick vegetation. Secretive and can be difficult to observe (best located by voice). Call is a scratchy, accelerating series (like a bouncing marble vibrating to a quick stop), *cheer-r-r-r'r'r'r.* Honduras to Peru.

RUFOUS-BREASTED SPINETAIL *Synallaxis erythrothorax*

6 in. (15 cm). Grayish head contrasts with **rufous breast, sides, and wings**; throat finely streaked black; also note black border to lower throat. Uncommon on Caribbean Slope; rare to uncommon on Pacific Slope; to 4,100 ft. (1,250 m). Found in coastal scrub and disturbed habitats. Often near water's edge. Forages at low levels in thick vegetation. Can be difficult to see (best located by voice). Call is a nasal *weet!-weet!-weet!-Wur'r'r'r'r*; also an agitated trill (similar to long call of Long-billed Gnatwren [p. 312]). Mex. and NCA.

SCALY-THROATED FOLIAGE-GLEANER
BUFF-THROATED FOLIAGE-GLEANER
RUDDY FOLIAGE-GLEANER
juvenile
SLATY SPINETAIL
adult
RUFOUS-BREASTED SPINETAIL

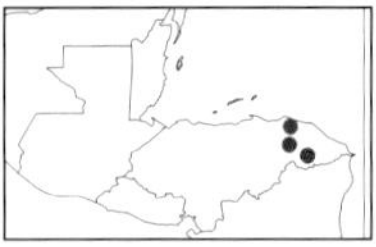

STRIPED WOODHAUNTER *Automolus subulatus*

7 in. (18 cm). Large, with a streaked backed, rufous tail, and **streaked buffy underparts**. Pale bill is slightly decurved. Rare in e. Honduras. Found at lower to midlevels in rainforest. Frequent call is a nasal *kip-kip-kip*. Honduras to Ecuador. Also known as Western Treehunter (*Hyloctistes virgatus*).

TYRANNIDAE (Order: Passeriformes). The largest family of birds on Earth. Members are "flycatchers" but some are also known as elaenias, tyrannulets, pewees, phoebes, kingbirds, attilas, mourners, spadebills, flatbills, tyrants, pygmy-tyrants, and kiskadees. Most are characterized by upright posture; short, rounded wings; and long tails. They are insectivorous (making short sallies from a perch to catch prey items), but a few species have specialized diets of small fruits or mistletoe berries. Vocalizations are an important key to their identification. **68 species (37 genera)**

YELLOW-BELLIED TYRANNULET *Ornithion semiflavum*

3.5 in. (9 cm). A tiny flycatcher; **underparts yellow**; note dark face with **broad white supercilium**. Uncommon on Caribbean Slope; to 4,920 ft. (1,500 m). Found in rainforest, taller semi-deciduous forest, and occasionally more disturbed habitats. Forages at midlevel to canopy. Call is a high-pitched whistle (*weeauuuu* or *peauuuu*), sometimes doubled; also an agitated "rubber duck" quality series of whistles, *pip'a'pip'a-pip-pip-peauuu-peauuu-pip'a-pip'a'pip'a*. Mex. to Costa Rica.

NORTHERN BEARDLESS-TYRANNULET *Camptostoma imberbe*

4 in. (10 cm). A tiny grayish flycatcher with a **short crest**; inconspicuous **supercilium**; **2 brownish wing bars**; small bill with **pink mandible**. Uncommon to fairly common in NCA; to 4,920 ft. (1,500 m). Found in thorn forest, disturbed habitat, and pine savanna. Forages at edges at low to midlevels. Frequently pumps or wags tail. Common call is a single *peaauuu*; also an excited *pity'yeeeww!*; song is a whistled *peaaa-pee'pee'pee'pee'peepeepee* (accelerating at end). U.S. to Costa Rica.

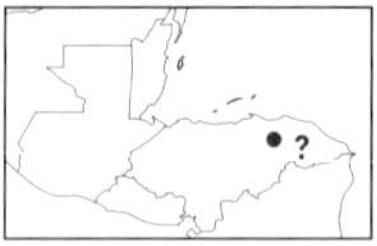

YELLOW TYRANNULET *Capsiempis flaveola*

4 in. (10 cm). A **tiny yellowish flycatcher**. Olive-yellow above; wings darker with 2 pale yellowish wing bars**; supercilium and underparts brighter yellow**. Dark bill short and thin. Recently recorded in e. Honduras, where it's apparently rare and local; to 1,700 ft. (500 m). Found in scrubby edge of rainforest or riparian forest; low second growth. Forages at low levels. Sometimes difficult to detect; rather silent, except when agitated. Calls include a squabbling "rubber duck" *pweep-pweep-pweep* often run into a longer agitated series. Honduras to Argentina.

PALTRY TYRANNULET *Zimmerius vilissimus*

4 in. (10 cm). A minute flycatcher with **broad white supercilium**; tail relatively long; bill short and stubby. Uncommon to fairly common on both slopes in NCA; to 5,910 ft. (1,800 m). Found in semideciduous forest, rainforest, coffee plantations. Forages at all levels (but generally mid- to subcanopy); often at edge. Feeds on mistletoe berries. Call is a 2-part *peuu-tip* or a single *peuuu*; also a repeated *peeep* and a short trill. Some authors treat populations of Honduras southward (east of Sula Valley) as a separate species, Mistletoe Tyrannulet (*Z. parvus*). Mex. to Venezuela.

STRIPED WOODHAUNTER

YELLOW-BELLIED TYRANNULET

NORTHERN BEARDLESS-TYRANNULET

YELLOW TYRANNULET

PALTRY TYRANNULET

GREENISH ELAENIA *Myiopagis viridicata*

5.5 in. (14 cm). A drab flycatcher; greenish yellow below with **faint gray streaking on chest**; head grayish, but note **pale white supercilium and dark eye line**; **bill thin** and mainly dark with pinkish base to mandible; crown has thin strip of yellow (rarely seen); **eyes dark.** Similar to Yellow-olive Flycatcher (p. 252), but has thinner, darker bill, and dark eyes; also note differences in calls. Fairly common in NCA, including on some of the Bay Is.; to 4,590 ft. (1,400 m). Found in a variety of taller forests: semideciduous and riparian forest, rainforest; coffee plantations, and even disturbed habitat; rarely in pine savanna. Forages at mid- to upper levels; sits patiently and calls irregularly. Call is a thin, slightly buzzy *tzeeee'eaauuu*; dawn song is of similar quality but notes repeated every 4 sec. Mex. to Argentina.

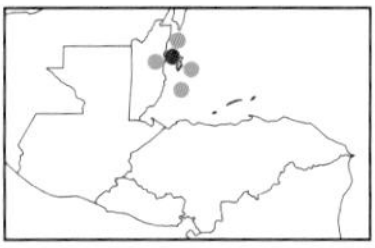

CARIBBEAN ELAENIA *Elaenia martinica*

5.5 in. (14 cm). Grayish olive above; **short crest with white base**; lacks eye-ring; 2 whitish to yellowish wing bars; pale underparts; pink mandible. In region, only on Caye Caulker (resident) and Ambergris Caye (winter visitor); vagrant to mainland; to 160 ft. (50 m). Found in coastal scrub. Forages at low to midlevels. Calls include an emphatic *peeeau!* or a lower, slightly descending *peeaauuu*; song (?) is an excited *peeea'pi'pip'pip!* (repeated every 2.5 sec.). Caribbean islands and Belize.

YELLOW-BELLIED ELAENIA *Elaenia flavogaster*

6 in. (15 cm). A medium-sized flycatcher with **large crest** (crest erected when agitated, exposing white base); **belly, vents, and undertail coverts pale yellow**; 2 whitish wing bars; bill fairly short with pale mandible. Similar to Caribbean Elaenia, but shows more extensive yellow below and larger crest; calls are different. Also similar to Mountain Elaenia, but has crested appearance (not rounded head) and yellow underparts; different calls. Fairly common on Caribbean Slope; uncommon on Pacific Slope (but rare and local in El Salvador); to 5,580 ft. (1,700 m). Found in semideciduous forest, thorn forest, coastal scrub, and disturbed habitat; also in towns and gardens. Generally at edges where it forages at low to midlevels. Often perches in the open. Calls include a screaming, drawn-out slightly buzzy *we'e'e-ruuuuu*; also an agitated *ta'wee'eauu-wee'eauu-ta'wee'ta'wee'ta'wee'eauuu*. Mex. to Argentina.

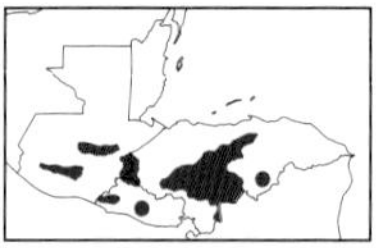

MOUNTAIN ELAENIA *Elaenia frantzii*

6 in. (15 cm). **Rounded head and pale eye-ring**; olive-brown above and grayish olive below; 2 pale wing bars and note **tertials broadly edged in white**; mandible pinkish orange. Compare with Yellow-bellied Elaenia, but has rounded head (not crest), more grayish olive below (not yellow); different calls. Uncommon in NCA; 2,460 to 7,220 ft. (750–2,200 m). Found in higher elevation woodlands: cloud forest, pine-oak forest, semideciduous forest, coffee plantations, and even gardens. Forages at midlevels. Migrates to lower elevations (Nov.–Mar.) in response to fruiting trees; feeds on small fruits. Call is a slightly buzzy *peeeer'r'r'r!*; song is an emphatic 2-part *wee'chup!* Guatemala to Venezuela.

GREENISH ELAENIA
CARIBBEAN ELAENIA
YELLOW-BELLIED ELAENIA
MOUNTAIN ELAENIA

OCHRE-BELLIED FLYCATCHER *Mionectes oleagineus*

5 in. (13 cm). Fairly drab-looking flycatcher. Olive-brown above with grayish face; **chest and remaining underparts tawny**; mandible yellowish orange. Uncommon to fairly common in NCA; to 5,910 ft. (1,800 m). Can be confused with some female manakins (p. 278) but note longer tail; also similar to juvenile Rufous-capped Warbler (p. 358). Found in understory of rainforest, semideciduous forest, riparian forest, coffee plantations. Calls include a repeated, nasal *wreeep*; also a repeated *pi'tah!* (both calls may be combined into a longer series). Mex. to Brazil.

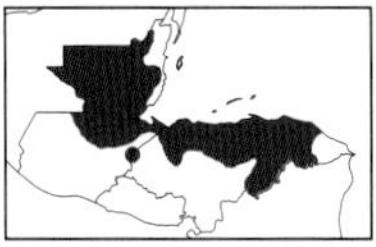

SEPIA-CAPPED FLYCATCHER *Leptopogon amaurocephalus*

5 in. (13 cm). **Dark brown cap, dark crescent on face**; 2 orange-yellow wing bars; **pale eyes**; thin warblerlike bill. Uncommon on Caribbean Slope; to 4,270 ft. (1,300 m). Found in rainforest and taller semideciduous forest where it forages at low to midlevels. Generally in forest interior, but occasionally at edge. Call is a rapid, accelerating trill, *pip'p'p'p'p'p'p'p'r'r'rrreeeel* (somewhat resembles call of Northern Bentbill). Mex. to Argentina.

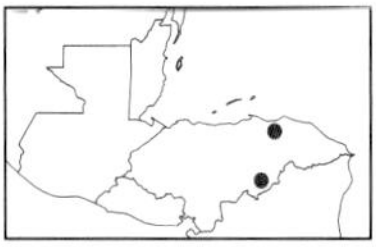

SCALE-CRESTED PYGMY-TYRANT *Lophotriccus pileatus*

3 in. (8 cm). A minute flycatcher. Rufous-tipped black crest feathers (seldom raised) form a **point at back of head**; 2 white wing bars; pale eyes; small bill. Rare in e. Honduras (few records); status unclear; to 3,940 ft. (1,200 m). Found in interior rainforest where it forages at low levels. Call is a sharp, repeated *peep!* or *pit!* or *prreeet!* Honduras to Peru.

NORTHERN BENTBILL *Oncostoma cinereigulare*

4 in. (10 cm). Small. **Short bill has curved culmen.** Similar to Slate-headed Tody-Flycatcher (p. 252), but has different bill structure, lacks pale supercilium, has more vertical feeding posture, and occupies different habitat. Fairly common in NCA; to 4,920 ft. (1,500 m). Found in semideciduous forest, rainforest, coffee plantations. Forages at low to midlevels. Call is rapid toadlike trill, *turrrrrrrrrrr*, and a trilling *prrrr're'e'e'eat!* (resembles call of Sepia-capped Flycatcher), also a single *turp!* and a *turp!-purrrrrrrrr* (similar to call of Slate-headed Tody-Flycatcher). Mex. to Panama.

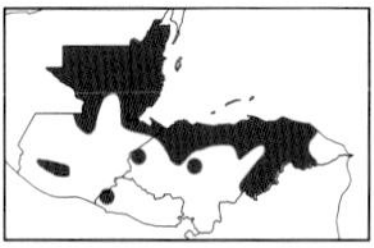

STUB-TAILED SPADEBILL *Platyrinchus cancrominus*

3.5 in. (9 cm). A minute flycatcher with a wide bill. **Distinctive face with pale whitish supercilium, dark ear patch, and broad dark malar stripe.** Similar to Golden-crowned Spadebill, but is more olive-brown on upperparts, crown also appears olive-brown (with concealed yellow patch), and underparts whiter. Uncommon on Pacific Slope; fairly common on Caribbean Slope; to 4,920 ft. (1,500 m). Found in a variety of mature woodland forests: semideciduous forest, riparian forest, rainforest. Forages at low levels in understory vegetation. Difficult to see. Call is an excited *whip'ip'ip* or *whip'ip* (softer than call of Bright-rumped Attila [p. 262]). Mex. to Costa Rica.

GOLDEN-CROWNED SPADEBILL *Platyrinchus coronatus*

3.5 in. (9 cm). Similar to Stub-tailed Spadebill, but note more olive upperparts (not olive-brown), **rufous-orange crown bordered by black** (yellow crown stripe on male often concealed; more yellow-orange on female), and buff yellow face and underparts (not whitish as in Stub-tailed). Fairly common in e. Honduras; to 3,610 ft. (1,100 m). Found in rainforest where it forages at low levels in understory vegetation. Difficult to see. Call is a thin rattling trill. Honduras to Brazil.

OCHRE-BELLIED FLYCATCHER

SEPIA-CAPPED FLYCATCHER

SCALE-CRESTED PYGMY-TYRANT

NORTHERN BENTBILL

STUB-TAILED SPADEBILL

GOLDEN-CROWNED SPADEBILL

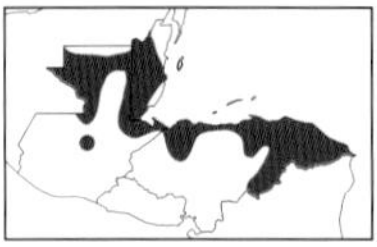

SLATE-HEADED TODY-FLYCATCHER *Poecilotriccus sylvia*

3.5 in. (9 cm). A minute flycatcher. Yellowish upperparts contrast with **grayish head and short pale supercilium**; 2 yellow wing bars; eyes pale. Similar to Northern Bentbill (p. 250), but smaller with different bill structure, pale supercilium (absent in Northern Bentbill), more horizontal feeding posture, and occupies more open habitat. Uncommon to fairly common on Caribbean Slope; to 3,610 ft. (1,100 m). Found at edge of semideciduous forest and in shrubby disturbed habitat. Forages low in understory vegetation. Can be difficult to see. Call is a 2-part *tip!—purrrrrrrr* (similar to call of Northern Bentbill). Mex. to Brazil.

COMMON TODY-FLYCATCHER *Todirostrum cinereum*

4 in. (10 cm). A minute flycatcher; dark **slaty black upperparts (crown slightly darker)**; 2 thin yellowish wing bars; **lemon yellow underparts**; **bill straight and black**; **eyes pale yellow**. Fairly common to common in region; to 3,630 ft. (1,100 m). Found in a variety of open woodlands, hedgerows, second growth, coffee plantations, coastal scrub, and mangroves. Forages at midlevels; often at edge; foraging posture is horizontal. Call is a rich *tip*; song is loud, repeated *tip'ip'ip'ip!* (similar to call of Tropical Kingbird [p. 272]). Mex. to Brazil.

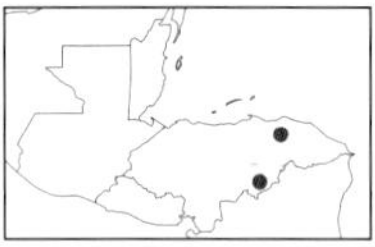

BLACK-HEADED TODY-FLYCATCHER *Todirostrum nigriceps*

3 in. (8 cm). A minute flycatcher with a short tail. From below, note **white throat** contrasting with **bright yellow underparts**. Above, **head black** with **dark eyes**. Rare to uncommon in e. Honduras; to 2,000 ft. (600 m). Forages in canopy or near canopy levels in rainforest. Very difficult to observe owing to very small size and location in forest treetops. Almost always first detected by loud, ringing voice, *tip!-tip!-tip!-tip!-tip!-tip!-tip!* Honduras to Ecuador.

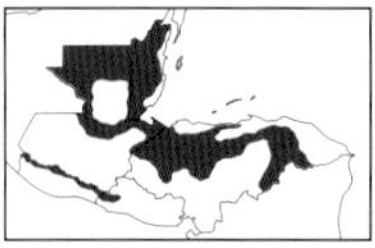

EYE-RINGED FLATBILL *Rhynchocyclus brevirostris*

6.5 in. (17 cm). Greenish overall; large round head with **bold white eye-ring**; **bill wide and flat**; mandible pink. Uncommon in region; to 6,950 ft. (2,100 m). Found in rainforest to cloud forest, including riparian forest and more humid semideciduous forest. Forages at low to midlevels. Secretive and can be difficult to locate. Calls include a thin, buzzy, insectlike *zweeeeeeee-zweeeee* (each part slightly rising) or *zeeeee-zeeeee-zeeeee-zweeeeee!*; or just a single *zeeeeee* (qualities of these calls very similar to those of Yellow-olive Flycatcher); also a high-pitched whistle, *sweeeeet!* Mex. to Ecuador.

YELLOW-OLIVE FLYCATCHER *Tolmomyias sulphurescens*

5 in. (13 cm). Yellow-olive above with contrasting **grayish head**; weak white eye-ring; **bill wide and flat**; mandible pink; **eyes pale gray**. Similar to Greenish Elaenia (p. 248), but has pale eyes (not dark), lacks streaking on chest, and has wide bill (not thin); also note different calls. Fairly common in NCA; to 6,070 ft. (1,850 m); however, generally below 5,090 ft. (1,550 m). Found in a variety of taller woodland habitat: rainforest, semideciduous forest, and riparian forest, usually at edges or in highly fragmented landscapes. Forages at mid- to upper levels. The compact, hanging nest is distinctive; it is usually constructed of fine blackish fibers and hangs from small branches over trails and open spaces in the midstory near forest edges. Call is a series of 4 thin insectlike buzzes, *zeee-Zeee-Zeee-ZEEEE!* Mex. to Brazil.

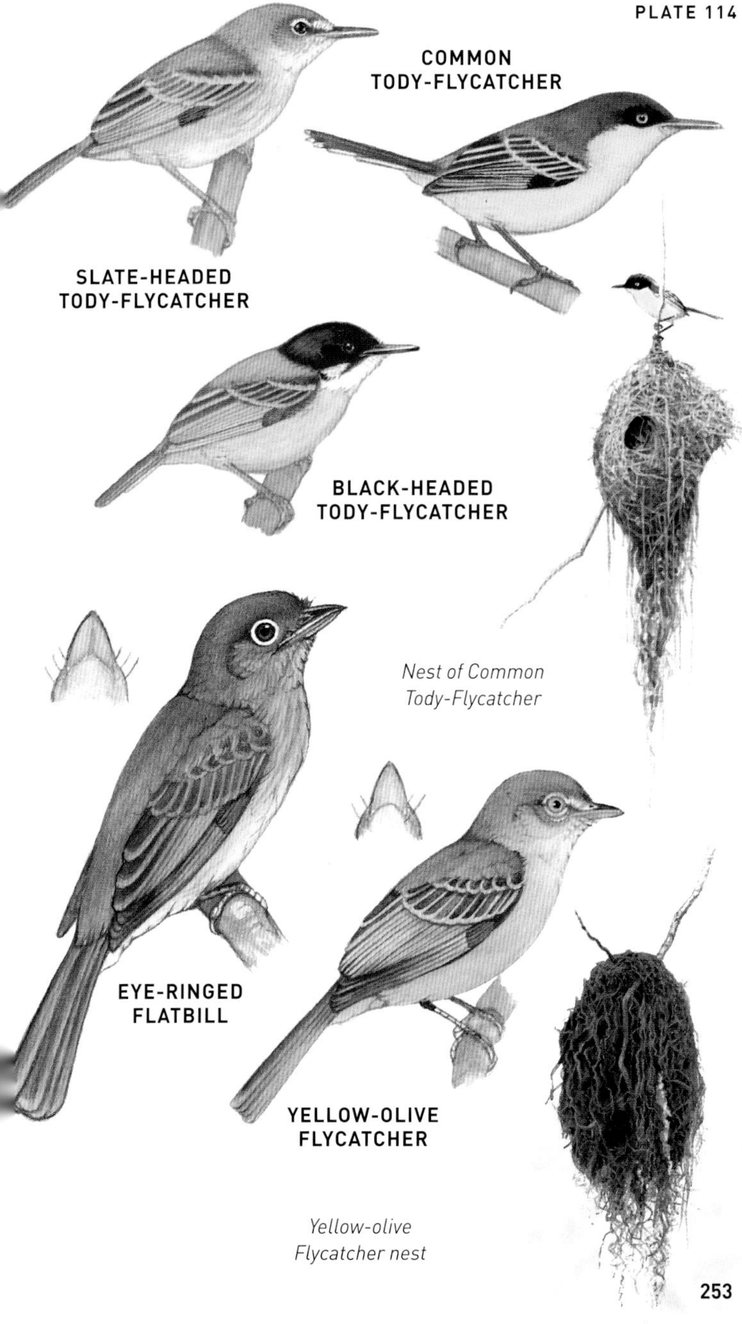
COMMON
TODY-FLYCATCHER
SLATE-HEADED
TODY-FLYCATCHER
BLACK-HEADED
TODY-FLYCATCHER
*Nest of Common
Tody-Flycatcher*
EYE-RINGED
FLATBILL
YELLOW-OLIVE
FLYCATCHER
*Yellow-olive
Flycatcher nest*

OTHER TROPICAL FLYCATCHERS

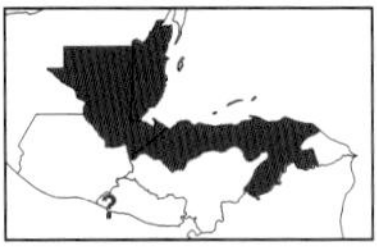

ROYAL FLYCATCHER *Onychorhynchus coronatus*
7 in. (18 cm). Brownish upperparts contrast with tawny rump and rufous tail; **head shape is pointed in back as large fanlike crest is normally held flat** (gaudy crest rarely seen open, but includes bright red [male] or orange [female] feathers tipped with iridescent blue). Very rare (extirpated?) on Pacific Slope; uncommon to rare on Caribbean Slope; to 3,940 ft. (1,200 m). Found in taller woodland forest: semideciduous forest, rainforest, riparian forest. Forages at low to midlevels. Large hanging basket-shaped nest is often located over a stream. Call is an emphatic, scratchy *pea'up!*; also an agitated *pea'pea'pea'pea'pea'up!* Mex. to Brazil.

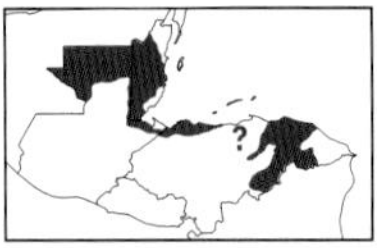

RUDDY-TAILED FLYCATCHER *Terenotriccus erythrurus*
3.5 in. (9 cm). A minute flycatcher with grayish head, and **contrasting tawny rufous tail, rump, and chest**; tiny bill. Rare to uncommon on Caribbean Slope; to 2,620 ft. (800 m). Found in interior of rainforest and taller semideciduous forest. Forages at midlevels in interior of forest. Often flits both wings at same time. Call is a 2-part, thin, high-pitched *peauu-teet!* Mex. to Brazil.

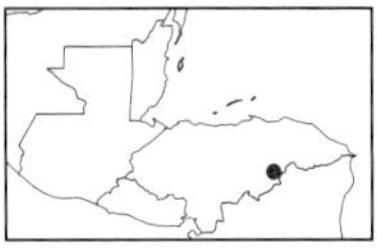

TAWNY-CHESTED FLYCATCHER *Aphanotriccus capitalis*
5 in. (13 cm). **Tawny chest** contrasts with yellow underparts; **gray head** also contrasts with olive upperparts; tawny wing bars. Apparently rare and local in e. Honduras; to 3,270 ft. (1,000 m). Found in rainforest. Forages at low levels. Calls include a sharp *Pee'u!* or *Peew!* and trilling *pip'pip'pip'pip'Pee'u'u'u.* Honduras to Costa Rica.

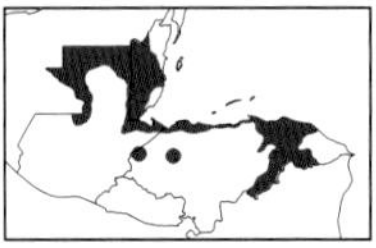

SULPHUR-RUMPED FLYCATCHER *Myiobius sulphureipygius*
5 in. (13 cm). **Lemon yellow rump contrasts with black tail**; note **tawny wash to chest**; plain face with dark eye. Uncommon on Caribbean Slope; to 4,920 ft. (1,500 m). Found in rainforest where it actively forages in understory, often near water. Frequently droops wings and spreads tail. Call is a hard *pik!* Mex. to Ecuador.

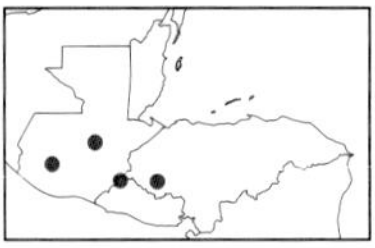

BELTED FLYCATCHER *Xenotriccus callizonus*
5 in. (13 cm). Grayish head with **sharply pointed crest** and whitish **teardrop-shaped eye-ring**; tawny wing bars; underparts washed yellow with **broad tawny chest band**. Rare and local at mid- and higher elevations; from 4,920 to 6,560 ft. (1,500–2,000 m). Found on vegetated semiarid slopes and pine-oak forest. Forages low. Secretive. Calls include emphatic nasal *peeurrr!* (similar to Tufted Flycatcher); also a 2-part *pee'wierr!;* song is a rolling nasal *pip-pip-pi'pi'pi'pi'pweee!* Endemic to region.

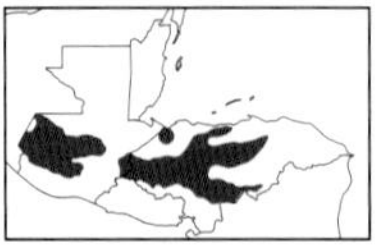

TUFTED FLYCATCHER *Mitrephanes phaeocercus*
5 in. (13 cm). Olive-brown upperparts contrast with **paler tawny underparts**; **pointed crest**; tawny brown wing bars. Fairly common in highlands of NCA; from 3,940 to 9,840 ft. (1,200–3,000 m). Found in cloud forest, pine-oak forest, and rarely in pine savanna. Actively forages at midlevels in forest, where it perches at end of bare branch, making frequent sallies (often flicks wings, shakes tail, and calls upon returning to perch). Call is a nasal, reedy *tweet-tweet* or *tweet-tweet-tweet'tee*; also a single rich *pip!* and *peeurrr!* (not as buzzy as Belted Flycatcher). Mex. to Bolivia.

ROYAL FLYCATCHER
female
male
raised crest rarely seen
RUDDY-TAILED FLYCATCHER
TAWNY-CHESTED FLYCATCHER
SULPHUR-RUMPED FLYCATCHER
BELTED FLYCATCHER
TUFTED FLYCATCHER

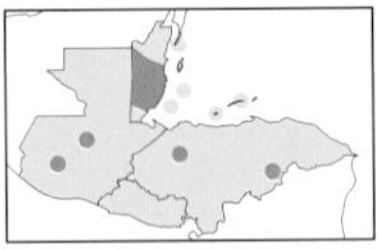

OLIVE-SIDED FLYCATCHER *Contopus cooperi*

7.5 in. (19 cm). Note **"vested" look; long primaries project well down tail** (making tail look short). From other pewees by size, more obvious vested look, and longer primary projections. Uncommon migrant and rare winter resident to highlands of NCA (late Aug.–late Apr.); from 1,970 to 9,190 ft. (600–2,800 m); during migration found down to sea level. Found in pine-oak forest and pine savanna; also taller semideciduous forest and disturbed habitat. Forages at canopy levels where it perches at end of tall bare branch. Calls occasionally: a sharp *pip-pip-pip!* or a single *pip*; song (heard Mar.–Apr.) best rendered as *quick-three'beeers!* AK (breeding) to Brazil (winter).

GREATER PEWEE *Contopus pertinax*

8 in. (20 cm). Similar to Olive-sided Flycatcher, but lacks strong vested look, has more **prominent crest**, and shorter primary projection. Fairly common resident in highlands of NCA; 1,310 to 10,990 ft. (400–3,350 m) but generally above 4,270 ft. (1,300 m). Found in pine savanna or pine-oak forest where it forages at canopy levels. Perches on open bare branches. Call is a repeated *pip!* or *pip-pip!*; song is a sweetly whistled *ho-Say-MaRIA!*; also a rolling *whee-di'reet* and a single note similar to call of Dusky-capped Flycatcher (p. 264). U.S. to Nicaragua.

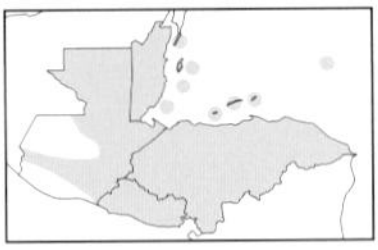

EASTERN WOOD-PEWEE *Contopus virens*

6.5 in. (17 cm). Similar to Western Wood-Pewee, but shows more **olive tones above, whitish wing bars are broader and more even in breadth**, and **mandible usually only one-third to slightly dusky tipped**. Also similar to Tropical Pewee but with more olive above (vs. brownish olive) and has longer primary projections. Common to abundant migrant on both slopes, including Bay Is. (mid-Mar.–early June; mid-Aug.–late Nov.); to 8,860 ft. (2,700 m). Found in a variety of lowland to foothill habitats. Forages at edge and in clearings where it perches at low to midlevels on exposed branches and snags. Call in NCA is a rich, slightly rising and usually 2-part *peee'eaaa* (not buzzy like Western). U.S. (breeding) to Bolivia (winter).

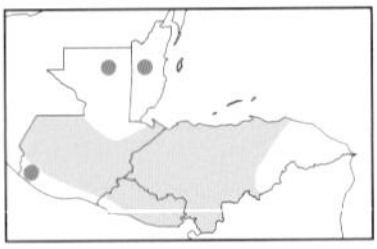

WESTERN WOOD-PEWEE *Contopus sordidulus*

6.5 in. (17 cm). **Sooty gray above; lower wing bar bolder than upper one; mandible completely or two-thirds dark**; long primary projection. Similar to Eastern Wood-Pewee, but generally colder above (sooty gray vs. olive), with darker mandible, and thinner upper wing bar. Also similar to Tropical Pewee, but grayer above (vs. brownish olive), has darker mandible, and longer primary projections. Common transient (mid-Apr.–mid-Oct.); to 9,350 ft. (2,850 m); migrants found at lower elevations, residents generally above 4,920 ft. (1,500 m). Suspected breeding in highlands is unconfirmed; migrants found in virtually any habitat. Call in NCA is a buzzy, slightly rising *peeeeaaa*; song is a *t'tew-ti'tip!* followed by a buzzy *BEEEurrrr!* AK (breeding) to Bolivia (winter).

TROPICAL PEWEE *Contopus cinereus*

5.5 in. (14 cm). Similar to both Western and Eastern Wood-Pewees, but smaller, **more brownish olive above** and has **shorter primary projections**; mandible generally pale but can be dusky tipped (like some Eastern Wood-Pewees). Fairly common in NCA; to 5,910 ft. (1,800 m). Found in a variety of open habitat; at edge of semideciduous forest, disturbed habitat, and coastal scrub, often near water. Forages at low to midlevels, where it perches in open on bare branch or snag. Call is a sharp and quick *peeaaa!* or a short liquid trill. Mex. to Argentina.

Contopus. *A genus of similar flycatchers known as pewees (for their calls), with "vested" appearance (whitish underparts with darker flanks). All perch on snags, making frequent sallies to catch flying insects and returning to the same perch. For identification, note differences in calls, primary projections, and mandible color. Some individuals may not be separable in the field. Larger than* Empidonax *flycatchers (p. 258), with longer primary projections and almost no eye-rings.*

EMPIDONAX FLYCATCHERS I

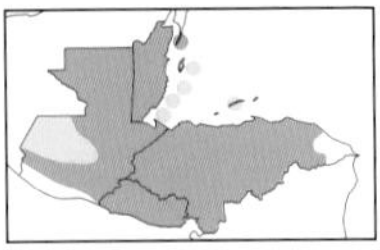

YELLOW-BELLIED FLYCATCHER *Empidonax flaviventris*

5.5 in. (14 cm). Rich yellowish olive above; medium length primary projection; **thin whitish eye-ring, often thicker at back**; underparts, including **throat, washed dull yellow**; medium-length bill with mandible yellowish pink. Most similar to Acadian Flycatcher, but has yellowish wash to throat and chest, and smaller bill. Common winter visitor in NCA (late Aug.–late May); to 9,510 ft. (2,900 m); generally below 6,560 ft. (2,000 m). Found in interior of rainforest, semideciduous forest, riparian forest, and coffee plantations. Forages at low to midlevels. Calls often on wintering grounds, a rich liquid *peeup!* or *peeep!* Occasionally sings a husky nasal *che-bunk*. Canada (breeding) to Panama (winter).

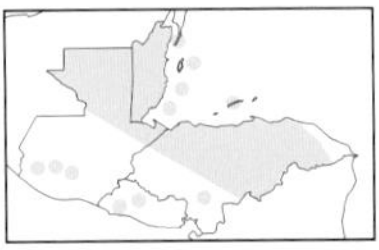

ACADIAN FLYCATCHER *Empidonax virescens*

6 in. (15 cm). Similar to Yellow-bellied Flycatcher, but larger, **plainer white below (throat whitish)** and **bill longer and wider** with yellowish pink mandible; also longer primary projection. Rare transient on Pacific Slope; fairly common on Caribbean Slope, including Bay Is. (late Aug.–Nov.; mid-Mar.–early May); some may overwinter; to 2,950 ft. (900 m). Found mainly in rainforest and semideciduous forest, occasionally in more open habitats. Forages at low to midlevels. Call is an emphatic sharp *pweep!* or *peep!* U.S. (breeding) to Ecuador (winter).

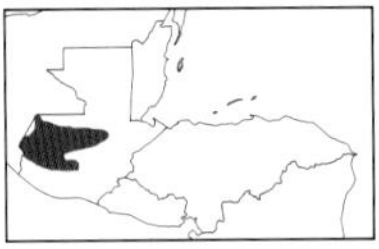

PINE FLYCATCHER *Empidonax affinis*

5.5 in. (14 cm). Olive-brown upperparts; teardrop-shaped, whitish eye-ring; **throat grayish white**; **bill medium in length, but narrow with little or no dusky tip**; medium primary projection. Rare to uncommon resident in w. highlands of Guatemala; 5,740 to 10,990 ft. (1,750–3,350 m). Found at edge or in clearings of pine savanna and pine-oak forest. Forages at low to midlevels. Call is a liquid *wit!* or *pit!*; song is a 2-part whistled *pit-WEEET!* (from n. Mex.; song apparently undescribed in NCA), also a *pit-pit-WEEEEE!* Mex. to Guatemala.

YELLOWISH FLYCATCHER *Empidonax flavescens*

5.5 in. (14 cm). **Yellowish green upperparts with 2 bold buffy-yellow wing bars**; **bold teardrop-shaped whitish eye-ring**; **throat washed yellowish gray**; bill medium in length and width with yellowish pink mandible; short to medium primary projection. Common in highlands of NCA; 2,130 to 9,840 ft. (650–3,000 m) but generally above 4,600 ft. (1,400 m). Found in cloud forest and pine-oak forest; also mature semideciduous forest. Forages at low to midlevels where fairly active. Call is a sharp, high-pitched, ringing *PEEEP!*; also a sharper *seeet!* (this call repeated to form a longer song). Mex. to Panama.

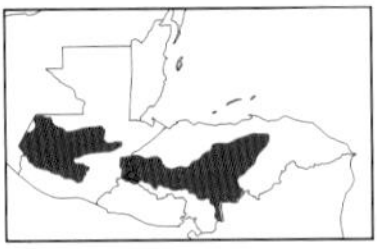

BUFF-BREASTED FLYCATCHER *Empidonax fulvifrons*

5 in. (13 cm). A small *Empidonax* flycatcher. **Orange-olive upperparts**; obvious teardrop-shaped whitish eye-ring; **underparts buffy orange (throat slightly paler)**; short to medium primary projection. Fairly common in highlands of NCA; 1,970 to 10,500 ft. (600–3,200 m). Found at edge within pine savanna and pine-oak forest; also in highland scrub with scattered trees or recent fire burns. Forages at low to midlevels. An active flycatcher that gives frequent flicks of wing and tail. Call is a soft, liquid *wit*; song is a rapid *ti'beuu!* or *pi'dew!* U.S. to Nicaragua.

Empidonax. *A flycatcher genus of infamous repute, as many individuals are difficult to identify. Key identification aids include vocalizations, habitat, throat color, and length of primary projection. Smaller than pewees, with blacker flight feathers and more distinct eye-rings. Some individuals may be best left identified as* "Empidonax sp." *Migratory species vocalize in migration and on their wintering grounds.*

ALDER FLYCATCHER *Empidonax alnorum*

6 in. (15 cm). Grayish olive above; medium to long primary projection; **thin whitish eye-ring nearly absent**; **whitish throat**; bill large in length and width with yellowish pink mandible (little or no dusky tip). Very similar to Willow Flycatcher. Uncommon migrant in NCA (late Aug.–Oct.; Apr.–mid-May); in spring it migrates more commonly along Pacific Slope; to 4,270 ft. (1,300 m). Found at edge in open woodlands, including semideciduous forest, coastal scrub, and coffee plantations. Forages at low levels. Call is an emphatic *pip!*; song is a buzzy, dry *reee'beee!* or *way-bey!-o*. AK (breeding) to Argentina (winter).

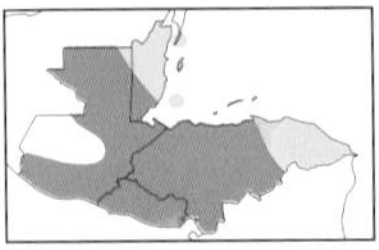

WILLOW FLYCATCHER *Empidonax traillii*

6 in. (15 cm). Very similar to Alder Flycatcher, but generally browner above (vs. grayish olive). Uncommon migrant and winter resident (late Aug.–mid-May); to 5,580 ft. (1,700 m). Found in coastal scrub and at edge of mangroves, but also in open woodlands, including semideciduous forest and coffee plantations, usually near water. Forages at low levels. Call is a liquid *wit!* or *wip!*; song is a buzzy, emphatic *reee'bew!* or *fitz'bew!*; also a *rreEEeep!* Canada (breeding) to Panama (winter).

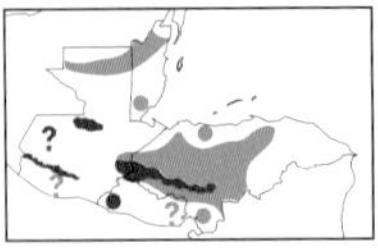

WHITE-THROATED FLYCATCHER *Empidonax albigularis*

5 in. (13 cm). Brownish olive above with dull wing bars; **dusky chest sets off white throat**; **rump slightly paler than lower back**; bill medium with yellowish pink mandible; thin, even eye-ring; short to medium primary projection. Uncommon and local in NCA; movements in region poorly known, but appears to winter in lowlands and breed at higher elevations; to 8,200 ft. (2,500 m); but breeding above 1,970 ft. (600 m). Found in meadows and grassland with scattered trees; at edge of lagoons; also in coastal scrub and freshwater marshes. Forages at low levels in thick vegetation where it's secretive and difficult to observe. Call is a harsh, raspy, somewhat nasal *rreeaah!* or *eaaahh!*; song is a slightly 2-part *rrrreea'ah!* Mex. to w. Panama.

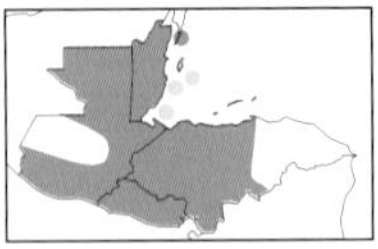

LEAST FLYCATCHER *Empidonax minimus*

5 in. (13 cm). Round-headed appearance useful in identification. Grayish brown above; slightly teardrop-shaped whitish eye-ring; medium primary projection; **whitish below, including throat**; **bill small, but fairly wide with dusky tip to mandible**. Common migrant and winter visitor to NCA (late Aug.–early May); to 9,510 ft. (2,900 m) but most common below 3,937 ft. (1,200 m). Found at edge in a variety of open woodland habitats. Forages at low to midlevels, where it's fairly active, often giving flicks to wing and tail. Call is a dry *wit*; song is an emphatic *chi'bet!* Canada (breeding) to Costa Rica (winter).

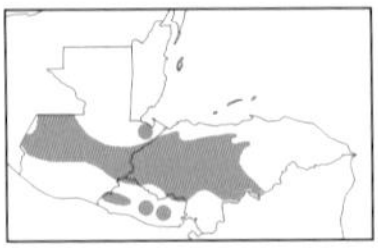

HAMMOND'S FLYCATCHER *Empidonax hammondii*

5.5 in. (14 cm). **Often appears big-headed and stubby-billed.** Grayish olive upperparts; usually obvious teardrop-shaped whitish eye-ring; **throat grayish**; **bill short, narrow, with dark-tipped mandible; long primary projection**. Possibly confused with Least Flycatcher, but note differences in bill structure and primary projection; also call and habitats. Common migrant and winter visitor to highlands of NCA (late Sept.–mid-Apr.); from 3,280 to 9,510 ft. (1,000–2,900 m). Found in pine-oak forest and pine savanna. Forages at all levels to subcanopy, where it's fairly active, often giving flicks to wing and tail. Call is a rich *peep!* AK (breeding) to Nicaragua (winter).

ALDER FLYCATCHER
WILLOW FLYCATCHER
WHITE-THROATED FLYCATCHER
LEAST FLYCATCHER
HAMMOND'S FLYCATCHER

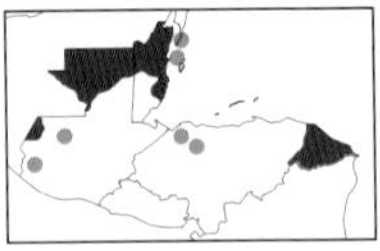

VERMILION FLYCATCHER *Pyrocephalus rubinus*

6 in. (15 cm). Male unmistakable. **Brilliant red** with dark eye line connecting with dark back. Female lacks red and instead shows **brown streaks on chest** and **pinkish belly**. Immature similar to female, but with yellowish belly. Fairly common to uncommon in Belize; rare to uncommon in rest of NCA; to 8,200 ft. (2,500 m). Found in pine savanna, savanna grasslands, and coastal scrub at low levels; often perched at top of small bush. Call is a fairly sharp *Peet!*; song is a rapidly delivered trill, *p'p'p'p'p'preeet!* U.S. to Argentina.

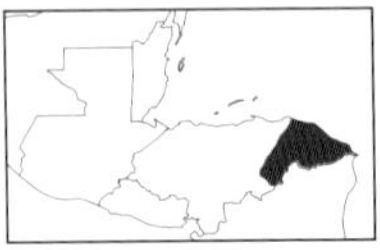

LONG-TAILED TYRANT *Colonia colonus*

10 in. (26 cm). Blackish plumage overall with **gray crown and white down back**; **tail has long, thin central tail feathers**. Fairly common in e. Honduras; to 1,970 ft. (600 m). Found at edge or near clearings of rainforest and riparian forest. Perches at mid- to upper levels, often on bare exposed branches. Calls include a rising *pweeet!* or *pa'pweeet!*; also a 3-noted *pweet!-pi'peuuu*. Honduras to Argentina.

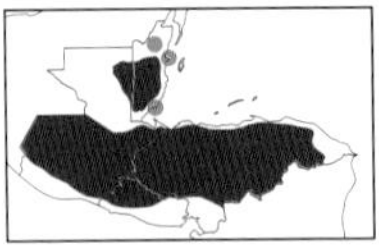

BLACK PHOEBE *Sayornis nigricans*

7 in. (18 cm). **Blackish plumage overall**; dusky wing bars barely noticeable; **belly, vent, and undertail coverts white**. Uncommon to fairly common in NCA; to 7,220 ft. (2,200 m). Usually found resting on a rock or partly submerged stick in a river or along a stream. Actively forages on rocks and boulders. Call is a rich *teep!*; dawn song is a repeated *tii'weep!—tii'wheeuu* (the last syllable buzzy and descending). U.S. to Argentina.

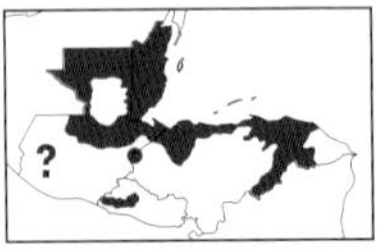

BRIGHT-RUMPED ATTILA *Attila spadiceus*

8 in. (20 cm). Tawny-brown upperparts with **golden yellow rump**; wing bars edged tawny; **tail rufous**; paler face and underparts lightly streaked; **eyes reddish brown**; large pinkish bill with **prominent hooked tip**. Fairly common on Caribbean Slope; rare on Pacific Slope; to 6,890 ft. (2,100 m). Found in interior of rainforest, taller semideciduous forest, and riparian forest, where it forages at mid- to upper levels. Longer calls include an excited *atila, atila, atila! Atila! ATILA! ATILA! Wheu!*; also a *kip* call (similar to Stub-tailed Spadebill [p. 250]). Mex. to Brazil.

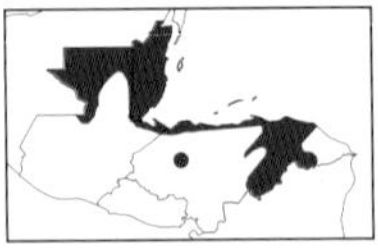

RUFOUS MOURNER *Rhytipterna holerythra*

8 in. (20 cm). Head fairly round and large; **tawny overall** with dark eyes; **bill pinkish based**. Very similar to Rufous Piha (p. 276), but smaller, lacks obvious eye-ring, has smaller bill and darker throat, and different voice. Also compare to Speckled Mourner (p. 280), but smaller, doesn't have contrasting darker wing coverts, and lacks scaling on breast. Uncommon to fairly common on Caribbean Slope; to 3,940 ft. (1,200 m). Found in interior of rainforest and taller semideciduous forest, where it forages at mid- to upper levels. Sits quietly for long periods. Call is a pair of clear rising, then descending whistles. Mex. to Ecuador.

VERMILION FLYCATCHER
male
female
LONG-TAILED TYRANT
BLACK PHOEBE
BRIGHT-RUMPED ATTILA
RUFOUS MOURNER

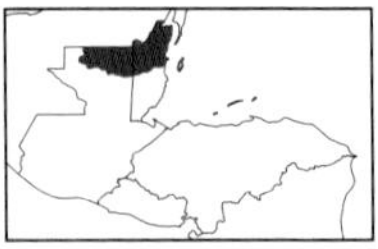

YUCATAN FLYCATCHER *Myiarchus yucatanensis*

7.5 in. (19 cm). Similar to Dusky-capped Flycatcher, but larger, **wing coverts mostly gray-brown (lack rufous)**, crown lighter, **head more rounded**, and undertail rufous. Fairly common in n. Guatemala and n. Belize (including Ambergris Caye); to 980 ft. (300 m). Found in open woodland such as pine savanna and at edge of semideciduous forest, where it forages at midlevels. Calls include a pleasant whistled *wuueeee!* or a more drawn-out *wuuueeeep!*; also a more agitated *wee'wee'wee'wee'wee'weeeur* and a *prrrrrt*. Endemic to region.

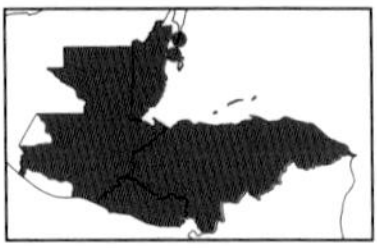

DUSKY-CAPPED FLYCATCHER *Myiarchus tuberculifer*

6.5 in. (17 cm). The smallest *Myiarchus* flycatcher in NCA. **Dark crown** contrasts with paler gray face; **wing coverts heavily edged rufous**; **undertail dusky with no rufous webbing**; **bill thin and dark**. Compare with Yucatan Flycatcher where ranges overlap, but is smaller, has contrasting dark crown, and heavy rufous edging to wing coverts; also distinct voice. Fairly common to common in NCA; to 9,350 ft. (2,850 m). Found in a variety of woodland habitats, including semideciduous forest, some disturbed habitats (like coffee plantations), riparian forest, rainforest, mangrove forest, and pine-oak forest. Forages at midlevels. Calls include a drawn-out, slightly mournful whistle; an excited *weeuu'p'p'p'p'p'p*; other contact calls include *pea'wheer!* and *whir'r'rrrrrr* (often the last 2 calls are combined in a longer excited or agitated series). U.S. to Argentina.

Myiarchus. *A confusing and difficult group of flycatchers. Some individuals may be best left unidentified to the species level. Important field marks include vocalizations, the pattern of dark webbing on undertail, pattern of rufous and yellow edging on folded wing, and bill structure (heavy or thin). Habitat can also be useful for ID when combined with field marks.*

Myiarchus flycatcher undertail patterns

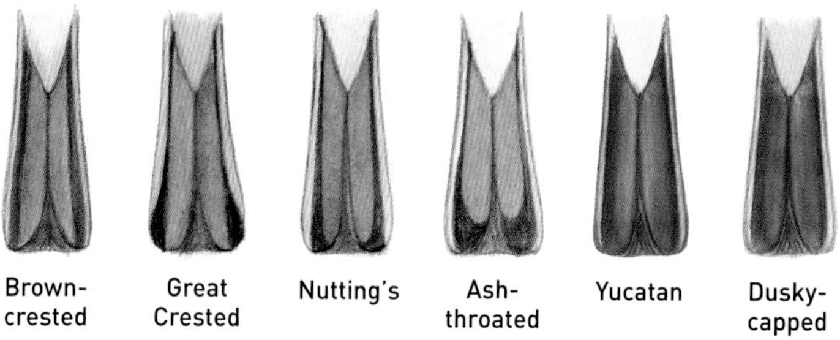

MYIARCHUS FLYCATCHERS II

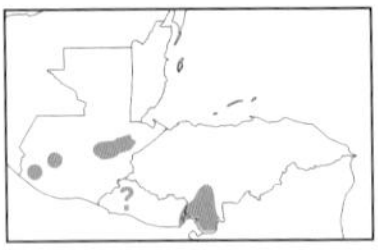

ASH-THROATED FLYCATCHER *Myiarchus cinerascens*

7.5 in. (19 cm). Face pale gray, contrasting somewhat with brownish crown; **note rufous-edged primaries and contrasting yellow-edged secondaries**; lightly washed lemon yellow belly and vent; **undertail rufous with dark outer edge forming broad dark tips to tail**; medium-sized bill mainly dark. Rare winter resident on Pacific Slope (Oct.–May), but probably is underreported; to 5,580 ft. (1,700 m). Found in arid and semiarid habitats such as coastal scrub and thorn forest. Forages at low to midlevels. Calls include a short whip, similar to Brown-crested Flycatcher call; a burry, excited *prik!* or *kibrik!*; also a *ki'breer!* U.S. (breeding) to Nicaragua (winter).

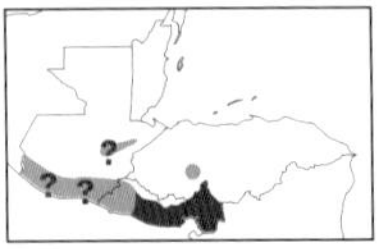

NUTTING'S FLYCATCHER *Myiarchus nuttingi*

7.5 in. (19 cm). On folded wing, **rufous-edged primaries blend gradually into more yellowish-edged secondaries**; bright lemon yellow belly and vent; **undertail rufous with dark outer edge (but not tip)**; medium-sized bill may show pinkish base. Quite similar to Brown-crested Flycatcher, but smaller, and note differences in calls. Mouth lining yellow-orange (pinkish in Brown-crested). Uncommon to fairly common on Pacific Slope; to 5,910 ft. (1,800 m). Found in semiarid habitats including thorn forest and coastal scrub, but also at edge of semideciduous forest. Forages at low to midlevels. Call is a low whistle that rises initially and then descends, *wEEeeeuuu* (similar to Dusky-capped Flycatcher [p. 264] but brighter in tone); also a similar, but shorter *wEEeuup* (this call similar to Great Crested Flycatcher, but higher-pitched and less hoarse); also a whistled whinny, and agitated nasal calls, *pee'up!* or *wi'wi'uh!* and a scratchy *rrheeaa*. Mex. to Costa Rica.

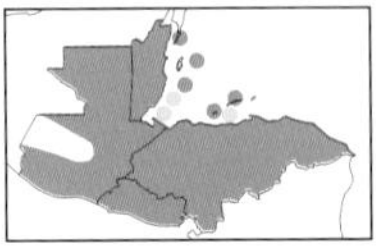

GREAT CRESTED FLYCATCHER *Myiarchus crinitus*

8.5 in. (22 cm). Dark gray-brown above; gray **throat and chest** contrast with bright lemon yellow belly and vent; **bright rufous-edged primaries and inner secondaries**; **bright rufous undertail**; bill stout with pinkish base. Common winter visitor including Bay Is. (mid-Sept.–early May); to 6,560 ft. (2,000 m). Found within a variety of lowland and foothill habitats: rainforest, semideciduous forest, taller disturbed habitats, and mangroves. Forages at all levels. Call is a scratchy, slightly forced *whheeeaak!* or can also be more disyllabic, *weeeaa'up!* (similar in quality to Nutting's, but lower pitched and hoarser). Canada (breeding) to Ecuador (winter).

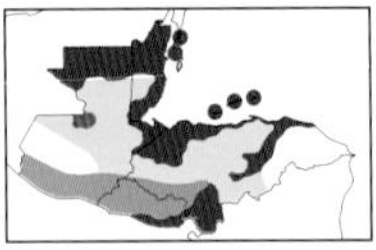

BROWN-CRESTED FLYCATCHER *Myiarchus tyrannulus*

8.5–9.5 in. (22–24 cm). Size varies between smaller resident (*brachyurus*) and migratory subspecies in NCA. In general, this species is a larger version of Nutting's Flycatcher; **on folded wing, rufous-edged primaries and inner secondaries blend gradually to yellow-edged outer secondaries**; belly and vent bright lemon yellow; **undertail rufous with fairly broad dark outer edging (but not tip); bill large and stout (generally all-dark)**. Mouth lining pinkish (yellow-orange in Nutting's). Resident (*brachyurus*; Pacific Slope of El Salvador and Honduras) is smaller, bill less stout, and has less dark edging on undertail. Fairly common resident and winter visitor to NCA; status of subspecies movements in region confusing and requires more study; to 6,070 ft. (1,850 m). Found in a variety of woodland habitats: semideciduous forest, coastal scrub, thorn forest, coffee plantations, pine savanna. Resident *brachyurus* nests in mangroves. Forages at all levels in forest. Call is an emphatic *whip!*, sometimes *ha'whit!* or *ha'weet!*; also agitated, complaining *wee'e'e'e'r'r'r'rrr* or *eear'r'r'rrrrr*. U.S. to Bolivia.

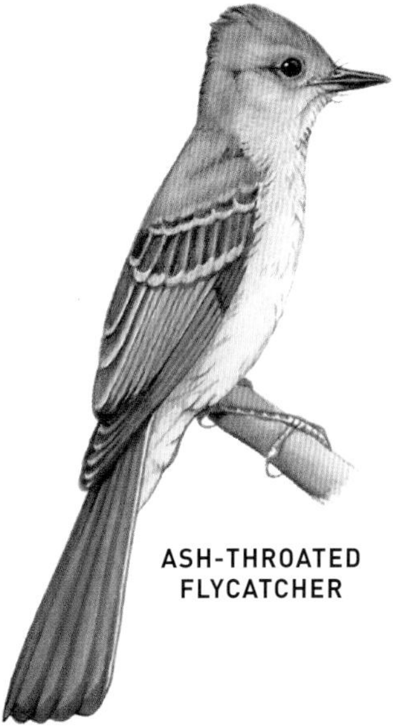

ASH-THROATED FLYCATCHER

NUTTING'S FLYCATCHER

GREAT CRESTED FLYCATCHER

BROWN-CRESTED FLYCATCHER

KISKADEE-LIKE FLYCATCHERS

GREAT KISKADEE *Pitangus sulphuratus*

9.5 in. (24 cm). Similar to Boat-billed Flycatcher, but note **rufous wings and tail** and **straight culmen**. Common in NCA; to 6,070 ft. (1,850 m). Found at edge in a variety of freshwater aquatic settings: lagoons and ponds, reservoirs and treatment plants, and along riverbanks. Also in urban areas. Forages at all levels, usually perched on exposed open branch. Calls include an often heard, husky *kis-ka-dee!*; also a simple *deeee!* TX to Argentina.

BOAT-BILLED FLYCATCHER *Megarynchus pitangua*

9.5 in. (24 cm). Quite similar to Great Kiskadee, but **culmen heavily arched** (bill appears more massive), and **lacks rufous edging to wings and tail**. Common in NCA; to 6,070 ft. (1,850 m). Found in a variety of woodland habitats, including semideciduous forest, rainforest, taller disturbed habitat, and mangroves. Forages at mid- to upper levels and often perches on exposed branches. Call is a nasal, vibrating rattle, *EHHhr'r'r'r'r'r'rrrrr*; dawn song is a 3-part *peer'brrrr'riit!*; also just a harsh, burry *peerrrr!* Mex. to Argentina.

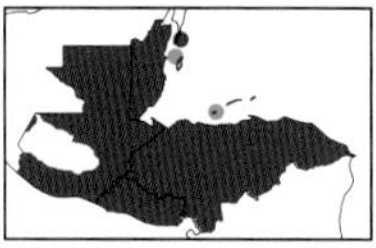

SOCIAL FLYCATCHER *Myiozetetes similis*

6 in. (15 cm). **Crown grayish** (with concealed reddish stripe); broad white supercilium; **grayish face** and white throat; remaining underparts bright yellow. Similar to White-ringed Flycatcher but has shorter bill, gray crown (with reddish stripe, not yellowish), is grayer in face (not black), and superciliaries usually do not connect at nape. Also similar to Gray-capped Flycatcher, but darker in face, has broader supercilium, dark eyes (not pale), and doesn't have gray nape. Abundant in NCA; to 6,070 ft. (1,850 m). Found at edge in a variety of open and disturbed habitats: second growth, plantations, around cities and towns; forages at low to midlevels. Calls include an emphatic *cheeeeo!* or *seeeu-suu!* or *sue!-sue!-sue!-brrreee!*; a longer *sue'su-sue'su-sue'su-sue'su-sue*; dawn song is a repeated *sue'bree!* Mex. to Argentina.

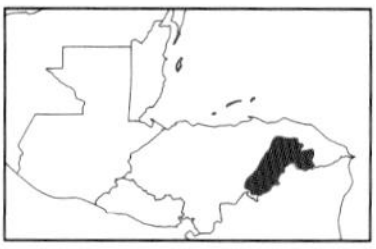

WHITE-RINGED FLYCATCHER *Conopias albovittatus*

6 in. (15 cm). Similar to Social Flycatcher, but crown (with concealed yellowish stripe) and face blacker; **broad white superciliaries connect in back of head**; bill also longer than Social Flycatcher. Rare to uncommon in e. Honduras; status unclear; to 2,460 ft. (750 m). Found in rainforest where it forages at mid- to upper levels. Call is an excited *wiii!'pea'd'd'd'd'd'd* (sputtering at the end); or just a single *wheeerr*. Honduras to Ecuador.

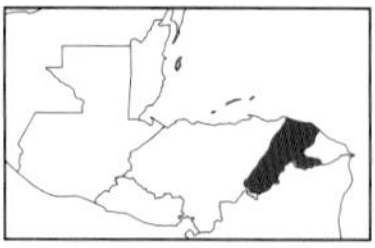

GRAY-CAPPED FLYCATCHER *Myiozetetes granadensis*

6 in. (15 cm). Crown (with concealed reddish stripe) and **nape grayish**; thin white supercilium (widest in front) barely extends beyond eyes; **eyes pale grayish white**. Social and White-ringed Flycatchers lack gray napes, have broader white superciliaries, and dark eyes. Uncommon to common in e. Honduras; to 5,910 ft. (1,800 m). Found at edge or clearings within rainforest and along riverbanks; generally stays close to water. Forages at low to midlevels in trees. Call is a short *wick* or *pic*; also an agitated, squeaky *bee-be-dee* and a *kyew-kyew!* Honduras to Brazil.

GREAT
KISKADEE
BOAT-BILLED
FLYCATCHER
SOCIAL
FLYCATCHER
WHITE-RINGED
FLYCATCHER
GRAY-CAPPED
FLYCATCHER

STREAKED FLYCATCHERS AND SCISSOR-TAILED FLYCATCHER

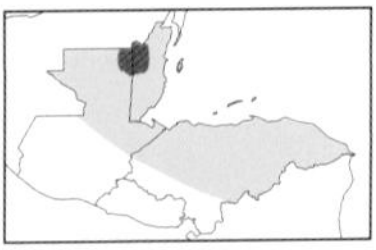

STREAKED FLYCATCHER *Myiodynastes maculatus*

9 in. (23 cm). Brownish upperparts streaked black; broad black eye line and yellow supercilium; **thin black malar stripe**; **whitish chin relatively unmarked**; whitish underparts streaked with narrow brown chevrons and generally washed with very pale yellow; tail rufous; **mandible has pinkish base**. Very similar to Sulphur-bellied Flycatcher, but has yellow supercilium (not white), thin black malar stripe (not broad), whitish chin (not dark), larger bill with pinkish base to mandible, and paler underparts. Transient and uncommon breeding resident on Caribbean Slope (mid-Mar.–Sept.); to 4,920 ft. (1,500 m). Found at edge or interior within pine savanna, semideciduous forest, and disturbed habitats. Forages at mid- to upper levels. Call is a squeaky, harsh *pik!* (often repeated); also an emphatic *pit-teeur!* Mex. to Argentina.

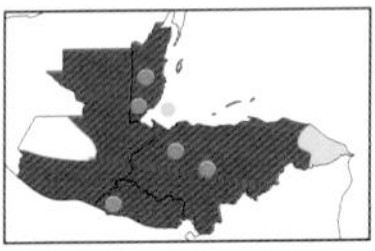

SULPHUR-BELLIED FLYCATCHER *Myiodynastes luteiventris*

8 in. (20 cm). Very similar to Streaked Flycatcher, but note **broad black malar stripe**, **dark chin**, stronger yellowish wash below, whitish supercilium (not yellow), and **smaller bill with dark base to mandible**. Fairly common to common breeding resident on both slopes (early Mar.–early Oct.); very rare in winter (Nov.–Feb.); to 5,910 ft. (1,800 m). Found generally at edge or in clearings within semideciduous forest, rainforest, or taller disturbed habitats. Calls include a squeaky, rubber ducky–like *sweee'yeuu!*; also a somewhat agitated *pip*, often given as *pip'pip'pip'pip'pip'pip'pip* . . . ; dawn song is a repeated *peaa!'tah'wreee*. U.S. (breeding) to Brazil (winter).

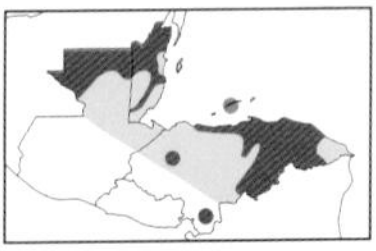

PIRATIC FLYCATCHER *Legatus leucophaius*

6.5 in. (17 cm). Brownish gray upperparts; dark face mask contrasts with white supercilium; **thin dark malar stripe**; lightly **streaked underparts**; faint yellowish wash to belly and vent; 2 weak wing bars; small bill. Fairly common migrant and breeding resident on Caribbean Slope (late Feb.–mid-Sept.); rare on Pacific Slope close to Nicaraguan border; very rare in winter (Nov.–Feb.); to 3,630 ft. (1,100 m). Found at edge or at clearings within rainforest, semideciduous forest, and disturbed habitats (like gardens and plantations). Forages at mid- to upper levels. Named for habit of driving other birds (especially caciques and oropendolas) from their completed nests. Call is a euphonia-like *wee-o-dee!*, given constantly from high perch; also a trilling *wee'e'e'e'e'e'e'*. Mex. (breeding) to Argentina (winter).

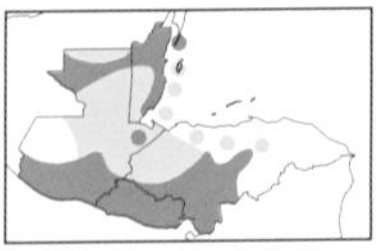

SCISSOR-TAILED FLYCATCHER *Tyrannus forficatus*

7.5–14 in. (19–36 cm); includes longer tail of male. A distinctive-looking flycatcher of open country. Dark gray wings contrast with pale gray back, **white head** and breast; **belly and underwing coverts are washed pink; long, black-and-white forked tail** (males have the longest tails). Similar to Fork-tailed Flycatcher (p. 274), but lacks black crown, is pinkish below, and tail is usually shorter and less deeply forked. Rare to uncommon transient and winter visitor on Caribbean Slope; common to abundant on Pacific Slope (mid-Aug.–early May); to 6,560 ft. (2,000 m). Found in a variety of open and disturbed habitats: along hedgerows and at edges of agricultural fields, in coastal scrub or thorn forest; also plantations. Perches in open and forages at low to midlevels. Large nighttime roosts of thousands of individuals have been recorded in mangroves and in urban centers. Diurnal migration includes small groups (5–10 individuals) or flocks of hundreds. Call is a sharp, nasal *pick!* U.S. (breeding) to Panama (winter).

STREAKED FLYCATCHER
SULPHUR-BELLIED FLYCATCHER
PIRATIC FLYCATCHER
male
SCISSOR-TAILED FLYCATCHER
Scissor-tailed Flycatchers often perch on fences

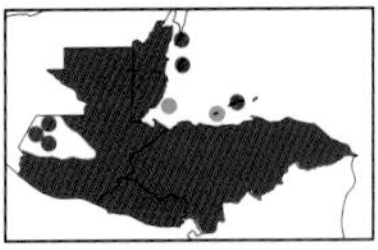

TROPICAL KINGBIRD *Tyrannus melancholicus*

8.5 in. (22 cm). Yellowish olive back with **contrasting grayish head**; faint dark mask; throat whitish; **chest yellowish olive** and remaining underparts bright yellow; 2 faint wing bars; **tail brownish olive and notched**. Extremely similar to Couch's Kingbird (nearly indistinguishable in the field where the 2 species overlap in Belize and n. Guatemala), but smaller, and has longer, thinner bill, and darker back; note differences in calls. Common resident in region; to 5,910 ft. (1,800 m). Found in a variety of open and disturbed woodland habitats, including cities, towns, and gardens, and along roadsides (often seen perched on power lines), where it forages at low to midlevels. Call is a short trill (similar to Common Tody-Flycatcher [p. 252], but longer and more rolling); dawn song is an excited, repeated *pit'teah'reee'reee!* U.S. to Argentina.

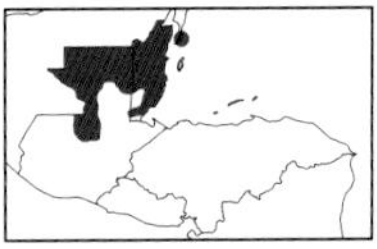

COUCH'S KINGBIRD *Tyrannus couchii*

9 in. (23 cm). Almost identical to Tropical Kingbird (nearly indistinguishable in the field), but slightly larger overall, and with smaller bill (shorter and broader), and greener back; differences in calls are the best clues. Uncommon to common in n. Guatemala and Belize (including cayes); to 4,430 ft. (1,350 m). Found at edge or in clearings within semideciduous forest, pine savanna, and taller disturbed habitats. Forages at all levels. Calls include a *pip-pip-weeeerrr!* (buzzy at the end) or just *weeeeerrrr!* U.S. to Belize.

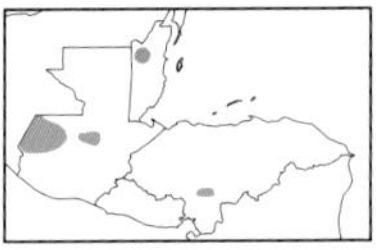

CASSIN'S KINGBIRD *Tyrannus vociferans*

8.5 in. (22 cm). Dark gray hood with darker mask and **contrasting white malar stripe**; **chest gray** with remaining underparts lemon yellow; **blackish tail squared with thin whitish tips**. Similar to Western Kingbird, especially when pale tips to tail have worn off, but hood and chest are darker gray, and white malar stripe is more obvious. Rare and local winter resident (mid-Oct.–early May); 2,970 to 8,200 ft. (900–2,500 m). Found in open country along hedgerows and agricultural fields, in grasslands; also in pine savanna. Forages at low to midlevels. Call is a 2-part *Kah-BEER!* U.S. (breeding) to Nicaragua (winter).

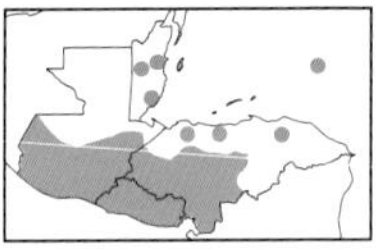

WESTERN KINGBIRD *Tyrannus verticalis*

8.5 in. (22 cm). Very similar to Cassin's Kingbird, but grayish hood and chest paler overall, malar stripe less contrasting, wings narrower, and squared black tail has **thin white border to outer tail feathers**. Common winter resident (mid-Oct.–mid-May) in NCA mainly on Pacific Slope; to 5,910 ft. (1,800 m). Found in a variety of open habitat types, such as coastal scrub, thorn forest, and along hedgerows and in agricultural fields. Large numbers found roosting in coastal mangroves. Forages at low to midlevels. Calls include a sharp, nasal *pik!* and agitated squabbles. U.S. (breeding) to Costa Rica (winter).

TROPICAL KINGBIRD/
COUCH'S KINGBIRD

Tropical Kingbird on roadside power line

CASSIN'S
KINGBIRD

WESTERN
KINGBIRD

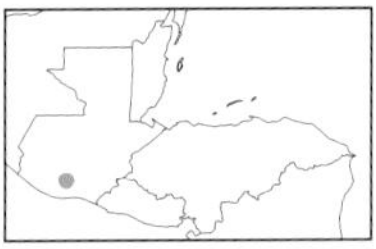

THICK-BILLED KINGBIRD *Tyrannus crassirostris*

9.5 in. (24 cm). Grayish olive upperparts; slightly contrasting **dark crown and blackish mask**; **throat and chest whitish**; remaining underparts washed lightly in lemon yellow; **stout black bill**. Juvenile has rusty tail and edging to wing coverts. Winter vagrant visitor to Guatemala; to 1,480 ft. (450 m). Found in open areas and at forest edge; also in riparian forest. Forages at mid- to upper levels. Call is a loud, emphatic, and excited *purr'reeeet!* or *purr'reeeet'rr*. U.S. (breeding) to Guatemala (winter).

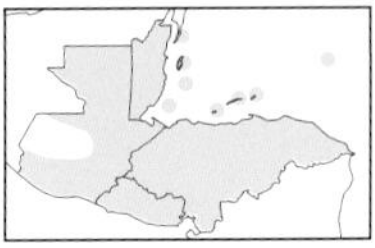

EASTERN KINGBIRD *Tyrannus tyrannus*

8.5 in. (22 cm). **Two-toned appearance** with grayish black upperparts and white underparts; gray smudge on sides of breast; **black tail has broad white tips**. Common transient on Caribbean Slope, including Bay Is., and rare to uncommon on Pacific Slope (mid-Mar.–late May; mid-Aug.–early Nov.); very rare winter visitor (Dec.–Feb.); to 6,560 ft. (2,000 m). Found at or flying over almost any habitat. Perches often in tops of trees; however, forages at all levels. Migrates by day in small groups (5–10 individuals) or dispersed flocks of hundreds. Call is a thin, buzzy *kzeeer!*; also gives other wiry, swiftlike twitters in migration. Canada (breeding) to Argentina (winter).

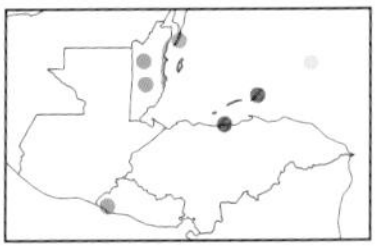

GRAY KINGBIRD *Tyrannus dominicensis*

9 in. (23 cm). **Gray upperparts, including crown, with contrasting dark mask** (ruby red crown patch rarely visible); underparts whitish with **faint dusky gray wash on chest**; **tail notched**; 2 pale wing bars; size and structure similar to Tropical and Couch's Kingbirds (p. 272), but note gray upperparts (not yellowish olive) and whitish underparts (not yellow). Rare transient and winter visitor to cayes and Swan Is. (late July–mid-May); recently bred (mid Apr.–mid Sep.) in n. Honduras (Ceiba) and at Guanaja (Bay I.); very rare on mainland but known to cross the isthmus to the Pacific Coast (in El Salvador). Found in coastal scrub, mangroves, and near towns where it perches in open, often on exposed branches or power lines. Forages at all levels. Calls (similar to calls of Tropical Kingbird) include a quickly delivered, liquid rolling trill *tea'rrreaa!* and a *ta'tea'rrreeea!* (this second call repeated as a dawn song). U.S. and Caribbean to Venezuela.

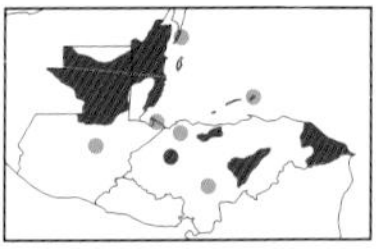

FORK-TAILED FLYCATCHER *Tyrannus savana*

7.5–16 in. (19–41 cm); includes longer tail of adult. A striking appearance. **Black crown** and blackish wings contrast strongly with pale gray back and white underparts; **very long tail, deeply forked**. Similar to Scissor-tailed Flycatcher (p. 270), but has black crown, no pinkish wash below, and shallower, fluttering wingbeats. Uncommon resident on Caribbean Slope and virtually absent from Pacific Slope; movements and distribution of local populations and of austral migrants in NCA is poorly understood; to 4,920 ft. (1,500 m). Found in open country such as grasslands, pine savanna; freshwater marshes; also along pastures and roadside where it often perches on barbed wire or fenceposts, and on or near the ground. Forages at low levels. Call is a raspy, harsh *chick* or *tic*; also a rapid *chick-chick-chick-chick* and metallic twittering. Mex. to Argentina.

migrating Eastern Kingbirds
THICK-BILLED KINGBIRD
EASTERN KINGBIRD
FORK-TAILED FLYCATCHER
GRAY KINGBIRD

COTINGAS

COTINGIDAE (Order: Passeriformes). The cotingas are medium-sized oddly proportioned Neotropical birds with relatively small heads, rounded bodies, and short tails. Bellbirds have 3 stringlike wattles hanging over their bills, giving them an even stranger appearance. All species in this family are frugivorous, and depend on the existence of large forest patches. The 2 cotingas rarely vocalize, while the piha and especially the bellbird have voices among the loudest in birds. **4 species (4 genera)**

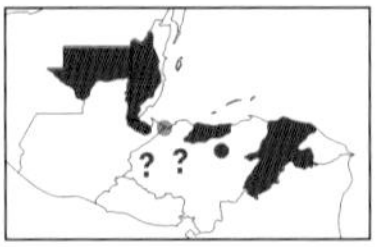

LOVELY COTINGA *Cotinga amabilis*

7.5 in. (19 cm). **Turquoise blue adult male** is unmistakable. Grayish female **heavily scalloped overall**. Rare on Caribbean Slope; to 4,920 ft. (1,500 m). Found in interior of rainforest or taller semideciduous forest where it forages at mid- to upper levels; often perches on exposed limbs protruding above canopy. Appears to be seasonal in some areas, as it follows seasonal fruit production of its favorite trees. Generally silent. Mex. to Costa Rica.

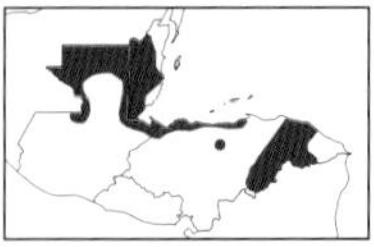

RUFOUS PIHA *Lipaugus unirufus*

10 in. (26 cm). A large, fairly drab cotinga of forest interior. **Rufous or tawny brown overall**; slightly paler yellow on throat and belly; **thin grayish eye-ring; short, but stout bill has pale base to mandible**; eyes dark. Very similar to Rufous Mourner (p. 262), but larger, with eye-ring and heavier bill. Also similar to Speckled Mourner (p. 280), but has weaker eye-ring, lacks scaling on chest, and less obvious tawny wing bars. Uncommon to rare on Caribbean Slope; to 3,610 ft. (1,100 m). Found in rainforest, where it forages and perches at mid- to upper levels. May be easily overlooked as it perches for long periods without moving, but easily detected by loud voice. Call is a very loud, scratchy, electric-sounding *WIIII'WERRRE!* or *Peuuur-WIIII'WERRRRE!*; or just a single *peeuuurr.* Mex. to Ecuador.

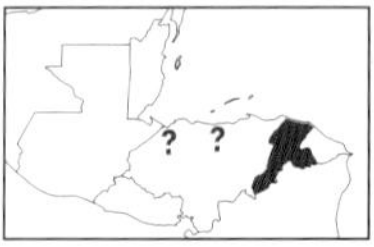

SNOWY COTINGA *Carpodectes nitidus*

8 in. (20 cm). **Adult male all-white** with short tail and dark bill. Female grayish above with faint eye-ring; fairly broad white wing bars. Very rare to rare in e. Honduras; to 2,460 ft. (750 m). Found in interior of rainforest, where it forages at mid- to upper levels; often perches on exposed bare limbs at canopy level. Generally silent. Honduras to Panama.

THREE-WATTLED BELLBIRD *Procnias tricarunculatus*

10–13 in. (26–33 cm). Adult male chestnut brown with white head and breast, with **3 long black caruncles hanging from its face**. Female smaller; greenish yellow overall with streaking on underparts, and lacks caruncles. Uncommon to fairly common and local in e. Honduras; seasonal movements within the region, moving among very large forest patches; to 7,710 ft. (2,350 m). Found in interior of rainforest, where it forages at mid- to upper levels. Males perch conspicuously and call at canopy level on exposed branches. Call is a loud, far-carrying electric bell-like *EENK!*; also a high-pitched *sheeeaaa*. Honduras to Panama.

Lovely Cotinga perched above canopy
male
female
LOVELY COTINGA
male
SNOWY COTINGA
female
RUFOUS PIHA
male
female
THREE-WATTLED BELLBIRD

PIPRIDAE (Order: Passeriformes). Neotropical birds known for enchanting courtship displays. Male manakins perform at leks (display grounds or avian "dance floors"). Performances include wing snaps (created by modified wing feathers), flight displays, and dancing movements on perches. Adult males are brightly plumaged, whereas females are uniformly olive or yellowish. Males can take several years to acquire adult plumage as they "learn" the sophisticated courtship necessary to attract females. **5 species (5 genera)**

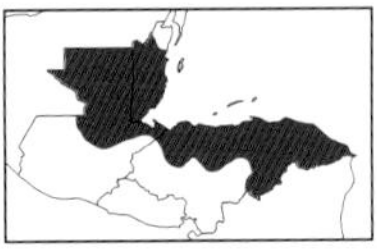

WHITE-COLLARED MANAKIN *Manacus candei*

4.5 in. (11 cm). Male has white upper body contrasting with **blackish wings and crown**; belly and vent bright yellow. Female yellow-olive overall. **Legs orange on both sexes.** Fairly common on Caribbean Slope; to 2,460 ft. (750 m). Found in rainforest, semideciduous forest, and disturbed habitats, where it forages at lower levels. Lek is a cleared area on the forest floor. Males at lek move quickly from one perch to the next with rapid buzzing noise of wings. At perch they make loud snapping noise with wings. Call is a rapid *meear'r'r'r'r'r'r!* Mex. to Panama.

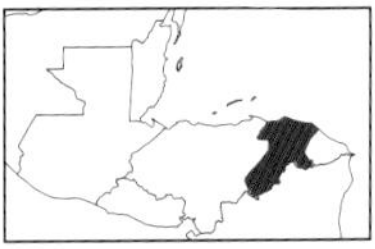

WHITE-RUFFED MANAKIN *Corapipo altera*

4 in. (10 cm). Adult male **glossy blue-black overall** with **bright white throat**. Female yellowish olive with **contrasting paler gray throat**. Legs grayish. Female similar to female Red-capped Manakin, but throat grayish. Rare in e. Honduras; to 4,100 ft. (1,250 m). Found in rainforest interior, where it forages at low to midlevels. Call is a trilling, bell-like *zeeu'u'u'u'u'u'u*. Honduras to Venezuela.

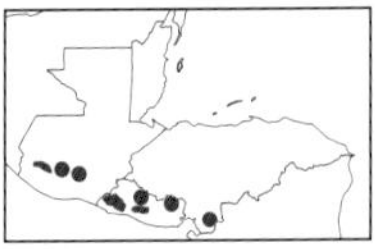

LONG-TAILED MANAKIN *Chiroxiphia linearis*

6–9.5 in. (15–21 cm). Male takes 5 years to acquire adult plumage. Immature male starts off as overall olive green with varying amounts of red on crown, and short central tail feathers; gradually acquires distinctive adult plumage with **long central tail feathers**. Female all olive green with no red on crown. **Yellow-orange legs in all plumages**. Common but very local on Pacific Slope; to 4,920 ft. (1,500 m). Found in interior of semideciduous forest, taller disturbed habitat, and riparian forest, where it forages at low to midlevels. At lek, adult males lead young males in coordinated leapfrogging display and butterfly flight. Calls include a nasal, insectlike *jeew'ah-jeew'ah-jeew'ah-jeew'ah* and *TO-LE-DO!* (given in unison during display); also a *pip* (sometimes as *pip-pip-pip-pip'pip'pip*) and *weee'oh!* Mex. to Costa Rica.

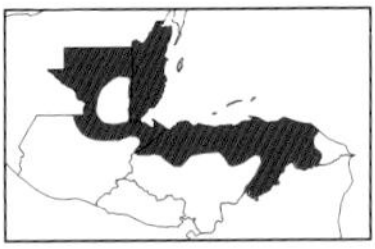

RED-CAPPED MANAKIN *Ceratopipra mentalis*

4 in. (10 cm). Adult male has **bright red head**; **pale eyes**; yellow thighs difficult to see. Juvenile male and female overall olive. Both sexes have grayish legs. Female and young male similar to female White-ruffed Manakin except throat is yellower. Uncommon to fairly common on Caribbean Slope; to 5,250 ft. (1,600 m). Found in rainforest, where it generally forages at midlevels. Lekking males make loud wing snaps and sophisticated aerial loops, wing flutters, and dance a "moonwalk." Calls include a rapid buzz, *eeeh'h'h'h'h'h'h'h*; also a *pip* and a long, high-pitched thin whistle, *weeeeuuuuuuuuu*. Mex. to Ecuador.

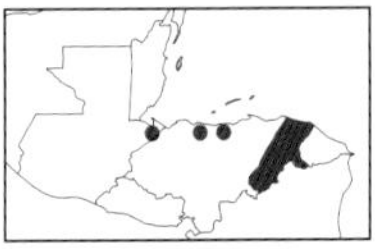

GRAY-HEADED PIPRITES *Piprites griseiceps*

5 in. (13 cm). Yellowish olive upperparts contrast with **grayish crown and face**; note **thin white eye-ring**; **head rounded**. Rare on Caribbean Slope; to 3,610 ft. (1,100 m). Found in rainforest, where it forages at midlevels, often in mixed-species flocks. Seldom seen in NCA. Call is a *Myiarchus* flycatcher–like *whit!* or *wip!*; also a *wip-wip'pr'r'eet*. Guatemala to Costa Rica.

male Red-capped Manakin "moonwalks" for a female

TITYRAS

TITYRIDAE (Order: Passeriformes). A family whose members were once scattered among the families Tyrannidae, Cotingidae, and Pipridae. However, recent genetic and morphological studies show that *Schiffornis*, tityras, and becards are best included in their own family. Species in this family are found in a variety of forest types throughout the New World tropics. Most have relatively short tails and large, rounded heads. **8 species (4 genera)**

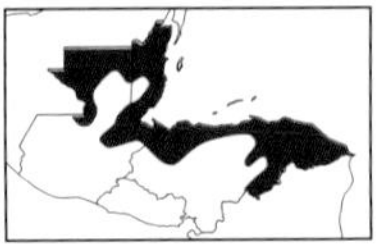

BLACK-CROWNED TITYRA *Tityra inquisitor*

8 in. (20 cm). Patterned similarly to Masked Tityra, but **crown completely black** and **bill on both sexes all-black**; eyes dark; **lacks bare skin around eye and lores**; smaller overall than Masked Tityra. Uncommon on Caribbean Slope; to 3,940 ft. (1,200 m). Found in a variety of woodland habitats, including taller disturbed habitats (plantations), semideciduous forest, and rainforest. Forages at mid- to upper levels; often perches in the open on exposed branches at canopy level. Usually in pairs; nests in cavities. Call is a nasal, scratchy *drrrrriit* or *drrriit-drrriit-drrriit*. Mex. to Argentina.

MASKED TITYRA *Tityra semifasciata*

9 in. (23 cm). Adult male distinctive in nearly **all-white plumage** with **contrasting black wings, tail band, and face**; bare **red skin around eyes and lores**; **heavy bill has pinkish red base**. Adult female and immature patterned similarly to adult male, but overall duller (brownish gray on back and face). Eyes reddish brown. Similar to Black-crowned Tityra, but all ages and sexes have bare red face and base to bill, and reddish brown eyes (not dark). Fairly common to common on both slopes; to 8,200 ft. (2,500 m). Found in a variety of woodland habitats, including taller disturbed habitats (plantations), semideciduous forest, and rainforest. Forages at mid- to upper levels; often perches in the open on exposed branches at canopy level. Usually in pairs; nests in cavities. Call is a nasal, piglike grunt. Mex. to Brazil.

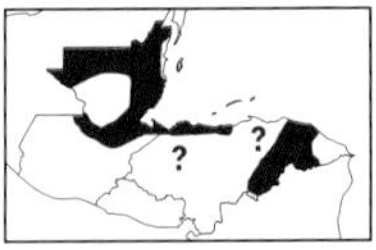

NORTHERN SCHIFFORNIS *Schiffornis veraepacis*

6.5 in. (17 cm). **A drab, nondescript tityra of forest interior**. Golden olive-brown upperparts; underparts slightly paler and wings more rufous; **rounded head**; eyes grayish brown. Uncommon to fairly common on Caribbean Slope; to 3,940 ft. (1,200 m). Found in rainforest and taller semideciduous forest, where it forages at midlevels. Easily overlooked unless calling. Call is a belting, clear whistled *heeeeeeey'RIcky!* . . . Mex. to Ecuador.

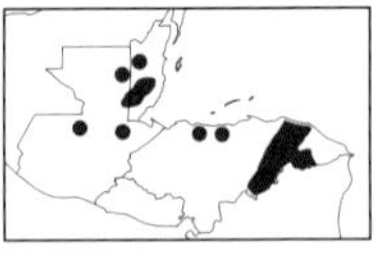

SPECKLED MOURNER *Laniocera rufescens*

8.5 in. (22 cm). Similar to Rufous Piha (p. 276), but paler tawny overall with **dark wing coverts edged tawny**; **weak scaling on chest**; **bold whitish eye-ring**; also yellowish wash to sides of chest often concealed by folded wings. Rare on Caribbean Slope; to 2,460 ft. (750 m). Found in rainforest, where it forages at mid- to upper levels. Solitary; perches quietly for long periods and easily overlooked. Call is a series of very high pitched, thin whistles, *seeeeeeu-seeeee-seeeee-seeeee-seeeee-seeeee*; also a mournful whistle, *weeeeeeuuu* (somewhat resembling call of Dusky-capped Flycatcher [p. 264]). Mex. to Ecuador.

BLACK-CROWNED TITYRA
male
female
MASKED TITYRA
male
female
NORTHERN SCHIFFORNIS
SPECKLED MOURNER

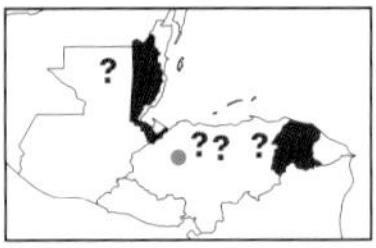

CINNAMON BECARD *Pachyramphus cinnamomeus*

5.5 in. (14 cm). **Tawny brown overall** with pale tawny supraloral stripe. Rare to uncommon on Caribbean Slope; to 1,640 ft. (500 m). The rarest NCA becard; apparently has declined or disappeared from extensive parts of its range, and any sightings in n. Petén and north coast of Honduras should now be documented. Can be confused with female Rose-throated Becard, but note different face patterns and tail shape. Found at edge of rainforest and semideciduous forest; also plantations. Forages at mid- to upper levels. Call is a high-pitched, thin, whistled *tseeeuuuu-tu'tu'tu'tu'tu'tu*. Mex. to Ecuador.

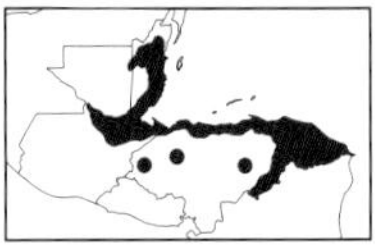

WHITE-WINGED BECARD *Pachyramphus polychopterus*

5.5 in. (14 cm). **Adult male black on crown, nape, and back**; **broad white scapular band**; graduated blackish tail has white tips. Adult female olive-brown above, **including on nape**; dull yellowish below; pale supraloral; and tawny edging to wing coverts. Adult male similar to Gray-collared Becard, but has black nape (not gray), lacks pale supraloral, and tail darker. Adult female similar to adult female Gray-collared Becard, but has dark nape showing little contrast with crown. Uncommon to rare on Caribbean Slope; to 3,610 ft. (1,100 m). Found in open woodlands or at edge: taller disturbed habitats, semideciduous forest, and rainforest. Forages at mid- to upper levels. Call is an accelerating *teu!-teeuuu-teu'teu'teu'teu''tu'tu'tu*; also a slightly lower pitched *teu-teu-teu-teu-teu*. Guatemala and Belize to Argentina.

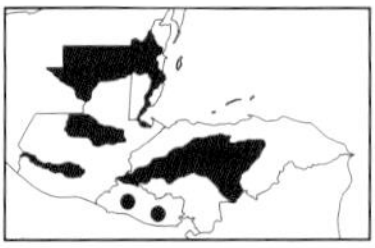

GRAY-COLLARED BECARD *Pachyramphus major*

6 in. (15 cm). Adult male similar to adult male White-winged Becard, but note pale **gray nape**, **pale supraloral**, and grayer tail. Adult female has **creamy buff nape, which contrasts with darker crown**. Rare to uncommon on Caribbean Slope; rare and local on Pacific Slope; to 8,200 ft. (2,500 m). Found at edge of semideciduous forest, pine savanna, and pine-oak forest, where it forages at mid- to upper levels. Call is a begging-like *eeuup-eeuup-eeuup*; also occasional squabbles and nasal agitated notes. Mex. to Nicaragua.

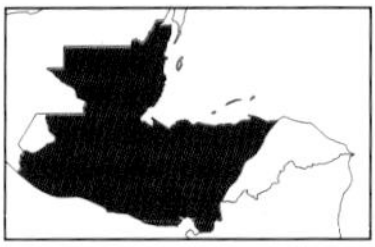

ROSE-THROATED BECARD *Pachyramphus aglaiae*

6.5 in. (17 cm). Regional variation in plumage. (*P.a. sumichrasti*; w. Guatemala to w. El Salvador) Adult male has dark crown and grayish upperparts; throat deep rose red. Adult female has grayish crown and tawny-brown upperparts. (*hypophaeus*; Belize and Caribbean Slope of Honduras) Adult male very dark overall; rose throat is normally lacking, but if present (n. Belize) much reduced and color is deep, purplish rose. Adult female deep tawny above. (*latirostris*; Pacific Slope of Honduras and e. El Salvador) Adult male much paler gray overall than other subspecies; shows sharp contrast between dark crown and paler gray upperparts; pale rose throat is sometimes lacking. Adult female has dark crown and rich tawny upperparts. Females in general can be confused with Cinnamon Becard, but note contrasting dark crown (absent in a tiny percentage of females), different face pattern and tail shape. Fairly common in NCA; to 6,560 ft. (2,000 m) although rarely above 4,900 ft. (1,500 m). Found at edge of taller disturbed habitat, semideciduous forest, pine savanna, and coastal scrub, where it forages at all levels. Often builds its bulky globular nests hanging above roads. Calls include high, thin whistles (some similar to Spot-crowned Woodcreeper [p. 240] and Fan-tailed Warbler [p. 358]); long call is a *wit-wi'wi'wi'wi'wi'wit'wit'wit'witsseeeeu!* U.S. to Panama.

CINNAMON
BECARD
male
WHITE-WINGED
BECARD
female
male
GRAY-
COLLARED
BECARD
female
ROSE-
THROATED
BECARD
female
male
female
Rose-throated
Becard at nest

SHRIKES AND SHRIKE-VIREOS

LANIIDAE (Order: Passeriformes). Shrikes are sit-and-wait predators renowned for impaling large insects, small birds, and mice on thorns or barbed-wire fences and returning later to consume them. Shrikes have stout, hooked bills used for tearing at flesh. The genus name *Lanius* means "butcher." Most shrikes live in the Old World. **1 species (1 genus)**

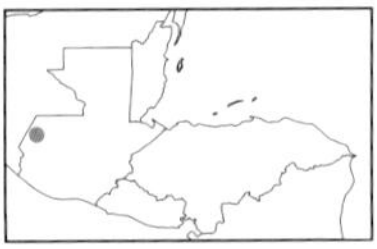

LOGGERHEAD SHRIKE *Lanius ludovicianus*

9 in. (23 cm). Distinctive black, white, and gray plumage; also **stout hooked black bill**. Sharply defined mask helps distinguish shrike from larger Tropical Mockingbird (p. 324). Vagrant in winter to w. Guatemala; to 9,840 ft. (3,000 m). Found in open country such as grasslands and savanna. Often perches on fenceposts or barbed-wire fences. Solitary. Has a direct, fluttering flight. Generally silent on wintering grounds. Canada to Mex.

VIREONIDAE (Order: Passeriformes). This is a New World family whose members resemble temperate wood-warblers (family: Parulidae) but are actually not closely related. Vireos are stockier with heavier, hooked bills and strong legs and feet. Vireos lack many of the bold colors of wood-warblers and behaviorally are often more lethargic, passive foragers. Sexes are generally similar. Several members of the genus *Vireo* are highly migratory. **19 species (5 genera)**

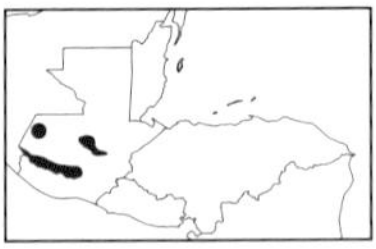

CHESTNUT-SIDED SHRIKE-VIREO *Vireolanius melitophrys*

7 in. (18 cm). A distinctive-looking bird with **yellow supercilium**, **broad blackish eye line**, and **chestnut collar and sides**. **Eyes white.** Rare to uncommon and local on both slopes of Guatemala; 3,940 to 11,480 ft. (1,200–3,500 m). Found in pine-oak and oak-dominated forest at upper levels near canopy. Call is an emphatic *vha'reeaaaar!* (like a distant store alarm), which can be heard from a great distance. Mex. to Guatemala.

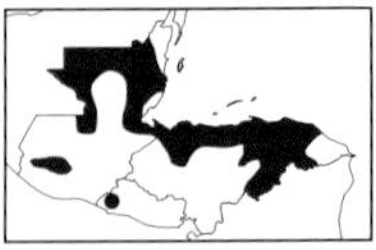

GREEN SHRIKE-VIREO *Vireolanius pulchellus*

5.5 in. (14 cm). Striking **bright green plumage and yellow throat** distinctive; **crown a brilliant aqua blue** (difficult to see). Juvenile drab olive-brown above; yellow supercilium and malar stripe; yellowish below. Rare and local on Pacific Slope; uncommon on Caribbean Slope; to 5,910 ft. (1,800 m). Found in semideciduous forest, shaded coffee plantations, and rainforest, where it forages at upper levels near canopy. Difficult to see well, but often heard calling. Song is a repeated sweet *peter-peter-peter* or *peer-peer-peer* (generally 3 notes, but occasionally more); also a *he-da-weer* (El Salvador); call is a raspy *djehr-djehr-djehr-* . . . Mex. to Panama.

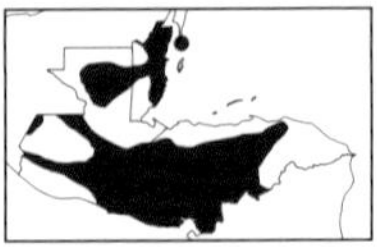

RUFOUS-BROWED PEPPERSHRIKE *Cyclarhis gujanensis*

6.5 in. (17 cm). Large and stocky. Gray nape and face contrast with **broad rufous supercilium**; **underparts yellow**; **eyes yellow-orange** (brown in immatures); **heavy pinkish gray bill**. Fairly common in NCA; to 6,230 ft. (1,900 m). Found in a variety of wooded areas: dry forest, taller semideciduous forest, riparian forest, and rainforest; also in mangroves and coffee plantations. Usually forages at mid- to upper levels near forest canopy. Vocalizes frequently, but often difficult to locate individual. Songs quite varied, but fall into 2 categories: females give lower-pitched songs, and males give higher-pitched songs. Lower-pitched song is generally of 5 to 10 long sad whistles descending in pitch; higher-pitched song is a fast, jumbled series of loud notes, highly variable. Calls include a repeated *pip!* Mex. to Argentina.

LOGGERHEAD
SHRIKE

CHESTNUT-SIDED
SHRIKE-VIREO

GREEN
SHRIKE-VIREO

RUFOUS-BROWED
PEPPERSHRIKE

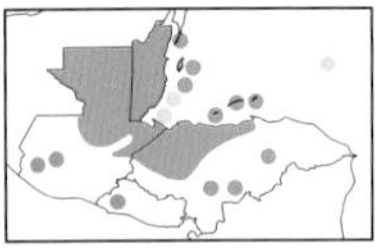

WHITE-EYED VIREO *Vireo griseus*

5 in. (13 cm). **Yellow spectacles; eyes white in adult**, dusky-brown in immature. Compare with Mangrove Vireo, but note contrasting gray nape and all-dark bill; voice different. Fairly common visitor (Sept.–Apr.) on Caribbean Slope; up to 2,950 ft. (900 m). Found in brushy forest understory and in disturbed habitat. Calls include nasal, harsh scolding; song is an explosive *chick-wheat-a-where-tik!* U.S. (breeding) to Nicaragua (winter).

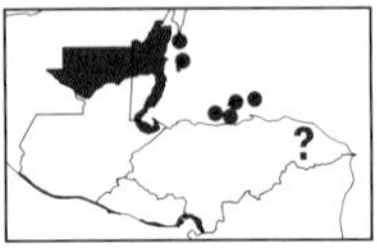

MANGROVE VIREO *Vireo pallens*

5 in. (13 cm). Regional variation (see 3 illustrated subspecies). Note **yellow lores** and **postocular spot; eyes pale gray**; bill with **pink mandible**. Compare with White-eyed Vireo. Locally uncommon on both slopes, except on Bay Is., where abundant; generally near sea level, but up to 820 ft. (250 m) on Caribbean Slope. Found at lower levels in mangroves, coastal swamps; and in semideciduous forest (Caribbean slope). Variable song repeats elements: *jear-jear-jear-jear-jear,* or a higher-pitched *wie-wie-wie-wie-wie-wie*; calls include an agitated chatter and a soft *jeeeeeear*. Mex. to Costa Rica.

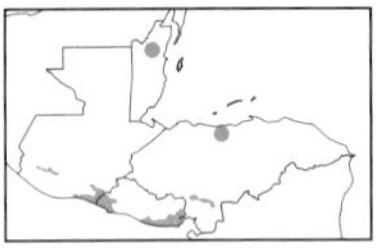

BELL'S VIREO *Vireo bellii*

5 in. (13 cm). **Weak whitish spectacles; upper wing bar less obvious than lower**; eyes dark. Underparts variable from dull to fairly bright yellow. Rare visitor (Oct.–May), mostly on Pacific Slope; up to 4,430 ft. (1,350 m). Forages low in coastal scrub, thorn forest, and disturbed habitat. Song is a rapid scratchy warble lasting about 1.5 sec. U.S. (breeding) to Nicaragua (winter).

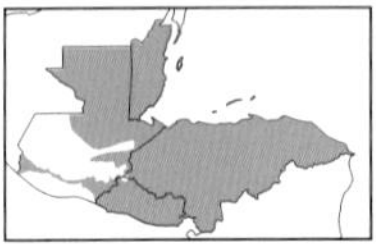

YELLOW-THROATED VIREO *Vireo flavifrons*

5.5 in. (14 cm). **Yellow spectacles, throat and chest** contrast with **white belly and undertail coverts**. Common visitor (Sept.–May) on both slopes; to 5,910 ft. (1,800 m) but generally below 3,940 ft. (1,200 m). Found at mid- and upper levels in a variety of woodland habitats. Frequent call is an accelerating chatter lasting about 1.5 sec. (like Blue-headed Vireo). Sings in spring: series of slow, slurry phrases with a hoarse quality. Canada (breeding) to Ecuador (winter).

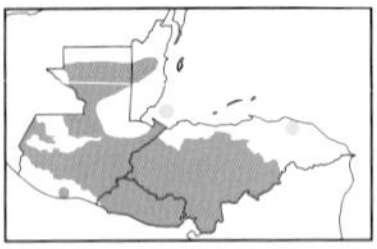

BLUE-HEADED VIREO *Vireo solitarius*

5.5 in. (14 cm). **Slate blue head contrasts with olive back and white throat; strong yellowish wash to sides, flanks, and vent.** Female/immature duller overall; similar to Plumbeous Vireo, but shows stronger contrast between gray cheeks and white throat; also stronger yellowish wash below. Fairly common visitor (Oct.–May) on Pacific Slope; generally 2,130 to 8,200 ft. (650–2,500 m). Found in a variety of woodland habitats. Forages at mid- to upper levels. Calls and song like Yellow-throated Vireo; song lacks hoarse quality. Canada (breeding) to Nicaragua (winter).

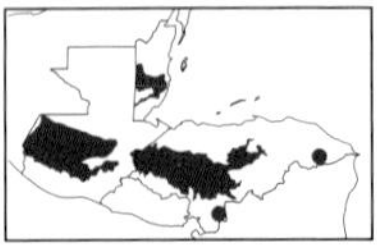

PLUMBEOUS VIREO *Vireo plumbeus*

5.5 in. (14 cm). Resident populations (*montanus*) have gray-olive back and gray head; **yellowish sides, flanks, and vent.** Migrants (*V.p. plumbeus*) grayer overall and lack yellow on underparts. Similar to Blue-headed Vireo immature, but shows less contrast between gray cheeks and white throat. Residents locally fairly common above 2000 ft. (600 m), or below 1000 ft. (300 m) in e. Honduras. Migrants very rare (Oct.–May). Found in pine savanna and pine-oak forest. Call is an agitated chattering; song is a slow series of 1 or 2 repeated notes, some burry. U.S. to Nicaragua.

WHITE-EYED VIREO

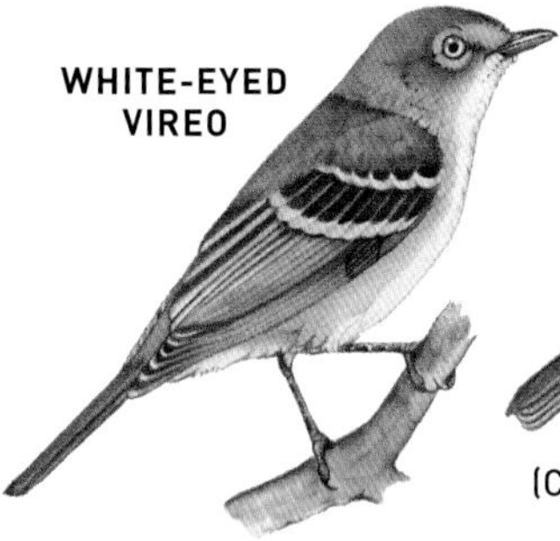

semiflavus
(Caribbean Slope and Bay Islands)

pallens
(Southern Honduras)

BELL'S VIREO

MANGROVE VIREO

ochraceus
(Pacific Slope: Guatemala and El Salvador)

YELLOW-THROATED VIREO

BLUE-HEADED VIREO

PLUMBEOUS VIREO

plumbeus

montanus

VIREOS WITHOUT WING BARS I

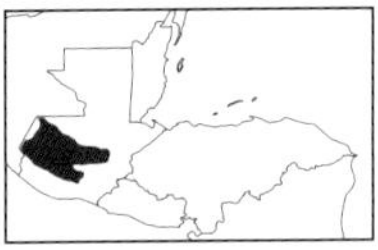

HUTTON'S VIREO *Vireo huttoni*

5 in. (13 cm). Similar to Ruby-crowned Kinglet (p. 314) (rare in NCA), but larger with heavier bill, and lacks black border to lower wing bar. Uncommon to fairly common in Guatemala; 3,940 to 11,500 ft. (1,200–3,500 m). Found at midlevels and higher in pine savanna and pine-oak forest. Can be difficult to see well. Call is a repeated *tzurreee*; song is slightly buzzier, *zeeeer* or *zeeerup* (also repeated). Canada to Guatemala.

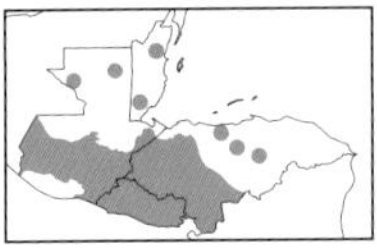

WARBLING VIREO *Vireo gilvus*

5 in. (13 cm). Olive-gray above with **slightly grayer crown**; **pale supercilium and lores**; white underparts with pale yellowish sides, flanks, and vent; **relatively small bill has pale base to mandible**. Similar to Brown-capped Vireo but generally found at lower elevations and grayer above, especially on cap. Also similar to Philadelphia Vireo, but lacks dark eye line and is white, not yellowish, on breast. Eastern birds darker overall than Western birds, but many individuals may not be separable in the field. Common winter resident (Nov.–May) on Pacific Slope; rare winter visitor on Caribbean Slope. Up to 8,200 ft. (2,500 m); however, most often between 2,300 and 4,270 ft. (700 and 1,300 m). Found in semideciduous forest, thorn forest, pine-oak forest, pine savanna, and coffee plantations. Forages at midlevels, often within mixed-species flocks. Frequent call is a repeated scolding; song is an extended pleasant warble sometimes heard during spring migration (very similar to song of Brown-capped Vireo). Canada (breeding) to Nicaragua (winter).

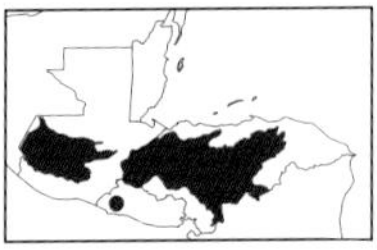

BROWN-CAPPED VIREO *Vireo leucophrys*

5 in. (13 cm). Compare with Warbling Vireo, but is browner overall (not gray) and has **brown cap**; also note elevation. Uncommon year-round in NCA; above 5,090 ft. (1,550 m); rarely lower. Found in cloud forest and pine-oak or oak forest, where it forages mainly at mid- to upper levels. Song is a short, sweet 2.5- to 3-sec. warble, similar to Warbling Vireo song; also a nasal, rising *rreih*. Mex. to Bolivia.

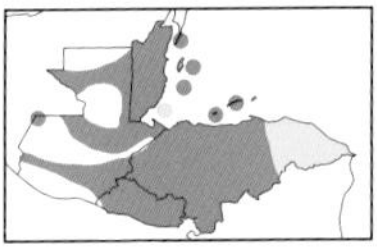

PHILADELPHIA VIREO *Vireo philadelphicus*

5 in. (13 cm). White supercilium bordered below by **dark eye line**; **throat and underparts washed yellow, often heavily** (especially in first-year birds). Confused with Warbling Vireo (above), but note dark eye line and warmer appearance with yellowish wash on breast. Also compare with Tennessee Warbler (p. 340), but has heavier bill (less pointed), shows more olive-gray above (vs. yellowish olive), and is a less active forager. Fairly common transient and winter visitor on Caribbean Slope; much less common on Pacific Slope (Nov.–Apr.). to 6,560 ft. (2,000 m). Mostly found in midelevation pine-oak forest, semideciduous forest, and coffee plantations, where it forages at midlevels. Generally silent in NCA. Canada (breeding) to Colombia (winter).

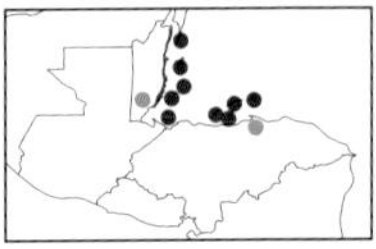

YUCATAN VIREO *Vireo magister*

6 in. (15 cm). **Grayish brown upperparts, including crown**; **bold pale supercilium**; dark eye line; heavy bill with pinkish base to mandible. Common on offshore Belizean cayes and Bay Is. (Honduras); fairly common but local on mainland in Belize; near sea level. Found in coastal scrub, mangroves, and at edge of disturbed habitats. Song is a rich warble, evenly paced, usually with 3 to 5 notes, *cheer up sweet* or *cheer up why not sweet* (last note slightly inflected); another variation in song is *beer-here alright!-wheo*. Yucatán Peninsula and western Caribbean Islands.

HUTTON'S VIREO
eastern group
WARBLING VIREO
western group
BROWN-CAPPED VIREO
PHILADELPHIA VIREO
YUCATAN VIREO

RED-EYED VIREO *Vireo olivaceus*

6 in. (15 cm). Olive upperparts contrast strongly with **gray crown**; **strong white supercilium bordered above and below with black**; underparts white, often with faint yellowish wash to vent; **eyes red** in adult (brown in juvenile); bill generally all-dark. Similar to Yellow-green Vireo, but has black border to supercilium and shows much less yellow on underparts, and has smaller bill. Uncommon to fairly common transient on Caribbean Slope (early Aug.–Nov.; late Mar.–May); rare transient on Pacific Slope; to 5,250 ft. (1,600 m). Found in semideciduous forest, dry forest, and pine-oak forest, where it forages at all levels. Call is a quick *rheeee* (like call of Yellow-green Vireo). Canada (breeding) to Brazil (winter).

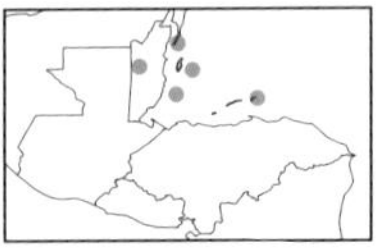

BLACK-WHISKERED VIREO *Vireo altiloquus*

6 in. (15 cm). Note **dark submalar stripe ("whisker")**. Separated from similar Red-eyed Vireo by black whisker. Very rare transient in spring and fall on offshore cayes and islands in the Caribbean (most records for NCA from Belize); near sea level. Found in coastal scrub, mangroves, and at edge of disturbed habitat. Song is a repeated *sweat john phillip*; call is a scolding *rheeee* (like Red-eyed Vireo). U.S. and Caribbean (breeding) to Brazil (winter).

YELLOW-GREEN VIREO *Vireo flavoviridis*

6 in. (15 cm). Similar to Red-eyed Vireo, but generally **warmer appearance overall (yellow flanks, sides, and vent)**, gray borders to supercilium (not dark as in Red-eyed), and pale base to mandible; bill larger than Red-eyed's. Common summer resident and transient (late Mar.–Oct.); to 4,430 ft. (1,350 m). Found in dry forest, semideciduous forest, and pine-oak forest; also riparian forest and coffee plantations. Forages at mid- to upper levels. Song (heard all day long) consists of 5 to 8 short repeated elements given in almost random order; call is like call of Red-eyed Vireo. Mex. (breeding) to Brazil (winter).

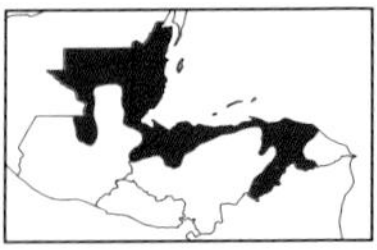

TAWNY-CROWNED GREENLET *Tunchiornis ochraceiceps*

5 in. (13 cm). **Rufous-olive upperparts**, including wings and tail; **tawny crown**; **face grayish**; underparts whitish, but chest edged tawny; **pale eyes**. Fairly common on Caribbean Slope; to 4,270 ft. (1,300 m). Generally found in rainforest, where it forages at low to midlevels, often in small groups or pairs and in mixed-species flocks. Common call is a high-pitched double-noted whistle, *wi-seeeeee* or *wi-heeeeee* (second part similar to call of White Hawk [p. 172]); also a liquid *tu'tu'tu'tu'tu wi-heeee*; scolding notes include a *vrrr'vrrr'vrrr'vrrr* mixed with soft *wit* notes. Mex. to Venezuela and Colombia.

LESSER GREENLET *Pachysylvia decurtata*

4.5 in. (11 cm). **Olive-yellow upperparts** contrast with **gray head and white eye-ring**; underparts white with yellowish wash to sides, flanks, vent, and undertail coverts; mandible pinkish; overall a chunky bird with a **short tail.** May be mistaken for a warbler; similar to Nashville Warbler (p. 340) but chunkier, tail shorter, and plumage is paler overall. Common on both slopes; to 4,590 ft. (1,400 m). Prefers taller semideciduous forest, riparian forest, and rainforest. Often forages in groups of 2 to 3 individuals at mid- to upper levels. Song is a doubled *chweet-chweet* or *siva-siva*; call is a complaining, thin chatter. Mex. to Ecuador.

RED-EYED VIREO
BLACK-WHISKERED VIREO
YELLOW-GREEN VIREO
TAWNY-CROWNED GREENLET
LESSER GREENLET

CORVIDAE (Order: Passeriformes). Corvids are medium to large songbirds with blue, white, and black plumage; sexes look alike. They have loud, raucous vocalizations and are social, intelligent, and curious creatures. They are omnivores and opportunists. Widespread; they can be found from sea level to the highest elevations in the region. **10 species (7 genera)**

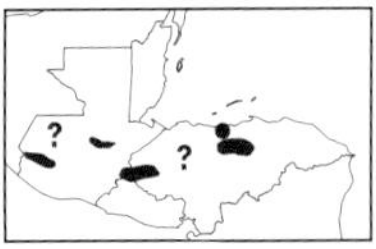

UNICOLORED JAY *Aphelocoma unicolor*

13.5 in. (34 cm). **Overall deep turquoise blue**; note **blackish facial mask**; eyes and bill dark. Rare to uncommon and local in NCA; from 5,740 to 10,010 ft. (1,750–3,050 m); rarely down to 980 ft. (300 m). Found in pine-oak forest, pine savanna, and cloud forest, where it forages at all levels. Travels in small groups. Often heard before seen. Calls include a thin, reedy *reeap-reeap*; also a harsher *rrek!-rrek!* Mex. to Honduras.

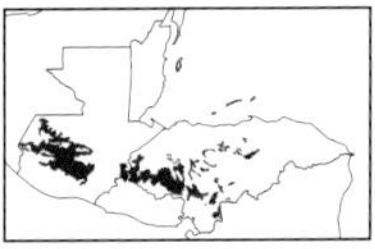

STELLER'S JAY *Cyanocitta stelleri*

11.5 in. (29 cm). **Body overall is purplish blue**; note lighter blue **short crest**; **face blackish with bold white slash above eye** and smaller white crescent below (Central American races differ in plumage from N. American races). Fairly common in highlands of interior NCA; above 2,950 ft. (900 m). Found in pine-oak forest and pine savanna, where it forages at all levels, often in family groups. Loud and raucous. Calls include a scolding, raspy *shreeah-shreeah-shreeah-shreeah*; also a series of clicks. Canada to Nicaragua.

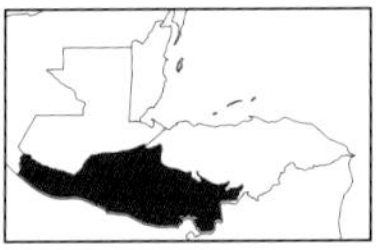

WHITE-THROATED MAGPIE-JAY *Calocitta formosa*

22 in. (56 cm). **Large, long-tailed, and distinctive looking.** Common on Pacific Slope; to 5,900 ft. (1,800 m). Found at edge in semideciduous forest, thorn forest, pine-oak forest, coastal scrub, and disturbed habitat (like coffee plantations and along roadsides). Forages at all levels where it often travels in family groups. Loud and raucous. Calls include a loud, scratchy *reaaahh!-reaaahh!-reaaahh!*, sometimes followed by a liquid gurgling. Mex. to Costa Rica.

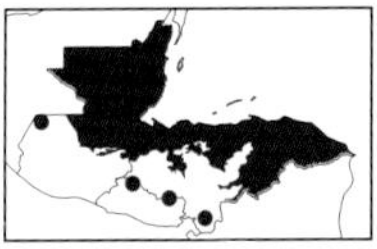

BROWN JAY *Psilorhinus morio*

16 in. (41 cm). Adult **chocolate brown above with dark hood**; underparts whitish; also note **broad white tips to tail feathers**. Immature has yellow eye-rings and varying amounts of yellow on bill and legs (these parts all-dark in adult). Common on Caribbean Slope; rare and local on Pacific Slope; to 5,250 ft. (1,600 m). Found at edge of disturbed habitats, semideciduous forest, rainforest, and thorn forest, where it travels in family groups. Very loud and raucous (often heard long before seen). Calls include a repeated loud, piercing *Peahhhhrrrr!* U.S. to Panama.

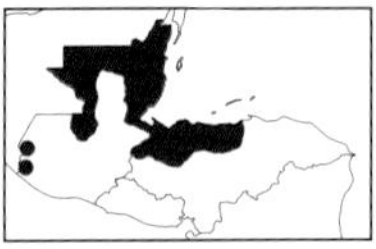

GREEN JAY *Cyanocorax yncas*

11 in. (28 cm). A striking jay. **Lime green upperparts**; **crown and parts of face purplish blue**; **remaining underparts and outertail feathers yellow**; eyes yellow. Uncommon on Caribbean Slope; rare on Pacific Slope in Guatemala; to 6,560 ft. (2,000 m). Found at edge of rainforest and taller semideciduous forest; also occasionally in pine savanna. Forages at all levels in family groups. Fairly quiet and a bit secretive. Calls are varied and include scolds, clucks, and growls; some with a scratchy electric or liquid quality. Common calls include a harsh, scratchy *reeahh-reeahh-reeahh-reeahh* or a thinner *eeh!-eeh!-eeh!-eeh!*; also a *chit'chit'chit'chit—chit'chit'chit'chit* . . . U.S. to Bolivia.

UNICOLORED
JAY
adult
immature
STELLER'S
JAY
WHITE-THROATED
MAGPIE-JAY
a group of
magpie-jays along
the Pacific Slope
adult
immature
BROWN
JAY
GREEN
JAY

JAYS II AND RAVEN

BUSHY-CRESTED JAY *Cyanocorax melanocyaneus*

12 in. (31 cm). Adult has **black hood; remaining plumage a fairly uniform turquoise blue** (birds in e. Honduras and n. Nicaragua show more black below); **eyes yellow**. Immatures have varying amounts of yellow on bill, and dark eyes. No range overlap with similar Yucatan Jay. Common in NCA; from 330 to 8,040 ft. (100–2,450 m) but generally above 2,950 ft. (900 m). Prefers pine-oak and oak-dominated forest; also, cloud forest, taller semideciduous forest, and occasionally in thorn forest. Forages at low levels (often on ground) to midlevels, where it's loud and obvious. Travels in groups up to 20 individuals. Calls include double-noted *cha-ra!* and *chee-tup!*; also an agitated, scratchy *eehhh!-eeh!-eeh!-eeh!-eeh!-eeh!-eeh!-eeh!-eeh!*; also a soft whisper song that includes a mix of regular calls, whines, and soft warbles. Endemic to region.

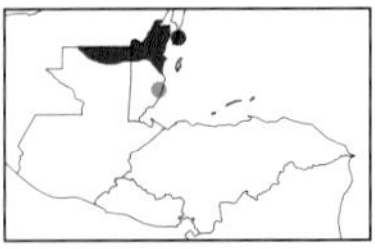

YUCATAN JAY *Cyanocorax yucatanicus*

12.5 in. (32 cm). **Upperparts, including wings and tail, a bright turquoise blue; head and underparts black**; legs yellow; eyes dark. Immature has yellow eye-rings and yellow bill. Juvenile plumage is distinctive with head and underparts white. No range overlap with similar Bushy-crested Jay. Uncommon to fairly common in n. Guatemala and Belize; to 820 ft. (250 m). Found at edge of thorn forest and semideciduous forest; also in pine savanna and pine-oak forest. Travels in groups. Calls include a harsh *chet'chet'chet'chet'chet'chet'chet'chet* and a distorted liquid *whe'wit*. Endemic to region.

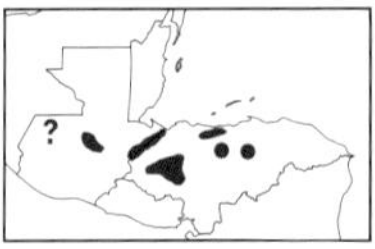

AZURE-HOODED JAY *Cyanolyca cucullata*

11.5 in. (29 cm). Deep purplish blue overall; throat and face black; **crown and nape light blue, blending below to silvery white edges**. Immature duller overall. Rare to uncommon and local in NCA; from 2,950 to 6,890 ft. (900–2,100 m). Found in pine-oak forest and cloud forest, where it forages generally at low to midlevels. A bit secretive and often solitary. Call is a loud, slightly nasal *reeiiik!-reeiiik!*; also a tinny *pip-pip-pip*. Mex. to Panama.

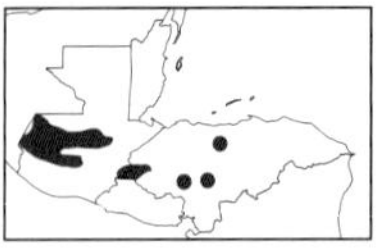

BLACK-THROATED JAY *Cyanolyca pumilo*

10 in. (26 cm). Overall deep blue; **throat and face black bordered above in white** (wrapping around forecrown). Rare to uncommon and local in NCA; from 3,940 to 10,010 ft. (1,200–3,050 m). Found in understory of pine-oak forest and cloud forest. Secretive. Solitary or in family groups. Calls include a shrieking *shreeaa'shreeaa—shreeaa'shreeaa—* . . . ; also a harsher, drawn-out *rhrrrrr or rhrrrreee!* Endemic to region.

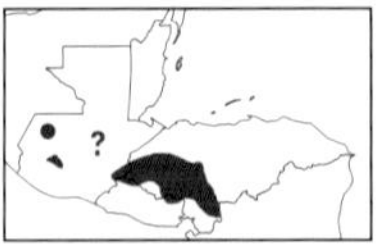

COMMON RAVEN *Corvus corax*

24.5 in. (62 cm). **A large black bird, the size of a hawk.** In flight, note **wedge-shaped tail**; heavy strong black bill. Rare in NCA; 2,600 to 12,000 ft. (800–3,650 m). Found in a variety of habitat types, but generally a montane species; oak and pine-oak forest, pine savanna, and grasslands with nearby cornfields. Forages on the ground and generally solitary or in pairs. Often heard calling in flight. Call is a throaty *rawwhh-rawwhh-rawwhh*. U.S. and Canada to Nicaragua.

adult with raised crest
BUSHY-CRESTED JAY
immature
adult
juvenile
adult
YUCATAN JAY
immature
AZURE-HOODED JAY
BLACK-THROATED JAY
COMMON RAVEN

HIRUNDINIDAE (Order: Passeriformes). Martins and swallows are small insectivorous passerines that are excellent fliers and aerial performers. Often confused for swifts (order: Apodiformes), they are more colorful and have broader, shorter wings and slower flight. North American species winter in large numbers in Cen. and S. America, where roosts may contain thousands of individuals. Mixed-species flocks are common. The migration patterns and wintering grounds of a few species are still a mystery. Sexes similar in most species. **15 species (8 genera)**

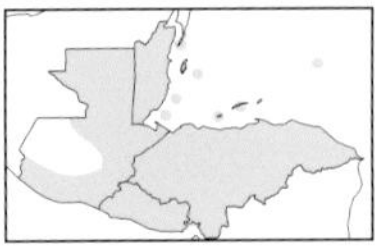

BANK SWALLOW *Riparia riparia*

5 in. (13 cm). Brown upperparts and white below with **brown chest band**. Fairly common transient in NCA (mid-Sept.–mid-Nov.; late Mar.–mid-May); to 6,560 ft. (2,000 m). To be looked for in migration within mixed-species flocks of swallows. Often found near water: rivers, lakes, and along the coast. Calls include a *vvriiit* and other churring, electric chatter. Canada and U.S. (breeding) to Argentina (winter); also Europe and Asia (where it's called "Sand Martin").

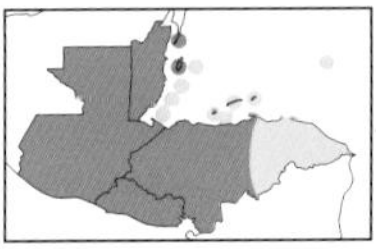

BARN SWALLOW *Hirundo rustica*

6.5 in. (17 cm). Dark blue upperparts with **chestnut or buffy forecrown and throat; underparts tawny rufous or cinnamon**, but paler in female and immature (some may appear more whitish); **long tail deeply forked with pale white band**. Tail shorter in immature. Common transient and winter visitor to NCA, but present nearly year-round (late June–early June); to 6,560 ft. (2,000 m). Found at edge or in clearings within a variety of habitats, but frequently in disturbed habitats (over agricultural fields), also along reservoirs and large lakes, estuaries, and coastal scrub. Often near human habitation. Nighttime roosts difficult to find but often contain hundreds or thousands of birds. Call is a distinctive *viit*. U.S. and Canada (breeding) to Argentina (winter); also Old World.

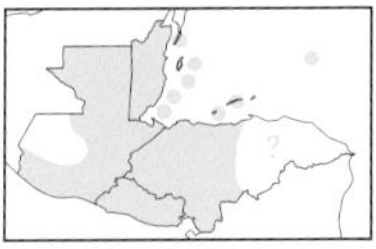

CLIFF SWALLOW *Petrochelidon pyrrhonota*

5.5 in. (14 cm). Similar to Cave Swallow, but has **dark rusty throat** (not pale tawny) and most (but not all) have **pale forecrown** (not dark); also paler rump. Common transient in NCA (late July–late Nov.; Feb.–mid-May); to 6,560 ft. (2,000 m). Found in open areas often near bodies of water or along the coast. Singly or in large groups of greater than 50 individuals. May mix with other species of swallows. U.S. and Canada (breeding) to Brazil (winter).

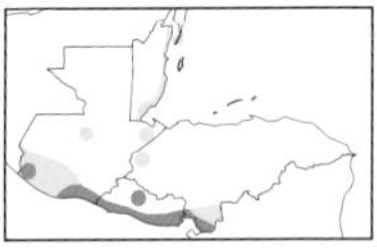

CAVE SWALLOW *Petrochelidon fulva*

5.5 in. (14 cm). Two subspecies found in NCA. The migratory population from s. Texas and ne. Mex. (*P.f. pallida*) has **dark chestnut forecrown and pale tawny throat**; also in flight note dark tawny rump. The resident population (*P.f. fulva*, of se. Mex. and Caribbean) is similar, but has **darker cinnamon throat and flanks, and darker chestnut rump**. Both subspecies similar to Cliff Swallow, but show dark forecrown and paler throat; also darker rump. Uncommon winter visitor to Pacific Slope (early Nov.–late Mar.); rare transient on Caribbean Slope (*pallida*). The *fulva* race is vagrant to Belize and presumably n. Guatemala; to 2,300 ft. (700 m). Feeds over coastal agricultural fields such as sorghum and sugarcane, where it roosts in flocks of thousands. Also found over semideciduous forest, coastal scrub, and estuaries. Calls include thin electric buzzes and chatters. U.S. and Caribbean (breeding) to Costa Rica (winter).

BANK
SWALLOW
BARN
SWALLOW
CLIFF
SWALLOW
CAVE
SWALLOW

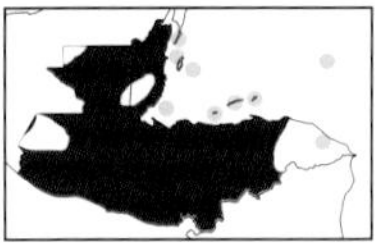

NORTHERN ROUGH-WINGED SWALLOW

Stelgidopteryx serripennis

5.5 in. (14 cm). **Upperparts brown; throat lightly washed with brown**; underparts whitish. Juveniles have bright cinnamon wing bars. Tail is squared. "Ridgway's Rough-winged Swallow" (*S.s. stuarti*; s. Mex. to Belize and n. Guatemala) is slightly larger and **darker brown above with white supraloral spots**; the undertail coverts are tipped blackish. Northern Rough-winged Swallow similar to Southern Rough-winged (overlap in e. Honduras), but has drabber throat and dark rump. Common year-round in NCA (population augmented by visitors from the north, Aug.–Apr.); to 10,170 ft. (3,100 m). Found in a variety of open habitat types. Nests in cavities (natural or manmade), often in cities. In nonbreeding season, large roosts form at night on city buildings. Call is a slightly liquid *prrrlliiit* (similar to Southern Rough-winged Swallow's). Canada and U.S. to Panama.

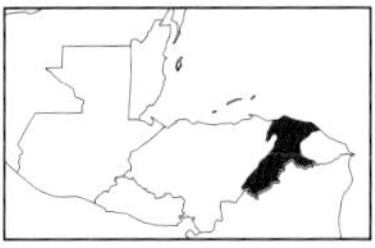

SOUTHERN ROUGH-WINGED SWALLOW

Stelgidopteryx ruficollis

5 in. (13 cm). Similar to Northern Rough-winged Swallow, but has **tawny throat and pale rump**. Fairly common in e. Honduras; to 3,940 ft. (1,200 m). Found at edge and in clearings of rainforest and riparian forest. Habits similar to Northern Rough-winged Swallow's, and they may forage together. Call is similar to Northern Rough-winged Swallow's. Honduras to Argentina.

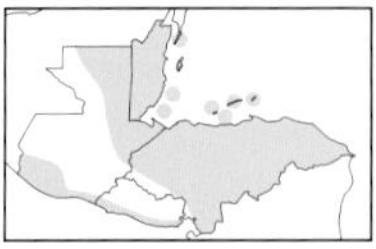

PURPLE MARTIN

Progne subis

8 in. (20 cm). **Male deep purple overall.** On female, **head and sides of nape are washed grayish** (female Gray-breasted Martin is uniformly dark on head and sides of nape). Fairly common transient on Caribbean Slope, including cayes and Bay Is. (late June–late Oct.; early Feb.–mid-Apr.); rare on Pacific Slope; to 9,350 ft. (2,850 m) but generally below 2,620 ft. (800 m). Found over a variety of open habitats, generally along coastlines. Migrates in small flocks; occasionally larger flocks with thousands of individuals. Calls in flight include a buzzy *zzzzzeeert*. Canada (breeding) to Argentina (winter).

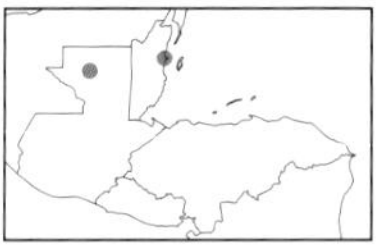

CARIBBEAN/SINALOA MARTIN

Progne dominicensis / sinaloae

7 in. (18 cm). Two species in which the adult males are nearly identical: **Deep purplish blue above**; **striking contrast between chest and white belly**; Caribbean Martin has less white on belly and dark spots on undertail coverts. Females of both species have dusky brownish face, chest, and flanks, with sharp contrast between darker chest and whitish belly; female Caribbean Martin has more extensive pale throat. Very rare transient (*sinaloae*) or vagrant (*dominicensis*) in NCA; status uncertain. Calls of both species like Purple Martin's. Mex. and Caribbean (breeding) to unknown wintering grounds.

GRAY-BREASTED MARTIN

Progne chalybea

6.5 in. (17 cm). Deep bluish purple above, **including sides of nape and forecrown** (which separate it from female Purple Martin); **chest washed grayish**. Fairly common resident (Pacific Slope) or breeding visitor (much of Caribbean slope) in NCA; to 4,920 ft. (1,500 m). Found over cities and towns, disturbed habitats often near water, and mangroves. Nests in tree cavities or in manmade holes in urban areas. Forms large roosts of hundreds or thousands of birds, often in cities. Calls include a *zeeeeeep!* and a *zeeeeeer*. Mex. to Argentina.

stuarti/
Ridgway's
NORTHERN ROUGH-WINGED
SWALLOW
SOUTHERN
ROUGH-WINGED
SWALLOW
male
PURPLE
MARTIN
female
male
female
GRAY-BREASTED
MARTIN
CARIBBEAN/
SINALOA MARTIN

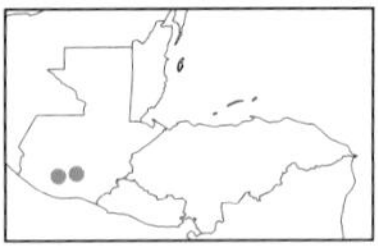

BLUE-AND-WHITE SWALLOW *Pygochelidon cyanoleuca*
5 in. (13 cm). Uniformly iridescent metallic blue above (dark blue in poor light) and clean white below; note **blackish undertail coverts and deeply notched tail**. Compare adult with adult Tree Swallow, but note dark undertail coverts (white in Tree); also, tail more deeply notched. Immature uniformly dark brown above; similar to Black-capped Swallow, which has longer forked tail and darker cap. Vagrant to NCA; most likely from 2,950 to 4,920 ft. (900–1,500 m); likely in cities and towns. Costa Rica to Uruguay.

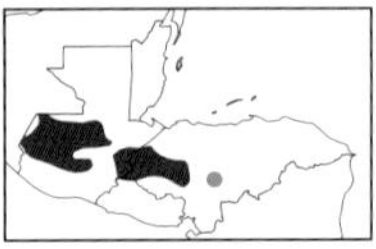

BLACK-CAPPED SWALLOW *Atticora pileata*
5 in. (13 cm). Brown upperparts contrast with **blackish cap**; **undertail coverts dark brown or blackish**; **note relatively long, black forked tail**. Uncommon to fairly common in interior highlands of NCA; from 2,460 to 8,690 ft. (750–2,650 m). Found at edge or in clearings of pine-oak forest and cloud forest. Nests in road cuts, embankments, and cliff faces. Often soars above forest in small flocks of 3 to 10 individuals, occasionally perching on exposed bare branches. Calls include a buzzy, electric *pzzzzzeeet!* and a more liquid *pweeet-pweeet*. Endemic to region.

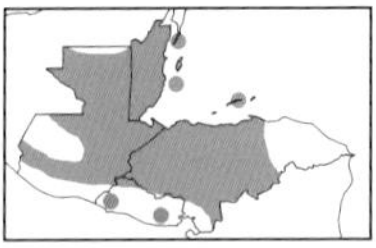

TREE SWALLOW *Tachycineta bicolor*
5.5 in. (14 cm). Adult has **iridescent blue-green upperparts** (appears dark in poor light), including face; **clean white underparts** create striking contrast with upperparts. Immature brown above, but still shows dark face. Very similar to Mangrove Swallow, but has completely dark rump (white in Mangrove). Compare with Violet-green Swallow, but does not show white above eye or on cheek, and sides of rump are relatively dark. Fairly common to common transient and winter visitor on Caribbean Slope, including Bay Is. (late Oct.–late Apr.); rare transient and winter visitor on Pacific Slope in lowlands; to 8,200 ft. (2,500 m). Generally found along the coast over coastal scrub and marshes, and at large inland lakes and reservoirs. Often perches on wires or power lines. Winter roosts may number in the thousands of individuals. Call is a liquid, slightly electric *tseeep* or *tzeeep*. U.S. and Canada (breeding) to Costa Rica (winter).

MANGROVE SWALLOW *Tachycineta albilinea*
5 in. (13 cm). **Rump white** (immature also shows white rump); also note **white edging on tertials** and **thin white line over eye**. Similar to Tree Swallow, but has white rump. Similar to Violet-green Swallow, but is larger, has more extensive white on rump and darker face and different feeding habits. Fairly common in NCA; to 3,940 ft. (1,200 m). Found at inland lakes and reservoirs, sewage lagoons, mangroves, also along rivers; always near water. Call is similar to Tree Swallow's, but slightly buzzier, *tzzzeep*. Mex. to Peru.

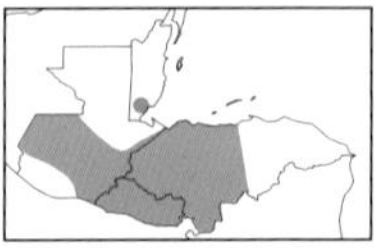

VIOLET-GREEN SWALLOW *Tachycineta thalassina*
4.5 in. (11 cm). In good light, **bright green back** contrasts with **purplish blue wings and rump**; also **note white above eye and white sides to rump ("saddlebags")**. Similar to Tree Swallow, but shows white above eye and on cheek and has white saddlebags on rump. Similar to Mangrove Swallow, but is smaller, tends to fly higher and in larger groups, and has more white on face. Fairly common transient and winter visitor to NCA (late Sept.–mid-Mar.); to 10,990 ft. (3,350 m). At edge of forest clearings in pine-oak forest or semideciduous forest; also around reservoirs or lakes, and in mangrove estuaries. Calls include a *tzzzeep* (similar to Mangrove Swallow) and a richer *seeuuu*. U.S. and Canada (breeding) to Nicaragua (winter).

BLUE-AND-WHITE SWALLOW
BLACK-CAPPED SWALLOW
TREE SWALLOW
MANGROVE SWALLOW
VIOLET-GREEN SWALLOW

AEGITHALIDAE (Order: Passeriformes). A primarily Old World family, the bushtits (or long-tailed tits) are among the smallest of passerine birds. Only one species inhabits the New World. **1 species (1 genus)**

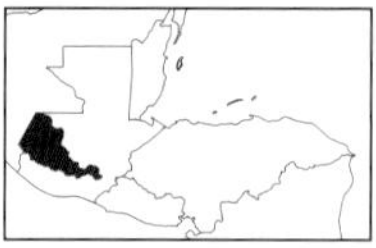

BUSHTIT *Psaltriparus minimus*

4.5 in. (11 cm). A tiny bird. Adult male grayish overall with **black cheeks** and dark eyes. Adult female has **brownish cheeks, black stripe over eye**, and pale eyes. Uncommon in Guatemala; from 4,920 to 10,990 ft. (1,500–3,350 m). Found at all levels of pine-oak forest and pine savanna, where often in family groups. Calls include high-pitched twitters, *tip!* or *tip'tip'tip* and *pseet!* U.S. and Canada to Guatemala. Formerly known as Black-eared Bushtit (*Psaltriparus melanotis*).

CERTHIIDAE (Order: Passeriformes). An Old World family with 1 representative in the New World. Creepers forage on bark-dwelling insects while hopping up tree trunks, similar to woodcreepers (Furnariidae) and woodpeckers (Piciformes: Picidae). Taxonomic studies suggest more than 1 species of creeper inhabits N. America. **1 species (1 genus)**

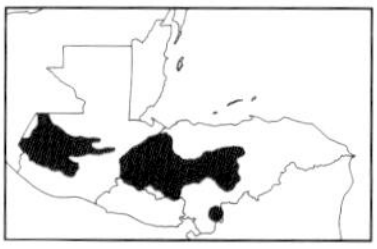

BROWN CREEPER *Certhia americana*

5 in. (13 cm). Upperparts **cryptically patterned**; whitish underparts; thin decurved bill. Uncommon in interior highlands; from 1,650 to 10,990 ft. (500–3,350 m) but generally above 5,090 ft. (1,550 m). Found in pine savanna and pine-oak forest. Hitches up trees like a small woodcreeper; often on main trunk. Forages at all levels. Generally solitary. Nests in crevices in tree bark. Song has a thin, buzzy introductory note, followed by several high-pitched clear whistles that rise and fall: *tzzeeeee—tsee-teuu-dee-dew*; call is a single high-pitched (slightly rattling) *tseeeeet!* and in flight a shorter, sharp *tseet!* U.S. to Nicaragua.

TROGLODYTIDAE (Order: Passeriformes). Active and vocal, wrens are small birds with cryptic plumage. They have short, rounded wings; thin bills; and most species have a white supercilium. There is little or no sexual dimorphism. Most species forage in dense undergrowth, vine tangles, and epiphytic growth, and a few species are adapted to living in urban areas. Several species have complex social breeding systems, and song duetting is common. **19 species (12 genera)**

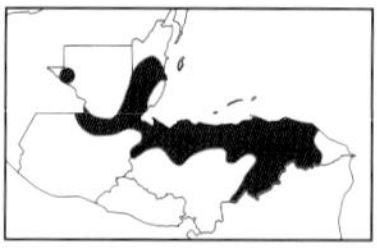

NIGHTINGALE WREN *Microcerculus philomela*

4.5 in. (11 cm). **Dark overall**; **wing coverts with small pale tips**; grayish underparts with **weak scaling**; **tail is extremely short**. Uncommon to fairly common on Caribbean Slope; to 5,910 ft. (1,800 m). Found in rainforest, semideciduous forest; generally in lowlands. Difficult to see; stays near the ground in debris piles and in shadows. May sit for long periods when singing. Song is a series of rising and falling sweet clear whistles, each on a single pitch; 1 series lasts 5 sec. or longer, but series may be repeated during many minutes, often without pauses. Mex. to Costa Rica.

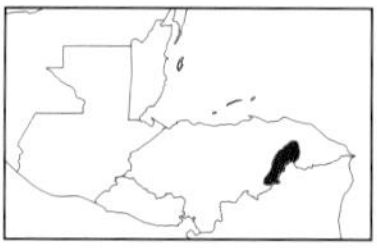

SONG WREN *Cyphorhinus phaeocephalus*

5 in. (13 cm). **Orbital skin is pale blue in shape of teardrop**; **face, throat, and chest are tawny**; remaining underparts are dark. Fairly common in e. Honduras; to 2,460 ft. (750 m). Found in rainforest understory, foraging among leaf litter on the ground. Sometimes in small groups. Song is a repeated mix of short clear whistles and agitated chatter; call is a nasal *crip'crip'crip'crip'crip'* . . . (similar to calls of Rufous-naped Wren [p. 310]). Honduras to Ecuador.

male

female

BUSHTIT

BROWN CREEPER

NIGHTINGALE WREN

SONG WREN

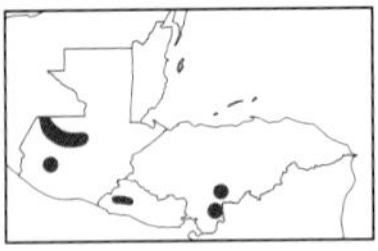

ROCK WREN *Salpinctes obsoletus*

5.5 in. (14 cm). Two distinctive subspecies in NCA. The northern form (*S.o. neglectus*; Mex. and Guatemala) is generally paler. Upperparts are gray-brown with dark and white flecking; rump cinnamon; weak white supercilium; **underparts whitish with small brown streaks and cinnamon on flanks**; tail with black subterminal band and pale cinnamon tips. The southern form (*S.o. guttatus*; El Salvador and se. Honduras) is generally darker. **Underparts heavily spotted and barred in dusky gray-brown.** Uncommon to fairly common in Guatemala (*neglectus*) but rare and local in El Salvador and Honduras (*guttatus*); 2,460 to 10,990 ft. (750–3,350 m). Found in rocky grasslands and on barren rocky landscapes, such as old lava flows. Flies low; most often seen perched on rocks. Song is a loud series of 3 to 12 repeated phrases similar to song of Tropical Mockingbird (p. 324), *pea'pea'pea'pea'pea'pea-pier'pier'pier'pier-sawee'sawee'sawee'saweee-ti'ti'ti'ti'ti'- . . .* ; also loud alarm note, *peep!* (repeated). Canada to Nicaragua.

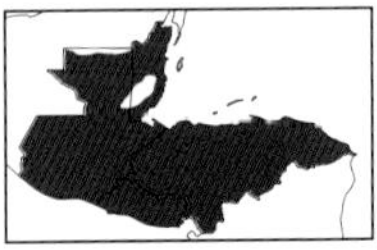

HOUSE WREN *Troglodytes aedon*

4.5 in. (11 cm). Dark brown above with **light black barring on wings and tail**; inconspicuous supercilium; below **buffy brown on chest, sides, flanks, and vent**; undertail coverts barred black. Similar to Rufous-browed Wren, but supercilium is pale, not rufous, tail is longer, and is found in more disturbed habitats; vocalizations are different. Common in NCA; to 9,510 ft. (2,900 m). Found in a variety of open habitats and at forest edge; an active wren, frequently bobbing with tail cocked upward. Song quite variable; usually a liquid jumble of trills and repeated elements lasting roughly 2 sec.; calls include a chatter *chit'chit'chit'chit . . .* ; also a nasal, agitated *cheeeeez*. Populations from s. Mex. to Argentina sometimes are treated as "Southern House Wren" (*T. musculus*). U.S. to Argentina.

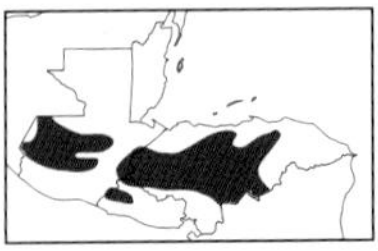

RUFOUS-BROWED WREN *Troglodytes rufociliatus*

4 in. (10 cm). A small wren; **deep chestnut above** with wings and tail barred lightly black; also note small white tips to wing coverts; **supercilium and face a rich rufous-edged buff**; throat and chest also a buffy-rufous; flanks, belly, and vent spotted or barred black; **tail is short**. Compare with House Wren. Fairly common in NCA; from 5,580 to 10,500 ft. (1,700–3,200 m). A bird of highland forests, where it's difficult to see in dark shade; forages in vine tangles and fallen trees; also highly arboreal, often found probing bromeliads. Song a variable tinkling jumble of notes (some high-pitched and others buzzy) lasting about 2 sec.; call a distinctive chatter, *zzzree-zzzree-zzzree . . .* Endemic to region.

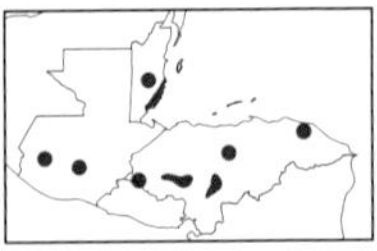

SEDGE WREN *Cistothorus platensis*

4.5 in. (11 cm). A small wren with mottled upperparts of buff-brown, black, and white. **Back mainly black with fine white streaks**; nape buff-brown with small black spots; **crown is dark with brown and white streaks**; wings and tail are buff-brown with dark barring; whitish throat and underparts contrast with **tawny flanks, vent, and undertail coverts**; mandible is yellow. Locally fairly common in Belize and in NCA highlands; to 6,560 ft. (2,000 m); on Pacific Slope generally above 3,950 ft. (1,200 m). Found in wet grasslands, meadows, and short scrub. Often seen with tail cocked. Song is a variable buzzy chatter: *chit-chitwa'zzzee'zzzee'zzzee*. Canada to Argentina.

PLATE 140

neglectus
ROCK
WREN
guttatus
HOUSE
WREN
RUFOUS-BROWED
WREN
SEDGE
WREN

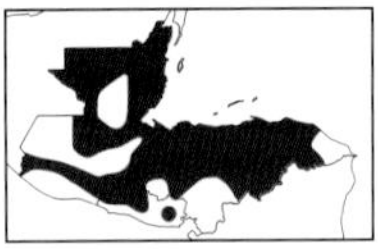

SPOT-BREASTED WREN *Pheugopedius maculipectus*

5 in. (13 cm). Brown upperparts contrast slightly with chestnut crown; white supercilium; white auriculars streaked black; underparts are white with dense **black spots across lower throat and chest extending down to undertail coverts**; tawny flanks; tail above has fairly broad dark bands; eyes red (brownish gray in immature). Compare with juvenile Rufous-and-white Wren (p. 308) and with Stripe-breasted Wren. Common in NCA; to 4,270 ft. (1,300 m). Inhabits lower levels of rainforest and semideciduous forest; somewhat arboreal. Song is series of clear whistles rising and falling in pitch, lasting around 1 sec., *ter'swee'awii'peter* (sometimes repeated as a longer series); pairs often duet (which can sound similar to duetting of Gray-breasted Wood-Wren [p. 310]); call is a dry *svit'svit*. Mex. to Costa Rica.

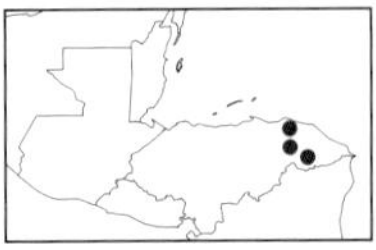

STRIPE-BREASTED WREN *Pheugopedius thoracicus*

5 in. (13 cm). Brown upperparts and crown; thin white supercilium; white auriculars and sides of neck with black streaks; **white underparts heavily marked with black streaks on chest, belly, and sides**; flanks and vent tawny; eyes red. Compare with Spot-breasted Wren. Locally common in e. Honduras; to 980 ft. (300 m). Found at edge in rainforest and riparian forest, where it forages at lower levels. Song is a loud series of short clear whistles *wee-meet'her* (repeated often in duet) or *tour-meet'gable*; calls include an emphatic repeated lower-pitched *peer* and a liquid *chirp*; also a soft chatter. Honduras to Panama.

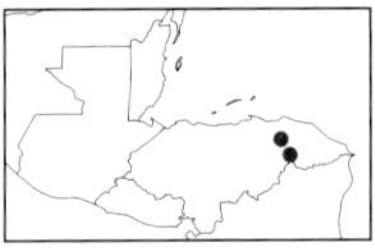

BLACK-THROATED WREN *Pheugopedius atrogularis*

6 in. (15 cm). Rufous-brown overall; **face, throat, and chest black**; thin white supercilium; faint white streaking on auriculars. Locally uncommon in e. Honduras; to 490 ft. (150 m). Forages in dense, overgrown vegetation at edge of rainforest. Variable song begins with a couple of clear whistles followed by a machine gun–like trill: *weear-wow'pow tr'tr'tr'tr'tr'tr'tr'tr'tr*. Honduras to Panama.

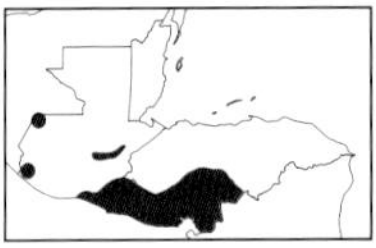

BANDED WREN *Thryophilus pleurostictus*

5.5 in. (14 cm). Adult brown above; white supercilium bordered in black; white auriculars and sides of neck streaked black; white underparts with **heavy black barring along sides and flanks**; undertail coverts, wings, and tail above with black barring; eyes brownish red. Immature plumage similar to that of adult Rufous-and-white Wren (p. 308), but note smaller size, brown upperparts on Banded Wren (not rufous), and broader black bands on upper tail. Fairly common to common along Pacific Slope of NCA; to 4,920 ft. (1,500 m). Found at edge of semideciduous forest and in dry forest. Song (variable) is a sweet series of repeated notes and clear whistles lasting for approximately 3 sec., *wip-wip-wip-tahhh-tweeeet'titah-peer'peer'peer' peer'peer'wheat!*, accelerating and inflected at end (song phrases given in 7- to 8-sec. intervals); chatter is a repeated *tik* similar to Cabanis's Wren (p. 308), but not as hard; also a *wip-tah* and a harsh *chareeee*. Mex. to Costa Rica.

SPOT-BREASTED
WREN
juvenile
STRIPE-BREASTED
WREN
BLACK-THROATED
WREN
BANDED
WREN
juvenile

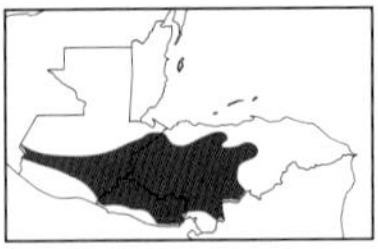

RUFOUS-AND-WHITE WREN *Thryophilus rufalbus*

6 in. (15 cm). Adult has **rich rufous upperparts**; supercilium white bordered in black; **black submalar stripe**; **underparts white** with dingy sides and flanks. Juvenile diffusely splotched below, reminiscent of adult Spot-breasted Wren, but on immature note yellow gape and base to bill, and brownish gray eyes. Locally rare to fairly common in NCA; to 6,070 ft. (1,850 m). Found at edge in a variety of woodlands, including rainforest, semideciduous forest, riparian forest, and pine-oak forest. Variable song is a pleasant series of soft hoots and whistles with a flutey quality, often starting and ending with a short high note; call is a thin *svit'svit* (similar to call of Spot-breasted Wren) also run into a longer chatter; immatures learning to sing make a variety of soft thin whistles different from adult song. Mex. to Colombia.

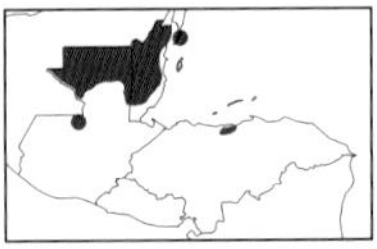

WHITE-BELLIED WREN *Uropsila leucogastra*

4 in. (10 cm). **A small wren** with **bold white supercilium** and **dark brown post-ocular line**. Possibly confused with Cabanis's Wren, but is much smaller, has a shorter tail, and is often arboreal; also note vocalizations. Fairly common to common in NCA; Honduras population limited to the Aguán Valley; to 1,640 ft. (500 m). Found in semiarid woodlands, such as semideciduous forest and thorn forest, where it's often found at midlevels or near canopy. Variable song is a whistled liquid *weeda-weed'her*; call a flat *chup* or *check*; also an agitated chatter *chi'chi'chi'chi . . .* Mex. to Honduras.

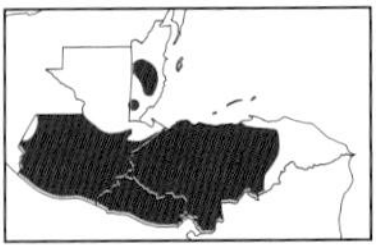

CABANIS'S WREN *Cantorchilus modestus*

5 in. (13 cm). Warm brown above **(contrasting crown is gray-brown)**; **generally has a plain face**, but sometimes with weak dark streaking; white underparts have extensive **buff-brown to chestnut flanks and undertail coverts**; eyes in adult are red (brownish gray in immature). Similar to Carolina Wren, but note gray-brown crown and little or no streaking on face; also different vocalizations. Possibly confused with White-bellied Wren, but is larger with a longer tail and less arboreal; also note vocalizations. Common on Pacific Slope and in interior; uncommon and local along both coasts and in Belize; to 6,250 ft. (1,900 m). Prefers drier habitats, including dry forest and semideciduous forest, and some disturbed habitats (such as coffee plantations). Forages at lower levels. Song is a short, high-pitched *tsee-see-a-wee*; duetting song is a loud, up-and-down series of repeated elements; call is a heavy *thick-thick*. Mex. to Panama.

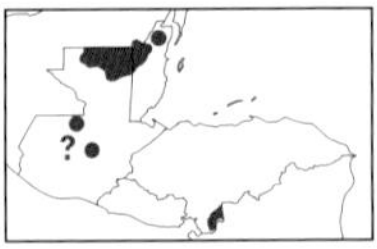

CAROLINA WREN *Thyrothorus ludovicianus*

5 in. (13 cm). Upperparts and crown rich brown; **underparts white with some buffy brown on sides and lower belly** (more extensively cinnamon belly south of Belize); flanks and undertail coverts with dark barring. Similar to Cabanis's Wren but warmer brown on upperparts, including crown, and barring on side of neck; also songs are different. Oddly disjunct range in NCA; locally fairly common in Belize and n. Guatemala; rare in s. Honduras; to 3,280 ft. (1,000 m). Found in dry forest or at edge of semideciduous forest, where it forages at lower levels in thick undergrowth. Song is a rolling *tweet'tweet'tweet'tweet'tweet'tweet* (Honduras) or *teacher'teacher' teacher'teacher'teacher'* (Belize); calls include a liquid *pr-di-rit*, a hollow *p-r-r-r-r-t*, and a Morse code–like *d-d-dit*; also loud, harsh scolds. Some authorities treat the NCA populations as "White-browed Wren," *T. albinucha*. U.S. to Nicaragua.

juvenile
RUFOUS-AND-WHITE WREN
WHITE-BELLIED WREN
CABANIS'S WREN
CAROLINA WREN
albinucha (Belize and northern Guatemala)
subfulvus (interior Guatemala and southern Honduras)

WHITE-BREASTED WOOD-WREN *Henicorhina leucosticta*
4 in. (10 cm). A small wren. **Chestnut back; dark crown** contrasts with **thin white supercilium; face marbled in black and white**; broad black submalar stripe; **throat and chest white**, but sides gray; **tail extremely short**. Juvenile similar but with gray wash on chest. Similar to Gray-breasted Wood-Wren (especially juvenile), but throat unstreaked and whiter; also differences in vocalizations and elevation. Common in NCA (except most of Pacific Slope); to 6,070 ft. (1,850 m) but rare above 4,590 ft. (1,400 m). Found in rainforest; also in coffee plantations. Forages on or near the forest floor. Secretive. Song a musical, clear-whistled, 3-noted *purr-pretty-peat!* or *tea-were-ready!* repeated several times; call is a slightly buzzy *beep* or a sharp *pink*; also a rapid machine gun–like chatter. Mex. to Peru.

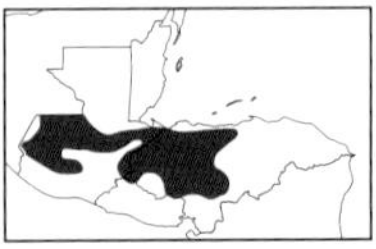

GRAY-BREASTED WOOD-WREN *Henicorhina leucophrys*
4.5 in. (11 cm). Similar to White-breasted Wood-Wren, but note streaked, gray throat and grayer chest; also differences in elevation and vocalizations. Uncommon in NCA; usually above 5,900 ft. (1,800 m) but occasionally as low as 3,940 ft. (1,200 m). Found in cloud forest, humid pine-oak forest, and rarely semideciduous forest, where it forages near forest floor. Sings a musical series of rapid elements, *wheater'or'wheat'beer-wheat'it'be* (often repeated or sung in duet); when duetting, song is similar to duetting Spot-breasted Wren's (p. 306); call a thin *chit'chit'chit'chit . . .* ; also a rapid chatter. Mex. to Bolivia.

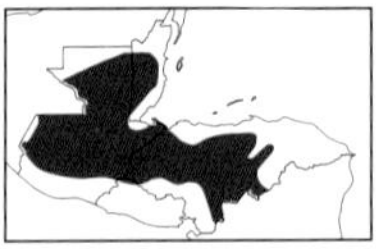

BAND-BACKED WREN *Campylorhynchus zonatus*
8 in. (20 cm). **Dark bands** on upperparts; **black spots on breast**; cinnamon belly, vent, and undertail coverts. Fairly common to common in NCA; to 9,840 ft. (3,000 m). Found within pine savanna, pine-oak forest, semideciduous forest, and disturbed habitats. Most often in family groups. Forages higher in trees than other wrens. Vocalizations include a noisy, nasal chatter, *chi-chi-chow chi-chow chi-chow*, and *chiv-chewie chiv-chewie chiv-chewie*; pairs often duet. Mex. to Ecuador.

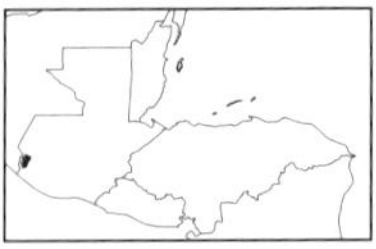

GIANT WREN *Campylorhynchus chiapensis*
8.5 in. (21 cm). **A large wren.** Similar to Rufous-naped Wren, but larger; wings and back are unmarked. Uncommon and local in w. Guatemala; to 650 ft. (200 m). Found at low to midlevels in coastal scrub, riparian forest, and disturbed habitat. Usually in small groups. Vocalizations similar in quality to Rufous-naped Wren (liquid phrases, nasal buzzes, and chatters); call a harsh, scratchy *reee-eh!* Endemic to region.

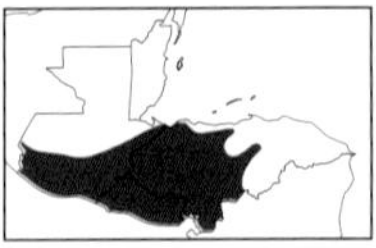

RUFOUS-NAPED WREN *Campylorhynchus rufinucha*
7 in. (18 cm). A large, noisy wren. Similar to Giant Wren, but smaller; wings and back are barred and spotted. Underparts white. W. Guatemala form (*C.r. nigricaudatus*) differs from other subspecies by solid rufous upperparts and blacker tail. Common in NCA; to 4,920 ft. (1,500 m); occasionally up to 5,250 ft. (1,600 m) on volcanoes. Found along edges of semideciduous forest, dry forest, and in disturbed habitats such as urban gardens and parks. Highly social (usually in family groups), inquisitive, and vocal. Vocalizations include liquid phrases, nasal buzzes, and chatter, often repeated 3 to 5 times: *toe-uh'oh-eh'awop toe-uh'oh-eh'awop toe-uh'oh-eh'awop . . .* ; also a prolonged, nasal, agitated chatter. Mex. to Costa Rica.

GRAY-BREASTED
WOOD-WREN

WHITE-BREASTED
WOOD-WREN

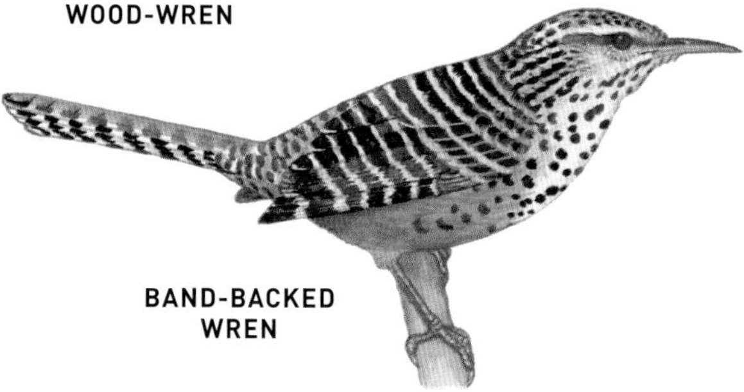

BAND-BACKED
WREN

GIANT
WREN

RUFOUS-NAPED
WREN

*duetting family of
Rufous-naped
Wrens in town*

GNATWRENS AND GNATCATCHERS

POLIOPTILIDAE (Order: Passeriformes). This strictly New World family, closely related to wrens, includes nearly 20 species (4 of which occur in NCA). Gnatcatchers are small passerines patterned in grays and whites, with short wings and long tails. The brown and buff gnatwrens also have short wings, a slightly shorter tail, and very long bills. Species in this group are insectivorous and active foragers, feeding in the crowns of bushes and trees. The gnatwren prefers to forage in vine tangles and dense understory vegetation. **4 species (2 genera)**

LONG-BILLED GNATWREN *Ramphocaenus melanurus*

5 in. (13 cm). **Nape, face, and chest tawny**; remaining underparts buffy white; **note long bill**. Tail often cocked. Fairly common on Caribbean Slope; rare to uncommon and local on Pacific Slope; up to 5,910 ft. (1,800 m) but generally below 3,280 ft. (1,000 m). Found in brushy understory to midcanopy of rainforest and taller semideciduous forest, where it forages among vine tangles and within dead leaf clusters. Typical call is a long, fast trill, lasting 2 to 4 sec. (sometimes changing pitch toward the end); also an agitated scratchy chatter. Mex. to Brazil.

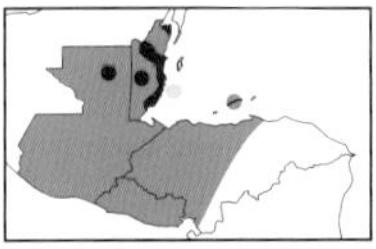

BLUE-GRAY GNATCATCHER *Polioptila caerulea*

4.5 in. (11 cm). Nonbreeding males and all females have **weak white eye-rings** on plain faces. Breeding males (Mar.–Aug.) show **black eyebrows**. Common resident in Belize; fairly common to uncommon winter visitor on Caribbean Slope (Sept.–May); uncommon to rare winter visitor on Pacific Slope; up to 12,300 ft. (3,750 m). Found in a variety of habitat types, including at edge of rainforest, riparian forest, semideciduous forest, and in interior of thorn forest, pine savanna, and coastal scrub. Forages at all levels. Song is a rapidly delivered series of thin wheezy notes, including short trills and buzzes that are often repeated and jumbled. Call is a thin nasal *wheeeeez* (similar in quality to calls of other gnatcatchers). U.S. and Mex. (breeding) to Honduras (winter).

WHITE-LORED GNATCATCHER *Polioptila albiloris*

4.5 in. (11 cm). Breeding male has **black crown**; nonbreeding male similar, but with **thin white supercilium and dark lores**. Female has **gray crown with thin white supercilium**. Nonbreeding male is similar to Tropical Gnatcatcher, but lores dark (not pale) and supercilium thinner; also note habitat and location. Common on Pacific Slope; common on Caribbean Slope in interior dry valleys of Guatemala (Motagua) and Honduras (Aguán); up to 5,910 ft. (1,800 m). Found in thorn forest and at edge of semideciduous forest, where it forages at lower levels. Common call is a nasal, scolding *cheeeez*; male gives a variety of calls, including a soft *tip* and *reeeeah*; also *tch-tch*. Female gives a soft *peep*. Song is a soft series of jumbled buzzes. Mex. to Costa Rica.

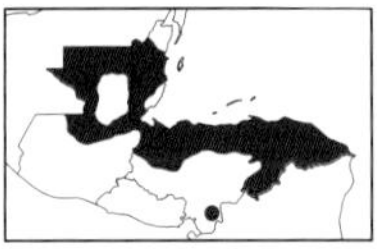

TROPICAL GNATCATCHER *Polioptila plumbea*

4 in. (10 cm). Male has **black crown**, **broad white supercilium, and pale lores**. Female similarly patterned but with gray crown. Male most similar to nonbreeding male White-lored Gnatcatcher, but note pale lores (not dark) and broader supercilium; also note differences in habitat and location. Fairly common on Caribbean Slope; up to 3,610 ft. (1,100 m). Found in rainforest, riparian forest, and taller semideciduous forest, where it forages at mid- to upper levels. Song is a descending whinnylike trill; call is a nasal *schweeee* (similar to calls of other gnatcatchers). Mex. to Brazil.

BLUE-GRAY
GNATCATCHER
breeding
male
nonbreeding male/
female
LONG-BILLED
GNATWREN
breeding male
WHITE-LORED
GNATCATCHER
nonbreeding
male
female
male
female
TROPICAL
GNATCATCHER

DIPPERS AND KINGLETS

CINCLIDAE (Order: Passeriformes). A nearly cosmopolitan family found on 5 continents, each with a single species. Dippers are the only passerines that dive and swim underwater. Adaptations for living in aquatic environments include a nictitating membrane (which allows them to see underwater), scales that cover the nostrils when diving, and a large preen gland for keeping their plumage waterproof. **1 species (1 genus)**

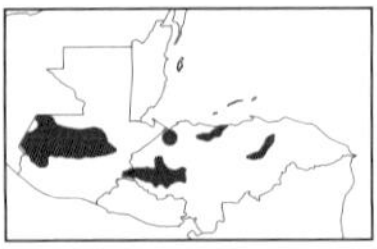

AMERICAN DIPPER *Cinclus mexicanus*

8 in. (20 cm). **Rotund with a short tail** and pinkish legs; **slate gray overall** with slightly browner wash to head and upper chest. Uncommon and local in NCA; 2,300 to 10,010 ft. (700–3,050 m). Found along swift-moving mountain rivers and streams. Forages among large boulders and rocks, where it feeds at bottom of stream- or riverbed. Constantly bobs. Song is a long series of repeated shrill and buzzy notes: *tzzzee-tzzzee-preeep-preeep-trrrrr-trrrrr-trrrrr-cheeeez-tip-tip-tip*. AK to Panama.

REGULIDAE (Order: Passeriformes). The warblerlike kinglets are very small, active foragers, feeding mainly on small insects; they occasionally feed on small fruits. There is slight sexual dimorphism. This family has 6 representatives worldwide (2 in the New World), all mainly in temperate climates. **2 species (1 genus)**

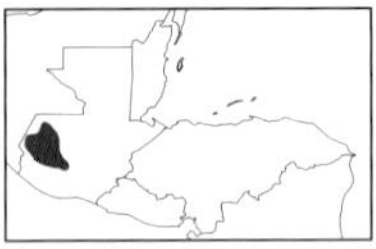

GOLDEN-CROWNED KINGLET *Regulus satrapa*

4 in. (10 cm). Very small. Olive upperparts; nape is gray; **black lateral crown stripes and broad white supercilium**; **crown yellow** (orange-yellow in adult male); underparts whitish; single white wing bar bordered below in black; yellowish edging to wings. Uncommon resident in highlands of w. Guatemala; between 7,550 and 10,500 ft. (2,300 and 3,200 m). Found in pine-oak forest and pine savanna, where it forages at mid- to upper levels in family groups. Calls are high-pitched *tseeet* or *tseet-tseet*; high-pitched song is an accelerating *tsee'tsee'tsee'tsee'see'see'see'see'sisisisisisrrrrr*. U.S. to Guatemala.

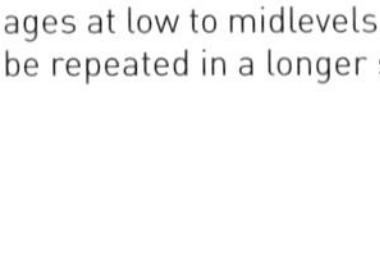

RUBY-CROWNED KINGLET *Regulus calendula*

4 in. (10 cm). Olive-brown upperparts; **broken white eye-ring**; **red crown** rarely seen (but raised when agitated); underparts gray-olive; white wing bar bordered below in black; secondaries and tail edged in yellow; yellow feet contrast with dusky legs. Vagrant winter visitor to Guatemala; between 6,560 and 10,010 ft. (2,000 and 3,050 m). Found in pine-oak forest and pine savanna, where it forages at low to midlevels. Often in mixed-species flocks. Call is a thin chatter, *chit'it* (may be repeated in a longer series). U.S. (breeding) to Mex. (winter).

AMERICAN DIPPER

female

GOLDEN-CROWNED KINGLET

male with raised crest

RUBY-CROWNED KINGLET

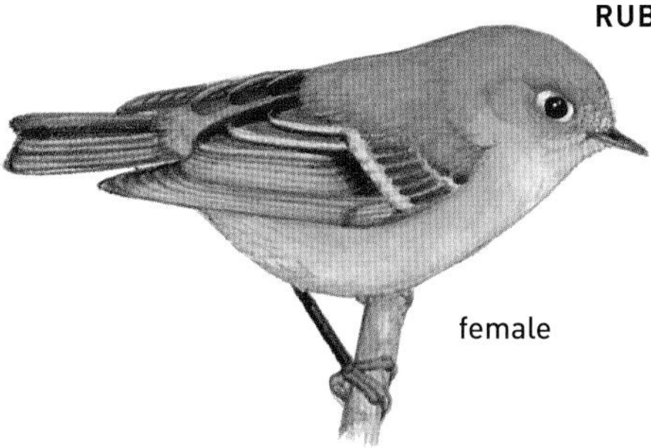

female

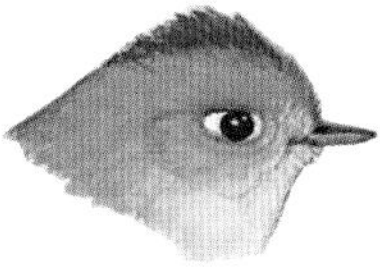

male with raised crest

NIGHTINGALE-THRUSHES

TURDIDAE (Order: Passeriformes). Thrushes and robins are medium to large-sized, round-bodied passerines with thin bills and horizontal postures. Bluebirds and solitaires are similar but with vertical postures. All are omnivores, often feeding on fruits and berries, and capable of dispersing great distances in search of fruiting trees. They feed in trees and on the ground. Sexes are generally similar, while juveniles show buffy spotting across the body and buffy tips to wing coverts. Most species are accomplished vocalists. **18 species (5 genera)**

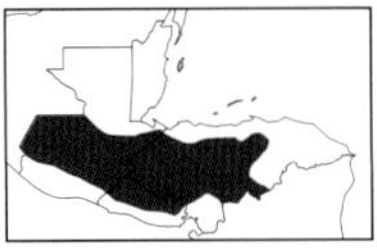

ORANGE-BILLED NIGHTINGALE-THRUSH

Catharus aurantiirostris

6 in. (15 cm). Warm rufous-brown upperparts contrasting with grayish underparts; **eye-ring, bill, and legs bright orange**. Immatures have buffy spots on chest and back. Common in NCA; from 1,970 to 9,350 ft. (600–2,850 m). Found at edge or in scrubby understory within semideciduous forest, disturbed habitat (such as coffee plantations), and pine-oak forest. Forages at lower levels and on ground. Somewhat secretive, but easily detected by voice. Song is variable, but individuals tend to repeat exactly the same phrase over and over, a scratchy warbling series of sharp whistles and buzzes: *chit-TSEE!-tah'wert-PEE'tseee-Cheet* or *TSIP!-Tseee-cheet-tsee'weet* (lasting approximately 2 sec.); calls include a sharp, high-pitched whistle, *tsseeeeeee*, or a catlike contact call, *rreeahhhh*. Mex. to Colombia.

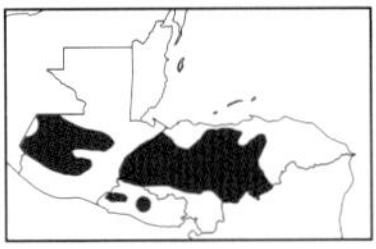

RUDDY-CAPPED NIGHTINGALE-THRUSH *Catharus frantzii*

6.5 in. (17 cm). Upperparts, including wings and tail, brownish olive with **contrasting ruddy crown**; **face and underparts grayish**; maxilla is dark while **mandible is orange-pink**. Uncommon in NCA; from 4,920 to 10,010 ft. (1,500–3,050 m). Found in understory of pine-oak forest and cloud forest, where it forages at low levels and on ground. Secretive, but will occasionally forage at edge in open. Often first detected by voice. Song is a sweet, fluid, melancholy series of organlike whistles, in question-and-answer fashion, the notes rising and falling in pitch, with short, well-separated phrases; distinctive call is a low-pitched, nasal, reedy whistle, *wuueeeeee!* and a short nasal *rank* similar to call of White-throated Thrush (p. 320). Mex. to Panama.

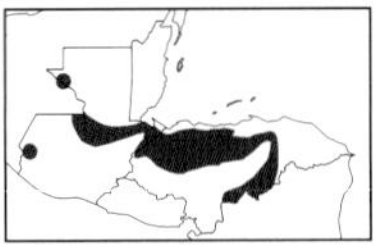

BLACK-HEADED NIGHTINGALE-THRUSH

Catharus mexicanus

6 in. (15 cm). Patterned similarly to Orange-billed Nightingale-Thrush, but with **contrasting black crown**. Female head pattern duller than male. Rare and local in Guatemala and uncommon in Honduras; 2,460 to 5,910 ft. (750–1,800 m). Found in pine-oak forest and cloud forest. Forages at low levels in shady undergrowth. Secretive and difficult to observe. Song is similar in quality to Orange-billed Nightingale-Thrush's, but faster, *Pseeee'cheaaah'wee'tu!* (lasting approximately 1 sec.); call is a scratchy, nasal *reeeaaahh!* Mex. to Panama.

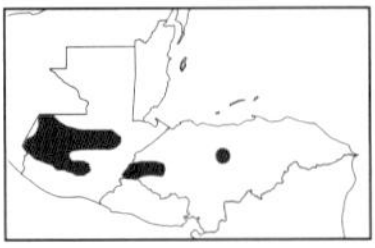

SPOTTED NIGHTINGALE-THRUSH *Catharus dryas*

7.5 in. (19 cm). Olive upperparts contrast with **black head**; **underparts washed yellow with light olive spotting on underparts**; bold **orange eye-ring, orange bill, and orange legs**. Rare to uncommon and local in NCA; from 3,940 to 9,350 ft. (1,200–2,850 m). Found in shady understory of pine-oak forest, cloud forest, and taller humid semideciduous forest; also in higher-elevation coffee plantations. Secretive and difficult to observe well. Detected most often by voice. Song is a sweet series of organlike whistled phrases, well separated, with just 2 or 3 notes per phrase; call is an agitated, scratchy, catlike *Reeeeeaaa'eh!* Mex. to Argentina.

ORANGE-BILLED
NIGHTINGALE-THRUSH

RUDDY-CAPPED
NIGHTINGALE-THRUSH

BLACK-HEADED
NIGHTINGALE-THRUSH

male

SPOTTED
NIGHTINGALE-THRUSH

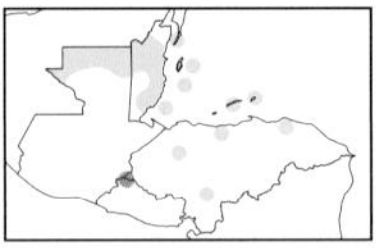

VEERY *Catharus fuscescens*

7 in. (18 cm). Eastern populations (*C.f. fuscescens*) are **warm reddish brown above**; face paler gray; **chest washed buff with small reddish brown spots**. Western populations (*C.f. salicicolus*) are darker brown overall. Compare *salicicolus* with Swainson's Thrush, but lacks bold buff eye-ring and malar stripe. Uncommon transient on Caribbean Slope, including cayes and islands (mid-Sept.–late Nov.; mid-Apr.–late May); vagrant to Pacific Slope; to 6,230 ft. (1,900 m) but generally below 2,460 ft. (750 m). Found in understory within a variety of woodland types. Generally silent in NCA. Call is a sliding, slurring *veeeer*. Canada and U.S. (breeding) to Brazil (winter).

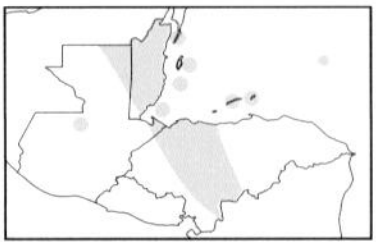

GRAY-CHEEKED THRUSH *Catharus minimus*

7 in. (18 cm). **Cold grayish brown upperparts**; **face washed grayish with partial thin whitish eye-ring** (slight teardrop behind eye); gray flanks and heavy black spotting on chest. Uncommon transient on Caribbean Slope, including islands (late Sept.–mid-Nov.; mid-Apr.–late May); to 4,920 ft. (1,500 m). Vagrant on Pacific Slope. Found in understory within a variety of woodland types. Generally silent in NCA. Call is a distinctive *Pweeer!* U.S. and Canada (breeding) to Colombia (winter).

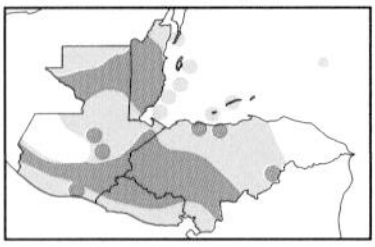

SWAINSON'S THRUSH *Catharus ustulatus*

7 in. (18 cm). Two groups found in NCA: "olive-backed" (*swainsoni*; eastern) and "russet-backed" (*ustulatus*; western). Olive-backed group has **bold buffy eye-ring and buffy wash to face and malar**; dense spotting on chest. Russet-backed group is similar, but with rufescent tones above, eye-ring less bold, and less spotting below. Like Veery (*salicicolus*), but with more buff in face. Common transient and winter visitor to NCA (mid-Sept.–late May); *swainsoni* is found primarily on the Caribbean Slope (to 4,920 ft. [1,500 m]); *ustulatus* in the central highlands and on Pacific Slope (1,970–9,350 ft. [600–2,850 m]), but distributions overlap. Found in a wide variety of woodland types. Forages at low to midlevels and on ground. In NCA, sings frequently during northward migration. Song is an upward spiraling series of fluting notes. Call is liquid *whip*. Canada and U.S. (breeding) to Argentina (winter).

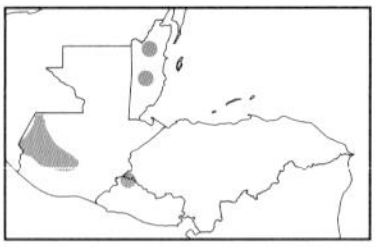

HERMIT THRUSH *Catharus guttatus*

6.5 in. (17 cm). Cold grayish brown upperparts contrast with **rufous brown tail**; **complete whitish eye-ring**; buffy wing stripe visible in flight. Uncommon in winter in Guatemala highlands (late Nov.–Mar.); rare in nw. El Salvador (and adjacent Honduras?); from 3,940 to 11,980 ft. (1,200–3,650 m). Found in understory of pine-oak forest. Forages low and on ground. Has distinctive habit of pumping tail. Call is a distinctive, low *tchup*. U.S. and Canada (breeding) to NCA (winter).

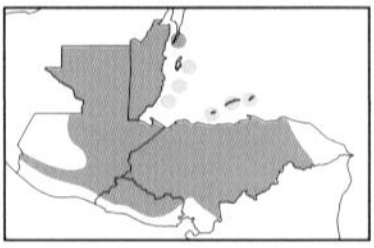

WOOD THRUSH *Hylocichla mustelina*

8 in. (20 cm). A larger, round-bodied thrush. **Bright rufous-brown upperparts**; **heavy black spotting and chevrons below**. Common winter visitor on Caribbean Slope (late Sept.–early May). Uncommon to rare on Pacific Slope; to 7,220 ft. (2,200 m). Found in a wide variety of woodland types. Forages in understory and on ground. Call is a sharp *whip!-whip!-whip!* U.S. (breeding) to Colombia (winter).

VEERY
fuscescens
GRAY-CHEEKED THRUSH
SWAINSON'S THRUSH
ustulatus
HERMIT THRUSH
WOOD THRUSH

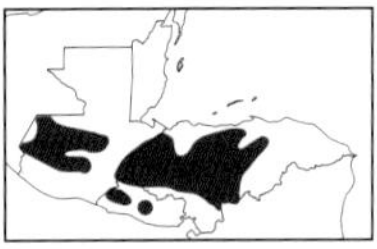

BLACK THRUSH *Turdus infuscatus*

9 in. (23 cm). Male **blackish overall** with **yellow bill, eye-ring, and legs**. Female dark brown overall with blackish bill, but **note yellowish brown legs** (Mountain Thrush has dark legs). Immature male is like female, but shows yellowish bill and eye-ring. Uncommon in highlands of NCA; from 3,280 to 10,000 ft. (1,000–3,050 m). Found in semideciduous forest, pine-oak forest, and cloud forest. Arboreal; forages at mid- to upper levels. Most often detected by voice. Song is a long, varied series of well-spaced, sweet clear whistled phrases: *chaao—sit!—peer!—tleeet—pip'pip—peeeer!—seeet!—weeeer!—peeer'peeer'peeer . . .* , given over several minutes from a high perch in the canopy; also a dry *che'che'che'che'* and in flight a thin *ssi*. Mex. to Nicaragua.

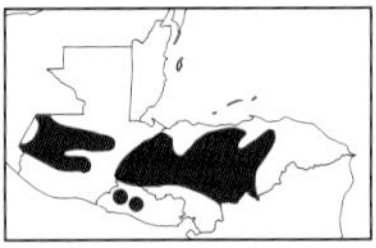

MOUNTAIN THRUSH *Turdus plebejus*

9.5 in. (24 cm). An all-dark gray-brown thrush with **dark bill and dark legs**. **Undertail coverts dusky with white edges, giving a scaled appearance**. Compare with female or immature Black Thrush (which always have lighter legs). Uncommon in highlands of NCA; from 4,270 to 10,500 ft. (1,300–3,200 m). Found in pine-oak and oak-dominated forest, and cloud forest. Forages at low to mid-levels, often at edge. Song is similar in quality to Rufous-collared Robin (p. 322), a warbling series of repeated elements (2–3 times), lacking the higher-pitched whistles and buzzes of Black Thrush: *churee-churee-tea'rrr-clearer-clearer-cheer'up-cheer'up-here!* (with roughly 3 sec. between each series); call is a high-pitched, sharp *pseeeeep!* Mex. to Panama.

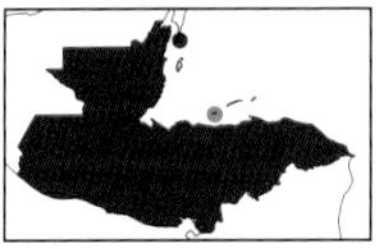

CLAY-COLORED THRUSH *Turdus grayi*

10 in. (26 cm). The most widespread *Turdus* thrush. **Light brown above and paler buffy brown below**; note **yellowish or yellow-green bill**, pink legs. Immature has buffy tips to wing coverts and smudgy spots on underparts. Common in NCA; to 6,890 ft. (2,100 m) but generally below 4,920 ft. (1,500 m). Found at edges of woodlands and in disturbed areas, such as coffee plantations, urban parks, and gardens. Forages at low to midlevels. Song is a sweet warbling series of evenly spaced elements with less immediate repetition than other *Turdus* species: *Tur-nup-cheerie!-hear'hee-hear'wee!-Sa'weeet!-pa'weeer-turn'up'turn'up-pa'weereea!- . . .* (each series lasting approximately 5 or 6 sec. with pauses of approximately 3 sec. between series); calls include a ringing *Churr'eeee*, and a harsher *chut'chut'chut* (similar to call of Rufous-collared Robin [p. 322]). Mex. to Colombia.

WHITE-THROATED THRUSH *Turdus assimilis*

10 in. (26 cm). **Throat has black streaks**, while chest and sides are washed dirty brown; note **small white collar**; also, **bill, eye-ring, and legs yellow**. Immature shows buffy tips to wing coverts and buffy spotting on back, crown, and chest. Uncommon to fairly common in NCA; appears to make altitudinal migrations and wanders in search of fruiting trees; to 6,890 ft. (2,100 m) but mostly above 2,450 ft. (750 m). Found in a variety of woodland types: rainforest, semideciduous forest, pine-oak forest, riparian forest, and coffee plantations. Forages at all levels. Song is a sweet warble of evenly spaced notes, richer with more trills, more repeated notes, and slower in tempo than Clay-colored Thrush but faster than Black Thrush: *Sa'wheet!—peurti—tear'wee'wee—peurti—tea'weu—weu'weu—Pureee!—pea'a'a'a'a—peur'weet!— . . .* ; call is distinctive, a harsh, nasal, slightly grating *rrreeuh* or *wrehnk*. Mex. to Ecuador.

BLACK THRUSH
male
female
MOUNTAIN THRUSH
CLAY-COLORED THRUSH
adult
juvenile
WHITE-THROATED THRUSH

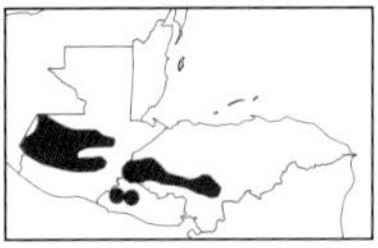

RUFOUS-COLLARED ROBIN *Turdus rufitorques*

10 in. (26 cm). Adult male blackish with **strongly contrasting rufous collar and chest**; bill and legs yellow along with weak yellow eye-ring. Female and immature drabber overall. Note white streaks on dark undertail coverts in all plumages. Fairly common in highlands of NCA; from 4,920 to 10,990 ft. (1,500–3,350 m). Found at edge in pine-oak forest and cloud forest; also at edges of open fields and in urban parks and gardens. Forages at all levels. Song quality is similar to Mountain Thrush (p. 320) with evenly spaced high-pitched warbling whistles and trills, but note little repetition and added "echo" to ending of many elements: *tre'e'e'e'e—chur'e'e'e'e'e'e'—We'dirt!—Tea'a'a'a!—pretty'dirt'pretty'dirt'irt'irt'irt'irt—We'dirt!—tseet!—Tea'Tea'ear'ear'ear'ear'ear—* . . . ; call is a *chut'chut'chut*. Endemic to region.

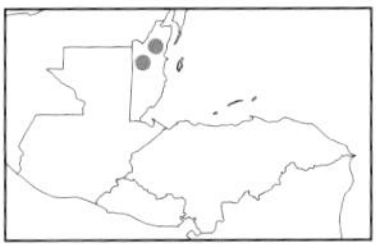

AMERICAN ROBIN *Turdus migratorius*

10 in. (26 cm). On adult male, gray upperparts contrast with **black head and rufous underparts**; also note streaked throat and **bold broken whitish eye-ring**. Bill is yellow. Female is drabber overall with less contrasting colors. Very rare winter visitor to NCA (recorded Jan.–Mar.); to 6,730 ft. (2,050 m). Found at forest edges and in urban gardens. Forages at all levels. Call is a rapid, *tuc'tuc'tuc'tuc'tuc* and a sharp, slightly metallic *pweep!* Canada to Mex. (and NCA).

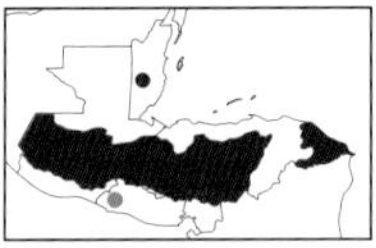

EASTERN BLUEBIRD *Sialia sialis*

6.5 in. (17 cm). Adult male **bright sky blue on head and upperparts,** including wings and tail; note **rufous collar, chest, and sides**. Female drabber overall. Juvenile has large whitish spots on back, crown, and underparts. Fairly common in NCA; to 10,660 ft. (3,250 m) and generally above 1,970 ft. (600 m), but at sea level in e. Honduras. Found in semiarid open country: grasslands, pine savanna, and at clearings in pine-oak forest. Forages at all levels. Sallies from exposed perch (such as fencepost) for insect prey and will also feed on ground and on berries. Song is a varied short burry warble, *Churt!-weeere-chu!* or *Chur-weee*; also, a scratchy *Wit-chi'chi'chi'chi*. U.S. to Nicaragua.

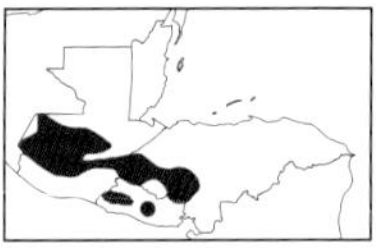

BROWN-BACKED SOLITAIRE *Myadestes occidentalis*

8 in. (20 cm). Grayish overall with **reddish brown back and wings**; also note **broken white eye-ring** and buffy wing stripe in flight. Juvenile is heavily spotted with buff. Fairly common in NCA; 1,970 to 10,000 ft. (600–3,050 m) but generally above 4,760 ft. (1,450 m). Found in pine-oak forest and some cloud forests; also taller humid semideciduous forest and coffee plantations. Forages at mid- to upper levels. Easily detected by loud, distinctive song, a liquid, cascading metallic jangling that starts slowly, but finishes in a jumbled crescendo (lasting around 11 sec.). Call is a sharp, metallic *Scheeet!* (as if pulling a sword from its scabbard). Mex. to Honduras.

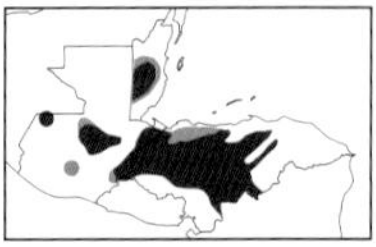

SLATE-COLORED SOLITAIRE *Myadestes unicolor*

8 in. (20 cm). **Back and wings are slaty gray**; in flight note buffy wing stripe. Fairly common in NCA; 2,950 to 8,860 ft. (900–2,700 m); in winter (Dec. to Mar.), regularly makes altitudinal migrations in search of fruiting trees, to near sea level. Found in humid pine-oak forest and cloud forest, occasionally rainforest. Forages at all levels. Frequently detected by loud, distinctive voice, a ringing metallic phrase, repeated regularly with little variation. Mex. to Nicaragua.

RUFOUS-COLLARED
ROBIN
male
female
female
male
AMERICAN
ROBIN
male
female
EASTERN
BLUEBIRD
juvenile
BROWN-BACKED
SOLITAIRE
adult
juvenile
adult
SLATE-COLORED
SOLITAIRE
juvenile

MIMIDS (Mockingbirds and Catbirds)

MIMIDAE (Order: Passeriformes). This group is best known for its diverse repertoire of vocalizations and its use of vocal mimicry, although NCA species rarely mimic other birds. Species are long-tailed, short-winged, and spend most of their time skulking in understory vegetation, the exception being the Tropical Mockingbird. **4 species (4 genera)**

BLUE-AND-WHITE MOCKINGBIRD *Melanotis hypoleucus*

10 in. (26 cm). Adults show **striking pattern of steely blue above and clean white below**; **black mask**. Juvenile dark smoky gray overall, with variable white streaking on breast. Fairly common in highlands of NCA; 3,940 to 9,510 ft. (1,200–2,900 m). Found in scrubby vegetation within clearings and at edges of pine-oak forest and cloud forest; skulking. When singing, may perch in open at tops of trees. Song is a rapidly delivered series of chirps, trills, and whistles, thrushlike, repeated every 10 or 20 sec. (occasionally mimics local bird sounds). Endemic to region.

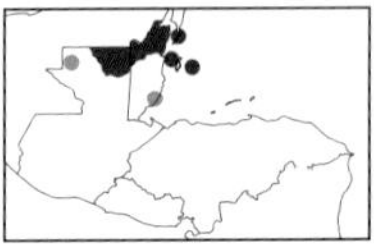

BLACK CATBIRD *Melanoptila glabrirostris*

8 in. (20 cm). **Blackish overall with a bluish gloss or sheen.** Fairly common in n. Belize; rare to uncommon in n. Guatemala; 2 historical records from n. Honduras; to 330 ft. (100 m). Found at edge of semideciduous forest and within scrubby woodland, where it forages at low to midlevels; skulking. Song is a tinkling, musical *sii-tink-leeer* (similar in tone and quality to White-bellied Wren [p. 308]); calls include a *pa'teeer* and a scratchy, agitated *rheeeeaaa*. Endemic to region.

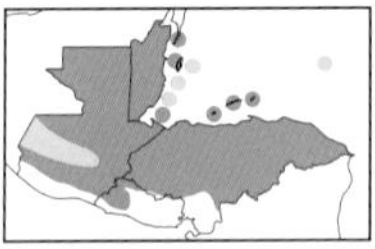

GRAY CATBIRD *Dumetella carolinensis*

8.5 in. (22 cm). Dark gray overall with **black crown** and tail; **rusty undertail coverts**. Common winter visitor (late Sept.–early May) on Caribbean Slope, including cayes and Bay Is.; rare on Pacific Slope; to 6,560 ft. (2,000 m). Found in scrubby vegetation, along hedgerows, in semideciduous forest; also gardens. Generally forages at lower levels, near ground; also frequents crowns of fruiting trees. Call is a nasal, catlike *wreeeeahhh*; also a nasal, thin *eeaahh*. Canada (breeding) to Panama (winter).

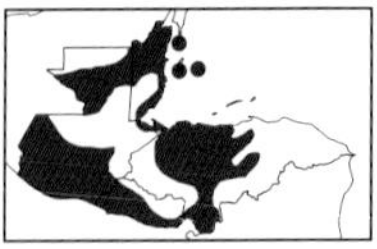

TROPICAL MOCKINGBIRD *Mimus gilvus*

10 in. (26 cm). Gray above and paler below; wings blackish with variable amounts of white—some birds have 2 thin white wing bars, and a few even have small white patches at the base of the primaries (especially near the Gulf of Fonseca); **long, rounded tail with broad white tips to outer tail feathers (flashed in flight)**. Compare with smaller Loggerhead Shrike (p. 284). Fairly common to common locally in NCA; to 7,870 ft. (2,400 m) but mostly in lowlands. Found in a variety of open habitats, along hedgerows, in agricultural areas, and along beaches. Often perches conspicuously in open, sometimes on wires. Calls and sings frequently: song is a long musical series of repeated elements and phrases: *teer-teer-teer-teer-teer-teer—here-here—wiir-wiir-wiir-wiir-wiir—tip-tip-tip-tip-tip-tip-tip-tip-tip—he'dee'weeir-he'dee'weeir-he'dee'weeir-...* (elements in series can be repeated 2 to 10 times or more); rarely mimics local bird sounds; call is a harsh *Tchit!* and a single or doubled *peeip*. Mex. and Caribbean to Brazil. **Northern Mockingbird (*Mimus polyglottos*)**, not illustrated, is a vagrant to NCA; it is similar to Tropical Mockingbird, but has large white wing patches, outer tail feathers are white from base to tip, and tail is squared (not rounded).

adult
BLUE-AND-WHITE MOCKINGBIRD
juvenile
BLACK CATBIRD
GRAY CATBIRD
TROPICAL MOCKINGBIRD

MOTACILLIDAE (Order: Passeriformes). A cosmopolitan family of mainly temperate, ground-dwelling passerines with lean bodies, relatively long legs, long claws on feet, and thin bills. Pipits are active foragers with a nervous temperament, rarely standing or sitting still. They have bounding flight and undertake long-distance migrations. **1 species (1 genus)**

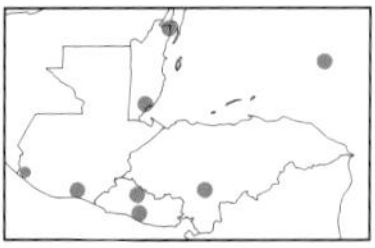

AMERICAN PIPIT *Anthus rubescens*

6 in. (15 cm). A fairly drab-looking bird, but note **pale ill-defined supercilium**; **whitish underparts with dull streaking on chest, sides, and flanks**; short bill with **pinkish yellow base to mandible**. Rare winter visitor to NCA (Nov.–Apr.); to at least 7,500 ft. (2,300 m). Found in open habitats like coastal beaches, short grassland, and agricultural fields; forages on ground. Flight call is a rapid *sipip* or *sipipi*. U.S. and Canada (breeding) to Mex. and NCA (winter).

BOMBYCILLIDAE (Order: Passeriformes). Waxwings are named for the brightly colored feather tips on their wings that appear as if dipped in wax. This temperate Holarctic family includes 2 New World frugivores, both of which occasionally make large-scale, massive irruptions to regions farther south in search of fruiting bushes and trees; only 1 species has reached NCA. **1 species (1 genus)**

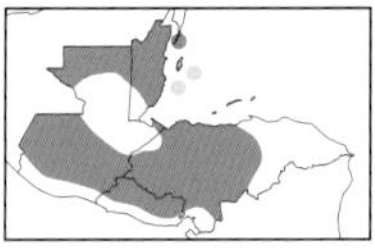

CEDAR WAXWING *Bombycilla cedrorum*

7 in. (18 cm). Tawny-brown above; **pointed crest**; **thin black mask bordered narrowly in white**; pale lemon yellow on belly and vent; **secondaries have waxy red tips**; gray **tail tipped broadly with yellow**. Rare to uncommon transient and winter visitor (Dec.–May) to NCA; absent some years; irruptions approximately every 4 years; to 9,510 ft. (2,900 m). Found in a variety of woodland types, including disturbed habitats (coffee plantations, gardens, cities and towns), cloud forest, and semideciduous forest. Forages at all levels; almost always in search of fruiting trees; flies in tight groups of 10 to 20 individuals. Call is a thin, high-pitched, slightly wavering *seeee*, given while perched and in flight. Canada (breeding) to Panama (winter).

PTILOGONATIDAE (Order: Passeriformes). The silky-flycatchers are found only in N. America. They are closely related to waxwings (Bombycillidae) with soft silky plumage, long tails, crests, and small bills. Silky-flycatchers are known for their aerial foraging techniques, hence the "flycatcher" name, but they feed on both insects and berries. **1 species (1 genus)**

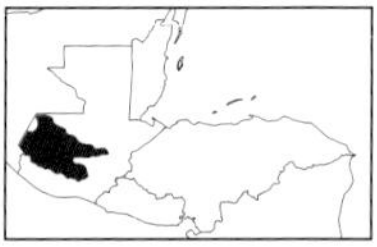

GRAY SILKY-FLYCATCHER *Ptiliogonys cinereus*

8 in. (20 cm). Fairly long tail, crest, and white eye-ring on both sexes. Male is grayish above on head, chest, and upperparts, with **yellowish belly and undertail coverts**, and **black band across base of undertail**. Female and juvenile browner overall with reduced yellow on underparts mainly limited to undertail coverts. Fairly common in Guatemala; from 3,940 to 10,010 ft. (1,200–3,050 m) but generally above 5,580 ft. (1,700 m). Found along edges in pine-oak forest and pine savanna; also less commonly in cloud forest. Perches in open on tops of tall trees; often detected by voice overhead in bounding flight. Frequently seen in groups of 5 to 15 individuals. Calls include chattering chips and chirps, *tik!-tip!* (the common flight call), and a more rapid *tik-tik-tik-tik-tik-tik-* . . . Mex. to Guatemala.

AMERICAN PIPIT

Cedar Waxwings form large, tight flocks

CEDAR WAXWING

male

female

GRAY SILKY-FLYCATCHER

HOUSE SPARROW AND MUNIAS

PASSERIDAE (Order: Passeriformes). The only representative of this family in NCA is an introduced Old World species now well established in much of N. and S. America. Originally native to the Middle East, the House Sparrow, or "English" Sparrow, colonized Europe with the advance of human settlement. It was introduced in New York City in 1852 and quickly spread through the Americas, becoming a familiar part of both urban and farmland avifauna. **1 species (1 genus)**

HOUSE SPARROW *Passer domesticus*

6.5 in. (16 cm). Adult breeding male has **gray crown bordered below with chestnut nape that reaches behind eye**; **black throat and chest**; also 2 small white wing bars. Nonbreeding male duller overall with reduced black on throat and chest. Female dull buffy brown overall with **buffy supercilium and dark postocular stripe**. Female similar to female Dickcissel (p. 390) but lacks malar stripe and yellow wash to breast. Common in NCA (but absent from n. Belize and n. Guatemala); to 10,170 ft. (3,100 m). Never found far from human habitation. Found in cities and towns, agricultural fields (especially around farm buildings), along roadsides, and in pastures. Forages at low to midlevels, often on the ground in small flocks. Call is a liquid *chirrup*. Worldwide.

ESTRILDIDAE (Order: Passeriformes). Introduced species that are native to India, China, and Southeast Asia. The munias are now found in various locales throughout the Caribbean and Cen. and S. America. **2 species (1 genus)**

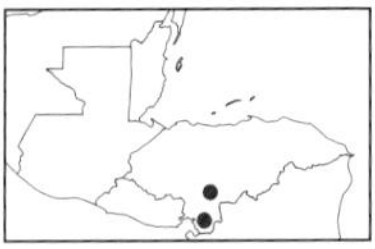

SCALY-BREASTED MUNIA *Lonchura punctulata*

4 in. (10 cm). Adult has chestnut face, dark brown head and upperparts contrasting with **bold black scalloping on underparts**. Note stout bill and short tail. Female and immature brownish overall, slightly paler buff below, similar to female Ruddy-breasted Seedeater (p. 370) but with shorter tail and larger bill. Rare and local in Honduras, and not yet well established; first recorded in 2009; to 3,940 ft. (1,200 m). Found in agricultural fields, hedgerows, and scrubby, abandoned lots. Generally in small flocks of 3 to 5 individuals. Calls include a disyllabic *pa'peep!* and a longer *peeep!* Native to India and Southeast Asia.

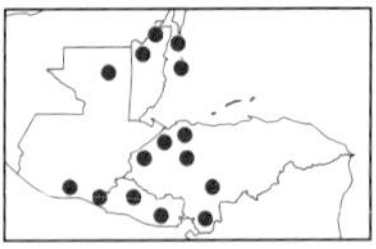

TRICOLORED MUNIA *Lonchura malacca*

5 in. (13 cm). Adult male has **black hood and belly, chestnut upperparts, and heavy, conical-shaped silver-blue bill**. Female and immature olive-brown above with whitish underparts. Tail fairly short. Rare and local, but widespread in NCA; first detected in 2003; to 2,560 ft. (780 m). Found in agricultural fields of sorghum or wheat and in tall marsh grasses along freshwater lakes. Generally in small flocks of 3 to 5 individuals. Calls include a sweet *weet!* or *peet!* and a rail-like *pee'deep!* Native to India and Sri Lanka.

HOUSE SPARROW

SCALY-BREASTED MUNIA

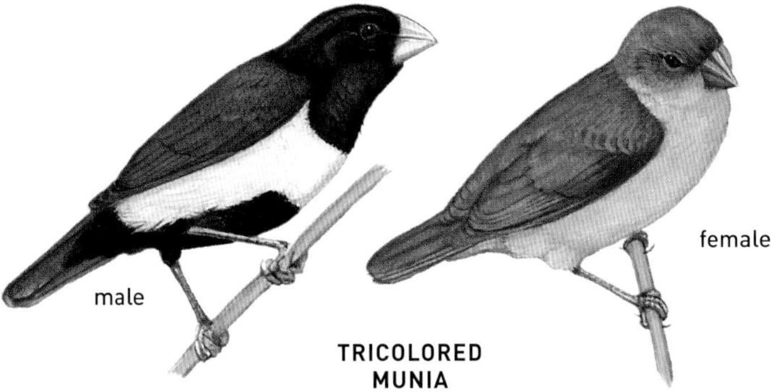

TRICOLORED MUNIA

CROSSBILLS AND OTHER FRINGILLIDS

FRINGILLIDAE (Order: Passeriformes). A group of small to medium-sized, berry-eating and seed-cracking passerines with conical-shaped or pointed bills. Euphonias specialize on mistletoe berries, while crossbills extract seeds from pine cones. In all NCA species, males are brightly colored and females are duller; juvenile males resemble females, and older immatures may show some features of the adult male plumage during extended molting. All Central American species breed locally, but may move or migrate as fruit or seed crops wax and wane. Local movements are still poorly understood and may not be predictable. Songs usually include complex warbles, scratchy or buzzy notes, and clear whistles. **13 species (5 genera)**

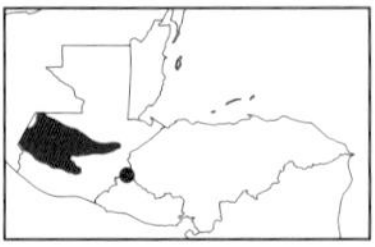

HOODED GROSBEAK *Coccothraustes abeillei*

7 in. (18 cm). Adult male has **black hood** and yellow body; **black wings and tail with bold white tertials**. Adult female duller yellow-olive with black crown. Uncommon on Pacific Slope and in interior; from 3,940 to 7,550 ft. (1,200–2,300 m). Found in pine-oak forest and cloud forest, also in taller semi-deciduous forest. Forages at mid- to upper levels. Often perches on tops of trees. Male call is a loud, ringing *peet!-peet!* and *peet!-peet!-peeeeeurrr* (ending slightly buzzy); female call is a ringing *pit!-preee!* and *peeeur'teee!* Mex. to NCA.

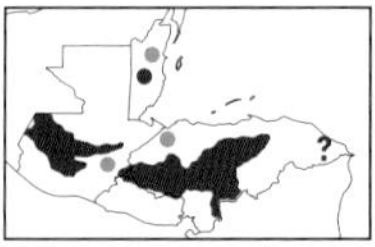

RED CROSSBILL *Loxia curvirostra*

6 in. (15 cm). **Unique bill with tip of maxilla and mandible crossed.** Adult male reddish to orange-red overall. Female and immature yellow-olive or grayish yellow overall (immature may show some red spotting). Uncommon in interior highlands; to 8,860 ft. (2,700 m). Found in pine savanna and pine-oak forest. Forages at mid- to upper levels. Occasionally found at "salt licks" on rocks. Generally in flocks of up to 15 individuals. Often detected by flight call. Calls are a chirping *tip'tip-tip-tip-tip'tip-tip-tip-tip-tip'tip- . . .* or a *chit-chit'chit'chit-chit-chit*. Canada to Nicaragua.

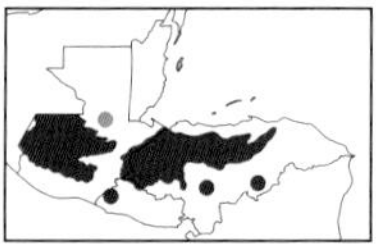

BLUE-CROWNED CHLOROPHONIA *Chlorophonia occipitalis*

5 in. (13 cm). Adult male shows sharp contrast between **bright yellow underparts and lime green upperparts**; **crown and collar sky blue**. Adult female shows less contrast and more green below. Generally uncommon and local in NCA highlands (not Belize); from 330 to 7,870 ft. (100–2,400 m); rare winter visitor below 1,970 ft. (600 m). Found in taller semideciduous and pine-oak forest to cloud forest. Forages at mid- to upper levels; often in clumps of mistletoe. Calls include a liquid, tinkling *where'my'shirt* or *two'eat!* and a nasal *wrap*; also a fairly low, mournful whistle, *peeeeewwww*. All calls may be used together in a longer series. Mex. to Nicaragua.

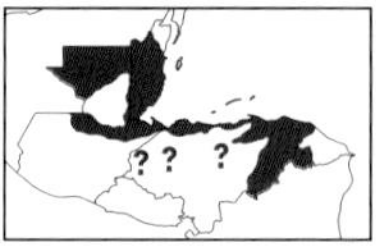

OLIVE-BACKED EUPHONIA *Euphonia gouldi*

4 in. (10 cm). Male has **chestnut belly, vent, and undertail coverts** and **yellow forecrown**. Female has chestnut undertail coverts and **small chestnut forecrown**. Fairly common on Caribbean Slope; to 4,270 ft. (1,300 m). Found in interior or edge of rainforest, where it forages at mid- to upper levels. Often in pairs. Song and calls are similar in quality to Yellow-throated Euphonia (p. 332). Song is a rapid jumble of chatters, buzzes, and harsh whistles; calls include a *chi'chi'chi'cheet* and a liquid *tsip'please-seeee'up!* Mex. to Panama.

HOODED
GROSBEAK
male
female
RED
CROSSBILL
male
female
BLUE-CROWNED
CHLOROPHONIA
male
female
OLIVE-BACKED
EUPHONIA
male
female

SCRUB EUPHONIA *Euphonia affinis*

4 in. (10 cm). Yellow on forecrown **extending just behind eye**. Adult female and juvenile show **slight grayish wash to cheeks and nape**. Adult male similar to Yellow-crowned Euphonia, but has less extensive crown patch. Also like White-vented Euphonia, but vent yellow. Female similar to female Yellow-crowned, but note grayish wash on head. Fairly common on both slopes; to 7,220 ft. (2,200 m) but generally below 4,270 ft. (1,300 m). Found at edge of semideciduous forest and rainforest; also in disturbed habitats, including open second growth, plantations, city parks, and gardens. Often in pairs or small flocks. Forages at mid- to upper levels; fond of mistletoe berries and palm fruits. Song is a rapid, jumbled warble of various tinkling elements and clear whistles. Call is a clear *dee-dee* or *dee-dee-dee*; also *tseeeu-dew*. Mex. to Costa Rica.

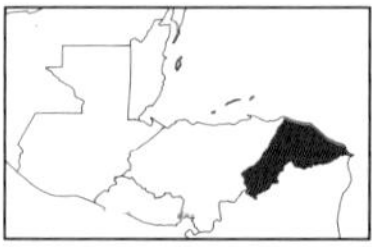

YELLOW-CROWNED EUPHONIA *Euphonia luteicapilla*

4 in. (10 cm). Adult male similar to adult male Scrub Euphonia, but **yellow forecrown more extensive and extends farther behind eye**. Adult female similar to female Scrub Euphonia, but **lacks grayish wash on head**. Uncommon in e. Honduras; to 3,940 ft. (1,200 m). Found at edge of rainforest. Forages at mid- to upper levels. Song usually begins with a sharp, whistled *Seeet!* followed by a jumbled warble of various tinkling elements and whistles. Call similar in quality and pattern to Scrub Euphonia, *weee-weee* or *we-we-we*. Honduras to Panama.

YELLOW-THROATED EUPHONIA *Euphonia hirundinacea*

4 in. (10 cm). Among euphonias, **bright yellow throat** is diagnostic. Adult female and immature male olive-yellow above with yellowish wash on sides and flanks, but **throat, belly and vent are grayish**. Fairly common on both slopes but absent from parts of the interior; to 6,560 ft. (2,000 m). Found in a variety of open and disturbed habitat, including forest edges and clearings, plantations, city parks and gardens. Song and calls are very similar to Olive-backed Euphonia's (p. 330). Song is a scratchy, complaining warble: *chit'chit'chit'chit-pretty'please!* or *tseet'tseet-cheer'up!*; occasionally mimics the songs of other songbirds; varied calls include a slightly ringing *peet!-peet!-peet!* or *peet!-peet!*, a buzzy, liquid *chit-cheeuu* or *pit!-seeeuu*; also a lower-pitched somber whistle, *preeeeaa*. Mex. to Panama.

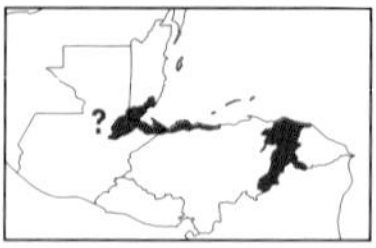

WHITE-VENTED EUPHONIA *Euphonia minuta*

4 in. (10 cm). Adult male similar to Scrub Euphonia, but note **white vent and undertail coverts**. Female **shows yellow across chest and contrasting grayish throat**. Uncommon on Caribbean Slope; to 3,280 ft. (1,000 m). Found in interior or at edge of rainforest, where it forages at all levels. Song is a tinkling, liquid warble; calls include a *tseeeu* and a *tsip*. Guatemala to Brazil.

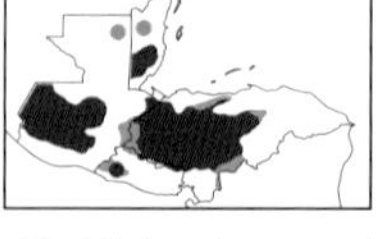

ELEGANT EUPHONIA *Euphonia elegantissima*

4 in. (10 cm). Adult male distinctive **with orange underparts; blue nape and crown**. Female and immature yellow-olive overall **with blue nape and crown**. Uncommon and seasonal in highlands and interior valleys; 1,650 to 10,010 ft. (500–3,050 m). Local movements not well understood. Found in a variety of habitats, wherever clumps of mistletoe are available. Forages at canopy levels. Often in pairs or small groups. Song is rapidly delivered liquid warble lasting up to several minutes with various complaining chatters, buzzes, and clear whistles; calls include a sharp *sip* or *suiit* and a nasal *ernt*. Mex. to Panama.

SCRUB EUPHONIA
male
female
YELLOW-CROWNED EUPHONIA
male
female
YELLOW-THROATED EUPHONIA
male
female
WHITE-VENTED EUPHONIA
male
female
ELEGANT EUPHONIA
male
female

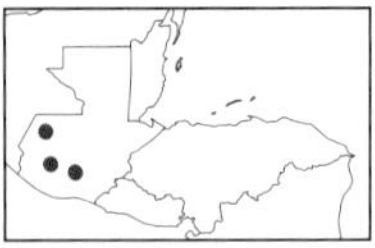

PINE SISKIN *Carduelis pinus perplexus*

4.5 in. (12 cm). Adult grayish overall with **fine or indistinct streaking on underparts**; contrasting **dark gray-brown cap (lightly streaked) and auricular**; back is streaked; **tail has bright yellow patches; small yellow patch at base of primaries**; bill small, pointed, and slightly decurved. Juvenile has coarser streaking below. Gray morph is pale gray overall with little or no streaking, and blackish cap; similar to Black-capped Siskin but has shorter bill, less black on cap, whitish vent, and lacks extensive olive tones (hybrids are possible). Rare in highlands of w. Guatemala; from 6,560 to 10,500 ft. (2,000–3,200 m). Found in pine savanna and pine-oak forest. Forages at all levels. Forms flocks of 5 to 20 individuals. Call is a whiny, thin buzz, *wheeeeeeee!*; song is not described for NCA. Canada to Guatemala.

BLACK-CAPPED SISKIN *Carduelis atriceps*

4.5 in. (12 cm). Adult male **yellowish olive overall**; contrasting **black cap**; blackish wings with yellow patch at base of primaries; tail also has large yellow patches. Female similar to adult male but duller. Juvenile washed yellowish below with heavy streaking, and dark cap. May occasionally hybridize with Pine Siskin. Uncommon in highlands of w. Guatemala; 5,250 to 10,170 ft. (1,600–3,100 m). Found at edge of pine-oak forest and in pine savanna. Forages at all levels. Generally in pairs or small flocks. Song is a varied buzzy, tinkling, liquid warble; calls include a buzzy *tzzzeeeeee!* and a *tzeep!* or double-noted *tzeep-cheet!*; also a chatter, *chit'chit'chit'chit'chit*. Endemic to region.

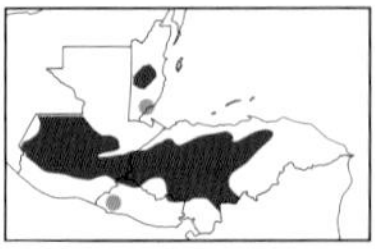

BLACK-HEADED SISKIN *Carduelis notata*

4.5 in. (11 cm). Adult male has **black hood**. Adult female lacks black hood and is duller overall. Fairly common in NCA; to 9,075 ft. (2,750 m). Found in weedy fields and at edge in a variety of woodland habitats, including semideciduous forest, pine-oak forest, taller second growth, and coffee plantations. Forages at all levels. Generally in pairs or small flocks. Song is a rapid, liquid, tinkling, buzzy series of repeated elements lasting up to 15 sec. Mex. to Nicaragua.

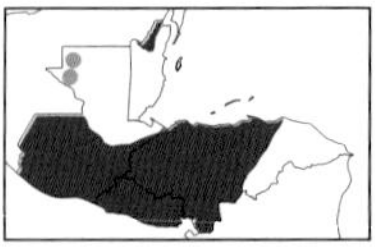

LESSER GOLDFINCH *Carduelis psaltria*

4.5 in. (11 cm). Adult male similar to several euphonias, with **bright yellow underparts contrasting with glossy black upperparts**; note **white patch, or "handkerchief," at base of primaries and white edges to tertials**. Female and immature male yellow-olive overall (brighter below), but **still shows white patch on wing like male**. Fairly common on Pacific Slope, less so on Caribbean; absent from most of Petén, La Moskitia, and Belize; to 7,050 ft. (2,150 m). Found in a variety of open and disturbed habitats, including city gardens and parks. Forages at all levels; often perches on flower heads. Generally in pairs, and may form flocks of up to 60 individuals. Song is a warbling series of clear whistles and scratches (less repetition than Black-headed Siskin and includes more chatter); calls include a clear, whistled *tseeeu!* and a chatter, *chi'chi* or *chi'chi'chi'chi* (also given in flight). U.S. to Venezuela.

PINE SISKIN
gray morph
BLACK-CAPPED SISKIN
female
male
BLACK-HEADED SISKIN
male
female
male
LESSER GOLDFINCH
female

WARBLERS I (Olive Warbler and Waterthrushes)

PEUCEDRAMIDAE (Order: Passeriformes). A single-species family that is more closely related to Old World accentors (Prunellidae) than to New World wood-warblers (Parulidae). The Olive Warbler is thought to share a common ancestor with all New World warblers, tanagers, sparrows, cardinals, blackbirds, orioles, and finches. **1 species (1 genus)**

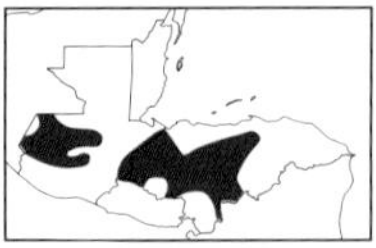

OLIVE WARBLER *Peucedramus taeniatus*

5 in. (13 cm). Adult male has **head and upper chest pumpkin orange with black mask**. Female and immature are duller (yellower on head). Fairly common from 3,280 to 9,000 ft. (1,000–2,750 m). Found in pine savanna and pine-oak forest canopy. Song is variable, with repeated elements: *vi-vi-vi-vi-vi-seeuuh!* (<1 sec.); call is a loud *teew.* U.S. to Nicaragua.

PARULIDAE (Order: Passeriformes). The "wood" warblers are a large family of small, colorful passerines that feed mostly on insects. Some species also eat berries and nectar during the nonbreeding season. A majority of the species in NCA (approximately 75 percent) are migrants that breed in the temperate north and winter in the tropics. The resident warblers are highly vocal during the reproductive period (Mar.–July) while most of the winter visitors or transients limit their repertoire to simple call notes (some may sing in early fall or spring). The visitors show marked sexual dimorphism as well as differences in nonbreeding (basic) and breeding (alternate) plumage; the breeding plumage can be seen in early spring prior to northbound migration. Most resident species do not have an alternate plumage, and have minor or no sexual dimorphism. **57 species (16 genera)**

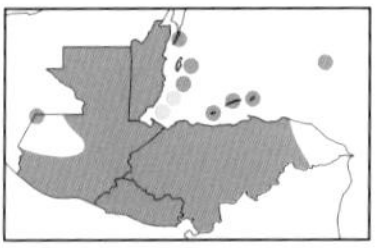

OVENBIRD *Seiurus aurocapilla*

5.5 in. (14 cm). Orange crown stripe (difficult to see) **bordered by black lateral crown stripes**; face with **bold white eye-ring**; **heavy black chevron streaking on white underparts**; legs pinkish. Similar to Northern and Louisiana Waterthrushes, which have eye stripes rather than eye-ring. Common visitor (mid-Aug.–mid-May); to 7,220 ft. (2,200 m). Prefers a variety of forest habitats, including shaded coffee plantations. Feeds on ants in leaf litter; often walks on ground with tail cocked. Calls include a sharp *chit*; also a high-pitched thin *tseet*. Canada (breeding) to Caribbean and Venezuela (winter).

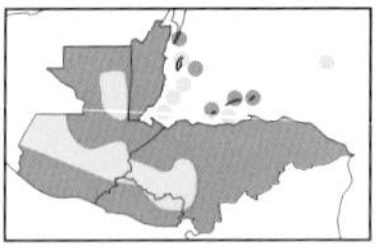

NORTHERN WATERTHRUSH *Parkesia noveboracensis*

5.5 in. (14 cm). Distinguish from Louisiana Waterthrush by narrower supercilium, streaked throat, heavier streaking on chest, smaller bill, and darker legs; also note habitat differences. Found closer to water than Ovenbird (which lacks supercilium). Common visitor (mid-Aug.–May); to 8,530 ft. (2,600 m). Generally near still or slow-moving water within swamp forests and mangroves. Walks on ground, constantly bobbing tail. Call is a rich slightly metallic *chip!* AK (breeding) to Caribbean and Peru (winter).

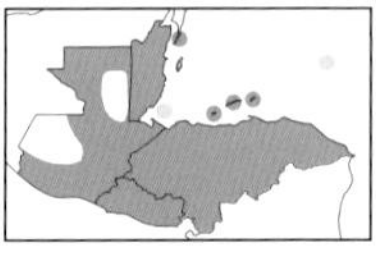

LOUISIANA WATERTHRUSH *Parkesia motacilla*

6 in. (15 cm). Distinguish from similar Northern Waterthrush by broader and longer supercilium, whiter supercilium and breast, buffy flanks, larger bill, unstreaked throat, and pinker legs; also note habitat differences. Found closer to water than Ovenbird (which lacks supercilium). Uncommon visitor (July–Mar.); to 6,560 ft. (2,000 m). Prefers swift-moving forest streams, where it walks on ground among rocks and boulders, constantly bobbing tail. Call is a sharp *tchip!* U.S. (breeding) to Caribbean and Colombia (winter).

OLIVE
WARBLER
female
male
OVENBIRD
NORTHERN
WATERTHRUSH
LOUISIANA
WATERTHRUSH

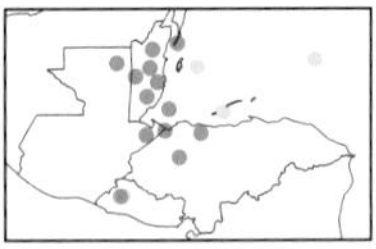

SWAINSON'S WARBLER *Limnothlypis swainsonii*

5.5 in. (14 cm). Brown upperparts; **crown is rufous-brown**; **whitish supercilium contrasts with dark eye line**; face and underparts buffy white; **heavy pointed bill**; legs pink. Uncommon winter visitor in n. Belize, including offshore cayes; rare on remaining mainland of Caribbean Slope; vagrant on Pacific Slope; from early Sept. to mid-Apr. Lowlands but occasionally to 5,910 ft. (1,800 m). Found in coastal scrub and swamp forest; also rainforest, more humid semideciduous forest, and rarely in shaded coffee plantations. Prefers deep shadows of forest, where it forages on ground. Difficult to see. Call is a rich *chip* or *tip*; flight call is a sharp, high-pitched *see*. U.S. (breeding) to Caribbean and NCA (winter).

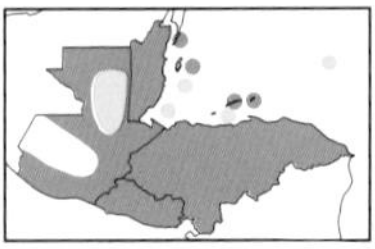

WORM-EATING WARBLER *Helmitheros vermivorum*

5 in. (13 cm). Brownish olive above; head buffy yellow with **black lateral crown stripes and eye line;** underparts also buff-yellow; legs pink. Uncommon winter visitor throughout NCA (Aug.–Apr.); to 6,560 ft. (2,000 m). Prefers more humid forest, such as taller semideciduous forest, rainforest, coffee plantations, and mangroves. Forages at low to midlevels, probing in dead leaf clusters and along vines. Call is a fairly rich *tsip* (similar to call of Black-and-white Warbler [p. 346]). U.S. (breeding) to Caribbean and Panama (winter).

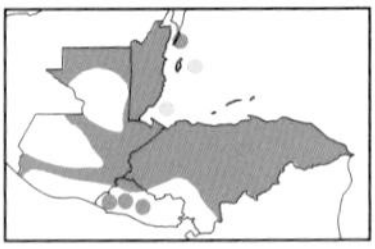

BLUE-WINGED WARBLER *Vermivora cyanoptera*

5 in. (13 cm). **Adult male body mainly yellow**; thin **black eye line**; wings blue-gray with **2 bold white wing bars**; outer tail feathers show extensive white. Female and immature similar, but duller overall. Uncommon to fairly common winter visitor on Caribbean Slope; rare on Pacific Slope (Sept.–Mar.); to 6,070 ft. (1,850 m). Found at edge in a variety of woodland types, including semideciduous forest, pine-oak forest, and disturbed habitats (coffee plantations and gardens). Forages in understory and midstory vegetation. Calls include a sharp *tchip*; and a buzzy *tzzii*, given in flight and often doubled. All sounds similar to Golden-winged Warbler. U.S. (breeding) to Panama (winter).

GOLDEN-WINGED WARBLER *Vermivora chrysoptera*

5 in. (13 cm). Adult male has **bold black auriculars and throat**; **bright yellow crown**; and **bright yellow wing patches**; outer tail feathers mostly white. Female and immature like male, but duller overall. Uncommon winter visitor on Caribbean Slope; rare on Pacific Slope (Sept.–Apr.); to 6,400 ft. (1,950 m). Found at edge in a variety of woodland types, including semideciduous forest, pine-oak forest, and disturbed habitats (coffee plantations and gardens). Forages in understory and midstory vegetation. Calls include a sharp *tchip*; also a buzzy *tzzii*, given in flight and often doubled. All sounds similar to Blue-winged Warbler. Canada (breeding) to Ecuador (winter).

Two hybrids of Blue-winged and Golden-winged Warbler are well known. The "Brewster's Warbler" (the dominant result of a pairing of pure parents) shows the face pattern of a Blue-winged and body of a Golden-winged, and, unlike both parents, shows a pure white throat. The rarer recessive form, "Lawrence's Warbler," is a striking yellow and black bird with general face pattern of a Golden-winged and body of a Blue-winged. Even rarer, back-crossed individuals (second- or third-generation hybrids) can have various combinations of features of either parent species.

WARBLERS III (*Oreothlypis* Genus)

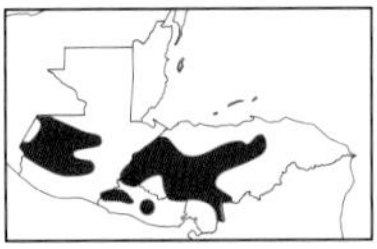

CRESCENT-CHESTED WARBLER *Oreothlypis superciliosa*

4.5 in. (11 cm). **Broad white supercilium**; weak **chestnut crescent on chest**. Immature paler. Fairly common in highlands; 4,000 ft. (rarely lower) to 10,500 ft. (1,200–3,200 m). Found in humid semideciduous forest, pine-oak forest, and cloud forest, where forages at mid- to upper levels, often within mixed-species flocks. Song is a rapid (1 sec.) insectlike rattle or trill; call is a high *tsit*. Mex. to Nicaragua.

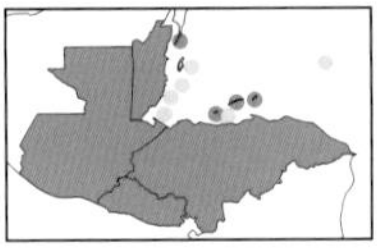

TENNESSEE WARBLER *Oreothlypis peregrina*

5 in. (13 cm). A relatively unmarked warbler. Adult male has **grayish head**; **face with dark eye line**; underparts whitish and **undertail coverts white**. Adult female, nonbreeding male, and immature show dull greenish yellow on head, chest, and sides; easily confused with Philadelphia Vireo (p. 288) but bill is finer; told from Orange-crowned Warbler by paler supercilium, unstreaked chest, and white undertail coverts. Common visitor (Sept.–May); to 10,330 ft. (3,150 m). Habitat includes a variety of woodland types, where it actively forages at mid- and upper levels, especially on flower nectar. Accompanies mixed-species flocks; migrant flocks can number in the dozens of individuals. Call is a sharp *tsip*; also a thin *tsii* given in flight. Canada (breeding) to Ecuador (winter).

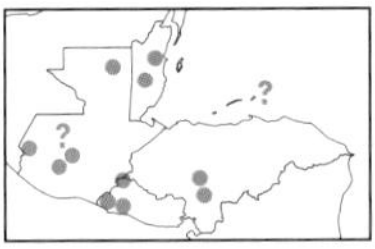

ORANGE-CROWNED WARBLER *Oreothlypis celata*

5 in. (13 cm). Overall **olive-yellow body**; orange patch on crown is usually concealed; face with **faint eye line**; **weak streaks on chest**; **yellow undertail coverts**. Some subspecies show grayer heads (*celata*), while others are washed more yellow overall (*lutescens*), but subspecific identification may be impossible in winter. Similar to Tennessee Warbler, but more olive-yellow body, weaker supercilium, streaked chest, and yellow undertail coverts. Uncommon winter visitor in cen. Guatemala (Oct.–Feb.); very rare elsewhere in NCA; to 9,510 ft. (2,900 m). Habitat is a variety of woodland forests (semideciduous), disturbed habitats, and scrub. Forages mostly low in understory vegetation. Call is a rich *tsick*. AK (breeding) to NCA (winter).

NASHVILLE WARBLER *Oreothlypis ruficapilla*

4.5 in. (11 cm). Adult male has **gray head with white eye-ring**; contrasting yellow throat; rufous crown patch often concealed; legs grayish with yellow feet. Female and immature similar but duller. Similar to Lesser Greenlet (p. 290), but sleeker, bill darker and thinner, and more extensive yellow on throat and breast. Uncommon winter visitor in Guatemala; rare elsewhere in NCA; to 6,890 ft. (2,100 m). Found in a variety of woodland types, including semideciduous forest, pine-oak forest, and disturbed habitats. Forages usually at mid- to upper levels, often in mixed-species flocks. Calls include a sharp, slightly metallic *plink*; also a clear *see* given in flight. NOTE: 2 distinct subspecies are possible: *O.r. ruficapilla* of e. N. America and *O.r. ridgwayi* of w. N. America ("Calaveras Warbler"); the latter occurs mainly in highlands; it is brighter above, especially on the rump and uppertail coverts; whiter on lower belly and vent, and pumps tail more frequently. Canada (breeding) to NCA (winter).

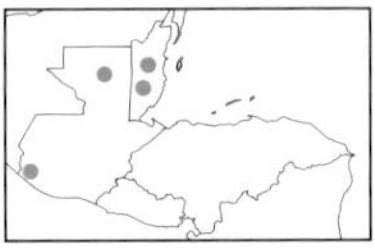

VIRGINIA'S WARBLER *Oreothlypis virginiae*

4.5 in. (11 cm). Overall gray; center of chest, **rump, undertail coverts yellow**; rufous crown patch often concealed; **bold white eye-ring**. Female and immature duller. Vagrant to NCA (Dec.–May); to 2,300 ft. (700 m). In NCA, recorded in roadside scrub and pine savanna. Forages low. U.S. (breeding) to Mex. (winter).

CRESCENT-CHESTED
WARBLER
breeding male
(spring)
TENNESSEE
WARBLER
female
immature
ORANGE-CROWNED
WARBLER
lutescens
celata
NASHVILLE
WARBLER
ruficapilla
ridgwayi
male
female
VIRGINIA'S
WARBLER

WARBLERS IV (*Geothlypis* Genus)

GRAY-CROWNED YELLOWTHROAT *Geothlypis poliocephala*

5.5 in. (14 cm). Forecrown grayish; **face with dark lores**; underparts usually bright yellow but variable; **heavy bill with pinkish mandible**. Fairly common in NCA (rarer in lowlands of Pacific Slope); to 5,740 ft. (1,750 m). Found in scrubby habitats, at forest edge and in hedgerows, grasslands, freshwater marshes, and pine savanna. Forages near ground. Song is a melodic warble lasting 2.5 to 3 sec. (similar to song of Blue Grosbeak [p. 388]); often sings from prominent perch; calls include a reedy *zeery-jer* and an agitated *tip'tip'tip'tip'tip'tew'tew'tew'tew*. Mex. to Panama.

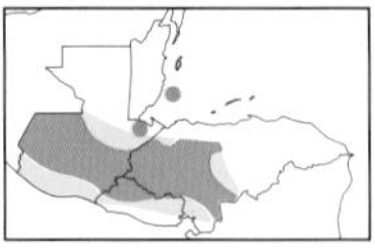

MACGILLIVRAY'S WARBLER *Geothlypis tolmiei*

5 in. (13 cm). Adult male has yellow-olive upperparts with contrasting **gray hood**; **bold white eye-arcs**; black patch on chest. Female and immature are similar, but drabber. Immature is similar to Mourning Warbler but note incomplete eye-ring; some individuals may not be separable in the field. Fairly common visitor to highlands (Sept.–mid-May); 1,500 to 10,330 ft. (450–3,150 m). Found in scrub; at edge of pine-oak forest, semideciduous forest, and pine savanna. Forages low, often near ground. Call is a hard *tip*. Canada (breeding) to Panama (winter).

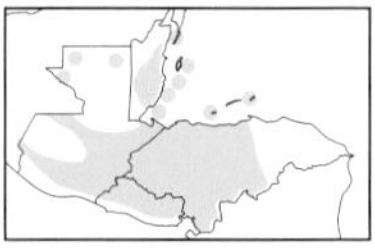

MOURNING WARBLER *Geothlypis philadelphia*

5 in. (13 cm). Adult male has yellow-olive upperparts with contrasting **gray hood**; lores are black; **lacks eye-ring**; **black patch on chest**. Adult female similar but has paler gray hood and throat. Immature even paler with **nearly complete eye-ring**; very similar to immature MacGillivray's Warbler, but note eye-ring (not eye-arc). Uncommon transient (mid-Sept.–mid-Oct., mid-Apr.–early June), including offshore cayes; to 5,910 ft. (1,800 m). Found in a variety of scrubby habitat; also at edge of semideciduous forest and in hedgerows. Forages low, often on or near ground. Call is a flat *tsip*. Canada (breeding) to Ecuador (winter).

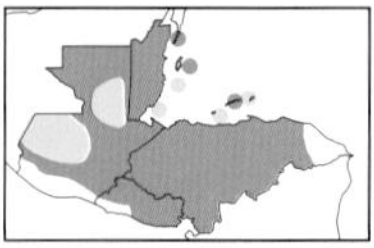

KENTUCKY WARBLER *Geothlypis formosa*

5 in. (13 cm). Crown is black with **black auriculars forming "sideburns."** Female and immature duller. Common winter visitor on Caribbean Slope; uncommon on Pacific Slope; from Aug. to Apr.; to 5,910 ft. (1,800 m). Prefers humid forest, such as rainforest, semideciduous forest, riparian forest. Forages low, often on the ground. Call is a sharp *chuck*. U.S. (breeding) to Venezuela (winter).

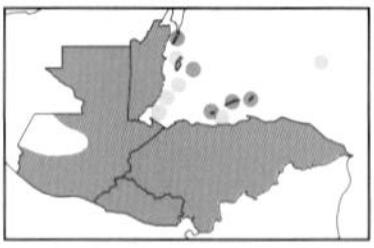

COMMON YELLOWTHROAT *Geothlypis trichas*

5 in. (13 cm). Adult male has **black mask bordered above in white**; **bright yellow on throat**. Female has brownish olive face and yellowish wash to throat. Immature male resembles female, but shows hint of black mask. Common winter visitor on Caribbean Slope; uncommon on Pacific Slope; from mid-Sept. to May; to 5,910 ft. (1,800 m). Found in grassy and scrubby habitats (often near water). Forages near ground. Call a distinctive *tchit*. Canada (breeding) to Panama (winter).

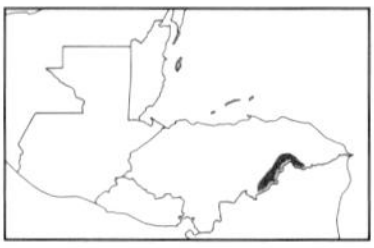

OLIVE-CROWNED YELLOWTHROAT *Geothlypis semiflava*

5 in. (13 cm). Adult male similar to adult male Common Yellowthroat, but more extensive yellow on underparts and lacks white border to mask. Rare in e. Honduras; to 3,940 ft. (1,200 m). Found in overgrown fields, grasslands, and at edge of disturbed habitats. Forages near ground. Song is a long (roughly 3.5 sec.), rich warble that accelerates toward a buzzy end; call is an agitated *tzzhere!*; also an alarm chatter. Honduras to Ecuador.

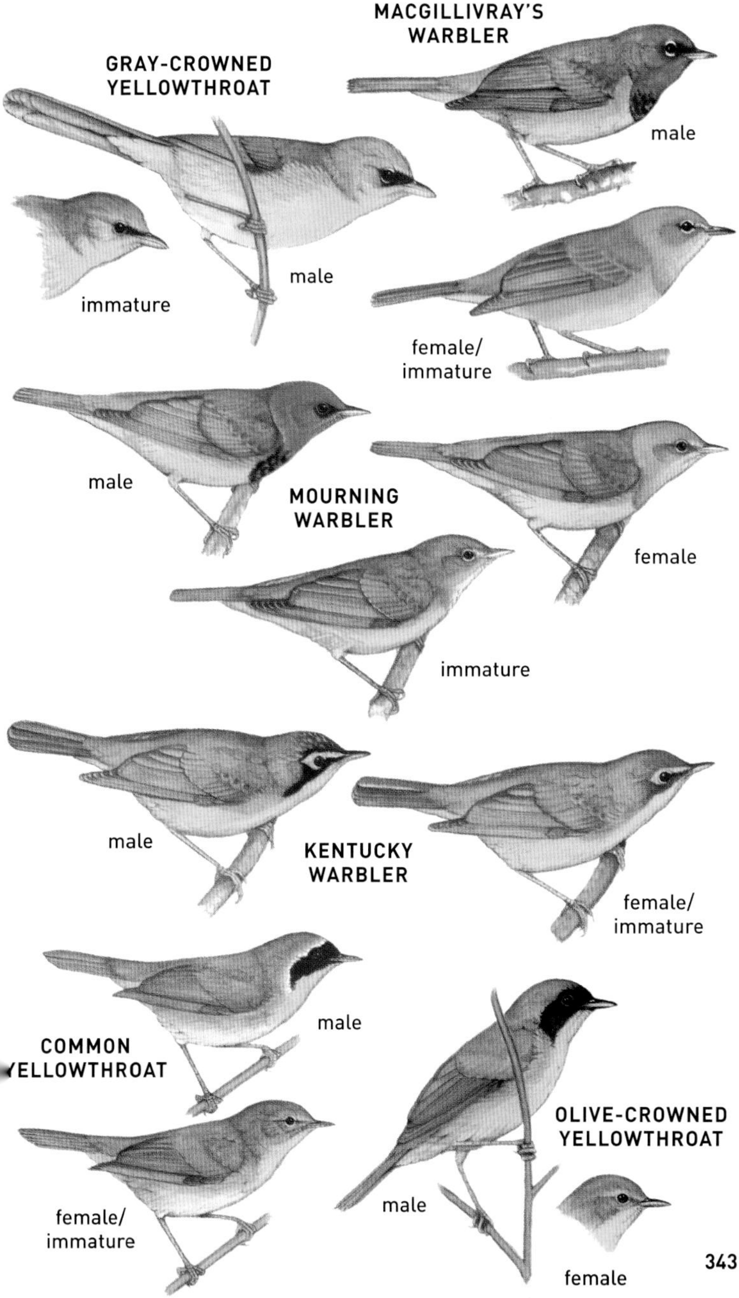
MACGILLIVRAY'S WARBLER
male
female/ immature
GRAY-CROWNED YELLOWTHROAT
male
immature
MOURNING WARBLER
male
female
immature
KENTUCKY WARBLER
male
female/ immature
COMMON YELLOWTHROAT
male
female/ immature
OLIVE-CROWNED YELLOWTHROAT
male
female

WARBLERS V (More Migrants from Eastern U.S.)

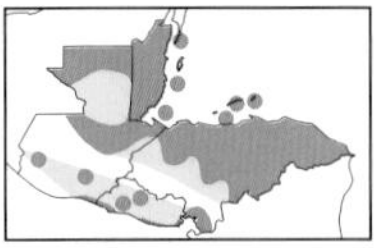

PROTHONOTARY WARBLER *Protonotaria citrea*

5.5 in. (14 cm). Adult male has **bright yellow head and black eyes**. Female and immature are similar but duller. Wings grayish, tail gray with white spots, undertail coverts white. Fairly common transient and local winter visitor in NCA (late July–Apr.); to 6,070 ft. (1,850 m) but generally below 3,610 ft. (1,100 m). Found in semideciduous forest, rainforest, coastal scrub, and mangroves, usually near water; forages low, including on ground. Call is a sharp, metallic *tseep*. U.S. (breeding) to Ecuador (winter).

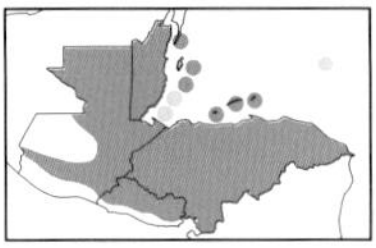

HOODED WARBLER *Setophaga citrina*

5 in. (13 cm). Male distinctive, with **yellow face and black hood**. On female and immature black hood is weakly defined, crown olive, and throat yellow. Distinguish from Wilson's (p. 350) and Kentucky Warblers (p. 342) by **white outer tail feathers**. Common winter visitor on Caribbean Slope; rare on Pacific Slope; from mid-Aug. to early May; to 7,220 ft. (2,200 m). Found in a variety of woodland types; however, females and immatures more likely than adult males in edges and open areas. Forages near ground. Call is a rich, ringing *tink*. Canada (breeding) to Panama (winter).

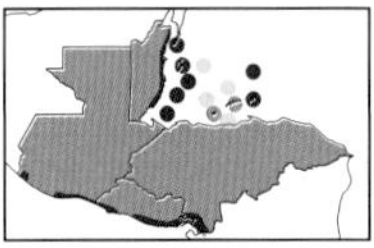

YELLOW WARBLER *Setophaga petechia*

4.5 in. (11 cm). Transients and winter visitors (the *aestiva* subspecies group): **adult male is bright yellow overall; underparts with chestnut streaking; underside of tail yellow**. Female and immature similar but duller overall; some washed with gray on back and head. Resident subspecies (*xanthotera* on Pacific Coast and *bryanti* on Caribbean coast) are known as **Mangrove Warbler**: adult male has **chestnut head**. Female and immature are difficult to separate from winter visitors. Juvenile plumage completely gray, sometimes with olive patches. Similar to Wilson's Warbler (p. 350), but tail yellow (not gray). Common winter visitor throughout NCA (Aug.–May); to 5,910 ft. (1,800 m). Winter visitors can be found in a variety of disturbed habitats; Mangrove Warbler is restricted to coastal mangroves. Winter residents give a rich *chip*, often repeated; Mangrove Warbler song begins with several rapid rich notes, intensifies and ends quickly; calls include a husky *chik*. AK (breeding) to Brazil (winter).

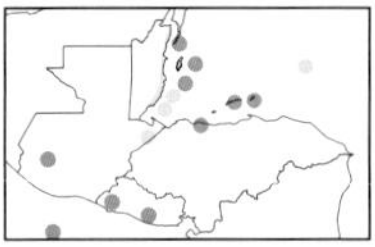

PRAIRIE WARBLER *Setophaga discolor*

4.5 in. (11 cm). Adult male upperparts yellow-olive with **rufous streaking**; supercilium and face yellow; **eye line and border to auricular black**; underparts yellow with dark streaking on sides and flanks. Female similar but duller, while immature is very pale and lacks obvious streaking. Female and immature recall Vitelline Warbler (p. 356) (Swan Is. only), but wing bars whitish (not yellow). All ages/sexes show white outer tail feathers. Rare transient and winter visitor (mid-Sept.–mid-Apr.) on Caribbean cayes and islands; vagrant on mainland; to 4,920 ft. (1,500 m). Prefers woodland habitats, where it forages at low to midlevels. Often pumps tail. Call is a fairly sharp *tsip*. U.S. (breeding) to Caribbean and Colombia (winter).

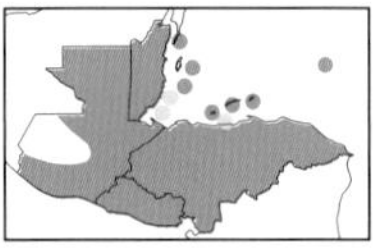

AMERICAN REDSTART *Setophaga ruticilla*

5 in. (13 cm). Adult male is **black overall with bright patches of orange on sides, wings, and base of tail**. Adult female and immature similarly patterned, but black replaced with gray on head, and orange patches replaced with yellow (immature males may show dark feathers on head and upper chest, and orange on sides). Common winter visitor (Aug.–Apr., rarely to early June); to 8,370 ft. (2,500 m) but mostly below 4,100 ft. (1,250 m). Found in a variety of woodland habitats. Forages at all levels. Call is a rich *tsip*. Canada (breeding) to Ecuador (winter).

male
PROTHONOTARY WARBLER
female
HOODED WARBLER
male
female/ immature
female/ immature
Mangrove Warbler (resident)
male
YELLOW WARBLER
male
male
PRAIRIE WARBLER
female/ immature
male
AMERICAN REDSTART
female
immature male

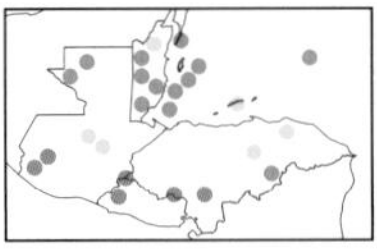

BLACK-THROATED BLUE WARBLER *Setophaga caerulescens*
5 in. (13 cm). Adult male striking in **steely blue, black, and white plumage**. Adult female and immature olive above and buff below with **white "handkerchief" on wing, dark face mask,** and white crescent below eye. Uncommon winter visitor on cayes (Belize) and Swan Is. (Honduras); rare winter visitor on mainland; from Sept. to mid-Apr. Found in coastal scrub, disturbed habitat, and a variety of woodland habitats. Forages at low to midlevels in forest. Call is a hard *tik*; also a high-pitched alarm call, *seet!* Canada (breeding) to Caribbean and Panama (winter).

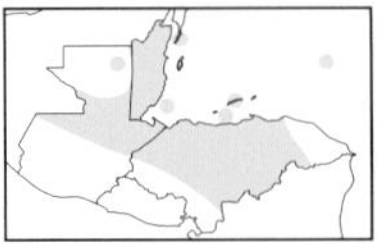

CERULEAN WARBLER *Setophaga cerulea*
4.5 in. (11 cm). Breeding adult male has **aqua blue upperparts**; 2 white wing bars; white underparts; **blue collar and dark streaking on sides and flanks**. On female and nonbreeding male plumage, note bluish green upperparts; pale supercilium; yellowish green wash to underparts; weak streaking on sides and flanks. Rare to uncommon transient (late Mar.–Apr., early Aug.–mid-Oct.) on Caribbean Slope; to 3,770 ft. (1,150 m), rarely higher. Found mostly in montane foothills of rainforest or semideciduous forest; also coffee plantations. Forages at mid- to upper levels. Call is a soft, fairly sharp *sip* or *tip*. Canada (breeding) to Bolivia (winter).

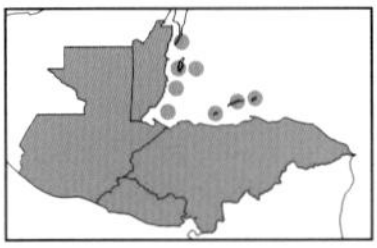

BLACK-AND-WHITE WARBLER *Mniotilta varia*
5 in. (13 cm). **Male has distinctive black and white plumage.** Adult female and immature similar but with less black in auriculars and on throat and duller streaking on flanks; immature with buffy wash to flanks and undertail coverts. Common visitor (July–May); to 8,370 ft. (2,550 m). Found in a variety of woodland habitats. Forages at all levels by creeping along tree trunks and branches; often in mixed-species flocks. May sing during migration; song resembles a squeaky wheel: *tsee tsee-a-tsee-a-tsee-a-tsee-a*; call is a flat *tsip*. Canada (breeding) to Peru (winter).

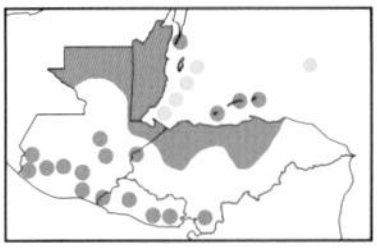

NORTHERN PARULA *Setophaga americana*
4 in. (10 cm). Upperparts bluish-gray except for olive patch on back. **2 white wing bars**; **white eye-arcs**; yellow throat and chest; in adult male, **chestnut and gray band crosses the upper chest** (absent in female and in many immatures, which are duller overall). Compare with Tropical Parula (p. 356). Fairly common winter visitor on Caribbean Slope; rare on Pacific Slope; late Aug. to May; to 3,940 ft. (1,200 m). Found in disturbed habitat (like coffee plantations), semideciduous forest, and mangroves. Forages at all levels, and often found in mixed-species flocks. Call is a rich *tsip*; song is a rapid accelerating trill, buzzy and inflected at the end. E. Canada (breeding) to NCA (winter).

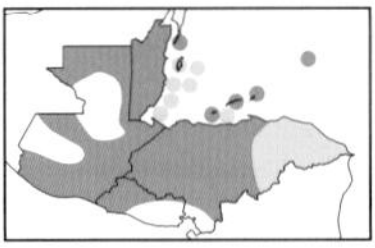

YELLOW-THROATED WARBLER *Setophaga dominica*
5 in. (13 cm). **Face with bold black-and-white pattern**; **throat is yellow**; underparts white with weak streaking along sides and flanks. Compare with Grace's Warbler (p. 356). Fairly common winter visitor on Caribbean Slope, and interior highlands (late July–late Apr.); rare on Pacific Slope; to 8,040 ft. (2,450 m). Found in a variety of woodland habitats; also disturbed habitats such as coffee plantations. Prefers foraging in palm trees when available. Generally gleans insects at mid- to upper levels, often in mixed-species flocks. May also feed on small fruits and berries or at nectar sources. Call a rich *tip*. U.S. (breeding) to Caribbean and Colombia (winter).

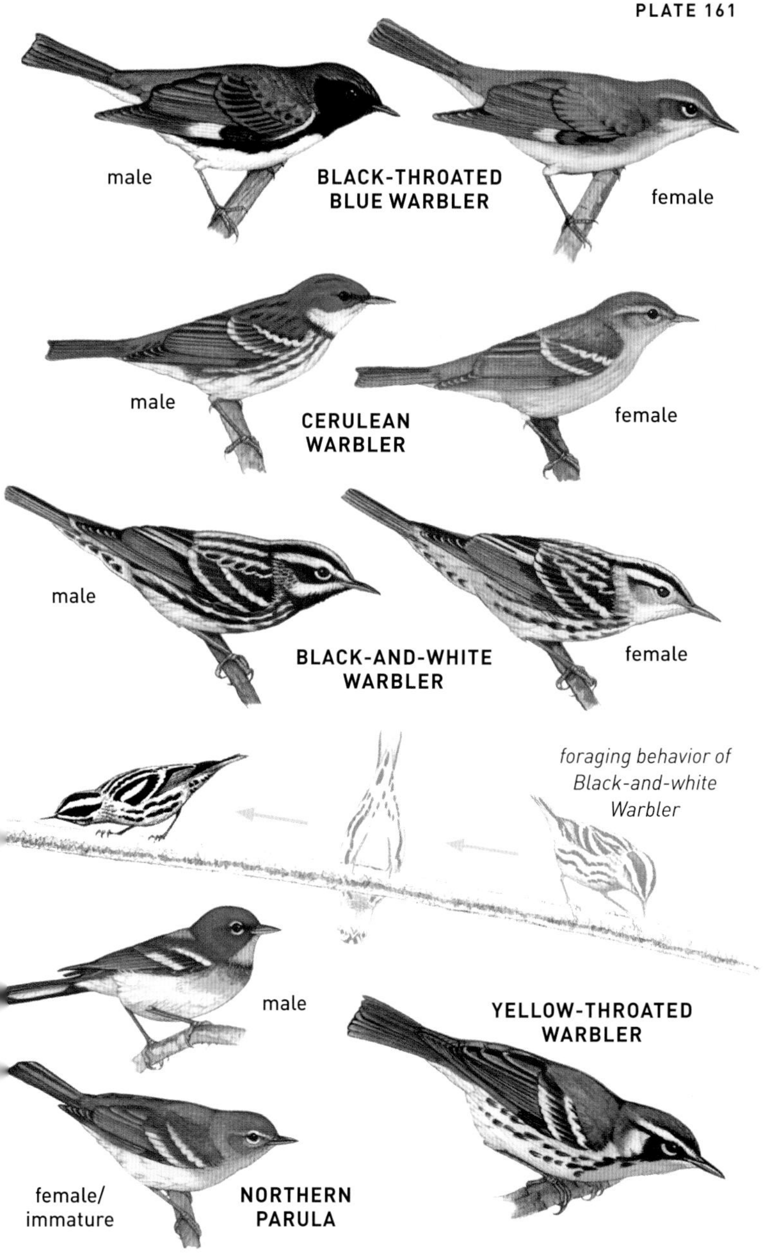
male
BLACK-THROATED
BLUE WARBLER
female
male
CERULEAN
WARBLER
female
male
BLACK-AND-WHITE
WARBLER
female
foraging behavior of
Black-and-white
Warbler
male
YELLOW-THROATED
WARBLER
female/
immature
NORTHERN
PARULA

WARBLERS VII (Migrants from the Boreal Forest)

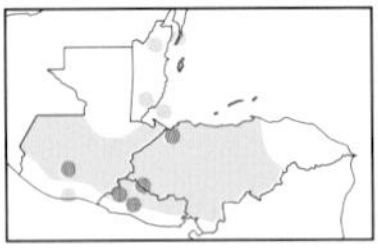

CANADA WARBLER *Cardellina canadensis*

5 in. (13 cm). Adult male shows striking **2-toned appearance**: slate blue-gray upperparts and bright yellow below. Note **yellow spectacles and black necklace across chest**. Female and immature duller overall. Legs pink. Uncommon transient (late Aug.–mid-Oct., early Apr.–mid-May); to 9,680 ft. (2,950 m). Prefers taller forest with thick understory; humid semideciduous forest, taller disturbed habitats like coffee plantations and botanical gardens. Forages at all levels in forest. Call is a hard, snappy *tip*. Canada (breeding) to Peru (winter).

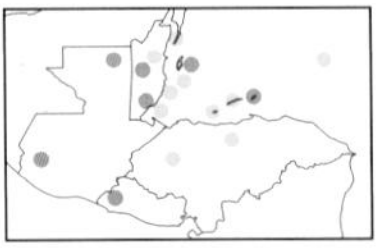

CAPE MAY WARBLER *Setophaga tigrina*

5 in. (13 cm). Nonbreeding individuals have grayish upperparts with light streaking; face lightly washed yellow with **grayish auriculars (washed orange-chestnut in males)**; yellowish or grayish below with **heavy dark streaking on chest, sides, and flanks**; some nonbreeding males have bold white wing panel; both sexes flash white in outer tail feathers; long primary projections. Uncommon winter visitor on offshore cayes and islands (Belize and Honduras); rare on Caribbean Slope mainland; vagrant to Pacific Slope; from late Sept. to late Apr.; to 2,130 ft. (650 m). Forages in disturbed habitats and coastal scrub, usually at mid- to upper levels. During winter, eats small fruits and berries, as well as flower nectar. Call a high-pitched *tseep*. Canada (breeding) to Venezuela and Caribbean (winter).

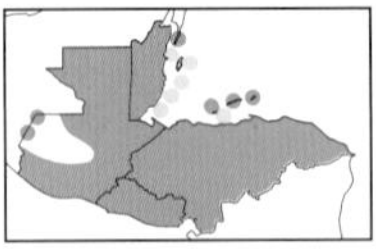

MAGNOLIA WARBLER *Setophaga magnolia*

5 in. (13 cm). **Head gray** contrasting with yellow-olive back streaked black; **note thin white eye-ring**; **contrasting yellow rump**; underparts yellow with **thin gray collar**. Adult male shows **heavier dark streaking on back, sides, and flanks**. Wide **black band on undertail** (outer half) is distinctive. In spring (Apr.–May), male shows black face with bold white stripe behind eye; bold white wing panel. Common winter visitor (mid-Sept.–mid-May); to 4,920 ft. (1,500 m). Found in a variety of woodland habitats, where it forages at all levels. Call is a distinctive nasal *iihk*, softer than Wilson's Warbler (p. 350). Canada (breeding) to Colombia (winter).

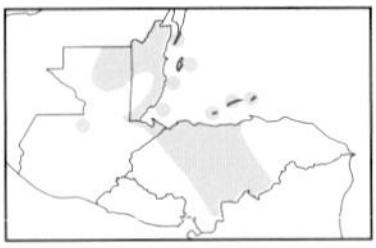

BAY-BREASTED WARBLER *Setophaga castanea*

5 in. (13 cm). Breeding male striking with **chestnut and black plumage**. Breeding female lacks black face and has less chestnut; immature washed **yellowish green above**; 2 bright white wing bars; dingy white below with **light wash of chestnut on sides and flanks** (sometimes absent). **Legs gray.** Nonbreeding individuals similar to nonbreeding Blackpoll Warbler, but lack streaking, and legs are gray (not yellow). Uncommon transient on Caribbean Slope (late Sept.–mid-Nov.; mid Apr.–May); to 4,600 ft. (1,400 m). Possible in a variety of woodland habitats, where it forages at all levels. Call a rich *tsip*. Canada (breeding) to Colombia (winter).

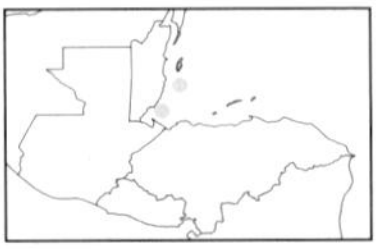

BLACKPOLL WARBLER *Setophaga striata*

5 in. (13 cm). Breeding male has grayish upperparts with heavy dark streaking; 2 white wing bars; **black crown and white face**; black submalar stripe connects with **black streaking on sides and flanks**. Breeding female streaked on crown and face and may show buffy-yellow wash below. **Legs on both sexes dark yellow.** Nonbreeding and immature plumages show buffy-yellow wash overall, especially on throat and chest; faint streaking on chest. Similar to nonbreeding Bay-breasted Warbler, but note light streaking on chest, and yellow legs. Accidental transient in spring and fall to Belize cayes; near sea level. Forages in coastal scrub and semideciduous forest at mid- to upper levels. Call is a sharp *tsip*. AK (breeding) to Brazil (winter).

CANADA WARBLER
male
female/
immature
underside of a
Magnolia Warbler
CAPE MAY WARBLER
male
female/
immature
MAGNOLIA WARBLER
breeding
male
(spring)
nonbreeding
immature
BAY-BREASTED WARBLER
breeding male
(spring)
nonbreeding
male/some
females
immature
BLACKPOLL WARBLER
breeding
male
(spring)
breeding
female
(spring)
nonbreeding/
immature

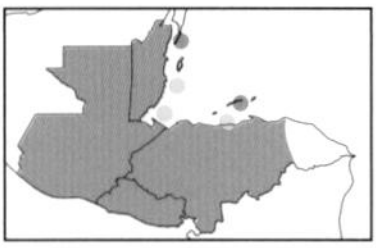

WILSON'S WARBLER *Cardellina pusilla*

4.5 in. (13 cm). Adult male is olive-yellow above; **small black crown spot, all-yellow below, tail completely gray**. Female and many immatures similar but lack extensive black crown (some show no black on crown). Legs pink. Distinguish from Hooded Warbler and Yellow Warbler (p. 344) by all-gray tail (lacking white or yellow patches). Common winter visitor; from mid-Sept. to early May; to 10,010 ft. (3,050 m) but less common below 1,970 ft. or 600 m. Found in a variety of woodland types. Actively forages at low to midlevels. Call is a distinctive *chit*. AK (breeding) to Panama (winter).

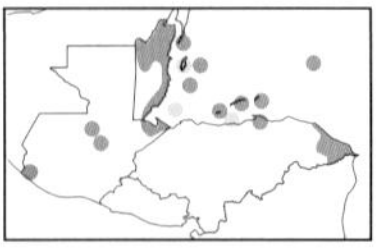

PALM WARBLER *Setophaga palmarum*

5 in. (13 cm). Two distinctive subspecies in NCA. [*S.p. palmarum*] Brown upperparts with black streaks; 2 faint wing bars; **crown rufous**; **supercilium and throat yellow washed**; remaining **underparts dingy white**; dark streaks on chest and sides; undertail coverts yellow. Nonbreeding plumage similar, but crown is brownish with light black streaks. [*hypochrysea*, not illustrated] Breeding plumage similar to above, but **underparts entirely yellow**. Nonbreeding plumage still retains large amount of yellow below. [*palmarum*] Uncommon to fairly common winter visitor along Caribbean coast, including cayes and islands (late Sept.–Apr.); [*hypochrysea*] vagrant to Belize cayes (2 records); near sea level. Found in open areas like beaches and at edge of coastal scrub; also gravel lots. Forages low, often on ground, and pumps tail frequently. Call is a sharp *tip*. Canada (breeding) to Caribbean and Nicaragua (winter).

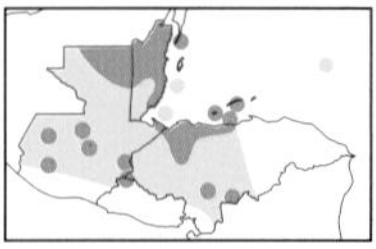

YELLOW-RUMPED WARBLER *Setophaga coronata*

5.5 in. (14 cm). Two subspecies possible in NCA: *coronata* (Myrtle Warbler) and *auduboni* (Audubon's Warbler). Nonbreeding Myrtle Warbler brownish gray above with dark streaking on back; yellow crown stripe usually concealed; 2 white wing bars; **weak supercilium**; pale broken eye-ring; **white throat**, whitish below with **yellowish wash to sides** and dark streaking on chest and sides; **rump yellow**; white flash in outer tail feathers. Audubon's Warbler similar, but note pale **yellow wash to throat** and lack of supercilium; also vocal differences. Compare female Audubon's Warbler with female Goldman's Warbler (p. 356), but Audubon's shows more yellow in throat with shorter bill and legs, and longer primary projections. Myrtle Warbler is a common although irregular winter visitor to Caribbean Slope and Bay Is.; rare on Pacific Slope; from Nov. to May. Audubon's Warbler is an uncommon winter visitor to highlands, and rare winter visitor to (mostly Caribbean) lowlands; from Nov. to May. Both subspecies found to 9,350 ft. (2,850 m). Possible in a variety of open woodland and open habitats. Forages at all levels. Calls between subspecies quite different: Myrtle a flat *tip*; Audubon's a richer *vip*. AK (breeding) to Panama (winter).

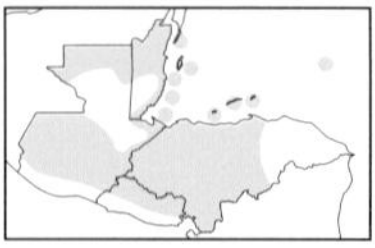

BLACKBURNIAN WARBLER *Setophaga fusca*

5 in. (13 cm). Nonbreeding adult male has dark back with messy light streaks, and dark crown with light center streak; 2 bold white wing bars that form a **white wing panel**; **obvious well-defined black auricular and yellowish orange face and throat**; white underparts have dark streaking on sides. Female and immature similarly patterned, but yellowish orange replaced with softer yellow, often lacking orange tones. Fairly common transient throughout NCA (mid-Aug.–mid-Nov.; mid-Mar.–mid-May); to 4,590 ft. (1,400 m). Found in a variety of woodlands, including disturbed habitats like coffee plantations, where it forages mostly at mid- and upper levels. Call is a fairly rich *chip* or *tip*. Canada (breeding) to Bolivia (winter).

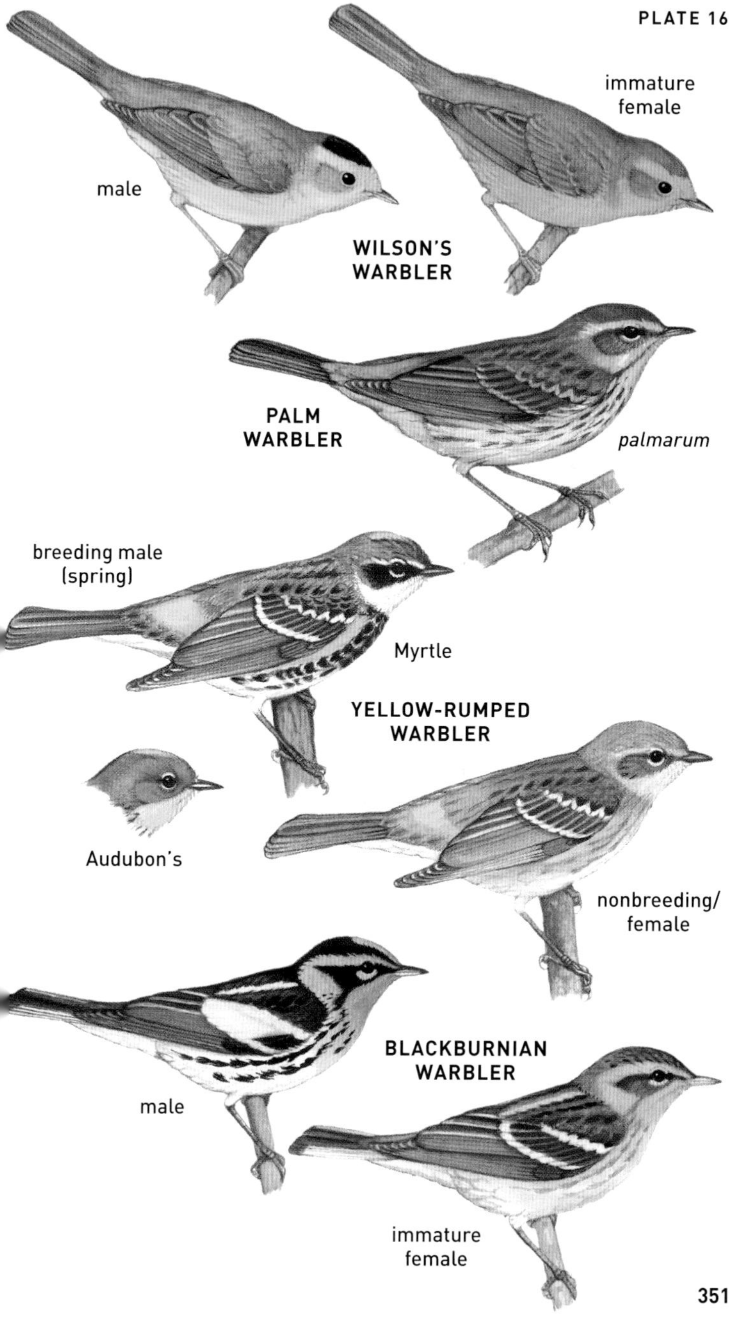
male
immature
female
WILSON'S
WARBLER
PALM
WARBLER
palmarum
breeding male
(spring)
Myrtle
YELLOW-RUMPED
WARBLER
Audubon's
nonbreeding/
female
BLACKBURNIAN
WARBLER
male
immature
female

WARBLERS IX

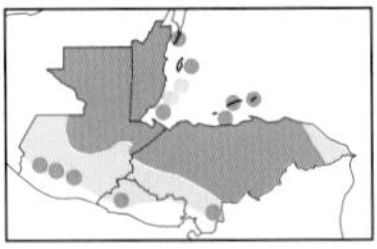

CHESTNUT-SIDED WARBLER *Setophaga pensylvanica*

5 in. (13 cm). Nonbreeding individuals are yellowish green above with **whitish face and underparts**; **white eye-ring**; 2 bold white wing bars; white outer tail feathers; both sexes can show **faint chestnut on sides and flanks** (often lacking). In spring, males molt into alternate plumage, with black streaks on back and face, bright yellow crown, and **deep chestnut stripe on sides**. Common winter visitor on Caribbean Slope; rare on Pacific Slope; from Sept. to May; to 4,920 ft. (1,500 m). Found in a variety of woodland habitats; usually forages at mid- to upper levels. Tends to keep wings drooped and tail slightly cocked. Call is a somewhat flat *chip*. Canada (breeding) to Colombia (winter).

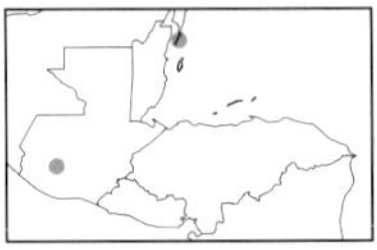

BLACK-THROATED GRAY WARBLER *Setophaga nigrescens*

5 in. (13 cm). Adult male has grayish upperparts, but **crown, auriculars, and throat black with yellow supraloral spot**; underparts are white with bold black streaking on sides and flanks. Female is duller gray overall with less black on throat. Similar to Black-and-white Warbler (p. 346), but has grayish upperparts (not streaked black and white), yellow supraloral spot, and differs in foraging behavior (gleans foliage near ends of branches). Winter vagrant in NCA; to 9,840 ft. (3,000 m). Possible in a variety of woodland types, including coastal scrub, semideciduous forest, and pine-oak forest, where it forages at mid- to upper levels, often in mixed-species flocks. Call is a fairly rich *tip* or *chip*. Canada (breeding) to Mex. (winter).

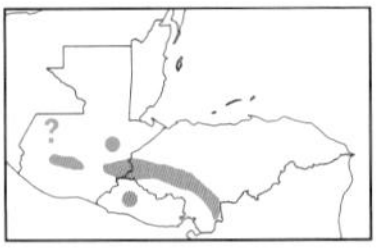

RED-FACED WARBLER *Cardellina rubrifrons*

5 in. (13 cm). Soft gray upperparts; white upper wing bar; **face striking** with black crown extending down into sides of face **and red forecrown, throat, upper chest, and sides of neck** (duller on female and immature). Fairly common (Guatemala) to rare (Honduras and El Salvador) winter visitor (late Aug.–Mar.); 2,130 to 8,690 ft. (650–2,650 m). Generally found in pine savanna and pine-oak forest (outside these habitats during migration). Forages at mid- to upper levels. Call a slightly flat *chip*. U.S. (breeding) to NCA (winter).

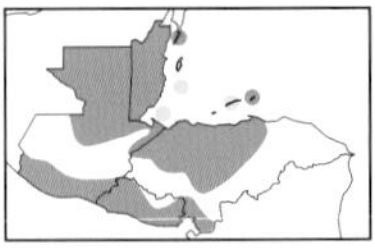

YELLOW-BREASTED CHAT *Icteria virens*

7 in. (18 cm). **Larger than all other warblers, with heavy bill**; **bright yellow on breast and throat**; upperparts yellow-olive to grayish; **white spectacles contrast with blackish lores** and dark gray auriculars. Fairly common winter visitor throughout NCA; to 5,250 ft. (1,600 m). Found in understory within a variety of scrubby habitat types; also coffee plantations. Calls include a nasal catlike *eaaaah* and a softer *chuck* (sometimes doubled). Canada (breeding) to Panama (winter).

CHESTNUT-SIDED
WARBLER
breeding male
(spring)
nonbreeding/
immature
BLACK-THROATED
GRAY WARBLER
male
female/
immature
RED-FACED
WARBLER
immature
adult
YELLOW-BREASTED
CHAT

WARBLERS X (The *Virens* Species Group)

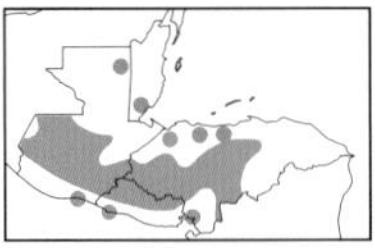

TOWNSEND'S WARBLER *Setophaga townsendi*

5 in. (13 cm). Adult male shows **black auriculars, crown, and throat contrasting with yellow face**; **upper chest and sides yellow with dark streaking**; 2 bold white wing bars. Female and immature similar but drabber, with less black on face, crown, and throat. Black-throated Green Warbler similar, but female Townsend's still shows darker crown and auricular, plus yellowish wash on chest. Common winter visitor (late Aug.–early May); very rare to Belize and n. Guatemala; 2,130 to 10,330 ft. (650–3,150 m). Found in semideciduous forest, pine savanna, and pine-oak forest, where it forages at mid- to upper levels, often in mixed-species flocks. Call is a *tip* (similar to Black-throated Green Warbler). AK (breeding) to Costa Rica (winter).

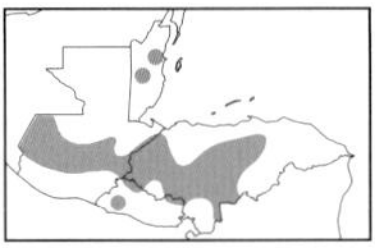

HERMIT WARBLER *Setophaga occidentalis*

5 in. (13 cm). Adult male shows **unmarked bold yellow face and forecrown** (female and immature show some auricular patch and gray forehead); male shows darker nape and hindcrown than female and has black throat; **white underparts with unstreaked sides and flanks**. Uncommon winter visitor (early Sept.–Mar.); 4,100 to 10,330 ft. (1,250–3,150 m). Habitats include pine savanna and pine-oak forest (much like habitats of Townsend's Warbler), where it forages at mid- to upper levels, often in mixed-species flocks. Call is a *tip* (similar to Black-throated Green Warbler). U.S. (breeding) to Nicaragua (winter).

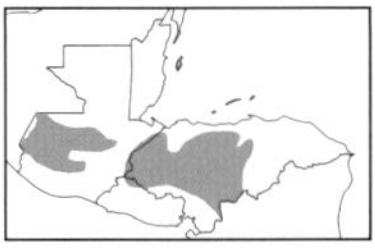

GOLDEN-CHEEKED WARBLER *Setophaga chrysoparia*

5 in. (13 cm). Adult male has bright yellow face with **black eye line that connects to rear of head**; **crown and back black**; throat black; white underparts with black streaks on sides and flanks; **vent and undertail coverts white**. Female and immature similar but crown and back olive-green; throat shows more white. Female and immature very similar to Black-throated Green Warbler, but crown darker, back with dull streaks, vent area bright white, and cheek bright yellow with dark eye line and no hint of auricular. Uncommon winter visitor (early Aug.–Mar.); mainly above 4,270 ft. (1,300 m). Found in highland pine-oak forest, where it forages at all levels. Often joins mixed-species foraging flocks. Call is a soft *tip*. TX (breeding) to Nicaragua (winter).

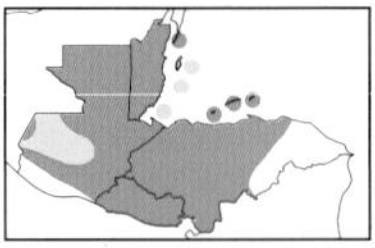

BLACK-THROATED GREEN WARBLER *Setophaga virens*

5 in. (13 cm). Adult male shows **olive crown and back**; 2 white wing bars; face yellow but **auriculars weakly defined in olive**; throat black, extending toward sides and flanks. Underparts mostly white. Female and immature similar but with paler throat; **vent on both sexes show yellowish wash**. Similar to female Golden-cheeked Warbler, but crown and back paler, auriculars darker (not bright yellow), and vent has yellowish wash (not white). Also similar to female and immature Townsend's Warbler, but auricular is paler and less defined, crown is more olive, and chest is whiter. Common winter visitor (mid-Sept.–May); to 7,870 ft. (2,400 m). Habitats include semideciduous forest and rainforest; also pine-oak forest and some disturbed habitats like coffee plantations. Forages at all levels. Call a fairly rich *tip*. Canada (breeding) to Panama (winter).

Virens *group:* *These 4 species are closely related and appear similar, especially females and immatures. For identification, focus on crown color (black vs. olive) and face (presence of eye line, extent of auricular patch), and extent of yellowish wash on chest and vent.*

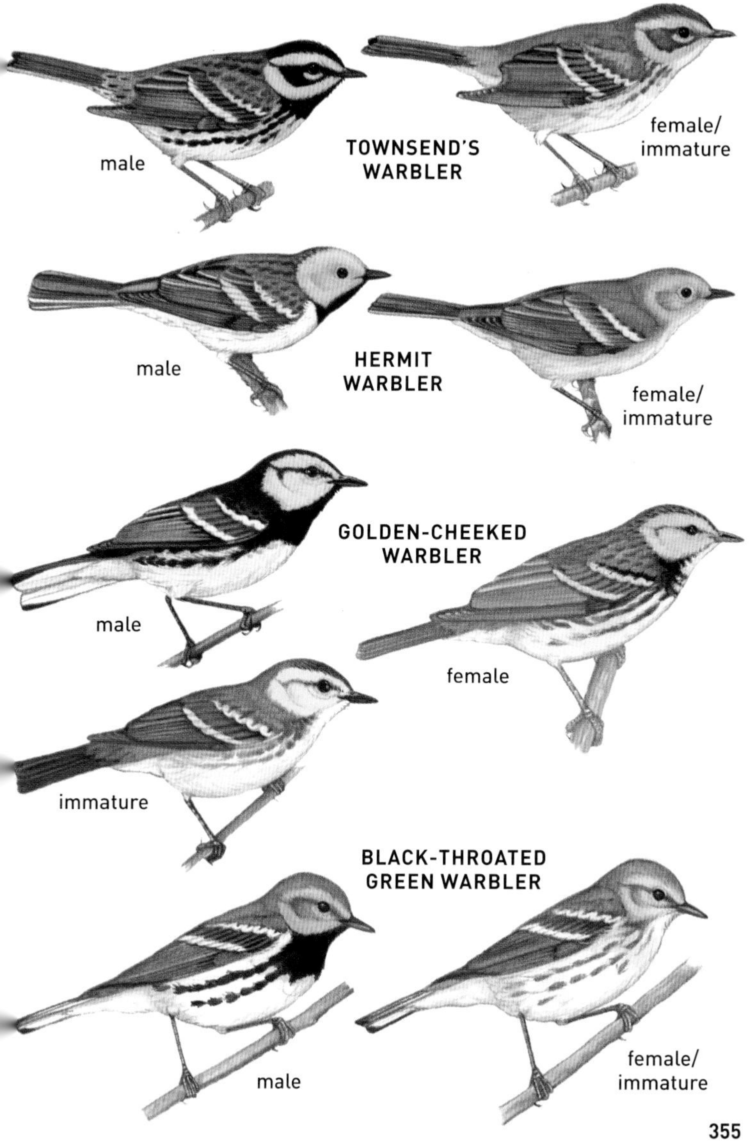

WARBLERS XI (Resident *Setophaga* Warblers)

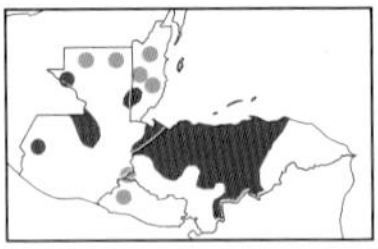

TROPICAL PARULA *Setophaga pitiayumi*

4 in. (10 cm). Similar to Northern Parula (p. 346) but darker blue-gray above, shows more extensive yellow below, has darker face, and lacks white eye-arcs. Uncommon on Caribbean Slope and adjacent areas of Pacific Slope; to 5,910 ft. (1,800 m). Found in a variety of forest types, including disturbed habitats (gardens and plantations), rainforest, semideciduous forest, thorn forest, pine-oak forest, and even cloud forest. Variable song is an accelerating series of trills lasting roughly 2 sec., inflected at the end; similar to Northern Parula, but less buzzy and includes more elements; call is sharp, rich *tsip*. Mex. to Argentina.

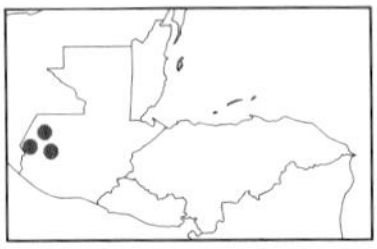

GOLDMAN'S WARBLER *Setophaga goldmani*

5.5 in. (14 cm). Adult male has **black upperparts, including head** (back with blue-gray edging); crown stripe and rump yellow; **note large white wing patch**; **white eye-arc under eye**; chin and border of throat white; **center of throat yellow**; **underparts mainly black with yellow patches on side**. Female brown overall, showing soft yellow on throat (but still has whitish chin and border to throat) and yellow on sides. Female similar to female and immature Audubon's (Yellow-rumped) Warbler (p. 350) but, in general, is larger, has longer bill and longer legs, and shorter primary projections. Uncommon in w. Guatemala; 5,910 to 11,480 ft. (1,800–3,500 m). Found in pine savanna and pine-oak forest, where it forages at mid- to upper levels. Song is a pleasant warble, *tweeta'wie-tweeta'wie-see-see* (the last part dropping off slightly); call is a flat *tip*. Endemic to region. Considered by some authors a subspecies of Yellow-rumped Warbler (p. 350).

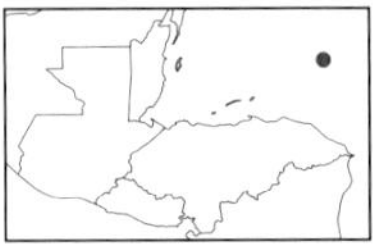

VITELLINE WARBLER *Setophaga vitellina*

5 in. (13 cm). Adult male has yellowish olive upperparts; **2 yellow wing bars**; **dark eye line and border to auricular** recalls facial pattern of Prairie Warbler (p. 344); yellow underparts; **weak olive streaking on sides**. Female and immature similar but duller (often grayer above). On all ages and sexes note small white patches on outer tail feathers. Similar to female Prairie Warbler, but markings on face, sides, and flanks are less distinctive; wing bars yellow (not white), and lacks rufous streaking on back. Swan Is.; near sea level. Found in arid coastal scrub, thickets, and other open habitats, where it forages at lower levels. Sings a harsh 4- to 5-syllable song, *szwee-szwee-szwee-zee*. W. Caribbean (Cayman and Swan Is. only).

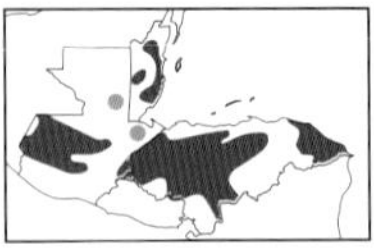

GRACE'S WARBLER *Setophaga graciae*

5 in. (13 cm). Bluish gray upperparts; **bright yellow supercilium and throat; face gray**; black streaking on sides and flanks contrasts with white underparts. Compare with Yellow-throated Warbler, but Grace's has yellow supercilium (not white) and lacks the bold black-and-white face pattern. Common resident in NCA on both slopes; to 8,200 ft. (2,500 m). Found in pine savanna and mixed-pine forests, where it forages at upper levels. Song accelerates through a 2-part trill often inflected at the end: *sip'sip'sip'sip'sip'sip'sip'sip'titititititititi!*; call a mild *tip*. U.S. to Nicaragua.

TROPICAL PARULA
GOLDMAN'S WARBLER
male
female/
immature
VITELLINE WARBLER
GRACE'S WARBLER

WARBLERS XII (*Basileuterus* Genus)

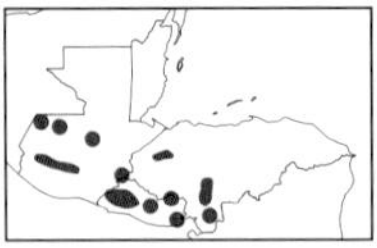

FAN-TAILED WARBLER *Basileuterus lachrymosus*

6 in. (15 cm). **Face distinctive, with white supraloral spot and white eye crescents**; tail broadly tipped white. Juvenile sooty dark with pale wing bar and pale tips to outer tail feathers. Fairly common at midelevations on Pacific Slope and in some interior Caribbean-slope valleys; 820 to 6,070 ft. (250–1,850 m). Found in understory of humid semideciduous forest, pine-oak forest, wooded ravines, and during nonbreeding season in shaded coffee plantations. Forages low, often on or near ground. Droops wing and fans tail; also small groups follow army ant swarms and foraging mammals, such as armadillos. Song a pleasant sharply whistled *see'sah'see'sah'see'seew'seew* (the last notes dropping in pitch); call a thin, high-pitched *seeeuh* (resembles call of Rose-throated Becard [p. 282]). Mex. to Nicaragua.

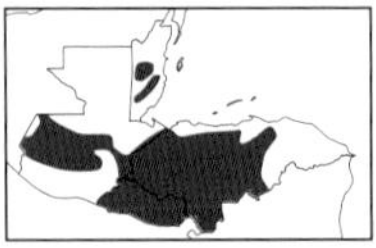

RUFOUS-CAPPED WARBLER *Basileuterus rufifrons*

5 in. (13 cm). Two distinctive groups in NCA. [*salvini* group] Adult has **grayish olive upperparts**; chestnut crown and **small chestnut ear patch; white below eye;** throat and chest yellow**; remaining underparts grayish white** (in Belize, yellow on underparts is more extensive). Fairly common in Belize and Guatemala (north of Motagua River Valley); 1,500 to 7,100 ft. (450–2,150 m). Found in dry scrub vegetation; in understory or edge of pine-oak forest, pine savanna, thorn forest, and disturbed habitats. [*delattrii* group] Adult similar to *salvini* but has **yellow-olive upperparts**; **chestnut auriculars extend below eye**; **underparts bright yellow**. Juveniles (of both groups) are olive-brown overall with yellow edging to wings and tail, and paler underparts, similar to Ochre-bellied Flycatcher (p. 250). Common south of Motagua River Valley (e. Guatemala) to Honduras and El Salvador; elevation range similar to *salvini*, but occasionally to near sea level. Found in understory of semideciduous forest, pine-oak forest, pine savanna, thorn forest, and coffee plantations. Both forms forage low; active often in pairs or family groups. Tends to droop wings and cock tail. Song (variable) is a sweet warble of repeated elements, *tsip-tsip-tsip-three'three'three'sea'sea'tawhee!*; calls include a 2-part *pit-tsew!* (*delattrii*); or a hard *chik*, also a high *tsi* (*salvini*). Mex. to Venezuela.

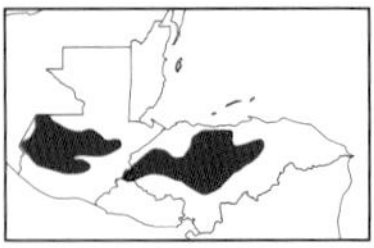

GOLDEN-BROWED WARBLER *Basileuterus belli*

5 in. (13 cm). Adult has striking face: rufous-chestnut auriculars, **broad bright yellow supercilium**, and rufous-chestnut crown stripe. Juvenile sooty olive overall with yellowish tones to supercilium and underparts. Locally fairly common in highlands; 3,940 to 10,010 ft. (1,200–3,050 m) but generally above 6,560 ft. (2,000 m). Found in understory of cloud forest and pine-oak forest, where it forages low, and often in pairs or small groups. Song is a rich warble with several repeated elements, *three'three'three'two'two'three'three'tzee'tzee'two'tzee!*; call is a sharp, high-pitched *seet!* Mex. to Honduras.

GOLDEN-CROWNED WARBLER *Basileuterus culicivorus*

5 in. (13 cm). Broad median crown stripe yellow (edged reddish orange in males), often difficult to see; **face with broad lateral crown stripes, broad pale supercilium, and dark eye line**. Juveniles are brownish overall with buff on belly and 2 pale cinnamon wing bars. Fairly common resident on Caribbean Slope; uncommon on Pacific Slope; to 6,070 ft. (1,850 m) but generally above 2,130 ft. (650 m) on Pacific Slope. Found in understory of humid forest, such as taller semideciduous forest, rainforest, and shaded coffee plantations. Forages near the ground. Usually in pairs or small groups. Song is a pleasant warble lasting roughly 1.5 sec., *see'see'see'seesah'wee!* (the last note inflected); call is a dry, electric *tik*, often repeated as *tik'tik'tik'tik'tik* . . . Mex. to Argentina.

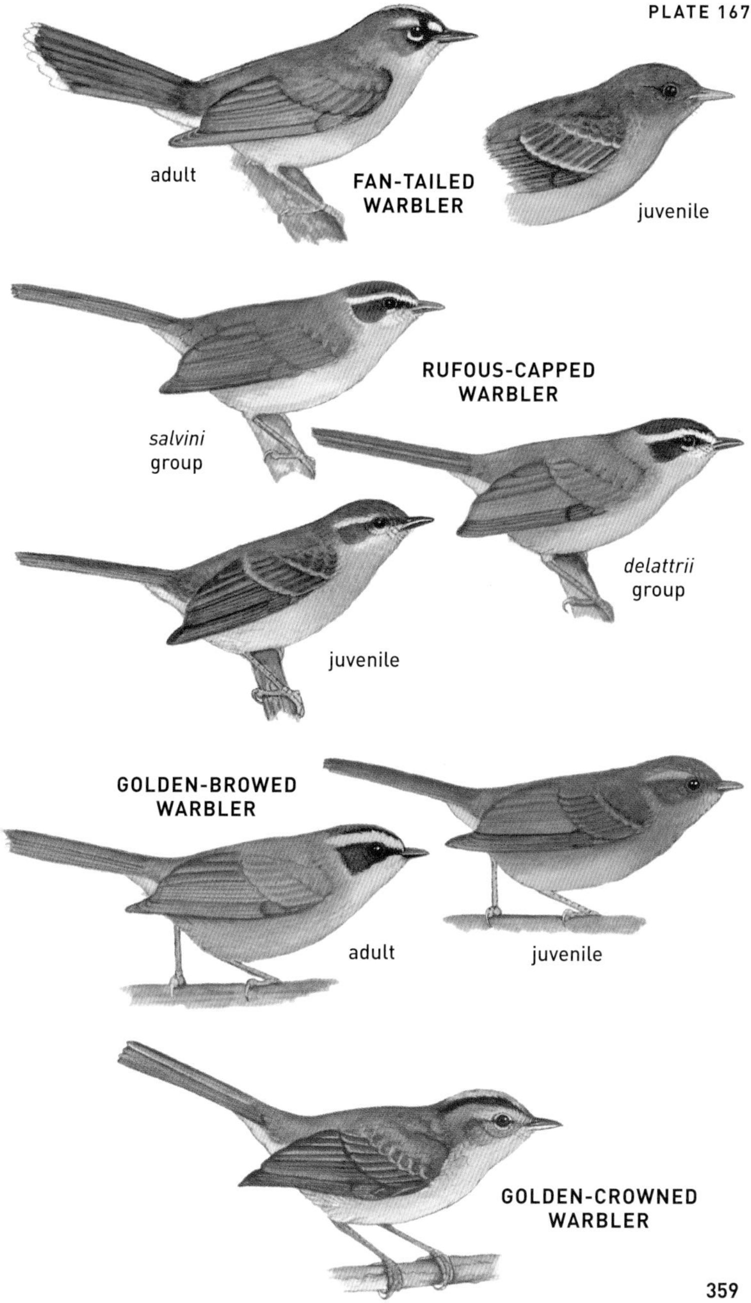
adult
FAN-TAILED WARBLER
juvenile
RUFOUS-CAPPED WARBLER
salvini group
delattrii group
juvenile
GOLDEN-BROWED WARBLER
adult
juvenile
GOLDEN-CROWNED WARBLER

WARBLERS XIII (More Resident NCA Species)

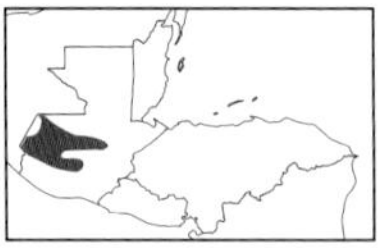

PINK-HEADED WARBLER *Ergaticus versicolor*

5 in. (13 cm). **Frosty pink hood**; rest of body reddish. Fairly common in Guatemala, but local and seemingly absent from suitable habitat; 6,070 to 10,990 ft. (1,850–3,350 m). Found in pine savanna and pine-oak forest. Forages at low to midlevels. Song (variable) is a rapid, trilling warble with a slightly accelerated ending, *sea'sea'sea'tea'tea'tea'tutututu'tawee!*; call is a distinctive ringing *tschink!* Endemic to region.

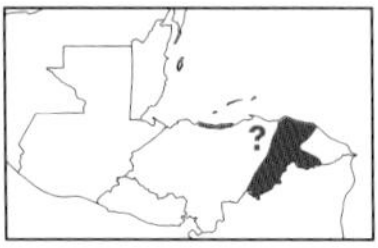

BUFF-RUMPED WARBLER *Phaeothlypis fulvicauda*

5 in. (13 cm). Upperparts brownish olive; **uppertail coverts and base of tail tawny-buff**; head mainly gray; pale supercilium; dark eye line; buffy white underparts with dingy sides and flanks; legs pink. Uncommon in n. and e. Honduras; to 3,280 ft. (1,000 m). Found along swift-moving streams and rivers in rainforest, where it forages among boulders and rocks. Song is a crescendo series of rich, repeated elements lasting roughly 4 sec., *sawee-sawee-tee-tee-tee-tee-see-see-TEW'TEW'TEW'TEW'TEW'TEW'TEW'TEW'TEW'TEW'TEW*; call is a hollow *peak!* Honduras to Brazil.

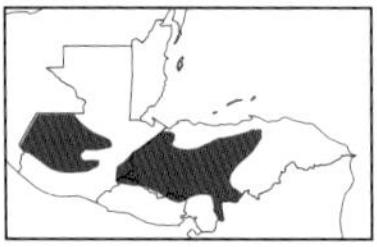

PAINTED REDSTART *Myioborus pictus*

5.5 in. (14 cm). Black overall with **white wing panels** and **red belly**; also note white lower eye crescent. Juvenile dark below, lacks red. Compare with Slate-throated Redstart, but Painted has obvious white wing patch and red belly (not orange). Uncommon in highlands of NCA; 3,280 to 10,990 ft. (1,000–3,350 m); rarely lower. Found in pine savanna and pine-oak forest. A very active warbler that generally forages at low to midlevels; often fans tail with wings drooped. Song a sweet warble lasting about 2 sec.: *weeta'weeta'weeta'weeta'swee'swee'swee'weeta* (similar to song of a *Geothlypis* yellowthroat [p. 342] or Grace's Warbler [p. 356]); call is a siskinlike, disyllabic *pseeuuu*. U.S. to Nicaragua.

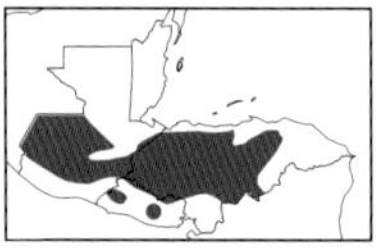

SLATE-THROATED REDSTART *Myioborus miniatus*

5.5 in. (14 cm). Adult is slate gray above with **chestnut cap** and black throat; **underparts orange**; outer tail tipped white. Juvenile has dark crown and orange replaced with sooty-brown. Compare with adult Painted Redstart, but lacks white wing patches and is orange (not deep red) below. Common in NCA (absent from Belize); 160 to 9,350 ft. (50–2,850 m) but generally above 1,800 ft. (550 m). Found in rainforest, semideciduous forest, cloud forest, and pine-oak forest; also shaded coffee plantations. An active warbler that forages at lower levels, often near the ground, with tail fanned and wings drooped. Tends to make short sallies for small flying insects from low perch. Song a soft sweet warble lasting about 2 sec.: *seesee-sweeswee-sisis-wee*; call a sharp, high-pitched *tseet*. Mex. to Peru.

PLATE 168

PINK-HEADED WARBLER

BUFF-RUMPED WARBLER

Buff-rumped Warbler among streamside rocks

PAINTED REDSTART

SLATE-THROATED REDSTART

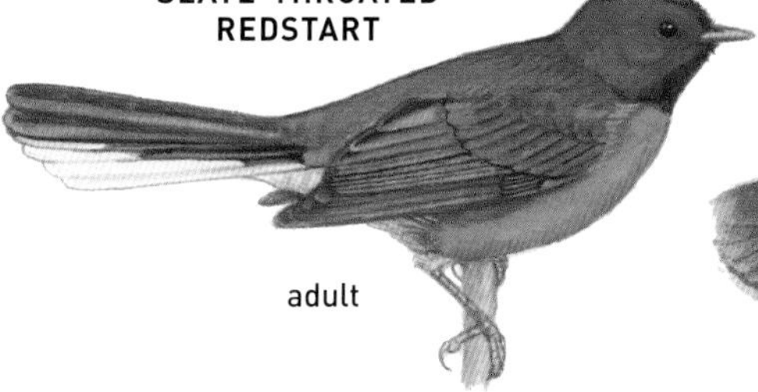

adult

juvenile

TANAGERS I

THRAUPIDAE (Order: Passeriformes). A mainly tropical family, tanagers are mostly frugivores with striking patterns and bright colors, and though quite vocal, song is rather limited to high-pitched whistles and chatters. Honeycreepers and dacnises are smaller tanagers with thinner bills and colorful legs. Grassquits and seedeaters are small granivores (seed-eating birds) that were long thought to be sparrows (Emberizidae family), but were placed into the tanager family in 2015 based on genetic studies. Sexes similar in many species. **31 species (17 genera)**

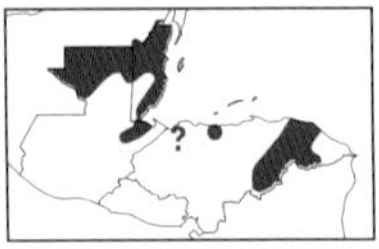

GRAY-HEADED TANAGER *Eucometis penicillata*

7 in. (18 cm). **Gray head contrasts with bright yellow underparts**; also note yellow-olive upperparts. Uncommon to fairly common on Caribbean Slope; to 2,460 ft. (750 m). Compare female with female White-shouldered Tanager, but brighter overall, larger, and head shows more gray. Found in interior of rainforest and taller semideciduous forest. Forages in understory, where it often attends ant swarms. Song is a rapid series of chatters and squeaks, *teep'tsee'u'cheu-teep'tsee'u'cheu-teep'tsee'u'cheu!* Mex. to Brazil.

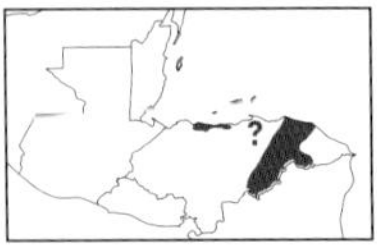

WHITE-SHOULDERED TANAGER *Tachyphonus luctuosus*

5 in. (13 cm). **A warbler-sized tanager.** Adult male is **black** with a **white shoulder patch.** Female is yellowish green overall with head washed in gray. Female is similar to Gray-headed Tanager, but duller overall, shows less gray on head, and is smaller. Uncommon in e. Honduras; to 2,460 ft. (750 m). Found at edge of rainforest and semideciduous forest; also some disturbed habitats. Forages at mid- to upper levels, often in mixed-species flocks. Calls include a thin, whiny *tzee!-tzee!-tzee!-tzee!* . . . Honduras to Brazil.

TAWNY-CRESTED TANAGER *Tachyphonus delatrii*

6 in. (15 cm). Male is **all-black** with **tawny-orange crest** (sometimes difficult to see). Female is **chocolate brown overall**. Fairly common in e. Honduras; to 2,460 ft. (750 m). Found in rainforest. Forages at all levels. Often in mixed-species flocks. Calls include a high-pitched *tzeeet!* and a scratchy *chit* and *pweet* (often mixed with an agitated chatter). Honduras to Ecuador.

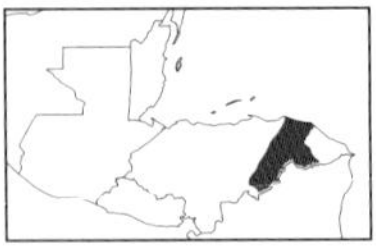

WHITE-THROATED SHRIKE-TANAGER *Lanio leucothorax*

8 in. (20 cm). Structure and plumage pattern similar to that of Black-throated Shrike-Tanager (below; no range overlap), but has **white throat and white slash (variable) on wing**. Uncommon in e. Honduras; to 3,610 ft. (1,100 m). Found in interior of rainforest, where it forages at mid- to upper levels, often in mixed-species flocks. Call is a repeated *peeuuu* (shorter than whistle of Black-throated Shrike-Tanager); also *peet-teeuu!* Honduras to Panama.

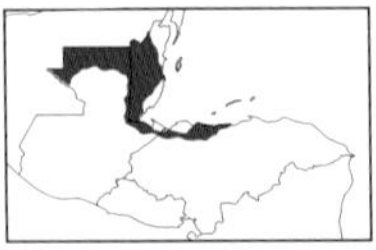

BLACK-THROATED SHRIKE-TANAGER *Lanio aurantius*

8 in. (20 cm). Adult male has **yellow body with contrasting black head and throat, wings, and tail.** Variable white spots on wing coverts. Female brownish olive above, washed yellow below. **Heavy black bill.** Uncommon to fairly common on Caribbean Slope in Guatemala, Belize, and nw. Honduras; to 3,940 ft. (1,200 m). Found in interior of rainforest and taller semideciduous forest, where it forages at mid- to upper levels. Often first detected by voice. Song is a loud, 2-part, *cheep-two!* or *peep-two-tu'tu'tu'tu'tu'tu'tu* (quality similar to call of Summer Tanager [p. 382]); also a clear whistled *peee'uuuu*. Mex. to Honduras.

GRAY-HEADED TANAGER
male
TAWNY-CRESTED TANAGER
female
WHITE-SHOULDERED TANAGER
male
female
male
female
WHITE-THROATED SHRIKE-TANAGER
BLACK-THROATED SHRIKE-TANAGER
male
female

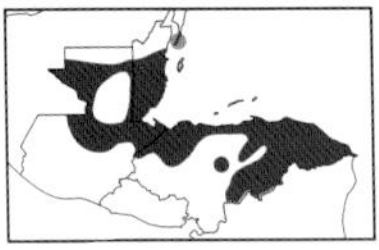

CRIMSON-COLLARED TANAGER
Ramphocelus sanguinolentus

7.5 in. (19 cm). A striking tanager. **Deep red crown, nape, and chest contrast with black face and body**; rump and undertail coverts also red; **red eyes and silver bill**. Fairly common on Caribbean Slope; to 3,940 ft. (1,200 m). Found in a variety of disturbed habitats, including botanical gardens and plantations; also at edge of rainforest and semideciduous forest. Forages at midlevels. Call is a slurring whistle, *tseeeu'weep!* Mex. to Panama.

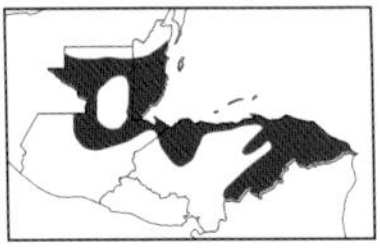

PASSERINI'S TANAGER
Ramphocelus passerinii

6 in. (15 cm). Male has **velvet black body** with **bright red rump**. **Silver bill**. Female yellowish brown overall with buffy-orange breast and grayish crown. Fairly common on Caribbean Slope; to 3,940 ft. (1,200 m). Found in a variety of disturbed habitats, including botanical gardens and plantations; also at edge of rainforest and semideciduous forest. Calls include a harsh chatter, *chiv'chiv'chiv'chiv'chiv* . . . or a single *chet*; song is a series of high-pitched whistles, *tseet-tseuu-sip-sip-tseeu-seep'seu-* . . . Mex. to Panama.

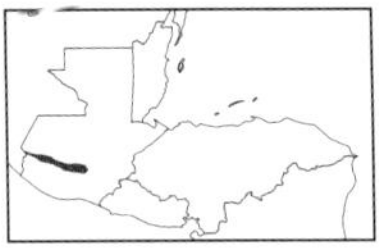

AZURE-RUMPED TANAGER
Tangara cabanisi

6 in. (15 cm). A small tanager. **Pale sky blue overall** with **small black mask and light black spotting on chest** (can be difficult to see); wings black, edged in blue. Uncommon and local in highlands on Pacific Slope of Guatemala; from 4,920 to 6,560 ft. (1,500–2,000 m). Found in taller semideciduous forest and cloud forest, often at edge, and in shaded coffee plantations. Forages at mid- to canopy levels, often on fruits of fig (*Ficus* spp.) trees. Song is a soft, high-pitched, and thin *tseu'weeee*; also sharp call, *tseet*. Endemic to region.

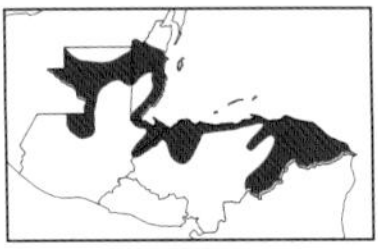

GOLDEN-HOODED TANAGER
Tangara larvata

5 in. (13 cm). A warbler-sized tanager. **Golden crown and neck contrast with turquoise blue forecrown and cheek, and black mask**; back and chest black. Flanks bright blue and vent white. Fairly common on Caribbean Slope; to 3,610 ft. (1,100 m). Found at edge of forest and in a variety of disturbed habitats, including gardens and plantations. Call is a scratchy *chit-chit-chit-* . . . ; also a rapid *ti'ti'ti'ti'ti'ti'ti'ti'ti'ti* . . . Mex. to Ecuador.

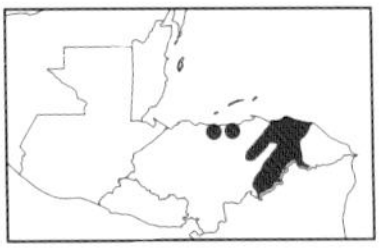

RUFOUS-WINGED TANAGER
Tangara lavinia

5 in. (13 cm). A warbler-sized tanager. On male **rufous wings and head** contrast with green body. Female duller green with light wash of rufous-brown on wings. Rare on Caribbean Slope of Honduras; to 2,460 ft. (750 m). Found in interior of rainforest. Forages at mid- to upper levels. Calls include a rapid *tit'tit'tit'tit'tit'tit'tit'tit*; also a whiny, thin, and complaintive *eeeaahhht!* and a high-pitched *seeet*. Honduras to Ecuador.

CRIMSON-COLLARED TANAGER
PASSERINI'S TANAGER
male
female
GOLDEN-HOODED TANAGER
AZURE-RUMPED TANAGER
RUFOUS-WINGED TANAGER
male
female

TANAGERS III (And Honeycreepers)

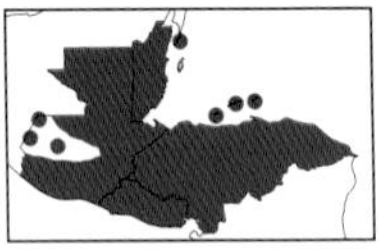

BLUE-GRAY TANAGER *Thraupis episcopus*

7 in. (18 cm). **Bluish gray overall.** Head paler than body. Common on both slopes up to 3,300 ft. (1,000 m), less common to 6,070 ft. (1,850 m). Found in a variety of disturbed habitats; also at edge of rainforest and semideciduous forest. Song is a complicated mix of thin, whiny, electric whistles, lasting around 3 sec.; call is a thin *tseee!* Mex. to Brazil.

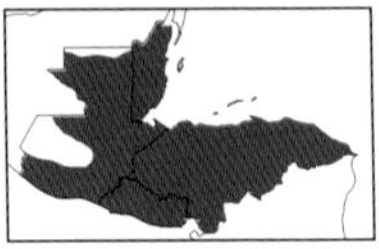

YELLOW-WINGED TANAGER *Thraupis abbas*

7 in. (18 cm). Note **contrasting small blackish mask and yellow patch on wing** (not always visible). Juvenile is overall olive-gray with just a hint of the yellow wing patch. Common in NCA; to 6,230 ft. (1,900 m). Found in a variety of disturbed habitats; also at edge of rainforest and semideciduous forest. Call (also given in flight) is a thin, high-pitched whistle, *seeeeaa'uh* or *tsseee'ah*, similar to Blue-gray Tanager; song is a drawn-out liquid trill. Mex. to Costa Rica.

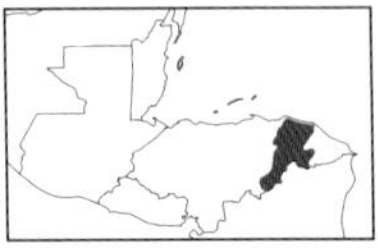

BLUE DACNIS *Dacnis cayana*

5 in. (13 cm). Male has **bright blue head and underparts** contrasting with **black throat, back, and wings**. Female yellowish green overall with a **bluish head**. Uncommon in e. Honduras; to 2,460 ft. (750 m). Found in rainforest or taller semideciduous forest; often at forest edge, where it forages at mid- to upper levels. Generally in pairs, and often joins mixed-species flocks. Calls include a high-pitched *seeet!* or *seeet-seeet*. Honduras to Argentina.

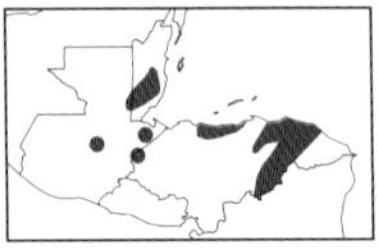

SHINING HONEYCREEPER *Cyanerpes lucidus*

4 in. (10 cm). Male **deep purplish blue overall** with black throat and bright **yellow legs**. Female has olive upperparts, paler face, with **dark streaking or scaling on chest**. Bill thin and decurved. Compare male with Red-legged Honeycreeper, but has purplish blue back and yellow legs. Rare to uncommon on Caribbean Slope; to 4,920 ft. (1,500 m). Found in rainforest and taller semideciduous forest; often at forest edge, where it forages in upper canopy. Call is a high-pitched *tseeeet!* Mex. to Colombia.

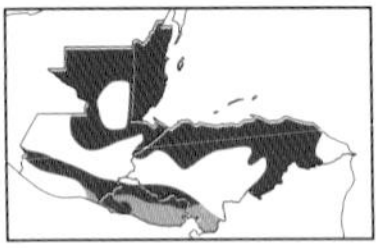

RED-LEGGED HONEYCREEPER *Cyanerpes cyaneus*

4.5 in. (11 cm). Breeding male **purplish blue overall with black back and wings**; **crown iridescent blue**; **legs bright red**. Nonbreeding male yellow-olive overall with black wings. Female pale olive overall. In flight, both sexes flash yellow wing linings. Breeding male similar to Shining Honeycreeper, but has black back and red legs. Common on both slopes; to 5,740 ft. (1,750 m), but absent or transient in parts of interior. Seasonal (nonbreeding) visitor in Pacific lowlands. Found in a variety of forest types; often at forest edge, where it forages at midlevels. In nonbreeding season, often in groups of up to 50 individuals. Call is a thin, whiny *chee'eeez* (similar in quality to a gnatcatcher). Mex. to Brazil.

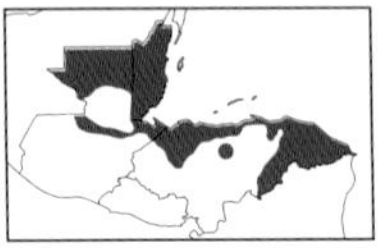

GREEN HONEYCREEPER *Chlorophanes spiza*

5.5 in. (14 cm). Male **overall turquoise-green with black hood**; **bright yellow mandible**. Female bright yellowish green. Fairly common on Caribbean Slope; to 4,920 ft. (1,500 m). Found in rainforest and semideciduous forest; also disturbed habitats, such as plantations. Often at forest edge, where it forages mostly at mid- and upper levels. Generally in pairs, and often in mixed-species flocks. Calls include a rich *tsip* and a higher-pitched *tseeep*. Mex. to Brazil.

BLUE-GRAY
TANAGER
YELLOW-WINGED
TANAGER
male
BLUE
DACNIS
female
male
female
SHINING
HONEYCREEPER
breeding
male
nonbreeding
male
female
RED-LEGGED
HONEYCREEPER
male
GREEN
HONEYCREEPER
female/
immature

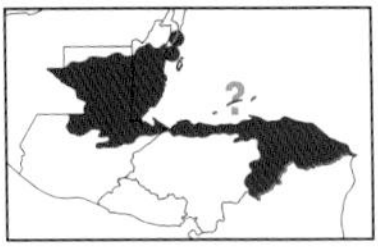

BANANAQUIT *Coereba flaveola*

4 in. (10 cm). **Broad white supercilium** and pale gray throat contrast with **black head and yellow underparts; white "handkerchief" in wing**; small bill is sharply pointed and decurved. Uncommon to rare on Caribbean Slope; to 3,280 ft. (1,000 m). Status on Roatán uncertain; possibly a regular winter visitor. Found at edge of rainforest, in gardens, and other disturbed habitat. Forages at all levels, where it feeds at flowering bushes and trees. Usually solitary. Song is a sharp, electric *wi-seee-wi-seee-wi-seee-wi-seee-tzzzeeeee!* Mex. and Caribbean to Argentina.

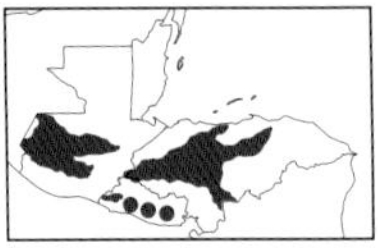

CINNAMON-BELLIED FLOWERPIERCER *Diglossa baritula*

4.5 in. (11 cm). On adult male, **dark blue-gray upperparts** contrast with **dark reddish brown underparts**. Female and immature overall olive-brown; may show faint buffy wing bars. Note **odd-shaped bill with hooked maxilla**. Fairly common in highlands; from 4,920 to 10,170 ft. (1,500–3,100 m). Found in clearings and at edge of cloud forest and pine-oak forest, where it uses hooked bill to steal nectar from the base of tubular flowers. In parts of range, breeds during dry season when nectar resources are most abundant. Song is rapid, high-pitched, soft tinkling series, *ti'ti'ti'ti'ti'ti'tseee'tu'tu'tu'tu'tu'tu.* Mex. to Nicaragua.

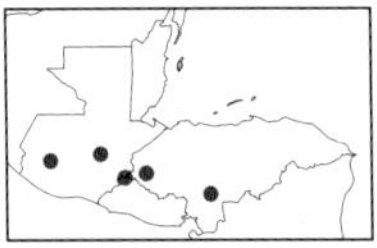

SLATY FINCH *Haplospiza rustica*

5 in. (13 cm). Adult male is **dark gray with a bluish tint**. Female is buffy brown with **light streaking below**. **Bill is sharply pointed in both sexes.** Very rare in NCA; between 4,430 and 9,510 ft. (1,350–2,900 m). Found in bamboo or thick understory of highland pine-oak forest and cloud forest. Status, distribution, and movements in region are poorly known. Song is a scratchy, buzzy series, *tzzzzeee'cheee-tip-tzzzzeee'cheee*; call is a soft, high-pitched *seeet!* Mex. to Bolivia.

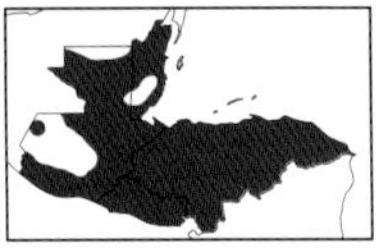

BLUE-BLACK GRASSQUIT *Volatinia jacarina*

4 in. (10 cm). Breeding male **glossy blue-black overall**. Nonbreeding male mottled black and brown on upperparts. Juvenile and female brownish overall and **streaked below**. Common in NCA; to 5,910 ft. (1,800 m). Found in disturbed habitats such as farm fields, along hedgerows, and in gardens. May nest in high densities in temporarily available grassy habitat, and forms loose foraging flocks of dozens of individuals. Male displays by jumping vertically a few feet and returning immediately to perch, singing while in the air. Song is a buzzy, insectlike *zeeee'ur!* Mex. to Argentina.

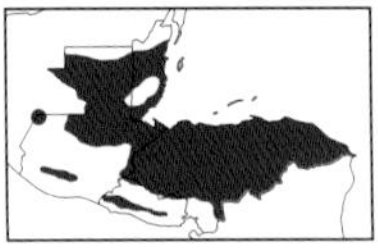

YELLOW-FACED GRASSQUIT *Tiaris olivaceus*

4 in. (10 cm). On male, bright **yellow supercilium and throat, contrasts with black face and chest**. Female and immature drab olive-brown overall. Fairly common in highlands and on Caribbean Slope; to 6,560 ft. (2,000 m); more common above 1,970 ft. (600 m). Found in open and disturbed habitats. Song is a high, squeaky, mechanical trill. Mex. and Caribbean to Venezuela.

GRASSLAND YELLOW-FINCH *Sicalis luteola*

4.5 in. (11 cm). Adult male **bright yellow below**; darker upperparts streaked. Female and immature browner and more streaked above. Locally fairly common in Belize and e. Honduras; to 4,430 ft. (1,350 m). Found in fallow fields and pine savanna. Usually in small flocks of 2 to 5 birds. Often heard calling in flight overhead (a thin, high-pitched *tsee-seut!*); song is a series of rapid trilling elements. Mex. to Argentina.

BANANAQUIT
male
CINNAMON-BELLIED
FLOWERPIERCER
female
robbing
nectar from
flowers
SLATY
FINCH
female
nale
LUE-BLACK
GRASSQUIT
male
female
Male Blue-black
doing flight display
while singing
GRASSLAND
YELLOW-
FINCH
male
YELLOW-FACED
GRASSQUIT
female

SEEDEATERS (*Sporophila* Tanagers)

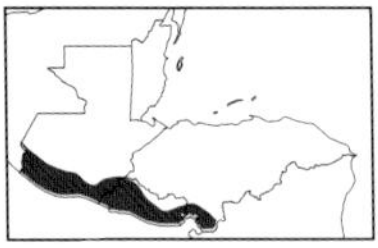

RUDDY-BREASTED SEEDEATER *Sporophila minuta*

4 in. (10 cm). Breeding male **gray above** and **rich tawny orange below**; small conical bill black. Nonbreeding male and female have pale brown upperparts and pale buffy or tawny-gray underparts; bill pale grayish orange. Fairly common in Pacific Slope floodplains; to 1,640 ft. (500 m). Prefers open or disturbed habitats. Song is more complex, with less repetition than White-collared Seedeater's; also includes buzzes: *see-seu-seu'a'whee-wip-tsee-you-ti'ti-trrrrrr-teat-chew-tip!*; call is a rich *tseeeu* (recalls Lesser Goldfinch [p. 334]). Mex. to Argentina.

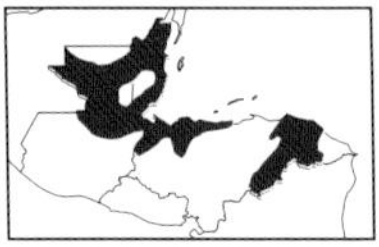

THICK-BILLED SEED-FINCH *Sporophila funerea*

5 in. (12 cm). Adult male very similar to Variable Seedeater, but larger overall with heavier, thicker bill. Female **chocolate brown** (slightly paler below). Both sexes told from Variable Seedeater by nearly **straight edge to culmen**. Uncommon to fairly common on Caribbean Slope; to 3,610 ft. (1,100 m). Found in open and disturbed habitats. Song is a musical, complex series lasting up to 5 sec., reminiscent of Gray-crowned Yellowthroat (p. 342); call is a doubled, buzzy *tzee-tzee*. Mex. to Ecuador.

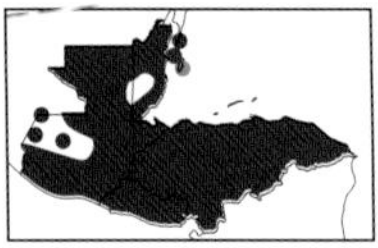

WHITE-COLLARED SEEDEATER *Sporophila torqueola*

4.5 in. (11 cm). Some geographic variation between Caribbean and Pacific slopes. Breeding-plumage male has black head, white collar, white patch at base of primaries, 2 white wing bars, **black breast-band**; underparts and rump white (Pacific) or pale buffy to cinnamon (Caribbean). Pacific Slope birds also show darker throats. Nonbreeding plumage warm brown above, buffy below and on rump, lacks breast-band (Caribbean); head, wings, and tail blackish; bright buffy wing bars. Female and immature brown overall, but show white wing bars and (on some) white wing patch. Common in NCA; to 8,040 ft. (2,450 m). Found in a variety of open and disturbed habitats. Song is a musical, variable series of repeated elements: *ti'ti'ti' ti'titea'tea'tea'teateu'teu'teu'teu*; calls include *pseeut!* (similar to calls of Yellow-throated Euphonia [p. 332] and Elegant Euphonia [p. 332]), and female also gives a whiny, scratchy *che-che-che-che-che* (similar to Lesser Greenlet [p. 290] scold). U.S. and Mex. to Panama.

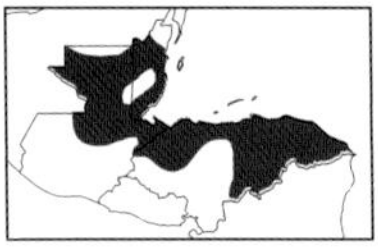

VARIABLE SEEDEATER *Sporophila americana*

4.5 in. (11 cm). Adult male **black overall** with **small white patch on wing**; heavy black bill with **curved culmen**. Female olive-brown above, slightly paler below. Both sexes similar to Thick-billed Seed-Finch, but smaller overall with smaller and more curved bill. Compare female with female Slate-colored Seedeater, but darker below and has smaller bill. Fairly common on Caribbean Slope; to 3,280 ft. (1,000 m). Found in a variety of open habitats; also at forest edge. Song is a musical series of repeated elements, each element repeated 2 to 3 times: *wi'teeu-wi'teeu-chewy-chewy-chewy-pizza-pizza-pizza-* . . . ; call is a whiny *cheeeu* or *cheeu-wee*. Mex. to Peru.

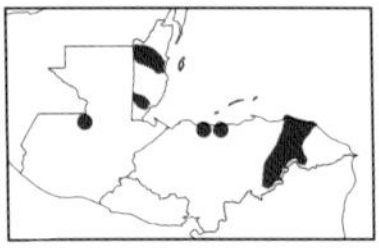

SLATE-COLORED SEEDEATER *Sporophila schistacea*

4.5 in. (11 cm). Adult male **gray overall** with white belly and vent; white malar stripe (often not visible); thin white upper wing bar; **white patch on wing**; **heavy yellow bill**. Female brown overall, slightly paler below with black bill; lacks wing bar. Female most similar to female Variable Seedeater, but paler below with heavier bill. Rare on Caribbean Slope; to 2,460 ft. (750 m). Found at rainforest edge in canopy or midlevels; also in or near thick patches of native cane or exotic bamboo when producing seeds. Song is an accelerating series of high-pitched *tsee* notes: *ti'ti'ti'ti'ti'ti'ti'ti'ti-tsee-tsee-tsee-tsee'tsee'tsee'tseetseetsee*. Belize to Brazil.

RUDDY-BREASTED SEEDEATER
male
female
male
female
THICK-BILLED SEED-FINCH
WHITE-COLLARED SEEDEATER
Pacific Slope
nonbreeding male
male
VARIABLE SEEDEATER
male
female
nonbreeding male
Caribbean Slope
male
female
male
female
SLATE-COLORED SEEDEATER

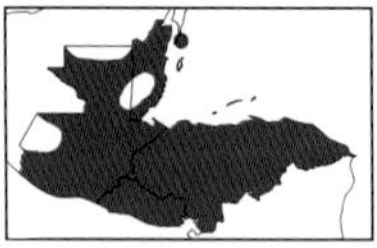

GRAYISH SALTATOR *Saltator coerulescens*

9 in. (23 cm). **Sooty gray overall** (head darker), but with tawny undertail coverts and **white supercilium**. Common in NCA; to 5,910 ft. (1,800 m). Found in open country and disturbed habitats, including second-growth scrub, along hedgerows, coffee plantations, and in gardens and city parks; also at edge of semideciduous forest and pine-oak forest. Saltators frequently consume fresh leaves in bushes and trees (unusual behavior in birds). Perches in open and often located by its loud and frequent song. Song is a 3- or 4-part series ending in a long clear upslurring whistle, *teeurt-peeur-weeeeeeeet!* Mex. to Brazil.

BLACK-HEADED SALTATOR *Saltator atriceps*

10.5 in. (27 cm). Similar to Buff-throated Saltator, but larger, **crown is black**, and has **all-white throat** (in Honduras, some have buff or tawny throat), and has less extensive black bib; note also differences in calls and distribution between the 2 species. Common in NCA; to 6,230 ft. (1,900 m). Found at edge in a variety of habitat types: semideciduous forest and rainforest, thorn forest, coffee plantations, gardens and parks, and mangroves. An active and loud forager and generally found in small groups of up to 10 individuals. Often consumes flowers or foliage. Call is a series of loud, electric chatters, *TSEEUT-SEET-TEEU-TU-TU'TU'TU'CH'CH'CH'E'E'E'E'E'E*; also single calls, *reeaah!* and *SEEET!* Mex. to Panama.

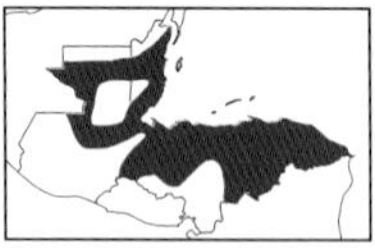

BUFF-THROATED SALTATOR *Saltator maximus*

8.5 in. (22 cm). Golden green upperparts (including wings and tail); **crown and face grayish**; limited white in throat is heavily bordered with black bib; **lower part of throat tawny-brown**; white supercilium. Similar to Black-headed Saltator, but smaller, gray crown (not black) and tawny-brown throat (not white); very different calls and distribution. Fairly common on Caribbean Slope; to 4,920 ft. (1,500 m). Found at edge of semideciduous forest and rainforest; also in disturbed habitat, such as gardens and plantations. Forages at mid- to upper levels on flowers and young leaves. Call is a 2-part *seet!-churr*; also a single, high-pitched *seeeet* (often given in flight). Mex. to Brazil.

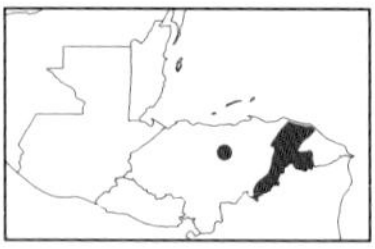

SLATE-COLORED GROSBEAK *Saltator grossus*

8 in. (20 cm). Slate gray overall with **blackish head and border to white throat**; **large, heavy bill is orange-red**. Juvenile similar but with whitish bill. Uncommon in e. Honduras; to 2,460 ft. (750 m). Found at edge of rainforest. Forages at mid- to upper levels. May join mixed-species flocks. Song is a series of 3 to 4 sweet, rich musical whistles (somewhat mournful in quality), *pwit-seeur-seeur-see'ehh!* or *pwit-seeeur-Peee'weur*; call is a nasal, whining *eeeeiirrr*. Honduras to Brazil.

GRAYISH
SALTATOR

tawny-throated
individual
(Honduras)

BLACK-HEADED
SALTATOR

BUFF-THROATED
SALTATOR

SLATE-COLORED
GROSBEAK

EMBERIZIDAE (Order: Passeriformes). A diverse family of small to medium-sized granivores with rounded bodies and long tails. Most species forage for seeds on the ground. Sparrows have strong legs and feet for kicking the ground for seeds and small insects, and their conical bills are designed for opening pods or crushing seeds. Several species are rare winter visitors from the north, but most NCA species are sedentary. **21 species (15 genera)**

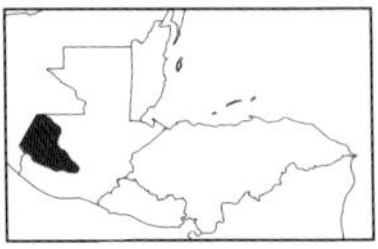

YELLOW-EYED JUNCO *Junco phaeonotus*

6.5 in. (17 cm). The subspecies endemic to the region, *J.p. alticola,* is known as "Guatemalan Junco." **Reddish brown upperparts**; **dark lores; eyes yellow to yellow-orange**; large, pointed bill with dark maxilla and silver-pink mandible. Juvenile has buffy flanks and dull streaking on underparts. Uncommon in interior highlands; 5,580 to 11,810 ft. (1,700–3,600 m). Found in a variety of open habitats. Song is a varied trill, *peuu-peuu-ti'ti'ti'ti'ti'ti'ti'teu'teu'teu*. U.S. to Guatemala.

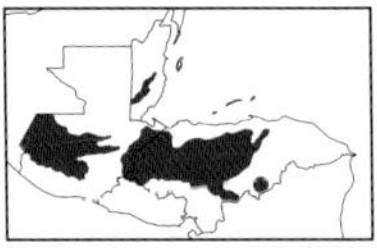

COMMON CHLOROSPINGUS *Chlorospingus flavopectus*

5.5 in. (14 cm). **Dark gray cap** contrasts with olive yellow back and white throat; **white postocular spot**; underparts are white with **yellowish wash to chest, sides, and flanks**. Common in highlands; 4,920 to 9,840 ft. (1,500–3,000 m), locally down to 660 ft. (200 m) near Caribbean coast. Found in pine-oak and cloud forest; also taller humid semideciduous forest. Forages at mid- to upper levels. Often in groups of 3 to 20 individuals. Song is a thin, high-pitched twitter; calls include an agitated rapid chatter; begging young give a thin, buzzy call, *zzzeeeep*. Mex. to Argentina.

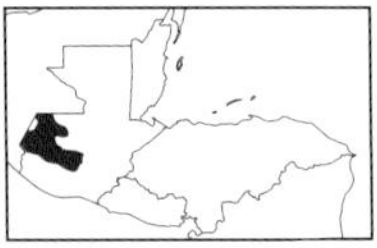

SPOTTED TOWHEE *Pipilo maculatus*

8.5 in. (22 cm). Adult male has **black hood**; **sides and flanks bold chestnut**. Female similarly patterned, but washed browner overall. Fairly common in highlands of Guatemala; 5,610 to 10,500 ft. (1,700–3,200 m). Found in clearings within pine-oak forest or pine savanna. Forages at low to midlevels. Song generally begins with a whistle followed by a trill, *seee!-twi'wi'wi'wi'wi'wi'wi'wi'wi'* or *weer-teet'ti'ti'ti'ti'ti'ti'ti'ti*; call is a buzzy, catlike *REEEeeeaah!* U.S. to Guatemala.

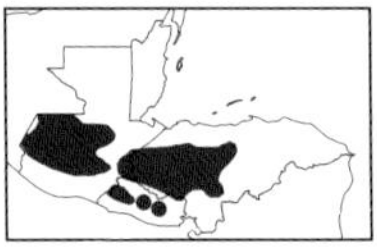

PREVOST'S GROUND-SPARROW *Melozone biarcuata*

6.5 in. (17 cm). Striking facial pattern: **white face with chestnut crown and ear patch**. Uncommon to fairly common in NCA; 2,300 to 9,510 ft. (700–2,900 m). Found in thick understory of pine savanna and pine-oak forest; also brushy hillsides and coffee plantations. Generally prefers more arid environments. Forages on or near ground. Song is a rich, fluid *tit-see'weet-teu-teu*; calls include a distinctive metallic *tip!*; also an agitated chatter, *cheee'cheee'cheee'cheeew'cheeew'cheeeew* . . . (similar to agitated scold of White-eared Ground-Sparrow). Mex. to Costa Rica.

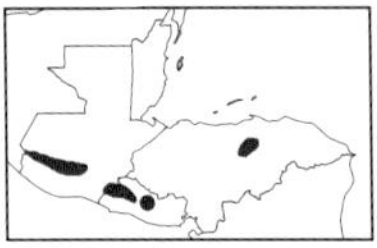

WHITE-EARED GROUND-SPARROW *Melozone leucotis*

7.5 in. (19 cm). Striking facial pattern is distinctive. Black breast spot contrasts with light gray underparts. E. Honduras population lacks eye stripe and has more extensive black on breast. Uncommon and local on volcanoes of Guatemala and El Salvador and mountains of e. Honduras; 2,130 to 6,070 ft. (650–1850 m). Found in thick understory of semideciduous forest, pine-oak forest, and coffee plantations. Generally prefers more humid environments. Forages on or near ground. Song is a ringing, slightly metallic *seet!—teet-teea-teu'teu'teu'teu*; also an agitated, buzzy scold, *seee-seeee-zeeee'zeeee'zeeeee'zeeeeu'zeeeeu'zeeeeu* . . . (higher-pitched and buzzier than scold of Prevost's Ground-Sparrow). Mex. to Costa Rica.

COMMON CHLOROSPINGUS
YELLOW-EYED JUNCO
male
SPOTTED TOWHEE
female
PREVOST'S GROUND-SPARROW
Eastern Honduras
Guatemala and El Salvador
WHITE-EARED GROUND-SPARROW

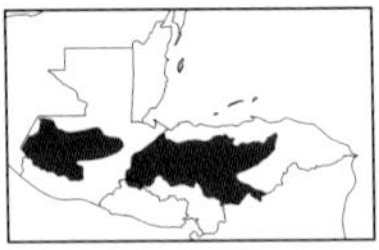

CHESTNUT-CAPPED BRUSHFINCH *Arremon brunneinucha*

7 in. (18 cm). Crown and nape chestnut, but **white throat is striking**, bordered below with black collar. Common in NCA; 4,270 to 10,170 ft. (1,300–3,100 m). Found in dense understory of pine-oak forest and cloud forest. Often stays hidden in dark tangles. Forages on or near ground. Song is fairly slow, high-pitched series of sharp whistles: *tseeee-tseeu-pseee-tzzzeeee*; call is a sharp *tseeeep*. Mex. to Peru.

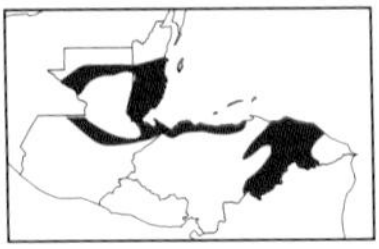

ORANGE-BILLED SPARROW *Arremon aurantiirostris*

6 in. (15 cm). **Distinctive black-and-white facial pattern**; also, **bright orange bill** (no other similar species shares this mark); shows yellow at bend of wing. Uncommon to fairly common on Caribbean Slope; to 2,950 ft. (900 m). Found in dense rainforest understory, often stays hidden in dark tangles. Forages on or near ground. Song is extremely high-pitched series of sharp whistles lasting about 2 sec.; call is a smacking *tsiit!* Mex. to Ecuador.

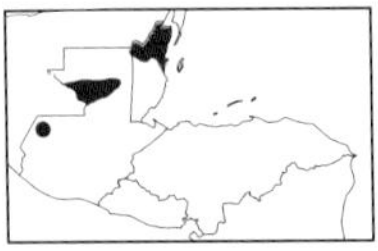

OLIVE SPARROW *Arremonops rufivirgatus*

6 in. (15 cm). **Dark brown eye line and lateral crown stripes**; **upperparts grayish olive**; buffy undertail coverts. Very similar to Green-backed Sparrow (sympatric in n. Belize); note differences in song, dark brown head stripes (not black). Fairly common in n. Belize; rare in n. Guatemala; to 3,280 ft. (1,000 m). Found in semiarid habitats (like savannas and tall grasslands and scrub); also at forest edge. Song is an accelerating series (bouncing ball–like), *peep!-seerip-seerip-seerip-seerip-seerip'seerip-see'rip'see'rip'see'tu'tu'tu'tu'tu'tu'tutututututu*. U.S. (TX) to Costa Rica.

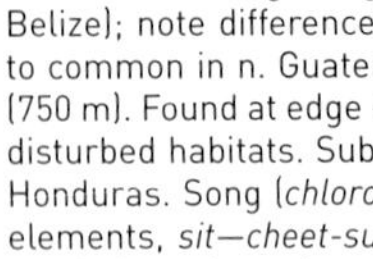

GREEN-BACKED SPARROW *Arremonops chloronotus*

6 in. (15 cm). [*A.c. chloronotus*; n. Guatemala, Belize, and nw. Honduras] **Black eye line and lateral crown stripes**; **upperparts olive-green**; **buffy-olive undertail coverts**. [*A.c. twomeyi*, not illustrated; Aguán and Agalta Valleys in Honduras] Paler (grayish white) on head; buff on chest (vs. gray on *chloronotus*); and brighter green upperparts. Very similar to Olive Sparrow (sympatric in n. Belize); note differences in song, black head stripes (not dark brown). Fairly common to common in n. Guatemala and Belize; uncommon and local in Honduras; to 2,460 ft. (750 m). Found at edge of semideciduous forest, in savanna, and thorn forest; also some disturbed habitats. Subspecies *twomeyi* is found locally in arid thorn forest of n. and e. Honduras. Song (*chloronotus*) is of even pace (not accelerating) with well-spaced song elements, *sit—cheet-sueew-sueew-sueew-sueew-sueew* or a slightly faster *sueet!-wip-seet!-chew-chew-chew-chew-chew-chew-chew-chew-chew-chew-chew*. Song (*twomeyi*) is a longer series overall and slightly accelerating, *pseee—suet-suet-suet-suet-tip'tip'tip'tip'tip'tip'tip'tip*; call is a soft, high-pitched *tit* or *tip*. Endemic to region.

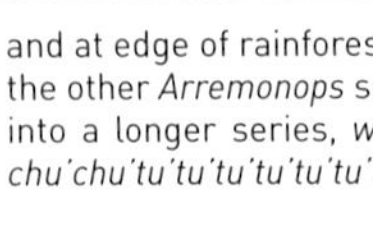

BLACK-STRIPED SPARROW *Arremonops conirostris*

6 in. (15 cm). Very similar to Green-backed Sparrow (not normally sympatric but both species have local populations in n. Honduras); note grayer face with contrasting white throat and differences in song. Rare in nw. Honduras but fairly common in ne. Honduras; to 1,970 ft. (600 m). Found in dense tangles and at edge of rainforest and taller disturbed habitats (prefers more humid habitat than the other *Arremonops* sparrows). Song begins with several rich calls before accelerating into a longer series, *wareep—weep!—warih—weep!—chu-chu-chu-chu-chu'chu'chu'chu'chu'chu'tu'tu'tu'tu'tu'tu'tu'tu-weep!* Honduras to Brazil.

CHESTNUT-CAPPED BRUSHFINCH

ORANGE-BILLED SPARROW

Arremonops. *This genus of sparrows (3 species) are very similar in appearance. They differ subtly in color of head stripes (brown vs. black) and color of upperparts (grayish olive to olive-green). Their ranges barely overlap, however, and vocalizations are quite distinctive. More studies are needed on taxonomy and species limits for the disjunct* twomeyi *(Green-backed) populations in interior Honduras.*

OLIVE SPARROW

BLACK-STRIPED SPARROW

GREEN-BACKED SPARROW

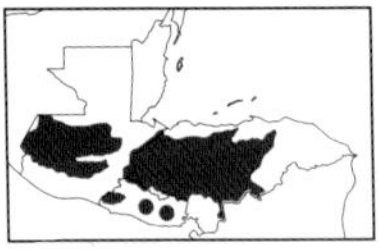

WHITE-NAPED BRUSHFINCH *Atlapetes albinucha*

7 in. (18 cm). **Distinctive black face and yellow throat**; thin white stripe through crown and nape. Fairly common in NCA; 2,950 to 10,170 ft. (900–3,100 m). Found in highland clearings and at forest edges. Often hidden in dense tangles. Forages near ground. Song is a series of high-pitched notes and trills: *tseee'up-tseee'ew-ti'ti'ti'ti'ti'ti'ti . . .* ; also a single *tseee'ew*. NCA population is part of the *gutteralis* group, known as Yellow-throated Brushfinch, found from Mex. to Colombia.

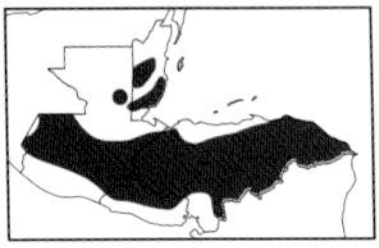

RUSTY SPARROW *Aimophila rufescens*

7 in. (18 cm). A large, long-tailed sparrow with a **chestnut lateral crown stripe, whitish eyebrows, and thin black submalar stripe**. Fairly common in NCA; to 8,530 ft. (2,600 m) but rare below 1,000 ft. (300 m). Found within arid to semiarid scrub, thorn forest, or at edge of pine savanna or pine-oak forest and even rainforest (on Caribbean Slope). Forages at low to midlevels. Song is a rich, liquid *cheet-cheet-swing-you!* or *sweet-sweet-to'you!*; also an agitated, sputtering scold, *seeeee!-peu'peu'peu'peu'peu'peu'peu . . .* Mex. to Costa Rica.

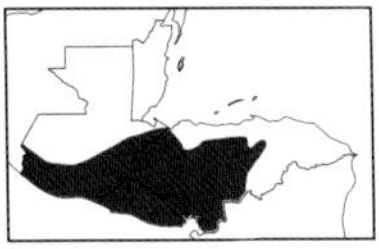

STRIPE-HEADED SPARROW *Peucaea ruficauda*

7 in. (18 cm). **Black face with broad white supercilium and black lateral crown stripes**. Uncommon to fairly common on Pacific Slope (locally in interior dry valleys of Caribbean Slope); to 4,590 ft. (1,400 m). Found in a variety of disturbed habitats. Forages near ground, often in family groups. Song is a varied scratchy warble lasting several seconds; also a rapid *tip-tip-tip-tip-tip-tip-tip-ti'ti'ti'ti'ti'ti-tip-tip-tip . . .* ; call is a soft, high-pitched *seeet!* Mex. to Costa Rica.

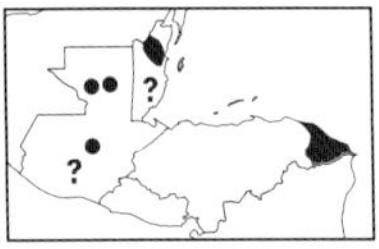

BOTTERI'S SPARROW *Peucaea botterii*

5.5 in. (14 cm). A dull grayish brown sparrow with a **long tail and heavy bill**. **Heavy dark streaking on upperparts**; note **weak postocular stripe.** Fairly common in Belize and e. Honduras; rare in Guatemala; to 4,920 ft. (1,500 m). Found in clearings and open grasslands within pine savanna and pine-oak forest. Forages on or near ground. Song consists of several high-pitched thin elements ending in an accelerating trill: *tseet-tseet-pwi'i'i'i't-pweet-pweet-teu'teu'tue'tue'tuetuetuetue*. U.S. to Costa Rica.

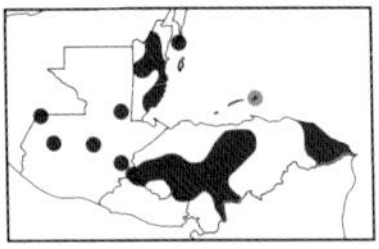

CHIPPING SPARROW *Spizella passerina*

5 in. (13 cm). Breeding adult has **bright chestnut crown, broad white supercilium, and dark eye line**; also note 2 white wing bars and **grayish rump**. Nonbreeding adult has buffy face and a finely streaked brown crown. Differs from very rare Clay-colored Sparrow by weak malar pattern, dark lores, and gray rump. Fairly common resident in Belize and Honduras, uncommon and local in Guatemala and El Salvador; also very rare winter visitor away from breeding sites; to 8,200 ft. (2,500 m). Breeds in pine savanna. Forages at all levels. Sings at mid- to upper levels in forest. Song is a dry mechanical trill; call is a thin *tsit*. Canada to Nicaragua.

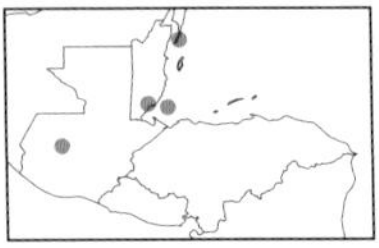

CLAY-COLORED SPARROW *Spizella pallida*

5 in. (13 cm). Very similar to nonbreeding Chipping Sparrow, but has pale lores, stronger malar pattern, and buff rump. Vagrant winter visitor (Sept.–Mar.); to 3,940 ft. (1,200 m). Found in disturbed habitats such as open second-growth scrub; also in grassland. Forages on or near ground. Call is similar to Chipping Sparrow. Canada (breeding) to Mex. (winter).

WHITE-NAPED BRUSHFINCH
RUSTY SPARROW
BOTTERI'S SPARROW
STRIPE-HEADED SPARROW
CLAY-COLORED SPARROW
breeding
nonbreeding
CHIPPING SPARROW
comparison of rump patterns of Chipping (left) and Clay-colored

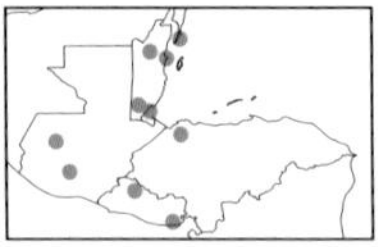

LARK SPARROW *Chondestes grammacus*

6.5 in. (17 cm). **Unique face pattern.** Rufous color on face is duller brown on immature. Very rare winter visitor (Sept.–Feb.); to 3,940 ft. (1,200 m). Found in grasslands, fallow fields, around scrubby second growth, and on beaches. Call is a hard, high-pitched *tsit!* Canada (breeding) to NCA (winter).

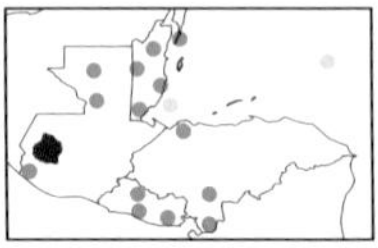

SAVANNAH SPARROW *Passerculus sandwichensis*

5.5 in. (14 cm). Resident and winter visitor. [*P.s. wetmorei*; w. Guatemala] Upperparts brownish gray and heavily streaked (note pale median crown stripe); **broad whitish supercilium is washed yellow**; underparts white with **crisp dark streaks on chest and sides**; short tail with **white outer tail feathers** (visible in flight); legs and bill pink. Rare and local in highlands of w. Guatemala; 4,920 to 10,990 ft. (1,500–3,350 m). Migratory races are similar to *wetmorei* but lack white outer tail feathers. Rare transient and winter visitor throughout including Swan Is. (late Oct.–early May); to 1,970 ft. (600 m). Resident in highland pine savanna with large bunch grass. Winter visitors found in grasslands, fallow fields, and around scrubby second growth. Forages on or near ground. When flushed, stays low and settles quickly. Call is a soft, high-pitched *seeet!*; song of *wetmorei* is undescribed. U.S. to Guatemala.

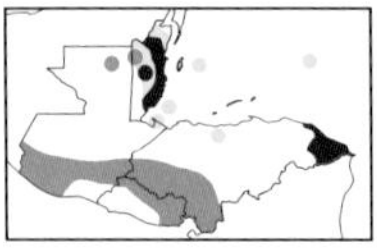

GRASSHOPPER SPARROW *Ammodramus savannarum*

5 in. (13 cm). A delicate sparrow with a **short, spiky tail and relatively flat head**. Face has **ochre supraloral spot**, thin white eye-ring, and a thin white median crown stripe; **nape is grayish with thin purplish red streaks**; chest is buffy and mostly unmarked. Fairly common resident in Belize and e. Honduras; uncommon winter visitor in NCA (mid-Oct.–mid-May); to 7,050 ft. (2,150 m). Forages on or near ground. A secretive sparrow preferring to scurry like a mouse rather than fly. When flushed, appears to be a weak flier, with its spiky tail held down; flies low and drops quickly to cover. Resident in pine savanna grasslands. Winter visitors occupy open fallow fields, and grassy edges to agricultural fields. Sometimes forms small or dispersed flocks. Song is an insectlike trill, beginning with a short liquid warble; call is a thin, buzzy *tzzeeet*. Canada to Panama.

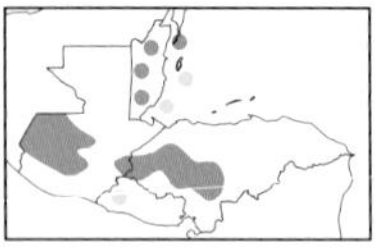

LINCOLN'S SPARROW *Melospiza lincolnii*

5.5 in. (14 cm). A fairly chunky, long-tailed sparrow. Note **grayish head**, reddish brown eye line, with **creamy buff malar stripe**; **chest and flanks washed buff** with **crisp dark streaking**. Compare with juvenile Rufous-collared Sparrow, but note less prominent crest and buffy malar stripe. Uncommon winter visitor in interior highlands, rare on Caribbean Slope (mid-Oct.–Apr.); to 8,530 ft. (2,600 m). Found in a variety of scrubby habitat. Forages at low levels; tends to stay hidden. Call is a sharp *tsip*. U.S. (breeding) to Honduras (winter).

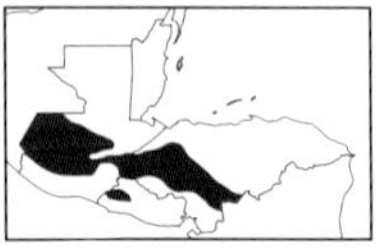

RUFOUS-COLLARED SPARROW *Zonotrichia capensis*

5.5 in. (14 cm). Note **broad rufous collar** and **chest has black smudges edged rufous**. Juvenile similar, but has crisp streaking on chest; lacks obvious rufous collar. Juvenile similar to Lincoln's Sparrow, but note more prominent crest and lack of buffy malar stripe. Fairly common in interior highlands; 2,950 to 10,990 ft. (900–3,350 m); uncommon and local below 4,950 ft. (1,500 m). Found in open habitats; also in cities and town. Forages at low to midlevels. Song is a pleasant, short series of clear whistles, *weee-weeuu-teeeuuu* (repeated every few seconds) or a *weee'pit-peeeuuu-peeet!*; call is a melancholy *tseeu*. Mex. and Hispaniola to Argentina.

LARK SPARROW
SAVANNAH SPARROW
GRASSHOPPER SPARROW
LINCOLN'S SPARROW
RUFOUS-COLLARED SPARROW
adult
juvenile

CARDINAL TANAGERS I (*Piranga* Genus)

CARDINALIDAE (Order: Passeriformes). A diverse group of insect-, fruit-, and seed-eating passerines, most with conical-shaped bills (exceptions are the *Piranga* "tanagers") and colorful plumages. Half of the group are migrants that breed in temperate N. America and spend the winter in the tropics. Plumages differ between the sexes (excepting 2 tropical grosbeaks). **25 species (11 genera)**

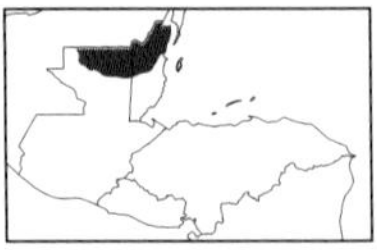

ROSE-THROATED TANAGER *Piranga roseogularis*

6.5 in. (17 cm). Adult male has **rosy red throat, crown, wings, and undertail coverts**; note **broken eye-ring**. Female similarly patterned, but red areas **replaced with yellow**. Rare to uncommon in n. Guatemala and n. Belize; to 820 ft. (250 m). Found at edge of semideciduous forest, where it generally forages at mid- to upper canopy levels. Song is a series of 4 to 6 sweet, clear whistles, *tseat-tsee'reu-wear'see'eh*; calls include a scolding, scratchy *Eh'eh'ehhhh!* Endemic to region.

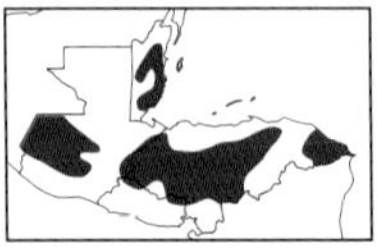

HEPATIC TANAGER *Piranga flava*

8 in. (20 cm). Distinguish from similar Summer Tanager (both sexes) by **grayish cheeks** and **grayish bill**. Juvenile similar to female, but has streaked back and crown. Fairly common in central highlands and in lowlands of Belize and e. Honduras; to 8,200 ft. (2,500 m). Found in pine savanna and pine-oak forest. Forages at mid- to upper levels. Song is a slightly burry series, sluggish, of evenly paced clear whistles generally including 5 to 6 distinctive elements; frequently call is a rich, hollow *chirt!* (often repeated in a longer series). U.S. to Argentina.

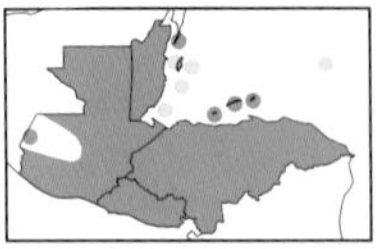

SUMMER TANAGER *Piranga rubra*

8 in. (20 cm). Both sexes have **yellowish bills**. Immature male similar to female, and may have large patches of red on head and back. Told from Hepatic Tanager by colorful cheeks and yellowish bills. Common winter visitor (mid Sept.–mid-May); to 8,530 ft. (2,600 m). Found in a variety of habitat types, including disturbed habitat (coffee plantations, city parks) up to pine-oak forest in highlands. Forages mostly at midlevels and often at edge. Call is a rapid *pi'tea'tuck!* U.S. (breeding) to Brazil (winter).

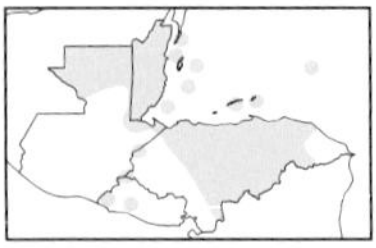

SCARLET TANAGER *Piranga olivacea*

7 in. (18 cm). In nonbreeding season (Aug.–Feb.), sexes similar: **greenish yellow overall** with **wings and tail darker** (black in male). Bill smaller than Summer Tanager's and pinkish to horn color with dark culmen. From Mar. to July, **male bright red with black wings**. Fairly common transient on Caribbean Slope, including Bay Is. (mid-Sept.–late Nov.; late Mar.–mid-May); rare on Pacific Slope (Oct. and Apr.). Found in taller semideciduous forest, pine-oak forest; also coastal scrub or even thorn forest. Forages at mid- to upper levels, often at edge. Call is an emphatic 2-part *chick!-pang* or a rich, liquid *tchip!* U.S. and Canada (breeding) to Bolivia (winter).

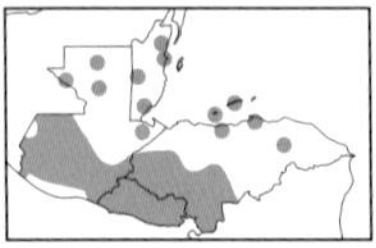

WESTERN TANAGER *Piranga ludoviciana*

7 in. (18 cm). On male note **bright yellow underparts, black back and wing**, and **orange-red wash on face** (brighter in breeding males, Mar.–May); bill is pinkish with darker maxilla. Female dull grayish yellow (brighter yellow below) with 2 yellowish gray wing bars. Common winter visitor to Pacific Slope (late Sept.–early May); to 10,010 ft. (3,050 m). Rare in Caribbean lowlands. Found in a variety of habitats. Forages at mid- to upper levels at edge. Call (similar to other tanagers, but with different ending) is a rapid, sputtering *pit'tea'weat!* U.S. and Canada (breeding) to Panama (winter).

ROSE-THROATED
TANAGER
male
female
HEPATIC
TANAGER
male
female
male
SUMMER
TANAGER
female
breeding
male (spring)
breeding male
(spring)
SCARLET
TANAGER
nonbreeding
male
WESTERN
TANAGER
nonbreeding male
(female and immature similar)
female

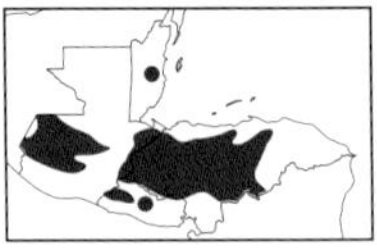

FLAME-COLORED TANAGER *Piranga bidentata*

8 in. (20 cm). Adult male **overall orange-red** with **dark streaking on back**; 2 white wing bars; note white-tipped tertials; strong bill is silver-gray. Female and immature similarly patterned, but **yellow overall**. Uncommon to fairly common; from 3,280 to 9,020 ft. (1,000–2,750 m). Found in pine-oak forest and cloud forest. Song is a burry warble, notes evenly spaced: *three-weep—cheerie—cheer-wee'wee*; call is a rapid, sputtering *pit'tea'wait!* Mex. to Panama.

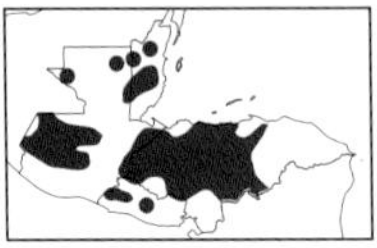

WHITE-WINGED TANAGER *Piranga leucoptera*

5.5 in. (14 cm). Male **deep cherry red; small black mask**; black wings with **2 bright white wing bars**. Female and immature similarly patterned, but **yellow overall**. Uncommon in NCA; 1,000 to 6,560 ft. (300–2,000 m). Found at edge in a variety of habitat types, including semideciduous forest, pine-oak forest, and coffee plantations; occasionally in cloud forest. Forages at midlevels. Song is a series of 2 to 3 high-pitched clear whistles, *pit-tseu-weet* or *pit-weet!* Mex. to Brazil.

RED-CROWNED ANT-TANAGER *Habia rubica*

7.5 in. (19 cm). **Adult male reddish brown overall**; bright red on throat and on crown stripe (difficult to see). **Female yellowish brown overall with lighter yellow throat.** Heavy black bill. Very similar to Red-throated Ant-Tanager, but lacks dark lores and face, has less contrasting throat, and slightly smaller bill; male has dark borders to the red crown stripe; also note higher-pitched calls and elevation. Uncommon to fairly common in NCA; on Caribbean Slope, to 4,920 ft. (1,500 m); on Pacific Slope, restricted to higher elevations, from 2,130 to 4,920 ft. (650–1,500 m). Found in understory of semideciduous forest and rainforest. Forages at low to midlevels, often in small family groups; also found at army ant swarms. On Pacific Slope, little overlap with Red-throated, which occurs at lower elevations; more range overlap on Caribbean Slope. Song is a slightly mournful, slurred *chuuer-chuuer-chuuer-chuuer-chuuer*; call is a complaining, thin *chit'chit'chit'chit'chit'chit'chit.* Mex. to Argentina.

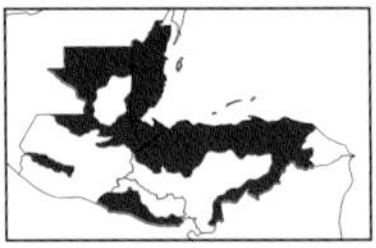

RED-THROATED ANT-TANAGER *Habia fuscicauda*

8 in. (20 cm). Adult male very similar to Red-crowned Ant-Tanager, but larger overall, **with dark lores and face, brighter red throat**, and heavier bill; also note differences in elevation and calls. Female yellowish brown overall, but shows **bright yellow throat that contrasts with darker face and underparts**. Fairly common in NCA; to 4,270 ft. (1,300 m), but on Pacific Slope usually below 1,960 ft. (600 m). Found in understory of semideciduous forest and rainforest, also coffee plantations. Forages at low to midlevels, often in small family groups; also found at army ant swarms. Song is a sweet, rising *tee'tu-tee'tu-Tee'tu-tee'tu-tee*; call is a scratchy *chueer-chueer-chet'chet'chet'Chet'Chet'chet'chet* (quality similar to that of shredding paper). Mex. to Colombia.

CARMIOL'S TANAGER *Chlorothraupis carmioli*

6.5 in. (17 cm). **Dusky olive overall**; also note **stout black bill**. Common in e. Honduras; to 3,280 ft. (1,000 m). Similar to female Hepatic Tanager (p. 382), but has olive cheeks (rather than dusky) and different habits, habitat, and vocalizations. Found in interior of rainforest; forages at mid- to canopy levels; often in mixed-species flocks and in small groups of 3 to 10 individuals. Groups can be quite vocal (often first detected by voice). Calls include nasal, scratchy, distorted chatters, *Peeeuu!-Peeeuu!-Peeeuu!*; song is a long series of sweet, clear, melodic whistles and buzzes (accelerating and rising in volume at end). Honduras to Colombia.

FLAME-COLORED TANAGER
male
female/ immature
WHITE-WINGED TANAGER
male
female/ immature
RED-CROWNED ANT-TANAGER
male
female/ immature
RED-THROATED ANT-TANAGER
male
female/ immature
CARMIOL'S TANAGER

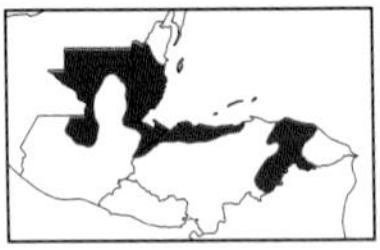

BLACK-FACED GROSBEAK *Caryothraustes poliogaster*

7 in. (18 cm). **Overall mustard yellow with a black mask**; grayish below; large conical bill with a silver base. Uncommon to fairly common on Caribbean Slope; to 3,940 ft. (1,200 m). Found in rainforest and along edges of pine savanna. Forages at mid- to upper levels. Loud and active, generally travels in small groups of 3 to 5 individuals. Call is a series of buzzy, ringing, and electric elements: *tzeeet!-pwee!-pwee!* or *tzeeet!-pee'pee-pee'pee!*; also just a single *tzeeet!* Mex. to Panama.

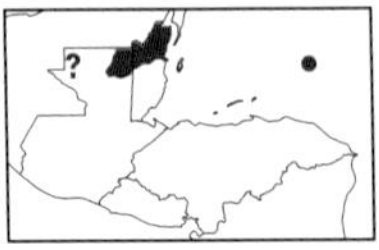

NORTHERN CARDINAL *Cardinalis cardinalis*

8.5 in. (22 cm). **Male distinctive.** Females olive brown overall with red in wings, tail, and crest. Rare to uncommon in n. Guatemala and n. Belize; also Swan Is. (Honduras), where it has bred; to 820 ft. (250 m). Found in pine savanna and second-growth scrub. Forages at low to midlevels in understory. Often in pairs. Song is a repeated or trilled series of sweet whistles (second part may be accelerated): *tue-tue-tue-tue-tue-tue-tue-tea'tea'tea'tea'tea'tea'tea'tea'tea'tea* or *twee-twee-twee-tweu-tweu-tweu-tweu-tweu-tweu*; call is a sharp, metallic *teep*. U.S. to NCA.

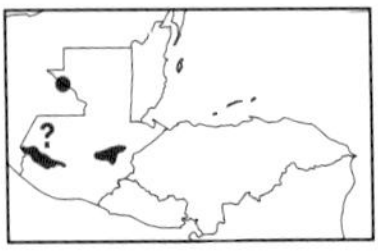

YELLOW GROSBEAK *Pheucticus chrysopeplus*

9 in. (23 cm). Male **golden yellow overall**; 2 white wing bars; also white patch at base of primaries and broadly white-tipped tertials. Female similarly plumaged but yellow (less orange) with streaked back and crown. Both sexes have **heavy, large conical silver-gray bill**. Uncommon in dry valleys of Guatemala; from 980 to 6,070 ft. (300–1,850 m). Song is a short, sweet warble lasting 2.5 sec., *where'wee-here'weat-ta'weee-here'weat-ta'weee*; call is a loud, explosive *Peeek!* Mexico to NCA.

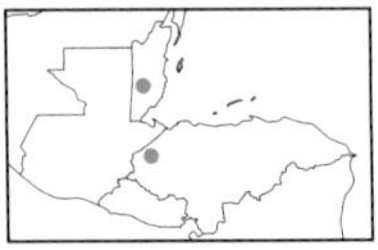

BLACK-HEADED GROSBEAK *Pheucticus melanocephalus*

8.5 in. (22 cm). Adult male distinctive. Immature male lacks black head, head pattern similar to female; however, **chest unstreaked**. Adult female has broad white supercilium; buffy orange wash below with **fine, crisp streaking on sides of chest**. Bill is always **bicolored with dark maxilla**. Female similar to Rose-breasted Grosbeak, but note finer, crisp streaking on sides of chest, bicolored bill (not pinkish), and yellowish underwings (immature male Rose-breasted underwing is pinkish red). Very rare winter visitor to NCA; to 3,940 ft. (1,200 m). Found at edge of pine-oak forest and semideciduous forest. Forages at all levels. Call similar to call of Rose-breasted Grosbeak, but slightly thinner. Canada (breeding) to Mex. (winter).

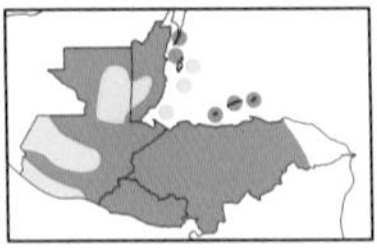

ROSE-BREASTED GROSBEAK *Pheucticus ludovicianus*

8 in. (20 cm). Adult male has striking black-and-white plumage and **cherry red smudge on chest**. Female and immature lack red smudge, have **dark, coarse streaking on chest** (some immature males with buffy wash); broad white supercilium; in flight, female shows yellow underwing. On both sexes, note **large pinkish white conical bill**. Compare female with female Black-headed Grosbeak, but note heavier, coarse streaking on chest and less buffy orange wash; also, bill on Rose-breasted is pinkish (not bicolored). Immature male is more difficult to separate from female Black-headed, but note pinkish bill and pinkish red underwing. Common winter visitor to NCA; to 9,350 ft. (2,850 m). Found in a variety of woodland habitats, including second-growth scrub and coffee plantations, semideciduous forest, rainforest, and pine-oak forest; also in city parks and gardens. Forages at all levels, on seeds and berries; often in groups of 5 to 10 individuals. Call is a loud, sharp *Peeek!* (like sneakers across a gym floor). Canada (breeding) to Peru (winter).

BLACK-FACED GROSBEAK
NORTHERN CARDINAL
male
female
YELLOW GROSBEAK
male
female
male
BLACK-HEADED GROSBEAK
female/ immature
grosbeaks in flight, (top) immature male Black-headed, (middle) female Rose-breasted, (bottom) immature male Rose-breasted
breeding male
immature male (fall)
ROSE-BREASTED GROSBEAK
female

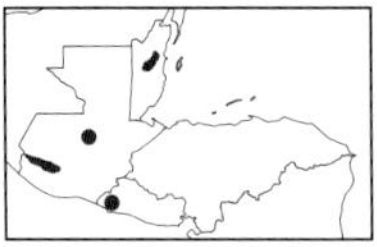

BLUE SEEDEATER *Amaurospiza concolor*

5 in. (13 cm). Adult male **dark slaty blue** (dark gray in poor light). Female tawny-brown. **Conical bill on both sexes silver-gray.** Female very similar to female Blue Bunting, but note difference in bill shape. Rare and local in NCA; to 6,890 ft. (2,100 m) but generally above 2,300 ft. (700 m). Found in taller semideciduous or broadleaf forest within understory of native bamboo thickets. Song is a high-pitched whistled *tseep!-peet-we-peet-ta'dee!* (dropping off in volume at the end); call is a distinctive, hard *pchit!* or *pwit*. Mex. to Ecuador.

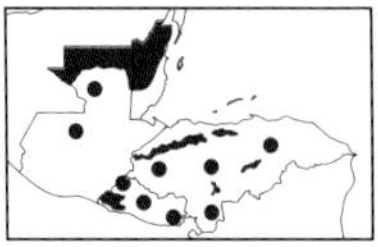

BLUE BUNTING *Cyanocompsa parellina*

5.5 in. (14 cm). Adult male dark blue with **iridescent turquoise blue on crown, nape, malar, and shoulder**. Female and juvenile male **tawny-brown overall**. Both sexes have medium-sized conical bill, larger than bill of Blue Seedeater. Uncommon on Pacific Slope; fairly common on Caribbean Slope; to 5,910 ft. (1,800 m). Found in understory of semideciduous forest, in thorn forest, and at edge of pine-oak forest. Song is short, sweet warble that falls off in volume toward the end, *Sa'weet—teee-teeu'tu'tu'tee'tee'tee'tee'tee*, or a shorter *Sa'weet—teee-tee'teeu*; call is a sharp, rich *tsip!* Mex. to Nicaragua.

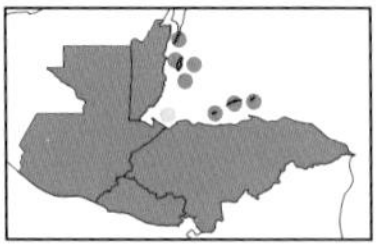

INDIGO BUNTING *Passerina cyanea*

5.5 in. (14 cm). Nonbreeding male and female (mid-Sept.–Mar.) **yellowish brown overall** (paler below with **faint streaks on chest**) and show **2 faint wing bars**; wings and tail often tinged blue. Nonbreeding male may have **varying amounts of indigo blue on body** (head, back, and chest). Breeding-plumaged male (Mar.–May) **bright indigo blue** with darker wings. Small, conical bill is silver-gray with a darker culmen (pale yellowish base in female and immature male). Fairly common in NCA as winter visitor (mid-Sept.–mid-May); to 7,550 ft. (2,300 m) but generally below 4,270 ft. (1,300 m). Found in a variety of open and disturbed habitats, including scrub, coffee plantations, hedgerows, brushy fields, and thorn forest. Often in flocks of up to 100 individuals. Call is a buzzy *zzzzrt*. U.S. (breeding) to Panama (winter).

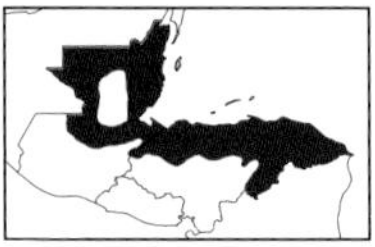

BLUE-BLACK GROSBEAK *Cyanocompsa cyanoides*

7 in. (18 cm). Adult male **dark blue overall**. Female and juvenile male **chocolate brown**. Both sexes have heavy dark conical bill. Uncommon to fairly common on Caribbean Slope; to 3,610 ft. (1,100 m). Found in shady understory of rainforest and taller semideciduous forest. Generally solitary or in pairs. Song is a rich, sweet warble lasting roughly 3 sec. that ends in a confusing garble, *Sweet-Seet-Seeee-Seeur-Seeur-sa'wee-pa'weet'ta'weet'ta'weet*; call is sharp *Peeak!* Mex. to Brazil.

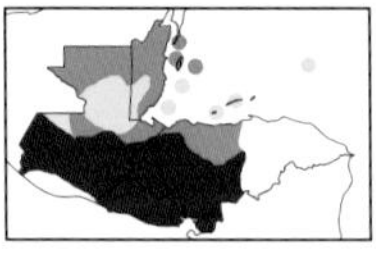

BLUE GROSBEAK *Passerina caerulea*

6.5 in. (17 cm). Adult male is blue overall with **chestnut shoulder and tawny wing bar**. Adult female and juvenile male tawny-brown overall (paler below) with **a light wing bar**. **Large, heavy bill is silver-gray** with black border at base. Uncommon in NCA; resident on Pacific Slope and interior; fairly common on Caribbean Slope as transient and winter visitor, including Bay Is. (early Sept.–late Apr.); to 7,550 ft. (2,300 m) but generally below 4,590 ft. (1,400 m). Found in pine savanna, thorn forest, second-growth scrub, and along hedgerows. Often perches in open. Song is a quickly delivered burry warble lasting roughly 2 sec. (shorter and burrier than song of Gray-crowned Yellowthroat [p. 342]); call is a sharp metallic *peek!* U.S. to Costa Rica.

Blue-black Grosbeak
Blue Grosbeak
Blue Bunting
Indigo Bunting
Blue Seedeater
male
BLUE SEEDEATER
female
male
BLUE BUNTING
female
molting male
female/immature
breeding male (spring)
INDIGO BUNTING
BLUE-BLACK GROSBEAK
male
female
BLUE GROSBEAK
male
female/immature

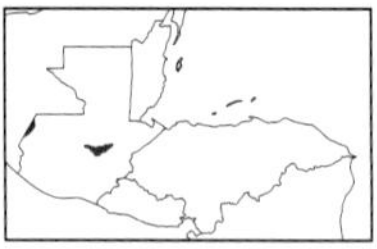

VARIED BUNTING *Passerina versicolor*

5.5 in. (14 cm). Adult male dark blue overall with **burgundy-brown back and chest, reddish purple nape and crown, and black face**; note 2 faint wing bars. Female yellowish brown overall, slightly paler below (similar to Indigo Bunting female [p. 388], but lacks streaks on chest). On both sexes, small, conical bill has a curved culmen. Uncommon in Motagua Valley (Guatemala); from 820 to 1,970 ft. (250–600 m). Found in understory of thorn forest. Song is a slightly burry, pleasant warble of sweet, buzzy whistles lasting roughly 2.5 sec., rising in volume toward the middle and jumbled at the end; call a liquid *plik!* U.S. to Guatemala.

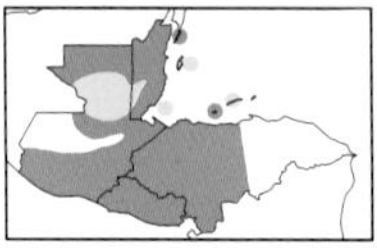

PAINTED BUNTING *Passerina ciris*

5.5 in. (14 cm). **Adult male distinctive.** Adult female **olive above and paler yellow below**. Immature male similar to female, but overall brighter. On both sexes, small, conical bill has a slightly curved culmen. Fairly common winter visitor to NCA (late Sept.–late Apr.); to 6,070 ft. (1,850 m) but generally below 4,270 ft. (1,300 m). Found in a variety of open and disturbed habitats, including scrub, plantations, hedgerows, brushy fields, and edges of forest. Call is a sharp, liquid *wheet!* or *peet!* U.S. (breeding) to Panama (winter).

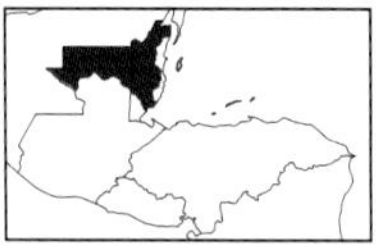

GRAY-THROATED CHAT *Granatellus sallaei*

5 in. (13 cm). Adult male has bluish gray upperparts and face; **broad white postocular stripe**; **chest and belly cherry red**. Adult female similarly patterned, but postocular stripe, throat, chest, and undertail coverts tawny-buff. Fairly common in Belize and n. Guatemala; to 4,920 ft. (1,500 m). Found in understory of semiarid brush, at edge of semideciduous forest, and in thorn forest. Secretive, can be difficult to see. Song is series (approximately 2 sec.) of sweet whistles, *sawhee'three'tawhee'here!*; call is *vit*. Mex. to NCA.

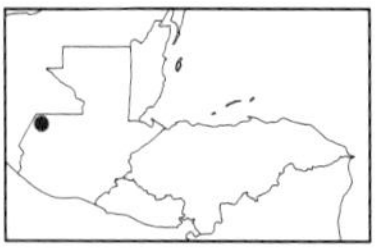

RED-BREASTED CHAT *Granatellus venustus*

6 in. (15 cm). Male has **broad white postocular stripe**, black face, **black collar**, white throat, and **cherry red chest and belly**. Female has face and underparts washed buff and lacks collar and red below. On both sexes, note **long tail with white outer tail feathers**. Rare and local in w. Guatemala; to 3,280 ft. (1,000 m). Found in semiarid brush; also at edge of pine savanna and pine-oak forest. Forages at low to midlevels, often with tail cocked and fanned. Secretive; seen singly or in pairs. Song is a variable sweet warble, *too'ta'weet-too'ta'weet-sweet'so'sweet-ta'weet'ta'weet'ta'weet*; call is a flat liquid *pweeet!* Mex. to Guatemala.

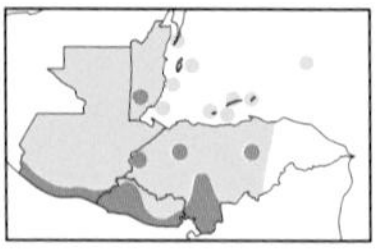

DICKCISSEL *Spiza americana*

6.5 in. (17 cm). Male has **broad white supercilium** and **chest washed with yellow**; **bold black "V" on throat**, and rufous shoulders. Female has less yellow wash on face and lacks black "V" on throat. Silver-gray bill is broad based and pointed. Common transient on Caribbean Slope, including Bay Is. (mid-Aug.–mid-Nov.; late Mar.–mid-May); uncommon winter visitor on Pacific Slope and locally elsewhere (late Aug.–mid-Apr.); to 4,920 ft. (1,500 m). Found in open and disturbed habitats, including scrub, brushy fields, and along hedgerows and in grain fields. Usually in flocks of up to 50 individuals; in migration may form huge flocks of thousands. Flight call is a distinctive, buzzy *dzzzzrt!* U.S. (breeding) to Guyana (winter).

male
female
VARIED BUNTING
male
PAINTED BUNTING
female
male
female
GRAY-THROATED CHAT
RED-BREASTED CHAT
male
female
male
DICKCISSEL
female

COLORFUL BLACKBIRDS

ICTERIDAE (Order: Passeriformes). Medium-sized passerines with relatively straight, pointed bills. Some are brightly patterned in orange and yellow (orioles), while others have darker plumage of glossy blue or black (grackles and cowbirds). Sexes are generally similar in tropical species, but different in temperate species. Males are often larger than females, which is obvious in grackles and oropendolas. Most icterids are omnivores, but blackbirds eat lots of grains, and orioles often feed at flowers. Cowbirds are brood parasites, laying eggs in nests of other species (frequently other icterids), which raise their young. **27 species (12 genera)**

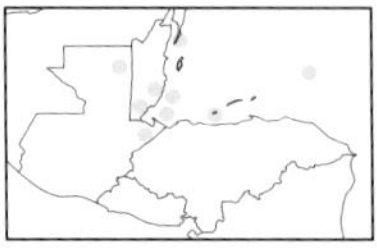

BOBOLINK *Dolichonyx oryzivorus*

6.5 in. (16 cm). Nonbreeding adult and female similar (Sept.–Nov.): overall **warm golden brown with heavily streaked upperparts, dark postocular stripe, and short spiky tail**. Breeding male (Apr.–June) quite distinctive in **black plumage and buffy yellow "pom pom" on head**. Rare transient to offshore Caribbean cayes and islands; occasional on mainland of Caribbean Slope (early Sept.–late Oct.; early Apr.–early June); to 660 ft. (200 m). Found in disturbed habitats, such as overgrown fields, along hedgerows, and in coastal scrub and savanna. Often perches on tops of tall grass stems. Generally in small groups of 3 to 10 individuals. Call is a raspy *chink*. U.S. and Canada (breeding) to Argentina (winter).

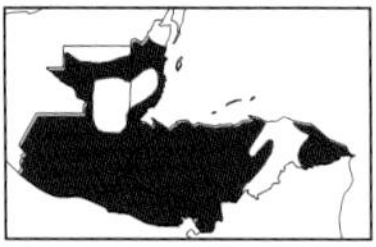

EASTERN MEADOWLARK *Sturnella magna*

9.5 in. (24 cm). **Bright yellow supercilium, throat, and underparts** with **large black "V" on chest**; short tail has 3 white outer tail feathers (obvious in flight). Uncommon to fairly common in NCA; to 10,170 ft. (3,100 m). Found in open country: grasslands and savanna, fallow fields, agricultural areas, and pastures. Often sits on exposed perch, such as a fencepost. Song is a quick *tzeeet'zeezee'churdle'dee!* (the first part buzzy, the second part a liquid warble) or a more pleasant, less harsh *tseee'teee'diddle'dee*; calls include a buzzy *tzeeeet* followed by a sputter, *tee'pi'pi'pi'pi'pi'pi'pi'pi'pi*. Canada to Brazil.

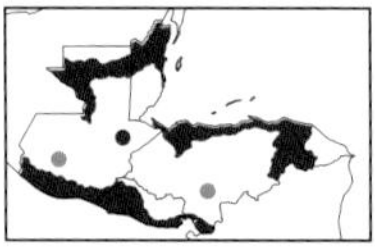

RED-WINGED BLACKBIRD *Agelaius phoeniceus*

Male: 9 in. (23 cm). Female: 7 in. (18 cm). Adult male **black** with **broad red epaulets on shoulders** bordered below in yellow. Female and immature brownish overall and **heavily streaked, with broad pale supercilium**; face occasionally washed with yellow or pink. Fairly common but local in NCA; to 2,790 ft. (850 m). Breeds in freshwater marshes along coast or inland, but foraging flocks may be found in agricultural areas. Flocks (often of just one sex) may include hundreds of individuals. Song is a 2-part liquid, ringing *turr'reeeeeeeeee*; calls include a tinny *kip!* and a lower, mournful *wheeeeeer!* U.S. and Canada to Costa Rica.

YELLOW-HEADED BLACKBIRD *Xanthocephalus xanthocephalus*

Male: 9.5 in. (24 cm). Female: 8 in. (20 cm). On adult male, **bright yellow hood and chest** contrasts with otherwise black plumage; in flight, **white patch on primary coverts is obvious**. Female and immature blackish brown overall; yellowish supercilium, throat, and chest. Vagrant from N. America to Belize (Sept. and Oct.) and to s. Central America; recorded near sea level. Found in open country: grasslands and savannas, fallow fields, agricultural zones, and pastures. Forages on or near ground. Call is a harsh *kri'i'i'i'i't*. Canada (breeding) to Mex. (winter).

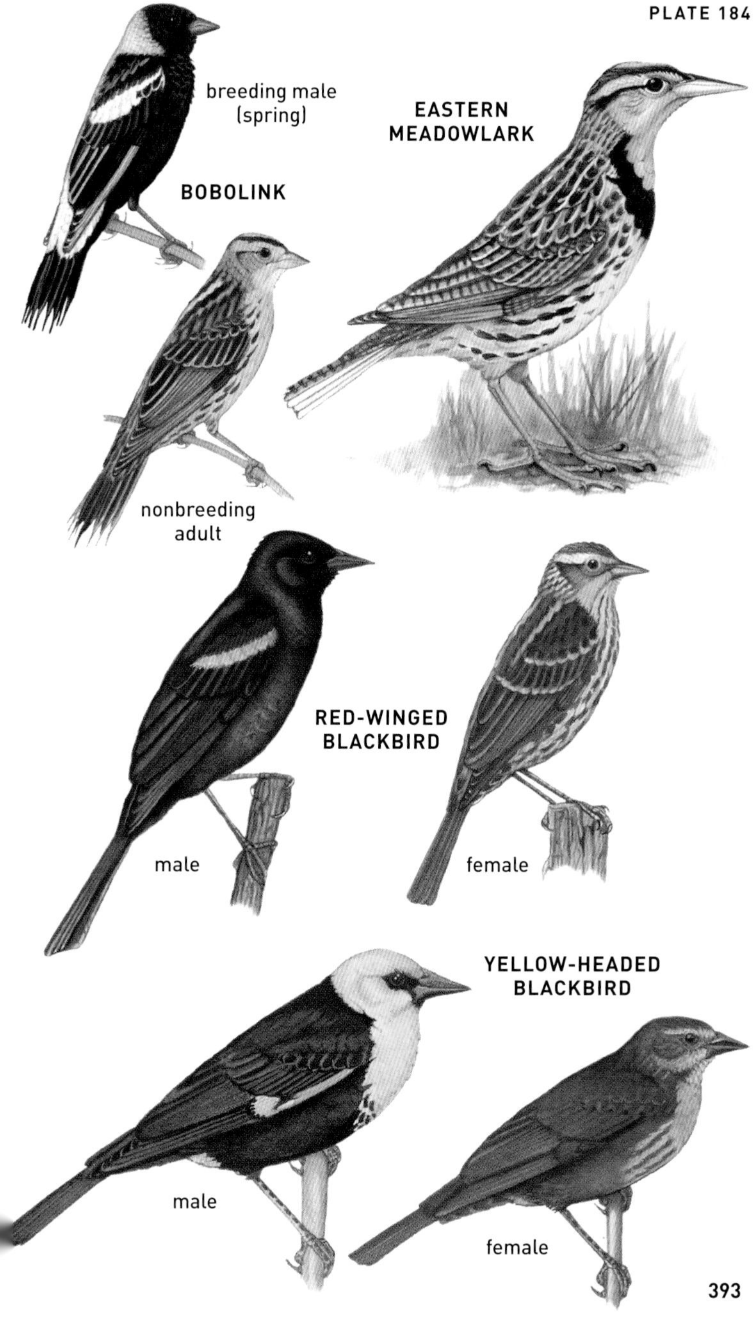
breeding male
(spring)
BOBOLINK
nonbreeding
adult
EASTERN
MEADOWLARK
RED-WINGED
BLACKBIRD
male
female
YELLOW-HEADED
BLACKBIRD
male
female

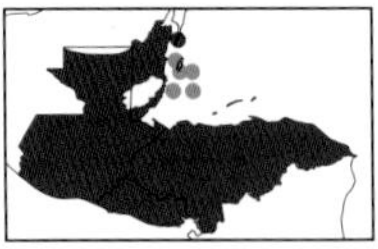

MELODIOUS BLACKBIRD *Dives dives*

10 in. (26 cm). **Glossy black plumage**; sleek looking and fairly long-tailed. Common in NCA; to 6,890 ft. (2,100 m). Found in a variety of open and disturbed habitats, including plantations, city parks and towns, and second-growth forest. Forages at all levels, sometimes on ground. Sings from an exposed perch, with pumping movements that appear almost like a dance. Loud song is ringing, slightly liquid *Wheeeee'Teeuu!* (often repeated into a longer series); calls include a sharp *Pit!* and a *Pit-tseeu!* Mex. to Costa Rica.

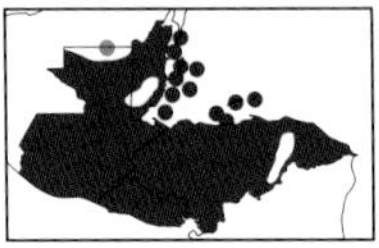

GREAT-TAILED GRACKLE *Quiscalus mexicanus*

Male: 18 in. (46 cm). Female: 12.5 in. (32 cm). Adult male has **purplish blue glossy plumage**, a flat crown, and a distinctive, **long, keeled tail**. Female and immature dirty brown overall, with paler supercilium and throat. On both adults, **eyes bright yellow** (dark on immatures). Common to abundant in NCA; to 7,550 ft. (2,300 m). Found in a variety of open and disturbed habitats almost always near human habitation. Generally in small groups of mixed males and females. Males often perch in open to call and display. Forages at low to midlevels. Gives a series of varied, electric whistles and grating screams. U.S. and Mex. to Peru.

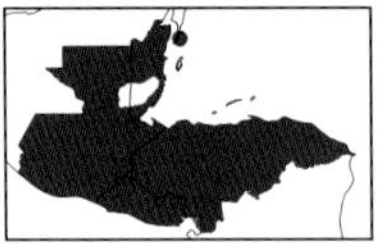

BRONZED COWBIRD *Molothrus aeneus*

Male: 8.5 in. (22 cm). Female: 7.5 in. (19 cm). Adult male has **glossy bluish black plumage**; male has neck ruff that expands during courtship displays. Female brown overall. Both sexes have **red eyes**. Juvenile dusky gray, has dark eyes and yellowish bill; often accompanied by foster parents, typically sparrows or orioles (cowbirds are strictly brood parasites). Fairly common in NCA; to 10,170 ft. (3,100 m). Found in open country, including savanna, fallow fields, agricultural zones, and pastures; also on lawns in city parks and towns or subdivisions. Male creates harem with 10 to 15 females. Courtship display includes "butterfly" flights, in which male hovers a few feet off the ground, above female. Song is a high-pitched, thinly whistled *t't't't't't'zzzzeu-tseeee'zzzzeuuu!*; call is a slightly descending *tew*. U.S. to Panama.

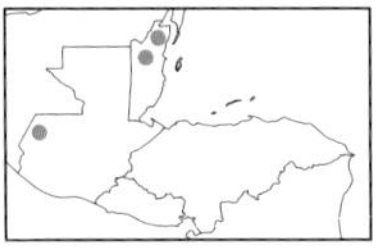

BROWN-HEADED COWBIRD *Molothrus ater*

Male: 8.5 in. (22 cm). Female: 6.5 in. (16 cm). Adult male has **chocolate brown head**; dark eyes. Female paler brown overall, but note **contrasting paler supercilium, malar stripe, and throat**. Bill **slightly conical and decurved**. Vagrant to NCA; to 2,460 ft. (750 m), but could show up at higher elevations. Found in open country, including savanna, fallow fields, agricultural zones, and pastures. Call is a high-pitched, liquid whistle, *tsseeeee'teeee!*; also a rattle, *tip'tip'tip'tip'tip'tip'tip'tip'tip*. Canada to Mex.

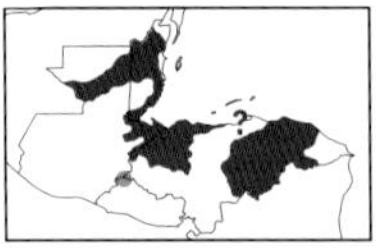

GIANT COWBIRD *Molothrus oryzivorus*

Male: 14 in. (36 cm). Female: 11 in. (28 cm). **A large, heavy-bodied blackbird.** Male has **glossy bluish black body**, long tail, and **reddish eyes**. Female browner overall. Characteristic head shape, with flat head and narrow face. Wings longer and more pointed than in other blackbirds, and flight pattern (with alternating flapping and gliding) is distinctive. Fairly common on Caribbean Slope; to 2,460 ft. (750 m). Found at edge of rainforest, taller semideciduous forest, taller second growth, and plantations. Parasitizes oropendola nests. Song is a loud, ringing *Peeeeet!-peeee'dee'deeet!*; calls include a *pit!* and *peet!* Mex. to Argentina.

male grackles
in flight
MELODIOUS
BLACKBIRD
female
juvenile
male
GREAT-TAILED
GRACKLE
adult
male
BRONZED
COWBIRD
male
female
Male Bronzed Cowbird in "butterfly" flight with females
BROWN-HEADED
COWBIRD
Giant Cowbird has bounding
woodpecker-like flight
juvenile
GIANT
COWBIRD
adult
male

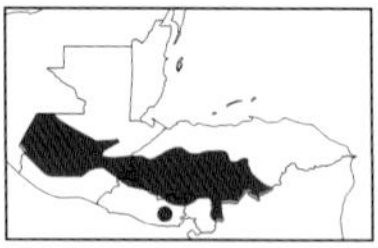

BLACK-VENTED ORIOLE *Icterus wagleri*

8.5 in. (22 cm). Adult has **black hood, upperparts, and undertail coverts; scapulars and remaining underparts yellow**. Immature yellowish overall with varying amounts of black on wings and tail; **generally with black throat**. Adult similar to adult Black-cowled Oriole, but larger and has black undertail coverts (not yellow); also note elevation and distribution. Fairly common in interior highlands of NCA; from 1,640 to 7,220 ft. (500–2,200 m). Found at edge of semideciduous forest and pine-oak forest to near cloud forest. Forages at mid- to upper levels. Frequently feeds at flowers. Call is a distinctive nasal *eeeaahnk!* Mex. to Nicaragua.

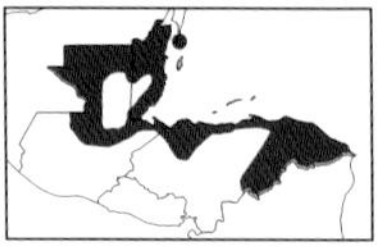

BLACK-COWLED ORIOLE *Icterus prosthemelas*

8 in. (20 cm). Similar to Black-vented Oriole, but smaller, leaner, and has **yellow undertail coverts**; also note habitat and elevation differences. Immature has black face and throat, also blackish wings and tail. Fairly common on Caribbean Slope; to 3,280 ft. (1,000 m). Found at edge of rainforest, semideciduous forest, and taller second growth, including plantations and gardens. Often found feeding in palms. Forages at midlevels. Song is a complicated, rich, liquid series of electric chatters and whistles; call is a nasal *eeaahnk*, and *chur'chur'chur*. Mex. to Panama.

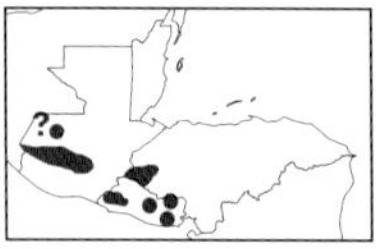

BAR-WINGED ORIOLE *Icterus maculialatus*

8.5 in. (22 cm). Adult male has black hood, back, and wings; **single white wing bar**; remaining body parts yellow, including undertail coverts. Female and immature olive-yellow overall with dark wings (**faint trace of a wing bar**); black face and throat. Uncommon at midelevations on the Pacific Slope; from 2,310 to 6,105 ft. (700–1,850 m). Found in semideciduous and pine-oak forest, and shaded coffee plantations. Forages at mid- to upper levels. Frequently feeds at flowers. Song is a bouncing series of rich, sweet whistles, *sa'weet-so'sweet-sa'weet-so'really'sweet-so'saw'weet*; call is scratchy, harsh *chiiirrrrr!* Endemic to region.

YELLOW-BACKED ORIOLE *Icterus chrysater*

8.5 in. (22 cm). **Yellow back** contrasts with black wings and tail, black mask and throat. Fairly common in NCA; to 7,710 ft. (2,350 m); however, generally above 2,620 ft. (800 m). Found in taller semideciduous forest, pine-oak forest, pine savanna, and occasionally in cloud forest. Forages at mid- to upper levels. Usually one of the first sounds of the forest dawn chorus; an accomplished singer. Song is a rich, pleasant series of sweet evenly spaced whistles lasting roughly 5.5 sec.; calls include a nasal *reeahh*, and *eeeahnk*. Mex. to Nicaragua and Panama to Colombia.

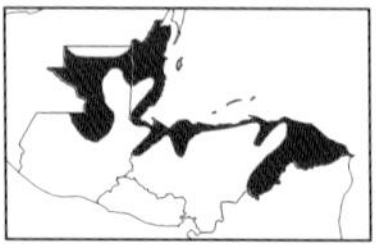

YELLOW-TAILED ORIOLE *Icterus mesomelas*

8.5 in. (22 cm). Yellow overall with black back, wings, and tail; **outer tail feathers and scapulars yellow**. Immature has yellow-olive upperparts and tail, bright yellow head and underparts, and yellowish bill. Fairly common on Caribbean Slope (rare in Honduras); to 3,940 ft. (1,200 m). Generally found near water: gallery forest, or in scrub or brushy areas along edges of marshes or swamps; also at edge of taller semideciduous forest. Forages at all levels. Song is a slightly harsh but pleasant 3- to 5-part *weeurr'cheer!-tip'weee'her!* (repeated into a longer series) or *tip-cheeer'her!*; calls include a nasal, chirpy *turp-turp-turp*. Mex. to Peru.

BLACK-VENTED ORIOLE
adult
immature
BLACK-COWLED ORIOLE
adult
immature
BAR-WINGED ORIOLE
immature
male
female
YELLOW-BACKED ORIOLE
YELLOW-TAILED ORIOLE

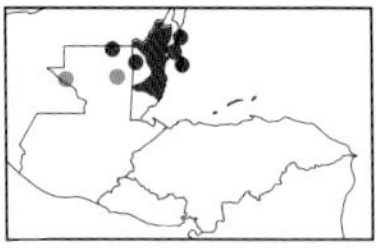

HOODED ORIOLE *Icterus cucullatus*

8 in. (20 cm). Adult male **orange-yellow with black mask and throat**; black wings have **2 obvious white wing bars** and edging to primaries. Adult female golden-yellow overall with 2 white wing bars; upperparts tinged olive. Immature male similar, but with black mask and throat. Female and immature similar to female Orchard Oriole (p. 400), but larger, with more decurved bill, longer tail, and more richly colored. Common in n. Belize; to 1,650 ft. (500 m). Found in a variety of disturbed habitats, including plantations, gardens, savanna, and coastal scrub. Forages at mid- and low levels. Sings a rapid series of chatters and clear whistles: *puuur'teee'weeurrrr-chi'chi'chi'chi'teeezz'weeur*; calls include a loud, clear whistle, *wheeat!*, a short *chut* (similar to *chuck* call of Orchard Oriole), and a thin chatter. U.S. to Belize.

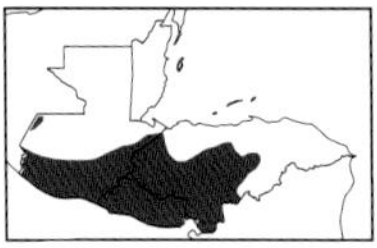

STREAK-BACKED ORIOLE *Icterus pustulatus*

8.5 in. (22 cm). Black back has **orange streaks or scalloping (on some individuals may appear entirely black)**; wings black with a **white lower wing bar, white edging on secondaries, and white "handkerchief" at base of primaries**. Adult female and immature yellower overall. Similar to larger Altamira Oriole (p. 400), but usually shows streaked back (entirely black in Altamira), smaller bill with a larger area of blue at base of mandible. Common on Pacific Slope; to 5,090 ft. (1,550 m). Found at edge of semideciduous forest, thorn forest, mangroves, and in disturbed habitats, such as plantations as well as city parks and gardens. Forages at midlevels. Song is a pleasant series of sweet, clear whistles (some elements repeated); calls include a *saweet!-taweee!—tawee-tawee*; a soft *churr'teee* and harsh chatters. Mex. to Costa Rica.

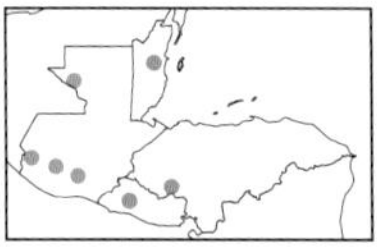

BULLOCK'S ORIOLE *Icterus bullockii*

8.5 in. (22 cm). Adult male orange-yellow overall with black back, crown, **black eye line and chin**; wings have **large white patches in wing coverts** and heavy white edging in primaries, secondaries, and tertials; also note **inverted "T" pattern on tail** (compare with tail pattern of Baltimore Oriole). Adult female has **grayish back** with darker streaking and is **paler orange-yellow on head**; **belly, vent, and undertail coverts grayish**. Immature male similar to female, but with **black throat and thin dark eye line**. Adult female very similar to female Baltimore Oriole (p. 400), but has gray back, paler gray below, and shows brighter orange-yellow face (lacks black splotches); some individuals difficult to separate. Hybrids (Baltimore x Bullock's) have been documented in Guatemala. Very rare winter visitor; to 9,190 ft. (2,800 m). Found at woodland edges, in second-growth scrub, parks and gardens. Forages at midlevels. Call is a chatter similar to Baltimore Oriole's. U.S. (breeding) to NCA (winter).

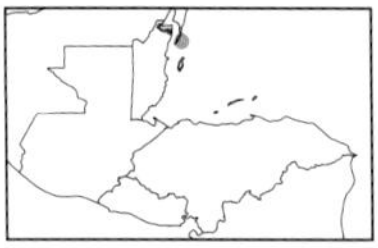

ORANGE ORIOLE *Icterus auratus*

7.5 in. (19 cm). Adult male has **orange-yellow back**; black mask, throat, and tail; note **broad white patch on upper wing coverts**. Female yellowish overall, has black throat, 2 **thin white wing bars**, heavy white edging on secondaries and primaries. Uncommon in n. Belize and winter visitor on Ambergris Caye (Oct.–Apr.); near sea level. Found at edge of semideciduous forest and in other open areas. Forages at mid- to upper levels. Song described as *peet—chur-chert'chert'chert'chert* (the last part often repeated several times); calls include a hard, nasal *nyehk*, a drawn-out *wheet*, and a clear *choo*; also dry chatters. Endemic to region.

male
female
worn individuals may show darker backs
HOODED ORIOLE
STREAK-BACKED ORIOLE
male
immature
male
female/ immature
BULLOCK'S ORIOLE
ORANGE ORIOLE
male
female/ immature

ORANGE ORIOLES II

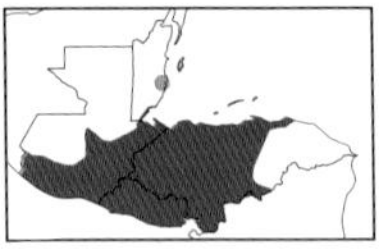

SPOT-BREASTED ORIOLE *Icterus pectoralis*

9 in. (23 cm). Adult has variable amount of **black spotting on sides of upper chest** (may be difficult to see), and a **large white "triangle" in secondaries (wings otherwise black)**. Juvenile pale yellow overall and variable, but shows same wing pattern as adult. **Basal two-thirds of mandible is silver-blue** (more extensive than on similar species). Fairly common in interior and on Pacific Slope; local and spreading on Caribbean Slope; to 5,250 ft. (1,600 m). Found at edge of a variety of forest types including parks and gardens. Forages at mid- and low levels. Song is a sweet, melodic rising and falling series of repeated clear whistles: *eeeep!-weu'peeer-eeeep!-weu'peeer-eeeep!-weu'peeer-eeeep!-weu'peeer . . .* ; calls include a harsh, scratchy, nasal *raannk* (similar to call of Altamira Oriole) and a hoarse chatter (similar to call of Streak-backed Oriole). Mex. to Costa Rica.

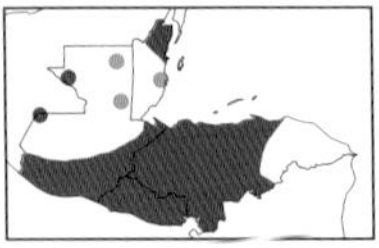

ALTAMIRA ORIOLE *Icterus gularis*

9.5 in. (24 cm). The **largest oriole**. Adult **back solid black**; black wings have **single white wing bar, white edging to secondaries, and white "handkerchief" at base of primaries** (similar pattern to Streak-backed Oriole). Adult female and immature similar, but yellower on head and underparts. Note large, heavyset bill and **small rectangle of silver-blue at base of mandible**. Larger than Streak-backed Oriole (p. 398), and larger bill shows less blue on mandible. Fairly common in most of NCA; to 6,230 ft. (1,900 m). Found at edge in a variety of habitat types including coffee plantations and gardens. Forages at midlevels. Song is a slow, evenly spaced series of 3 to 4 clear sweet whistles: *seeurt—seeat—Saa'wheeet!*; may be extended into a longer series; call is a nasal, jaylike *raank!*, often repeated (similar to call of Spot-breasted Oriole). U.S. and Mex. to Nicaragua.

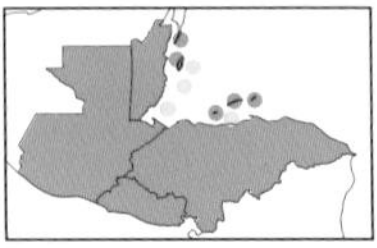

BALTIMORE ORIOLE *Icterus galbula*

8.5 in. (22 cm). Adult male has **black hood; bright orange rump; black "T" on an otherwise orange tail**. Adult female paler yellow-orange overall; grayish yellow edging to back; **black splotches on head**. Immature similar to female, but drabber still and lacks black on head; grayish wash to belly and vent. Female similar to female Bullock's Oriole (p. 398), but has yellowish tones on back, more yellow below, and shows darker face; some individuals difficult to separate. Hybrid Baltimore x Bullock's individuals have been documented. Common winter visitor; to 8,530 ft. (2,600 m). Found in all wooded habitats and disturbed habitats such as coffee plantations, city parks, and gardens. Forages at mid- to upper levels. Often in groups of 5 to 15 individuals (forms larger groups at nighttime roosts). Calls include sweet, rich whistles, *sa'weet-chup'chup'chup—sa'weet'tee'tee* and *two'wee*; and a harsh chatter (similar to Streak-backed Oriole [p. 398]). Canada (breeding) to Colombia (winter).

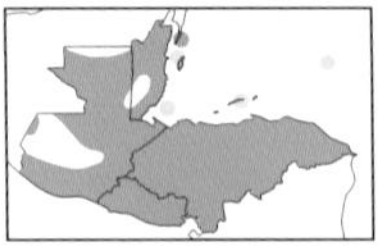

ORCHARD ORIOLE *Icterus spurius*

7 in. (18 cm). The **smallest oriole**. Adult male **chestnut brown** with **black black and hood**. Female olive-yellow (lemon yellow on underparts) with 2 thin white wing bars. Immature male similar to female, but with **black throat**. Bill thin and slightly decurved. Female similar to female Hooded Oriole (n. Belize) (p. 398), but smaller overall, and has straighter bill, shorter tail, brighter yellow belly and vent, and broader lower wing bar. Common winter visitor (late July–mid-Apr.); to 6,560 ft. (2,000 m). Found at edge in a variety of open and disturbed habitats. Forages at midlevels, often in groups up to 30 individuals. Feeds frequently at flowers. Call is a distinctive, nasal *eeeeuh*, or a ringing *eeeank*; also a flatter *chuck*. U.S. (breeding) to Colombia (winter).

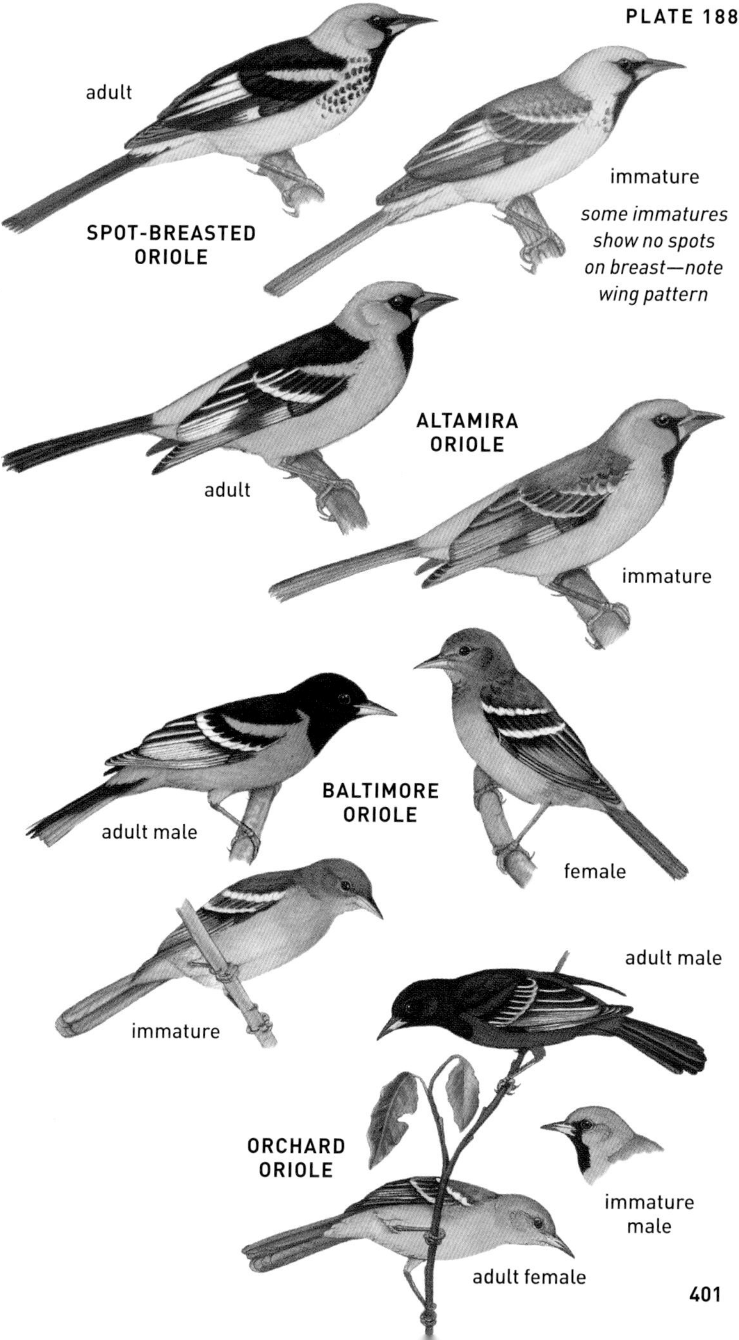
adult
SPOT-BREASTED ORIOLE
immature
some immatures show no spots on breast—note wing pattern
ALTAMIRA ORIOLE
adult
immature
BALTIMORE ORIOLE
adult male
female
immature
adult male
ORCHARD ORIOLE
immature male
adult female

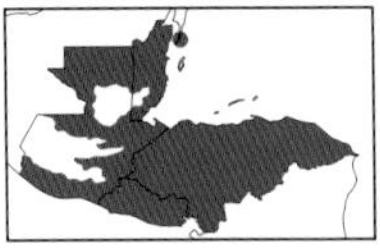

YELLOW-BILLED CACIQUE *Amblycercus holosericeus*

Male: 10 in. (26 cm). Female: 8.5 in. (22 cm). All-black plumage with **horn-colored bill** and **pale yellow eyes**. Uncommon on both slopes; to 7,050 ft. (2,150 m). Found in understory and edge of semideciduous forest and rainforest, also pine-oak forest and second-growth scrub, coffee plantations. Secretive. Generally heard, but difficult to see. Pairs duet. Male song is a loud *Teeer—purr'weeuur!-Teeer—purr'weeurr-Teeer—purr'weeurr-Teeer—purr'weeurr . . .* or *Peeeur-Peeeur-weeer!—Peeeur-Peeeur-weeer!*; while male sings, female gives a long down-slurred whistle, followed by a harsh nasal chatter. Calls include a husky, burry scolding, often given in doublets. Mex. to Bolivia.

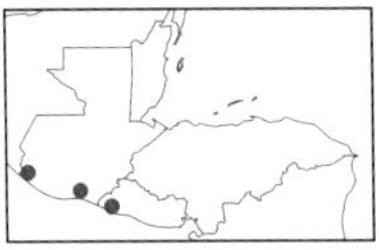

YELLOW-WINGED CACIQUE *Cassiculus melanicterus*

Male: 12.5 in. (32 cm). Female: 10 in. (25 cm). A long-tailed black bird with contrasting **yellow patch on scapulars, yellow rump, and yellow outer tail feathers; bill horn-colored**; also note small crest. Female similarly patterned, but duller overall and smaller. Uncommon and very local on Pacific Slope of Guatemala and El Salvador; to 660 ft. (200 m). Found in open, disturbed country along the coastal plain: agricultural areas with scattered large trees and wooded riparian corridors. Forages in small groups at mid- to upper levels. Nests colonially in large trees (like oropendolas). Varied calls include harsh electric chatters, bell-like screams, and clear whistles. Mex. to El Salvador.

SCARLET-RUMPED CACIQUE *Cacicus uropygialis*

9 in. (23 cm). All-black plumage with **bright red rump, horn-colored bill**, and **pale blue eyes**. Rare to uncommon in e. Honduras; to 2,460 ft. (750 m). Forages in small groups at mid- to upper levels in rainforest. Song is a loud, ringing *peer'peer'peer'peer'Peer'Peer'Peer'PEER'PEER'PEER!*; call is a *peeur!* Honduras to Peru.

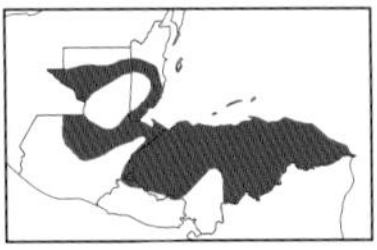

CHESTNUT-HEADED OROPENDOLA *Psarocolius wagleri*

Male: 14 in. (36 cm). Female: 11 in. (28 cm). **Rich chestnut body and head**; black back, wings, and tail (**outer tail feathers yellow**); **pale horn-colored bill** and **soft blue eyes**. Fairly common on Caribbean Slope; rare to uncommon in interior highlands; to 5,580 ft. (1,700 m). Found at edge in rainforest, in open second-growth forest, plantations, and less commonly around openings or edges in pine-oak forest. Forages at mid- to upper levels. Almost always in groups of 5 to 15 individuals, sometimes larger groups. Nests colonially in a single tree, typically with 10 or 20 hanging nests placed in a tree. Calls include a scratchy, liquid, electric *whaaakka*. Mex. to Ecuador.

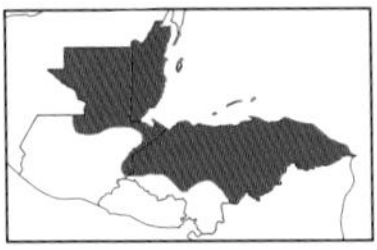

MONTEZUMA OROPENDOLA *Psarocolius montezuma*

Male: 20 in. (51 cm). Female: 16 in. (41 cm). **Pale blue patch on face and orange and black bill pattern are distinctive.** Common on Caribbean Slope; to 3,610 ft. (1,100 m). Found at edge of rainforest, in open second-growth forest, and plantations. Forages at mid- to upper levels. Almost always in groups of 5 to 15 individuals. Breeding colonies often have more than 100 hanging nests, all in a single emergent tree. Song (given by male as part of courtship display, in which male appears to fall over and call while upside down) is a liquid, electric *walla'walla'walla'walla'walla'yreeeeahh!*; calls include a scratchy, nasal *kwar*. Mex. to Panama.

YELLOW-BILLED CACIQUE

YELLOW-WINGED CACIQUE

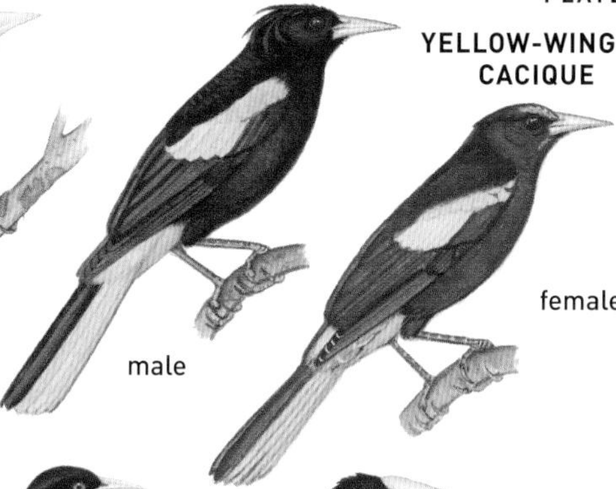

male

female

SCARLET-RUMPED CACIQUE

CHESTNUT-HEADED OROPENDOLA

MONTEZUMA OROPENDOLA

hanging nests in an oropendola colony

APPENDIX: ADDITIONAL SPECIES

ACKNOWLEDGMENTS

REFERENCES

PHOTO CREDITS

INDEX

Vagrant Species of NCA

The following species have been recorded and adequately documented one or two times in NCA, but are not included in the main body of the text. We do not consider them part of the regular NCA avifauna. They have been included in the total species count for NCA. The source of most of these reports since the year 2000 has been the quarterly roundup of observations in Central America, published in the journal *North American Birds*. Earlier reports were published in one or more of the ornithology monographs or field guides mentioned in the References list (p. 415). Several other vagrants, which we expect are likely to occur again or have been found more than twice, are treated directly in the text and illustrated in the plates.

1. **Magellanic Penguin (*Spheniscus magellanicus*):** One individual collected at Barra de Santiago (Sonsonate Department), El Salvador, on June 7, 2007.
2. **Greater White-fronted Goose (*Anser albifrons*):** One specimen from Canton Farm (Belize District), Belize, on January 15, 1973.
3. **Canada Goose (*Branta canadensis*):** One individual visited Crooked Tree Wildlife Sanctuary (Orange Walk District), Belize, in October and November 2007. Another report from near Choluteca, Honduras, on October 28, 2012.
4. **Greater Scaup (*Aythya marila*):** One adult male observed and photographed at Cattle Landing (Toledo District), Belize, on November 17, 2014.
5. **Hooded Merganser (*Lophodytes cucullatus*):** Records from Crooked Tree (Orange Walk District), Belize, in 1990 and 1991.

6. **Steely-vented Hummingbird (*Amazilia saucerottei*):** One photographed at Cerro Izopo (Francisco Morazán Department), Honduras, on August 29, 2015.
7. **Peruvian Pelican (*Pelecanus thagus*):** One individual observed and photographed flying with Brown Pelicans (*Pelecanus occidentalis*) at La Libertad (La Libertad Department), El Salvador, on December 21, 2012.
8. **Scarlet Ibis (*Eudocimus ruber*):** One individual with White Ibis (*Eudocimus albus*) from Punta Ycacos (Toledo District), Belize, on March 17, 1999.
9. **Piping Plover (*Charadrius melodus*):** Photographed on beach at Tela (Atlántida Department), Honduras, on October 16, 2012.
10. **Ruff (*Calidris pugnax*):** One basic-plumaged female collected on Pacific Coast of Guatemala at La Avellana (Santa Rosa Department) on April 16, 1974.
11. **Great Skua (*Stercorarius skua*):** One adult found dead near San Pedro (Belize District), Ambergris Caye, Belize, on March 20, 1971.
12. **Black-legged Kittiwake (*Rissa tridactyla*):** One adult recorded from Caye Caulker (Belize District), Belize, on January 9, 2000.
13. **Black-tailed Gull (*Larus crassirostris*):** One breeding-plumaged adult from Dangriga (Stann Creek District), Belize, on March 11, 1988.
14. **Manx Shearwater (*Puffinus puffinus*):** One beached carcass near Dangriga (Stann Creek District), Belize, on February 9, 1990.
15. **Great Shearwater (*Ardenna gravis*):** One photographed at sea off of Guanaja Island (Islas de la Bahía Department), Honduras, on December 15, 2015.
16. **Flammulated Owl (*Psiloscops flammeolus*):** One adult photographed in Todos Santos Cuchumatan (Huehuetenango Department), Guatemala, in March and April 2016.
17. **Short-eared Owl (*Asio flammeus*):** A mummified carcass found in Belize (Toledo District), March 4, 1999. Also, old reports (prior to 1970) from Agua Volcano (Sacatepéquez Department) in Guatemala.
18. **Northern Mockingbird (*Mimus polyglottos*):** One photographed at El Jicarito (Choluteca Department), Honduras, on April 19, 2003.

19. **White-throated Sparrow (*Zonotrichia albicollis*):** One record from Half Moon Caye (Belize District), Belize, on May 18, 2005.
20. **White-crowned Sparrow (*Zonotrichia leucophrys*):** One record from Ambergris Caye (Belize District), Belize, on October 28, 1988. A second was at Lighthouse Reef (Belize District), Belize, on November 15, 2006.
21. **Vesper Sparrow (*Pooecetes gramineus*):** One recent record from Cattle Landing, Toledo District, Belize, on August 26, 2001. Old records (prior to 1970) from Guatemala and El Salvador.
22. **Brewer's Blackbird (*Euphagus cyanocephalus*):** One specimen from Hacienda Chancol (Huehuetenango Department), Guatemala, prior to 1970.

Hypothetical Species

These species have been reported by reliable observers in NCA, but without adequate documentation such as a photograph, voice recording, or specimen. They should be watched for in NCA. We have not included these in the species totals for NCA.

1. **White-naped Swift (*Streptoprocne semicollaris*)**
2. **South Polar Skua (*Stercorarius maccormicki*)**
3. **Murrelet sp. (*Brachyramphus/Synthliboramphus* sp.)**
4. **Heermann's Gull (*Larus heermanni*)**
5. **Gray-hooded Gull (*Chroicocephalus cirrocephalus*)**
6. **Large-billed Tern (*Phaetusa simplex*)**
7. **Parkinson's Petrel (*Procellaria parkinsoni*)**
8. **Townsend's Shearwater (*Puffinus auricularis*)**
9. **Wilson's Storm-Petrel (*Oceanites oceanicus*)**
10. **Ashy Storm-Petrel (*Oceanodroma homochroa*)**
11. **Slaty-backed Forest-Falcon (*Micrastur mirandollei*)**
12. **Crimson-fronted Parakeet (*Psittacara finschi*)**
13. **Bay Wren (*Cantorchilus nigricapillus*)**
14. **Slate-throated Gnatcatcher (*Polioptila schistaceigula*)**
15. **Aztec Thrush (*Ridgwayia pinicola*)**
16. **European Starling (*Sturnus vulgaris*)**
17. **Connecticut Warbler (*Oporornis agilis*)**
18. **Palm Tanager (*Thraupis palmarum*)**
19. **Lazuli Bunting (*Passerina amoena*)**
20. **Shiny Cowbird (*Molothrus bonariensis*)**

More Species to Watch For in NCA

Below we list more species that we expect are likely to occur in the future (in addition to the hypothetical list above). Some may have already occurred in the past, without being observed or documented. For example, the Horned Lark, a highly migratory North American bird, colonized Colombia in the past and now has a resident population in that country's montane grasslands. It must have passed through Central America and may do so again in the future. The Craveri's Murrelet may occasionally reach NCA during the winter, nonbreeding season; a flock of unidentified murrelets reported offshore of Guatemala in the last century were more likely this species than other, more northern murrelets. Some of the other species are increasing in neighboring countries (Savanna Hawk, Red-breasted Meadowlark). We also include a suite of species that habitually wander north from the Galápagos Islands during El Niño events, typically reaching Costa Rica and occasionally Nicaragua. We expect these will eventually be recorded in Pacific waters of NCA: Peruvian Booby, Swallow-tailed Gull, and Inca Tern.

1. **Violaceous Quail-Dove (*Geotrygon violacea*)**
2. **Pacific Golden-Plover (*Pluvialis fulva*)**
3. **Craveri's Murrelet (*Synthliboramphus craveri*)**
4. **Western Gull (*Larus occidentalis*)**
5. **Yellow-footed Gull (*Larus livens*)**
6. **Swallow-tailed Gull (*Creagrus furcatus*)**
7. **Inca Tern (*Larosterna inca*)**
8. **Tahiti Petrel (*Pseudobulweria rostrata*)**
9. **Galapagos Petrel (*Pterodroma phaeopygia*)**
10. **Black-capped Petrel (*Pterodroma hasitata*)**
11. **Ainley's Storm-Petrel (*Oceanodroma cheimomnestes*)**
12. **Townsend's Storm-Petrel (*Oceanodroma socorroensis*)**
13. **Band-rumped Storm-Petrel (*Oceanodroma castro*)**
14. **Markham's Storm-Petrel (*Oceanodroma markhami*)**
15. **Peruvian Booby (*Sula variegata*)**
16. **Savanna Hawk (*Buteogallus meridionalis*)**
17. **Green Parakeet (*Psittacara holochlorus*)**
18. **Brown-chested Martin (*Progne tapera*)**
19. **Horned Lark (*Eremophila alpestris*)**
20. **Red-breasted Blackbird (*Sturnella militaris*)**

Future Splits and Taxonomic Changes

Every year, ornithologists and systematists discover new information about species relationships and their evolution. This new information often justifies taxonomic changes, including the splitting of a species into two or more recognized taxa. Once a year, the Clements Checklist (taxonomy used in this guide) is updated on a website managed by the Cornell Laboratory of Ornithology. The last published changes incorporated in this book were published in 2016.

The order of the families, genera, and species in the field guide generally follow the taxonomic order that has been approved by the American Ornithologists Union. The order is meant to represent, as best as possible, the evolutionary relationships of birds at many levels. Often, if two species are adjacent on a plate, they are their closest relatives and are believed to have evolved from a common ancestor. We have made some exceptions in order to place birds with similar ecology, distribution, or plumages together for field identification purposes, but for the most part, we have followed the widely accepted taxonomic order.

In 2016, the American Ornithologists Union published major changes in the taxonomic order for the birds of North America. Many of those changes are reflected in this book, but the publication came too late to accommodate all of the changes. The changes in taxonomic order that were not made include the following:

The Caprimulgiformes (nightjar family and potoo family), which appear in this book between owls and trogons, should be placed much closer to the beginning of the book, after cuckoos (Cuculiformes) and before swifts and hummingbirds (Apodiformes). The nightjars and potoos are now considered to have shared a common ancestor with the Apodiformes. The Sunbittern (Eurypygiformes), placed before the shorebirds (Charadriiformes), should follow the shorebirds (including gulls and jaegers). The tropicbirds (Phaethontiformes) should follow the gulls and terns and the Sunbittern, and precede the shearwaters and petrels (Procellariiformes). The storks and herons (Ciconiiformes) should follow the shearwaters and petrels, and the boobies, cormorants, anhingas, and frigatebirds (Suliformes) should follow the storks and herons. Finally, the flamingo (Phoenicopteriformes) should directly precede the grebes (Podicipediformes).

Within the songbirds in the second half of the book (Passeriformes), the AOU has also rearranged the order of several bird families. Again, we were able to make some of the changes just before going to press. Three families, each represented by just one species, could not be moved. One such species is the American Pipit (Motacillidae) which should appear after the House Sparrow (Passeridae), and before the crossbills, fringilline and cardueline finches, and euphonias (Fringillidae). Another misplaced species is the Olive Warbler (Peucedramidae), which should appear after the Gray Silky-Flycatcher (Ptilogonatidae) and before the munias (Estrildidae). The third out-of-place species is the House Sparrow (Passeridae), which should directly follow the Estrildidae rather than precede that family.

Use the space below to note the taxonomic changes made in 2017 and later years, or newly recognized species for the NCA area:

The authors wish to thank several people who were instrumental in the development of this book. We are especially grateful to the artists: Robert Dean, who illustrated virtually all of the 827 species depicted, and Peter Burke, who prepared the illustrations of the jaegers, several flying shorebirds, and more than 100 vignettes that supplement the principal illustrations. Vladlen Henríquez, Rafael Alberto Maeshiro Watanabe, and Rocio Avila helped with map layout, design, and preparation. The authors are extremely grateful to the HMH editorial team for their hard work on this guide: Lisa White, Beth Burleigh Fuller, Eugenie Delaney, Brian Moore, Jill Lazer, Emily Neeves, Katrina Kruse, Dan Janeck, Loma Huh, Connie Binder, and Taryn Roeder.

We acknowledge the contributions of hundreds of active or occasional bird observers in the NCA region, many of whom shared their information through eBird.org. Worthy of special mention are the country correspondents for the *North American Birds* quarterly roundup summaries, many of whom double as local reviewers for eBird. This select group of dedicated field ornithologists includes H. Lee Jones (Belize), Knut Eisermann (Guatemala), Roselvy Juárez (El Salvador), and John van Dort (Honduras).

We are also grateful for the editorial contributions of the staff at Zona Tropical Publications (John McCuen and Robin Kazmier). In addition, we acknowledge the support we have received from our employers during the development of the book: Field Guides Inc. (Jesse Fagan) and Zamorano University (Oliver Komar).

Jesse Fagan would like to thank his family and friends who have supported him throughout his many life endeavors, but especially his mom. Also, Claudia M. De La Cruz (and CC), who introduced him to the amazing NCA region. In addition, he would like to personally thank the following people and institutions for their support and help over the years spent studying the birds of NCA. In El Salvador: Carlos Funes, Karla Lara, Museo de Historia Natural de El Salvador (MUHNES; Ana María Rivera), Vicente "Chente" Rodríguez, Roselvy Juárez, and SalvaNATURA. In Guatemala: Jason Berry, John Cahill, Mario Castillo, Renato Fernández-Ravelo, Bitty Ramírez-Portilla de Fernández, Hugo Haroldo Enríquez Toledo, Josue de León (Finca Los Tarrales), Miguel Marín (Tikal), and Universidad del Valle de Guatemala (Claire Dallies de Masaya and Gabriela Palomo). In Honduras: James Adams (The Lodge at Pico Bonito), Dave Anderson, Mark Bonta, and Jorge Emilio Salaverri.

Oliver would like to acknowledge Jed Burtt, his ornithology professor at Ohio Wesleyan University, who encouraged him and many others to pursue careers in ornithology and tropical ornithology. Oliver also thanks Town Peterson, his dissertation advisor at the University of Kansas, and his colleagues at the KU Natural History Museum and the Department of Ecology and Evolutionary Biology, who helped expand his interests in avian ecology and conservation.

Thank you to Louisiana State University Museum of Natural Science (J. Van Remsen and Daniel F. Lane) and University of Kansas Natural History Museum (Mark Robbins and A. Townsend Peterson) for access to their wonderful bird collections. George L. Armistead, Alvaro Jaramillo, Chris Benesh, John Cahill, Steve N. G. Howell, Lee Jones, Daniel F. Lane, and John van Dort all provided us with useful information, insights, and ideas about NCA birds.

We would also like to thank several people who motivated us or helped directly over the years to complete this guide. Tom Jenner was with Jesse on his first road trip through Honduras in 2003 and they made several trips together throughout El Salvador during Tom's time in that country (2000–2006). It was during the 2003 trip to Honduras that the idea for a regional NCA guide was born. Leticia (Lety) Andino accompanied Jesse through several years of travels in El Salvador, Honduras, and Guatemala. Her expertise, local knowledge, and general help were greatly appreciated. We are grateful to Bret Whitney for his permission to use several illustrations by Peter Burke, from Bret's forthcoming guide to Brazil.

Finally, we thank Terry Chesser, Marshall Iliff, and Tom Schulenberg, all of whom graciously collaborated with information about the latest taxonomic changes planned by the ornithological taxonomy authorities, before they were published.

REFERENCES

Whether you are living in NCA or planning a visit, we encourage you to consult useful references that delve into more detail about local birds than we can in this guide. In addition to the publications listed below, consider searching the social networks to find groups dedicated to discussion (or photography) of local birds. For example, Facebook groups of local bird clubs exist in each of the four NCA countries. Often, searching for "Birding [Country]" or "Aves [Country]" will help you locate these groups. In Honduras and El Salvador there are several groups that begin with the acronym COA, which stands for *Club de Observadores de Aves*. We also encourage you to visit the Central American eBird portal, which includes notices and articles intended for birders in Central America, available in Spanish and English. More about eBird is presented in the Introduction (p. 22).

FOR THE REGION

Howell, Steve N. G., and Sophie Webb. 1995. *The Birds of Mexico and Northern Central America*. Oxford University Press.

Jones, H. Lee, and Oliver Komar. 2000–2015. Central America regional summaries, published quarterly in the journal *North American Birds*.

GUATEMALA

Eisermann, Knut, and Claudia Avendaño. 2007. *Lista Comentada de las Aves de Guatemala* (*Annotated Checklist of the Birds of Guatemala*). Barcelona: Lynx Edicions.

Land, Hugh C. 1970. *Birds of Guatemala*. Wynnewood, PA: Livingston Publishing Company.

BELIZE

Jones, H. Lee. 2003. *Birds of Belize*. Austin: University of Texas Press.

EL SALVADOR

Dickey, Donald R., and A. J. van Rossem. 1938. *The Birds of El Salvador.* Zoological Series 23. Chicago: Field Museum of Natural History.

Komar, Oliver, and Juan Pablo Domínguez. 2001. *Lista de Aves de El Salvador*. San Salvador: SalvaNATURA.

Thurber, Walter A., J. F. Serrano, A. Sermeño, and M. Benitez. 1987. *Status of Uncommon and Previously Unreported Birds of El Salvador*. Proceedings of the Western Foundation of Vertebrate Zoology 3(3).

HONDURAS

Bonta, Mark, and David L. Anderson. 2002. *Birding Honduras: A Checklist and Guide*. Tegucigalpa, Honduras: EcoArte S. de R.L.

Gallardo, Robert J. 2014. *Guide to the Birds of Honduras*. Mountain-Gem Bird Tours.

Monroe, Burt L., Jr. 1968. *A Distributional Survey of the Birds of Honduras*. Ornithological Monographs 7. American Ornithologists' Union.

PHOTO CREDITS

JAMES ADAMS: Page i, Collared Aracari; Page ix, Lovely Cotinga; Page x, Yellow-eared Toucanet; Page 20, Rainforest, Pico Bonito National Park, Honduras; Page 404, Keel-billed Toucan; Page 406, Scarlet Macaws; Page 417, Spectacled Owl

ALEXANDER ALVARADO: Page 418, Ocellated Quail

JOHN P. CAHILL: Page vi, Spot-breasted Oriole; Page viii, Pink-headed Warbler

JESSE FAGAN: Page 21, Pine savanna, Rus Rus, Honduras

RENATO FERNÁNDEZ: Page ii, Resplendent Quetzal

CARLOS FUNES: Page 17, Lake Güija, El Salvador; Page 17, Talgua River, Honduras; Page 19, Coastal scrub, Icacal Beach, El Salvador; Page 21, Riparian forest, Araute River, Morazán, El Salvador

OLIVER KOMAR: Page 17, Swamp forest, Jeannette Kawas National Park, Honduras; Page 18, Lake Yojoa marsh, Honduras; Page 18, Punta Condega mudflat, Honduras; Page 18, Red Mangroves, Jeannette Kawas National Park, Honduras; Page 18, Black Storm-Petrel, Gulf of Fonseca, Honduras; Page 19, Thorn forest, El Progreso, Guatemala; Page 19, Semideciduous forest, Finca Los Tarrales, Guatemala; Page 20, Cloud forest, Uyuca Biological Reserve, Honduras; Page 22, Pine-oak forest, Teupesenti, Honduras; Page 407, Crimson-collared Tanager

JAN MEERMAN: Page 21, Savanna, Belize

WILLIAM ORELLANA: Page 415, Honduran Emerald

JOHN VAN DORT: Page 1, Striped Owl; Page 24, Wine-throated Hummingbird; Page 413, Rufous-collared Robin

INDEX

Page references in **bold** refer to illustrations.